Business Monitor International
Guide to the World's Major Emerging Economies: Country Analysis and Forecast Reports 2000 - 2002

Volume I

First published in the USA and UK 2000

FITZROY DEARBORN PUBLISHERS
919 North Michigan Avenue - Suite 760
Chicago, IL. 60611
USA

AND

310 Regent Street
London
WIB 3AX
England

ISBN 1-57958-283-4

Library of Congress Cataloging in Publication Data and British Library Cataloguing in Publication Data are available.

Contents

Preface v

Introduction: Global Assumptions vii

Volume I

Asia

China 15

Indonesia 97

Malaysia 181

Philippines 253

Thailand 335

Vietnam 415

Emerging Europe

Hungary 493

Poland 571

Russia.. 657

Volume I

Asia
China
Indonesia
Malaysia
Philippines
Thailand
Vietnam

Emerging Europe
Hungary
Poland
Russia

Volume II

Latin America
Argentina
Brazil
Chile
Colombia
Mexico
Venezuela

Middle East and Africa
Egypt
Iran
Saudi Arabia
South Africa
Turkey
UAE

Preface

Business Monitor International Guide to the World's Major Emerging Economies: Country Analysis and Forecast Reports is comprised of two volumes specifically designed to suit the research needs of library and academic communities. It offers a detailed and authoritative appraisal of political risk, macroeconomic performance and outlook, leading industry sectors, capital markets and business environment for 21 emerging markets countries in four global regions. A detailed forecast for each of the years 2000, 2001 and 2002 provides full analysis of the key issues, both foreign and domestic, and assessment of the principal risks. Information is correct as of June 2000.

Written by acknowledged country experts, this comprehensive overview is based on market intelligence obtained through Business Monitor International's (BMI) exclusive network of public and private sector sources, backed by their emerging markets economics team and proprietary databases. It offers specialist advice on the impact of government and economic policy changes on the business operating environment.

Established in London in 1984, BMI is recognised as a leading source of specialist news analysis, data and forecasts on financial, economic and political developments across emerging markets worldwide.

BMI today serves the business information needs of senior executives at leading multinational companies, banks, research centres and governments in over 125 countries, in recognition of which the company has been honoured with the Queen's Award for Export Achievement.

Introduction: Global Assumptions

Global Growth Outlook

Slowdown Ahead

The global economy is still performing well and there is a good chance that GDP growth in 2000 will be the strongest for a decade. The most favourable phase is, however, now drawing to a close and there are significant challenges over the forecast period. US interest rates are at a nine-year high of 6.5% and, in Q2 00, the European Central Bank (ECB) increased rates more aggressively than expected with a 50 basis points hike to 4.25%. The tightening over the past year has finally had a significant impact on shares, reversing the sharp upward spike in technology prices seen in Q1 00. The Nasdaq index at one point dropped over 40% from its peak and there were also sharp falls in European technology indices.

Broader stock market values have not been seriously affected and tech stocks have largely recovered from the bout of turbulence during April. Valuations, however, remain historically stretched and there is the risk of an extended downturn in stock prices. There is also an increased danger that property markets will weaken across the G7 states. These factors combined may slow consumer demand and have a dampening effect on the global economy as a whole. One of the key uncertainties is whether global financial markets can avoid the sort of instability seen in 1998. In conditions of rising interest rates and falling liquidity, there is a higher threat of systemic financial failure. This could pose a significant risk to the global economy.

Economic Imbalances Remain Serious

There are signs that the balance of growth between the US and Europe is improving. The European economy is continuing to make steady progress and there is some evidence that the US economy is starting to slow. However, a further slowdown in the US is still required and the global economy faces a difficult transition period. Europe will be important, but the key relationship is between the US and Japan. The two countries are mutually dependent, with the US needing excess Japanese savings, just as Japan needs excess US

The global economy remains strong and GDP growth is likely to be at least 4% in 2000. There will, however, be a slowdown over the next 18 months, reflecting reduced liquidity and less robust asset prices as central banks continue to increase interest rates.

There is some evidence that the US economy is starting to slow, but a difficult transition period lies ahead.

Supply Remains Tight
Brent Crude (US$/b)

Source: Reuters/BMI.

There is a risk that countries will adopt protectionist measures if growth slows.

spending. The danger is that faltering growth in either of these two economies will impact negatively on the global economy.

Oil prices remained surprisingly strong during Q2 00, despite Opec action to increase output in March. Prices initially fell to approximately US$20/b, but then rallied. At the meeting, Opec agreed an informal target range of US$22-28/b, planning an "automatic" 500,000b/d output increase or decrease if the 20-day moving average price fell outside of this band. The oil price approached US$30/b in June – a level that should have triggered extra output – but increases did not occur until Opec ministers met on June 21. However, despite the high cost of crude, developed states are less dependent on oil than in the 1970s and the inflationary impact is expected to be limited.

Trade Momentum Needs To Be Maintained

There have been more positive developments on international trade. The US House of Representatives approved permanent normal trade relations (PNTR) with China in the face of intense lobbying against the proposals. China is also close to WTO entry and, following these two decisions, there will be greater optimism that the proponents of free trade can regain the momentum lost over the past two years. There are, however, still significant hurdles ahead, especially as the WTO has struggled to function effectively since its creation in 1995. The greatest risk is that countries will adopt protectionist measures if growth slows. This is a threat in Latin America, especially with the Mercosur trading block facing another testing year.

GLOBAL ASSUMPTIONS		1997	1998	1999	2000	2001	2002
Real GDP growth (%)	USA	3.9	4.3	4.0	4.0	3.0	3.1
	Euro-zone	2.7	2.7	2.2	3.3	3.1	2.6
	Japan	1.4	-2.8	0.3	1.0	1.4	2.1
Consumer inflation (average)	USA	2.3	1.6	2.1	3.0	2.8	2.5
	Euro-zone	2.0	1.2	1.2	2.0	2.1	1.7
	Japan	1.4	0.6	-0.4	0.6	0.7	1.2
Current account (US$bn)	USA	-144	-221	-330	-420	-350	-290
	Euro-zone	95	87	60	60	50	40
	Japan	95	121	100	105	100	70
Short-term interest rates (three-mth average)	USA	5.6	5.4	5.2	6.6	7.3	6.1
	Euro-zone	3.3	3.5	3.0	4.1	5.2	4.0
	Japan	0.6	0.7	0.3	0.1	0.5	1.0
Long-term interest rates (10-yr average)	USA	6.3	5.3	5.6	6.5	7.0	6.3
Exchange rates (end year)	US$/EUR	1.13	1.18	1.00	1.07	1.25	1.18
	JPY/US$	121	113	102	105	95	120
Commodity prices (average)	Gold - US$/oz	331	294	279	290	300	290
	Oil - Opec basket US$/b	18.77	12.28	17.47	23.50	20.00	18.00
	Copper - US cents per lb	103.1	75.0	71.4	80.0	85.5	90.0

Source: BMI.

United States

Fed Acts More Aggressively

The US economy grew at an annualised rate of 5.4% in Q1 00 and consumer spending expanded at a very strong 7.5%. At the beginning of Q2 00, inflation concerns increased. The headline inflation rate rose above 3.0%, reflecting, to a large extent, higher wages. Total labour costs rose 4.3% in the year to March, the fastest rate of increase for eight years. This suggests that strong demand and the very tight labour market are finally feeding through to wage inflation. In response, the Federal Reserve tightened monetary policy more aggressively, with the Fed Funds rate raised to a nine-year high of 6.5% in mid-May. In early June, there were tentative signs that the rate of growth was starting to slow. Industrial orders weakened and there has also been a drop in housing starts. Employment growth slowed and the unemployment rate rose to 4.1% from 3.9%. Consumer confidence is high, however, and this will tend to underpin spending growth. It is certainly too early to conclude that a sustained slowdown is under way.

Private Savings Need To Rise

Over the past few years, there has been a major shift in the private sector's behaviour, with a rapid increase in debt. The financial balance (private savings net of borrowing) has moved to a deficit of around 5% of GDP in 2000, compared with a 5% surplus in 1992. The trade and current account deficits are still widening, with the latter heading for at least 4% of GDP in 2000. This will need to be corrected over the forecast period. The Fed continues to face the very difficult task of achieving the necessary correction without triggering a deep recession. This has been made more difficult by the resilience of asset prices over the past two years. There is a high risk that markets will assume that the Fed will reverse monetary policy and cut interest rates if asset prices do drop significantly. If this is the perception, then there will need to be a more aggressive use of interest rates to stem excess demand. This, in turn, would increase the risk of recession.

Overall, the Fed is likely to tighten policy again, especially as it is not yet particularly restrictive. Short-term interest rates are likely to rise to around 7.5% in H2 00. On balance, this should be enough to slow the economy to a more sustainable rate. However, if Fed chairman, Alan Greenspan, concludes that rates need to be raised above 7.5% then the chances of recession would increase sharply.

A more aggressive monetary stance will slow the US economy. Fed chairman, Alan Greenspan, retains the confidence of the market, but there remains a high risk that the record-breaking expansion will be followed by recession.

Wide trade and current account deficits will need to be reined in over the forecast period.

US Prices Still Under Control
consumer price index - change, % y-o-y

* less food and energy ; Source: Bureau of Labour Statistics.

In the presidential election campaign, Republican candidate George W. Bush probably has the edge over Democrat rival Al Gore, but the contest is still wide open. If Bush does win, there will undoubtedly be conflict with congress, but he would pursue a policy of tax cuts. However, either candidate is unlikely to significantly alter government economic priorities. In the longer term, the president will have to appoint a new Fed chairman, together with at least four new Reserve governors. These will be important for the longer-term economic prospects.

Cyclical Dollar Downturn Likely

It will be increasingly difficult to maintain the strength of the US dollar over the forecast period.

The dollar's performance will be important over the next year, reflecting the need for orderly depreciation. The currency has remained remarkably strong, with optimism over the economy and investment inflows allowing the current account deficit to be easily financed. It will, however, be increasingly difficult to maintain this strength during the forecast period and the currency has already fallen significantly. The trade-weighted index dropped around 6% between early May and mid-June. A slowdown in the economy, coupled with weaker asset price growth, will erode currency strength. The Fed will not lift interest rates aggressively just to support the dollar and any sharp currency decline would tend to damage the prospects for European growth.

Euro-Zone

ECB Gets Tough

The euro-zone economy is continuing to expand. The Purchasing Managers' Index remained close to 60 last month, suggesting further significant growth in the industrial sector. Consumer spending is also expanding at a comfortable pace. Demand is rising very strongly in the smaller and more peripheral countries. In particular, rapid growth in Ireland is causing serious inflation problems.

The European economy should still be able to record strong growth over the forecast period. The ECB's determination to curb inflation could, however, damage the recovery, leaving unemployment at historically high levels.

The ECB has continued to tighten monetary policy, reflecting general inflation concerns. The ECB is concerned over euro weakness, the fresh increase in oil prices and the acceleration in money supply growth to 6.5% in April from 5.3% in January. The June 0.5% increase in the repo rate was more aggressive than expected and there is a small risk that this will choke off the recovery. The ECB's judgement has also been called into question again. GDP growth should still be at least 3.0% over the next two years, but this assumes that interest rates peak at 5.0-5.5%.

Euro Still Faces Structural Concerns

The ECB and European policymakers have become more unified in their opposition to the weak euro. The ECB has always been wary of the inflationary impact of currency weakness, but finance ministers were previously ambivalent over euro declines due to the beneficial impact on growth. The slump to below EUR0.90/US$ appears to have prompted a change in attitude. So far, there has been no direct intervention to support the currency, but officials have been keen to stem the decline seen in H1 00.

There is the risk of renewed division among individual countries over the strength of the euro.

Judged against the euro-zone's economic fundamentals, the currency's fall appears unjustified. Signs of a slowdown in the US economy have helped the euro rally back to around EUR0.95/US$ by mid June. There are, however, still significant hurdles for the euro. There is the risk of renewed division among individual countries, reflecting their divergent policy needs. For countries such as Ireland, further interest rate rises are needed, but growth in Germany and Italy is still relatively subdued and there could be opposition to further monetary tightening. Any division would also sap international confidence in the currency.

The Only Way Is Up
EUR/US$ exchange rate

Source: Reuters

A key factor behind the euro's weakness since launch has been the outflow of investment capital, primarily in search of improved growth prospects in the US. In Q3 00, this should be reversed, but there will be concern that European policymakers are not addressing the region's structural problems.

Japan

Sustained Growth Still Lacking

There have been some encouraging signs, but the economy is still unable to achieve strong self-sustaining growth. Performance is likely to remain disappointing during the forecast period.

GDP rose by an impressive 2.4% in Q1 00. There have been some slightly more encouraging figures on consumer spending, with a 1.3% increase in the year to April and unemployment has dropped slightly. There is, however, no sign of a sustained increase in domestic demand and there have been warnings from officials that GDP could contract in Q2 00. Leading indicators suggest that the economy may even slip back into recession. There are still serious concerns over the quality of official statistics and the savings rate will remain high, reflecting economic uncertainty and fear of unemployment. Japan remains dependent on budget spending to achieve growth and one of the key members of the ruling coalition recently admitted that the government had run out of policy options. Official debt is continuing to expand rapidly and the rate of debt growth experienced since 1998 is not sustainable in the medium term.

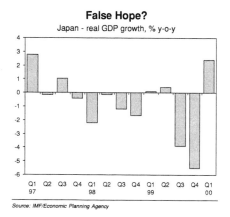

False Hope?
Japan - real GDP growth, % y-o-y

Source: IMF/Economic Planning Agency

The IMF has recommended that the government should continue the current policies, with another fiscal stimulus this autumn. The central bank has warned that interest rates could rise in July, but this would risk flipping the economy back into a prolonged downturn and only a slight rise in interest rates is likely.

LDP Weakness Prevents Policy Shift

Despite its unpopular leader, the LDP is likely to win the parliamentary elections on June 25. This will weaken the coalition and may impact upon economic policy.

General elections will be held on June 25. The Liberal Democratic Party (LDP) is now led by Yoshiro Mori, following the death of Keizo Obuchi. Mori, however, has suffered a fall in opinion poll ratings, after a series of well-publicised gaffes. His approval ratings are currently at less than 20% compared with 40% on election. There is a strong probability that Mori will be replaced as party leader after the election. The LDP are unlikely to perform well in the general election, but the probability is that they will retain power. A weaker coalition government would struggle to provide the necessary political leadership over the forecast period. The legislative programme would continue to be dominated by factional politics. Economic and political reform is, therefore, liable to be delayed further, aggravating the extended period of weak growth.

ASIA

CHINA 2000

Analyst: Lucy Elkin

Editor: Sara Matchett

Contents

Political Outlook _____ 19

Domestic Political Outlook 19
Foreign Policy 22

Profile and Recent Developments _____ 24

The Political System 24
Foreign Policy 29

Economic Outlook _____ 33

Introduction 33
Economic Activity 34
Fiscal Policy 36
Monetary Policy 37
Exchange Rate Policy 39
Balance Of Payments 40
Foreign Direct Investment 42

Profile and Recent Developments _____ 45

Characteristics Of The Economy 45
Economic Activity 48

Key Economic Sectors _____ 51

Introduction 51
Computers 52
The Internet 53
Agriculture 55

Profile and Recent Developments _____ **57**

Introduction 57

Industry And Manufacturing 58

Electronics 60

Agriculture And Food Processing 62

Mining 63

Construction 65

Telecommunications 66

Banking And Financial Services 69

Business Environment _____ 75

Introduction 75

Infrastructure 76

The Domestic Market 78

The Labour Market 79

Industrial Policy 80

Foreign Investment Policy 84

Foreign Trade Policy 86

Bureaucracy And Corruption 88

Environmental Regulation 88

Capital Markets _____ 91

Introduction 91

Equity Markets 91

Bond Markets 95

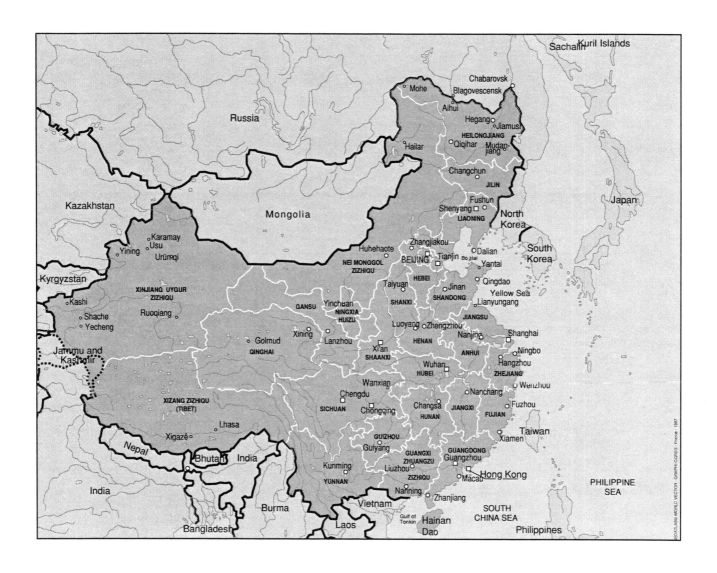

CHINA: MACROECONOMIC DATA AND FORECASTS

	1993	1994	1995	1996	1997	1998	1999	2000f	2001f	2002f
Population (bn)	1.20	1.21	1.22	1.23	1.24	1.25	1.26	1.27	1.28	1.29
Nominal GDP (US$bn)	598.77	541.74	700.61	821.85	903.46	964.52	1,013.81	1,083.53	1,161.04	1,158.29
GDP per capita (US$)	500.47	448.16	573.57	667.03	726.43	772.86	803.88	851.08	907.06	897.93
Real GDP growth (%)	13.49	12.66	10.55	9.54	8.80	7.80	7.10	7.40	7.50	7.50
Oil production (mn b/d)	2.9	2.9	3.0	3.1	3.2	3.2	3.2	3.2	3.2	3.3
Retail price inflation (an. avg % y/y)	13.2	21.7	14.8	6.1	0.8	-2.6	-2.9	-0.5	2.5	4.0
Consumer price inflation (an. avg %)	14.7	24.1	17.1	8.3	2.8	-0.8	-1.3	0.8	3.0	5.0
Bank rate (% pa)	10.1	10.1	10.4	9.0	8.6	4.6	3.2	4.5	7.5	7.3
Deposit rate (% pa)	11.0	11.0	11.0	7.5	5.7	3.8	2.3	1.9	3.5	3.9
Lending rate (% pa)	10.98	10.98	12.06	10.08	8.64	6.39	5.85	4.85	5.85	6.85
CNY/US$ (eop)	5.8	8.4	8.3	8.3	8.3	8.3	8.3	8.3	9.0	10.0
CNY/US$ (period average)	5.8	8.6	8.4	8.3	8.3	8.3	8.3	8.3	8.5	9.5
Merchandise exports (US$bn)	91.0	121.0	148.8	151.2	182.9	183.6	194.9	215.0	247.3	264.0
Merchandise imports (cif, US$bn)	103.1	115.7	129.1	138.9	142.2	140.3	165.8	190.0	224.2	240.0
Trade balance (customs, US$bn)	-12.1	5.4	19.7	12.3	40.7	43.3	29.1	25.0	23.1	24.0
Current account (US$bn)	-11.61	6.91	1.62	7.24	29.72	29.32	16.02	15.04	8.02	7.20
Current account (% GDP)	-1.94	1.28	0.23	0.88	3.29	3.04	1.58	1.39	0.69	0.62
Foreign reserves (US$bn) *	22.39	52.91	75.38	107.04	142.76	149.19	154.70	157.00	145.37	140.00
Import cover (mths) **	2.6	5.4	5.9	7.4	9.2	9.5	8.6	7.7	6.1	5.4
External debt (US$bn)	83.6	92.8	110.4	116.3	131.0	146.0	145.0	160.0	175.0	190.0
External debt (% exports)	91.6	74.3	72.4	65.0	62.2	68.5	63.9	62.5	60.3	56.9
External debt (% GDP)	14.0	17.1	15.8	14.1	14.5	15.1	14.3	14.8	15.1	16.4

f = BMI forecast, eop = end of period, * excluding gold, ** no. of months imports covered by FX reserves + gold. Sources: State Statistics Bureau/World Bank/BMI.

Business Monitor International Ltd

Domestic Political Outlook

Jiang Indicates He Will Step Down In 2002

In early May the *South China Morning Post* reported that the president, Jiang Zemin, had informed key party members that he would step down as the Communist Party's general secretary at the next party congress, in 2002. This was the first time that Jiang had made clear his intention not to seek a third term. He must also step down as state president in early 2003, as he has already had two terms in the post (the maximum allowed under China's constitution). Jiang reportedly called for a complete revamp of the party's most powerful body, the Politburo Standing Committee, urging the replacement of all but the youngest two members (Hu Jintao, 57, the current vice president, and Li Ruihuan, 65, chairman of the Chinese People's Political Consultative Conference.)

President Jiang Zemin has crystallised his intention to begin handing over key posts, but he will retain a strong behind-the-scenes influence.

THE STATE COUNCIL			
Prime Minister	Zhu Rongji		
Vice premiers	Li Lanqing, Qian Qichen, Wu Bangguo, Wen Jiabao		
State Councillors	Luo Gan, Chi Haotian, Wu Yi, Ismail Amat, Wang Zhongyu		
Secretary-general of the State Council	Wang Zhongyu		
Key Ministers			
Ministry of Agriculture	Chen Yaoban	Ministry of Civil Affairs	Doje Cering
Ministry of Communications	Huang Zhendong	Ministry of Construction	Yu Zhengsheng
Ministry of Culture	Sun Jiazheng	Ministry of Defence	Chi Haotian
Ministry of Education	Chen Zhili	Ministry of Finance	Xiang Huaicheng
Ministry of Foreign Affairs	Tang Jiaxuan	Ministry of Foreign Trade and Econom	Shi Guangsheng
Ministry of Health	Zhang Wenkang	Ministry of Information Industry	Wu Jichuan
Ministry of Justice	Gao Changli	Ministry of Land and Resources	Zhou Yongkang
Ministry of Labour and Social Security	Zhang Zuoji	Ministry of Personnel	Song Defu
Ministry of Public Security	Jia Chunwang	Ministry of Railways	Fu Zhihuan
Ministry of Science and Technology	Zhu Lilan	Commission of Science, Technology	Liu Jibin
Ministry of State Security	Xu Yongyue	State Development Planning Commis	Zeng Peiyan
State Economic and Trade Commission	Sheng Huaren	State Family Planning Commission	Zhang Weiqing
State Ethnic Affairs Commission	Li Dezhu	Ministry of Water Resources	Wang Shucheng
Ministry of Supervision	He Yong	Auditor General of the State Auditing	Li Jinhua
Governor of the People's Bank of China	Dai Xianglong		
Source: Embassy of the People's Republic of China, Washington DC.			

However, Jiang is highly unlikely to fade away just yet. There is a strong chance that he will retain his third key post – that of chairman of the Central Military Commission. He can also be expected to step up efforts to secure top party and government posts for protégés, with the intention of continuing his influence on power through them. The current favourite to succeed Jiang as state president is the vice president, Hu Jintao. However, other senior party leaders – some rivals to Jiang – will play a similar game, pushing their own supporters forward. Hence the run up period to the 2002 congress – which in a sense has already begun – will see intensive backroom manoeuvring.

Falun Gong Just Won't Go Away

There have been further peaceful protests by the quasi-religious Falun Gong group, despite a continued crackdown by Beijing.

In April and May the Falun Gong organisation – a quasi-religious group that mixes Buddhist and Taoist practises with *qigong* breathing and meditation techniques – staged repeated small-scale protests of up to several hundred members, unfurling banners and performing meditation exercises in Tiananmen Square, before being removed by security police. An intensive official crackdown on the group began in April 1999, when some 10,000 members staged a peaceful protest in central Beijing. The group was banned as an "evil cult" in July 1999, since when tens of thousands of ordinary Falun Gong members have been detained, key leaders have been given long jail terms, and an officially-backed media campaign has sought to warn ordinary Chinese away from the "superstitious" group.

Yet despite these efforts, Falun Gong continues to show a surprising capacity to organise gatherings even in central Beijing. The crackdown is believed to have reduced overt support for the group – but it has also left a hardened core of believers, who continue to protest. The group's supporters in the US have also been successful in courting international followers – some of whom have been able to help organise a sophisticated PR campaign raising awareness of Falun Gong within the US congress. Thus Beijing has found the spotlight of international attention focused on its security forces and their treatment of a group that claims to be a religious minority – at a time when relations with the US are already sensitive (*see Foreign policy*). As **BMI** stated in its last report, Falun Gong members seem to have no political agenda and have so far not attempted to galvanise anti-CPC sentiment. However, harsh treatment at the hands of the authorities could change this.

Rising Unemployment Will Bring More Protests

As unemployment rises and pensions and wages continue to go unpaid, another jump in labour protests is expected this year.

Although reports rarely filter out into international news media, China has experienced a surge in labour and other protests in the last two years. Even security officials expect this to intensify this year, as state-owned enterprise reform gathers pace, resulting in further job losses and continued wage freezes and unpaid pensions. In April reports came to light of a massive riot in the north-eastern town of Yangjiazhanzi, when the closure of a state-owned mine prompted 20,000 miners to take to the streets, protesting the level of redundancy payments. The protesters went on the rampage, breaking windows and damaging cars until several hundred riot police were called in to restore order. Also in April, 500 workers blocked a railway line in Sichuan, to protest the rumoured closure of the mine that employed them; again, police had to be brought in. Then in mid-May around 1,000 factory workers blocked the main road to the northern rust-belt city of Shenyang and besieged local government offices until the government promised to meet a backlog of unpaid wages and pensions.

These protests are just the tip of the iceberg. Officials from Fujian province reported 31 "mass" protests in the first half of 1999, up from just four in the first half of 1998. For the most part the protests remain peaceful – and tend to be isolated, as the authorities deal harshly with any labour leaders who attempt to join forces with groups in other areas. And there have been few signs of politically motivated dissent. In late May a rare student protest was reported, when more than 1,000 students at Beijing University gathered. However, there was no political motivation for the protests – rather, the students had been angered by the university's handling of the murder of a fellow student – and the protests swiftly ended.

The Anti-Corruption Drive Nets Some Bigger Fish

One of the party elite's biggest concerns is that public disgust at official corruption will erode public support for the party, perhaps even paving the way for new civil or political groups to spring up. As a result, the anti-corruption campaign begun two years ago continues in full swing. The most recent high-profile victim was Chen Kejie, the vice-chairman of the Standing Committee of the China's parliament, the National People's Congress. Chen, who was sacked and then arrested in late April, was accused of taking US$4.5mn in bribes during his years as head of the local government of Guangxi province. Claims that Chen's downfall is a sign that no one is immune are probably overstated. Despite Jiang's call for all corrupt party members – however high up – to be weeded out, there is a widespread popular perception that those with friends in high places are often spared. Chen's fall may have come because he had been abandoned by powerful backers.

Yet while the top leadership are calling for a clean-up of the party, outside criticism is still not tolerated. For example, in April an anti-corruption campaigner, An Jun, was sentenced to four years in prison for organising a

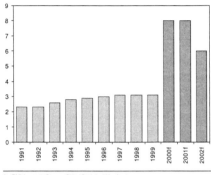

Seeds Of Discontent
China - urban unemployment rate, %

f = BMI forecast; Source: China Statistical Yearbook.

The party-backed anti-corruption campaign is still in full swing, but outside criticism is dealt with harshly.

Better Than Some
Corruption Perception Index - a regional comparison

World Ranking	Country	CPI Score*
7	Singapore	9.1
16	Hong Kong	7.8
29	Malaysia	5.3
29	Taiwan	5.3
43	South Korea	4.2
52	**China**	**3.5**
55	Philippines	3.3
61	Thailand	3.0
66	India	2.9
71	Pakistan	2.7
74	Vietnam	2.5
80	Indonesia	2.0

*10 = highly clean; 0 = highly corrupt. Source: Transparency International.

300 member corruption monitoring group, and for writing articles about corruption which the authorities feared could incite "public discontent" with the government. The media are encouraged to unveil official corruption – one of China's most popular television shows focuses on corruption scandals – but this is tolerated, even encouraged, by the authorities, because it is censored by officials and also because it does not involve any organisation of public groups. It is gatherings of people, and "uncontrolled" news, that frighten Beijing.

Foreign Policy

Growing Uncertainty Over Taiwan

On May 20 Chen Shui-bian, the candidate of the pro-independence Democratic Progressive Party (DPP), was inaugurated as president of Taiwan. Chen's election is a major headache for the government in Beijing, which fears he will seek a referendum on independence for Taiwan at some point during his time in office. Chen has sought to soothe Beijing's nerves, while ahead of Chen's inauguration, Beijing extended an olive branch of its own, suggesting that the two sides could hold talks on an "equal status", rather than insisting that Taiwan must negotiate as a mere province of China. But despite efforts to calm troubled waters, there is no getting away from the fact that Chen does not support reunification. Chen ignored Beijing's demand that Chen should recognise the "one China" principal during his inaugural speech as president. However, Chen did promise not to declare independence or hold a referendum on the issue, or even change Taiwan's formal name (the Republic of China), as long as China did not attack.

Military hawks in Beijing want to step up the war of words, but the top politicians want to take a wait-and-see approach – while also continuing to make threats to try to keep Chen in line. Beijing has long made clear that it will act militarily if Taiwan makes any move towards declaring independence. In late May Beijing held week-long military exercises on the coast opposite Taiwan. DPP party officials have held several policy meetings to try to hammer out an acceptable stance on independence that will not provoke Beijing further. A formula of Taiwan as a "sovereign country" but without a name change or formal declaration of independence has been proposed, but any clear statement that Taiwan is anything other than part of China would be unacceptable to Beijing. The DPP is expected to discuss this further at a mid-year party congress.

The new president of Taiwan, Chen Shui-bian, took office in late May. Chen's pro-independence background has left Beijing very uneasy, and tensions have remained high.

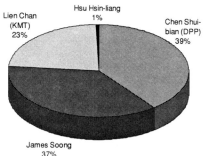

Beijing's Least Favoured Outcome
Taiwan - presidential elections, 18/3/00

Lien Chan (KMT) 23%
Hsu Hsin-liang 1%
Chen Shui-bian (DPP) 39%
James Soong 37%

Source: Taipei Times.

The US Agrees A Key Trade Pact

On May 24 the US House of Representatives approved a key proposal granting China "permanent normal trade relations" (PNTR). Members of the World Trade Organisation (WTO) are required to grant all other WTO members PNTR. Previously, the US had voted annually on whether or not to grant China normal trade relations status. If congress had not passed the bill, China would have been able to withhold the new trading privileges agreed with the US in November 1999 in a bilateral WTO pact. The vote was fairly close, although not as close as expected: many Democrats opposed extending PNTR, fearing that it would reduce US leverage over China on issues such as human rights. To soothe Democrat opponents of PNTR the bill included provision for a new commission that will monitor human rights in China – a move that angered Beijing.

Despite the passage of the PNTR bill, relations between China and the US remain strained. As ever, differences over human rights issues remain a problem. The quasi-religious Falun Gong movement has been able to win considerable sympathy in the US for what is seen as needless repression by the authorities in China. Perhaps more critically, the US government is alarmed at heightened tensions between China and Taiwan since the election of Chen Shui-bian in March (*see above*).

The US congress has approved permanent "normal trade relations" status for China, a key vote that clears the way for China to join the WTO. Yet China-US relations continue to be overshadowed by tensions over Taiwan.

Profile and Recent Developments

The Political System

One-Party Rule Continues

The Chinese Communist Party (CCP) has ruled China since 1949. In theory, there is a separation between the CCP, the government and the judiciary, but in reality all branches of government are under the control of the CCP. For example, the CCP general secretary, Jiang Zemin, also holds the less powerful position of state president. This is mirrored throughout the power structure, with local governments at provincial, county and city levels matched by local party organisations. At its apex, the CCP has a structure of small, internally selected committees, culminating with the Politburo and its Standing Committee: the latter are the most important political bodies, and shape all key policy decisions. The CCP has close to 60mn members. Membership can still be useful for career advancement, notably in government or administrative positions (where in some instances party membership is a necessity), although to a much lesser degree than in the past. China's constitution enshrines a leading role for the CCP, and the eight other legally permitted parties are all small in membership and subject to very tight control. Hence China is, in all practical senses, a one-party state. Attempts to register new political parties have been consistently crushed by the authorities, the most recent example being the crackdown in 1998-99 on the fledgling China Democracy Party; its attempts to register as an official party failed, and key leaders were jailed on charges of trying to "overthrow the state".

The CCP Structure

The CCP usually holds a Party Congress every five years, at which broad policy direction is presented and changes to the top party posts are made. The next Congress is due to be held in late 2002. Policy is, for the most part, formulated before the congress itself; the actual congress is used as a vehicle for announcing and legitimising decisions made at higher levels. The last gathering, the 15th Party Congress, was held in September 1997, and attended by more than 1,500 delegates from around China. Important changes in line-up were made, and Jiang Zemin strengthened his position through the promotion of supporters and by the enforced retirement of a potential rival, Qiao Shi, then number three in the party and chair of the legislature, the National People's Congress. Significant changes in line-up at the top may be made at the next, 2002, Congress. Jiang's five-year term as party general secretary will be up; he can stand for re-election but may choose not to as he and other top leaders are coming under pressure from some sections of the party to hand over to a younger generation.

The party's 153-member Central Committee holds a plenum each autumn to discuss policy direction, when changes or shifts in emphasis are announced. This is more than a talking shop, as its members are powerful party figures, who use the event to air views and concerns. However, the main agenda is, once again, set beforehand. The last plenum, held in September 1999, was used to highlight continued support for state-owned enterprise reform and restructuring. The Central Committee is in theory selected by the Party Congress, although some party posts (such as the heads of key provinces or cities, such as Shanghai) carry almost automatic membership, and the top party leaders also manoeuvre their protégés onto the Central Committee. In addition to the 153 full members, there is also a 191 member 'shadow' body of so-called 'alternate' members. The Central Committee also has numerous departments that oversee various areas, including propaganda and foreign affairs.

Power is concentrated further in the Central Committee's Political Bureau (known as the Politburo), which currently has 22 members, again shadowed by 'alternate' members. Its members are elected by the Central Committee, and are drawn from among the top party and government posts, as well as representatives of the military. The apex of power within the CCP and China as a whole is the Politburo Standing Committee, currently comprising the seven highest-ranking members of the politburo. This small committee is China's top level decision-making body. It is headed by the party general-secretary (currently Jiang Zemin, who is referred to as being at the "core" of these highest leaders). Jiang also heads the Secretariat that is the administrative and bureaucratic support for the Politburo and Central Committee. The Secretariat prepares policy papers and overseas the implementation of Politburo decisions by the government machinery.

Other Party Bodies

The seven-member Central Military Commission (CMC) forms a link between the state and the People's Liberation Army (PLA) and the People's Armed Police (PAP). The PLA, which includes the navy and airforce, is the only other organisation besides the party-bureaucracy structure with a national reach, and the support of the PLA is considered to be vital to the survival of the party. In Deng Xiaoping's day, the CMC was regarded by some as his real power base. Jiang is chairman of the CMC, while his allies Generals Zhang Wannian and Chi Haotian are vice chairmen.

Much less influential is the Chinese People's Political Consultative Conference (CPPCC), which groups representatives of the CCP, ethnic minorities and the eight permitted non-communist political organisations. It meets once a year, while its regional committees meet more often. It has a nominal advisory role to the party, but has limited influence. The eight political parties are all interest groups, with relatively small membership, and are under tight CCP control. Officially, they are described as being neither parties of office, or of opposition.

At the local level, the party's influence used to be felt through a network of work units and neighbourhood committees which at one stage controlled much of everyday life, allocating jobs, housing, education, providing health care and meals, and checking up on people's activities and their loyalty to the party line. Deng weakened this system with the introduction of the household responsibility system. More recently, more rapid economic reforms have brought greater labour mobility and less general state interference in everyday life, as the old structures of enforcement and control have weakened.

The Government

In tandem with this party structure is a government that is organised along similar lines, and which at the top at least is run by most of the same key party figures. The nominal head of state is the president (currently Jiang Zemin, who also holds the top party post, that of general secretary). Jiang's second (and final) five-year term of office as state president ends in 2003; a successor is expected to be confirmed by the March 2003 meeting of China's parliament, the National People's Congress (NPC). Jiang is regarded as "the core of the leadership of the third generation", that is of the crop of leaders that succeeded Mao Zedong and Deng Xiaoping, through his occupation of the country's three top posts – he is head of state (president), head of the party (party general secretary), and head of the Central Military Commission. Despite the likely hand-over of some or even all of these posts in the next few years, Jiang is expected to maintain a strong behind-the-scenes presence, and to use the next few years to place loyal protégés in key posts – as Deng Xiaoping did before him.

The executive, or cabinet, is called the State Council. This comprises the prime minister (also known as the premier), currently Zhu Rongji, as well as the vice-premiers, state councillors and heads of the government ministries and commissions. It holds a full meeting each month, and a weekly meeting of its smaller Standing Committee. The members of the State Council are in theory chosen every five years by the NPC (although appointments are first approved by the CCP Central Committee). The State Council makes many policy decisions and oversees the day-to-day government of the country through its various ministries and commissions. The major commissions tend to have a greater policy-formulation role than the ministries, but are otherwise similar in scope. There are in addition some small commissions formed for a specific purpose, such as the commission overseeing the construction of the Three Gorges dam. When he came to office as prime minister in March 1998, Zhu announced a sweeping reorganisation of the administrative bureaucracy, cutting the number of ministries and commissions from 40, to 29, to improve efficiency (*see below*).

China also has a legislature, the 3,000 or so member National People's Congress (NPC). The NPC meets every year in March for two to three weeks, and its members are selected for five-year terms from among regional congresses. The NPC also has a Standing Committee that meets more regularly, as well as some small committees with their own permanent staff. In theory, the NPC is the highest power in the land, passing laws and selecting ministers. In reality, the NPC used to be almost entirely a rubber stamp organisation. Its previous head or chair of the NPC Standing Committee, Qiao Shi, did push for a larger role for the NPC in monitoring the government, and NPC members do use their votes to show dissatisfaction with the government or particular key officials. The NPC does not yet provide an independent check on the CCP, or challenge the State Council's decisions. However, it is slowly becoming bolder in exerting a supervisory role over the government. For example, at the March 1999 session, the NPC formed a small committee to assess the budget before it was passed. At the most recent March 2000 NPC session, the NPC passed a law requiring the State Council and all regional assemblies to register new laws with the NPC, where they would pass through three review committees. This gave some teeth to the NPC's role, already enshrined in the constitution, although not enforced – previously, local assemblies were not required to send new legislation to the NPC for approval provided that it did not clash with the constitution. However, the new law does not include decisions by the party, and the current NPC chairman, former prime minister Li Peng, stated recently that the NPC should "follow the line and policies of the party".

The Judiciary

The highest court in the land is the Supreme People's Court, while People's Courts are established at the provincial level. Below these are intermediate and basic level People's Courts, while small mediation committees are widely used to settle civil cases. Many cases are tried publicly, but despite significant efforts to tighten up in recent years, abuses are very common. The quality of the judiciary is still low: many officials are unqualified, nepotism and corruption are rampant, and there are reports of widespread police brutality. Cases involving dissidents or others perceived as a threat to the state are often carried out in secret and justice is peremptory, a reflection of the fact that the judiciary is not independent of the CCP.

Policy Making And Implementation

There are a wide range of additional, important bodies which are not captured on official organisational charts of the Chinese government. Some of these are informal and are established on an *ad hoc* basis to respond to a specific situation. Numerous working groups consist of a core of senior leaders and a small staff. These bodies oversee broad areas such as foreign affairs, security, and the role of the party, encompassing the activities of a number of ministries and commissions. In addition, some functional groups, such as the group overseeing party affairs, have long vertical lines of authority from the Politburo at the top, all the way down to party representatives in state-owned enterprises and other local-level organisations. Formal and informal structures at different levels have complex systems of vertical and horizontal linkages that make the policy-making process hard to discern. However, major policy choices are undoubtedly handled at the very highest levels – within the Politburo and the CCP Central Committee. For example, the budget and major policy and personnel changes are presented by the State Council to the NPC for approval, but only after the key decisions have already been taken by the CCP Central Committee. A vast range of day-to-day decisions and policy implementation is then handled by the government ministries and commissions, and related administrative units. Policy has to be implemented through the network of nation-wide party and local government bodies, while many key ministries also have their own vertical chains reaching local government level.

This complex system of both formal and less well-known party and government bodies results in a complex and fragmented decision-making system, lacking in transparency. There is a web of vertical and horizontal linkages between government and party, necessitating much bargaining and passing of decisions up and down the chain of command. Unsurprisingly, conflicts of interest between the various bodies occur frequently and lines of responsibility are difficult to untangle, sometimes resulting in stasis. Perhaps even more common, provincial-level units and their sub-branches prefer to go their own way, and policy set by the centre is watered down, changed or even blocked altogether as it filters down the system. A final, but critical, constraint on the system is the paucity of reliable information. Despite Zhu Rongji's tough calls for improvements in official statistics, local officials still often make sure that their numbers match official targets. Accordingly, at the March 2000 NPC congress, Zhu broke with tradition and did not announce an official growth target for the year.

Two changes begun in 1998 were intended to boost the transparency and efficacy of this party-state machinery. First, following his promotion to the post of prime minister, Zhu Rongji brought a range of skilled technocrats into cabinet (State Council) posts. Second, Zhu announced a major overhaul of the bureaucracy. The number of ministries and commissions was cut from 40 to 29. Several massive industrial ministries were merged to form 'super ministries', in a bid to reduce conflicts between ministries and to streamline decision-making, while focusing these bodies more clearly on economic reform and bringing them more under the control of Zhu and his team. Among the most powerful of the new bodies is the State Economic and Trade Commission (SETC), which has absorbed the coal, metallurgy, machine-building and internal trade ministries. In addition, the State Planning Commission was renamed the State Development Planning Commission (SDPC), and made answerable to the prime minister's office. The second change begun in 1998 was the trimming of the bureaucracy; progress here has been slower, as the cuts have been strongly resisted and many people have simply been moved into new quasi-official bodies. As official concern over the level of unemployment rises, reluctance to push vocal civil servants out of their jobs is likely to prevent full implementation of these cuts.

The government remains enormous and complex, an added difficulty for foreign investors, who often need to get to grips with a number of local and central bodies that often lack clear lines of authority. In addition, improvements in the quality of governance have been slow in coming. In his annual report to the March 2000 NPC meeting, Zhu Rongji made clear that much remains to be done. He took aim at the bureaucracy, citing poor management, chaotic implementation of regulations, smuggling, tax evasion, and the falsification of statistics as factors that had "severely impeded" policy implementation. Zhu announced that teams would be sent out to inspect government departments, and called again for party and government members to avoid corruption.

A growing trend will be the move towards a separation between the regulatory and commercial interests of key ministries and commissions. This is driven by a number of diverse factors, including efforts to reduce graft, and to meet the entry requirements of the World Trade Organisation. For example, there are plans to turn the Ministry of Information Industry (MII) into a regulating body without links to commercial operations. In addition, **State Power Corp** (SPC), the sole owner of the national grid, has started buying a portion of its electricity through a bidding system, with the ultimate aim of introducing competition through the entire system, and separating the grid operation from SPC's power plants.

Foreign Policy

China's Changing Role

Foreign policy under Deng and now Jiang has been primarily shaped by the desire to ensure smooth regional and wider international relations in order to create a suitable background for developing economic ties. In line with this policy, many disputes with neighbouring nations have been settled, and China has started to play a fuller role in regional and international associations. China has taken steps towards meeting international norms, including signing and ratifying several key arms control agreements (such as the Comprehensive Test Ban Treaty on nuclear testing in 1996) and has worked with the USA in talks on the future of the Korean peninsular. However, China's behaviour in the international community is still at times driven by somewhat unsubtle self-interest. For example, China vetoed a UN peace-keeping force to Macedonia in February 1999, because Macedonia had diplomatic ties with Taiwan.

Beijing also feels that China's growing economic importance should result in greater international recognition and respect. Its own foreign policy is governed by five principals which include "non-interference in the internal affairs" of another country, and it is exasperated at the frequent western criticism of what is sees as internal matters. In 1998, Beijing lost few opportunities for portraying itself as a responsible regional power when it maintained the stability of the renminbi at a time when a devaluation could have sparked another regional currency crisis. However, at a time of deepening domestic problems, Beijing may seek to bolster domestic support by intensifying nationalistic policies, including a tougher stance on Taiwan and on territorial disputes in South China Sea.

Taiwan – The Number One Problem

Following the return of Macau to Chinese rule in December 1999, there is a new urgency in Beijing's desire to push for the reunification of Taiwan with China. However, the two sides remained far apart in 1999, when the outgoing president, Lee Teng-hui, caused a furore in July by calling for any cross-Straits dialogue to be conducted on a "state to state" basis, apparently rejecting Beijing's "one China" policy. Jiang desperately wants to oversee moves towards re-unification as part of his own personal legacy, and also to spur patriotic support for the CPC. In addition, hawks within the military are pushing for a tough stance. Accordingly, in late February 2000 China's State Council issued a policy paper that called for force to be used to against Taiwan if it continued to resist reunification talks. Previously, Beijing has only threatened to use force in the event that Taiwan made any step towards independence.

On March 18, 2000 Beijing had to face the outcome it had least desired when Chen Shui-bian, the candidate of the pro-independence Democratic Progressive Party (DPP), won the Taiwan presidential election with 39% of the vote. Chen immediately took a conciliatory line, suggesting that the resumption of direct trade and investment ties between Taiwan and the mainland, and military "confidence building" measures, were all up for discussion. He also said that he would welcome a visit from Jiang, Zhu and the mainland's top Taiwan negotiator, Wang Daohan, and proposed that he should make a "peace visit" to Beijing before his inauguration on May 20. Chen has long held that independence is a long-term, rather than an immediate, goal, and is not likely to make any move to call for a referendum on independence until he is well established. Just before the election he even hinted that he could become a "non-partisan" president, withdrawing from the DPP – an effort to distance himself from his party, which has the formation of an independent Taiwan as a gaol of its party charter. However, despite these efforts to make conciliatory statements, Chen still does not accept "one country, two systems", and has said that "Taiwan must never become a second Hong Kong."

The question of how to react to Chen has caused heated debate for the government in Beijing. Immediately after the Taiwan vote, it seemed that the moderates (who include Zhu Rongji) were in control. The State Council's Taiwan Affairs Office issued a fairly modest statement saying that it would wait and see what happened (although, not surprisingly, reiterating that "any form" of independence would "absolutely not be permitted.") But hardliners, including senior figures within the military, may press for a show of force, such as war games and missile tests across the Taiwan strait (as in the run-up to Taiwan's last presidential election in 1996) in an effort to pre-empt any move towards independence. Some extremists may hope that such a move would destabilise Taiwan, preventing Chen from taking up office. It is most likely, however, that Beijing will try to leave the ball in Chen's court until he has assumed office. Yet it is clear that Chen's election create a new period of heightened tension and greater uncertainty; the rules of the game are changing.

Tough Relations With The USA Could Jeopardise The WTO Deal

China-US relations reached a low in May 1999 with the bombing of the Chinese embassy in Belgrade by NATO, sparking officially sanctioned anti-US protests in Beijing. Ties did begin to improve late in the year; military exchanges have resumed, and a major breakthrough came in November 1999 when China and the USA at long last signed an agreement on China's accession to the WTO. Under the terms of the deal, access is to be granted to many sectors including agriculture, and services such as finance, telecommunications, retail trade and distribution. However, the USA continued to criticise China for human rights abuses through 1999 and into 2000, while anti-China sentiment in the US congress may yet derail the WTO deal. The US congress must still approve permanent Normal Trade Relations (NTR, formerly called Most Favoured Nation trading status) for China. NTR is currently approved each year in an annual debate which focuses on whether China has complied with human rights, labour and other standards. All WTO members must extend permanent NTR to each other; hence without the vote, China would have the right to withhold from US companies the market access measures agreed in November. The Clinton administration wants to get the vote out of the way well ahead of the presidential election in November, as it will be a very tough call, given congressional concerns over human rights and other issues, including China's treatment of Taiwan. Beijing's belligerence towards Taiwan in early 2000 has strengthened the hand of congress members who oppose granting permanent NTR.

China Fears A US-Japan Axis

China's threats to Taiwan could seriously undermine relations with the USA and its regional allies, particularly Japan. The USA has defence treaties with Japan and South Korea, and a continued heavy military presence in the region; both factors are viewed by China as heavy-handed and threatening. This situation deteriorated in 1998-99, as Japan and the USA moved steadily towards greater military cooperation. Following a long-range missile test by North Korea in 1998, the USA proposed the development of a 'theatre missile defence' (TMD) system together with Japan, ostensibly to protect US troops and allies in Asia. China reacted angrily, fearing that TMD could be extended to include Taiwan. Although TMD is still years away from becoming a reality (if it ever does), in 1999 Beijing continued to protest stridently against Taiwan's inclusion, saying that such a step would bolster Taiwan's pro-independence movement.

The extent of Japanese and US support for Taiwan is left deliberately vague. In September 1997 the USA and Japan revised their defence treaty, and the new terms included a pledge for Japanese troops to "support" the USA in "areas surrounding Japan", but this did not explicitly include Taiwan. However, given the recent election victory of the DPP's candidate in Taiwan, some hawks in the Chinese military are calling for China to force Taiwan to the negotiating table, before TMD is created. China fears that the inclusion of Taiwan in the TMD would drastically reduce China's ability to use the threat of force to keep Taiwan from breaking free, as China's main threat to Taiwan is from its missiles ranged on the Chinese coast.

If Taiwan were to be included in the TMD, military analysts expect that this would prompt China to upgrade its own, currently rather modest, nuclear arsenal, although the more dire predictions of an Asian arms race and new Cold War seem premature. However, China's access to "dual use" technology from the USA did blow up into a big issue in 1999. The partial declassification of a US Congressional Committee report, known as the Cox report, detailed damage to US national security resulting from China's attempts over two decades to obtain military technology and information, including through the misuse of dual-use technology. The report charged that two US satellite companies, **Hughes Electronics** and **Loral**, had inadvertently helped China to improve its rocket launching systems by participating in the enquiry which followed the explosion of a Chinese Long March missile. The report urged tighter control over sensitive exports such as super-computers and stricter monitoring of US investment in China in defence-related industries. Following the Cox report, in March 1999 the US government reversed a 1996 decision to allow a US$450mn export of telecommunications satellite equipment by Hughes, to a joint Chinese-Singaporean consortium, **Asia-Pacific Mobile Telecommunications Satellite**. The Cox report also came at the same time as allegations were leaked to the press that information stolen by China in the 1980s from a US nuclear laboratory at Los Alamos, enabled China to develop smaller nuclear warheads. China vigorously denied the charge, but one US scientist, Wen Ho Lee, was charged in

December 1999 in connection with the allegations, apparently for breach of security procedures.

China Eyes Japan With Caution

Against this background, relations with Japan remained tricky in 1999. Policy towards Taiwan and Japan's relations with the USA are the major hurdle in developing closer relations with China. Efforts to deepen ties have made little progress. In February 2000 China's foreign ministry stated that it would not attend the G8 meeting to be held in Japan in April, scotching rumours that Japan wanted China to attend, and possibly even to join the grouping. The rebuff was seen as reflecting China's distaste for Japan's efforts to deepen its regional diplomatic role (other factors include China's dislike of the G8's intervensionist stance on issues such as Kosovo, and concern that bolstering the G8 would undermine the UN Security Council on which China already sits).

Tensions between Japan and China may also flare from time to time over territorial disputes. The two nations, along with Taiwan, all claim sovereignty over a group of uninhabited islands in the East China sea, known as Diaoyu in China and the Senkaku in Japan, and the islands have in recent years been the scene of repeated small-scale protests. Again, if Beijing attempts to stoke patriotic/ nationalistic sentiment in China, such incidents could intensify and become more difficult to contain – although outright armed conflict remains highly unlikely.

China's Claims In The South China Sea

Another regional dispute centres on the Spratly islands, an oil-rich group of islands in the South China Sea which are claimed outright or in part by six Asian nations – China, Taiwan, Vietnam, the Philippines, Malaysia and Brunei. China claims "indisputable sovereignty" over the entire chain (known as the Nanshas in China). Although China has stated its commitment to resolving the problem through talks, there have been a number of stand-offs resulting from Chinese naval incursions in the area. According to the Philippines, China has built permanent military structures on one island, Mischief Reef, sending in naval patrols in late 1998 while the work was being completed. China claims that the buildings are facilities for fishermen, and has offered access to the Philippines. The Philippines has complained of what it calls China's "talk and take" policy (that is, China's increased presence in the area, even while it is engaging in regional discussions). There is growing concern within the Association of South East Asian Nations (Asean) that China is becoming more aggressive in pushing its South China Sea claims, and that as Chinese naval capabilities are strengthened over the next few years, it will be able to back up these claims militarily. In late 1999 Asean drafted a 'code of conduct' on the South China Sea, but China did not agree to all the provisions, and has yet to sign the code. Certainly work on the code has not done much to reduce tensions; in March this year the Philippines made another formal complaint when Chinese fishing vessels entered disputed waters around Scarborough Shoal, another disputed area to the north of the Spratlys.

2 Economic Outlook

Introduction

Demand Is Still Weak

Good first quarter growth figures – real GDP rose by a higher-than-expected 8.1% y-o-y – have led some commentators, including **BMI**, to revise up growth forecasts for the year. However, growth is being driven by a rebound in exports, and deep structural problems persist. Consumer demand is still slack; the result of high unemployment and unpaid wages and pensions. Continued restructuring of state-owned enterprises (SOEs) and increased competition as China reduces tariffs and opens sectors following WTO entry, will ensure further job losses in 2000-2001. In a bid to lift growth, an expansionary fiscal policy will continue at least through 2000 (*see fiscal policy*). The government plans to continue selling large quantities of bonds to fund pension payments, a clean-up of the ailing state-owed banks, and state infrastructure projects designed to lift GDP growth. The fiscal deficit still remains low, but government debt is rising rapidly, and Beijing will not want to continue pump-priming beyond 2001.

Against this backdrop, consumer demand is unlikely to stage a strong recovery in 2000-2001, and state fixed investment will slow from 2001. Hence **BMI** does not expect a strong upturn in growth in 2000-2002, when restructuring of the SOEs and the banking sector will drag on. However, there are some bright spots – most notably, China's entry into the WTO, likely in late 2000 or H1 2001. WTO entry will lift foreign investment inflows and stimulate exports – although the gains will be partially offset by rising imports and a painful shakeout in many sectors faced by greater foreign competition. Over the longer term, the quality of growth will slowly improve, with less reliance on state spending, and a steady levelling of the playing field for private firms as WTO entry forces the pace of deregulation.

There were signs of stronger economic growth in the first quarter, but unemployment is expected to rise again this year as state sector reform continues, and hence consumer demand will remain very weak.

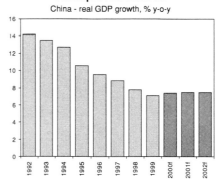

An Improved Outlook
China - real GDP growth, % y-o-y

f = BMI forecast; Source: State Statistical Bureau.

Economic Activity

Q1 Growth Was Better Than Expected...

Growth was stronger than expected in the first quarter, lifted by surging exports rather than a strong recovery in domestic demand.

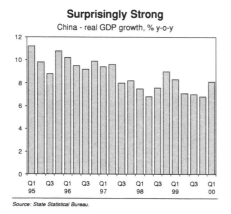

Surprisingly Strong
China - real GDP growth, % y-o-y

Source: State Statistical Bureau.

Official figures vastly underreport the degree of unemployment in China.

Real GDP growth picked up by a surprisingly strong 8.1% y-o-y in the first quarter, according to data from the State Statistical Bureau (SSB), driven by a 10.7% increase in industrial output, and an 8.5% rise in fixed asset investment. The later was driven by continued heavy state spending: billions of dollars have been poured into regional infrastructure projects and into soft loans for state-owned firms wishing to investment in new equipment. Industrial output was lifted by a strong performance by the manufactured export sector: exports jumped by just over 39% y-o-y in the first quarter, boosted by high export tax rebates and strong demand from regional markets and from the buoyant US economy. A research institute of the State Development and Planning Commission suggested after the first quarter figures were released that real GDP growth could reach 7.5% this year, compared with the official forecast of 7%. **BMI** has revised up its own forecast for the year to 7.4%, but believes that the momentum of the first quarter is not sustainable while private consumption remains slack.

...But Unemployment Is Still A Big Headache...

In a report out in April the Asian Development Bank (ADB) estimated that the urban unemployment rate had reached 9.5% by the end of 1999 – compared with an official estimate of a mere 3.1%. (The official unemployment rate only includes people registered with the Ministry of Labour, thus leaving out millions of people who are still registered as being employees of ailing SOEs, but who are in reality no longer being paid.) Further, the ADB estimated that some 30% of the rural workforce was under or unemployed (official unemployment figures do not include rural areas). The ADB forecast that the urban unemployment rate would rise further to 10.5% in 2000, as another 5mn state workers are expected to lose their jobs this year. The ADB's unemployment forecast was based on the assumption that GDP growth would slow as low as 6.5% this year, a forecast compiled before the strong first quarter GDP figure was published. But even if overall GDP growth is stronger than the ADB expects, it is clear that unemployment is going to remain a critical issue for this year.

...And Consumer Demand Remains Weak

China is still trying to pull itself out of a deflationary spiral, in which heavy job losses have reduced demand and dampened prices. Yet signs are beginning to emerge that the economic slowdown which has persisted for the last seven years may be bottoming out. Retail sales are starting to pick up (rising 10.4% y-o-y to CNY839.4bn in the first quarter), and consumer prices posted one month of positive growth during the first quarter. The government even granted an unusual week-long holiday for May Day, hoping that a prolonged holiday period would give a further boost to spending. However, most of the strong first quarter GDP performance was the result of heady export growth; consumer demand is still fairly weak. Without a sustained, strong upturn in consumer spending, the government will have to rely once again on its massive fiscal stimulus programme to lift GDP growth for the year.

While China may be seeing the end of deflation, consumer demand remains anaemic.

GDP, OUTPUT & EMPLOYMENT									
	1993	1994	1995	1996	1997	1998	1999	2000f	2001f	2002f
Real GDP growth (% y/y)	13.5	12.7	10.5	9.5	8.8	7.8	7.1	7.4	7.5	7.5
Industrial production (% y/y)	-	-	13.4	13.2	11.1	8.9	9.6	8.5	10.0	11.0
Urban unemployment rate (%)	2.6	2.8	2.9	3	3.1	3.1	3.1	8.0	8.0	6.0

f = BMI forecast; Source: IMF; Reuters; official press reports.

Fiscal Policy

Revenues Are Rising Strongly...

Further pump-priming will be required to lift growth this year, and the budget deficit will rise, despite strong revenue growth.

Government revenues surged 27.7% to CNY280.86bn in the first quarter of 2000, according to the State Administration of Taxation (the figures are for all levels of government, both local and central). Central government revenues alone rose by 34.6% y-o-y to CNY163.5bn, while local government revenues rose 19.2% y-o-y to CNY117.4bn. The massive jump reflects a pick-up in first quarter economic growth (boosting corporate profits), as well as a sharp rise in stamp duties on stocks, thanks to buoyant trade. In addition, the surge in exports lifted customs revenues by 27.5% y-o-y through the first four months of the year, to CNY64.1bn.

This strong first quarter performance suggests that revenue growth may be a little higher than expected in 2000. The budget for 2000, approved in March, targets a rise in central government revenue of 8% y-o-y to CNY690.4bn, while expenditure is forecast to increase 12.3% to CNY920.3bn, leaving a deficit of CNY229.9bn. The rate of growth of revenue through the first quarter suggests that revenues may be higher than planned – although the growth rate was boosted by the low base period. However, WTO admission will force Beijing to cut import tariffs and re-examine some preferential tax policies starting later this year, which will eat into customs and other revenues.

GOVERNMENT FINANCE (CNYBN)										
	1993	1994	1995	1996	1997	1998	1999	2000f	2001f	2002f
Total revenue	434.9	521.8	624.2	740.8	865.1	985.4	1137.7	1200.0	1190.0	1250.0
Total expenditure	464.2	579.3	682.4	793.8	923.4	1077.2	1313.7	1450.0	1480.0	1650.0
Budget balance	-29.3	-57.5	-58.1	-53.0	-58.3	-91.8	-176.0	-250.0	-290.0	-400.0
Budget balance (% of GDP)	-0.9	-1.2	-1.0	-0.8	-0.8	-1.1	-2.1	-2.8	-2.9	-3.6

f = BMI forecast; Source: IMF; BMI.

...But Reforms Impose A Heavy Burden

The finance ministry has made clear that heavy government expenditure will continue to be used through this year in an attempt to lift GDP growth. The government has forecast a budget deficit for 2000 of CNY229.9bn, up from CNY179.1bn in 1999. In addition to continued heavy spending on infrastructure projects, the cost of reforming the welfare system will impose an added burden. As many as 10% of the urban workforce and up to 30% of the rural workforce are now unemployed or underemployed (*see above*). In theory, contributions from workers and enterprises fund existing pension and other welfare payments, but many struggling state-owned enterprises have been unable to keep up their payments, and some CNY40bn in pension payments are outstanding. The 2000 budget forecast social welfare payments for the year at CNY70.7bn – compared with spending on education, for example, of CNY16.5bn. In April, the *China Daily Business Weekly* reported that officials had agreed on the introduction of a new social security tax, but that it had not yet been decided whether the new system would replace the old contributions system or run in tandem with it.

Monetary Policy

Some Signs Of A Weak Recovery In Prices...

Consumer price inflation (CPI) turned positive – just – in the first quarter of the year, rising by 0.1% y-o-y. (Since the start of this year the CPI has replaced the retail price index as the measure officially tracked by the government.) Consumer prices turned positive in February, rising 0.7% y-o-y – after almost two solid years of deflation – boosted by heavy spending around the time of the Chinese New Year. The rise was helped by a weak base period, and also by the unexpectedly strong surge in exports in the first quarter, which helped to soak up some excess capacity, while retail sales also picked up. (Another factor is that, after two solid years of deflation, firms have little further scope to cut prices.) However, the CPI dipped again in April, falling 0.3% y-o-y. Prices in April were pushed down by falling food prices, as the spring harvest resulted in increased availability, and hence lower prices, for foods such as vegetables and meat. As a result, consumer prices averaged zero change during the first four months of the year compared with the same period of 1999. Retail prices have continued to fall, dropping by an average of 2% y-o-y for the period January-April.

The government has cut interest rates repeatedly and introduced a tax on interest earnings in November 1999, measures intended to get savings out of

The government has weighty spending commitments this year.

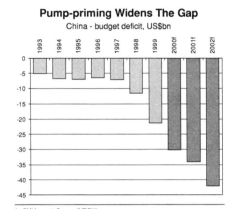

Pump-priming Widens The Gap
China - budget deficit, US$bn

f = BMI forecast; Source: IMF/BMI.

Inflation has risen briefly, as demand picks up a little and excess capacity problems start to ease. Rising prices are better news for industry, and suggest China may be able to avoid a deflationary spiral – although the price pickup is certainly not strongly established.

the banks and into the shops. They have even extended public holidays, in the hope that longer holidays will both encourage higher spending and also slow production, reducing high inventories. The government is also planning to hike fees for housing, education and rents this year in order to boost the services component of CPI – although this will have to be carefully managed if it is not to backfire and dampen consumer confidence. These measures will start to be felt through H2, pushing inflation more firmly into positive territory by the end of the year, and **BMI** expects annual average consumer price inflation to pick up modestly through 2001-02.

...But M2 Stays Sluggish

Growth of China's broad money supply (M2) has continued to slow. M2 growth moderated fairly steadily through the second half of 1999 to 14.7% y-o-y at end-December, just below the 15% y-o-y target. The M2 growth target for 2000 remains at 14-15% y-o-y, but M2 rose by only 13.7% y-o-y at the end of April. The government has already cut interest rates seven times since May 1996, and has lowered bank reserve ratios and increased open market operations. However, these measures have not translated into stronger lending as banks remain burdened by bad debts and prefer to buy low risk government paper. Hence **BMI** expects the central bank, the People's Bank of China, to make another quite aggressive cut in lending and deposit rates in 2000, in a bid to get real interest rates down and stimulate borrowing. Lending rates and deposit rates will pick up thereafter, as inflation rises and interest rates are slowly liberalised.

BMI *expects the central bank to make another cut in lending and deposit rates in 2000.*

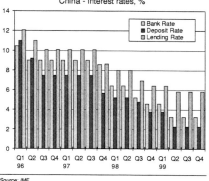

Failing To Stimulate Lending
China - interest rates, %

Source: IMF.

INTERNAL RATES & INFLATION										
	1993	1994	1995	1996	1997	1998	1999	2000f	2001f	2002f
Lending rate (local currency, % eop)	11.0	11.0	12.1	10.1	8.6	6.4	5.9	4.9	5.9	6.9
Deposit rate (local currency, % eop)	11.0	11.0	11.0	7.5	5.7	3.8	2.3	1.9	3.5	3.9
Consumer price inflation (% an. avg)	14.7	24.1	17.1	8.3	2.8	-0.8	-1.3	0.8	3.0	5.0
Retail price inflation (% an. avg)	13.2	21.7	14.8	6.1	0.8	-2.6	-2.9	-0.5	2.5	4.0

f = BMI forecast; eop = end of period; Source: BMI.

Exchange Rate Policy

Wider Currency Band Under Consideration

Concerns that China may devalue its currency, the renminbi, have receded since exports began to pick up strongly in late 1999. China has little to gain from moving the renminbi lower at the moment: exports are already surging, while a devaluation would increase the cost of vital imported inputs. However, WTO entry will increase pressure for a more flexible exchange rate system, in order to boost export competitiveness and to make the economy more flexible. The renminbi currently trades within a very narrow band set by the central bank, the People's Bank of China (PBOC). Since the last report there have been further hints that the authorities are considering widening the band – although no timetable has been given. On three occasions in April and May, the renminbi closed outside its trading band. Although the movements were very small, the fact that the PBOC did not intervene was taken as a sign that the central bank was testing the waters before allowing the renminbi a little more freedom. Under the current "previous day plus" trading system, the renminbi is permitted to fluctuate a mere 0.3% above and below the previous day's average rate. **BMI** expects that the current "previous day plus" trading bands will be formally widened perhaps as early as late 2000 or early 2001 – although probably by only a few basis points. Following such a widening, the initial pressure on the renminbi could be on the upside, but by late 2002 the erosion of the current account surplus could push the renminbi down to CNY10/US$.

BMI expects a widening of the trading bands and a modest devaluation of the renminbi by end-2002.

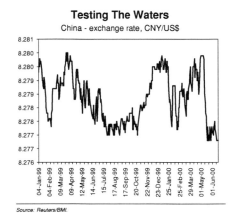

Testing The Waters
China - exchange rate, CNY/US$

Source: Reuters/BMI.

EXCHANGE RATES & RESERVES									
	1993	1994	1995	1996	1997	1998	1999	2000f	2001f	2002f
CNY/US$ (an. avg)	5.76	8.62	8.35	8.31	8.29	8.28	8.28	8.28	8.50	9.50
CNY/US$ (eop)	5.80	8.45	8.32	8.30	8.28	8.28	8.28	8.28	9.00	10.00
Foreign exchange reserves (US$mn)*	22.39	52.91	75.38	107.04	142.76	149.19	154.70	157.00	145.37	140.00

*f = BMI forecast; eop = end of period; *excluding gold; Sources: IMF, International Financial Statistics; BMI.*

Balance Of Payments

WTO Entry May Be On The Cards This Year

WTO entry will boost both exports and imports.

On May 19 China signed an agreement with the European Union (EU) on admission to the WTO. The EU was the last really important bloc yet to have reached agreement with China. The deal, which came after weeks of tense negotiation, secured improved terms in some areas compared with the US deal reached in November 1999. In particular:

- foreign firms will now be permitted a maximum 49% stake in mobile and fixed-line telecommunications services within three years of accession (compared with six years under the US deal). Firms will be permitted a 25% stake on accession, rising to 35% after one year, and to 49% in the third year;

- seven EU insurance firms are to be granted licenses before WTO entry;

- foreign firms will be allowed to import up to 20% of China's oil imports;

- restrictions on foreign joint ventures in large retail stores are to be removed on accession;

- tariffs on 150 key EU exports are to be cut to 8-10% on accession (the items include ceramics, textiles, glass, footwear, machinery, leather goods, cosmetics, wine and spirits).

Another potential stumbling block was cleared on May 24 when the US House of Representatives approved so-called "permanent normal trade relations" status (PNTR) for China. Normal trade relations status was previously approved each year in an annual debate that focused on whether China has complied with human rights as well as labour and other standards. As all WTO members must extend permanent NTR to each other, if congress had rejected the bill, China would have been had the right to withhold from US companies the market access measures agreed in November.

Clearing these two major hurdles makes it more likely that China will be admitted to the WTO later this year – although there is still much to be done. China has still to reach agreements on WTO entry with Mexico, Ecuador, Guatemala and Switzerland. It also has yet to complete the binding schedules required by the WTO working party on China's accession. However, with the EU and US deals in the bag, the pace may pick up, and **BMI** still expects

China to be admitted to the WTO perhaps by end-year, or early 2001 at the latest.

Exports Are Booming...

One reason for the good overall growth performance in the first quarter was the strong recovery in merchandise exports, which jumped 39.1% y-o-y in the first quarter, to a huge US$51.72bn. Exports were lifted by a variety of factors including strong demand in the US (a key market for China's goods, accounting for around 20% of all exports). Exports to the US rose almost 33% y-o-y to US$10.5bn in the first quarter. Another factor was a sharp recovery in demand from key Asian markets, including Hong Kong (where China's exports were up 48% y-o-y in the first quarter), Japan (up 30.4%), South Korea (up 57%) and Taiwan (up 32.2%). In addition, export growth was boosted by the low base period; exports sagged in the first months of 1999, picking up strongly towards the end of the year. An opposite pattern is expected this year, with export and import growth rates likely to slow towards the end of the year, because of a higher base period.

The flip-side of the surge in exports is that imports rose even more rapidly, up 41% y-o-y in the first quarter, to US$46.5bn. China is heavily reliant on imported inputs for many key manufactured goods, such as electronics. In addition, inventories in some sectors are at last starting to run down. For example, crude oil imports reached their highest level since end-1993 in March (at 6.8mn tonnes), thanks to stronger industrial production combined with lower domestic inventories.

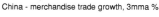

Exports have surged on the back of strong US and regional demand.

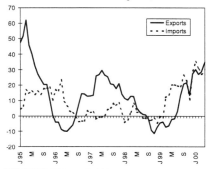

Exports Drive Growth
China - merchandise trade growth, 3mma %

Source: State Statistical Bureau.

	1993	1994	1995	1996	1997	1998	1999	2000f	2001f	2002f
BALANCE OF PAYMENTS (US$BN)										
Merchandise exports (fob)	75.66	102.56	128.11	151.08	182.67	183.53	194.90	220.00	250.00	275.00
Merchandise imports (fob)	-86.31	-95.27	-110.06	-131.54	-136.45	-136.91	-165.80	-190.00	-225.00	-250.00
Trade balance	-10.65	7.29	18.05	19.54	46.22	46.61	29.10	30.00	25.00	25.00
Current account balance	-11.61	6.91	1.62	7.24	29.72	29.32	16.02	15.04	8.02	7.20
Current account (% of GDP)	-1.94	1.28	0.23	0.88	3.29	3.04	1.58	1.39	0.69	0.62

f = BMI forecast; Sources: IMF; BMI.

Rising imports will erode the current account surplus.

Imports Will Squeeze Surplus
China - current account balance, US$bn

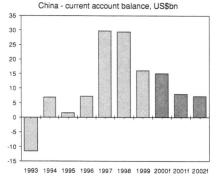

f = BMI forecast; Source: IMF/BMI.

But The Current-Account Is Set To Erode Further

For the time being, the balance of payments position is looking healthy. According to the latest figures from the State Administration of Foreign Exchange (SAFE), out in late May, despite a smaller current account surplus the capital account (which includes investment flows and debt) posted a US$7.6bn surplus in 1999, a marked turnaround compared with a deficit of US$6.3bn in 1998. Part of the improvement came from a crackdown by SAFE on illegal outflows of foreign exchange and unregistered borrowing. As a result, reserves picked up US$9.7bn by end 1999, to US$154.7bn, rising slightly further to US$156.8bn by the end of March.

However, there are worries over the longer term. Entry to the WTO will bring much lower tariffs and trade barriers over the next few years, boosting imports. In addition, stronger GDP growth and lower inventories are likely to lead to even stronger demand for imports from 2001, including imported inputs for export sectors given a new lease of life by WTO entry (such as textiles). Hence the merchandise trade surplus is likely to continue to run down gradually, resulting in an erosion of the current-account surplus. Eventually, the current-account surplus may tip into deficit, making it vital that China continues to attract large flows of long-term capital.

Foreign Direct Investment

FDI Approvals Are Up

Entry into the WTO should boost FDI inflows in some key sectors, although the implementation of opening will not be smooth.

WTO Entry Will Boost Inflows
China - foreign direct investment, US$mn

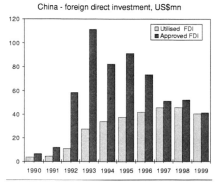

Source: China Statistical Yearbook.

Actual FDI fell by 11% to US$40.4bn in 1999. FDI inflows continued to fall steeply, dropping some 12% y-o-y in January-February, but a strong rise in March meant that actual FDI inflows averaged a more modest 2.7% y-o-y fall for the quarter. Yet approved FDI rebounded strongly, up 27% y-o-y in the first quarter, to US$11.08bn. FDI approvals are likely to rise still further now that a deal has been struck with the EU on WTO entry and the US has approved PNTR, making it more likely that China will be admitted to the world trade body by year-end (*see above*). Some commentators have predicted a massive surge in FDI approvals and inflows, suggesting annual inflows could reach as much as US$100bn, adding half a percentage point each year to GDP growth. However, while **BMI** has forecast a rise in FDI thanks to WTO entry, such a huge rise seems to be overplayed. Foreign firms are facing an extremely tough market in China, hampered by weak demand, slowing growth, an opaque legal and regulatory environment, and widespread problems with piracy.

The west of China lags far behind in attracting FDI. In 1998 close to 97% of all FDI went to the east coast and central regions. This year, the government is striving to boost investment, including FDI, into the less developed central and western regions of the country. To kick-start this process, some major infrastructure projects are planned, while the government is also offering tax holidays and other incentives. However, there is little that western officials have not already offered in a bid to try to tempt investors inland. Among the many problems hampering investment in the west are poor infrastructure, lower incomes, and distance from comparatively affluent eastern markets.

FOREIGN INVESTMENT (US$MN)									
	1993	1994	1995	1996	1997	1998	1999	2000f	2001f	2002f
FDI approvals	111.4	82.7	91.3	73.3	51.0	52.1	41.2	45.0	43.0	35.0
FDI inflows	27.5	33.8	37.5	41.7	45.3	45.6	40.4	39.0	41.0	39.0

f = BMI forecast; Source: China Statistical Yearbook; BMI.

Exports Lead Growth
China - merchandise trade, US$bn

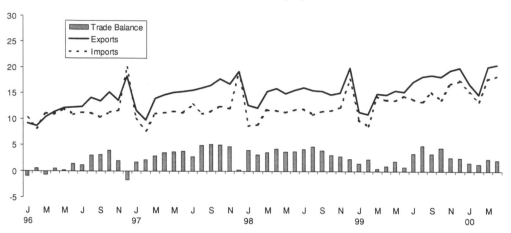

An End To Deflation?
China - consumer price inflation, % y-o-y

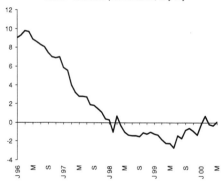

A Drag On Growth
China - GDP and consumer price inflation, % y-o-y

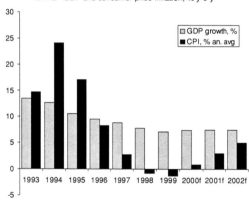

Pumping Growth
China - fixed asset investment growth, % y-o-y

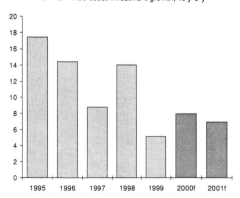

Boosted By Smuggling Crackdown
China - foreign exchange reserves minus gold, US$mn

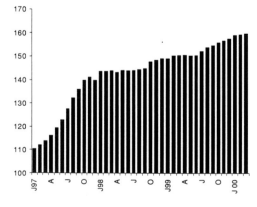

f = BMI forecast; Source: China Statistical Yearbook 1999; IMF; BMI.

Profile and Recent Developments

Characteristics Of The Economy

A Huge Domestic Market

The economic reforms of the 1980s and 1990s, combined with a massive influx of foreign capital, have helped to propel China into the ranks of the world's largest economies. In 1994-98, China recorded an impressive average GDP growth rate of 9.8% in real terms. At the same time, population growth has slowed steadily. As a result, average GDP per capita has more than tripled since 1990 in local currency terms, reaching CNY6,413 in 1998 (on an expenditure basis), up from only CNY1,601.6 in 1990. In the mid-1990s, GDP per capita jumped by around 25-35% per year for several years. However, this rate of growth has now slowed to single figures, in 1998-99 it was 7.4% on an annual average basis, as growth in domestic demand slowed. Although a sharp drop in inflation has smoothed the slowdown in growth in GDP per head in real terms, disposable incomes are being eroded as massive reform of the welfare system has resulted in rising unemployment and the cost of housing, education and healthcare has increased.

It is easy to forget the speed at which China has been catapulted into the global economy as both a massive market and a key player. The opening of the economy really began to accelerate in the early-1990s, when China started to attract huge inflows of foreign direct investment (FDI), initially focused primarily on producing low-tech manufactured exports. Driven by the expansion of foreign-funded enterprises and the rapid growth of the non-state sector, in the last 10 years China has become one of the world's largest exporters of a range of items such as toys, footwear, consumer electronics and, increasingly, more high-tech items. In dollar terms, exports were equivalent to 19% of GDP in 1998, up from less than 9% in 1985. The structure of exports has shifted dramatically: primary goods accounted for only 11.2% of exports in 1998, down from 50.6% in 1985, while manufactured goods rose to account for 88.8% of exports in 1998, from 49.4% in 1985. In addition, China itself has become a leading world market for western companies in a wide range of sectors, such as mobile phone equipment, aircraft, power generation equipment and computers.

Natural Resources

China has achieved this growth without a massive endowment of natural resources. According to the State Statistical Bureau (SSB), 33% of the land area is classified as mountainous, much of it in the west and north of the country, where conditions can also be very arid. Only 10% of China's total land area is cultivated (according to 1997 estimates). Hence, although land is used intensively and irrigation is extensive, China may be unable to keep pace with growing demand for foodstuffs such as meat and even cereals, and may become a major world importer of some agricultural and food products within the next 10-20 years.

China does have considerable reserves of oil and natural gas, both onshore and offshore, among the world's largest reserves of coal, and extensive deposits of many metals and minerals such as copper, iron ore and phosphates. With an eye to securing long-term supply of raw materials, efforts are being made to exploit new finds, many in remote inland regions, while Chinese firms are also seeking mining and energy concessions overseas. Finally, China's vast river networks have given it considerable potential as a producer of hydroelectric power, which the authorities are now seeking to exploit.

An Industrial Economy

Unlike many middle- to low-income emerging markets, China's economy is dominated by the secondary sector (manufacturing, construction, mining and energy), partly as a legacy of several decades of central planning, which favoured the development of heavy state-controlled industry. By 1998, the secondary sector accounted for 48.7% of nominal GDP. Light export-oriented manufacturing industries have grown particularly rapidly in the 1990s, eroding the traditional domination of heavy industries such as mining and steel. The coastal areas have seen particularly fast growth in such industries, while heavy industry (including coal mining, oil and steel production) is concentrated more in the north. By comparison, the share of the primary sector (agriculture, forestry and fishing) in total output declined steadily throughout the 1990s, dropping from 24.5% of nominal GDP in 1992, to 18.4% of GDP by 1998. The primary sector still accounts for a disproportionate share of employment (49.8% of total employment in 1997, compared with 23.5% in the secondary sector and 26.7% in the tertiary sector). This is beginning to change as a result of rapid urbanisation and increasing labour mobility and the proportion of the labour force engaged in primary industry is exaggerated by the continuance of the household registration system that classifies as rural all those not actually legally resident and employed in towns. Millions of people defined as rural labourers have migrated to towns and cities in search of informal work. During the 1990s, the share of the tertiary (services) sector remained fairly steady at around 31-33% of nominal GDP. Its share in both output and employment is likely to increase, as the government is encouraging the formation of small-scale service enterprises in a bid to create jobs, while continued steady liberalisation will give a boost to key service industries such as retail, insurance and banking.

Looking at the expenditure breakdown of GDP is problematic for China, as the official data give only the net contribution of exports and imports of goods and services. Bearing this caveat in mind, SSB data show that private consumption is the largest component of GDP, accounting for 46.2% of the total in 1998; government consumption for 11.9%. This is actually fairly low, for both developing and developed countries. China is notable for the large share of investment (calculated as fixed assets plus stocks), which typically accounts for just under 40% of GDP; in 1998 it accounted for 38.1% of GDP, of which stocks accounted for 2.3%. Looking at the external sector, exports are often referred to as one of the 'engines' of growth in China. The SSB does not provide a breakdown of the contribution of exports and imports of goods and services in national accounts terms, stating only that the net contribution of foreign trade to GDP in 1998 was 3.8%. According to World Bank data, exports and imports of goods and services (in national accounts terms) tend to each account for around 20-25% of GDP – about twice the level of the USA, but well below the levels seen in more open trading economies such as Malaysia. Hence, whilst export-oriented industries have been growing very fast in recent years, China remains only a moderately open economy, in which the outlook for domestic markets also remains critical.

The Declining Role Of The State Sector

Another issue in China is the role of the state-owned sector. As of 1998, China still had 64,700 industrial enterprises which were wholly state-owned or majority state-owned (as well as many other non-industrial ones). However, there has been a quite profound shift in the last decade or so, in which the share of the non-state sector in output has rapidly overtaken that of the state-owned sector. In 1998, state-owned enterprises (SOEs) accounted for only 28.2.% of the gross output value of industry, down from close to 65% in 1985. The share of the collective owned sector, meanwhile, rose modestly from 32.1% in 1985, to 38.4% in 1998, while the private sector, including the foreign-funded sector, expanded to fill the gap. The SOE sector still accounted for 20% of total urban employment in 1997, down only slightly from 18% in 1985. But the large-scale closures and mergers of 1998 brought this figure down to 13.2% in 1998. The SOE sector also still takes the bulk of all loans, and (including non-industrial SOEs) accounted for 54.1% of all investment in 1998 (down from 66.1% in 1985). Thus in 1998, SOEs received the majority of capital and accounted for more than half of all investment, but managed to produce less than one-third of industrial output. Another radical shift can be seen in the domestic trade sector: SOEs accounted for 28.8% of all domestic sales of consumer goods in 1995, but by 1998 this had dropped to 20.7%. However, large SOEs remain dominant in a number of sectors, particularly capital-intensive heavy industries.

State Enterprise Reforms, And A New Look At The Private Sector

The SOE sector faces problems including massive oversupply in some sectors, poor products, outdated technology and weak management. In a major policy shift, the authorities have recognised that the problems of many SOEs can only be solved by radical restructuring, and now accept that SOEs will not play a dominant role in some sectors of the economy – although a central role for the SOE sector is still enshrined in the constitution, and SOEs are expected to dominate 'national interest' sectors such as energy. In keeping with this new stance, a key priority announced at the 15th Party Congress in September 1997, was the reform of the SOE sector within three years. The 1997 announcement heralded a wave of selling, in which many thousands of small SOEs were merged, sold or closed. The authorities focused on the idea of 'letting go of the small' while developing the largest 500-1,000 SOEs into key global players. The resulting chaotic sell-off of smaller SOEs, which resulted in heavy job losses and asset stripping, alarmed Beijing, which began to place greater emphasis on restructuring and improved management at remaining SOEs. Now in the third and final year of this reform programme, at the March 2000 NPC conference Zhu Rongji claimed that the policy has already helped to return to profit SOEs in some sectors, such as textiles. However, progress in setting up a welfare system – which will allow much of the burden of pensions, healthcare and other 'social' costs to be removed from the SOEs – has been sluggish.

At the same time, there seems to be a growing realisation that increased competition from the private sector could both force restructuring of the SOEs and also provide jobs. Hence a number of steps have been taken to level the playing field for the private sector, including an amendment to the constitution in March 1999 recognising the role of private enterprise, as well as efforts to improve private sector access to capital. Most recently, in early 2000, the minister of the State Planning and Development Commission (SPDC), Zeng Peiyan, announced that all discriminatory regulations in the areas of taxation, land-use, business start-ups, import and export, would be removed, and that private firms would be given equal opportunity to list on the stock market (*see Industrial Policy*). However, progress in reforming the SOEs and levelling the playing field for private enterprise will be very patchy.

Economic Activity

The Government Tries Fiscal Stimulus

The reform period in China has been characterised by 'boom' periods of high growth and high inflation, followed by sharp, policy-induced downswings of one to two years of slower growth. By 1997, it seemed that China had achieved a 'soft landing', as credit tightening helped to slow GDP growth from 14.2% in 1992, to 9.6% in 1996 and 8.8% in 1997. However, when real GDP growth slid to 7.2% y-o-y in Q1 98, the authorities began to worry that the slowdown had overshot. Hence in March 1998, the government announced a fiscal stimulus package aimed at lifting growth in 1998-2000. Initially, the government pledged to spend US$750bn on infrastructure over three years. Subsequent official spending targets ranged as high as US$1.3trn, but these employed a broad definition of "infrastructure" that included a range of wide fixed asset investment. Whatever the final figure, it was clear that China began a massive pump-priming exercise in H2 98 that continued through 1999. To raise funds, the government issued CNY100bn (US$12bn) in 10-year bonds in 1998 with a further CNY60bn in 1999, and called on the state banks to extend another CNY100bn in lending to state projects. Spending was targeted on projects ranging from road and rail expansion, to dams, grain storage and telecommunications. The policy is to be continued this year, funded by a further CNY100bn in special infrastructure bonds.

Weak Domestic Demand Holds Down Growth

However, there are signs that gains from the massive pump-priming effort are slacking. Despite the surge in state spending, GDP growth slackened to 7.8% in 1998 and 7.1% in 1999. In 1999 real fixed investment growth dipped to 5.2% y-o-y, down from 14.1% in 1998. Private and collective investment remained sluggish, because of slack domestic demand. There is some evidence for a recovery in private consumption in 1999. Nominal retail sales of consumer goods rose by 6.8% y-o-y in 1999, 10.1% in real terms, after a sluggish 5.9% growth in private consumption expenditure in 1998. But these data are somewhat surprising in view of the anecdotal accounts of weak consumption and there are fears that this recovery may not be sustained. Continued deflation (partly a result of massive oversupply in some sectors) resulted in consumers delaying purchases, waiting for further price reductions. The signing in late 1999 of a deal with the USA was a further factor; some consumers choose to delay purchases of big-ticket items such as cars, expecting slashed import tariffs to bring lower costs and greater consumer choice within the next year or so.

At the same time, there was a further rise in unemployment (although this was not reflected in the official figures), while efforts to reform the housing, medical and education systems – ending decades of free provision by the state – caused consumers to save rather than spend. Personal savings reached a massive CNY6trn (US$724.8bn) at the end of January 2000, equivalent to 70% of GDP. Repeated interest rate cuts and the imposition from November 1, 1999 of a 20% tax on interest earned from savings have not yet managed to ignite spending. Evidence of this weak consumer demand could be seen in falling prices – retail prices fell by an average 2.6% y-o-y in 1998 and a further 2.9% in 1999 – while the broader measure of consumer prices fell by an annual average of 0.8% y-o-y in 1998 and by 1.3% in 1999.

Supply Factors – Sluggish Industrial Production

In 1993-97, GDP growth was led by the industrial sector (including manufacturing, construction, mining and energy). Excluding construction, industry rose by an average 15.2% y-o-y, boosted by large foreign investment inflows, and a jump in export-oriented manufacturing along China's coastal 'special economic zones'. The services sector also expanded rapidly, particularly transport and telecommunications. Industrial output continued to lead growth in 1998-99, although the overall growth rates slowed. Although heavy fixed investment spending boosted growth in industrial output of such items as cement and steel in the last few months of 1998 and through 1999, this was offset by the impact of weak consumer demand. However, in H2 99, stronger demand from recovering Asian markets and a recovery in domestic consumption helped to lift growth in the export-oriented manufacturing sector. Further, strong state investment in areas such as transport and telecommunications may have been behind the pick-up in the services sector through 1999. Industrial value-added grew by 8.5%, close to the 8.9% growth of 1998.

Data Problems

The conventional wisdom among the major multilateral institutions is that annual GDP growth in China is overstated by between one and two percentage points. The SSB has admitted that there is still a tendency for provincial bodies to pad out their data – combining provincial GDP data typically give China an overall growth rate several percentage points higher than the official growth rate. The SSB undertakes its own sampling to try to get a clearer picture, but the size of the task suggests that data are still suspect. In recognition of the problem, at the March 2000 NPC meeting Zhu Rongji broke with tradition, and did not issue an official growth forecast for the year. The deflators used to convert nominal industrial output and the components of GDP into real terms may be inaccurate, overstating the measured rates of growth. Certainly the real rates of industrial output growth and GDP are released with surprising speed, a speed which casts further doubt on their veracity.

3 Key Economic Sectors

Introduction

Greater Competition Will Force Shakeout

With a deal agreed with the EU, another obstacle to China's entry to the WTO has been removed. Vested interests can be expected to resist some market opening measures, and progress is unlikely to be smooth. Hence the full benefits of market opening may not be felt for some time. However, Chinese firms in many sectors will be exposed to much greater foreign competition within the next one to two years. The review below looks at three key areas where massive change is expected following WTO entry. For computing, Chinese firms currently dominate the domestic market, but WTO entry will bring lower tariffs on imported products, while technological changes are reducing barriers between computing, telecoms and the internet. The big Chinese players are seeking to move away from being mere hardware producers, in a bid to become integrated computing and communications firms. A related sector, the internet, will also undergo massive changes. Again, major Chinese players are currently the key portals, but WTO entry will gradually permit increased foreign participation in both service and content provision. Firms – both Chinese and foreign – are seeking new ways to encourage internet use in China, including the use of "set top" boxes and Wireless Access Protocol (WAP) mobile phones.

Domestic players in agriculture, are in a much weaker position. Officials fear that, thanks to lower tariffs and cheap international prices, China is set to become the world's largest importer of many commodities, with grave implications for employment and incomes in rural areas. Even here, however, there are opportunities for foreign investors, as China seeks to upgrade farming techniques, transport and refrigeration, and food processing.

The full benefits of market opening following WTO entry may not be felt for some time. However, Chinese firms in many sectors will be exposed to much greater foreign competition within the next one to two years.

Computers

Chinese PC Manufacturers Are Shaping Up

China's computing industry (PCs, peripherals, IT and software) was worth CNY172bn (US$20.7bn) in sales in 1999 (of which hardware accounted for close to 76%). According to some official estimates, by 2002, annual PC sales could reach 10.2mn units, making China the third largest market after Japan and the USA. Currently, the hardware market is dominated by local firms, that have benefited from good connections to government (a massive market comes from ministries and departments that are upgrading their hardware or investing in computers for the first time), and the ability to market and provide after-sales service. In 1999 the top three places in terms of hardware sales were held by local firms **Legend Holdings**, **Founder** and **Great Wall**, led by the state-owned **Legend Holdings.**

However, Chinese firms will be in for a tough time following China's entry into the WTO. Tariffs on computers are set to drop from 13% to zero within five years of WTO entry. Further, restrictions on foreign retail and distribution will be removed. Major international players such as **IBM**, **Compaq**, **Hewlett-Packard** and **Dell** are gearing up to expand into consumer markets and to target e-commerce through software and services. To counter this, the government has already drawn up a range of incentives, such as tax rebates, to assist both hardware and software producers.

The top companies are also restructuring. For example, in April it was announced that Legend would split into two. **Legend Computer Systems** will concentrate on hardware, but will aim to move into wireless devices, as well as into internet services and portals. Meanwhile, **Legend Digital China** will develop software and services for e-commerce. Legend has placed internet access and services - rather than simply hardware development – at the heart of its new strategy. For example, Legend has already begun producing set-top boxes that enable internet access through TVs – targeting the millions of Chinese who do not own a computer. Legend is also working with **Motorola** to produce palmtops with wireless access to the internet. A number of other key Chinese PC makers, such as **Founder Holdings**, **Great Wall**, **Star** and **HiSense** plan to follow a similar route.

The Internet

Official Uncertainty Has Delayed Listings

Last quarter's report discussed the government's ambivalent attitude to the internet. There are concerns that foreign players will introduce "unsuitable" content, and that they will also out-compete local players in both content and service provision. A raft of new rules on content was introduced in January, while new rules in encryption were also introduced. This official uncertainty was also seen when a number of China's top portals sought listings on the US stock markets this year. Approval is needed from the Ministry of Information Industry (MII), which is known to favour state control over internet companies, as well as the China Securities Regulatory Commission (CSRC). (Content providers also need approval from the State Council, China's cabinet). MII in particular dragged its feet, alarmed at the idea that Chinese content-providers could raise funds overseas. Eventually, **Sina.com**, China's most popular portal, listed on the NASDAQ exchange on April 13 - although technology stocks had already begun to plummet, Sina managed to raise close to US$70mn. However, to win permission to list, Sina had to spin off its mainland portal into a separate holding firm, listing its non-mainland sites (targeted at overseas Chinese). This method, in which mainland assets are de-linked from listing units, is expected to be dissolved once China joins the WTO, which permits foreign investment in up to 49% of internet content and service providers.

Continued regulatory problems have delayed overseas listings by several key internet firms.

INTERNET & TELECOMMUNICATIONS (MN, END-YEAR)			
	1997	1998	1999e	2000f
Mobile subscribers	15	25	40	70
Internet users	0.4	1.5	7.5	15.0

e/f = BMI estimate/forecast; Source: State Information Centre/BMI.

Big Hopes For WAP And Cable

Rapid growth in interactive services provided via WAP and Cable TV is expected. More Chinese currently have access to mobile phones and Cable TV than to PCs.

In March, MII gave permission to **China Mobile Communication Group** (the mobile units of the main state telecom firm, China Telecom) and **China Unicom**, permission to trial WAP services in six major cities (Beijing, Tianjin, Shanghai, Hangzhou, Guangzhou and Shenzhen). The mobile market is already much bigger than the internet market (with some 40mn mobile users by end-1999, a figure which some expect to more than double by end-2000), compared with around 8-9mn internet users. The relatively cheap price of a WAP phone compared with a PC may mean that WAP phones become the main method of accessing the internet for many Chinese. The deputy director of the MII has estimated that there will be 65mn internet subscribers by 2002, of whom 30mn will access the internet via WAP phones, with the remainder accessing via either PCs or set-top boxes.

Tempted by such estimates, both foreign and Chinese firms are leaping into the fray. For example, Finland's **Nokia** signed an agreement in March with China portal **Sohu.com** to provide WAP services covering stock markets, news and entertainment. **Motorola** has signed an agreement with business-to-business site **Alibaba.com** to provide connections to Alibaba's on-line trading site through WAP. **Netease**, another major China portal, has already developed WAP services. It is still early days, however. Question marks over WAP range from new technology standards, the cost of WAP phones, and the type of services and information being developed for them.

However, the introduction of WAP phones is still in the early stages, while Cable TV networks will need massive investment to make them data-compatible.

The integration of internet services with cable TV is another exciting area. There are some 90mn cable subscribers in China – more than double the current number of mobile users (although mobile subscribers are growing rapidly). Some 50% of all urban residents are estimated to have access to cable TV, compared with only around 20% who have a PC. The problem is that only around 10% of China's cable network is estimated to be capable of carrying two-way data, allowing people to 'log on' through special TV "sets top" devices to access the internet, home shopping and other services. In a recent report on the sector **Indosuez WI Carr** estimated that upgrading China's cable network would require investment close to US$50bn. One way around the problem is for people to use set-top boxes to send messages out via normal telephone land-lines, while receiving data back via cable - but this is currently regarded as "convergence" between sectors, and is banned by the government. Upgrading is made still more problematic as China currently has more than 1,000 cable TV operators across the country. Their systems will need to be linked up and made compatible. Several regions have already started, but it will be a time-consuming process.

Agriculture

Big Changes Lie Ahead

All is not well in China's farming sector. Massive environmental problems, such as acute shortages of water, soil erosion, frequent flooding and overuse of pesticides, cause problems in many areas. Oversupply affects sectors such as wheat, corn, rice, sugar and cotton. Things are expected to get much worse following WTO entry. According to the US Chamber of Commerce in China, average tariffs for agricultural products are to be cut to 17% from 21.2% following WTO entry, with the average tariff for US priority products falling to 14.5%, and further cuts to follow. According to the State Council, China could overtake Japan as the world's largest importer of agricultural produce by 2010, and WTO entry could increase agricultural imports by US$1bn a year.

Some agricultural sectors have already been affected. In late March, China removed import restrictions on a range of US agricultural products, including wheat from the US northwest, and meat, and citrus fruit from a number of states. China is currently the world's third largest grower of citrus fruits, after the US and Brazil. But the sector is gearing up for a drastic increase in foreign competition, now that the restrictions have been removed.

Officials fear that China's agricultural sector will have a tough time competing with a flood of cheap foreign imports. For one thing, many Chinese farms are small scale, with limited use of new techniques. The State Council fears that some 9.6mn farmers may loose their jobs as a result of increased competition following WTO entry (although it was not clear over what time period they expected the job losses to table place). New jobs will be hard to find; in rural areas, so-called township and village enterprises, which boomed through the 1980s and much of the 1990s, are now being hit by massive oversupply of many of the products they churn out (such as consumer electronics). Officials estimate that some 70mn people have already left rural areas to try to find work elsewhere, but other estimates put this so-called "floating population" as high as 120mn. Millions are scraping a living in low-wage jobs such as construction in the east-coast cities, while millions more have been unable to find permanent work.

The agriculture sector gets relatively little attention, but it will still employs close to half of the workforce. Yet WTO entry will bring real problems for the sector – as well as new opportunities for foreign exporters and investors.

It is not all gloom however. Officials are hoping that they can attract increased foreign investment into some agricultural sectors, to upgrade technology and improve efficiency. They are particularly interested in labour-intensive sectors such as fruit and vegetables that can use China's ready supply of cheap labour. Other areas where greater investment will be sought include agro-processing, packaging, storage and transport.

AGRICULTURAL OUTPUT ('000 TONNES)				
	1994	1995	1996	1997	1998
Rice	175,930	185,230	195,103	200,735	198,713
Wheat	9,930	102,210	110,569	123,289	109,726
Sugarcane	60,927	65,417	66,876	78,897	83,438

Source: State Statistical Bureau.

Profile and Recent Developments

Introduction

Industry Structure: A Continued Role For SOEs

The state-owned enterprise (SOE) sector dominates China's industrial output. As noted, SOEs accounted for 54.1% of total fixed investment in 1998, compared with 14.7% for collectives, 6.8% for enterprises which have issued shares, known as joint-stock enterprises (which may be part state-owned, as are many collectives) and 5.8% for FIEs. The smaller collective and private sector (including FIEs) is typically more vibrant, and plays a large role in higher growth non-traditional sectors such as consumer electronics and IT. As a result, despite its dominant share in fixed investment, SOEs' share of industrial value-added was only 32.8% in 1999, while collectives' share was 9.8% and FIEs' was more, at 11.9%.

These figures highlight the relative inefficiency of the SOE sector, which is burdened by outdated technology, overstaffing and huge welfare-related costs. In early 1998, the government announced a three-year plan of far-reaching SOE reform, including the sell-off, merger or even closure of smaller loss-making SOEs, and the restructuring of larger ones. In 1999, the constitution was changed to recognise the importance of the private sector, and in early 2000 the end of discriminatory measures against the private sector was announced. However, SOEs will remain dominant players in many key sectors throughout the forecast period. In the short term, continued heavy government spending on fixed investment and infrastructure has artificially boosted SOE investment and industrial output. In addition, for the next few years at least the state sector will continue to benefit disproportionately from access to state-directed credit, access to the domestic and international capital markets, and government subsidies and protectionist policies. From 2002 onwards banking reforms required by WTO membership are likely to start levelling the playing field for the non-state sector. However, the government remains committed to a strong role for SOEs. It has started trying to 'pick winners' – consolidating the largest 500-1,000 SOEs through mergers, and nurturing them through a range of measures – in order to create globally competitive companies that will also take dominant shares in some key domestic markets.

Manufacturing And Services Are The Key Sectors

The share in total GDP of the primary sector – agriculture, forestry and fishing – has been steadily declining throughout the 1990s, dropping from 24.5% of nominal GDP in 1991, to 18.4% of GDP by 1998. Secondary industry (manufacturing, construction, mining and energy), on the other hand, has grown much more rapidly; and as a result, it accounted for 48.7% of nominal GDP in 1998 compared with 42.1% in 1991. This trend is likely to accelerate following WTO accession, which will cause severe disruption for China's protected agricultural sector.

Within industry, the bias towards heavy industry remains, although light industry has grown rapidly, and has come to dominate exports. China is now both a key market and important exporter of a range of consumer goods, such as TVs, refrigerators, PCs and telephone equipment. The more mature of the light industries, such as textiles, have lost some of their price competitiveness, thanks to falling regional prices, the strength of the renminbi, and outdated technology. The share of the services sector in GDP, which remained fairly steady through the 1990s at around 31-33% of nominal GDP, is likely to rise over the next few years. The government will encourage small-scale service industries through tax incentives, easier licensing and financial support, in the hope that the sector will generate an increasing share of employment. Consumer spending is expected to shift towards services and more value-added products, away from basic consumer goods. WTO accession will also open many services to foreign investment for the first time, giving the sector a further boost.

Industry And Manufacturing

Textiles And Garments – Still Among The Top Exports

Textiles and garments are among China's top exports, but the sector was hit hard by the Asian crisis, as Chinese firms were forced to cut prices to maintain sales to recession-hit regional markets. According to revised customs data, 1999 saw a modest recovery, with textile and garment exports up 2% y-o-y in 1999, to US$41.27bn, 21% of total exports for the year. Textile exports rose US$11.7bn during the first 11 months of 1999, up 11.7%, although garment exports continued to sag, dipping 0.8% y-o-y to US$27.1bn during the first 11 months. Drastic restructuring of the sector – which is dominated by outdated SOEs – also continued. According to the State Textile Bureau some 9.1mn spindles were taken out of commission in 1999, and 1.16mn workers were laid off. Partly as a result of these cutbacks, and boosted by stronger demand from Asia in H2 99 (and reduced Asian competition as other regional currencies recovered against the renminbi), China's textile industry as a whole made a modest profit in 1999, ending six consecutive years of losses. The outlook for the textile sector will improve considerably when China joins the WTO, as quotas to key markets such as the USA will be phased out.

Oil Refining Remains A Difficult Market

According to the SSB, in 1999 160mn tonnes of crude oil were processed, down 0.1% on 1998. Demand for refined oil products began to pick up in H2 99, boosted by stronger domestic demand, the continued crackdown on smuggling, and the closure of a number of small refineries. These factors helped to offset the rise in the cost of inputs (boosted by surging world oil prices). Further consolidation of the refining industry is planned for this year; another 30 small refineries (each processing less than 1mn tonnes of crude a year) are to be closed, following the closure of 70 small refineries in 1999. Industry analysts expect the remaining refineries to boost throughput to around 183mn tonnes in 2000 – still well below total processing capacity of 250-260mn tonnes.

In 2000 China's two main state-owned energy exploration, production and refining companies, **China National Petroleum Corporation** (CNPC)**,** and **China National Petrochemical Corp** (known as **Sinopec**), will continue restructuring in order to face increased competition once China joins the WTO. China currently protects crude output with high domestic prices and imposes import restrictions on many oil products. CNPC is the main exploration and production company, while Sinopec is the main refiner, although the two were restructured in 1998 to create two huge vertically integrated companies. CNPC was given responsibility for both upstream and down-stream activities in the north and west of the country, the location of China's largest onshore oil and gas reserves; hence CNPC still controls around 67% of national crude production. Sinopec was given the south and east. Staff and cost-cutting measures are being used to streamline the two firms. Early in 2000, **PetroChina**, a unit of CNPC raised US$3.1bn in a lisiting on the New York stock exchange. The offer, scaled back from a planned US$10bn, was received with some reluctance, both because market conditions were not favourable and because of investor doubts and plans by Sinopec to list later in the year may have been derailed.

Iron And Steel – Further Consolidation

According to the State Statistical Bureau, steel output rose by 6.2% in 1999 to 124.4mn tonnes. Price floors imposed since H2 98 helped to boost prices, while massive state investment also increased demand for steel and steel products. However, the iron and steel sector remains beset by over-capacity and efficiency problems, made worse by heightened competition from other Asian countries. Hence the State Economic and Trade Commission intends to cap output at around 110mn tonnes in 2000, hoping to reduce inventories. The restructuring of the sector begun in 1998 – including cuts in the workforce and the replacement of open-hearth furnaces and rolling equipment – is to continue. Some 2,500 smelters and mills with annual capacity of less than 100,000 tonnes will be closed in 2000.

The government has also indicated that it would like to see the emergence of a handful of major, internationally competitive steel producers within the next few years. Accordingly, the construc-tion of new steel smelters has been banned, and stronger firms have been encouraged to take over loss-making ones. For example, **Wuhan Iron and Steel**, the third most profitable steel maker in 1997, took over the loss-making **Xiangfan Iron and Steel** in October 1998. Then in late 1998 the largest iron and steel maker, **Baoshan Iron and Steel**, merged with two state-owned firms, **Shanghai Metallurgical Holding** and **Meishan Co**, to form **Shanghai Baosteel Group**, with a production capacity of 20mn tonnes a year. At the time of the merger, analysts suggested that Baoshan had only agreed to the merger in exchange for permission to seek a stock-market listing, to meet its capital needs for technical upgrading. Shanghai Baosteel is indeed planning to seek a US listing this year for a unit called **Baoshan Iron and Steel**, and may also list domestic A-shares.

The companies expected to survive as key players are Shanghai Baosteel and Wuhan as well as **Anshan Iron and Steel**, **Capital Groups Iron and Steel** and **Handan Iron and Steel**.

Electronics

High-End Electronics Are Increasingly Important To China

The electrical appliance sector took off in China when rising incomes in the early 1990s prompted a wave of spending on such goods as refrigerators and TVs. A multitude of township and village enterprises (TVEs) sprang up to meet the demand. As a result of this proliferation of domestic producers, as well as considerable foreign investment in some areas, China is now one of the world's largest producers and exporters of a range of consumer electronics. According to the Ministry of Foreign Trade and Economic Cooperation (MOFTEC), China now leads the world in output of a range of goods including colour TVs, stereos and telephones, while sales of PCs and mobile phones are rising sharply. Continued foreign interest and official encouragement suggest that electronics will remain among the fastest growing industrial sectors throughout the forecast period. A shift has already begun to more high-tech items (such as computers and IT) and away from basic household electrical appliances, where there is now considerable excess capacity. According to MOFTEC, information technology exports were worth US$39bn in 1999, half of all machinery and electronics exports, and 20.6% of total exports, up from 14.7% of total exports in 1998. However, despite rapid growth in sectors such as computers, China has yet to move far up the value-added chain, and remains reliant on imports for many complex inputs. For example, in 1999 China's imports of integrated circuits totalled US$7.5bn, compared with exports of US$1.9bn.

Electrical Appliances Hit By Excess Capacity

Following heavy investment in the 1990s, it is estimated that that around two-thirds of home appliances are now in oversupply, and price wars have driven many smaller producers into the red. Large home appliance groups such as **Guangdong Kelon Electrical Holdings**, **Haier Group**, and **Little Swan** are expected to retain their market lead, but considerable consolidation will reduce the overall number of appliance groups substantially. The larger firms are already positioning themselves to gain from this shakeout. For example, in October 1998, Kelon joined forces with another major refrigerator producer, **Huabao**, boosting annual capacity to more than 3mn units. In a bid to build market share, some are even moving overseas; for example, in early 2000 Haier was building a US$30mn plant in the USA. In addition to these key domestic players, some big foreign corporations have entered the market, setting up local production facilities. For example, a US$383mn joint venture between **Samsung** and **Tianjin Electronic Corporation** began production of colour TV tubes in late 1998. Samsung is also a key player in the refrigerator market, while **Hitachi** is one of the market leaders in air-conditioning. However, foreign entry into TV production has been limited since 1996.

In the short term, the anti-smuggling drive begun in Q4 98 has stemmed price falls for some appliances. Over the medium term, however, there has been considerable debate over whether China's market for basic home appliances has now matured (suggesting weak prices in the longer term). Successful firms will have to hunt out niches to lift sales. Rural areas where penetration is still far from complete are likely to be the new prime growth market for electrical goods, such as TVs, refrigerators, washing machines, microwave ovens and electric rice cookers. Product penetration is still often lower in rural areas, and appliance use will be encouraged by reductions in rural electricity prices and an expansion of the rural grid network. In higher income urban areas on the other hand, there is likely to be a rise in demand for higher quality "replacement" products, including washer-dryers, computers, environmentally friendly refrigerators, and wide-screen TVs (in 1999 production of TVs with a screen size of more than 25 inches accounted for more than half of total output for the first time). A rise in relatively new purchases such as dishwashers is also expected. In December 1998, Little Swan and Italy's **Merloni Corp** formed a US$30mn joint venture, **Wuxi Little Swan Corp**, to produce dishwashers – China's first domestic dishwasher manufacturer. Eventual annual production capacity was targeted at 800,000 units, which would make it one of Asia's largest dishwasher manufacturers.

Information Technology – Still Growing

Sales for the entire computing industry (PCs, peripherals, IT and software) rose by 16.2% y-o-y in 1999, to CNY172bn (US$20.7bn). Of this, hardware jumped by 13% y-o-y to CNY130bn. According to some official estimates, by 2002, annual PC sales could reach 10.2mn units, making China the third largest market after Japan and the USA. Chinese manufacturers have tended to outstrip foreign brands and imports in many areas. In 1999, the top three places in terms of hardware sales were held by local firms **Legend Holdings, Founder** and **Great Wall**. The state-owned **Legend Holdings** is now China's dominant PC maker. Legend has led a massive price war, overtaking **IBM** of the USA as local market leader in 1997. Legend has benefited as some of China's huge ministries have computerised their operations; around 25% of Legend's sales are government contracts. After WTO accession, foreign companies will benefit from being able to set up their own marketing and after-sales services, which may help them increase market share.

Sales of software and information services rose by 27.5% y-o-y in 1999, to CNY41.4bn. The State Information Centre (SIC) estimates that China now has 2,000 software companies, employing around 100,000 software developers. The Ministry of Information Industry (MII) is keen to support local software manufacturers through the provision of loans and incentives, while foreign companies will also continue to expand local development facilities. For example, **Microsoft** of the USA will invest US$80mn over six years in a research lab in Beijing, only its second such lab outside of the USA (the other is in the UK). The government has also introduced tax breaks for high-tech firms; in a package unveiled in late 1999, software producers will receive VAT rebates (reducing the level of VAT from 17% to 6%), while software distributors will pay even lower rates, and firms that transfer technology will be VAT-exempt. However, piracy is still a massive problem, and will continue to hold back growth in the software industry. The China Software Alliance estimates that for popular products pirated versions outnumber legitimate ones by three to one. WTO entry will provide a further challenge; lower tariffs and reduced barriers to entry by foreign firms will narrow the price gap between domestic and foreign brands, suggesting Chinese firms will have to concentrate on ensuring high quality marketing, services and development of new products if they are to retain their market share.

BMI expects that there will be significant opportunities for foreign firms providing new technological solutions for communications and other business problems. For example, the French company **Schlumberger** provides more than 50% of the "smart cards" used in banking and other areas in China; in November 1998 the company won a contract from **Nanjing Commercial Bank** to supply another 500,000 cards. Another growth area will be cheaper alternatives to PCs, including so-called 'set top boxes' that allow internet access; **Microsoft** launched its Venus product to enable internet access via TVs in 1999, capitalising on the massive TV-owning market in China, which still dwarfs PC ownership.

Agriculture And Food Processing

Major Liberalisation Is On The Cards

China is a major producer of cereals, including rice and wheat and exporter of maize. China has experienced several years of bumper harvests for some key crops such as grain and cotton and this has reduced the need to import grain to supply the eastern seaboard. The grain storage and distribution system is undergoing reform, but is still highly inefficient. According to the SSB, grain output fell slightly to 508mn tonnes in 1999. China's cotton output dropped almost 15% y-o-y to 3.83mn tonnes in 1999 as prices fell following the scrapping of protected state pricing, a move intended to reduce the massive cotton reserves. Other key crops include oil-bearing crops, and some industrial raw materials, such as sugarcane and rubber.

Domestic prices for most key commodities have been protected behind fairly high tariffs, quotas and other non-tariff barriers for years. This will change following WTO accession. For example, the quota for wheat imports will jump immediately to over 7mn tonnes a year, from less than 2mn tonnes currently, and tariffs on a portion of the new quota will be cut steeply (*see Foreign Trade Policy*). Increased competition from imports and the resulting downwards pressure on commodity prices has significant implications for rural livelihoods. The Communist Party's Central Committee plenum, held in October 1998, concentrated on rural development issues, acknowledging that rural incomes lagged behind the rest of the country. The plenum approved plans to extend household land use rights – granted in 1978 – for another 30 years. Yet the government has also already started to dismantle state procurement and pricing systems, as with cotton, when the guideline price of cotton was moved down in 1998, and textile companies were permitted to buy direct from farmers, ending the state-owned cotton supply and marketing cooperatives. However, this liberalisation may be watered down in order to protect farmers' incomes, if prices fall too steeply following WTO entry.

Changing Food Trends

Rising incomes are likely to alter food consumption patterns. Typically, as incomes rise, demand for items such as meat increases, while among the higher income bracket, greater demand develops for package and convenience foods. The International Food Policy Research Institute estimated recently that meat demand in China would jump to an annual 85mn tonnes by 2020, up from only 38mn tonnes in 1993. At the same time, China's relatively small area of usable agricultural land is being rapidly eroded and diverted to other uses. According to the *China News Service*, China lost a net 135,000ha in 1997, and a further net 200,000ha in 1998. This erosion of arable land will continue, despite a likely tightening of policy on land use, as farmland is eaten up by the building of roads and factories. As a result, there are 'doomsday scenarios' in which China becomes a net importer of cereals on a scale sufficient to affect world prices. However, the government is seeking to encourage more efficient production; future trends include the probable extension of longer land-use rights, as well as greater use of high quality seeds, improved harvesting and storage facilities, and increased mechanisation. The latter is already resulting in demand for farm machinery including large tractors, which at present China has little capacity to produce, offering opportunities to foreign investors.

Food Processing: A Priority Sector

Another area where foreign investment is likely to be encouraged is food processing. According to the UK Department of Trade and Industry, China currently only processes around 20% of its food, compared with a typical figure of around 80% for a developed country. Accordingly, the 1996-2000 Five Year Plan has targeted the development of the food processing sector, focusing on raw materials processing, convenience foods, processed foods for export and soft drinks. FIEs already in China include **Coca-Cola** and **Swire Beverages**, which together opened a US$35mn extension to the **Swire Guangdong Coca-Cola** bottling plant in late 1998.

Mining

Coal Output Has Fallen

Coal is China's primary energy source, accounting for around 75% of electricity production (although this has fallen from around 97% in the 1950s), and according to World Bank estimates, in 1995, China accounted for one in every three tonnes of coal burnt in the world. However, coal output has been static or falling throughout the 1990s. The SSB coal output in 1999, at 1.045bn tonnes, represents a 16.4% drop compared with 1998. Further cuts are planned for 2000. Coal demand has been reduced partly as a result of the steady upgrading of technology and improved energy efficiency at state-owned and other industrial firms – reducing demand for electricity (and hence coal). In addition, large coal reserves have left a considerable oversupply.

However, the under-development of oil and gas resources means that coal is expected to remain China's single most important energy source for the foreseeable future. Once GDP growth starts to pick up, coal output is likely to rise again – heavy government spending on infrastructure has boosted energy demand from sectors such as steel and other construction materials. There is an imbalance in coal output and demand; the top four coal producing provinces – Shanxi, Henan, Shandong, and Inner Mongolia, which together produce almost half of national total – are all located in the north. As a result, coal accounts for the largest share of freight volumes, placing a huge strain on the rail network.

More Emphasis On Oil And Gas

China has large onshore and offshore reserves of both oil and gas (although offshore resources are much less developed, and account for only a small proportion of total oil output). Both oil and gas have been relatively under-exploited in comparison with coal. Natural gas has been particularly under-used, accounting for only around 2% of domestic energy in the 1990s. The state-owned firm **China National Petroleum Corporation** (CNPC) dominates onshore production, although there has been some foreign investment, and **Sinopec** too is now involved in upstream production.

According to the State Statistical Bureau (SSB), crude oil production totalled 160.2mn tonnes in 1999, a drop of 0.5%, compared with output of 162.6mn tonnes in 1998. China's main fields – including Daqing, Liohe and Dagang – are all maturing. Output at the key Daqing oilfield dipped to 54.5mn tonnes in 1999, from 55.7mn tonnes in 1998. Experts hope that production at the key Daqing field will remain above 50mn tonnes per year until 2010. According to the SSB, natural gas output rose 10.4% to 24.6bn m³ in 1999. The main natural gas fields are located in four regions in the far west: in the Xinjiang autonomous region; in an area crossing the Shaanxi, Gansu and Ningxia provinces; in Sichuan province; and in the far western province of Qinghai. In addition, total offshore natural gas reserves are estimated at 8.4trn m³.

Energy policy through the forecast period will focus on ways to boost the exploration and development of new fields, encouraging greater use of natural gas for environmental reasons, and boosting the efficiency of the major energy players. Exploration efforts have concentrated on the western regions and offshore. **BP Amoco** and **Enron Development** are among the foreign companies believed to be interested in investing in a US$12bn pipeline project to bring gas from the north-western Xinjiang province to Shanghai. Looking at offshore developments, **China National Offshore Oil Corp** found five large oil and gas bearing fields in 1999 (four in Bohai Bay, including the huge Penglai 19-3 field). After lacklustre performance in the 1990s, recent offshore finds have started to stimulate foreign interest; foreign investors involved in recent finds include **Philips Petroleum** of the USA (which plans a joint venture in Bohai bay with CNOOC). As these fields come on stream, CNOOC is aiming to double its oil and gas output to 40mn tonnes by 2005.

The oil and gas sector will also have to face up to sweeping changes following WTO entry. All import duties on crude oil and gas are to be lifted immediately on WTO accession, while tariffs on fuel and oil products are to be cut to 6% from 9% within two years. The massive state oil and gas exploration/production companies are taking steps to improve management, slash staff numbers, and raise international financing. For example, **China National Petroleum Corporation** (CNPC) has raised US$3.1bn in a dual listing on the Hong Kong and New York exchanges this year for a unit called **PetroChina**.

Construction

Continued Heavy Spending On Infrastructure

The government's massive infrastructure spending spree, begun in 1998, continued through 1999. The government has pumped billions of dollars into rail, road, irrigation, grain storage and energy projects, lifting growth in the construction sector. At the March 2000 National People's Congress, Zhu Rongji outlined plans to direct billions more in state investment into the central and especially the least-developed western regions of the country. A major recipient of the increased spending has been the railway sector; the government plans to spend a further CNY56bn (US$6.8bn) on expanding track and electrifying lines in 2000. Foreign involvement in construction remains modest; according to a report by the *Construction Daily,* by early 2000 China had 178 foreign construction firms, 81 of which were from Hong Kong.

The Property Sector – Signs of Life?

Commercial property remained in the doldrums in 1999. Several years of rapid growth have left oversupply of office space in many cities, resulting in a slump in commercial rents and purchase prices. The problems were compounded by the Asia crisis, as Hong Kong, Japanese and other Asian investors put major property projects on hold, and as foreign firms from crisis-hit countries delayed expansion plans or entry to China. Rents for offices and warehouses continued to fall through 1999, dropping by 5.3% y-o-y in the fourth quarter of the year. The resulting slump has hit building materials sectors such as cement and glass; these sectors are expected to suffer further following WTO entry, when the price of higher-quality imported materials will fall.

The outlook for residential property is somewhat better. A survey by the State Development Planning Commission and the State Statistical Bureau found that residential housing prices rose slightly in the fourth quarter of 1999, up by 0.6% y-o-y, and residential rents rose 2.4% y-o-y. However, residential land prices continued to fall, dropping 0.1% y-o-y in the fourth quarter. The government is trying to stimulate demand for private housing, and has encouraged banks to begin mortgage lending. The high cost of mortgages, uncertainty about the future and poor quality housing stock have held back growth; in the whole of 1999, according to *China Securities,* mortgages totalled only CNY126bn – around 1.3% of total loans worth CNY9.4trn. Mortgage-backed securities are to be introduced soon and this will deepen the lending market by spreading the risks. According to a recent survey of 14 major cities, urban residents are expected to purchase 1.3mn units of privately-built housing in 2000, up from 860,000 units in 1999; purchases of public housing (including housing previously attached to SOEs) will total 850,000 units this year.

Telecommunications

Continued Rapid Expansion Of Fixed Lines...

The telecoms sector is one of the key areas targeted by the government's three-year infrastructure spending plan. In April 1998, MII said that it would oversee spending of around CNY450bn (US$54.2bn) in three years (some of which may come from private and foreign investors). A massive expansion of landlines is planned; MII plans to have 1bn lines by 2020 – up from 141m in late-1999, with a target of 166mn lines by the end of 2000, and 379mn by 2010. Network expansion picked up strongly in H2 99, boosting demand for equipment.

...And In The Mobile Sector

Growth in the mobile sector has outpaced fixed lines, and by late 1999 the number of mobile subscribers had reached 40mn, up from 25mn at the end of 1998. Analysts believe this figure could jump to 70mn by the end of the year, and that China could soon become the second largest mobile market in the world, after the USA, with demand boosted as greater competition following WTO entry forces down connection fees. The mobile services market is currently dominated by the key state-owned player, **China Telecom**. However, **China United Telecommunications Corp**, known as **Unicom** (which was established in 1994 to provide some competition) managed to increase its share of the mobile market to 11% at end-1999, up from 5% at end-1998. In early 2000 **China Unicom** signed a preliminary patent deal with **Qualcomm** of the USA, permitting the widespread use of CDMA (Code Division Multiple Access) wireless technology in China. Up until now China's mobile market has been dominated by the GSM (Global System for Mobile communications) system. China Unicom hopes to challenge this with the Qualcomm deal, building a network of 10mn users in 250 cities by end-2000, and adding an additional 10mn users each year from 2001.

The mobile equipment sector remains dominated by foreign manufacturers. According to **Deutsche Bank**, only around 1-2% of all handsets were local brands by mid-1999, with the market dominated by Finland's **Nokia** as well as **Ericsson** of Sweden and **Motorola**. Nokia estimated that China was its second largest market in 1999 after the USA. Motorola forecasts that demand will be particularly strong for phones with Chinese interfaces. The MII wants to reduce foreign domination of the mobile equipment sector; it has set a target of local brands to make up 50% of the market within five years, and has provided cash grants to a number of local manufacturers. However, foreign suppliers of CDMA equipment will be the first to benefit if the CDMA deal goes ahead. **Motorola**, **Lucent Technologies** of the USA, and Canada's **Nortel Networks** already have ventures licensed to make and sell CDMA equipment in China; other contenders are **Ericsson**, South Korean firms **Samsung** and **LG information**, and Japan's **NEC**. In early 2000 **Ericsson** announced that it was seeking permission to expand the number of mobile handsets it makes this year to 8mn, double last year's output (output of units by foreign companies is regulated). The key Chinese telecoms equipment manufactures, **Datang** and **Huawei Technology**, have only a small market share; future contracts are likely to go to foreign companies willing to transfer technology and to cooperate with Chinese firms.

WTO Entry Will Speed Deregulation

There are plans to turn the Ministry of Information Industry (MII) into a regulating body without links to commercial operations, and to break up the dominant service provider, the state-owed **China Telecom**, into fixed line, pager, mobile and satellite companies to improve competition. China Telecom has already been forced to hand over pager operations to **China Unicom**. In late 1999 a third major telecommunications company, **China Netcom**, was set up; it has plans to build a 15-city fibre optic network to sell broadband network access (suitable for multimedia functions). The WTO deal signed with the USA is expected to speed up this process, by permitting foreign participation in telecoms services (foreign manufacturers already dominate the mobile equipment market), and requiring the establishment of an independent regulatory body. The key points of the USA WTO deal for telecommunications are as follows:

- Foreign firms will be permitted a maximum 49% stake in mobile and fixed-line telecommunications services within 5-6 years of accession; 49% ownership for most other related telecommunications services will be allowed immediately on accession, rising to 50% within two years.

- Geographical restrictions on paging and value-added telecommunications services will be phased out within two years of accession; similar restrictions on mobiles will be phased out within five years, and on landlines within six years.

- The Beijing-Shanghai-Guangzhou telecoms corridor will be opened immediately for all telecommunications services.

These deals may be further improved upon. A key sticking point in EU-China WTO negotiations is the EU demand that foreign firms be allowed a majority stake in mobile firms. However, the introduction of foreign competition in the telecoms sector remains very sensitive, and may be resisted by key ministries. The MII has taken a dim view of earlier efforts to increase foreign participation; 45 deals signed by China Unicom with foreign firms were declared to be "irregular" in 1999 by the Telecoms Administrative Bureau (under MII), which ordered China Unicom to divest any foreign joint ventures or investments. The decision affected around US$1.4bn worth of foreign investment in leasing and consultancy agreements, and negotiations on unwinding the deals were still continuing in early 2000.

Internet Services – Explosive Growth Expected

According to official estimates, the number of net users reached 7-8mn at the end of 1999, up from 1-2mn in 1998. There are varied estimates available however; the China Internet Network Information Center (CNNIC) estimated net users to have reached 8.9mn by end-1999, up from 2.1mn at the end of 1998. Although exact figures are difficult to pin down, the number of users may now be doubling every six months. This rate of growth may slow, but the market is still set for massive expansion through the forecast period; the major providers plan to invest US\$1bn in 2000 on upgrading their systems to cope with growing demand. China Telecom remains the largest service provider, accounting for 80% of users. Its 300-centre network now covers most of the country.

Foreign firms have been investing heavily in the China internet market: for example **AOL** of the USA has a cooperative venture with **China Internet Corporation** (CIC) to develop Chinese and English language web sites. In late 1998, the US company, **Yahoo**, signed an agreement with **Infoshare**, a state-owned company owned by MOFTEC's **China International Electronic Commerce Centre**. WTO entry will clarify foreign ownership of internet companies. Under the terms of the US WTO deal, both internet content providers and service providers (ICPs and ISPs) will be permitted 49% ownership initially, rising to 50% within two years. Unclear rules mean that some foreign firms already have larger stakes; the MII has made clear that these investments will have to be unwound.

The government, alarmed at the likely increase in foreign participation in internet services (both as service providers and content providers), issued new regulations on internet content in early 2000, requiring all web sites to undergo security checks, and making it a crime to release 'state secrets' on the web. The definition of 'state secrets' is extremely broad, in theory raising doubts over most information not already explicitly cleared for publication. In one sense the rules introduce nothing new, but they suggest a new determination to police the internet. In addition, new rules were announced in January 2000 requiring all foreign and Chinese users of encryption technology – embedded in much commonly used software as well as mobile phones, cable TV networks and so on – to register with the official State Encryption Management Commission. However, after a storm of protest, the new rules were watered down, exempting many products including mobiles, internet browsers and Windows software. Rules on overseas listings by internet firms have also been somewhat unclear, and uncertainty over the exact approvals needed has delayed several planned US listings by key Chinese internet companies. However, in mid-March, one major portal, **Sina.com**, was given official approval to go ahead with its planned listing on the US NASDAQ exchange.

As internet use expands, an explosion of e-commerce is expected, albeit from a tiny base. According to the MII, e-commerce sites in China had total revenues of CNY200mn (US\$24mn) in 1999, double the 1998 figure, and sales could reach more than US\$1bn by 2002. Other estimates suggest that e-commerce business-to-business sales had already reached US\$40mn in 1999. Firms are looking for ways to broaden the e-commerce market through link-ups with existing wireless technology. For example, **MeetChina.com** has teamed up with China's **Legend** and **Motorola** to expand its export/import service to mobile phone users (currently a market more than four times the size of internet users).

Banking And Financial Services

The Structure Of The Domestic Banking Sector

There has been considerable reorganisation of China's banking sector in the 1990s. A major step was taken in 1994 with the creation of three so-called policy banks – the **Export-Import Bank of China**, the **State Development Bank** and the **Agricultural Development Bank of China**. The government intended that these new banks would take over the bulk of state-directed lending, allowing the existing "big four" state banks – **Bank of China** (BOC), **Industrial And Commercial Bank of China** (ICBC), **China Construction Bank** (CCB) and **Agricultural Bank of China** (ABC) – to commercialise their operations. A number of state- and publicly-held banks have also been established, including **CITIC Industrial Bank** and **China Everbright Bank**, as well as a range of locally-owned urban and rural cooperative banks, savings banks and provincial development banks. There is also one majority private-owned domestic bank, **Minsheng Bank**, established in 1995.

The "big four" dominate the banking sector. According to a speech by the governor of the central banks, Dai Xianglong, in January 1999, total assets of all financial institutions (excluding securities and insurance firms) totalled CNY15.3trn at the end of 1998; of this, the assets of the big four banks accounted for CNY9.5trn (62% of the total), while the policy banks accounted for another CNY1.4trn (9.2% of the total). Other commercial banks had CNY1.7trn (11.1%), urban and rural credit cooperatives another 11.1%, trust and investment companies CNY540bn (3.5%) and foreign banks CNY280bn.

Non-Performing Loans: A Big Problem

The banks are governed by a banking law that took effect in July 1995. This law set out a comprehensive framework for commercial banking, requiring the state banks to sever links with SOEs, to pull out of securities, property and investment trust operations, to safeguard deposits and to meet capital adequacy requirements and bad debt provisions. The law also called for loans to be made on commercial criteria only, and for credit checks to be used. In practice, however, limited headway has been made in efforts to put the banks on a stronger, more commercial footing. The main problem is that the banking sector remains burdened by a long history of politically-directed lending to shaky SOEs and priority sectors, as a result of which the biggest banks are now burdened by massive non-performing loans (NPLs). The central bank governor, Dai Xianglong, has estimated that NPLs were in the region of 26% of all loans, of which around 6% was unrecoverable. By early 2000, Dai was quoted at a news conference saying that unrecoverable (bad) loans totalled 8-9% of all loans.

The real situation is even worse: China does not define a loan as being non-performing until after six months, compared with the international standard of three months. New classification rules should have been adopted by end-1999, but Dai Xianglong has admitted that the new standards are still not being widely used, partly because of differences in accounting practises. In addition, poor auditing of the banks (some of which employ many thousands in thousands of branches scattered across the country, with poor record keeping) means that the true level of the problem is simply not clear. The World Bank and some international rating agencies have estimated that NPLs may be as high as 40% – much higher than the levels seen in Thailand before the 1997 crisis, for example. However, the banking sector is insulated to an extent, thanks to the relatively low level of external liabilities, and to continued central government support. It is also helped by the high savings rate: residents' savings reached CNY6trn by end-1999, around 70% of GDP. There are few investment vehicles open to savers, who continue to trust at least the large state-owned banks. A run on deposits at one of the big banks would be disastrous, but is highly unlikely: during recent failures of smaller investment trusts (*see below*), there was something of a flight of deposits to the larger state banks.

The Three-Year Reform Plan

In early-1998, Dai announced a clean-up of the banking sector, echoed by Zhu Rongji at the March 1998 NPC congress, when he called for a clean-up of the banks in tandem with the restructuring of the SOEs, to be completed within three years. As a priority, efforts have been made to improve regulation. Restructuring the central bank, the People's Bank of China (PBOC) began in 1998, when the network of 31 provincial offices was replaced with nine larger, regional offices, while 148 sub-provincial branches, 6% of the total, were closed. These measures were taken in a bid to improve efficiency and to minimise interference in PBOC regulatory and lending activities by provincial governments. In order to bolster the PBOC's regulatory capacity, responsibility for securities and insurance regulation was spun off in 1998, leaving the PBOC to focus on the banking sector. The big four banks themselves are also undergoing massive restructuring, slashing staff numbers and upgrading technology.

To send a signal about increased commercialisation, in January 1998 government-set loan quotas were officially abolished. The state banks had lent below their quota ceilings in 1997, seen by some as a sign that they were starting to make lending decisions on more commercial criteria, and were taking seriously the government's demands to pay more attention to loan quality. Further, in early 2000 Dai reiterated a promise to widen the band within which interest rates are set; some progress is expected within 1-2 years.

Direct steps have also been taken to improve the financial health of the banks. The government is setting aside increasingly large amounts of funds to help the banks write off bad debts, while in 1998 the reserve requirement was cut from a very high 13%, to 8%, with a further cut to 6% in 1999 (freeing up more funds for lending). In addition, CNY270bn (US$32bn) in government bonds was issued to the banks in 1998 to start recapitalising them. Then in 1999 another major step was taken with the formation of four Asset Management Corporations (AMCs) to take over, securitise and re-sell the bad loans (classified as loans on which no payment has been received for the last two years) of the big four banks. The four AMCs, each with an initial registered capital of CNY10bn, are: **Cinda Asset Management**, **Dongfang**, **Great Wall** and **Huarong**. Each is assigned to a particular state bank; for example, Cinda is to take over the problem loans of the China Construction Bank (CCB). The main method being used is debt-for-equity swaps. According to *China Securities* news, around 600 SOEs will be given permission in 2000 to conduct debt-for-equity swaps on debts of CNY400bn. Progress has been slow – by the end of 1999 only around 30 firms had signed debt-for-equity deals – but the pace is expected to quicken this year. Problems include the lack of a secondary market for the assets, as well as the massive cost to the government. In early 1999 a CCB official estimated that as much as CNY500bn (US$60bn) of the bad loans transferred to the AMCs would not be recoverable during the next five to ten years. Hence, the cost to the government of this restructuring will be substantial.

WTO Will Bring More Competition

These measures will undoubtedly mean that, by the end of the forecast period, China's banking sector will be leaner and better regulated. The banks' close ties with the SOEs mean that reducing NPLs will be a more intractable problem. However, impending entry into the WTO will force the pace of banking reform, as China faces up to a big increase in foreign competition. During the last two decades, China has cautiously permitted foreign banks to enter the market and to expand their activities. However, to date the scope of foreign banking activity and the geographical areas in which it is permitted have been heavily restricted. For example, foreign banks are permitted to operate in 23 cities and Hainan Island only. Currently, banks are limited to foreign exchange business (deposits and loans, and dealing with remittances and import and export settlements) for FIEs, foreigners and SOEs. Modest participation in renminbi business has been permitted since March 1997; by March 2000, licences for renminbi business had been granted to 24 banks in Shanghai and another eight in Shenzhen, including Germany's **Dresdner Bank**, Hong Kong's **Bank of East Asia**, the **Overseas Chinese Bank of Singapore** and the **Development Bank of Singapore**, as well as **Credit Suisse**, **Credit Lyonnais**, **Bank of America**, the Netherlands' **ABN-Amro** and Japan's **Sumitomo Bank** and **Sakura Bank**.

All that will change following WTO entry. Under the terms of the US-China trade agreement, all foreign banks will be able to conduct local currency transactions with Chinese enterprises within two years and with individual clients within five years. Foreign currency business with Chinese customers will be possible within one year of accession. Foreign firms will be permitted to invest up to 33% in fund management and underwriting firms. Geographic restrictions on banking will be removed within five years; while the big four banks support massive national branch networks and a huge staff, incoming foreign banks are likely to concentrate on the more affluent cities in the east.

Faced with the prospect of growing foreign competition, the banking sector is likely to undergo considerable consolidation, with mergers and acquisitions likely among the smaller banks. For example, **CITIC Industrial Bank** – wholly owned by China International Trust and Investment Corp (CITIC) – plans to merge with **Shenzhen Development Bank**. A raft of listings is also likely as banks seek capital to fund restructuring; **Everbright Bank**, **China Merchants Bank** and **China Minsheng Bank** were all considering listing in early 2000. Beijing may also relax the restrictions that currently separate out financial-sector activities (preventing banks, trust and securities firms and insurance companies from straying into each other's markets) in order to allow stronger, integrated financial firms to develop.

A Small And Weak Non-Bank Financial Sector

In addition to the largely state-owned domestic banking sector, China also has thousands of relatively small non-bank financial institutions. This includes a network of thousands of rural and urban credit cooperatives, as well as local International Trust and Investment Corporations (ITICs). Despite periodic efforts to clamp down on the ITICs, used as vehicles to raise overseas foreign funds by provincial governments and enterprises, their numbers proliferated in the 1980s and 1990s (although their share in total lending remained in low single figures). In addition to these institutions, there are also many leasing, securities and insurance companies, many with close ties to state banks. Many of these non-bank financial institutions suffer even more than the banks from weak regulation, and severe shortages of skills and technology.

GITIC Failure Prompts Financial Sector Shake-out

International attention focused on the ITICs in October 1998, when the **Guangdong International Trade and Investment Company** (GITIC) announced that it was unable to service some US$4.3bn in external debts. To the surprise of some in the international banking community, the central government did not step in to save GITIC, which was closed by the PBOC in October 1998, filing for bankruptcy in early 1999. In early 1999 another lending arm of the Guangdong provincial government, **Guangdong Enterprises** (GDE) announced that it could not service its US$2.9bn external loans. A rash of other ITICs – including **Guangzhou International Trust and Investment Corporation** (GZITIC) and **Guangdong Overseas Chinese Trust and Investment Corp** (GOCTIC) – then announced either delays in meeting payments or outright defaults. GITIC's closure changed assumptions about lending to China. It is clearly no longer enough to rely on state backing for local government guarantees (much of the ITICs' borrowing had not been registered, as required, with the State Administration of Foreign Exchange, relying solely on provincial government guarantees). However, the means of assessing credit risk are hindered in China by a lack of reliable financial information or established liquidation processes.

The government has made it clear that it expects a drastic consolidation of the non-bank financial sector. At least 12 urban credit cooperatives were quietly closed in 1998, and the government has stated that it expects many more of the remaining 239 ITICs to close. Little progress was seen in 1999, but in early 2000 the **Hainan International Trust and Investment Company** was closed, unable to service its debts. Officials indicated that more ITIC closures would follow.

The Insurance Sector Has High Growth Potential

The insurance sector is seen as a very high growth area, given the combination of low penetration, high levels of savings, a lack of state pensions and welfare provision and an increasingly uncertain employment and welfare situation. There are plans to set up a state medical insurance scheme this year that could reach 50mn people. However, the life sector is still underdeveloped, while the slower-growing property, health and accident sectors are very limited, with a poor product range. The Insurance Law which came into effect in October 1995 held the promise of more products and expanded competition, but the sector has remained rather chaotic, plagued by problems such as excessive commissions, poor management and fraud. To improve matters, a new agency, the China Insurance Regulatory Commission (CIRC) was set up in November 1998 to assume responsibility for regulation of the insurance sector, previously under the wing of the PBOC. The CIRC, which reports directly to the State Council, has already started to impose some order. CIRC approval is required for senior appointments at insurance firms, in a bid to improve management. The CIRC has also cracked down on the illegal selling of passengers' insurance by some airlines. In early 2000 the CIRC released new regulations governing minimum capital requirements for insurance companies and detailing the requirements for stock market listings by insurance firms. The trend for the forecast period will be tougher implementation of existing insurance regulations and closer scrutiny of insurance companies.

The *China Business Times* reported that insurance premiums rose by 10% y-o-y in 1999, to CNY139.3bn, of which life and health insurance accounted for CNY87.2bn, rising by 15% y-o-y. Property premiums rose by 3% to CNY52.1bn. Payouts by all insurance firms in 1999 totalled CNY51bn, down from CNY55.6bn in 1998, (of the 1999 total, CNY28bn went to property and CNY23bn on life and health policies). China has 30 insurance firms, including four state-owned firms. The state-owned **People's Insurance Company of China (PICC)** totally dominates the market; its life insurance arm accounted for 42.5% of total premiums in 1998, and its property arm accounted for another 32.2% of premiums. The only other sizeable players are **Ping'an Insurance Co** and **Pacific Insurance Co**, but some newer regional entrants, such as **Xinhua Life Insurance Co**, set up in Beijing, may emerge as national players over the longer term.

Foreign insurers on the other hand still have only a toehold in the market. The first foreign insurers licensed to operate in China were **American International Assurance** (AIA), part of **American International Group** of the USA, and **Tokio Marine and Fire Insurance of Japan**. Other entrants include the Swiss firm **Wintherthur** and the UK's **Royal and Sun Alliance**. Beijing has moved slowly to license new foreign entrants, partly in a desire to protect domestic players. However, WTO entry will bring much greater foreign competition; geographic restrictions will be removed within three years (currently foreign insurers are permitted only in Guangzhou and Shanghai) and foreign firms will be able to offer a broader range of products – including health and pensions – within five years. Life insurers will be permitted up to 50% ownership in joint ventures and will be able to select their own partners; 51% ownership in non-life firms will be permitted, with 100% ownership of reinsurance companies.

4 Business Environment

Introduction

Large-scale FDI Flows

China has become one of the largest recipients of foreign direct investment (FDI) in the world, with actual inflows of US$40.4bn in 1999. It is also a major trading nation, with imports of US$165.8bn in 1999. However, many foreign firms (known in China as foreign invested enterprises, or FIEs) and trade partners find operating conditions in China difficult. Distribution networks are inadequate, turnover of skilled labour can be high, and investors face continued problems with corruption and weak protection of intellectual property.

These problems are certainly not unique to China, and are encountered in many other emerging markets. However, the complexity and diversity of China's consumer market is often underestimated. Further, seven years of slowing growth have exacerbated the massive oversupply now affecting many sectors. Consumer demand is expected to pick up only modestly through 2000-2002, constrained by rising unemployment and acute uncertainty as China's welfare system is fundamentally reshaped.

These trends will have a mixed impact on policy towards foreign investors. On the plus side, the need to ensure continued high foreign capital inflows in order to help lift flagging growth and stave off balance of payments problems may push the government to extend or even improve incentives for investors in some priority sectors. Competition for funds among the myriad special investment zones will also result in them continuing to improve their infrastructure and cut back red tape. However, the government wants to boost investment in the west and central regions, and hence incentives are likely to be targeted in areas that remain unattractive to investors because of poor transport and distribution links. The government is also desperate to support some sections of the sagging state-owned enterprise (SOE) sector in a bid to stem the recent sharp rise in unemployment. As a result, there has already been a resurgence in protectionist and anti-competitive policies (such as the reintroduction of price floors.) The government intends to cut back its overall shareholding in state enterprises in the next few years – but will concentrate on beefing up control of what it sees as key sectors such as telecommunications and energy.

These policies do not sit easily with the market-opening measures required by the WTO. China has reached agreement with the USA on WTO membership, and a deal with the other remaining partners, including the EU, is probable this year, allowing entry late 2000, or 2001. The WTO deal is likely to result in a jump in FDI in financial and services sectors, such as telecommunications, retail and distribution services (as opposed to the current dominance of export-oriented manufacturing projects). However, strong vested interests will resist many market opening measures, and progress in deregulation and implementing the rules of law will be very uneven.

Infrastructure

Expanding Basic Infrastructure: A Priority

The government's Ninth Five Year Plan, which covers 1996-2000, emphasised the need for a massive expansion of infrastructure in five key areas – agriculture, water conservation and management, energy, transport and telecommunications. Opportunities in these and other areas have been opened up by the massive government pump-priming programme that began in 1998, and which is set to continue through 2000, financed by government bond issues and by state bank lending, although foreign participation is also being sought. Spending has concentrated on upgrading basic infrastructure – although the quality of some of the projects has been questioned.

China's road and rail services are inadequate for the volume of traffic and freight, and pose a considerable constraint on business activity. China has around 60,000km of railway track. Another 10,000km were to be added in 1996-2000, while the Ministry of Railways also wants to speed up services in order to win back freight and passengers. Also planned is a US$12bn, 1,300km high-speed rail-link between Beijing and Shanghai. China's road system reached 1.28mn km at the end of 1998; and 2672km of new express roads were added in 1999. The road system will be further expanded by the development of 12 national highway routes. China's airline services have expanded, with a proliferation of provincial services now competing with those run by the Civil Aviation Administration of China (CAAC). The 1996-2000 five-year plan outlined a massive programme of refurbishment, expansion and construction of airports; majority foreign ownership of such projects is not permitted, although foreign firms have been active in supplying aircraft and other equipment. China's inland waterways are an important means of transporting freight. One of the reasons for the massive and controversial Three Gorges project, which will dam the Yangtze river, is to enable larger ships to reach as far inland as the major industrial city of Chongqing. Capacity at Shanghai, China's main seaport, is being expanded.

In addition to expanding basic transport infrastructure, there will be an increased focus during the forecast period on upgrading technology and improving services for some utilities such as water and waste management, in an effort to cope with China's increasing environmental problems (*see Envrionmental Regulation*). Foreign technology and management are being actively sought in these sectors. There is considerable ambivalence about foreign participation in telecommunications, but entry to the World Trade Organisation will force open the telecommunications services market to foreign investors (*see Foreign Trade Policy*). The market for both telecoms services and equipment manufacturers is expanding rapidly – with much room for further growth.

Once GDP growth begins to pick up, capacity problems will re-emerge in power and other infrastructure sectors, suggesting that the authorities will again seek to make regulation and incentives more favourable to foreign investors. In addition, in the medium term, multilateral assistance to China for power and other infrastructure projects is likely to slow, further boosting the need for foreign capital. Likely changes include the final passage of the BOT law during the forecast period. In late 1997, a BOT agreement was awarded to **GEC Alsthom** (an Anglo-French conglomerate) for the Laibin B coal-fired power plant, suggesting that more such projects would follow, but other planned BOT projects were delayed, as doubts about growth in demand for energy mounted in the context of the economic slowdown. Full BOT regulations have yet to be issued.

Deregulation Of The Power Sector

In the early 1990s, it seemed that China's appetite for power was insatiable. However, the marked downturn in the economy since 1998 has raised the spectre of over-capacity in the power sector in the short term, a situation which most foreign investors had not anticipated, and which is doing nothing to encourage the government to improve regulations and incentives. For example, in late 1998 the government announced an end to guaranteed off-take and tariffs for foreign-funded power projects. Instead, the official focus is now on the expansion of electricity provision in rural areas (according to the World Bank, around 60mn rural consumers still do not have access to electricity) and upgrading the load capacity in urban areas.

At the same time, deregulation of the power sector will slowly be pushed forward. The **State Power Corp** (SPC), the sole owner of the national grid, has started buying a portion of its electricity through a bidding system, in a move that regulators hope will reduce electricity prices and boost rural energy demand. The new policy will be tried out first in Shanghai and the provinces of Zhejiang and Shandong. In these areas, SPC will buy around 15% of its electricity through the bidding system, with the remainder coming from existing contracts. The new policy will gradually be expanded throughout China, starting from late 2000. The ultimate aim – which could take a decade or more – is to introduce competition through the entire system, separating the grid operation from SPC's power plants. Some foreign investors are unhappy with the new scheme, as state power producers receive many subsidies, and so can continue to undercut on price. Hence the new move may result in delays to some foreign-back projects.

The Domestic Market

The Population Is Ageing

China's population reached an estimated 1.26bn in 1999. Population growth has not been above 1% in recent years, a modest rate compared with many countries at comparable income levels. The slowdown is mainly a result of the government's 'one child' policy, in force since the early 1980s (less strictly enforced outside urban areas). As a result of the slowdown, the age structure of China's population will shift markedly in the next decade or so. The World Bank expects that the proportion of those aged 65 years and above will rise from 6.4% in 1995, to 10.8% in 2020. The number of people of working age will fall from 10 for every person of pensionable age now, to six by 2020, and to three by 2050, with profound implications for incomes and spending patterns.

A Fragmented Market, With Rising Income Inequality

China's domestic market is also characterised by its uneven population density. The key coastal and central provinces are home to the bulk of the population, while the largest inland provinces are more sparsely populated, with poorer transport and distribution links. However, there are some major inland population centres, such as the 22mn-strong municipal area of Chongqing, and even in the remoter regions greater population mobility and the almost universal penetration of TV has increased product awareness.

Another major trend shaping China's domestic market is rising income inequality. There are already marked differences between rural and urban areas, as well as sharp disparities between regions. For example, in 1999, average rural incomes were CNY2,210, up only 3.8% in real terms, compared with an average of CNY5,854 for urban residents, a rise of 9.3% y-o-y in real terms Reducing this gap is now a government priority, as seen in the drive to attract more FDI into central and western regions announced at the March 2000 NPC congress. Slowing growth in private consumption has also made the overall consumer market much tougher. GDP growth has slowed, unemployment is rising, and the uncertainty created by the dismantling of the 'iron rice bowl' – China's cradle-to-grave welfare system for those employed in the state-sector – will encourage continued high savings rates. At the same time, oversupply will ensure that price competition remains keen in many key sectors.

As a result of these trends, the consumer market is becoming more fragmented, demanding a wider range of goods and services tailored to different income groups. Consumers are also expected to become more quality conscious and more interested in services. A higher proportion of spending is expected to be directed towards 'big ticket' items such as housing, cars, and higher value-added consumer goods such as PCs, and on services in areas such as education and finance, at the expense of more basic items such as refrigerators and TVs.

The Labour Market

Still Inexpensive, But Some Skills In Short Supply

Labour in China is still inexpensive, although wages have tended to rise more rapidly than inflation. China's labour-cost advantage was somewhat eroded in comparison to those Asian nations that experienced sharp currency falls in 1997-98, but most Asian currencies have now appreciated against the renminbi. Foreign firms find that introducing concepts such as performance-related pay can be a problem, and wage expectations need careful management. In addition, the welfare system is in a state of flux. A contributory pension scheme is being phased in; depending on current local policies, this could either lower or increase contributions. Shortages of skilled staff mean that wage pressures and turnover can be high for some sectors. For unskilled workers, a minimum wage is set, although enforcement can be lax.

The availability and quality of labour is varied. Unskilled labour is plentiful, and will remain so during the forecast period. However, it is a different story for skilled workers, and there is a particular shortage of staff with language and technical skills, and managerial skills in areas such as finance and marketing. Staff with IT skills commend particularly high salaries. Steady improvements are being made, however. The number of higher education institutions is being expanded and university curricula are being updated, while many foreign enterprises have invested in training.

Labour militancy is a relatively minor problem in China compared with some other low-wage Asian countries. Union activity is permitted under China's labour regulations, but all activity is overseen by an official body, which is under firm party control. However, the more difficult economic climate, combined with higher unemployment, has already resulted in a sharp rise in labour protests. Although little reported, such protests now occur in many cities on a regular basis. Most are orderly and peaceful. Foreign firms are unlikely to be singled out as targets, because the main causes for complaint are redundancies and pay freezes at SOEs. However, foreign firms may be affected in the longer term if a tradition of labour protests starts to become more entrenched.

Exit policy in China is a difficult area. The SOEs still tend to keep workers on basic pay for long periods rather than making large-scale redundancies, while the regulations for foreign firms are unclear. It is possible that concern over rising unemployment may result in some toughening up in this area. More generally, labour mobility will increase. The old system required workers, even college graduates, to take the job allotted to them, and movement between posts was difficult. However, this is already breaking down, even within SOEs, and the flexibility already permitted foreign firms will increase further as graduates are officially given more room to make their own career choices.

Industrial Policy

Restructuring The State-Owned Sector

China state-owned enterprise (SOE) sector faces massive problems, including oversupply in many key sectors, continued weak domestic demand, poor products, outdated technology and weak management (for example, many SOEs still favour stockpiling production in times of difficulty, rather than restructuring and retrenchment). Yet for years the state banks have been forced to keep on lending billions of renminbi to keep the SOEs afloat. The result: a massive, bloated and inefficient state sector, and a banking sector weighed down by non-performing loans. The authorities grasped the nettle at the 15th Party Congress in September 1997, when it was announced, somewhat optimistically, that the SOE sector would be reformed within three years (i.e. by late 2000). Although privatisation is still a taboo word, the 1997 announcement heralded a wave of selling, and many thousands of small SOEs under the control of local governments have already been merged, sold or closed. In early 2000 the government announced plans to reduce its overall shareholding in SOEs to 51%, from a current 62%, in part to raise funds for welfare reform.

As a result of the SOE restructuring that has occurred so far, millions of state workers have lost their jobs, or had pay and pensions frozen. Yet slowing economic growth and continued restrictions on the private sector have reduced employment opportunities elsewhere, resulting in a surge in unemployment. The registered urban unemployment rate was 3.1% at the end of 1999, but in some northern rustbelt cities the rate may be as high as 30%. Hence the authorities are now having to deal with perhaps the most severe economic and social problem that has emerged since the reforms began: how to restructure the SOEs without creating a level of unemployment that could result in severe social unrest. This problem is made worse because SOEs still provide pensions, healthcare, housing and education to millions of workers and their families. Efforts will continue to be made to put state-funded and private welfare schemes into place, but this will take time.

The government intends to retain the largest 500-1,000 SOEs in strategic sectors such as energy, transport and telecommunications, but with improved management and less direct government control. It also intends to create large conglomerates capable of competing on international markets. Large SOEs were in theory to have been removed from government control by end-1998, as a first stage in their being shaped into internationally competitive players. However, direct ministerial control has merely been replaced with management by a group of other government bodies. For example, personnel and welfare issues are now managed by a new Central Working Committee for Large-Scale Enterprises, while assets have been registered with the Finance Ministry. In late 1999 the Company Law was amended to allow the formation of supervisory committees, staffed by State Council appointees and SOE staff, to oversee the running of SOEs in a bid to improve management. This 'separation' is intended to weaken the SOEs' ties to particular ministries, which have in the past been exploited to obtain credit or contracts.

However, the SOEs will not be truly independent until the government ceases its policy of pressuring the state-owned banks to extend credit to keep even loss-making SOEs afloat. In early 2000 four of China's 'mega cities' – Beijing, Shanghai, Chongqing and Tianjin – announced new policies to choke off state funds to loss-making SOEs and banned the formation of new SOEs in some sectors. However, it remains to be seen how strictly these policies are enforced. There are concerns that another critical policy in strengthening the SOE sector – the transfer of billions of renminbi in bad debts to the asset management companies (AMCs) formed in 1999 – is merely being used to give struggling SOEs a new lease of life, rather than forcing fundamental restructuring. A number of factors, including SOEs' reluctance to buy-back unsold equity, have resulted in very sluggish progress to date in planned debt-for-equity swaps.

Supporting The Non-State Sector

The non-state sector – collectives, private and foreign-funded firms – are still dwarfed by the SOEs. In 1999, the non-state sector (comprising collectives, and private domestic and foreign enterprises) accounted for almost 72% of total industrial output and industrial output by the non-state sector is rising much more rapidly (despite slower growth in fixed investment). This pattern continued into 2000; in January-February value-added industrial output rose by a real 10.4% y-o-y – led by a 14.1% y-o-y rise in output by FIEs, followed by an 11.8 % rise in joint-stock enterprises. Collectives and SOEs lagged with growth of 7.1% and 7.6%. Private enterprises and FIEs now account for over 40% of exports. It should be noted that the role of the private sector may be somewhat overstated, in part because the ownership structure of the so-called township enterprises (TEs, previously known as township and village enterprise TVEs), which make up the bulk of the collective sector, is rather unclear. Many are part-owned by local or provincial governments, yet their output is included in that of the collective sector, and some may now be registered as private enterprises. Despite these statistical problems, it is clear that the non-state sector has become the engine of industrial growth.

The non-state sector is also providing a rising share of employment, although overall the figures remain relatively small. In January 2000 the *China Daily* reported that there are 1.49mn private firms employing a total of 19mn people, but this excludes enterprises employing less than eight people. There are a further 31.6mn such enterprises, employing 83.3mn people. The government hopes that, by correcting some of the legal and financial biases against the non-state sector, more rapid growth will help to soak up some of the millions of annual entrants to the job market. Hence there will be both greater formal recognition of the role of the non-state sector, and more efforts to remove some of the biases against such enterprises, especially their access to bank finance.

A number of steps have already been taken towards levelling the playing field for state and non-state firms. In March 1999 a carefully worded change to the constitution was approved, describing the non-state sector as an "important component" of the economy, rather than merely "complementing" the state-owned sector. Also in early 1999, the first private firms were granted licences by the Ministry of Foreign Trade and Economic Cooperation (MOFTEC) to undertake foreign trade. Previously, only state trading companies, selected state manufacturing companies and FIEs were permitted to conduct import and export business. Efforts have also been made to improve non-state sector access to credit. Also in early 1999 the State Economic and Trade Commission drafted regulations establishing institutions to provide guarantees for borrowing by small- and medium-sized enterprises, in a pilot scheme in 10 provinces. Then in January 2000 Zeng Peiyan, the minister of the State Planning and Development Commission (SPDC), took a step further, announcing that all "restrictive and discriminatory regulations" in the area of taxation, land-use, business start-ups, import and export, would be removed, and that private firms would be given equal opportunity to list on the stock market.

However, vested interests at the local and industry level are likely to continue to favour state-owned firms with government/party links for a long time to come. In addition, the non-state sector will continue to be hampered by lack of access to capital. State banks are ill-equipped to calculate commercial risk, and until interest rates are deregulated, will remain reluctant to lend to the faster growing but little-analysed private firms, with which they limited traditional links. But within the next few years, a gradual transformation of the banking sector – and the entrance of foreign competition – will start to improve matters.

WTO Membership Will Speed Rationalisation Of Industry

Since 1994, official industrial policy has centred on the promotion of the five so-called "pillar industries"–construction, automobiles, machinery, electronics and petrochemicals. The main aim is to boost the share of these sectors in world markets and as a proportion of China's industrial output. The government uses a range of measures to achieve these aims, such as tax and pricing measures and protection against imports. According to the World Bank, this policy mix often works at cross-purposes, distorting industrial development. In some cases, particularly automobiles, encouragement of new entrants (both domestic and foreign) has resulted in a proliferation of small ventures, and massive oversupply. Weak domestic and external demand, cheap imports including from crisis-hit Asian markets, and the growing presence of foreign firms have all exacerbated the oversupply problems which now affect many other key sectors. This is particularly acute in traditional sectors, such as textiles, coal, metals, and construction materials, as well as the light manufacturing sectors where TVEs have been active. In early 1999 the *China Economic Times* published a report estimating that 66.7% of 605 key manufactured products were oversupplied.

This is despite the fact that China has been undergoing a wave of merger mania since late 1997. SOE mergers are likely to continue, as healthier enterprises are married (sometimes reluctantly) to ailing partners. The government has also ordered production of some items (mostly outdated machinery) to halt, while reduced output targets are being set for commodities such as steel. FIEs are not exempt from these cutbacks. Another key measure intended to combat the effects of oversupply and growing competition, but which will also affect FIEs' profitability, was the introduction in the last quarter of 1998 of price floors for a range of products including glass, steel, cars, petrochemicals and farm machinery. (China's Price Law permits the use of such measures in exceptional circumstances.) Prices can be set and monitored in a number of ways, including through local government price bureaux, and by industry associations.

WTO membership will speed up the consolidation process. Certain sectors – such as banking, telecommunications and distribution – will have to face up to the chill winds of foreign competition for the first time. Oversupply in other sectors – such as cars – will be made even worse by the likely flood of cheap imports following the removal of protective tariff barriers. The result is expected to be a drastic consolidation of the auto sector, with many small producers forced out of business or into take-overs. The coal sector – which is also overrun by small players – faces a similar fate. However, there will be some winners. For example, the ailing textile industry, dominated by small SOEs, will receive a significant boost following the removal of export quotas by many key markets.

Corporate Taxation

China currently operates a several-tiered corporate tax band, with a range of tax incentives available to foreign funded firms. The standard corporate tax rate is 33% (including 3% local tax). FIEs in certain geographic zones or economic sectors benefit from lower tax rates in a range of 15-24% (*see Foreign Investment Policy*). The overarching direction for tax policy will be the unification of these rates, to level the playing field between Chinese and foreign firms. It is not yet clear how this is to be achieved, but the most likely option is probably for the corporate tax rate to be left in a 15-33% band, but with incentives extended to local firms (as has already started to happen in Shanghai, for example).

The widening budget deficit expected by **BMI** in the next few years suggests that the government will be unlikely to lower corporate tax rates significantly. Indeed, the 15% rate may eventually be phased out for all but the most high-priority sectors. However, concern that foreign investment inflows have peaked has made the government more reluctant to reduce incentives for FIEs in the short term. Indeed, some incentives for foreign firms are being extended (as with reduced taxes for FIEs investing in west and central regions, announced in early 2000).

Foreign Investment Policy

FDI Inflows Have Slowed

The recent rapid growth of China's export-oriented sector owes much to an influx of foreign direct investment (FDI). Between 1990-99 China has attracted around US$293bn in actual FDI inflows, dominated by small- and medium-sized firms from Hong Kong, Taiwan and the wider Chinese diaspora. Hong Kong still dominates, accounting for around 30% of actual FDI inflows in the first three quarters of 1998 (although these figures may be inflated by so-called round-tripping – funds diverted from mainland firms to their Hong Kong subsidiaries, before re-entering as FDI, in order to gain tax incentives and other privileges). Another problem is that some FDI inflows may actually be unregistered foreign loans.

Despite these distortions, it is clear that FDI inflows have played a massive role in China's recent economic success. In 1998, FDI was equivalent to 17% of total fixed investment, according to the State Statistical Bureau, and the FIE sector accounted for 44% of total exports. However, in 1999 FDI inflows totalled US$40.4bn in 1999, a drop of 11.4% compared with record inflows of US$45.6bn in 1998. Contracted FDI also dipped, reaching US$41.24bn, compared with approvals of US$52bn in 1998, itself below the previous year. Contracted FDI has been slowing steadily since 1993, when the value of contracts approved reached US$111.4bn. This slowdown in approvals points to a slowdown in actual inflows further down the line.

The 1999 fall in actual FDI inflows was blamed by the authorities on greater competition from elsewhere in Asia. But it also reflects uncertainty about emerging markets in 1997-98 as a result of the crisis. Other factors specific to China include acute overcapacity in some sectors, slowing growth and weak domestic demand. In addition, investors are facing slower decision-making by some ministries following reorganisation and staff cuts begun in 1998, and remain cautious ahead of key WTO agreements and a possible devaluation of the renminbi.

The Use Of Incentives

The pattern of FDI promotion in China mirrors the wider economic reforms, whereby the authorities use a system of trial and error, at first permitting new activities in only a few cities or specially-designated areas, before opening up across the country. Thus, after 6-10 years of heavy promotion of foreign investment, China has ended up with a plethora of different types of special investment zones offering a variety of incentives. The largest areas are the five Special Economic Zones (SEZs), each based around a coastal city. The first four opened in 1980, essentially as export processing zones, and were the first areas to offer specific investment incentives to foreigners. The next layer comprises the 452 open zones and cities, offering tax incentives and (in some cases) above-average infrastructure and other facilities. The most famous example is Shanghai's Pudong, itself home to five special sub-zones. There is also a range of other cities and zones where tax breaks are offered for investment in priority sectors.

The provinces, SEZs and other zones compete among themselves to attract FDI, and this competition has intensified as a result of the Asian economic crisis, pushing local officials to become more adventurous in offering incentives and seeking out new markets in the EU and USA. The attractiveness of SEZs and other zones offering special incentives to foreign investors will be affected when tax incentives are eventually phased out or unified for local companies (*see Industrial Policy*). However, the special zones intend to combat this by continuing to improve infrastructure and other facilities. In reality, the larger of the special zones and industrial parks are now well established, suggesting that they will remain favoured locations for FIEs. The inland provinces will continue to face an uphill struggle to attract foreign investment, although this will slowly improve as investor attention continues to shift towards exploiting China's domestic market. In order to speed up this trend, at the March 2000 National People's congress it was emphasised that priority would be given to foreign investment in these less-developed regions, including through a range of tax breaks for investors.

The Impact Of WTO

Policy towards foreign investment will be crucially shaped in the coming years by China's WTO commitments. In the agreement with the USA, China promised to open a wide range of financial and other services to foreign investment. For example:

- **Telecommunications**: Foreign firms – previously prevented from direct investments in telecoms services – will be permitted a maximum 49% stake in mobile and fixed-line telecommunications services within 5-6 years of accession; 49% ownership for most other related telecommunications services will be allowed immediately on accession, rising to 50% within two years. Geographical restrictions on paging and value-added telecommunications services will be phased out within two years of accession; similar restrictions on mobiles will be phased out within five years, and on landlines within six years.

- **Insurance**: Geographic restrictions will be removed within three years (currently foreign insurers are permitted only in Guangzhou and Shanghai). Permission will be granted for a broader range of products – including health and pensions – within five years. Life insurers will be permitted up to 50% ownership in joint ventures and will be able to select their own partners; 51% ownership in non-life firms will be permitted, and 100% ownership of reinsurance companies.

- **Banking and finance**: Geographic restrictions will be removed within five years. All foreign banks will be able to conduct local currency transactions with Chinese enterprises within two years and with individual clients within five years. Foreign firms will be permitted to invest up to 33% in fund management and underwriting firms.

- **Retailing, distribution and trading**: Removal within three years of extensive restrictions preventing foreign firms from owning or managing distribution networks, warehousing, transportation firms, wholesale or retail outlets, and from providing many after-sale, customer support and repair services. Within 3-4 years foreign firms will also be permitted to engage in related services, such as rental, leasing, freight, storage, advertising and packaging. Trading rights (for import and export) – currently highly restricted mainly to large state-owned firms – will be extended to foreign firms within three years.

- **Professional services**: Access to be granted to foreign professional firms including legal, accountancy, architecture, medical and computer-related services (with some restrictions – for example majority foreign ownership of law firms will not be permitted.)

- **Media**: Cinema ownership and video distribution will be permitted. There will be a modest increase in access for foreign films; China has committed to import 50 foreign films within three years.

- **Travel and tourism**: Majority ownership of hotel operators will be allowed on accession, with 100% foreign ownership possible within three years.

These measures are likely to stimulate a surge in FDI approvals following accession. However, for some sectors (such as cars), reduced tariffs following WTO accession may make it more viable to export to China, rather than setting up a local manufacturing base. Further, the impact on actual inflows (rather than simply approvals) will depend on how well WTO deregulation is implemented. While WTO membership will give China's market-opening and tariff reform an internationally recognised legal framework, with set deadlines, making it harder for China to backtrack, it will also result in severe dislocation for some sectors and regions. Vested interests are likely to resist implementation, and hence progress is unlikely to be totally smooth. Hence actual FDI inflows may well drop further this year, continuing to slide in 2001-2002 – despite a likely jump in approvals following WTO admission.

Foreign Trade Policy

WTO Entry Will Bring Further Tariff Cuts And Market Opening

The biggest story for China's trade policy in the coming years will be accession to the World Trade Organisation (WTO). As noted, a major hurdle was overcome in November 1999 when China finally signed an agreement on WTO membership with the USA. All the concessions accorded to US firms must also be accorded to all other WTO members – but each partner is able to negotiate bilaterally. As of March 2000, China had yet to conclude bilateral agreements with a few remaining partners – by far the most important being the EU. Talks with the EU stalled, partly over China's reluctance to improve on the telecoms offer made to the USA. An additional problem is that the US Congress has yet to approve permanent Normal Trade Relations (NTR) for China; failure to do so could prevent the concessions negotiated in November 1999 from being extended to US firms, although it probably would not prevent China's entry into the WTO. However, **BMI** expects these problems to be overcome this year, allowing China to join WTO perhaps in H2 2000 or early 2001.

WTO entry means adhering to a schedule of tariff cuts covering many key sectors. China has already made considerable progress in cutting tariffs in recent years – average tariffs were reduced to 17% from a previous 23% in October 1997, the last major round of reductions – and hence some sectors will not see drastic change. However, other long-protected sectors will be forced open. For example, the following (drawn from the US-China Business Council), delays key concessions accorded in the US deal:

- **Industrial products**: The average tariff will be reduced from 24.6% (1997) to 9.4% by 2005. Some quotas (such as on fibre optic cable) will be removed on accession.

- **The car sector**: Top tariffs will be cut from the current 80-100% to 25% within six years of accession. Quotas will be phased out by 2005. Foreign financing companies will be able to provide car loans on accession.

- **Chemicals**: Tariffs will be cut from 35%, to bands of 0%, 5.5% and 6.5%.

- **Electronics**: China will join the Information Technology Agreement, eliminating tariffs on semiconductors, computers and internet-related equipment within five years of accession (compared with an average pre-accession tariff on electronics of 13.3%.)

- **Agriculture**: China currently uses a range of quotas and non-tariff barriers (NTBs – such as pest, disease and sanitation controls); these measures must all be phased out. Average tariffs on agricultural products will be cut to 17% by January 2004, with an average of 14.5% for US priority products (such as citrus fruits) compared with an average of 31.5% now. There will be sharp increases in the imports of so-called 'bulk' commodities (such as wheat, barley and rice), and tariffs on a portion of these quotas will fall from over 120%, to 1-3%. Overall, there will sharp cuts in tariffs on dairy products, meat, fruit and wine.

In addition, market-opening of financial, communications and other services is expected. However, progress in implementing WTO provisions is not expected to be smooth. For example, continued use of 'hidden' subsidies for exporters (such as export tax rebates) is likely for some time.

Bureaucracy And Corruption

The Crackdown Continues

Corruption and excessive red tape are significant problems for foreign investors in China. Investors face the almost institutionalised charging of excessive fees and fines by local officials, while corruption has also permeated the police and judiciary. Smuggling has also been a major problem – cheap smuggled imports have exacerbated oversupply in some sectors – although the crackdown of 1998-99 has started to reduce this.

The government fears that such high levels of corruption within the Party and government threaten its legitimacy. As a result, a massive crackdown on corruption and smuggling is underway. Efforts have also been made to streamline the government, military and judiciary in a bid both to improve efficiency and to remove opportunities for graft. For example, the armed forces were ordered in 1998 to divest from their non-military commercial operations by the end of the year. These ventures were a major source of income for members of the armed forces as well as a hotbed of smuggling activity. However, there is evidence that some ties have not been fully severed (for example, **China Telecom** and military joint-ventures are already operating mobile 'CDMA' networks on an experimental basis in some key cities, in defiance of the ban on military-run companies). Enforcing the new anti-corruption policies is also proving problematic, because of both the size of the task and also endemic corruption within enforcing bodies.

Environmental Regulation

China Faces Massive Environmental Problems

China's environmental protection law was revised in 1989, requiring environmental impact studies for large projects and imposing fines for exceeding pollution limits. Foreign firms complain that environmental regulators unfairly target them. However, years of rapid growth, combined with outdated technology and weak implementation of this existing legislation, have left China facing severe environmental problems. The most critical issues are water shortages and pollution, air pollution and land degradation. Greater water use for both domestic and commercial purposes combined with inadequate pricing has resulted in quite severe water shortages in the north. In addition, according to the United Nations Development Programme (UNDP), an estimated 79% of the total population regularly drink polluted water.

Five of the world's 10 most polluted cities in terms of air quality are in China. China is the world's second largest source of greenhouse gases, and is expected to overtake the USA as the largest single source by 2020. The high level of air pollution reflects China's reliance on poor-quality sulphur-rich soft coal as a key energy source, while the rapid increase in vehicle use has exacerbated the problem. Finally, deforestation has resulted in massive soil erosion in the far north and west, adding to air-borne pollution. The UNDP estimates that lost production and other pollution-related costs (such as health problems) are currently equivalent to around 8% of China's GNP each year. Severe pollution makes some cities unpopular with both expatriate and Chinese staff.

Environmental Industries Offer Opportunities

These environmental problems offer opportunities to foreign investors in areas such as the provision of energy-efficient technology (a priority sector which offers tax breaks to foreign investors). There are also considerable opportunities for investors in key environmental projects, including the massive US$30bn Three Gorges dam, due for completion in 2009, and the wide range of environmental protection projects partly funded by the international donor community. The government plans to increase spending on environmental protection to 1.5% of GDP (from the current 0.8%) by 2005. Its priority sectors are:

■ water pollution in key river basins;

■ waste management;

■ conservation of biological resources (China is one of the world's 12 'mega biodiversity' countries);

■ conservation and cleaner use of coal, gas, oil, electricity, chemicals and metals;

■ improvement of environmental monitoring and management.

5 Capital Markets

Introduction

Relatively Undeveloped Markets

China's capital markets as a whole are relatively underdeveloped, and bank loans remain the main source of funding for most companies. This is partly the result of a reluctance to develop capital markets too rapidly while the banking sector remained unreformed. However, the government now realises that financially sound SOEs are a pre-requisite of a stronger banking system. Hence the government hopes that the capital markets will become a key source of funding for cash-strapped state-owned enterprises (SOEs) and, eventually, for private sector firms. Hence the next few years will see considerable efforts to develop institutional investment vehicles, in a bid to deepen the capital markets and reduce volatility. Improved regulation and supervision will be a vital aspect of these efforts; considerable improvements have already been made in regulation and information standards, boosted by the passage of a new Securities Law in 1999. Further regulatory changes are planned; in January 2000 the China Securities Regulatory Commission (CSRC) said that the quota system for A-share IPOs would be abandoned, with underwriters playing a bigger role in recommending new issues. However, China is still a long way behind international norms.

Equity Markets

Thin & Volatile

China's two main securities exchanges (located in Shanghai and Shenzhen) both trade A-shares (open to local investors only) and B-shares (theoretically open to foreign investors only). Trading now takes places on-line and there is a centralised settlement system. However, both markets are rather thin and volatile, as small-scale individual investors dominate trading. Secondary boards to trade in high-tech stocks are planned for this year, which may attract greater inflows of funds, although a rash of further listings by state-owned firms may depress the main boards. In addition, in late 1999 the government announced that it would gradually reduce its holdings in state-owned firms from a current 62% of total share capital, to 51%, in order to raise funds for social welfare spending. The placing of large quantities of such shares – altogether CNY200bn is expected to be sold – is expected to drive down the markets. In addition, the asset-management companies formed to convert the debts of state-owned enterprises into equity, are likely to try to offload some of those shares in the markets, further depressing prices. Plans to merge the A- and B-share markets, which could really stimulate foreign investment, seem to have been delayed.

The domestic bond market also remained undeveloped, as issuance is limited by state-set quotas and subject to fixed interest rates, although modest liberalisation of interest rates is expected to begin within 1-2 years. Overseas corporate bonds are also subject to quotas and regulated by the State Administration of Foreign Exchange (SAFE). Private companies complain that the quota system is heavily biased towards the state-sector, and are pushing for an easier approvals process. China returned to the international capital markets with a US$1bn 10-year sovereign bond in December 1998, partly to set a benchmark for future corporate issues.

Very limited use is made of derivatives. Treasury bond futures were banned in 1995 following a price rigging scandal, leaving only commodity futures. Even these were scaled back in 1999, when the number of commodity futures exchanges was cut back from 14, to three (leaving three exchanges, based in Shanghai, the northern city of Dalian, and the central city of Zhengzhou). Overseas futures trading is banned. The July 1999 Securities Law did not cover derivatives, as the authorities prefer to focus instead on improving the existing markets. However, as the stock markets expand, the lack of any hedging facilities will become more onerous, and in late 1999 reports emerged that the CSRC was considering the introduction of stock index futures, under pressure from institutional investors.

Market Structure And Size

China has two main securities exchanges, located in Shanghai (opened in 1990) and Shenzhen (opened in 1991). Both exchanges trade two classes of shares, called A- and B-shares Companies are permitted to list on both exchanges. According to press reports, total market capitalisation for both the Shanghai and Shenzhen exchanges reached CNY2.65trn (US$320bn) by end-1999, up 36% y-o-y. At this level, market capitalisation was equivalent to around 26% of GDP, indicating considerable scope for further deepening of the equities markets. The number of companies listed jumped from 851 at end-1998 to 949 at end-1999 (of which 108 were listed on the B-share markets). However, some companies are expected to have posted losses for three years running in 1999, and hence face de-listing.

At both exchanges, the local-currency A-share market, which is open to local investors only, is much larger and more liquid than the foreign-currency denominated B-share market. Daily trading volume tends to be much higher on the A-share market, and the range of sectors included is wider. In theory, the B-share market is open only to foreign investors. However, locals with access to foreign exchange are heavily involved in the B-share market (as much as 60-80% of trading may be by local investors). In 1999, both A-shares and B-shares recovered from a weak 1998; A-shares on the Shanghai exchange ended the year at 1,451.9, up 19% y-o-y, while Shenzhen A-shares closed 1999 at 431.8, up 16.7% y-o-y. B-shares – which had fallen steeply in 1998 as foreign investors worried about spread of the Asia crisis and a possible devaluation of the renminbi – showed an even stronger turnaround. Shanghai B-shares ended 1999 at 37.9, up 32% y-o-y, while

Shenzhen B-shares jumped by 58% y-o-y, to a close of 84.7.

In addition to the main exchanges, a rash of OTC exchanges sprang up in the 1990s, approved by local governments but not Beijing. After having mostly turned a blind eye for several years, in 1998 Beijing began to clamp down on the largely unregulated provincial securities industry as part of the ongoing drive to tighten up on financial sector regulation. According to the China Securities Regulatory Commission (CSRC), 42 OTC markets were closed in 1998, including one of the largest, located in the major industrial city of Wuhan. China permits only limited derivatives trading, concentrated on commodities and currency futures, and short selling is not permitted on the Shanghai and Shenzhen exchanges.

Merger of A- and B- Share Markets A Long-Term Goal

In 1997, it seemed that a merger of the A- and B-share markets was imminent; investors would like to see this step, as a way of deepening the market and boosting turnover. However, the authorities were alarmed by the role of foreign portfolio capital in triggering the Asia crisis, and have delayed merger of the two markets, as this would require making the renminbi at least partially convertible on the capital-account. The 1999 Securities Law did not specifically include the B-share market, rather stating that the State Council was empowered to issue regulations covering B-shares. Further, it emphasised that all registered A-share account holders must prove Chinese citizenship or that they were acting for a Chinese firm, suggesting that A-share and B-share markets are unlikely to be merged any time soon. In January 2000 the *Xinhua* news agency reported that merger of the A- and B-share markets was likely "within 10 years." However, access to B-shares may formally be broadened: in February 2000 officials discussed the formation of a China-foreign joint venture fund to invest in B-shares, officially giving local access to the B-share market, a move that would increase liquidity.

Two New 'High-Tech' Boards Are Planned

The Shanghai and Shenzhen exchanges are both expected to launch second boards for high-technology stocks in H2 2000, an idea first floated last year. The hope is that the new boards will be differentiated from the SOE-dominated main board, attracting fresh inflows of capital to the rapid growth high-tech sectors (such as telecommunications equipment, software and other IT firms.) The second boards will have easier listing requirements to encourage entry by smaller and newer firms, including firms from the private sector. According to the *China Business Times,* regulations governing the new boards will require listing firms to post only one year of profit – compared with the three years required on the main boards – with a lower minimum registered capital of CNY30mn (compared with CNY50mn for the main boards). A number of firms had applied to list of the new exchanges in early 2000, and hopes are high that the new boards will show strong growth this year. (The Shanghai Technology Stock Exchange, opened in late 1999, is a separate venture, allowing small high-tech firms to sell equity to institutional investors only; it is not linked to the main Shanghai exchange.)

The Clean-up Of The Securities Industry Will Continue

China's exchanges have been plagued by poor regulation, high volatility and rampant speculation. The surge in the number of individual shareholders (estimated at more than 40mn) has alarmed the authorities, fearful that a steep slide in shares could cause protests. The authorities do want to enlarge the markets, to give the corporate sector (both state-owned and private) an alternative source of capital, but recognise that this must be accompanied by further tightening up of supervision, and continued efforts to clamp down on irregularities. Accordingly, since mid-1998, the CSRC, rather than the central bank, has held sole responsibility for overseeing securities regulation. In 1999 a new Securities Law was approved. The law brought in tougher transparency requirements for listed companies; firms that violate the disclosure requirements of the 1995 Company Law will be suspended, as will firms which record losses for three consecutive years. The law also introduced a scale of fines for abuses such as false financial reporting and insider trading. In addition, banks, insurance companies and trust and investment firms were banned from running securities operations. Policing will get tougher, and even well-connected firms will be affected. The commitment to continued reform was underscored in early 2000 when sweeping personnel changes were made at key banks and regulatory agencies. Notably, a reformist ally of Zhu Rongji's, Zhou Xiaochuan, was appointed as chairman of the CSRC. Zhou had previously headed **China Construction Bank**, one of the 'big four' state banks.

As with so many other sectors, entry to the WTO will force further restructuring of the securities industry. Under the terms of the agreement with the USA, foreign financial companies will be able to take up to a 33% stake in fund management companies, rising to 49% within four years, while foreign underwriters will also be permitted to invest up to 33%. Such joint ventures will be able to trade in and underwrite domestic and foreign currency securities, on the same basis as wholly-owned Chinese firms.

H-shares And Red Chips

Since 1993, Chinese companies have been able to seek overseas listings, the favoured location to date being in Hong Kong. Mainland listings in Hong Kong comprise red chips (companies incorporated in Hong Kong but with a controlling interest in the mainland) and H-shares (incorporated in the mainland). Initially, both red chips and H-shares tended to underperform Hong Kong's Hang Seng index, in part because of concern over problems with transparency. This gave way to 'red chip fever' in 1997, boosted by investor optimism that, following the handover of Hong Kong to Chinese rule in July 1997, these companies would stand to benefit from their close ties to the mainland. However, slowing growth on the mainland and continued disclosure problems dampened enthusiasm in Hong Kong for mainland plays in 1998. Then, in late 1998, the failure of the **Guangdong International Trust and Investment Co** (GITIC) hit a number of Hong Kong banks and also raised concerns about the level of foreign debt held by some mainland companies, dampening the performance of mainland-linked shares throughout the first half of 1999. A steady recovery then allowed the red chip index to end 1999 up 40.7%, at 1,286.2 (although well below the 1997 peak of over 4,000), while H-shares rose by a more modest 14.1% to a year-end 454.3.

A number of big-name Chinese companies plan to list further afield in 2000. **China National Petroleum Corporation** (CNPC) raised US$3.1bn with a dual listing in Hong Kong and New York in April, for a unit called PetroChina. A number of factors including concerns that CNPC would use funds raised to pay laid off workers, rather than to upgrade infrastructure, have dampened overseas interest, and CNPC has had to scale down its planned listing from an initial US$7-8bn, to around US$3bn. China's second oil major, Sinopec, plans to follow with a listing for a new unit called **China Petrochemical** in Hong Kong, New York and London. In mid-March one major internet portal, **Sina.com**, was given official approval to go ahead with its planned listing on the US NASDAQ exchange.

Bond Markets

Domestic Bonds

China has a fledgling bond market on which a variety of state and corporate bonds are traded – although many big issues are placed with private investors. Primary issues are controlled by administrative fiat, although secondary trading is permitted to take place on the Shanghai and Shenzhen securities exchanges, and on two on-line electronic systems (the Securities Trade Automated Quotations System and the National Electronic Trading System). Annual quotas set by the State Council limit corporate bond issues; specific issues must be approved by the CSRC. Interest rates are regulated, being set in relation to the current bank deposit rates. Despite these factors, and competition from the government's large funding needs, the corporate bond market is likely to expand considerably in the 2000-2002 forecast period. The authorities realise that further development of institutional funds including pension funds will require a bond market with greater depth, while the funding needs of the SOEs suggest that corporate issuance may start to rise more rapidly. Some liberalisation of interest rates for corporate bonds is also expected within the next 1-2 years. China has an interbank money market, whose members comprise state banks, insurance firms and foreign bank branches. In addition to short-term funds, certificates of deposit, and commercial paper and bills of exchange are traded.

The most rapid growth has been in government debt, sold to the state banks. Since 1981, the government has issued increasingly substantial amounts of state bonds to fund the budget deficit; in 1999, the Finance Ministry issued CNY401.5bn (US$48.5bn) in bonds. It was not clear whether this figure included the CNY60bn in additional special infrastructure bonds. Bond issuance has been boosted by the need to fund the government's pump-priming projects and to underwrite the recapitalisation of the state banks. For example, in 1998 new state debt issues totalled CNY280bn, with a further CNY370bn in 'special' bonds – CNY270bn issued to start recapitalising the state banks, and CNY100bn issued as part-funding for the massive infrastructure spending programme.

The government began open market operations in 1996, but these were suspended until May 1998, partly because of a lack of tradeable bonds. However, in 1998 the central bank traded CNY176bn in bonds, rising to CNY707.6bn through open market operations in 1999. In early 2000 officials were rumoured to be considering allowing individuals and corporations to buy and sell treasury bonds through the 'big four' state banks (**Industrial and Commercial Bank of China, Agricultural Bank of China, Bank of China** and **China Construction Bank**), a move that would make the market more liquid. Further, the central bank was reportedly discussing the formation of an OTC debt market at commercial banks, to permit smaller enterprises to enter the market.

International Bond Issues

On December 10, 1998 China successfully launched a US$1bn sovereign 10-year bond, its first since the start of the Asia crisis. The issue, seen as something of a benchmark for investor appetite for Asian paper, was priced at 280 basis points over US Treasuries (50 basis points more than China's benchmark 2006 bond). The issue was oversubscribed, although there were some rumours in the market that the overseas branches of Chinese banks had bought heavily, in a bid to ensure that the offering was well received. The need for large amounts of capital (to fund bank, SOE and welfare reform) is likely to result in further international issues in the next few years.

Concerns over slowing economic growth and persistent deflation – and the impact of this on bank reform – led the rating agency Standard and Poors to downgrade China's sovereign rating to BBB, from BBB+, in July 1999. However, Moody's Investor Services left its rating at A3, two notches above the S&P rating, because of confidence in the government's commitment to economic reform, and the large size of China's reserves (giving it substantial debt-servicing capacity).

INDONESIA 2000

Analyst: Georgina Wilde

Editor: Sara Matchett

Contents

Political Outlook _____ 101

Domestic Political Outlook 101
Foreign Policy Outlook 106

Profile and Recent Developments _____ 107

Introduction 107
The Political System 110
Regional Tensions 113
Foreign Affairs 117

Economic Outlook _____ 121

Economic Activity 121
Balance Of Payments 126
Fiscal Policy 127
Monetary Policy 128
Exchange Rate Policy 129
External Debt 130
Foreign Direct Investment 131

Profile and Recent Developments _____ 133

Introduction 133
Indonesia And The IMF 135
Fiscal Policy 138
The Balance Of Payments 139
Monetary Policy 140
Exchange Rate Policy 140
Foreign Direct Investment 141

Key Economic Sectors _____ 143

Introduction 143
Manufacturing 144
Oil And Gas 146
Banking 149

Profile and Recent Developments _____ 151

Introduction 151
Metals And Mining 154
Oil And Gas 155
Manufacturing 158
Telecoms 160
Consumer Goods 160
Banking 161
Property 162
Tourism 163

Business Environment _____ 165

Introduction 165
Infrastructure 166
The Domestic Market 167
The Labour Market 168
Industrial Policy 169
Tax And Bankruptcy Policy 170
Foreign Trade Policy 172
Bureaucracy And Corruption 173
The Environment 175

Capital Markets _____ 177

Equity Markets 177
The Debt Market 178

INDONESIA: MACROECONOMIC DATA AND FORECASTS

	1993	1994	1995	1996	1997	1998	1999e	2000f	2001f	2002f
Population (mn)	187.6	190.7	194.8	196.8	199.9	204.4	206.1	209.2	212.5	215.0
Nominal GDP (US$bn)	158.0	176.9	202.1	227.4	215.0	94.2	136.9	150.4	159.2	175.9
GDP per capita (US$)	842.3	927.7	1,037.9	1,155.3	1,075.6	460.6	664.1	718.8	749.0	818.3
Real GDP growth (% y/y)	6.5	7.5	8.2	7.8	4.7	-13.2	0.3	4.5	4.7	5.7
Consumer price inflation (% an avg)	9.6	8.6	9.4	8.0	6.7	57.7	20.5	6.0	6.5	7.5
Consumer price inflation (% eop)	10.2	9.6	9.0	6.6	11.6	74.6	-0.3	9.8	7.0	8.0
Discount Rate (% eop)	9	12	14	13	20	38	13	15	14	13
Money Market Rate (% an avg)	9	10	14	14	28	63	24	16	18	16
Lending Rate (% an avg)	21	18	19	19	22	32	28	23	22	20
IDR/US$ (eop)	2,110	2,200	2,308	2,383	4,650	8,025	7,085	8,090	8,500	8,600
IDR/US$ (an avg)	2,087	2,161	2,249	2,342	2,910	10,014	7,855	7,900	8,300	8,500
Merchandise Exports (US$bn)	36.8	40.1	45.4	49.8	53.4	48.8	48.7	56.7	62.7	68.8
Merchandise Imports (cif, US$bn)	28.3	32.0	40.7	42.9	41.7	27.3	24.0	27.8	35.4	40.6
Trade balance (US$bn)	8.5	8.1	4.8	6.9	11.7	21.5	24.7	28.9	27.3	28.2
Oil/Gas exports (US$bn)	9.7	9.9	10.5	12.2	11.7	7.4	8.8	10.1	9.9	9.2
Oil output (mn b/d)	1.3	1.3	1.3	1.4	1.4	1.3	1.3	1.3	1.3	1.3
Current account (US$bn)	-2.1	-2.8	-6.4	-7.7	-4.9	4.1	5.6	6.4	5.3	2.5
Current account (% GDP)	-1.3	-1.6	-3.2	-3.4	-2.3	4.4	4.1	4.2	3.3	1.4
Foreign reserves (US$bn)*	11.3	12.1	13.7	18.3	16.6	22.7	24.0	28.0	30.2	32.0
Import Cover (mths)**	3.4	3.2	2.9	3.5	2.9	5.2	9.6	9.8	9.0	8.2
External debt (US$bn)	89.2	107.8	124.4	128.9	136.2	147.5	139.9	141.5	147.3	151.2
External debt (% GDP)	56.4	61.0	61.5	56.7	63.3	156.6	102.2	94.1	92.5	86.0
External debt (% exports)	214.4	234.1	229.4	222.3	209.2	259.8	272.2	236.2	221.5	212.4

e/f = BMI estimate/forecast, eop = end of period, * excluding gold, ** no. of months imports covered by FX reserves + gold. Sources: Bank Indonesia/IMF/World Bank//BMI.

Domestic Political Outlook

Wahid Under Siege

President Abdurrahman Wahid's fortunes plummeted in the second quarter of 2000, along with the rupiah and Jakarta stock exchange. Under attack from across the broad political spectrum that united to bring him to power in October 1999, the president now faces censure at the annual meeting of the the People's Consultative Assembly (*Majelis Permusyawaratan Rakyat*, or MPR) in August when the upper house will hear his annual progress report. He will almost certainly survive, but at the price of making concessions to his coalition partners.

Wahid, a liberal Muslim cleric, won the presidency last October as a compromise candidate, who had to reach out to other parties to form a government. His own political party, the National Awakening Party (PKB), controls only about 10% of seats in parliament (the *Dewan Perwakilan Rakyat*, or DPR). He built a coalition based on three main blocs: the Indonesian Democratic Party Struggle (PDIP) of his defeated rival, vice-president Megawati Sukarnoputri; Golkar, much reduced in strength though only slightly reformed since it ceased to be the political vehicle of former president Suharto and his successor, B J Habibie; and the Muslim Centre Axis, an alliance of Muslim parties. His loudest critic has been Amien Rais, leader of the National Mandate Party (PAN) and the moving force behind the Centre Axis, who has already announced that he intends to run for the presidency in 2004.

Other parts of the coalition have also begun to waver. The loss of cabinet seats has angered the PDIP, Golkar and the United Development Party (PPP), the largest party in the Centre Axis. Particular policies, such as the president's proposal to lift a ban on communism and his supposed indifference to the fate of Muslims in the Moluccas, have alienated followers of the more militant, "modernist" Islam that dominates the Centre Axis. The modernists have always been suspicious of the form of political Islam represented by the

President Abdurrahman Wahid faces censure in August as discontent with his leadership intensifies across the political spectrum.

The Forces At Play
Indonesia - 1999 general election results

Party	Number of seats	% of elected seats	% of DPR seats	% of MPR seats
DPR (National Assembly)				
PDI-P	153	33	31	22
Golkar Party	120	26	24	17
PPP	58	13	12	8
PKB	51	11	10	7
PAN	34	7	7	5
Crescent Star Party	13	3	3	2
Justice Party	7	2	1	1
Love The Nation Democratic Party	5	1	1	1
Nahdlatul Ulama Party	5	1	1	1
Justice & Unity Party	4	1	1	1
Indonesian Democratic Party	2	0	0	0
Appointed by the Military	38		8	5
Others	10	2	2	5
Sub-total DPR	500			71
Appointed by Provinces (5 per Province)	135			19
Appointed by the National Election Commission	65			9
Sub-total Appointed Members	200			29
Total MPR	700			100

MPR = Majelis Permusyawaratan Rakyat, DPR = Dewan Perwakilan Rakyat; Source: BMI.

The postponement of IMF funding and the sacking of two senior ministers on April 24 have raised doubts about Wahid's handling of the economy.

Bottom Of The Heap

Corruption Perception Index - a regional comparison

World Ranking	Country	CPI Score*
7	Singapore	9.1
16	Hong Kong	7.8
29	Malaysia	5.3
29	Taiwan	5.3
43	South Korea	4.2
52	China	3.5
55	Philippines	3.3
61	Thailand	3.0
66	India	2.9
71	Pakistan	2.7
74	Vietnam	2.5
80	**Indonesia**	**2.0**

10 = highly clean; 0 = highly corrupt.; Source: Transparency International.

Wahid's decision to sack two key ministers from opposition parties has attracted allegations of cronyism.

"traditionalist", liberal Wahid and backed him in his fight with Megawati for the presidency only as the lesser of two evils. Policy disarray, sometimes amounting to paralysis, in areas as vital as the economy and the regions, has further undermined support for the president. At the same time, signs that a new brand of authoritarianism and cronyism may be emerging has worried liberals, who together with the PKB and its parent Muslim social organisation, *Nahdlatul Ulama*, make up Wahid's core constituency.

Poor Economic Management

Two recent events in particular – the IMF's decision at end-March to delay disbursement of the latest tranche of its assistance package and the sacking of two senior ministers on April 24 – highlighted the difficulties the president is having in running his government. The IMF took its decision on the grounds that the government had failed to meet no less than 42 deadlines set out in its January Letter of Intent (LOI). By early June – after a flurry of ministerial activity allowed more deadlines to be met and a new LOI had been agreed that permitted the postponement of others – IMF funds started to flow again, but this did little to dispel doubts about the quality of economic management. The confused response to the fall of the rupiah in April-May, when senior officials, including the president, made contradictory statements about what the government would do to stem the currency's decline, contributed to a new crisis of confidence that overshadowed the IMF's guarded vote of confidence. Various presidential initiatives have not brought increased orderliness to economic management. His own more direct involvement in policy-making and the mushrooming of advisory and monitoring committees have, if anything, further weakened the already rocky position of the co-ordinating minister for economic affairs, Kwik Kian Gie, who looks likely to go in the major cabinet reshuffle now expected to take place after the August MPR session.

Mounting Allegations Of Sleaze

The cabinet changes of April 24 were ostensibly about improving economic management. In fact they raised wider questions about the president's management skills and integrity, while doing nothing to enhance the cabinet's economic competence. Wahid sacked two core members of his economic team, the minister of investment and state enterprises, Laksamana Sukardi of the PDIP, and the industry and trade minister, Yusuf Kalla of Golkar. In their place he installed two of his own circle: Rozy Munir to investment and state enterprises, and Lieutenant-General Luhut Panjaitan at industry and trade, thereby attracting charges of cronyism. His failure to give consistent reasons for the sackings – he veered between accusing the two ministers of poor teamwork and finding "indications" of "corruption, collusion and nepotism" (KKN) – only increased the suspicion that his motives had more to do with consolidating his own patronage network than improving the performance of his government. The changes also further upset the balance of political forces in the cabinet, which had already been disturbed by earlier reshuffles. The PDIP, Golkar and the PPP can now all claim to be underrepresented in the cabinet as a result of the changes (five in all) Wahid has made to the 34-member cabinet since he picked it last October.

Potentially most damaging for Wahid, his accusation that the two sacked ministers were corrupt has backfired, and has fed into the wider allegations of sleaze now lapping around his presidency. It is widely believed that Sukardi lost his post precisely because he had tried to fight corruption. He had tried to bring to book a well-connected conglomerate, **Texmaco**, which he had publicly accused of serious violations of banking regulations during the Suharto era, and had attempted to set more rigorous criteria for appointments to the boards of state-owned enterprises. Kalla's fall has been linked to a power contract won by a firm he controlled which was coveted by Wahid associates. Other disclosures have given credence to the view that the Wahid presidency is nurturing a new climate of KKN. The most serious of these is the so-called Buloggate scandal, centring on allegations that Wahid's former

THE INDONESIAN CABINET (AS OF JUNE 2000)	
DEPARTMENT	**NAME**
President	**Abdurrahman Wahid**
Vice-president	**Megawati Sukarnoputri**
Co-ordinating minister for economics, finance & industrial affairs	Kwik Kian Gie
Defence	Juwono Sudarsono
Co-ordinating minister for political & security affairs and home affairs	Lieutenant-General Surjadi Sudirja
Agriculture	Mohammad Prakosa
Co-ordinating minister for people's welfare and poverty alleviation	Basrii Hasanuddin
Attorney-general	Marzuki Darusman
Education	Yahya Muhaiman
Foreign Affairs	Alwi Shihab
Communications	Lieutenant-General Agum Gumelar
Finance	Bambang Sudibyo
Trade & industry	Lieutenant-General Luhut Panjaitan
Forestry & plantations	Nur Mahmudi Ismail
Law & legislation	Yusril Ihza Mahendra
Investment & state enterprises	Rozy Munir
Mines & energy	Lieutenant-General Bambang Yudhoyono
Public Works	Rozik Boediro Soetjipto
Central bank governor	Sjahril Sabirin
Source: BMI.	

masseur and possibly other close associates of the president were involved in the disappearance of IDR35bn (US$4.1mn) from the state commodities agency, Bulog.

Social Turmoil

Social and sectarian unrest intensified in the second quarter of 2000.

These developments have taken place against a background of continuing social and sectarian unrest across much of the archipelago, which the government appears powerless to stem. Christian-Muslim conflict is still most acute in the Moluccas, but has spread to other parts of the archipelago. A cease-fire agreement that came into force in Aceh on June 2 has not reduced either the level of violence or the strength of pro-independence sentiment in the province. In Irian Jaya (Papua), greater official tolerance has merely confirmed that the desire to separate from Indonesia may be unstoppable: an officially-sanctioned Papuan People's Congress in early June, bringing together thousands of delegates from throughout the province, ended with the endorsement of a 1961 declaration of independence. Regional policies designed to satisfy local grievances against central government are in disarray. Two Habibie-era bills, giving the regions greater governmental and budgetary powers, look like turning out to be another poisoned chalice for Wahid from his predecessors. The bills are due to come into force on January 1, 2001, but the process of handing over powers to the regions is just getting under way. No one expects the newly empowered provinces and districts to operate smoothly from Day One, and many fear that the new arrangements will be fiscally damaging and encourage corruption.

The Armed Forces Will Remain On The Defensive

Wahid will probably have to concede greater freedom of manoeuvre to the TNI to ensure its support in parliament and contain social unrest.

Political and social turmoil put the armed forces (TNI) in a position to claw back some of their lost power, but not very much of it and a return to the dominance they enjoyed during the Suharto years can be ruled out. The power of the TNI, in particular of its core service, the army, has been waning since Suharto's overthrow in May 1998. A host of recent reverses – the sacking of General Wiranto; ongoing investigations into alleged military abuses in East Timor, Aceh and elsewhere; its inability to control the various conflicts rocking the archipelago; the development of a new defence doctrine, giving internal security functions to the police and focusing on Indonesia's maritime strategic needs; and a squeeze on their budget and off-budget financing – continue to keep the TNI on the defensive. Wahid needs a supportive military, whether to combat social unrest or in parliament, and will probably have to concede greater freedom of manoeuvre to the TNI to ensure it. This will probably slow the TNI's return to the barracks but, barring a prolonged period of turmoil leading to social meltdown, will not reverse the military's loss of power and standing.

Impeachement Or Compromise?

The combination of policy failure, scandal and unchecked social turmoil has created the spectre of the PDIP and Golkar lining up with the Centre Axis at the August MPR session to impeach the president. This scenario has been encouraged by statements from Amien Rais, who argues that the PDIP-Golkar-Centre Axis alliance is fully entitled to withdraw its support from the president it had in effect created. The two other leaders whose backing Amien needs – Megawati Sukarnoputri and the Golkar chairman, Akbar Tanjung – have so far shown little enthusiasm for ousting the president so soon after his election. However, a move initiated by Golkar to summon the president to the DPR for questioning has succeeded in gaining the support of a majority of MPs. Some saw this "interpellation" of the president as the first step in his impeachment.

In fact, although talk of impeachment is unlikely to die down in the weeks leading up to the MPR session, for both procedural and political reasons Wahid is unlikely to be forced out of office. To impeach the president, the MPR would have to hold a special session rather than the regular annual session now envisaged, and to call a special session requires a resolution in the lower house, the DPR, supported by two-thirds of its members. Even then the MPR could call for Wahid's resignation only if it could show that he had breached the law or the constitution or seriously deviated from the MPR's Guidelines of State Policy. Hence the importance of the corruption allegations swirling around the presidency: if Wahid's involvement could be substantiated, they could form the basis for impeachment. However, even then the political will for impeachment probably would not exist. Wahid remains the closest thing to a unifying force in Indonesian politics. Ideological opposition – mainly from the Muslim right – to Megawati, who would automatically become president were Wahid forced to step down, is now supplemented by wider doubts about her capacity to do the job based on her poor performance as vice-president. Even the most hostile political parties look likely to shrink from the sort of internecine politics that could one day claim them.

The more likely outcome is a new political contract between the coalition partners. Two options are being mooted. Under the first Wahid has a freer hand in appointing his cabinet, although he would still presumably have to continue to pay political debts to his coalition partners. This would be the president's preferred option: as soon as he was appointed, Wahid made know his dislike of the "cattle auction" that had produced his cabinet, even

For both procedural and political reasons Wahid is unlikely to be forced out of office at the August session of the MPR.

claiming that some of his ministers were unknown to him. The second option would be to pay greater attention to the requirements of political balance by recasting the cabinet in conjunction with the main power brokers. Neither option would guarantee a stable political climate for long, but either could buy Wahid more time.

Foreign Policy Outlook

The Domestic Dimension

Foreign relations will continue to be heavily influenced by domestic politics.

Wahid came into office preaching a new foreign-policy doctrine for Indonesia based on a tilt away from the country's traditional Western allies, the US and Australia in particular, and towards "non-hegemonic" powers, such as India, China and Russia. In practice he has behaved differently, finding friends wherever he can through visits to more than 30 countries, mainly with an eye to shoring up support at home. Domestic politics will continue to dictate how much freedom of movement Wahid has in developing foreign policy. His delicate relationship with the military will largely determine how far he can go in mending relations with the West after the breach they suffered in the wake of last year's events in East Timor. Currently these pressures are most evident in the continuing difficulties in relations with Australia, but if Indonesia enters another political and economic downward spiral, the impact on its foreign policy could be more far-reaching.

Profile and Recent Developments

Introduction

The New Order

The Hindu and Buddhist kingdoms that developed in Sumatra and Java from the 7th century, succumbed in the 14th century to the slow advance of Islam. European incursions began in the 16th century, led by the Portuguese, who built fortresses in the Moluccas to protect their lucrative spice trade. The Portuguese were replaced in the 17th century by the Dutch, who achieved dominance in Java and the other islands in the 19th century. Dutch rule ended when Japanese forces occupied the archipelago in early 1942. On Japan's surrender, nationalist groups declared independence from the Netherlands on August 17, 1945. The Dutch only officially relinquished their power over most of the archipelago in December 1949. In 1963 Indonesia was given sovereignty over Dutch New Guinea (Irian Jaya), which was formally incorporated into Indonesia in 1969; in 1975 Indonesia invaded, and subsequently integrated the former Portuguese colony of East Timor, an annexation that was not recognised by the United Nations. In 1982, Indonesia was accorded international recognition of its sovereignty over the seas separating its many islands.

Sukarno was Indonesia's first president. A populist, he ruled from 1945 until an abortive coup in 1965 – blamed on the Communist Party of Indonesia and accompanied by large-scale bloodshed – led to his downfall. Sukarno left the country in economic chaos, but his poor record is fading in the Indonesian people's memory, and he is increasingly remembered as a socialist-populist-nationalist leader. Sukarno's daughter Megawati Sukarnoputri gained in stature as a result of this. He was replaced by Major-General Suharto who was inaugurated in 1967 and elected for six more five-year terms, the last beginning in March 1998. Suharto's New Order government focused on economic development. The economy was diversified, moving Indonesia from a dependence on oil and gas and commodities to a manufacturing-based economy. But the corruption and graft associated with Suharto have increasingly overshadowed his economic record.

Suharto's Iron Grip

Before Suharto took power in 1966, the Communist Party of Indonesia (PKI) was the world's third largest with around two million members. In the bloody upheaval which saw Sukarno ousted, as many as 500,000 suspected communists were slaughtered. For more than 30 years, Suharto maintained his grip on power in Indonesia by keeping a delicate balance between the major forces of the country, and making economic development the cornerstone of his policy. Economic growth averaged 8% a year in the first 15 years of his rule and poverty levels dropped from 65% in 1965 to about 10% two decades later.

The "New Order", as Suharto's administration was known, was largely supported by the West, even if it was associated with limited political and press freedom, no separation of powers and a judiciary system obedient to the executive. The "New Order" was virulently anti-communist and as the cold war intensified – and the Vietnam war became a major East-West ideological conflict – Indonesia found itself a key Asia Pacific ally. Consequently, the West closed its eyes to Suharto's suppression of opponents, including communists, supposed communists, Islamists and democrats.

Increasingly, as his country became richer, Suharto seemed unable to set priorities or separate the interests of his cronies and the nation. Economic growth remained strong, but the nature of the country's expansion shifted. Manufacturing grew in importance, fuelled by foreign investment that was increasingly associated with Suharto cronies. Banks lent on the basis of connections over economic fundamentals. The income gap between those who had and those who had not widened, and the legitimacy Suharto commanded in his early years weakened. Discontent became wider and deeper.

The economic crisis that began in 1997 was accompanied by increasingly bold opposition to the regime, opposition which culminated in riots in Jakarta in May 1998 and brought Suharto's reign to an end. He resigned and was succeeded by the vice-president, Jusuf Habibie. Habibie faced numerous political and economic pressures as economic crisis was compounded by unrest among Indonesia's diverse communities. Habibie's association with Suharto, his long-term patron, tended to discredit him. Most of the forces responsible for the end of the Suharto era distrusted the new president and in October 1999 the People's Consultative Assembly, (*Majelis Permusyawaratan Rakyat*, or MPR) voted to reject his account of his 18 months in office, effectively ending his political career.

The 1999 Elections

Meanwhile, under arrangements prescribed by the outgoing House of People's Representative (Dewan Perwakilan Rakyat, or DPR), Indonesia's first free election since 1955 was held in June 1999. Accepted by observers as free and fair – although the votes took a very long time to count and the results were not finally ratified by presidential decree until August – the elections failed to produce an outright winner. The Indonesian Democratic Party of Struggle (PDI-P) gained the most votes, 34% of the total, followed by Golkar, chaired by Akbar Tanjung, whose superior organisational and financial resources helped it to take 22% of the vote, despite the fact that many of its built-in advantages were stripped away before the election. The National Awakening Party (PKB), led by Abdurrahman Wahid, gained 13%, the United Development Party (PPP), led by Hamzah Haz 11%, while Aimien Rais's National Mandate Party (PAN) performed poorly, with only 7% of the overall vote.

The electoral arithmetic for the election of the president was complicated by the fact that the MPR, which elects the president, consists of the 500-member DPR (462 elected members, plus 38 military representatives under the new arrangements for the 1999 election) and 200 appointed members from regional and functional groups. As the leader of the party which gained the largest share of the popular vote in June election, Megawati Sukarnoputri started as the front-runner for the presidency. She had a claim as Sukarno's daughter. She also appeared to enjoy the support, somewhat grudging, of the armed forces and police faction in the MPR, although such support, and its reputation for involvement in money politics, was also a source of doubt about the PDI-P's commitment to reforms. Against her, moreover, was her gender. Also the fact that despite having the largest number of parliamentary seats it was difficult to find the necessary allies, her closest ally being the PKB. Nor was her personal style regarded as conducive to building support.

Habibie's prospects seemed to have been boosted by Golkar's surprisingly strong showing in the elections. The incumbent president hoped to attract Muslim and military support as well as the backing of a substantial proportion of the non-elected representatives to the MPR, thanks to the previously compulsory and now informal support of many local bureaucrats for Golkar. But Golkar itself had become disunited, with a reformist wing under Akbar Tanjung, a nationalist wing and a smaller Habibie wing, which was at odds with the other two. Habibie's chances were further dented by the Bank Bali scandal in August 1999, when it was suggested that funds intended for recapitalisation of Bank Bali had been diverted for his faction of Golkar. The humiliation surrounding the loss of East Timor (*see below*) helped to dash his hopes. General Wiranto, the then commander of the armed forces and the defence minister, widely seen as responsible for meddling in politics and for military excesses, turned down Habibie's invitation to run as vice-president shortly before the vote was due and the MPR rejected the president's speech (*see above*), with substantial desertions by Golkar. Humiliated, Habibie withdrew from the contest. Nor would either of those he asked to stand in his place – Amien Raias and then Akbar Tanjung – agree to do so.

Both of the latter decided to support the eventual victor in the presidential race: Abdurrahman Wahid (widely known as Gus Dur) was chosen as president on October 20, 1999. The base of his support came from the fact that he, like his father and grandfather before him, served as leader of Nahdlatul Ulama (NU), a Muslim social organisation with nearly 40mn members. He founded the PKB in July 1998. Having looked unlikely to win the presidency, he came in through the middle, with the strong support of the Centre Axis, a Muslim Coalition set up by the PAN leader, Amien Rais, in July 1999. A liberal, he appeared to be the only person able to bridge the divisions between the strands of Islam, between secular nationalism and the Muslim faith and between reformers and the still powerful heirs to Suharto's New Order. Megawati was elected shortly thereafter as vice-president, despite any misgivings he may harbour about her style.

Wahid's First Cabinet

The new president announced his first cabinet on October 26. Described as a cabinet of "national unity", it was a tribute to Gus Dur's political horse-trading skills, including representatives of virtually the whole political spectrum. A Habibie loyalist, representing so-called "black" Golkar,

Jusuf Kalla, was appointed as trade and industry minister and a Suharto-era trade unionist Bomer Pasaribu, was made minister of manpower. In a cabinet of 36 members, the Centre Axis parties gained the largest number of seats, with just under half, while Tentara Nasional Indonesia (TNI, the armed forces, formally ABRI) took six positions. Three powerful coordinating ministries were retained and went to the military (General Wiranto, coordinating minister for political and security affairs), a nationalist (Kwik Kian Gie of the PDI-P, economics, finance and industrial affairs) and a Muslim politician (Hamzah Haz of the PPP, people's welfare and poverty alleviation).

Widely criticised as unwieldy and lacking in cohesion, the cabinet quickly came under fire. Individuals – notably Hamzah, Borner Paribasu and Jusuf Kalla – were referred to the attorney-general on corruption related matters from the previous regime. It also became apparent that the ministries are becoming party fiefdoms, with the risk of replicating in their own way the cronyism of the Suharto era. Nor are the coordinating ministries proving notably successful and there is talk of abolishing them and creating a prime ministerial system. But Megawati, the vice president, whose public standing has not improved and is widely known as the "sleeping princess" is not seen as a suitable choice for such a role.

The Political System

The New Order System

The "New Order" was based on a vague ideology known as *pancasila*, which included five principles such as the belief in one god, calls for humanitarism, national unity and democracy through consensus and social justice. Only three parties were allowed to operate in Indonesia; the government party, *Golongan Karya* or Golkar, and two small "opposition" parties, the United Development Party (PPP), an amalgam of a number of Muslim organisations, and the Democratic Party of Indonesia (PDI), which was forged out of nationalist and Christian parties. Only these three parties were allowed to contest the parliamentary elections in May 1997. The PDI's decline in 1997 was due to the eviction of Megawati by a more docile rival. Most of the lost votes went to the PPP.

The system of government under Suharto was theoretically a democracy, but the country was in practice ruled by an oligarchy of around 2,000 Javanese individuals. The notion of separation of powers was completely ignored. The president was elected for a five-year term, and could be elected indefinitely. The cabinet was appointed by the president and was responsible to the chief executive. The president was in theory accountable to the MPR, *(Majellis Permuyawaratan Rakyat)*, the People's Consultative Assembly. This 1,000-member body was empowered with the highest authority of the state. The body consisted of 500 members of the House of Representatives, *Dewan Perwakilan Rakyat* (DPR) – 425 elected and 75 reserved for the military – and 500 presidential appointees. As a result, a majority of the MPR, which appointed the president, worked for the ruling party.

Towards A Federal System

Indonesia's political and constitutional institutions are in a state of flux. The passage of three bills covering the democratisation process shaped the conduct of democratic elections in 1999. The continued presence of military representatives was a thorny issue, but the key opposition parties accepted the reduction, to 38 from 75 military seats, viewing it as a first step towards ending the military's involvement in politics. It has been agreed, although not legislated for, that military representation in the DPR will be phased out by 2004. To avoid conflicts of interest, the new laws also banned members of the DPR and the MPR from holding positions in either the government or the judiciary, thus removing one of Golkar's key advantages. The laws covering the elections are due for review after three years, and the current system of proportional representation, which still gives additional weight to voters in outlying districts, is likely to be changed.

The Indonesian constitution is likely to evolve in the direction of a more truly federal system, although the process will be slow. New laws passed by the outgoing DPR in 1999 provided for devolution of the administrative and fiscal systems by 2001. These provide for a more district-based administration and will redistribute resource-based revenues more equitably. The government is offering resource-rich provinces 15% of the government's share of net oil revenue, 30% of gas and 80% of proceeds coming from forestry, mining and fisheries. A number of other constitutional changes are being considered by the MPR Standing Committee, including direct election of the president (whose term is now limited to two five-year periods), changes to the relative powers of the MPR and DPR (the MPR currently elects the president), establishment of a system of judicial review and redefinition and reduction in the role of the armed forces. A federal structure would lend itself to the existing cultural and ethnic diversity of Indonesia, and may help to placate separatist aspirations, Moreover, many provinces rich in natural resources, ranging from oil and gas to gold, copper and timber, have complained that Jakarta has ended up with the lion's share of revenue from these resources and want a greater say in running their own affairs.

The Changing Role of The Military

Indonesia's army, battered by charges of human rights abuses and dogged by calls to get out of politics, is not popular. Its prestige has been severely dented by its blatant involvement in the violent aftermath to the independence referendum in East Timor in September 1999 and by longstanding charges of abuse in Aceh and elsewhere. Despite its loss of prestige, however, the military remains the strongest and most unified institution in Indonesia. Although the number of seats allocated to the military in the DPR has been cut to 38 from 75, that still gives the military almost 8% of seats, more than all but a handful of the parties won in the June elections. In addition, the military holds 27 of the 135 seats in the MPR allocated to regional representatives.

The army's dual military and socio-political role, known as dual-function (*dwifungsi*), is rooted in the 1945-49 war of independence from the Dutch. The military has concentrated on combating perceived internal threats – such as in East Timor – and on contributing to the development of the country. Politics was crucial to both, and for three decades the army threw its political and military weight behind Suharto.

The attitude of the military during the last days of Suharto, including its involvement in the riots which hit Jakarta and human rights abuses in East Timor, Aceh and Irian Jaya, has discredited it in the eyes of many Indonesians. The fall of Suharto was accompanied by growing public demands that the military go back to the barracks and reassess its role and doctrine, including its *dwifungsi* role. The military understands that its links to Suharto's rule are becoming a major obstacle to its repositioning in a new, more democratic Indonesian society. But there are divisions about how to proceed to rebuild the army's prestige and the armed forces face stringent financial constraints in the new climate. A three-way split is discernible in the armed forces. The old Suharto-era elite is now largely in retreat, but its attitudes are well-entrenched. Reformers see the need for rapid disengagement of the army from politics and generally support the reformist cause. Professional soldiers put the army at the centre of their aspirations and are willing to compromise along reformist lines if this is expedient, although they have no particular enthusiasm.

In April 1999 the 180,000-strong police force (Polri) was formally split from the 220,000-strong TNI (armed forces). The then army chief General Wiranto acknowledged that the role of police should be different from the army. The new police force reports to the Defence Ministry, where a civilian minister of defence was installed by the new president. Wiranto stepped down as army chief when he joined the new government and was succeeded by Admiral Widodo Adisutjipto.

In early February 2000 it was announced that Wahid had asked former armed forces chief General Wiranto to relinquish his post as coordinating minister for political and security affairs. This decision came in the wake of a government-backed inquiry, which incriminated the former armed forces commander, along with five other senior officers, in the bloodshed in East Timor. The president signed a decree a few days before the findings of the official investigation were reported, ordering the general's early resignation from the Indonesian army, to take effect from March 31. Wiranto initially resisted, refusing to step down until his position was judicially clarified, but Wahid prevailed and Wiranto has now been sidelined.

Further moves to phase out the Old Guard from the armed forces came later in February with the announcement of a major armed forces reshuffle involving the transferral or retirement of 74 officers. The most notable change was the promotion of reformer Major General Agus Wirahadikusumah to the position of Army Strategic Reserve Command (Kostrad) chief, effective from March 1. He has been an ardent critic of the military's interference in politics and was moved from a regional command post. He takes over from Lieutenant General Djadja Suparman, a Wiranto ally. Anther important change was the removal of Lieutenant General Suaidi Marasabessy, another Wiranto crony from the post of Chief of General Staff, to be replaced by Lieutenant General Djamari Chaniago.

Almost all senior military posts are now filled with either moderate or radical reformers loyal to the civilian government. This will help in the process of diluting the military's 'dual function' role, as both socio-political ballast and defence force. Wirahadikusumah has been an outspoken opponent of this system, while chief of staff for territorial affairs, Lieutenant General Agus Wijaya, has said that he and many of his colleagues would like to move away from their non-military role when the civilian administration has been correspondingly strengthened.

Cleansing The System

Wahid's commitment to stamping out corruption, collusion and nepotism (*korupsi, kolusi dan nepotism, KKN*) has come under question as his own political and economic crony system has established itself. This is partly a function of the lack of robust public institutions in Indonesia. A new anti-corruption law was passed in July 1999, but the then attorney-general, Andi M. Gahib, used Suharto's ill-health as a reason for halting action against him in mid-1999. Ghalib himself resigned. Shortly thereafter Indonesian Corruption Watch charged him with accepting bribes. Nor has his successor, Marzuki Darusman, found any charges that have stuck against any of the Suharto family or cronies, despite widespread allegations of massive fortunes at home and abroad. The official investigation failed to find more than US$3mn in Suharto's Jakarta bank accounts when his fortune is estimated at more than US$15bn.

Regional Tensions

Ethnic Tensions Mount

Indonesia's size and ethnic and religious diversity offer huge potential, but also contain the seeds of fragility, discontent and violence. Indonesia's Chinese community comprises 3-4% of the population, but controls about three-quarters of the country's private economy. Over the years, it has been a frequent target of animosity and periodic violence from the Muslim majority. As the Chinese community is also Christian, this adds to ethnic tensions.

The Chinese community found itself the target of looting, violence and rapes during riots in 1998. The role of Suharto's son-in-law Prabowo remains unclear, but he is believed to have instigated the riots in order to foment civil war, which would have given him the opportunity to take Wiranto's position. His plans eventually failed, and he was demoted shortly after Suharto's resignation.

During the riots, many ethnic Chinese fled from the violence and took refuge in Singapore, Australia or further afield. Money from the Chinese community had begun to exit the country for Singapore when the rupiah started depreciating in autumn 1997, and any that remained had left by the time Suharto stepped down. Houses were bought in cities such as Perth or Singapore, assets that the Chinese hope would smooth the way towards citizenship if things were to go wrong again at home.

Ahead of the June elections, the Chinese community took no chances. Most sent their families to Singapore to wait for the outcome. They are hopeful that the anti-Chinese violence can be tackled and few are considering leaving Indonesia for good. But a permanent resolution will require better education for all Indonesians and a reduction in the wealth disparity between communities.

The Hot Spots

The economic crisis has highlighted ethnic, religious and social tensions in Indonesia. The following highlights Indonesia's hot spots:

The Moluccas, also known as the spice islands, has a population mix of Christians, Muslims and animists. The worst violence has taken place in Ambon, where several hundred people have been killed, mainly due to religious tensions. Long-time observers agree that Ambon was never the haven of religious harmony portrayed by the government. When Indonesia won independence in 1949, Christian separatists in Ambon sought to break away from the new republic, with the aim of creating their own Republic of the South Moluccas. The post-independence years saw an influx of devoutly Muslim migrants from other islands of Sulawesi. Over time, the new settlers ate away at Christian dominance. When an Ambonese Muslim became governor in 1992, Christians began to fear that they were under threat. The economic downturn has exacerbated competition for resources and added to the underlying tensions. Violence is now endemic.

West Kalimantan is a traditional hot spot. Violence erupted in 1997 in the provincial capital of Pontianak. The city has a violent history and diverse ethnic mix, including ethnic Chinese, Muslims, indigenous Dayaks and immigrants from the Indonesian island of Madura. This immigration was largely based on Suharto's past policy of "transmigration", which relocated large numbers of people into different parts of the country, regardless of their different cultures and religions. The Madurese became a target of violence from the rest of the Western Kalimantan population.

Violence also erupted in the West Timor capital of Kupang between Muslims and Christians. Southern Sumatra was also affected, especially in the Lampung area between local people and Java immigrants, also resulting from the government's transmigration programme.

Ethnic violence is clearly a by-product of the economic crisis and the unstable political situation. Many allegations have been made that Suharto's supporters were behind the outbreaks of unrest in Ambon and Western Kalimantan. There is a lack of solid evidence to prove that there was a conspiracy aimed at disrupting the June elections. But whether or not the violence was premeditated, it only required a spark to ignite the fire.

However violent and tragic these ethnic conflicts were, none of them threaten the integrity of Indonesia to the extent of the East Timor conflict and possibly Irian Jaya or Aceh. A federal structure might help to contain centrifugal forces.

The Loss Of East Timor

Annexed in 1976 as the Portuguese withdrew hastily from the remaining parts of their colonial empire, Indonesia has never been able to suppress a strong pro-independence movement in the territory. The East Timor problem reflects Indonesia's difficulty in integrating different ethnic groups, cultures and religions under a single centralised structure.

The United Nations continued to recognise Portugal as the official administrator of East Timor. The island has seen ongoing sporadic violence, which culminated with the 1991 Dili massacre when the Indonesian army shot at a crowd of protestors. The most influential leader of the East Timorese independence movement (*Fretilin*), Jose "Xanana" Gusmao, was captured and put in jail in 1992 and then transferred to house arrest until after the referendum on East Timor.

In a major shift in policy, Habibie offered East Timor autonomy through a referendum. Indonesia and Portugal agreed to the autonomy vote under the control of the United Nations, with Indonesia taking responsibility for security during the vote. If the referendum were to be rejected, East Timor would be free to secede. Anti-independence militias, reported to have been armed and trained by members of the Indonesian military, tried to scare the population into accepting autonomy and then went on a violent rampage when over three-quarters voted against it. The army believed that independence for East Timor would create a precedent for separatist movements in Aceh and Irian Jaya.

The aftermath of the East Timor vote, in which there was an overwhelming rejection of Indonesia by a population that had been oppressed for over 25 years, was deeply humiliating for the army and for President Habibie. Perhaps the greatest humiliation was the international pressure, which forced Indonesia to accept an Australian-led international peacekeeping force in East Timor in September 1999, and the withdrawal of the Indonesian army.

Irian Jaya: Next On The List?

Irian Jaya and East Timor are the only provinces added to Indonesia since its independence in 1945. Irian Jaya, as West Papua, was a Dutch colony until 1962 and transferred to Indonesia as part of the decolonisation process. Indonesia had promised to give the people independence by 1969, but instead, the traditional leaders were asked, under the gaze of armed Indonesian soldiers, if they wanted to be part of Indonesia. The result was a unanimous vote for integration. Since then, the OMP, or Free Papua Movement, has fought a low-level campaign against the Indonesian military, although it is reported to have been subverted.

Irian Jaya's independence movement does not have the funding, the network of international lobbyists or the support of Western governments that East Timor's activists enjoy. Moreover, Irian Jaya is vital to Indonesia's economy. Most of the country's gold and copper comes from the province. The Grasberg mine, operated by **Freeport McMoran,** is worth US$50bn in proven reserves of minerals. Oil and gas are abundant and most of the new discoveries are taking place in offshore Irian Jaya. The province has one of the world's largest virgin rain forests and its potential value is huge.

Irian Jaya does not have the cultural and ethnic unity of East Timor. Although the population is very different from the rest of Indonesia – from a Melanesian stock – the large number of tribes, languages and local ethnic groups makes a united front difficult to achieve. Although the Indonesian government has promised more autonomy for Irian Jaya, especially by giving the province more control of its revenues, it has also made clear that Irian Jaya will not be given the same treatment as East Timor.

But the independence movement has stepped up since Gus Dur came to power. In September 1999 the Habibie government declared that the province would be divided in three, provoking protests. The new government revoked this decision and changed the province's name to Papua, fuelling demands for independence and provoking fresh repression. Wahid visited Papua and issued promises for more autonomy, but pro-independence activists remain unsatisfied and are organising protests and mapping out an independence strategy.

Aceh Heats Up

At the northern tip of Sumatra, Aceh, a resource rich and staunchly Muslim province, may also take advantage of the East Timor referendum to obtain more autonomy. Indonesia's military set up a brutal campaign to crush the separatist Free Aceh Movement and it was only in 1998 that a five-year period of martial law was ended, leading to the exposure of massive human rights violations.

A referendum campaign has been gathering momentum since then and government business has ground to a virtual halt while the armed forces have been pressing for the reimposition of martial law. A pro-referendum rally in the provincial capital, Banda Aceh, in November 1999, attracted about 1mn people, nearly a quarter of the population, indicating a wellspring of support for independence and opposition to Indonesian rule, although the underground Free Aceh Movement is not well organised. Informal networks of religious teachers and students and the Aceh Referendum Information Centre were instrumental in organising the November rally. The various groupings are divided about strategy and the guerrilla movement is split into four hostile factions. But the government has not been able to take advantage of this and its efforts to establish dialogue with the various parties have so far failed, not least because Wahid has spoken of granting a referendum, but has now retreated from this position, saying that the approval of the MPR, the DPR and the military would be needed first. A human rights group, Rehabilitation Action for Torture Victims in Aceh, estimates that 30,000 people have been the direct or indirect victims of torture in the past six months. The minister of human rights, Hasballah Saad, has called for the trial of those charged with human rights abuses. But faith in the government's assurances is weak.

Foreign Affairs

The Fear Of Contagion

Indonesia's Asean neighbours, struggling to emerge from financial and economic crises of their own, were concerned by the fall of Suharto. Authoritarian regimes within the region were worried by the growing democratic pressures in Indonesia. Regional neighbours were deeply concerned about the centrifugal forces unleashed by the removal of the Suharto regime, fearing that turmoil in this vast country could destabilise the region.

Asia's financial crisis has shown the limits of the much-vaunted "Asian values" which had been trumpeted by some Asian politicians to defend their authoritarian rule and the denial of human rights and freedom. The system was justified by impressive economic development. But as the Asian economies fell into turmoil, authoritarian leaders lost this source of legitimacy and found themselves under fire. The fall of Suharto was a bad omen for many regional leaders. Things are already changing. Indonesia has lifted its anti-subversion law, which has been used to silence government critics for decades. The anti-subversion law carried the death penalty. In the region, only Malaysia and Singapore still have an Internal Security Act – left over from British rule – which is the main legal obstacle to more political freedom.

Asean countries were placed in a quandary in deciding how to react to the violence that broke out in East Timor after the referendum. Most kept their counsel, although Malaysia's Prime Minister Mahathir Mohamad was outspoken in his opposition to the involvement of an international force. Since his election, Wahid has travelled widely, including to Asean countries, and relations with Asean neighbours have been largely harmonious. However, Asean has expressed concern about the situation in Aceh, with the summit in November 1999 explicitly reaffirming its commitment to the sanctity of national borders.

Singapore is taking a cautious attitude towards developments in Indonesia, having held a close relationship with the Suharto family and cronies. The relationship between the two neighbours deteriorated somewhat when Habibie called Singapore a racist country that discriminates against its Malay minority. Singapore also worries about political and social spillover, with a potential flashpoint being the treatment of illegal immigrants. But Singapore knows that whatever it thinks of its neighbours, it has to live with them.

Asean has also changed. Its vision of becoming a dynamic organisation in which a group of small countries are able to find security together is increasingly looking elusive and so far attempts to forge a closer economic union have not been notably successful. The economic crisis and the regional political transformation has weakened Asean further. The idea of a group which would be able to contain China's expansion lacks credibility, and the US has moved towards taking a greater regional role to fill the vacuum created by a weaker Asean and a weaker Japan.

China: Keeping A Low Profile

When serious anti-Chinese riots took place in 1965 after the alleged Communist coup that allowed Suharto to take power, Jakarta accused Beijing of being involved. This time, although Beijing expressed concerns over the ethnic dimensions of the Indonesian crisis, the official view is that the Chinese living there are Indonesian citizens. China has been wary not to jeopardise the cordial ties established with Jakarta over the past few years.

Recent measures taken by the Indonesian government went towards appeasing ethnic Chinese, including lifting a 30-year ban on the use and teaching of the Chinese language. The use of Mandarin was banned by Suharto and Mandarin-language schools closed in a bid to assimilate the minority group.

China might not see a more democratic South East Asia as beneficial, but a weaker Asean is probably positive for China's long-term regional ambitions. However, regional stability is also in China's interests and China is seeking to project itself as a good neighbour, although it is reluctant to accept Indonesian offers of mediation over the disputed areas in the South China Sea, claimed by China and a number of other countries in the region.

Japan: A Fading Role

For 20 years Japan has been working at improving its regional ties from an economic angle, while keeping a low profile in politics. The memories of the war are still close to the surface. The past strength of the yen has driven Japanese companies to relocate their manufacturing operations in lower-cost Asian countries, establishing a force locally and building up market shares in rapidly growing local markets. Then suddenly, things changed. Economic crisis, both in Japan and in the rest of Asia, wiped out investments and market opportunities. Japan's role in alleviating the crisis has been widely criticised for being too timid and its aid has been more vocal than effective. As the Japanese economy is still far from what it used to be, Tokyo's role is unlikely to become more prominent in the near future.

Australia: Relations Are Poor

Few countries are more concerned about the stability of Indonesia than Australia. Australians are well aware that Indonesia's population exceeds theirs by 11 times and Indonesia has always remained the root of Australia's fear of invasion from the north. Australia's former prime minister Paul Keating sought to turn Australia into an Asian regional power and concluded a security agreement between the two countries in 1995.

Australia is also one of the few countries to have recognised Indonesia's claim to sovereignty over East Timor. The main reason is the nightmare prospect for Australia of uncontrolled violence from the north. When the pro-integrationist forces in East Timor ran amok, Australia and to a lesser extent New Zealand, found themselves at the forefront of international pressure on the Habibie government to accept an international peacekeeping force under Australian leadership. Indonesia accuses Australia of manipulating the referendum and then sending troops in for its own ends.

Bilateral relations have not improved since the new president took office; he has decided to delay a proposed visit to Australia, scheduled for March, partly because of a strong tide of anti-Australian feeling in Indonesia.

The US: A Gradual Improvement

The Clinton administration, while stepping up calls for Indonesian reform during last year's riots, never directly suggested that Suharto, a long-time US ally, step down. State Secretary Madelaine Albright offered praise for the ex-president's record but welcomed his resignation.

The Pentagon has been training Indonesian military forces since 1992, despite a congressional ban intended to curb human right abuses. But Indonesia is not as strategically important as it once was. The US has signed an agreement with Singapore for the use of deep-water facilities and is currently signing another agreement with the Philippines. East-Timor's Fretilin has long given up its Marxist economic doctrine and the only worry for the US could be the emergence of radical Islamic politics.

But the US was vocal in its condemnation of the actions of the militia, abetted by the Indonesian armed forces, and was critical of the Habibie government's slow response to the chaos and violence that errupted. Miltary cooperation was cut off as a mark of US disapproval of the Indonesian government's actions and has only been partially restored. But Indonesia, however irked by US criticism, badly needs the West's financial support and the new president has been quick to stress that an announced shift towards Asia (especially India and China) in Indonesian foreign policy, would not be at the expense of pursuing good relations with the US.

2 Economic Outlook

Economic Activity

A Broader, But Still Fragile Recovery

Real GDP grew by 3.2% y-o-y in Q1 2000, rather a disappointing perform-ance after the strong Q4 99 growth of 5.0% (all 1999: 0.3%). The first quarter result was depressed by revisions to the year-ago data, raising the base for comparison. Encouragingly, growth spread in terms of demand, encompass-ing investment (up 11.7% after falling 8.1% in Q4 99 and 20.0% in full-year 1999) and imports (up 4% after a fall of 14% in Q4 99 and 41% in the whole year). Export growth was sustained, edging down to 9% y-o-y, after growth of 9.6% in Q4 99 and a fall of 32% in 1999. Private consumption, by contrast, faltered, with growth slowing to 1.8% y-o-y, after growing 5.5% in H2 99 and 1.5% in the whole year, while government consumption showed positive growth, up 1.1% y-o-y in Q1 2000, after falling 2.8% in Q4 99 and rising 0.7% for the whole year. The recovery is extremely fragile, and sustained rupiah weakness and/or a return to high interest and inflation rates could stop it in its tracks.

Looking ahead through to 2002, **BMI** expects the economy to strengthen. But there are strong provisos. First, and possibly most heroic from the standpoint of mid-2000, is a return to political and macroeconomic stability, in particular to the currency markets. Second, and also problematic, is that the policy drift in evidence during 2000 gives way to progress on the corporate and financial sector restructuring front and development of a viable channel for financing the corporate sector. Without this, the recovery in investment will not continue. But if these provisos are met, as **BMI** believes they will be (*see Political Outlook* and *Fiscal Policy*), growth will gather momentum this year, reaching 4.5%, accelerating to an average 5.2% in 2001-02.

Private consumption has lost some momentum in Q1 2000, with doubts about political stability and a weak legal environment intensifying. The **Danareksa Research Institute**'s March survey of consumer confidence

Growth broadened out in Q1 2000, but the tentative recovery could flounder on sus-tained rupiah weakness and/or a return to high interest and inflation rates.

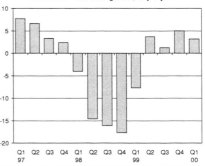

A Disappointing Performance
Indonesia - real GDP growth, % y-o-y

Source: Bank Indonesia.

The Slow Climb Back
Indonesia - GDP per capita, US$

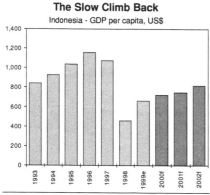

e/f = BMI estimate/forecast; Source: Bank Indonesia, World Bank.

showed falls in April and May, taking the index down to 8.8% below its November 1999 peak at 64.2 (although positive responses still outnumbered negative ones). Its quarterly index of confidence in the government fell by 14% from the previous three months, although the 125.2 point score showed that positive responses outnumbered negative ones. The survey also found that only 30% of respondents intended to buy durable goods over the next six months and that although respondents felt employment was less hard to find than three months ago, they still felt job prospects were poor. With the average annual rate of inflation falling back to 20.5% in 1999, the average increases in the minimum wage of around 25% in April, will help to restore some spending power (but there are likely to be exemptions). But the official minimum wage is still regarded as below the minimum subsistence level in most provinces. Farmers incomes, especially rice farmers, are being hit by poor prices and there is every prospect of further layoffs in urban centres, especially in financial services. So private consumption growth will be subdued this year, rising only 1.6% y-o-y. Better economic conditions in 2001-2002 will support a rebound, boosted by higher civil service wages and a tighter labour market: we expect private consumption to grow by 3.5% next year, rising to 4.1% in 2002.

Government consumption is constrained by pressure on resources, especially interest payments on rising government debt; it will grow by less than GDP over the three years to 2002. Prospects for external demand are bright, with continuing strength in the world economy and world trade boosted by the ongoing recovery in East Asia. Provided supply constraints and political uncertainties do not derail exports, **BMI** expects exports to accelerate from this year, growing at double digit rates of around 12% in 2001-2002, after 8.5% in 2000.

GDP AND POPULATION									
	1993	1994	1995	1996	1997	1998	1999e	2000f	2001f	2002f
Population (mn)	187.6	190.7	194.8	196.8	199.9	204.4	206.1	209.2	212.5	215.0
Nominal GDP (US$bn)	158.0	176.9	202.1	227.4	215.0	94.2	136.9	150.4	159.2	175.9
GDP per capita (US$)	842.3	927.7	1,037.9	1,155.3	1,075.6	460.6	664.1	718.8	749.0	818.3
Real GDP growth (% y/y)	6.5	7.5	8.2	7.8	4.7	-13.2	0.3	4.5	4.7	5.7

e/f = BMI estimate/forecast; Source: Bank Indonesia/IMF.

Investment Prospects Are Critical

Although there is significant importation of intermediates, so that higher export growth will suck in imports, the key factor propelling imports will be a recovery in investment. This is crucial to restore long-term growth. Foreign and domestic investment approvals were down 11.9% and 19.7% in dollar value in 1999, but figures for Q1 suggest a glimmer of hope. Data from the Investment Co-ordination Board (BKPM) show that foreign investment approvals rose to US$1.7bn for 412 projects in January-April, up from US$56mn in Q1 99.

In March, former minister of investment and state enterprises, Laksamana Sukardi, said the government would amend the 1967 law on foreign investment and the 1968 law on domestic investment. Bureaucracy and a lack of respect for the law, as well as political uncertainty, remain major obstacles to foreign investors. Public investment is constrained by budgetary factors and private domestic investment by the poor state of corporate balance sheets and banks' unwillingness to lend in the current climate. Although the successful sale of the Indonesian Bank Restructuring Agency's (IBRA's) 40% stake in the conglomerate **PT Astra**, to a consortium led by **Cycle and Carriage Ltd** of Singapore, is an encouraging sign of a more positive outlook, at least for portfolio investment, the immediate prospects are not bright. **BMI** does not expect the upturn in BKPM approvals in Q1 2000 to be sustained into the rest of the year and is forecasting overall growth of only 5% in gross fixed investment this year, followed by an accelerated recovery in a more conducive political and economic climate in 2001-2002, to average 9%. But investment will still be well below the 1997 level in 2002, demonstrating how serious the decline has been.

Manufacturing Will Lead The Recovery

In terms of supply, manufacturing is the key to growth in the short term. Output rose 7.2% in Q1 2000 (after 8.5% y-o-y growth in Q4 99 and 2.6% in the full year), as the recovery broadened into the export sector (*see Key Economic Sectors*). There was some concern that the y-o-y growth rate was slower in Q1 2000 than it had been in Q4 99 and politics and rupiah weakness suggest that this slowdown may accelerate in mid 2000. **BMI** expects growth in the 8% range over 2000-2001, with both domestic and export-oriented manufacturing entering a period of sustained growth from Q4 2000.

Forecasts for agriculture in 2000 suggest that the rice crop could be down as low prices (and high fertiliser costs) encourage diversion of land to other uses. Other crops may show only modest rises, as discussed by **BMI** in our Q2 2000 Quarterly Forecast Report, with growth constrained by under-

BMI does not expect the upturn in foreign investment approvals seen in Q1 2000 to be sustained into the rest of the year.

BMI expects domestic- and export-oriented manufacturing to enter a period of sustained growth from Q4 2000.

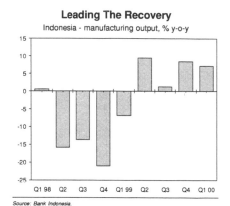

Leading The Recovery
Indonesia - manufacturing output, % y-o-y

Source: Bank Indonesia.

Weak domestic demand will keep a lid on inflation in 2000.

investment and disruption. Timber production will be hit by the heavy debts of plantation companies, and by attempts to bring former Suharto cronies to book and to regulate over-logging. We expect little growth in agriculture this year, and a mild recovery in 2001-2002. Mining output growth is also being curbed by long gestation periods and disruption to some important projects. A modest recovery in visitor arrivals and in overall business activity will help restore the trade, hotels and restaurants sector to growth in 2000 and onwards, and other services (including public services) will be stimulated by the decentralisation and devolution that the government is committed to implementing from 2001.

The financial services sector has been deeply in the doldrums – its value-added fell by 25.5% in 1998 and by 9.5% in 1999, before rising by 5.4% in Q1 2000. **BMI** expects a further decline of 2% in the sector in 2000, as bank restructuring is substantially completed, followed by the dawn of recovery from 2001, for average growth of 4.9% in 2001-2002, roughly in line with GDP growth.

Inflation Subdued, Unemployment Falling Slowly

Consumer price inflation accelerated to 0.84% m-o-m in May from 0.56% in April. The increase was attributed to further increases in administered prices (particularly transport and electricity prices), the weakness of the rupiah and the unattractiveness of deposit rates for prospective savers. The National Development Planning Board (*Bappenas*) is now forecasting inflation in the April-December financial year of 7-9%, as measures in the current budget, including higher civil service salaries, higher import duties on sugar and rice and the (delayed) decision to make substantial cuts to fuel subsidies feed through. Rupiah weakness will have some inflationary impact, but the weakness of domestic demand will temper this. **BMI** forecasts inflation at 6% in 2000 (with the fuel subsidy not being lowered until late in the year), rising to 7.5% in 2002 as the economy strengthens, more subsidies are lifted and moderate rupiah depreciation sets in.

CONSUMER PRICES										
	1993	1994	1995	1996	1997	1998	1999e	2000f	2001f	2002f
Consumer price inflation (% an. avg)	9.6	8.6	9.4	8.0	6.7	57.7	20.5	6.0	6.5	7.5
Consumer price inflation (% eop)	10.2	9.6	9.0	6.6	11.6	74.6	-0.3	9.8	7.0	8.0

e/f = BMI estimate/forecast; eop = end of period; Source: Bank Indonesia/IMF.

Around 3mn additional people come on the job market every year and it was already difficult for the Indonesian economy to absorb them with GDP growth of 7% per annum. Reliable data for unemployment are hard to come by, and estimates vary widely, Recent statistics, published by the Indonesian government, cite an unemployment rate of about 17.15% of the workforce, or 17mn people, for 1999. Whatever the true figure, there is little chance that demand for labour, especially in the urban areas hardest-hit by retrenchments, will recover rapidly, although the degree of open unemployment will be mitigated, as previously, by downwards flexibility in wages and by re-migration to rural areas. As the recovery broadens in 2001-2001, job opportunities will increase, especially in skilled areas, but pressure on wages will be minimal over the forecast period.

Despite this, labour unrest is on the rise in Indonesia, adding to the factors deterring inward investment. Reports of strikes are frequent, as workers take advantage of a new-found freedom to organise. The Ministry of Manpower reported 52 strikes in Q1 2000, after 125 in all of 1999. This is widely considered to be a gross underestimate. The conjuncture of a slack labour market with increased incidence of labour unrest can be explained partly by the lack of an effective regulatory framework within which labour and management can operate in the context of falling real wages and widely varying conditions in the archipelago. It is one aspect that the government will need to address to get FDI moving again and take advantage of cost competitiveness gains

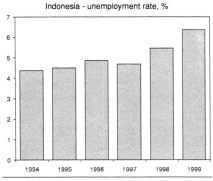

Seeds Of Discontent
Indonesia - unemployment rate, %

Source: BPS.

Balance Of Payments

External Sector Takes Off

Non-oil and gas exports grew strongly in the first four months and, while the high growth rate is unsustainable, the prospects for the external sector are bright.

In the first four months of 2000 the dollar value of exports was up 35.9% y-o-y, a dramatic improvement on the 0.8% rise in customs-basis exports in 1999. Oil and gas exports, propelled by higher prices, were up 23.2%. Encouragingly, non-oil and gas exports rose 23.2%. Imports were also up, but by only 15.2% (including oil and gas) and 5.7% (non-oil and gas), driven by intermediates and capital goods, up 19.7% and 21.4% y-o-y in Q1 2000. This increase bodes well for continuing export and investment growth over the full year. The trade surplus was up 61% y-o-y in the four months, at US$10.3bn.

With world trade growth strong, reinforced by a recovery in East Asia, prospects for export demand look bright. Provided that supply side problems do not disrupt export production, exports will be robust. The very fast growth of the first four months is unlikely to be sustained, but **BMI** believes that the dollar value of exports will rise very strongly in 2000, boosted by higher oil prices. After that, with oil prices likely to fall back next year, growth in nominal dollar terms will be less vigorous, but still robust. Imports will rise strongly, as the recovery in exports and investment gathers pace. But the trade surplus will rise in 2000 and will be above US$20bn in 2001-2001.

The current account surplus has been around 4% of GDP since the import compression of 1998. Over the period to 2002, the deficit on services and income, profits and dividends (IPD) will rise, fuelled by trade-related services imports and by outflows on IPD. **BMI** expects the current account surplus to be substantially eroded by the combination of a shrinking trade surplus and a rising deficit on the invisibles account, falling to 1.4% of GDP in 2002.

A Robust Outlook
Indonesia - merchandise trade growth, 3mma %

Source: Bank Indonesia.

BALANCE OF PAYMENTS (US$BN)									
	1990	**1991**	**1992**	**1993**	**1994**	**1995**	**1996**	**1997**	**1998**
Exports (fob, US$bn)	26.81	29.64	33.80	36.61	40.22	47.45	50.19	56.30	50.37
Imports (fob, US$bn)	21.46	24.83	26.77	28.38	32.32	40.92	44.24	46.22	31.94
Trade balance (US$bn)	5.35	4.80	7.02	8.23	7.90	6.53	5.95	10.07	18.43
Invisible trade balance	-8.76	-9.32	-10.37	-10.87	-11.31	-13.95	-14.55	-16.00	-15.67
Balance on goods and services	-3.41	-4.52	-3.35	-2.64	-3.41	-7.41	-8.60	-5.92	2.76
Current account balance	-2.99	-4.26	-2.78	-2.11	-2.79	-6.43	-7.66	-4.89	4.10
Current account (% GDP)	-2.8	-3.7	-2.2	-1.3	-1.6	-3.2	-3.4	-2.3	4.4

Source: Bank Indonesia.

Fiscal Policy

Limited By Politics And Debt

Fiscal policy will continue to be limited in its effectiveness by economic and political uncertainty and the constraints imposed by the demands of debt servicing. Debt servicing is expected to account for close to 40% of total expenditure over the next few years, and the World Bank thinks the government needs a primary surplus (before debt-servicing) of 2% of GDP. Whether or not the government can achieve that target, its capacity to spend on its employees' salaries and on public investment, both areas where greater expenditure is needed, will be severely limited.

This year's budget process highlighted the uncertainties surrounding government economic policy-making in an era of coalition government, greater parliamentary control and social turmoil. An unprecedentedly large number of changes were made to the budget in the DPR and the government itself has bowed to popular pressure not to introduce budgeted cuts in fuel subsidies. Among the changes made by the DPR were some tough projections for revenues from asset sales and debt recovery by the Indonesian Bank Restructuring Agency (IBRA) and from privatisation. The difficulties faced by both these programmes to date had already cast doubt on the government's ability to meet its initial targets in these areas, never mind the new, more ambitious ones.

A weak rupiah has undermined budgetary assumptions, although its impact will be partially offset by higher-than-anticipated oil prices.

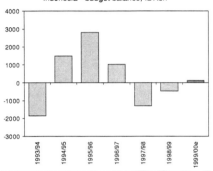

External Funding Masks True Deficit
Indonesia - budget balance, IDRbn

e = revised estimate; Source: Bank Indonesia.

GOVERNMENT FINANCE (IDRBN)							
	1993/94	1994/95	1995/96	1996/97	1997/98	1998/99	1999/00e
Total Revenue; of which:*	66,870	76,256	82,023	99,530	126,661	215,130	245,325
Oil and gas	12,503	13,537	16,055	20,137	35,357	41,254	56,303
Non-oil gas	43,610	52,881	56,969	67,493	72,827	111,556	145,390
Development Revenues	10,753	9,838	9,009	11,900	23,817	62,320	43,632
Programme Aid	-	-	-	-	-	36,403	-
Project Aid	-	-	-	-	-	25,917	-
Total Expenditure; of which:	68,718	74,761	79,216	98,513	127,969	215,586	245,192
Operational	40,290	44,069	50,435	62,561	84,607	147,717	N/A
Development	28,428	30,692	28,781	35,952	47,200	67,869	N/A
Budget Balance	-1,848	1,495	2,807	1,017	-1,308	-456	133
(% GDP)	-1	0	1	0	-0	-0	0

*e = revised official estimate; *Includes external funding; Source: Bank Indonesia.*

Adding to the budgeting uncertainties are domestic and international sources of instability. The collapse of the rupiah from late March took the currency into territory well outside the IDR7,000/US$ assumed in the budget. Meanwhile, increases in Opec production quotas have not succeeded in bringing the oil price down to the US$20/b projected in the budget (**BMI** projects an average oil price of US$23.5/b in 2000). Parliament's hopeful reduction of the projected cost of financing bank recapitalisation already looks likely to fall foul of rising interest rates. The government itself has been in some disarray over whether it needs to redo its budget calculations.

Many of these changes are mutually offsetting. The higher-than-expected oil price will both boost revenues and raise the cost of the fuel subsidy required to limit the increase in oil product prices to the 12% envisaged in the budget. The weak rupiah will raise interest costs, but will also further raise the value of dollar-based revenues, including those from oil and gas and from the foreign assistance used to cover the fiscal deficit.

Monetary Policy

Avoiding Higher Interest Rates

The government will want to avoid, as far as possible, exacerbating the tight fiscal policy by imposing a tight monetary policy. Spectacularly high interest rates during the depths of the economic crisis in 1997-98 are now believed to have made the downturn more severe than it needed to be. There are now understandable fears that a new round of interest rate increases will nip the nascent recovery of both the banking system and the broader economy in the bud.

But the government is in a dilemma, as there are strong upward pressures on interest rates that are likely to continue at least over the next year. Led by the US, interest rates are rising internationally. The need to prop up the weakening rupiah has already reversed the long, downward drift of interest rates, which had been underway since late 1998. Efforts to meet monetary targets agreed with the IMF will probably also put upward pressure on interest rates, although the Fund, having got much of the blame for the devastation caused by high interest rates in 1997-98, may be willing to be more flexible this time around. But at the same time, mounting inflationary pressures, primarily arising from the weak rupiah and subsidy cuts, will exert upward pressure on Indonesian rates.

The need to meet IMF monetary targets and rising inflation will put upwards pressure on interest rates.

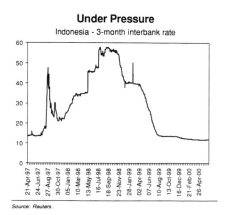

Under Pressure
Indonesia - 3-month interbank rate

Source: Reuters.

There is no way out of this dilemma. The outcome is likely to be rises in rates that that are moderated by a concern not to send the economy back into recession. This has been the pattern to date: although the benchmark rate on one-month Bank of Indonesia Certificates (SBIs) has been rising virtually since the currency started weakening in late March, adjustments have been quite modest, still leaving rates in low double figures.

Exchange Rate Policy

Rocky Rupiah

The rupiah will remain vulnerable to fluctuations of sentiment about the Indonesian economy and to global developments, which the government will be largely powerless to control. A fresh bout of turmoil on the foreign exchange markets since the IMF's decision in late March to delay disbursement of the latest instalment from its US$5bn Extended Fund Facility loan has been a reminder after a period of six months of relative stability that the rupiah's potential for volatility remains high. By mid-May, in the wake of further political and economic shocks, made worse by confused policy responses, the rupiah was nearly 20% below its level at the beginning of the year. After briefly steadying, the rupiah started sliding again in early June when the central bank governor, Syahril Sabirin, was named as a suspect in the **Bank Bali** case and subsequently detained. More such shocks will almost certainly rock the foreign exchange markets in the lead-up to the August session of the MPR.

Political uncertainty has unsettled the rupiah once again, but Indonesia is unlikely to introduce capital controls.

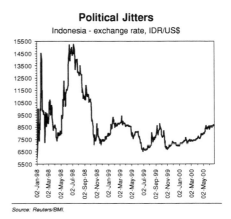

Political Jitters
Indonesia - exchange rate, IDR/US$

Source: Reuters/BMI.

INTEREST AND EXCHANGE RATES										
	1993	1994	1995	1996	1997	1998	1999e	2000f	2001f	2002f
Discount Rate (% eop)	8.8	12.4	14.0	12.8	20.0	38.4	12.5	15.4	14.1	12.5
Money Market Rate (% an. avg)	8.7	9.7	13.6	14.0	27.8	62.8	23.6	16.0	18.4	16.0
Lending Rate (% an. avg)	20.6	17.8	18.9	19.2	21.8	32.1	27.7	23.0	22.0	20.0
IDR/US$ (eop)	2,110	2,200	2,308	2,383	4,650	8,025	7,085	8,090	8,500	8,600
IDR/US$ (an. avg)	2,087	2,161	2,249	2,342	2,910	10,014	7,855	7,900	8,300	8,500

e/f = BMI estimate/forecast; Source: Bank Indonesia/IMF.

Various policies have been discussed as possible ways to limit this volatility. The resulting confusion of voices has only had the effect of further undermining confidence. Though canvassed by some government officials, capital controls can be ruled out as almost certain to be ineffective, although various incentives aimed at repatriating flight capital and exporters' foreign-exchange earnings are being put in place. Similarly there is unlikely to be a move from the current foreign-exchange regime, which allows the currency to float freely, to a fixed rate regime of some sort, even though the Coordinating Minister for Economics, Kwik Kian Gie, has in the past advocated a currency board system for Indonesia. Continuing political uncertainty will prevent the rupiah from approaching the IDR7,000/US$ envisaged in the budget. Instead, at best, **BMI** expects it to stabilise around IDR8,250/US$ after the MPR session and to depreciate only mildly thereafter.

External Debt

Falling Gently

Debt write-offs, debt-equity swaps and the non-renewal of short-term credit lines have led to a fall in private sector debt.

Indonesia's external debt has been falling modestly and its share of GDP will continue to drop during the next two years, although the absolute level will not. The fall in the debt stock was the result of a larger decline in private sector debt than the new bilateral and multilateral lending to the government. Debt write-offs, debt-equity swaps and the non-renewal of short-term credit lines accounted for the fall in private sector debt. The fall occurred despite the ineffectiveness of existing mechanisms such as the Jakarta Initiative Task Force (JITF), the Indonesian Debt Restructuring Agency (INDRA), the Indonesian Bank Restructuring Agency (IBRA) and the Bankruptcy Court, in settling the private debt. More determined efforts to give these agencies real bite, greater acceptance of debt write-offs ("haircuts") and growing enthusiasm among foreign investors to acquire Indonesian assets will accelerate the trend.

					GOVERNMENT DEBT					
	1993	1994	1995	1996	1997	1998e	1999e	2000f	2001f	2002f
External debt (US$bn)	89.2	107.8	124.4	128.9	136.2	147.5	139.9	141.5	147.3	151.2
External debt (% GDP)	56.4	61.0	61.5	56.7	63.3	156.6	102.2	94.1	92.5	86.0
External debt (% exports)	214.4	234.1	229.4	222.3	209.2	259.8	272.2	236.2	221.5	212.4

e/f = BMI estimate/forecast; Source: Bank Indonesia.

Meanwhile government borrowing will continue to rise, even though the official position is that it should be as constrained as possible. The modest net rise in overall external debt will bring the debt/GDP ratio down to 86% by the end of 2002, from more than 100% at the end of 1999.

The burden of government debt will be reduced by further reschedulings through the Paris and London Clubs, covering bilateral and multilateral debt and commercial debt respectively. The latest rescheduling agreement (reached in April) with the Paris Club has already covered US$5.8bn of debt coming due in the two years to March 2002 by extending its maturity by 11-20 years. In June a similar agreement covering US$340mn in commercial sovereign debt was reached with the London Club. These agreements will reduce Indonesia's looming debt obligations and hence its debt-service ratio, which we foresee falling from 38.2% in 1999 to 30.1% in 2002. However, this improvement could well be undermined by the continued inability of the private sector to sort out its debt problems, whether due to institutional ineffectiveness, political interference or the failure of the economy to grow.

Foreign Direct Investment

Investors Will Be Wary

Foreign investors will continue to be wary of Indonesia as a destination for their funds. We expect an upturn in investment approvals and realisation over the next two years, but both will remain well below pre-crisis levels. The sensitivity of FDI to political and economic uncertainty was evident in May, when in a month of turmoil FDI approvals dropped 84% below their April level. Until May approvals had risen in each successive month of the year, from US$100mn in January to US$1.1bn in April, and despite the drop in May, they reached US$2.06bn in total during the first five months of the year, a 27.2% increase on the US$1.62bn worth of approvals in the same period of 1999. The focus of foreign interest has shifted to natural resource development and processing, in such areas as palm oil and pulp and paper, fields that have been relatively unaffected by the downturn. Hence in 1999, when the overall value of approvals fell by nearly 20%, the value of projects approved for the resource-rich island of Sumatra rose by 440% to account for 70% of the total (compared with 14.4% of the total in the pre-crisis year of 1996).

The level of Foreign Direct Investment inflows remains highly sensitive to the political environment.

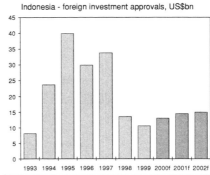

Confidence Wanes
Indonesia - foreign investment approvals, US$bn

f = BMI forecast; Source: Bank Indonesia.

The political uncertainty marked by such events as the dismissal of two cabinet ministers on April 24 and fresh outbreaks of violence, including in the major cities of Jakarta and Medan and affecting major projects such as the Arun gas field run by **Exxon-Mobil** in Aceh, will have given investors serious pause in May. In particular the sacking of the minister of investment and state enterprises, Laksamana Sukardi, an assiduous cultivator of foreign investors, who had working on an extensive set of amendments to the foreign investment law, will have sapped confidence.

A range of other factors adds to the current uncertainty. Nationalist objections are blocking the sale of shares in privatising state enterprises to foreign companies. Already fears about the impact of the devolution of power to regions (which is not due to take effect until the beginning of 2001) are being fanned by calls by local legislatures for the renegotiation of mining contracts. There are policy U-turns, such as the government's decision, now apparently rescinded, to lift the exemption on VAT that has been on offer to investors in the special industrial zone of Batam. Greater awareness of environmental concerns, as seen in the closure of the massive Indorayon plant in North Sumatra and the cutback in production agreed with**Freeport**, operator of the Grasberg mine in Irian Jaya, are also having a chilling effect. The uncertain legal environment adds to investors' tribulations: in late May a Jakarta court ordered the Indonesian subsidiary of the Swiss pharmaceuticals company, **Roche**, to pay US$33mn in compensation to a local distributor whose contract the foreign firm had annulled.

Profile and Recent Developments

Introduction

A Recovery Sets In

In 1998, Indonesia's GPP declined by 13.2%, as the effects of the crisis took a deep toll on domestic demand, especially investment demand. The decline would have been even more pronounced in the absence of a fairly strong performance by exports, which registered growth of 11.2%. In terms of supply, all the major sectors with the exception of utilities registered declines.

In 1999 a recovery began; growth turned positive in the first quarter and accelerated to 5.8% y-o-y in the fourth quarter. For the full year, GDP in demand terms rose by 0.3%. The recovery was limited to consumption; private consumption rose by 3.7% after a fall of 6.3% in 1998. Investment shrank again, falling by 20% after declining by 33% in 1998. Exports shrank, falling by 32%, but imports fell even more, by 41%, so the change in the foreign balance was strongly positive.

On the supply side, the recovery was led by agriculture (up 2.1%), manufacturing (2.6%), and utilities. Services, especially financial services, were depressed. Banks' value-added fell by 15.9%. Transport, construction and catering and hotels were all down in year-on-year terms.

What is more, the recovery in 1999 was only partial and tentative. Comparing GDP at 1993 prices with the 1997 level shows that only agriculture and utilities were above their 1997 level in terms of supply, and not by much. GDP in 1999 was 12.7% below its 1997 level. Private consumption was 2.9% down and investment was as much as 46.4% below its 1997 level.

Structural Change

The structure of the Indonesian economy has changed considerably since Suharto took power in 1965. In the late 1960s, the economy was largely dependent on agricultural production. The contribution of food, beverages and tobacco accounted for 65% of value-added manufacturing in 1970. In 1991 the share of manufacturing in GDP surpassed agriculture for the first time. Exports have played a key role in this process of industrialisation, the fall in oil prices from the early 1980s providing an additional spur to the development of export-oriented manufacturing.

The Role Of Oil And Gas

Oil and gas plays an important, though declining role in the economy, accounting for about 20% of government revenue and about 16% in exports in 1998. The sector typically generates about 8% of GDP, its importance having declined as the process of diversification has proceeded. The sharp increase in oil price was the main reason behind the growth acceleration to 7.2% for the 1973-1980 period, from 6.6% in 1965-1973. Reducing dependence on oil and gas has been a key policy of the government over the past decade.

The combination of a falling rupiah and, in 1999, rising oil prices has increased the contribution of oil and gas to budgetary revenues to over 30% in 1998/1999, against less than 16% the previous year. This was a welcome source of additional revenue at a time of economic difficulty. The 2000 budget, based on what is probably a conservative oil price estimate of US$18/b, predicts that revenues from oil and gas will reach 27% of the total for April-December.

Poverty Rises

In 1966, Suharto inherited a poor country with a chaotic economy and hyperinflation. GDP per capita was in the region of US$100, and the percentage of the population living in absolute poverty was close to 60%. Much progress was made in the intervening years, and there has been some success in reducing inequality, with the Gini index in 1996 at 36.5, according to World Bank data, lower than Thailand, Malaysia and the Philippines. The incidence of poverty, as measured by national data, fell sharply from about 40% below the national poverty line in the mid-1970s to 9.7% urban and 12.3% rural poverty in 1996. The economic crisis has caused a marked deterioration, with the total percentage of households falling below the poverty line rising from 11.3% in 1996 to 20.31% in 1999. Overall, the nominal Gini coefficient has changed very little over the crisis period. However, this masks important differences between urban and rural areas. Applying the Gini coefficient to household incomes deflated to reflect actual consumption patterns, urban inequality has decreased from 0.299 to 0.289 (principally because of a fall among richer urban households), while rural inequality has increased from 0.265 to 0.289 (apparently because of worsening conditions for landless rural labourers, not cushioned by the ownership of land). The rise in rural inequality is the result of increasing inequality in the bottom tail of the distribution (the poorest), while lower urban inequality is primarily driven by a collapse in incomes of the top half of the income distribution. This is consistent with trends in the severity of poverty, which increased substantially for rural households between 1997 and 1998.

There is some suggestion that poverty has fallen since February 1999 as real consumption expenditures in the national accounts have risen and the relative (and nominal) price of rice has fallen. Preliminary indications from an August 1999 household survey suggest that poverty rates may have fallen by as much as 2-3 percentage points from their February levels.

Indonesia And The IMF

The IMF Steps In

The US$43bn rescue package was put together under IMF auspices in late 1997 in the context of a collapse in the value of the rupiah and large-scale insolvencies provoking an international payments crisis. The condition was across the board reform. The fall of Suharto removed a major obstacle to progress, as the First Family had been involved at all levels of the economy.

As discussed below, Indonesia still has to speed up banking reform and proceed with restructuring corporate debt to the state banks. But there are many obstacles – economic, political and social – in the way of rapid reform and the restructuring of the financial corporate sectors in general and progress has consistently lagged the targets.

Relations with the IMF have not been smooth. In September 1999, the government's failure to act swiftly over the Bank Bali scandal (the discovery that large sums had been siphoned from Bank Bali when the bank paid a 60% commission to a company run by officials of President Habibie's Golkar party for the recovery from IBRA of IDR 904bn in loans) led to temporary rupture in relations between the IMF and Indonesia and the delay in disbursements, which did not resume until February 2000, (following agreement on a draft letter of intent in November) before being delayed from April, because of numerous missed targets. Balanced against the IMF's wish to see its approved programmes carried out to the letter, is its reluctance to put further pressure on an already shaky socio-economic structure.

The Challenges Ahead

Indonesia's bank reforms are gathering momentum, but these measures have a cost and their funding will be an important challenge. The reform programme was announced at a time when Indonesia's commercial banks had negative equity of more than IDR112trn (US$13bn). Getting the sector back on a viable footing will require substantial injections of foreign capital. Management contracts involving equity injections, such as the proposed **Standard Chartered/Bank Bali** deal, which collapsed in 1999 on the basis of strong local opposition, are difficult to consummate.

The issuance of recapitalisation bonds is placing a major strain on public sector funding and on the asset structure of the banks which have purchased them. The bank sector crisis could spill over into a public sector funding crisis, if interest rates rise too far and if the banks fail to sell the bonds on the secondary market in sufficient quantities.

The government has issued an effective guarantee to private bank deposit holders. By closing 38 banks on March 13, 1999, the government has assumed potential liability for deposits of IDR28trn. The problem is compounded by the fact that 85% of all private bank deposits have a maturity period of one month or less. This makes the banking system vulnerable to any additional shocks.

NPLs are still in the region of 40%, having peaked at 60-80% in 1998. Recapitalisation bonds will be the major source of interest bearing assets on bank balance sheets. The level of interest rates on bonds will be a mix of fixed rate bonds, variable rate bonds indexed to the benchmark SBI (Central Bank Certificate) and inflation-indexed bonds. Managing margins will be more complicated in the future, and there is increased risk that, until changes are made to the mix of new/performing and old/non-performing loans, banks may face periods of negative margins. This will slow the rebuilding of banks' equity bases.

Indonesia's weak legal system is a stumbling block to the establishment of functional bankruptcy laws. Currently, banks face major costs in gaining access to collateral. A stronger legal system will help attract foreign capital, but the courts continue to produce idiosyncratic verdicts in bankruptcy cases. The IMF has recently indicated that aid will be dependent upon state banks launching bankruptcy proceedings on their largest bad debtors.

Restoring confidence in Indonesia's banking system and capital markets is a pre-condition of economic recovery. Foreign capital beyond IMF/World Bank funds is likely to be required in large amounts. Early in 2000 total government debt – external and domestic – was US$134bn (83% of GDP) according to World Bank data, up from US$53bn before the crisis. Nearly three-quarters of the increase was to pay for the restructuring of the banking system. At the end of 1999, Indonesia had total external debt of about US$141bn, down from US$146.9bn at the end of 1998. The latter (which are the most recent such breakdown available) were broken down as follows: government liabilities were US$67.3bn, state-owned enterprises, US$5.6bn, bank external debt, US$10.8bn, and private non-banks, US$63.1bn.

Reforms, Reforms And More Reforms

The IMF-mandated reform programme has two broad objectives: damage-control policies to help minimise social unrest, and economic reforms to lay the foundations for recovery. As demonstrated in recent budgets, the government is heavily relying on assistance from the World Bank, ADB and other agencies.

The restructuring of the corporate sector is also crucial for economic recovery and for the development of a sound banking system. The government must encourage the tedious process of debt workouts between creditors and debtors by ensuring an adequate legal framework.

The acceleration of structural reform policies is also essential. Many inefficient cartels and state monopolies have been dissolved, but price subsidies on some items still need to be scaled down. Trade liberalisation, and the government's privatisation programme must also be accelerated to boost competition and enhance efficiency. In all spheres of business, transparency, accountability and disclosure must be strengthened and crony capitalism banished.

Corporate Debt Restructuring Is Slow

Progress in corporate debt restructuring in Indonesia has been slow. Among the major barriers are:

political uncertainty and interference; an inadequate bankruptcy mechanism which fails to induce debtors to enter voluntary workout agreements; the sheer magnitude and complexity of the corporate debt problem, compared with other East Asian countrie 60% of creditors are foreign banks; fragmentation among the institutions charged with the task of encouraging corporate re structuring and continued lack of support for their operations; poor corporate governance, especially with respect to disclosure of financial information and enforcement against offenders; the slow start in restructuring the banking system; the complex tax, legal and regulatory framework . All this has compounded lack of investor confidence, itself a major impediment to progress.

The August 1998 Frankfurt Agreement led to the creation of an institutional framework for corporate debt restructuring which depended on the government sponsored Jakarta Initiative Task Force (JITF), launched in November 1998 with help from donors. It provided a framework for voluntary out-of-court debt negotiations following guidelines known as the Jakarta Principles. The JITF was also intended to operate a regulatory facilitation group or "One Stop Shop" to speed the process of obtaining regulatory approvals for restructuring deals. The Indonesian Debt Restructuring Agency (INDRA) was also created in late 1998 and offers a facility for hedging against devaluation of the rupiah for restructuring agreements which are under implementation. At about the same time the DPR approved a new bankruptcy law and the Commercial Court was created. In late 1998 corporate debt was estimated at US$118bn (94% of GDP) More than 330 corporates (of which around 180 are SMEs), representing more than US$23bn in debts, have registered with the JITF, but it has led the restructuring of only six enterprises, with debts of less than US$1bn. A few debt restructuring agreements have been concluded outside the JITF framework, the most notable of which has been **PT Astra** which restructured debts of US$1.1bn. Only **PT Danareksa** has used the INDRA facility. The body could not recruit enough senior Indonesians to lead its case work and resignations have made the task more difficult.

Since its operating rules were approved in October, 1999, the Asset Management Unit of the Indonesian Bank Restructuring Agency (IBRA) has been playing a growing role in restructuring, foreclosing and disposing of the loan portfolio it has acquired. After taking over the portfolios of the failed banks, IBRA is now the largest domestic creditor in Indonesia. It has extraordinary powers (so-called PP17powers) to seize assets of non-cooperative debtors and, like any other creditor, it can also use the normal bankruptcy process. IBRA's role in corporate debt restructuring is growing rapidly.

Bank Restructuring Makes More Progress

Following the introduction of blanket guarantees of bank liabilities in January 1998, and the creation of the Indonesian Bank Restructuring Authority (IBRA), the systemic runs on the banking system were contained. This allowed for the closure of a total of 68 banks over the next two years without further undue disruption to the payment system. From June the government, with support from the multilateral organisations, designed a programme to evaluate all 77 private and state banks. The results of the audits were released in October 1998, after which IBRA was put under the supervision of the Ministry of Finance. In March 1999, it was announced that 38 private commercial banks would be closed, seven nationalised and nine recapitalised, if they could raise 20% of the capital. In return for the state's contribution, bank owners and management were required to enter into time-bound performance contracts designed to ensure the implementation of the operational restructuring contained in their business plans.

From the onset of the crisis, 65 banks have been closed, 13 nationalised, seven private banks recapitalised, and four of the seven state banks merged. The state has issued IDR500trn (US$58.bn) to support the deposit guarantee and recapitalisation programme, of which IDR178trn was required for the **Mandiri** merger of four banks alone. The total cost of the recapitalisation programme is still expected to be in the vicinity of IDR 670trn. The intention is to merge eight nationalised banks into **Danamon** by the end of September 2000 before privatisation in 2001 and to sell the government's shares in Bali and **Niaga** outright by end-June, 2000.

With the decision made to merge four state banks into a new institution (Mandiri), the focus shifted to the three remaining state banks (Bank Negara Indonesia, Bank Rakyat Indonesia, and Bank Tabungan Negara). These banks are behind with completion of their business plans, which are supposed to include the engagement of new management and international partners to assist in governance.

Fiscal Policy

Budgets Are Subject To Strains

The large sums being absorbed for recapitalisation represent a significant current and future obligation on the budget. The World Bank has recently suggested that Indonesia needs to run a primary surplus (before interest payments) of about 2% of GDP to finance US$134bn of government debt, most of which is the direct result of the issuance of recapitalisation bonds. While foreign borrowing and aid currently play a key financing role, this is not sustainable indefinitely, as domestic debt is also rising fast. Government debt is now about 100% of GDP, up from about a third before the crisis.

The budget outturn for 1998/99 (fiscal years ending March 31) was close to what was expected, with a deficit of IDR500bn (including foreign borrowing). Oil revenue was hit by low prices, but non-oil revenue rose by 62%, chiefly reflecting taxes on time deposits when interest rates were high. Spending was well below target, both on interest payments and subsidies and on development spending. The 1999/2000 budget and the 2000 budget (which has moved to a calendar year basis) got the IMF's approval, despite considerable backtracking on reforms such as the removal of tariff barriers and subsidies. The deficit in 1999/2000 is expected to have come in below the projected 6.8% of GDP (excluding foreign funding), at about 4%, largely thanks to higher-than-forecast oil prices, which outweighed a higher cost of fuel subsidies, but also because development spending was behind schedule once again. Targets for privatisation receipts were also missed.

A Social Safety Net

Development expenditure in 1999/2000 was set at IDR83.65trn, as social safety net programmes are a central focus of the budget. This measure was seen as populist, but the government had little choice, given that 80mn Indonesians are living on less than US$1 per day. As noted, the target was missed.

Other measures aimed at protecting living standards in the budget included the maintenance of fuel oil subsidies and higher wages for public officials. Civil servants' salaries were due to be increased by up to 50%, (against an inflation rate of about 20%) at a total cost of IDR2.6trn, and funding for small- and medium-sized businesses was raised by IDR300bn.

The need for foreign capital has intensified, but even before the Asian financial crisis, Indonesia was reliant on multilateral and bilateral lenders to close its budget deficit and fund development spending. These lenders, known as the Consultative Group for Indonesia (CGI), meet every year. The annual aid package was typically worth about US$5.5bn annually in 1992-97. A combination of aid and quick-disbursing loans valued at nearly US$14bn was pledged in 1998 and in 1999 US$9bn was required.

The Balance Of Payments

Imports Slump

The crisis produced a large contraction in imports. These fell in dollar terms by 34.2% in 1998, as investment and domestic demand slumped by another 12.2% in 1999. Exports fell by 8.6% in 1998 and by 0.7% in dollar terms in 1999, with a 24% rise in oil and gas exports not quite making up for a 5.5% contraction in non-oil exports. The merchandise trade balance (fob) rose to US$20.5bn in 1999, up from US$18.4bn in 1998.

Data on the destination of exports in 1999 show a mixed picture. Only Japan and South Korea registered strong growth among major markets and both are leading consumers of Indonesian oil and natural gas, two commodities whose prices were buoyant in 1999. By contrast, exports to the Asean region fell by 10.8%, mainly because of a 13.8% fall in exports to Singapore, whose share of Indonesian exports fell from 11.7% of the total to 10.1%. There were particularly dramatic falls in sales of pulp and paper and jewellery to Singapore, reflecting the weak performance of manufactured exports generally. Exports to the US and Germany also fell.

The collapse in imports in 1998/99 transformed what was normally a current account deficit of the order of about US$6bn (or some 3% of GDP), into a surplus of US$5-6bn. The services and invisibles accounts have remained in deficit, thanks to sizeable net outflows on transportation, travel and investment income.

Monetary Policy

Falling Inflation

Inflation peaked at 82.4% y-o-y in September 1998. In January 1999, inflation was still showing a 70.7% y-o-y rise, but it has been declining regularly since then, falling to 5.6% y-o-y in August, as demand fell and the rupiah recovered. Annual consumer price inflation in 1998 was 46.1%, easing to 20.5% in 1999.

Falling Interest Rates

At the height of Indonesia's economic chaos in August and September 1998, the interest rate on benchmark one-month *Sertifikat Bank Indonesia* (SBI) central bank certificates rate peaked at more than 70%, up from about 12% in 1997. As inflation subsided and the currency stabilised, interest rates have moved downward, although remaining strongly positive in real terms; the SBI rate fell to 35.06% in January 1999 and then gyrated around 37% before falling again and ending the year at about 12%. The fall was supported by the weakness in demand for credit, which helped the Indonesian authorities to stay within monetary targets set in agreement with the IMF.

Exchange Rate Policy

The Rupiah: Still Fragile

As well as being the hardest hit by the original currency crisis, the rupiah has been the slowest to recover. Not only was Indonesia involved in the Asian economic and financial crisis, but it has also been affected by serious disorder and political uncertainty, so the currency has been subject to periodic jitters and gyrations. Before the crisis the authorities ran a managed float, aiming to maintain competitiveness in export markets in the face of the inflation differential and the currency tended to slip by about 4% a year against the dollar. From an annual average of IDR2,910/US$ in 1997, the currency fell to IDR10,014/US$ in 1998 before recovering to IDR7,855 in 1999 and ending the year at IDR7085.

Monetary Growth: Recovering Slowly

Targets for the level of base money (currency in circulation plus bank deposits with Bank Indonesia) agreed with the IMF have generally been met. At the end of December 1999 M1 was 23.2% up on the year, with M2 up 11.9%, after falls or very small rises in mid-1998 and early 1999. The very sluggish demand for money was also reflected in slow growth in deposits and in lending. Domestic credit (in rupiah and foreign exchange) was 54% down at the end of 1999, at IDR225.1trn.

Reserves Rise

Gross foreign assets collapsed from a peak of US28.9bn at the end of June 1997 to a low of US$16.6bn at the end of March, when net reserves fell to US$13.2bn, as private capital fled the country. The IMF backed rescue programme stabilised the situation and reserves started to recover, reaching US$26.4bn at the end of 1999, providing 6.3 months of income cover. Foreign debt, meanwhile, had reached about US$141bn at the end of 1999, of which US$73bn was public medium- and long-term debt and the debt service ratio was about 35%, after reschedulings under the aegis of the IMF-backed programme.

Foreign Direct Investment

Dwindling Inflows

The past decade has seen a growing trend of foreign direct investment (FDI) inflows, which have translated into higher exports, especially non-oil exports. Attracting FDI was a key plank in Indonesia's policy to switch its economy into more value-added sectors. Japanese investment was a major component. The strengthening of the yen in the 1990s encouraged Japanese industrial groups to relocate their operations to South East Asia. The pro-business stance of the Suharto government, Indonesia's plentiful natural resources and the cheapness and abundance of labour, more than offset the graft and corruption prevailing in the country.

This picture has changed in the past few years. Economic difficulties in Japan, combined with a weakening yen, reduced the incentive for Japanese corporates to relocate. South Korean investment partly made up for this, but the regional crisis and Indonesia's deteriorating business environment did not augur well. There has always been a large gap between approved and realised FDI. Large oil refineries, telecommunication projects, power generation and petrochemical plants inflated the numbers for approved FDI, but most of these planned investments were not justified in terms of investment returns.

FDI approvals fell to US$10.6bn in 1999, down from US$13.6bn in 1998 and US$33.8bn in 1997. Realisation, on the other hand, rose to US$7.64bn in 1999 from US$5.77bn in 1998, suggesting that there is some improvement in Indonesia's standing as a location for FDI. But some US$80bn that left the country along with the many Indonesian-Chinese in 1998 has yet to return, chiefly from Singapore.

Domestic investments have been following a similar trend as a result of the credit crunch. The recovery will also be slow, given the large debt problem faced by the Indonesian private sector. In 1998, approved domestic investments declined to IDR60.7trn, from IDR119.9trn in 1997. They fell further in 1999, to IDR 53.6trn.

In its attempt to fight corruption, Jakarta is cutting red tape by permitting foreign investments valued at US$100mn or less to be approved directly by the Investment Coordinating Board. In the past, such investments needed final approval from the president. Investment proposals exceeding US$100mn in value will still require presidential approval. The new investment rules will also decentralise power by letting local authorities approve domestic investments of IDR10bn (US$858,000) or less.

3 Key Economic Sectors

Introduction

Recovery Will Broaden

Growth in Q1 2000 was led by manufacturing on the production side, expanding by 7.2% y-o-y. Prospects for a broader recovery are good, provided that the recent rupiah weakness does not prompt punitive increases in interest rates. While the recovery in manufacturing was concentrated in domestically-oriented industries in 1999, this is now spreading to the export sector. Other sectors, notably mining and financial services, are seeing little growth. The trade, hotels and restaurants sector and transport and communications sectors returned to growth in Q3. They grew faster in Q4, by 14.3% and 11.7% y-o-y respectively, thanks partly to the base year effect – Q4 98, was the low point of the recession – but still fell in y-o-y terms in 1999 as a whole. Mining edged up 0.2% in Q4, but fell by 1.7% for the whole year, with oil and gas down by 5.1%. Financial and business services also returned to positive growth in Q4, up by 5.2% y-o-y, but down 9.5% in the whole year. Agriculture failed to register growth in Q4, with output falling by 3% y-o-y after a 5% decline in Q3. But for the whole year, agriculture was up 2.1%, thanks to growth in the first half.

BMI expects the recovery to broaden and deepen during the forecast period, spreading into the export sectors as the financial sector stabilises during the course of 2000.

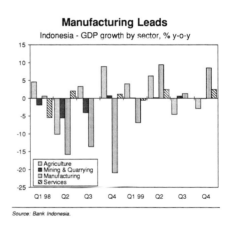

Manufacturing Leads
Indonesia - GDP growth by sector, % y-o-y

Source: Bank Indonesia.

GDP GROWTH BY SECTOR (% Y-O-Y)									
	1994	1995	1996	1997	1998	1999e	2000f	2001f	2002f
Agriculture, Forestry & Fishing	0.6	4.4	3.1	1.0	-0.7	2.1	0.5	1.4	1.3
Mining & Quarrying	5.6	6.7	6.3	2.1	-2.8	-1.7	1.2	1.3	1.5
Manufacturing	12.4	10.9	11.6	5.3	-11.4	2.6	8.0	7.8	8.5
Construction	14.9	12.9	12.8	7.4	-36.5	-1.6	5.0	8.5	9.5
Utilities	12.5	15.9	13.6	12.7	2.3	8.2	9.0	8.5	9.0
Financial Services	10.2	11.0	6.0	5.9	-25.5	-9.5	-2.0	3.8	6.0

e = BPS estimate; f = BMI forecast; Source: Bank Indonesia.

But the recovery in the real economy in 1999 was fragile. Comparing 1999 with 1997 shows how much output has been lost. Within a 12.7% fall in GDP (which was up by 4.7% in 1997), agriculture rose 1.4%, mining fell 4.4% and manufacturing was down by 9.1%. Even sharper falls were registered in service-oriented sectors: trade, hotels and restaurants were down 18.4%; transportation & communications by 15.7%, and finance, rental and leasing and business services fell 32.6%. Looking ahead, **BMI** expects the recovery to broaden and deepen during the forecast period, spreading into the export sectors as the financial sector stabilises during the course of 2000. Within an overall forecast of growth ranging around 5.0% over the three years 2000-2001, a strong rebound in manufacturing will lead, followed from 2001 by an accelerating recovery in financial services and domestic trade. Growth in the agriculture and mining sectors will be slower, curbed by capacity constraints.

Manufacturing

Exports Lead Recovery

The manufacturing recovery broadened out into export-oriented sectors in the first quarter, while domestic consumption appears to be slowing.

In terms of production, the nascent recovery in the Indonesian economy was concentrated in domestically-oriented manufacturing in Q4 99, when the manufacturing sector grew by 9% y-o-y, bringing annual growth in the sector to 2.6% in terms of GDP. This growth in manufacturing was not broad-based, being led by food, beverages and tobacco (up 4.2%), paper and printing (2.4%) chemicals and rubber (9.3%) and cement (4.1%), all items largely for domestic consumption. Export-oriented sectors, notably textiles, leather and footwear (up 0.9%), wood products (down 13.3%), iron and steel and transport equipment and machinery grew very little or not at all.

Q1 2000 has seen the recovery widen to export-oriented sectors, in the face of an apparent slowing in growth in consumer demand at home (*see Economic Activity*). Among the sub-sectors where this trend is apparent is automobiles. Domestic car sales recorded a rise of 78,739 units in the first 11 months of 1999, up 35% on the 1998 total of 58,303 units, according to the Association of Indonesian Automotive (Gaikindo). Gaikindo is forecasting a recovery to 240,000 units in 2000, up 255% y-o-y, but the current state of domestic demand makes this unlikely this year and **BMI** is expecting a sustained recovery in the sector to be delayed until 2001. The recent successful privatisation of PT Astra, the largest producer of automobiles and motocycles, will help spur recovery, after an evaluation phase and new plans have been drawn up. Domestic car sales fell in January, to 11,036 units from

15,348 units in December 1999. This may be due to seasonal factors, with the holiday season occupying a large part of January. PT Astra expects 44% growth in domestic motorcycle sales this year to 700,000 units. Q1 sales were 166,000 units.

The textiles sector is the largest earner of foreign exchange after and oil and gas. About 2,300 enterprises, of varying size and sophistication, employ over 1mn people. The sector (including footwear and leather) produced nearly 2% of GDP in the recession years and investment is needed to improve its competitive position and regain market share lost as foreign buyers became wary of unrest. Given better conditions and renewed investment, growth should be strong over the forecast period. Textiles exports (excluding footwear and leather) managed to rise to US$7.8bn in 1998, but fell to about US$6bn in 1999. The target for 2000 is US$8bn, which should be within reach.

Shoe exports are expected to rise to around US$2bn in 2000, from US$1.7bn in 1999, according to the Indonesian Footwear Association (Aprisindo). Its secretary-general, Djimanto, said that Wahid's extensive overseas travel had helped to restore confidence among foreign buyers. Order books are now bulging; with 35.8mn pairs of shoes ordered for H1. Full-year orders could be 130mn pairs, although financing exports is a serious problem for exporters because foreign banks are unwilling to accept Indonesian letters of credit. Exports fell from US$2.2bn in 1996 to US$1.2bn in 1998, with Aprisindo's membership down from 178 firms in 1996 to 91 firms in 1999 as companies succumbed to mounting debts and contracting orders. Aprisindo says about 10% of its members, mostly smaller producers based in the greater Jakarta area, planned to apply for exemption from paying the increased minimum wage after the new rates take effect in April.

Wahid's extensive overseas travel has helped to restore confidence among foreign buyers of Indonesian footwear.

For sustainable growth over the forecast period, with both domestic and export-oriented manufacturing returning to positive growth, a resolution of the logjam in financial sector reform is crucial. Without this, companies will not be able to finance production on a larger scale, much less investment.

MANUFACTURING OUTPUT (IDRBN)						
	1997	% of GDP	1998	% of GDP	1999	% of GDP
Manufacturing	108.8	25.1	94.8	25.2	97.8	25.9
Oil/gas industry	10.7	2.5	10.8	2.9	11.7	3.1
Non-oil/gas industry	98.2	22.6	84.0	22.3	86.1	22.8
Source: Bank Indonesia.						

Oil And Gas

Opec Quotas Up

Continuing high oil prices caused Opec to raise quotas by 1.45mn b/d in March and another small rise is expected this year. Analysts have said that Opec is seeking to hold the benchmark North Sea Brent Crude in a range of US$20-25/b. In early March it hit US$34/b, the highest level since the 1991 Gulf War. Prices as of June were still above the target range, continuing to provide windfall revenues for the budget, which forecast a price of US$20/b. Indonesia's new quota is 1.28mn b/d, up from 1.19mn, but it is thought that actual output has been a little above this. The budget assumed production of 1.52mn b/d in 1999/2000, and 1.46mn b/d in 2000. **BMI** expects oil prices to average US$23.5/b (Opec basket) in 2000, up 34.5% from US$17.5 in 1999, which was itself 42.3% above 1998. Indonesia's oil exports earned US$19.7/b in 1999, up from US$15.0/b in 1998.

Pertamina To Raise Oil Output

In February Wahid appointed Baihaki Hakim president-director of the state oil and gas company, Pertamina, replacing Martiono Hadianto. Mr Baihaki is a former president of **PT Caltex Pacific Indonesia**, a joint venture between the US firms **Chevron** and **Texaco**, which operates Indonesia's largest oilfield, Minas, in the province of Riau on Sumatra. Baihaki's task is to transform the lumbering state-owned company into a world-class global player and has set the goal of raising output from 70,000 b/d to 100,000 b/d within 2-3 years. He says most of the 30,000 b/d rise will come from higher output at Tepus and Sopa fields in South Sumatra, where Pertamina has recently discovered reserves with the potential to produce 24,000 b/d and 18,000 b/d respectively. The company's new finance director, Ainun Naim, a former research and electronics development programme co-ordinator at Gajah Mada University in Yogyakarta, has close political ties with Amien Rais's National Mandate Party (PAN).

Legislation that would have opened the sector to foreign and domestic players, ending Pertamina's monopoly control of production-sharing contracts, was turned down by the legislature in February 1999, after vigorous lobbying by Pertamina. The minister of mines and energy, Bambang Yudhoyono, said late last year that he intends to represent a modified version of the law, with the downstream market expected to be fully liberalised. As of mid-2000 it was reported that the new law, still under discussion, would be presented to the DPR soon.

*Despite a rise in Opec quotas, **BMI** expects oil prices to average US$23.5/b (Opec basket) in 2000, up 34.5% from the US$17.5 seen in 1999.*

Legislation that would have opened the oil and gas sector to foreign and domestic players, ending Pertamina's monopoly, was turned down by the legislature in February 1999.

Output Slumps
Indonesia - oil output, mn b/d

Source: Petroleum Economist.

The production of liquefied natural gas (LNG) at the Arun gas field in Aceh is to be cut back by 37%, due to declining reserves. **PT Arun**, a joint venture between **Exxon Mobil** of the US (35%) and Pertamina (55%), is Indonesia's second largest producer of LNG. Efforts to find more reserves at the site have been hampered by unrest in the province and in early May the company announced the temporary suspension of all exploration and administrative activities after violent incidents in which company employees and property were targeted by armed men. The separatist Free Aceh Movement (*Gerakan Aceh Merdeka*, or GAM) said it was not involved in the incidents.

Interregional Tensions Continue

Interregional tensions are complicating the decision about the future operation of the 70,000 b/d Coastal Plain Pekanbaru (CPP) oilfield in Riau, operated by **Caltex Pacific Indonesia**, (CPI) in a production-sharing agreement with Pertamina. When the current agreement ends in August 2001, CPI wants its share to rise from 12% of production, to equal ownership with Pertamina. Pertamina wants to keep more. The Riau provincial government is staking a claim to the concession and has reportedly won the support of Wahid, who has said that the central government is now in negotiation with the Riau government and delicate negotiations between Caltex and Pertamina over the future ownership of the concession have been cancelled. Caltex produces 70,000 b/d from its Coastal Plains Pekanbaru (CPP) oil block in the province and has operated the concession for 29 years under a production-sharing arrangement with Pertamina. There are fears that the precedent Wahid has set by supporting the Riau government's demands could spark many similar claims against foreign investment projects.

There are fears that the precedent Wahid has set by supporting the Riau government's claim for a concession in the Coastal Plain Pekanbaru oilfield, could spark many similar claims against foreign investment projects.

OIL AND GAS EXPORTS						
	1994	1995	1996	1997	1998	1999
Volume (mn tonnes)						
Crude oil	43.7	40.7	38.2	39.0	36.9	35.9
Oil products	8.8	11.2	10.7	10.2	8.4	7.8
Gas	29.3	28.2	29.3	29.0	28.9	30.1
Value (US$mn)						
Crude oil	5,072	5,146	5,712	5,480	3,349	4,517
Oil products	933	1,297	1,516	1,303	708	918
Gas	3,689	4,022	4,494	4,840	3,816	4,357
Total	9,694	10,465	11,722	11,623	7,872	9,792
% of total exports	24.2	23.0	23.5	21.8	16.1	20.1
Source: Statistics Indonesia.						

Uncertainties notwithstanding, there has been quite a lot of activity in the oil/gas sector in the most recent quarter, particularly offshore. Announcements include: **Premier Oil** of the UK has found offshore gas in Block A in its Naga-I well, close to its Gajah Puteri and Pelikan fields. The gas could be exported by pipeline to Singapore and/or Malaysia and gas from this find is expected to start flowing by mid 2001. The Naga-I field may be developed jointly with Gajah Puteri and Pelikan, via the Anona platform.

A subsidiary of **Tenggara Capital** of Malaysia is to invest US$24mn over three years to explore the Karapan block off Java. **Unocal**, the largest oil producer in Indonesia, together with **Mobil**, has been given permission to start a deepwater project in the West Seno and Merah Besar oil and gas fields in offshore Kalimantan; oil is expected to start flowing in 2002. Unocal, which is the most active explorer, has announced plans to spend an additional US$700mn over the next three years. Kuwait's ambassador to Jakarta, Jamal Al-Nesafi, has said that Kuwait will invest about US$4bn in the oil sector in Selayar island, on top of US$1.25bn already invested in Seram. **Phillips Petroleum** and its Australian and Japanese partners have announced that production from the Elang field has risen to 20,000 b/d, from 6,500. But sales contracts are getting shorter as buyers demand more flexibility. Separate talks between Pertamina and Japanese buyers are ongoing, to renew 25-year contracts that will expire in 2004 with the contracts also expected to be of five years' duration.

A fall-off in oil and gas revenues as prices come down will encourage the government to end fuel subsidies.

BMI does not expects oil and gas output to rise over the next two years and revenues will fall back as prices ease. This will help to stiffen the resolve of the government to end the fuel subsidies that are a drag on budgetary resources and distort the overall price level. Indonesia is reportedly producing at capacity and reduced output at Arun will constrain LNG. Most new capacity currently under development will come on stream after the end of the forecast period. Pertamina says oil reserves are expected to fall to 9.3bn barrels in 2000, down from 9.8bn in 1999, sufficient for about 19 years' production.

Banking

Banks Lose And Lend Less

Pre tax losses in the banking sector in 1999, though still large at IDR97.1trn (US$12bn), were 48.7% down on 1998 and losses from negative interest spreads have also fallen (*see Quarterly Forecast Report Q2 2000, Key Economic Sectors*). But non-performing loans (NPLs) continue to accumulate, as debtors default. They are now in the region of 30% of assets, down from about 50% in 1998. The banks' capital position has also improved: although the net equity position was still negative as of the end of 1999, at IDR41.2trn, this was better than the net position at the end of 1998-IDR129.7trn. March data show 112 banks with capital adequacy ratios (CARs) of more than 8%, 10 banks with CARs between 4-8%, and 39 banks with CARs less than 4%.

The still poor balance sheets of the banks are deterring lending: total credit outstanding from the banking sector was IDR228.9trn at the end of April, down 20.5% y-o-y, with loans to manufacturing down 21.4%, at IDR86.7trn. Only IDR270trn out of the IDR800trn in time deposits at commercial banks had been lent to the real sector, according to Bank Indonesia. Bank Indonesia is anxious to stimulate lending, although liquidity is tight and banks are content to buy government-issued bonds, a safer bet than new loans. The rules for calculating CARs are to be eased, to encourage lending. Other concessions to the legal lending limits have also been announced

More Recapitalisation Bonds

The government plans to issue another IDR105.65trn in bank recapitalisation bonds this year, raising the total outstanding to IDR655.37trn (about US$77bn) including the bonds issued to finance Bank Indonesia's liquidity support for ailing banks and credit programmes, according to a Ministry of Finance spokesman. The bonds will finance what is expected to be the final round of bank recapitalisation of five banks: IRD31.80trn for the second and final recapitalisation of **Bank Negara Indonesia** (BNI), (after IDR30trn worth of bonds in April); IDR29.17trn for state-owned **Bank Rakyat Indonesia** (BRI) (to complete a recapitalisation delayed by the ongoing tussle between Wahid and Bank Indonesia Governor Sjahril Sabirin); IDR11.2trn for state-owed **Bank Tabungan Negara** (BTN); IDR4.61trn for **Bank Bali** (delayed by a legal suit brought by Bank Bali's former owner Rudy Ramli).; and IDR28.87trn for the second recapitalisation of **Bank Danamon**, which

Non-performing loans continue to accumulate, as debtors default.

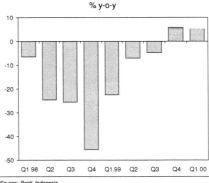

Lacklustre Growth
Indonesia - financial and business services growth, % y-o-y

Source: Bank Indonesia.

There are plans to issue another IDR105.65trn in bank recapitalisation bonds this year.

needs a second injection ahead of its merger with eight smaller banks which still have negative CAR levels.

BCA Privatised Amid IBRA Overhang

BMI expects substantial progress on banking sector reform this year, while the disposal of IBRA's portfolio will be much slower.

In May, the initial public offering (IPO) for a stake in **Bank Central Asia** (BCA), finally went through. The poor state of the stockmarket and weak foreign interest kept the price below what had been hoped, but it was a relief that the issue did not have to be delayed once again. IBRA meanwhile, continues to sit on huge assets (in book value at least) and faces ongoing problems with recalcitrant creditors. Nor is it being backed by the courts: all five of the bankruptcy cases it has brought to date have failed; in mid June the Supreme Court rejected the fifth, against palm oil producer **PT Sumi Asih**. The government has said it will strengthen IBRA's powers so that the agency can proceed towards its long-delayed privatisation targets. As of late March, IBRA was in control of assets worth a nominal IDR441trn (US$52bn) including non-performing loans, pledged assets from shareholder settlements and investments in the recapitalisation of seven private banks and four nationalised ones. Unwinding and disposing of these holdings will be a protracted affair, and the pace needs to be measured to avoid rocking or overwhelming the fragile capital markets.

Looking ahead, **BMI** expects substantial progress on banking sector reform this year, while disposal of IBRA's portfolio will be much slower. Until the banking sector resumes lending to finance the real economy, a sustained economic recovery cannot gain hold. Banks are expected to start lending again this year, but ongoing restructuring will prevent growth in the banking sector until 2001, despite Q1 growth of 8.4%. Recovery will gather pace from 2001.

COMMERICAL BANKS' OUTSTANDING CREDITS (IDRBN)									
	1995	% of total	change (% y-o-y)	1998	% of total	change (% y-o-y)	1999	% of total	change (% y-o-y)
State Banks	93,480	39.8	16.8	220,747	45.3	44.0	112,288	49.9	-50.9
Regional Government Banks	5,242	2.2	24.8	6,570	1.3	-12.8	6,793	3.0	3.4
Private National Banks	111,644	47.6	29.4	193,361	39.7	14.6	56,012	24.9	-29.0
Foreign and Joint-Venture Banks	24,245	10.3	32	66,748	13.7	37.3	50,040	22.2	-75.0
Total	234,611	100.0	24.2	487,426	100.0	28.9	225,133	100.0	-46.2

Source: Bank Indonesia.

Profile and Recent Developments

Introduction

Agriculture Is Still Important

Agriculture, which contributes 17% of GDP and employs around 40% of the labour force, has been comparatively sheltered from the effects of the economic crisis; food crop output growing by 1.4% in 1999 and plantation output by 3.3%. Forestry output was up 1.6% in GDP terms and fishery output was up 1.9%. But there are some serious problems. The food crop sector's structural weaknesses – chronically poor productivity and distribution – are a function of smallholder inefficiency and a lack of capital, compounded by ineffective government policies – and are not going to be solved immediately. The crisis has had a serious impact on investment in the agriculture sector; this fell by 65.4% in 1998, to IDR4757.7bn, and then again, by 66%, in 1999.

Rice Imports Are Needed

Annual rice production has been rising, to 49.9mn tonnes of unhusked rice in 1999, up by 1.3% on drought-affected 1998. But this is only just enough to meet current consumption, which is rising by about the same amount. Hence the large annual imports of 3.6mn tonnes in 1999 and 5.9mn in 1998 according to USDA figures – which have helped to depress domestic prices. In some areas these are reportedly below the IDR1400 (US$19)/kg current floor price which the state procurement agency, *Bulog*, has set and *Bulog* is reported to be unable to fully meet even this commitment, partly because of liquidity problems caused by the banking sector crisis. To counter falling prices and raise domestic production, the government has imposed a 30% import tariff on rice, effective until August 2000. Sugar imports will be subject to a 25% duty. Trade in both crops has been liberalised, removing *Bulog's* monopoly over imports of certain grades of rice. *Bulog* has said it will spend IDR8trn (US$800mn) in 2000 on supporting the rice price, but rice farmers have been hit by an IMF-mandated decision to scrap fertiliser subsidies and by low domestic prices.

Soybean output was 1.3mn tonnes in 1999, slightly down on the 1998 crop of 1.4mn tonnes, on a slight fall in yields. Corn output was stable between the two years, at 3.4mn tonnes. Indonesia expected to import between 3.3-3.5mn tonnes of wheat in 1999 compared with 4mn tonnes in 1998. In 1998, it also imported 1.7mn tonnes of sugar and 640,000 tonnes of soybeans.

IDR4.4trn (US$550mn) was allocated to agriculture in FY1999/2000. The government plans to boost production of basic commodities, such as corn, soybeans and rice, in order to reduce imports, the price of which was sent spiralling by the collapse of the rupiah.

Coffee: Robust Robusta

Coffee production and exports were up in 1999/00, the former by 23% to an estimated 470,000 tonnes, the latter by 9% to 360,000 tonnes, but depressed world prices limited the gains. In the first nine months of calendar 1999 foreign exchange earnings from coffee were down 16.2% to US$373mn. Meanwhile, data for Vietnamese coffee yields underline Indonesia's poor performance: yields in Vietnam average 1.2 tonnes/ha in the Central Highlands area, while in Indonesia's southern Sumatran provinces, the yield is a mere 650kg/ha. Coffee exports are expected to fall to around 300,000 tonnes (on production of about 430,000 tonnes) in 2000/01, according to the Indonesian Coffee Association, because rain has hit output.

Palm Oil And Cocoa

Indonesia is the world's second largest CPO producer after Malaysia and in a strong position to become the world's leader. Unlike Malaysia, where the additional supply of suitable land continues to shrink, Indonesia has a vast land bank available, especially in East Indonesia. Indonesia will also catch-up, as its plantations are less mature than Malaysia's. The CPO yield normally increases in line with the age of the trees and it is estimated that around 65% of Indonesia's palm oil plantations are mature against 90% in Malaysia. Moreover, the extraction rate – the quantity of oil generated from each palm oil fruit – is higher in Indonesia than in Malaysia, (23% versus 19%) due to Indonesia's low-cost labour, which allows greater specialisation. Moreover, Indonesia's palm oil facilities are generally newer and more efficient than Malaysia's.

Crude palm oil exports should have risen in 1999 on the back of another increase in the area cultivated. But the discovery, in November 1999, that a shipment of 85,000 tonnes of Indonesian CPO to Rotterdam had been contaminated with diesel oil, has damaged prospects in the short term, cutting export demand. Exports in 1999 were expected to have reached 2mn tonnes, without the contamination scandal, up from 1.5mn in 1998, but far below the record 3mn tonnes of 1997. Domestic stockpiles have risen, to as much as 500,000 tonnes, and the price has fallen. The 10% tax on CPO exports, which is intended to secure sufficient domestic supplies of cooking oil, is expected to be reduced to 3%, to boost exports in 2000. After the collapse of the rupiah, it was more attractive for Indonesian producers to export rather than sell to the local market and this created cooking oil shortages. As a result, the government imposed first an export ban and afterwards a 60% export tax, to deter exports. With the recent strengthening of the rupiah, producers have started selling locally again, pushing the local price down.

Cocoa production has been hit by the spread of a pest to the areas that account for about 75% of annual production. After rising by 4% to 350,000 tonnes in 1998/99 because of new plantings, the harvest is expected to fall to 438,000 in 1999/00 because of the pest, so Indonesia has not benefited fully from higher prices in late 1999/early 2000.

Rubber Prospects Improve

Indonesia is the third largest natural rubber producer after Malaysia and Thailand. Indonesia's output was expected to reach 1.55mn tonnes in 1998, up from 1.5mn tonnes in 1997. Most of this production is exported – an estimated 1.5mn tonnes in 1998 – particularly with domestic consumption falling in the past year. Rubber may be a bright spot in an otherwise bleak picture. Despite the imminent sale of the International Rubber Organisation (INRO) stockpile, in the wake of INRO's disbanding in October 1999, the more liberal market that will follow the end of INRO was expected to lift prices. But there has been a surge in output from Thailand, where annual yields are as high as 1,000kg per ha, compared with 400-700kg/ha in Indonesia. The effects of the 1998 drought linger on and Indonesian output in 2000 will stagnate at around last year's 1.6mn tonnes, according to **Gapkindo**, the rubber producers' association. So even if prices rise, the gains to Indonesia will be limited in the short term, although the longer-term outlook is now more favourable.

Timber, Pulp And Paper: Focusing On Exports

As a result of Suharto's fall, Indonesia's plywood monopoly, Apkindo, controlled by the former president's close friend, Mohammed "Bob" Hassan, has been dismantled. This may make the allocation of timber concessions more transparent. The country plans to increase its landbank for plantations from 2.4mn ha to 3.9mn ha, requiring large-scale deforestation. Investment in the forestry sector rose in 1998-99, by 228% in 1998 and further by 38% in 1999. Log production was up 2.5% in 1998 and is likely to rise further. Forest concessions of 51.5mn ha are controlled by conglomerates, the largest being **Barito Pacific**. Barito holds concessions estimated at around 2.7mn ha, and is expanding its operations into pulp and paper. One of its subsidiaries, **Musi Hutan Persada**, opened a US$1bn pulp factory in August 1999.

The Indonesian government has decided to impose progressive taxes on forestry companies, who hold concessions of more than 3.5mn ha. It is also considering a levy of US$2 per cubic metre of wood to be channelled into education. With an economic recovery in Korea and possibly Japan, demand for timber is poised to increase dramatically in the next few years. Barito Pacific will clearly benefit from it, although the group's bottom line will continue to be affected by high financial charges in line with its large borrowings.

The Indonesian pulp and paper industry is dominated by **Indah Kiat** and **Tjiwi Kimia** which together give their parent, the **Sinar Mas Group**, an estimated 80% market share. This monopolistic situation affects the smaller paper producers with the industry already among the world's lowest cost producers. Most the of companies in the sector have increased their exports in order to offset poor domestic demand, although some, such as **Asia Pulp and Paper**, have always relied on exports for the vast majority of their sales.

Metals And Mining

A Rich Resource Base

Indonesia is well-endowed with mineral resources and has encouraged foreign investment in the sector, in close collaboration with large state-owned conglomerates. Non-oil mining accounted for 2.7% of GDP in 1999 and grew by 6.6% in that year. The country is one of the world's leading producers of tin, deposits on and offshore being estimated at over 1m tonnes. State-owned PT Tambang Timah accounts for 80% of national production. Output has been depressed in recent years by poor prices, but rose in the wake of the demise of the supply scheme run by the Association of Tin Producing Countries, in 1996. Output reached 55,174 tonnes in 1997 and declined to 53,959 tonnes in 1998.

Indonesian mining output includes bauxite (output fell to 620,500 tonnes in 1998), nickel (1.9mn tonnes), and coal (38mn tonnes). Copper is also important; with Freeport Indonesia mining the large Grasberg mine in Irian Jaya from 1990, where gold is also extracted. But operations have been scaled back after a landslide exacerbated environmental problems and lent support to the long-standing opposition of environmentalists. Another large copper mine, on the island of Sumbawam, operated by PT Newmont Nusa Tenggara, came into operation in 1999. Nickel is also mined.

Metals prices were weak in 1998, falling by about 19% and then stagnant the following year. Currency depreciation in 1998 boosted the local currency revenues of Indonesian mine operators. But appreciation in 1999 offset this trend.

Indonesian Gold: Bright prospects

Indonesia ranked sixth in the world among gold producers in 1999, with output of 155 tonnes, up from 139 tonnes in 1998. Over 60% of the country's gold is generated as a by-product at the Grasberg mine, now the largest single gold-producing mine in the world. Output rose at Grasberg to 93 tonnes as the fourth concentrator operated for its first full year. Also, Minahasa's production was raised by three tonnes as Newmont began operating Indonesia's first heap leach pad. The Gosowong gold-silver project produced nearly four tonnes although the first gold was only poured in July and the mine was affected by local unrest. Meanwhile, the Batu Hijau operation started up at the end of the year and is expected to produce 15 tonnes annually as a by-product of copper mining. Gold prices were 5% down on average in dollar terms in 1999, at US$278.6/oz, a 20-year low, falling 28% in rupiah terms.

Oil And Gas

Indonesia's Oil Reserves: Urgent Refuelling

Indonesia is OPEC's sole Asian member. Its proven oil reserves are about 5.5bn barrels, with another 4.4bn barrels of probable reserves. Average daily demand was 920,000 b/d in 1997, but there are estimates that domestic production could decline to about 1mn b/d early next century. On this basis, Indonesia could become a net oil importer as early as 2005. At a time of severe recession and crisis in many sectors, Wahid's new government has good reason to be thankful for recent developments in the oil sector, which still accounts for about 9% of GDP and contributed 20% of total exports in 1999. Higher oil prices in fiscal 1999/00 helped to contain the budget deficit to 3.9% of GDP (but the net gains were cut by the continuance of domestic fuel price subsidies which will cost about US$3.7bn in fiscal 2000), and boosted oil and gas exports by 24% in calendar 1999, to US$9.8bn, thanks to oil exports of US$4.52bn, up 35%. Indonesia's Opec quota was reduced from 1.5mn b/d to 1.187mn in March 1999. Indonesia's oil exports earned US$19.7/b in 1999, up from US$15.0/b in 1998.

A recent discovery by **Unocal-Mobil** off the coast of East Kalimantan has raised hopes, but the Indonesian government might have to introduce a new oil contract before more exploration risks are taken by foreign oil companies. **Caltex Pacific Indonesia**, jointly owned by US oil giants **Chevron** and **Texaco**, produces about 50% of Indonesia's crude while other operators include **Arco** and **Total**.

Production sharing contracts have been the rule, although in 1994, new terms for deep-water areas gave exploration companies 35% of revenues instead of 20%. But operators have also asked for tax consolidation, which would allow expenditure in exploration blocks to be offset against tax on revenues from producing areas. Pertamina currently taxes producers on a contract-by-contract basis. The 85:15 revenue split in favour of Pertamina for non-frontier blocks has deterred most foreign oil companies to go ahead with costly wildcat exploration programmes.

Natural Gas: Too Valuable to Burn?

Pertamina estimates Indonesia's gas reserves at 140trn cf, of which about 80trn can be considered as proven reserves. Indonesia is already the world's biggest supplier of liquefied natural gas (LNG) and exports some 26.5mn tonnes per annum, mostly to Japan, Taiwan and Korea. With oil reserves stretched, natural gas could become Indonesia's future cash cow.

Indonesia's largest field is the giant Natuna field, located in the South China Sea, some 1,100km north of Jakarta. Natuna's reserves are believed to be 45trn cf. The western part of the field contains high quality gas, but its eastern part has a 70% ratio of unwanted carbon dioxide, which increases production costs through higher processing costs. Other smaller fields have been recently discovered, which may have a higher commercial value, such as Arco's Wiriager Deep, offshore from Irian Jaya, with estimated reserves of 7trn cf.

Natural gas is becoming increasingly attractive as an efficient and clean source of energy. Although Indonesia's natural gas can mostly be exported in LNG form, Pertamina has signed a contract with Singapore's **Sembawang Gas** to supply 325mn cf per day through a 640km pipeline to Jurong island. The US$4bn gas contract will allow the future Tuas II power plant to be fuelled in 2001 with natural gas coming from West Natuna. However, natural gas can be more value-added if it is used as feedstock for petrochemical downstream operations, rather than being burned. Downstream applications include produce of ethylene and propylene and further processing leads to production of PVC resin, polystyrene, polyethylene, polypropylene as well as phenolic and synthetic resin.

Pertamina's Restructuring: Slippery Road

Scandal has dogged Pertamina through the years. In 1976, the company required a massive government bailout after racking up US$10.5bn in debt through unwise investments. A decade later, lucrative subcontracting deals with the monopoly enabled Suharto's two sons to set up business empires. In 1993, the group started a restructuring programme that reduced production costs to US$5.1/b from US$11.7/b and scaled down the workforce from 45,540 to 30,000.

Since the fall of Suharto, the group has saved US$100mn by scrapping dubious supply and distribution contracts with 32 firms, most of them linked to the former president's family and friends. Pertamina claims that US$650mn savings were made in this way in calendar 1998. Oil projects have been delayed, awaiting a better pricing environment.

Petrochemicals: A New Beginning?

As already mentioned, Indonesia aims to increase the value-added element of its natural gas output through the development of a petrochemical industry. However, refinery building requires large capital expenditure and the credit crunch resulting from the crisis has set back the emerging industry. No less than eight refinery projects involving FDI were approved in 1995 and 1996 and Indonesia already had one olefin centre in operation in Merak, West Java. Since 1994, 15 companies have received licences from the government to build private refineries, but none has started construction. The government is therefore considering revoking the three-year licences, if the deadline for building the refinery has passed, or if the intentions of those involved are not judged to be serious.

The government acknowledges that there were few incentives to build a strong petrochemical industry. It is preparing a law aimed at liberalising the sector and opening the retail market for oil products. In 1989, the government opened the door for private investors to build refineries, but interest was dampened by regulations forbidding private refinery owners from selling their products on the domestic market. In addition, Pertamina gave no assurance it would provide crude oil supply to private refineries.

Former president Suharto eased the regulations in 1997 by allowing private refinery owners to enter into an off-take agreement with Pertamina for the sale of their products on the domestic market at a price agreed upon by both parties. Although many investors applied, Pertamina only made agreements with companies controlled by Suharto's family and friends. Pertamina operates nine refineries with a combined processing capacity of 1mn b/d.

The Indonesian government may acquire a stake in **Chandra Asri**, if the petrochemical firm fails to reach an agreement over debts totalling US$830mn. Chandra Asri is Indonesia's largest ethylene producer, controlled by Suharto's second son Bambang Trihatmodjo, but with other shareholders including **Showa Denko**, **Marubeni** and **Toyo Engineering**. Chandra Asri borrowed funds from local banks, which were later transferred to Indonesian Bank Restructuring Agency.

Power: Unplugged

Demand for electricity grew at an average of 15% per annum during the early 1990s. The economic crisis put a stop on Indonesia's power thirst and in 1998, demand for electricity is estimated to have declined by nearly 20%. Power supply in Indonesia is seen as a public service, not a commercial venture and the state-owned **PLN** sells electricity at less than it costs to produce. During recent years, it simply amassed debt.

The utility agency is facing a difficult future. Increasing the electricity tariffs can only be done slowly and gradually as it could cause social and political unrest. It will have to cut back on projects, reducing capital expenditure and other costs, as higher income will be difficult to achieve. PLN tried to back out of contractual obligations, such as **PT Unocal Geothermal**, a subsidiary of Unocal, by using an unrealistic exchange rate. However, such artifices are not applicable over the long run and the restructuring of PLN will be a long and costly process.

Indonesia's power reforms are estimated to cost US$1-1.5bn annually in 1999 and 2000 and US$4bn in 2001. The Asian Development Bank (ADB) has approved a total of US$400mn in loans for the country's power restructuring programme. The balance of the costs are expected to be met by direct budgetary outlays, loans from bilateral and multilateral sources and part of the proceeds from the sale of PLN's assets in Java and Bali.

Uncertainties For Oil And Gas

The oil and gas sector faces some problems and uncertainties. Interregional tensions are complicating the decision about the future operation of the 70,000 b/d Coastal Plain Pekanbaru (CPP) oilfield in Riau, operated by **Caltex Pacific Indonesia**, (CPI) in a production-sharing agreement with **Pertamina**, when the current agreement terminates in August 2001. CPI wants its share to rise from 12% of production, to equal ownership with Pertamina. Pertamina wants to keep more. The Riau regional administration reportedly wants a share in the field as well. **Mobil** is reported to have pulled some staff out of the troubled province of Aceh in December 1999 and there are fears among the oil majors that the government and the military will be less willing to prevent local communities disrupting their activities. A number of contractual disputes involving foreign oil companies remain unresolved.

Among the uncertainties is the future of Pertamina itself. After an audit by **PriceWaterhouseCoopers** found that corruption and inefficiency had lost the country about US$5bn in 1996-98, a new top management team was installed at Pertamina at the end of February 2000. Baihaki Hakim, previously president of CPI, is the new chief executive. He has pledged sweeping changes and a transparent regime and has been given the task of raising Pertamina's output to make it an international oil major. The goal is to raise production to 100,000 b/d from 70,000 now within two or three years. To do this, in time for Pertamina to gear up to compete with regional oil majors as the Asean free-trade area takes shape from 2004, he will have to be able to invest much more of its profits in exploration. Pertamina will need to become an independent player and no longer a cash cow for the government. The current production-sharing framework is expected to remain in place, and Baihaki Hakim has said he sees no immediate case to unify taxation rates, which currently vary across areas.

Central to the plans being contemplated to restructure the oil sector, with strong distaste felt in some quarters, is a new oil and gas law. Legislation that would have opened the sector to foreign and domestic players, ending Pertamina's monopoly, was turned down by the legislature in February 1999, after vigorous lobbying by Pertamina. The new minister of mines and energy, Liuetenant-General Bambang Susilo Yudhoyono, said late last year that he intends to represent a modified version of the law, with the downstream market expected to be fully liberalised.

Manufacturing

Recovery Begins

In terms of production, the nascent recovery in the Indonesian economy in 1999 was concentrated in domestically-oriented manufacturing. The sector grew by 2.2% in terms of GDP. This growth in manufacturing was not broad-based, being led by food, beverages and tobacco, paper and printing and chemicals, all items largely for domestic consumption. The economic crisis has hit the sector harder than agriculture, mining or oil and gas. Construction has been affected, causing a sharp drop in demand for steel and cement. Apart from basic items, such as food and cigarettes, demand for consumer goods has also slumped, especially for non-essential items such as cars, white goods or luxury items.

Cement Industry: Continuing Oversupply

The cement industry in Indonesia, and in many Asian countries, has benefited from easy and cheap financing and based its cashflow forecasts on unsustainable demand growth. With the region's appetite for cement overstated, the outcome was a production glut. Indonesia's cement industry is dominated by three major producers, **Semen Gresik**, **Semen Cibinong** and **Indocement**, which have a combined market share of over 90%.

Domestic demand plunged to about 15.30mn tonnes in 1998 against 27.40mn tonnes in 1997.

Exports rose, thanks to Indonesia's comparative advantage in terms of production costs as the rupiah collapsed. Indonesia's cash costs are around US$13-15/tonne. With export prices around US$20/tonne, the Indonesian producers – especially Semen Gresik – have been able to increase their market share. The main problem comes from a lack of infrastructure, such as port facilities.

Semen Gresik is in much better shape than its peers. Its debt structure was mainly in local currency with a bearable debt-equity ratio. The presence of Mexico's **Cemex** as a major shareholder will improve Gresik's prospects further.

Krakatau Steel: Undecided Fate, But Large Potential

The steel industry in Indonesia is dominated by state-owned **Krakatau Steel**, with an estimated 75% market share. Apart from some downstream operations, most of the balance was supplied from imports. Demand for steel was around 7mn tonnes in 1997, but is estimated to have declined by nearly 50% in 1998 to about 3.5mn tonnes. From a net importer, Indonesia switched to a net exporter, and Krakatau has been active at selling hot-rolled coils in the US, China and Europe.

The privatisation of Krakatau Steel has been postponed. In the last days of the Suharto rule, **Ispat International** was supposed to have reached an agreement with the Indonesian government for the acquisition of a 51% majority stake for US$430mn. However, the deal was quickly cancelled after Suharto's fall and Krakatau's future remains undecided. Korea's **POSCO** has stopped its joint venture for the production of 1mn tonnes HRC. However, Krakatau's potential remains as the sole integrated steel producer in a country of more than 200mn people, although it has to work on more restructuring before being sold.

Automotives: A Recovery

The sector is dominated by **PT Astra International**, a leading conglomerate and part of the **Salim Group**. It has licences to assemble and distribute vehicles for **Toyota**, **Daihatsu**, **BMW**, **Honda**, **Peugeot**, **Renault** and **Isuzu**. In 1997, 386,709 vehicles were sold in Indonesia, a 16.5% y-o-y increase. However, the crisis has hit the industry hard and in 1998, only 18,845 vehicles were sold. A recovery in domestic demand took place in 1999, with The Association of Indonesian Automotive Industries (*Gaikindo*) reporting that car sales reached 78,739 units in January-November 1999, up 35% from the same period of 1998. The association expected car sales of 85,000 for the full year and 160,000 in 2000.

Astra's market share is estimated at 50% for cars and motorcycles sold in Indonesia. When listed on the Jakarta Stock Exchange in 1990, Astra International was regarded as the bluest of the blue chips. Crony relations were a major asset, but after the fall of Suharto the tables turned. Astra's showrooms were looted and burned. Its debt – (US$1.6bn), mostly in US dollars – soared and, given falling cashflow, servicing became impossible. In April 1998, Astra International reported a net loss of IDR279bn, its first loss since founding in 1957. It became a prime candidate for restructuring.

Telecoms

Industry Domination

Two major companies dominate the telecommunication industry in Indonesia: local provider **PT Telkom** and international provider **PT Indosat**. Benefiting from a weak rupiah, Indosat, which dominates the international phone traffic, is sailing through the turmoil. Net profit rose 82% in 1998 to IDR1,166bn. Unlike many Indonesian companies, Indosat is not weighted down by heavy foreign borrowings and as a dollar earner, the company was able to book a IDR183bn foreign exchange gain. But a looming hurdle is an expected 50-60% increase in the fees Indosat pays to PT Telkom to use its infrastructure. The rise will put pressure on margins. In 1998, compensation to Telkom and non-Telkom services accounted for 36% of total operating expenses. Interconnection charges were 16-17% of Indosat's revenues.

Consumer Goods

Consumer Recovery

Indonesia's food sector, particularly the instant noodle market, is dominated by **Indofood**, part of the Salim Group. Shareholders are currently negotiating the sale of 60% of the group to Japan's **Nissin Food Products** and **First Pacific Co**, a unit of the Salim Group listed in Hong Kong. Indofood has annual production capacity of 13bn packs of instant noodles, which contribute 50% of sales. Retailers have been hit hard by the collapse in domestic demand, but the beginnings of an upturn in 1999, concentrated on consumer spending, has brought some relief. Thus, the upmarket supermarket chain **PT Hero Supermarket** reported a net loss of IDR69bn in 1998, despite a 36% rise in turnover, and a foreign exchange loss of IDR68bn. In 1999, PT Hero Supermarket made profits of IDR90.87bn (US$11.6mn) in 1999 and other retailers were expected to announce similarly improved results.

Tobacco Firms: Defying The Crisis

The sector is dominated by *kretek* makers, as the clove flavoured cigarettes are known. Listed companies include **Gudang Garam** and **Sampoerna**, which dominate the sector with respective market shares of 48% and 12%. Although the sector has also been hit by plunging purchasing power, most tobacco companies have remained profitable. The only major change has been a switch to less expensive brands. Gudang Garam is the leader in cheaper machine-rolled *kreteks* and has won business from consumers switching from other brands. Around 80% of Gudang Garam gross profit comes from machine-rolled cigarettes, while close to 90% of Sampoerna's gross profits come from hand-rolled *kreteks*. Gudang Garam is expected to post record profits both in 1998 and 1999, while Sampoerna is made a make a net loss in 1998 – mainly related to its US$400mn debt – before returning to profitability in 1999.

The Indonesian government is considering changing the tobacco industry's complicated tax structure, perhaps introducing a uniform tax, instead of setting different rates according to the size of the firm. The producers are currently categorised according to the number of cigarettes produced per year. Tax and excise duty are different depending on whether the cigarettes are hand- or machine-rolled.

Banking

Losses Are Falling

The banking sector posted a decline of 15.9% in value-added in 1999. According to Bank Indonesia, pre tax losses in the banking sector in 1999, though still large at IDR 97.1trn (US$12bn), were 48.7% down on the 1998 figure. But non-performing loans (NPLs) continue to accumulate, as debtors default. Total NPLs were put at 32.8% of assets in 1999, down from about 50% in 1998. The banks' capital position has also improved; although the net equity position was still negative as of the end of 1999, at IDR41.2trn, this was better than the net position at the end of 1998, at IDR129.7trn. By the end of January 2000, IBRA (the restructuring agency) was sitting on IDR 115trn (US$15bn) in NPLs from state-sector banks and was expecting to assume another IDR16.6trn in **Bank Mandiri** NPLs shortly.

Bank Mandiri was formed from a merger of four state banks in 1999, and its recapitalisation was completed in December 1999, when the government issued the second tranche of bonds worth IDR75trn, bringing the total cost of recapitalising the merged bank to IDR178trn (US$24bn). The bank is now embarking on a restructuring which will cause widespread job losses: its 19,000-strong workforce will be cut by 5,000 by the end of 2001.

Liquidity remains tight. IBRA has delayed payment of interbank claims worth IDR5trn due at the end of December 1999 until they have been verified by an international auditor and trading in government recapitalisation bonds has been restricted. The situation should improve now that trading in part of the recapitalisation bonds is being lifted, although there are doubts about the ability of the market to absorb large volumes of tradeable bonds. In 1999, the stock of commercial banks' outstanding rupiah credits fell by 55.1%, to IDR140.5trn, from IDR313.1trn at the end of 1998. Investment lending (rupiah and foreign exchange) fell by 52.8%, to IDR154.5trn: loans for working capital were down by 48.9% to IDR 95.7trn and consumption lending fell by 12.6% to IDR31trn. The closure of 39 private banks in 1999 (68 banks have been shut since mid-1997, the most recent, **Bank Putera Multikarsa**, the banking arm of the troubled **Texmaco** group, was shut in late January 2000), as well as the collapse in domestic and external demand, have depressed lending growth. Bank savings are reported to have held up well. Bank Indonesia has reported that depositors are moving funds into savings deposits because of their superior liquidity and a narrowing interest gap between savings and time deposits. Total time and savings deposits of commercial banks rose by 14% y-o-y between the end of 1999 and the end of 1998.

More bank closures are still possible in the private sector as the continuing weakness claims more victims and drives up NPLs. The government would prefer recapitalisation to closure, but resources are limited. As measures to strengthen Bank Indonesia's supervision of around 160 remaining commercial banks agreed as part of the latest Letter of Intent are implemented over the coming year, more closures and restructurings could be in the offing. Standard Chartered's withdrawal from its agreements to manage and invest in Bank Bali, late in 1999, damaged prospects for foreign investment in the sector. Meanwhile investigation into the Bank Bali interbank loan repayment scandal of August 1999 has been continuing.

Property

Recovery Delayed

Limited demand in Indonesia's property market and foreign debt repayment problems weighed heavily on the sector in 1998-99. Construction in GDP terms was down by 36.5% in 1998 and it fell again by 1.6% in 1999. Rising interest rates, weak public purchasing power and expensive raw materials have forced most firms in the property sector to the verge of bankruptcy. Most of them saw also their debt balloon as a result of rising rates and high forex exposure.

Of the three main property companies listed on the Jakarta Stock Exchange, only **Jaya Real** was expected to remain profitable in 1998-99, thanks to its limited exposure to foreign debt. **Ciputra**'s, which has foreign debt estimated at US$250mn, is currently working on a debt restructuring programme. The third largest company, **Jababeka**, is also expected to post losses. Nearly all property shares dropped below their book value. A pre-requisite for an improvement of the market – besides a better political environment – would be a fall in interest rates. Although they have already halved – from 70% to about 35% – it may not be sufficient. The market was already facing an oversupply, even before the crisis, and it will take at least two years before the excess office and residential space is absorbed.

Tourism

After The Smog, The Riots

The number of tourists visiting Indonesia dropped from 5.0mn in 1997 to 3.7mn in 1998. A recovery started in 1999, but it was nipped in the bud by a combination of political uncertainty and ethnic unrest. Total arrivals, at 3.9mn, ended the year 4.1% up on 1998. The tourism industry has not benefited as much as it should have done from rupiah weakness, simply because many hotels kept quoting their prices in US dollars, instead of taking advantage of the falling rupiah. Most of the good hotels in Bali are no cheaper than their equivalents in Phuket or Burakai. Continuing political troubles have also blighted prospects in the short term.

State-owned airline **Garuda** is expected to post a profit of US$30mn (IDR280bn) in 1999, compared with an estimated loss of IDR400bn in 1998. The airline has signed a management contract with Germany's **Lufthansa**, while **Deutsche Bank** is helping the airline to restructure its US$1bn foreign debt. Garuda has decided to concentrate on profitable routes and has returned several leased planes. It has also decided to cut its workforce by 2,000. Garuda was badly affected by the collapse of the rupiah as its revenues were mainly in rupiah, while about 80% of its costs were in US dollars.

4 Business Environment

Introduction

Suharto's Legacy: Progress And Graft

Suharto marched his sprawling country from overwhelming poverty to the brink of relative prosperity. The years of steady economic growth seemed to justify the title the former army general bestowed on himself in the 1980s: the "Father of Development". But the undeniable progress and the transformation of Indonesia left open the question of what could have been achieved without the rampant corruption, monopolies and crony capitalism that also marked the business environment in Indonesia during the Suharto years. It was those failings that helped push Indonesia to the brink of economic collapse and undermined Suharto's authority, ultimately forcing him to resign as president in the face of widespread protests, civil unrest and rioting.

Well into the 1970s, more than 60% of the population lived in poverty, per capita income hovered around US$70 a year and the country was the world's largest rice importer. By the mid-1990s, economic growth had averaged more than 6% annually and when adjusted to a purchasing-parity measurement, GDP per capita stood at more than US$3,000 per annum. At the same time, "foundations" established in Suharto's name were raking in fortunes estimated at up to US$3bn per year by the early 1990s. In addition, the regime allowed Suharto's six children to build a family empire worth billions more, largely through monopolies and tax-break arrangements over an estimated 260 separate companies.

In line with the development of the country, Suharto's children and friends became increasingly greedy, using their influence to penetrate practically every sector of the economy. The direct role of foreign investors in the build-up of the Suharto family's wealth is another consideration. At least 44 Western companies have gone into business with the Suhartos in Indonesia, plus another 15 from Japan and South Korea. Nineteen Suharto-linked companies were listed on the Jakarta Stock Exchange (JKSE). Listing has been a deliberate strategy to spread the ownership of their companies and thus increase the number of other investors with an interest in the maintenance of the family's privileges.

A very good example of this is provided by Suharto's middle son Bambang Trihatmodjo, whose flagship holding, the **Bimantara Group**, was listed on the JKSE. This means that members of the public have a share in each of the group's myriad of companies rather than one or two subsidiaries.

The Suharto assets are therefore very different to those accumulated by former Philippines strongman Ferdinand Marcos. The Suhartos have been integral to the founding and subsequent management of many of their companies, whereas the Marcos family restricted itself to large passive shareholdings in Philippine blue chips as well as cash kept overseas. So, ridding Indonesia's economy of the Suhartos and their cronies will not simply be a matter of transferring their equity, but would mean stripping them of their management as well.

The fall of Suharto, together with the political and economic turmoil in Indonesia, leads to several questions: Will the high level of corruption in Indonesia diminish in line with a more "liberal" and open government? Or will political and economic uncertainty more than offset any improvement on the corruption and graft front? There is certainly a strong current of popular resentment against "corruption, collusion and nepotism" (*korupsi, kolusi, nepotisme*, KKN), seen as pervasive in the Suharto-Habibie eras. The institutional and legal weakness left by Suharto make rapid change to a rules-based transparent system of governance more difficult. A recent survey undertaken by the **Political and Economic Risk Consultancy** (PERC) ranked Indonesia 7.43 on a scale of 1 to 10 for its responsiveness to foreign investors. Only China ranked worse in the poll of 500 expatriates working in Asia. The uncertain legal framework for contracts and erratic government policy also continues to impede investment

Infrastructure

Victim Of Corruption And A Survival Budget

Infrastructure was a key issue in Indonesia's development. The country's thirst for roads, power plants, ports and water plants seemed endless. Spending on infrastructure was supposed to reach US$55bn over the 1994-99 period. But IMF conditions stated that only projects considered vital for the country should go ahead. Soon after the fall of Suharto, eight projects were cancelled and seven more were put under review. The rationale was both political and economic.

It should come as no surprise that 39 government infrastructure projects were cancelled on the grounds of corruption. Other projects will have to be renegotiated. A typical example was the Tanjung Jati power plant project, a partnership between Suharto's daughter "Tutut" Siti Hariyanti Rukmana and **Hopewell Holdings**. Through her **Citra Lantoro Gung Group**, Tutut was involved in several toll roads and other infrastructure projects. Since the crisis began, 24 toll road projects have been dropped – nearly all of them involving Citra Lantoro – saving the government more than US$1bn.

Indonesia's state-owned power utility **PLN** is also renegotiating several projects, involving **Siemens**, **General Electric** and **Mitsui**, as a result of the economic crisis and the backlash against the business partners of the Suharto family. Many of Indonesia's 26 independent power projects were deemed unnecessary because of over-supply, and the collapse of the rupiah has rendered the dollar-denominated contracts hugely unprofitable for loss-making PLN.

Thames Water of the UK and France's **Suez Lyonnaise des Eaux** were among the first foreign companies to see their contracts cancelled as a result of an association with Suharto's family or friends. The separate concessions to develop and manage water supply systems for the eastern and western halves of Jakarta, worth US$120mn over 25 years, were initially cancelled, then re-awarded to the two groups. **Kati**, a company owned by Suharto's eldest son, Sigit Harjojudanto, has agreed to transfer its 20% stake in the concessionaire managing water supply in eastern Jakarta to Thames Water. Similarly, Suez Lyonnaise des Eaux agreed to buy back the 60% stake held by the **Salim Group**. Indonesia also announced that it would reallocate local companies' oil production sharing contracts, if it was shown their involvement stemmed from corruption during Suharto's rule.

As recovery sets in, infrastructure construction will once again become an important component of development spending. Like many Asian countries, Indonesia faces some serious infrastructural deficiencies, notably urban transport, water and waste disposal, as well as a continuing need to improve transport and communications networks.

The Domestic Market

Growing Population, Rising Poverty

The population of Indonesia was approximately 208mn at the end of 1999, and the country ranks as the fourth most populous country in the world behind China, India and the US. The average annual growth rate of the population was 1.9% in 1990-98, down from 3.2% in 1980-90. Indonesian estimates of the effects of the crisis on poverty are based on surveys carried out by the Central Statistics Agency. A December 1998 household expenditure survey showed poverty at 16.7% (the percentage of the population with consumption expenditure below the official poverty line), up from 11.3% in February 1996. Poverty rose to an estimated 20.7% in August 1998 and was still 20.3% in February 1999, according to similar surveys, suggesting a return to levels seen in the mid-1980s.

A recent World Bank study put the poverty level at about 14% of the population in 1998, a rise of 3 percentage points from 1997. This is based on an estimated income of less than US$0.5 per person per day.

Indonesia's population is young; with 33.9% below the age of 15 in 1995 and a further 19.2% between 15 and 24. Literacy rates are quite high, with 9% of men and 20% of women over 15 illiterate in 1997. The crisis has taken a toll on educational enrolment. The primary enrolment rate was close to 95% in fiscal 1997/98, taking advantage of free primary school provision. There is now a consensus that the crisis has not done too much damage at this level, but it may have had more impact on secondary and tertiary enrolment, because of the costs. The World Bank has concluded that enrolment levels have fallen, but only by four or five percentage points.

Although the decline in enrolment might have been overestimated, education remains a key issue in South East Asia and in Indonesia. Countries in the region will only be able to switch from labour-intensive to more capital-intensive economies if they give more attention to education. In this sense, the economic crisis has delayed this slow process. Even if it has been over-estimated, the impact of the crisis will have long-term consequences on the future of Indonesia.

The Labour Market

Open Unemployment Is Restrained

Unemployment or under-employment is always difficult to quantify in Indonesia, but has always been a major issue, often leading to social unrest. The first difficulty is to determine the unemployment rate in Indonesia. Government statistics mentioned an official rate of 7.5% in 1996, but including under-employment, the level was much higher. But in an economy where wages are downwardly flexible and social safety is minimal, the rise in open unemployment was restrained, with the slackening labour market putting pressure on real wages. In the mid-1990s over 40% of the labour force was still classified as agricultural, suggesting a high level of underemployment; manufacturing accounted for 13%, and trade, hotels and restaurants for 17%. It is difficult to quantify how much new unemployment resulted from the closing of hundreds of businesses, the destruction of shops, the interruption of construction activities and the collapse of the tourism industry. On top of that, given a labour force growth population growth rate of 3.1%, around 3mn additional people come on the job market every year and it was already difficult for the Indonesian economy to absorb them with GDP growth of 7% per annum. Recent statistics, published by the Indonesian government, cite an unemployment rate of about 17.15% of the workforce, or 17mn people for 1999.

Indonesia's workforce is estimated at 98mn people; agriculture accounted for nearly 49% of the total labour force in 1998, a greater proportion than in 1997, as people returned to the land to avoid urban poverty . This is a reversal of the trend in the previous decade, when many poor and unskilled workers were attracted by the glitter of large cities.

In the pre-crisis environment, organised labour was assuaged by wage increases and tolerated by the country's watchful military. Over the past couple of years, as unions have ceased to be constrained, labour demonstrations have become more disorganised, violent and likely to spark confrontation with government forces. Unskilled and poor workers were the first to be affected by factory closures, which increased the number of people living in poverty.

Minimal Minimum Wage Increase In 1999

As noted, real wages have fallen sharply as a result of the crisis. In February 1999 the government announced that the regional minimum wage would rise by 16.1% on April 1. Inflation in calendar 1999 was 20.5%, after 57.6% in 1998, so real wages remained under downwards pressure. One official said that the higher minimum wage would cover 70% of workers' daily minimum needs. Sectoral minima were set for the first time. The new minimum wages ranged from a low of IDR130,000 per month (US$14.80) in Yogyakarta to a high of IDR290,000 (US$32.95) on the industrial island of Batam, near Singapore. The old wages ranged from IDR122,500 (US$13.90) a month in Yogyakarta to IDR270,000 (US$30.70) in Batam. The awards were branded as inadequate by unions and non-governmental organisations (NGOs), which argue that the government is ignoring International Labour Organisation (ILO) Convention No. 115 on minimum wages, which Indonesia ratified in 1981. Under the convention minimum wages should take into account the provision of such items as clean water, education, healthcare, social security, family needs, shelter and clothing.

Enforcement of the new wages is the responsibility of regional administrations and companies can apply for exemptions on grounds of adverse impact on profitability if they agree to allow government and trade union officials to inspect their books. Decisions to award exemptions will be taken at regency level under the broader programme of decentralisation. In the past such decisions were taken by the central government.

Industrial Policy

Privatisation A Slow Process

Privatisation has been a key plank of the reform programme, but progress has been slow, hampered by bureaucracy and by the poor market conditions. Of the 14 companies originally slated for privatisation, stakes in just three – cement producer, **PT Semen Gresik**; noodle manufacturer, **PT Indofood Sukses Makmur**, and port operator, **PT Pelindo II** – had been sold by 1999, raising little more than US$200mn. As of the end of Q3 99, privatisation revenues had reached IDR6.7trn, about half way to the 1999/2000 goal, but it was not expected to be met.

In spite of the economic crisis and the badly needed proceeds, privatisation is not a popular theme in Indonesia. The issue of who can own strategic, state economic assets is still contested territory. Economic nationalism remains a wide banner under which many groups can gather. Cemex still has the option to acquire another 21% of Gresik from the government, which, added to the possible purchase of a further 16% on the open market, would give Cemex a strategic 51% interest. However, both the Indonesian government and Cemex have decided to allow time for passions to cool down before going further ahead.

Among the successful privatisations are:

- The government sold a 14% stake in **Semen Gresik** to **Cemex** of Mexico for US$115mn in September 1998.

- In April 1999 The government sold a 49% stake in **Jakarta International Container Port** (Pelindo II), the operator of Jakarta port, to **Grosbeaks Pte Ltd**, a unit of Hong Kong's **Hutchison Whampoa**, for US$215mn.

- The government has sold a stake in **Pelindo II** (Surabaya Port) for US$174mn to **P&O Australia** and in April 1999 it sold a 49% stake in the Jakarta container terminal, **Pelindo 1**, to Grosbeaks, a subsidiary of Hutchison Whampoa for US$215mn.

- In May 1999 the government sold 9.6% of Telekom to 80 institutional investors from Asia, Europe and the USA for US$404mn.

Krakatau Steel: Backtracking

Krakatau Steel is a different story. The Indonesian steel-maker has been on the privatisation list for a long time. However, Krakatau Steel is a debt-ridden inefficient company, and restructuring had to be completed before privatisation. In the last days of Suharto's rule, a memorandum of understanding was signed with **Ispat International** for the acquisition of a 51% stake for about US$400mn. Clearly the old links between Suharto and Ispat's chairman Lakhsi Mittal played a key role. The deal was cancelled soon after as a clear example of graft.

Tax And Bankruptcy Policy

Taxation

Indonesia revised its tax system on January 1, 1995, the first major change since 1983. The main changes were: corporate and personal income taxes lowered from the 15-35% range to 10-30%; value-added tax extended to cover electricity; the highest level of tax on luxury goods raised from 35% to 50%; and the income of charitable foundations to be taxed. The aim of the reform was to enlarge the revenue base in order to lessen reliance on oil and gas revenues, a constant theme of Indonesia's tax policies over the past 15 years. At present, only 3mn Indonesians pay taxes and the government hopes that its revenues will rise as the rate of tax avoidance falls.

New Anti-Monopoly Law

Indonesia's parliament approved a draft anti-monopoly law in 1999 which will affect many of the country's quasi-monopolistic conglomerates. The law, promised by Indonesia last year in its agreement with the IMF, may force many of Indonesia's most prized firms to reduce market share or sell profitable units. The law forbids two or three related companies from having a combined market share of more than 75%, while in monopoly industries, maximum market share was set at

50%. Related companies can be defined as firms making some sort of arrangement among each other to treat the market unfairly, while a monopoly industry is defined as an industry where there is only one dominant market player.

Firms affected by the new law include the world's largest noodle maker, **Indofood**, part of the **Salim Group**. Indofood has a 90% share of the domestic noodle market and a monopoly in wheat flour processing. Salim is currently in the process of selling 60% of Indofood to Japan's **Nissin Food Products** and **First Pacific Co**, a unit of the Salim Group listed in Hong Kong. Such a law should encourage foreign investors as it includes all the sectors of the economy including the pulp and paper industry dominated by the **Sinar Mas Group** and the iodised salt market dominated by the **Fiskaragung** group. Industries with near monopolies or oligopolies by state-owned companies include telecommunications, dominated by Telcom, and the oil industry, dominated by Pertamina. The government will appoint a commission to assess whether market share in different industries breaches the law. The maximum penalty has been fixed at IDR100bn (US$11mn) or six months in prison. The aim of the new law is also to have a more equal distribution of wealth and reduce potential social tension.

The Bankruptcy Law Remains Ineffective

Indonesia's new bankruptcy law, adopted in 1998, was designed to prove that Indonesian borrowers could be held accountable. However, lawyers and creditors have commented that few bankruptcies have been declared because judges fail to understand the nature of debt or lack the will to implement the law, implying that the courts are reluctant to declare against vested Indonesian interests in favour of foreign claimants. The new law established a new commercial court and obliged judges to rule on a petition within 30 days, which was supposed to give foreign bankers more leverage over local companies, unable or unwilling to repay their debts. But progress has been very slow.

The case brought by **American Express** and other creditors against **Ometraco**, a financial services conglomerate, ended in failure, as did another by the International Finance Corporation, the World Bank's Corporate lending arm, together with **ING Bank** of the Netherlands and **Bank Niaga** of Indonesia, against **Dharmala Agrifood**. Ineffective bankruptcy procedures are a deterrent to new international borrowings. Foreign companies are increasingly settling for debt-equity swaps or allowing debt to be bought back by the issuer at large discounts.

Recently Completed Major Foreign Investments

Several recent transactions suggest that foreign investors are interested in entering the Indonesian market, despite the many uncertainties:

They include:

■ In April 1999 **ANZ-Panin Bank** signed a binding agreement to acquire **Bank Papan**'s Visa credit card business for IDR39.3bn. Bank Papan is one of the 38 banks closed by the government in March.

■ **First Pacific** of Hong Kong recently announced that it intends to proceed with acquiring a 30% equity stake in **PT Indofood Sukses** for US$285mn.

Foreign Trade Policy

Apec Initiatives Founder

The Apec meeting which took place in Kuala Lumpur in November 1998 was supposed to discuss economic and trade issues, but was diverted by politics. Earlier in 1998, the Apec Vancouver meeting agreed to work on early tariff cuts that would open trade worth about US$1.5trn in nine sectors: environmental goods and services; fish and fish products; forest products; medical equipment; energy; toys; telecommunications; gems and jewellery; and chemicals. Japan refused to sign an immediate agreement on two sectors – fisheries and forestry products. A last minute compromise decided to refer the liberalisation programme to the WTO. Opening the nine sectors would be a step towards Apec's plans to become tariff-free by 2010 in developed countries and by 2020 for less developed countries.

Afta: Long Term

Indonesia is, in theory, backing the creation of a free trade zone within the Asean region, called the Asean Free Trade Association (Afta). Under Afta, officially launched as a preferential trading bloc, tariffs on most manufactured products should be cut to no more than 5% by 2000 and completely abolished by 2003. (Vietnam, which joined Asean in July 1995, has until 2006 to lower its duties to these levels). As a result, the average Asean tariff is expected to decrease from 7.1% in 1996 to 2.7% in 2003. Unprocessed farm commodities, including politically sensitive ones such as rice and sugar, are to have all tariffs removed by 2010. Indonesia is in theory a strong supporter of Afta, calling for an opening of Afta to all countries by 2000. At the meeting held in Bangkok in December 1995, Indonesia expressed reservations about meeting the 2010 deadline, although, under its agreement with the IMF, Jakarta agreed to dismantle the grain distribution monopoly, Bulog.

Trade Barriers And Indonesian Agribusiness

With its plentiful supplies of fish and palm oil, Indonesia should be a major exporter, but trade barriers have been set up in both directions. Jakarta kept items from entering the country through tight control of tariffs and other barriers, and it also limited the flow of other goods going out. Indonesia is the world's second largest palm oil producer with a 27% share of the world market. In 1998, the country's plantations yielded 4.5mn tonnes, double what Indonesia can use domestically. Yet the government imposed a 60% export tax to make palm oil uncompetitive overseas and ensure that producers maintain a steady domestic supply. An export tax was introduced in July 1998, replacing a 40% tax, which in turn had replaced an outright ban on palm oil exports introduced in December 1997. The tax has severely dented Indonesia's export earnings. Indonesia earned US$1.7bn from palm oil exports in 1997, but figures for the first eight months of 1998 show a 56% drop, to US$359mn. Meanwhile, the world price for palm oil is up 70%, although the increase is partly due to the reduced supply from Indonesia. The tax is unlikely to be lifted soon. The outcome is an increasing loss of market share to Malaysia, which is focusing on processing and exporting palm oil.

The fishing industry faces similar problems. Fish exports earned about US$1.5bn in exports in 1997, although commercial vessels ply only a tiny fraction of Indonesia's waters. For years, commercial fishing was discouraged because boats were so expensive. Jakarta imposed high tariffs on imported vessels to promote its own shipbuilding industry. That began to change in 1996 when the government allowed imports of up to 1,000 boats within four years, but conditions attached restricted the potential benefits.

Bureaucracy And Corruption

A History Of Corruption

According to the Political & Economic Risk Consultancy, Indonesia under Suharto was Asia's most corrupt country. In research published in 1998, stockbroker **Kleinwort Benson** highlighted similarities between Indonesia and Nigeria. After the fall of Suharto, will corruption decline in Indonesia? The Habibie family and friends had a distinctly lower profile than those of Suharto. But the Habibie family's business empire is well entrenched in Batam, the island 20km from Singapore. Twenty years ago, Suharto put his protégé, then minister of research and technology, Jusuf Habibie, in charge of the island's development and the Habibie family prospered with its growth. The main industrial park on Batam is run by a company called **PT Batamindo Investment Corp**. Batamindo's key shareholder is a company called **PT Herwindo Rintas**, involving Suyatim Abdulrachman "Timmy" Habibie, B.J. Habibie's youngest brother and Bambang Trihadmodjo, Suharto's middle son. But Habibie's dream was the development of a locally made jet through a company called **PT Industri Pesawat Terbang Nusantara** or IPTN. Imported parts for the project were halted when Habibie's son, Thareq, started to manufacture similar parts through his company.

Habibie's project to develop (another) national car was supposed to involve two Australian companies, **Orbital Engine** and **Millard Engineering**, but it was also clear that Thareq would be the part supplier. However, the project has been scrapped in the light of the economic crisis. Habibie's brother-in-law, retired army Major General Sudarsono Darmosuwito, used to run Batam. He now runs a build-operate-transfer contract for two of Batam's ferry terminals and a company, **PT Citra Lingkungan Lestari**, which undertakes environmental impact studies for any new construction on the island.

Can Suharto Be Charged For Corruption?

Ex-president Suharto has been questioned by the attorney general about seven charity funds, the national car project (Timor), involving his youngest son, Hutomo "Tommy" Mandala Putra, and his personal assets, including bank accounts and land. Suharto handed back the control of the charity organisations in November 1998 and has not been charged, nor even considered a suspect, but just a witness. Last November, Indonesia's highest legislative body named Suharto in a decree ending corruption. Suharto's interrogation has attracted demonstrators demanding political reform and his trial over corruption charges. Most of them believe that although Suharto was questioned on graft, there is practically no chance that he will be charged and condemned. It is believed that Habibie's government put on a show of investigating the former president in an effort to placate protesters, and had no intention of pursuing those guilty of corruption as several current government figures, including Habibie, served under Suharto and could therefore be implicated. New corruption laws were passed in 1999, but a mild stroke suffered by the ex-president was used as an excuse to stop the inquiry into his affairs before the election and despite anti-corruption rhetoric, the new government under President Wahid was slow to act against Suharto.

The Fall Of Suharto's Family And Friends

Some of Suharto's cronies are paying the price of their connections. One of the most famous is Mohamad "Bob" Hasan, who led Indonesia's plywood cartel, **Apkindo**. Golfing buddy, Hasan, has built his fortune on his personal 30-year friendship with Suharto. Hasan has also been questioned about his large forest concessions and the use of an official reforestation fund. Another casualty of Suharto's fall is the **Salim Group**, and more specifically his founder, Liem Sioe Liong. His friendship with Suharto helped him forge a conglomerate spanning dozens of industries, often in partnership with Suharto's now-reviled children. But the group's greatest asset – its link with the Suharto clan – has become a liability.

The campaign against Suharto and his friends has degenerated into a campaign against ethnic Chinese, and the Salim Group has become a visible target of angry mobs. The Salim Group is now run by Liem's son, Anthony Salim. *Forbes* magazine estimated Liem's personal fortune at US$4bn in February 1998, but said that it fell to US$1.7bn shortly after Suharto's downfall. The group's strategy to cope with its troubles is to sell stakes in its businesses to foreign firms, raising cash to repay its spiralling debts and at the same time winning some insulation from political attacks in Indonesia.

Suharto's children are also retreating from the limelight: Bambanng Trihatmodjo, Suharto's second son, has resigned as chief executive of **Bimantara Citra**, flagship of a diversified conglomerate and one of Indonesia's largest listed companies. Suharto's eldest daughter, Tutut, has also resigned from her top position in the **Citra Lantoro Group**.

Curbing The Military's Business

As in several Asian countries, the Indonesian armed forces became involved in business both to create wealth for the top brass and also to supplement an inadequate budget. Profits from military businesses are supposed to go to projects like housings for the troops and support the military's *dwifungsi* (dual-function) role of promoting national security and socio-political stability. But the military has its fingers in almost every industry. The army has a *yayasan* – a charitable foundation – with more than 64 companies, including one that is part-owner of Jakarta's Sudirman Central Business District. The navy, airforce, police and special forces have their own empires. In all, the corporate wealth is estimated at more than US$8bn, not counting the tens of thousands of distribution cooperatives across the country and security or debt-collection services.

The army's business ties have long been an open secret. It is only recently that the extent of the empire has been discovered and some question whether the military should be in business at all. The new Indonesian reformers are calling for transparency in the military's business dealings and the Wahid government has pledged to scrutinise military-run enterprises.

The Environment

Not On The Political Agenda

Environmental groups both in and outside South East Asia say the current pace of timber cutting in Indonesia is far in excess of a sustainable level. But the vested interests are far too powerful to be prosecuted. The forestry department found through its investigations that Suharto, his family and friends own or control about 9mn ha of rainforest, about the size of the main island of Java. The Indonesia plywood panel company, **Apkindo**, was controlled by Hasan, a crony of Suharto.

Habibie acknowledged problems in the country's forest management ordering a top-down review of forestry policies. However, the environment may be sacrificed to economic recovery. Although eco-labelling is gaining ground for exports to Europe and the US, the timber industry can ignore any certification when selling to other Asian markets. A recovery in Japan and Korea could mean more bad news for the Indonesian forests.

Instead of selective cutting, timber companies prefer to set fire to the jungle, clearing all the smaller trees and destroying all the indigenous flora and fauna. Gigantic forest fires caused a poisonous smog, known as "haze", all over South East Asia in 1997. The phenomenon was avoided in 1998, thanks to "*La Niña*" which brought heavy rains in the region. Fires were reported to have broken out again in 1999, although not on such a severe scale. The luck may not repeat itself in the coming years and South East Asia's population will probably suffer again from the effects of the "haze".

5 Capital Markets

Equity Markets

A Strong Recovery In 1999

Indonesia's stockmarket staged a strong recovery in 1999. Prices, as measured by the Jakarta Stock Exchange (JKSE) ended the year 70% higher than at the end of 1998, rising from 398.038 to 676.919. This was the third best performance after South Korea and Singapore. Capitalisation was up to IDR443.3trn, from IDR175.5trn, but the rise was driven by inflation-based adjustment. Foreign investment accounted for only 35% of the transactions, the lowest level for seven years. In US dollar terms, Indonesia was the worst-affected Asian stock market in 1998, as a result of the rupiah's collapse, itself exacerbated by political uncertainty. The recovery was, like the trajectory of the rupiah, a roller-coaster ride; political tension, the debacle in East Timor and the reverberations of the Bank Bali scandal caused severe sell-offs at various points.

Market Regulations

Adopted in 1990, one of the most important decrees providing coherence to financial regulation defined the role of the Capital Market Supervisory Agency (*Bapepam*). Contained within this decree was provision for the establishment of a fair market, with proper disclosure and insider trading regulations and the supervision and licensing of brokers and intermediaries. *Bapepam* was established in 1976 to run and regulate the stock exchange, although since the privatisation of the JKSE in 1992, it no longer runs it. The 1995 Capital Market Act reinforced *Bapepam*'s position, giving it the authority to investigate possible violations. The new regulations also provide minority shareholders with greater protection by requiring full disclosure by listed companies and offering a more level playing field for investors.

Restrictions On Foreign Investors Lifted

Foreigners could initially buy up to 49% of the shares of any listed company, but this restriction has been scrapped under the IMF agreement signed in 1998. Whenever the 49% limit was reached, foreigners could still buy and sell shares through a foreign board, which traded at a premium to the local price. The only foreign limits on stocks purchases are for banks – although foreigners are allowed to own up to 99%, *Bapepam* approval is required.

The Debt Market

Slow Recapitalisation Process

At the end of 1998, the government unveiled its initial estimate that it would take some IDR300trn (US$34bn) to clean up the sector. The true cost will be much higher, and is now estimated at IDR670trn (US$805bn at the 1999 annual average exchange rate).

The government will provide 80% of the funding through bond issues – preventing the scheme from becoming inflationary. Banks will issue preferred convertible shares, which will be convertible into common shares with limited voting rights. In return, the banks will be able to rectify their balance sheet problems by transferring their bad debts to the Asset Management Unit of Indonesian Bank Restructuring Agency at zero value. There are three types of bonds:

- Market-linked 20-year bonds (based on three-month SBI rates) for banks with capital adequacy ratios (CARs) that are either zero or negative. A redeemable option is also attached allowing the government to redeem the bonds upon recovery of bad assets.

- Fixed-rate five-year bonds for banks with CARs of 0-4%, carrying interest rates of 20-25%.

- Negative amortisation bonds to replace the IDR140trn in liquidity credits extended to the banking sector.

Indonesian Bank Classifications

As already outlined (see Key Economic Sectors), the Indonesian government has announced that banks will be recapitalised or liquidated. Only nine private banks were deemed eligible for recapitalisation, including some of Indonesia's largest and highest profile banks such as **Bank Internasional Indonesia**, **Bank Bali** and **Bank Niaga**. Thirty-eight mostly small banks were to be liquidated, with an additional seven banks to be taken over by the government.

The reason given for not liquidating these seven was the size of their deposit or depositor base. Another 73 private banks were deemed to be in "Category A", or able to raise their CARs to 4% without government assistance. To be eligible for recapitalisation, banks had to meet a minimum CAR of 25% and provide 20% of the new equity needed to raise this ratio to 4%. They also have to submit business plans demonstrating how they would raise their CAR to 8% in two years. The seven state-owned banks and the 27 government-owned provincial development banks, are all to be recapitalised.

Sovereign Debt: "Selective Default"

Indonesia has, for the first time, defaulted on its sovereign debt to the private sector, causing **Standard & Poor's** to downgrade the country's long-term foreign currency rating to "Selective Default" (SD). This rating is the lowest possible for a sovereign government and follows the country's default on a US$210mn loan to a syndicate of international banks led by **Tokyo Mitsubishi.**

S&P downgraded Indonesia four times in 1998 to CCC+, while **Moody's** downgraded Indonesia sovereign rating twice to B3. A plan for Japan to back Asian sovereign bond issues up to JPY2trn, giving its struggling neighbours access to international finance, came to nothing, but was additional to the US$30bn Japan pledged to its neighbours under the Miyazawa Plan. The **Export-Import Bank of Tokyo** also plans to support a new export financing agency with US$300mn.

Debt rescheduling

Indonesia is not expected to default on its external obligations, having successfully negotiated a grace period until March 2001 on repayment of its US$4.1bn in Paris Club debt (official debt, owed to bilateral and multilateral credit). Under the deal, US$3.5bn of loans falling due by December 2001 will be exchanged for loans with longer maturities and different interest rates – ranging from 2.25-2.75 percentage points over LIBOR. The agreement followed a similar deal in 1998 for US$9.2bn of loans falling due by March 1999. The latest agreement involved rates from 2.75-3.5% over LIBOR. Discussions on the rescheduling of London Club (private sector) debt, and on the renegotiation of private sector debt under the 1998 Jakarta Initiative have been ongoing.

SBIs

SBIs (Central Bank Short-Term Certificates) are sold by Bank Indonesia (BI) in daily and weekly auctions as a means of conducting open-market operations. Bids are made through the state and private banks that act as primary dealers. BI sets a maximum and minimum yield and bids outside this band are rejected. The maturities of SBIs for daily auction are seven days, 14 days and 28 days and for weekly auctions, 28 days, 91 days, 182 days and 357 days. A longer-term yield curve can be imputed through fixed rates of rupiah interest-rate swaps and maturity ranges between one and five years.

SBIs are the primary instruments with which BI manages liquidity in the country's money market. They also provide the base against which banks set their time deposits. SBI 30-day rates increased from 20% in 1997 to 68.8% in Q4 98, before falling back to 33.2% in mid-1999 and 11.93% at the end of December 1999. Since then rupiah weakness has stopped their decline.

Recapitalisation bonds, of which IDR500.1trn are in various maturities to the banks and to the central bank, had been issued by early 2000, 10% of which were due to become tradeable on the secondary markets from February. This, it is hoped, will help to develop a bond market, which will supplement and eventually replace the SBIs. The now moribund domestic corporate bonds used to be a benchmark. Indonesia could use a newly established bond market to finance its budget shortfall in the future, especially when market conditions are not favourable for privatisation.

Taxation, Trading And Settlement

Since January 1995, the New Taxation Law means that domestic investors are subject to a 15%

withholding tax on interest income. However, banks and pension funds are exempt from this withholding tax. For foreign investors, a 20% withholding tax is imposed unless there is a joint tax treaty.

High withholding tax and poor liquidity make rupiah bonds relatively unattractive to trade, in spite of high yields. The sharp depreciation of the currency has also deterred would-be investors. However, over the long run, and in a post-crisis context, a local pension fund base could promote the development of a local bond market, complemented by the emergence of a new Treasury market.

To enhance trading volumes and improve liquidity, the exchange has introduced an electronic monitoring system on bond transactions called the Parallel Information Bonds System (PIBS) which will be linked to Indonesia's depository and clearing agency, KDEI. This system would provide real-time information on bond prices and transactions executed on the secondary market.

MALAYSIA 2000

Analyst: Sara Matchett

Editor: Sara Matchett/Mathew Brooks

Contents

Political Outlook _____ **185**

Domestic Political Outlook 185
Foreign Policy 189

Profile and Recent Developments _____ **191**

The Political System 191
Political Parties 192
Institutions 194
Foreign Policy 195

Economic Outlook _____ **197**

Economic Activity 197
Balance Of Payments 199
Foreign Direct Investment 201
Monetary Policy 202
Exchange Rate Policy 203

Profile and Recent Developments _____ **206**

Characteristics Of The Economy 206
Economic Background 207
Exchange Rate Policy 209

Key Economic Sectors _____ **211**

Introduction 211
Property & Construction 212
Stockbroking 215
Rubber 217

Profile and Recent Developments _____ **220**

Introduction 220
Manufacturing 220
Agriculture, Forestry And Fishing 225
Mining 227
Oil And Gas Extraction 227
Construction 228
Utilities 229
Telecoms 229
Finance And Insurance 231

Business Environment _____ **235**

Introduction 235
Infrastructure 236
The Domestic Market 237
The Labour Market 238
Industrial Policy 240
Foreign Investment Policy 243
Foreign Trade Policy 245
Bureaucracy And Corruption 247
Environmental Regulation 248

Capital Markets _____ **249**

Equity Markets 249
Bond Markets 252

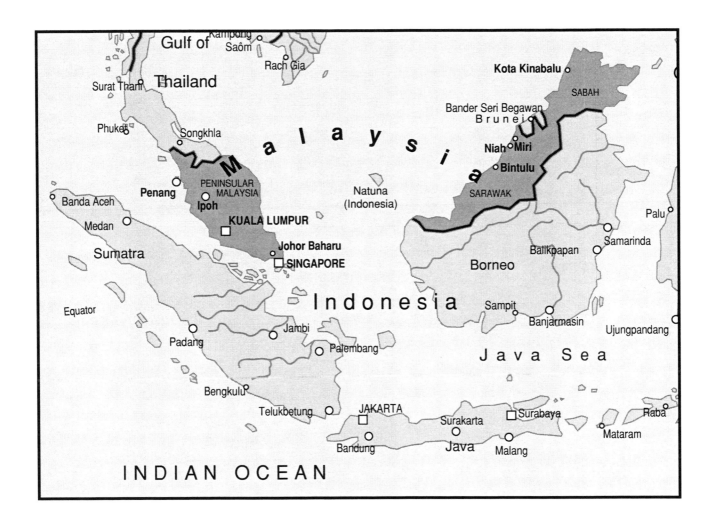

MALAYSIA: MACROECONOMIC DATA AND FORECASTS

	1993	1994	1995	1996	1997	1998	1999e	2000f	2001f	2002f
Population (mn)	19.2	19.7	20.1	20.6	21.0	21.4	21.8	22.2	22.6	23.0
Nominal GDP (US$bn)	66.9	74.5	88.8	100.8	100.2	72.5	78.9	87.0	101.8	115.5
GDP per capita (US$)	3,482	3,789	4,417	4,908	4,772	3,389	3,621	3,923	4,512	5,027
Real GDP growth (% y/y)	9.9	9.2	9.8	10.0	7.5	-7.5	5.4	6.4	6.0	6.5
Industrial output (% y/y)	9.6	12.4	13.1	11.0	10.6	-7.2	9.0	12.0	8.6	9.0
Unemployment rate (%, an. avg)	3.0	2.9	2.8	2.5	2.5	3.2	3.0	3.0	2.8	2.6
CPI (% y/y, eop)	3.4	5.4	3.2	3.3	2.9	5.3	2.5	3.5	3.6	2.7
CPI (% y/y, period avg)	3.5	3.8	3.4	3.5	2.7	5.3	2.8	3.0	3.6	2.8
3-month interbank rate (%, an. avg)	7.21	5.14	6.05	7.23	7.78	9.06	4.13	3.40	4.30	4.80
MYR/US$ (eop)	2.7	2.6	2.5	2.5	3.9	3.8	3.8	3.6	3.4	3.4
MYR/US$ (an. avg)	2.6	2.6	2.5	2.5	2.8	3.9	3.8	3.8	3.5	3.4
Merchandise exports (US$bn)	47.1	58.7	73.9	78.3	78.5	73.0	84.5	92.1	98.6	105.5
Merchandise imports (cif, US$bn)	45.6	59.4	77.6	78.4	78.5	58.1	65.5	76.0	85.1	93.6
Trade balance (customs, US$bn)	1.5	-0.8	-3.7	-0.1	-0.0	14.9	19.0	16.2	13.5	11.9
Current account (US$bn)	-3.0	-4.5	-8.5	-4.6	-4.8	9.4	12.5	10.0	7.0	5.0
Current account (% GDP)	-4.5	-6.1	-9.5	-4.6	-4.8	12.9	15.8	11.5	6.9	4.3
Foreign reserves (US$bn, eop)*	27.2	25.4	23.8	27.0	20.8	25.6	30.9	39.9	26.5	27.0
Import cover (mths)**	5.7	4.2	3.1	3.3	2.5	4.2	4.4	5.4	3.7	3.5
External debt (US$bn)	26.1	29.5	34.4	39.0	42.7	41.3	43.2	41.0	39.5	38.0
External debt (% GDP)	39.1	39.7	38.7	38.6	42.6	56.9	54.8	47.1	38.8	32.9
External debt (% exports)	47.8	43.1	39.9	41.4	44.7	49.0	44.2	43.3	40.1	36.0

*e/f = BMI estimate/forecast, eop = end of period, *excluding gold, ** number of months imports covered by FX reserves. Sources: Bank Negara Malaysia/IMF/BMI.*

1 Political Outlook

Domestic Political Outlook

By-Election Victory Boosts UMNO

The ruling United Malays National Organisation (UMNO)'s fortunes took a turn for the better early on in the second quarter. Prime Minister Mahathir Mohamad received a welcome psychological boost on April 1, when the UMNO candidate won the Sanggang by-election in Pahang state. The seat fell vacant following the death of state assemblyman Abdullah Kia on February 26. With 10,000 card-carrying *Barisan Nasional* members in Sanggang, 6,400 of whom support UMNO, victory was never really in doubt: The new electoral roll has 15,276 voters. But Mahathir has made much of winning candidate Redzwan Harun's 1,963 votes majority over the *Parti Islam se Malaysia* (PAS)'s Hishamuddin Yahaya. Abdullah had secured a majority of just 1,083 in November's general election. Mahathir predictably interpreted the results as "a sign that UMNO is undergoing rejuvenation after suffering a drop in support at the last election."

Mud-slinging has been rampant since the election, with PAS linking the UMNO victory to money politics, and Mahathir accusing PAS of a range of dirty tricks designed to disrupt voting. The prime minister has even proposed new laws to ensure that parties adhere more strictly to campaigning procedures; a move clearly aimed at discrediting PAS. But foul play aside, UMNO's emphasis on a "hands on" approach to resolving the constituency's problems looks to have swayed voters, unconvinced by a PAS campaign focussed primarily on discrediting the government rather than concrete policy initiatives. This should serve as a wake up call to PAS, which can not rely indefinitely on dissatisfaction with UMNO, and the Anwar issue in particular, to lure Malay voters.

The large majority secured by UMNO candidate Redzwan Harun in the Sannang by-election in April, comes as a warning to PAS that they cannot rely indefinitely on dissatisfaction with the government to lure voters.

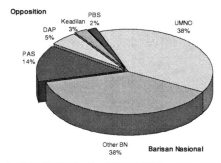

Dominated By National Front
Malaysia - seats in Dewan Rakyat, % of total 102

Source: Reuters.

Mahathir and Abdullah's virtual clean sweep of the nominations for leadership of UMNO, despite evidence of rising dissatisfaction with the leadership within the party, highlights the inability of the party to reform itself.

UMNO Elections Prove No Contest

Mahathir will have been further heartened by the failure of Kelantan prince and former finance minister, Razaleigh Hamzah, to secure sufficient nominations to run for either the leadership or deputy leadership posts in UMNO's internal elections in May. Of the 156 divisions that met the April 2 deadline for nominations, only one nominated Razaleigh for president and two for deputy president, while Mahathir and his deputy, Abdullah Badawi, gained 154 and 153 nominations respectively. Razaleigh did not even garner the 17 nominations required to run for the lower post of vice president, gaining the support of just 13 provinces. There are several reasons for his failure: The Kelantan prince was late to enter the fray, never officially declaring his candidacy and issuing conflicting and vague statements on his actual intentions. He proffered no policy initiatives, positioning himself as a reluctant candidate for the contest. And his rather lacklustre approach was insufficient to secure the support of party members, intimidated by the Supreme Council's "recommendation" that Mahathir and Abdullah stand unopposed for the leadership.

THE MALAYSIAN CABINET (AS OF MARCH 2000)	
DEPARTMENT	**NAME**
Prime Minister	Dr Mahathir bin Mohamad
Deputy Prime Minister/Home Affairs	Abdullah Ahmad Badawi
Finance Special Functions	Daim Zainuddin
Foreign Affairs	Hamid Jaafar Albar
Education	Musa bin Mohamad
Defence	Najib Abdul Razak
Energy, Communications and Miltimedia	Leo Moggie Anak Irok
Health	Chua Jui Meng
International Trade and Industry	Rafidah binti Aziz
National Unity and Social Development	Dr Siti Zaharah Sulaiman
Rural Development	Haji Azmi bin Khalid
Science, Technology and Environment	Law Hieng Ding
Transport	Dr Ling Liong Sik*
Works	Samy Vellu
Youth and Sports	Hishammuddin Hussein
Agriculture	Mohd Effendi Norwawi
Culture, Arts and Tourism	Abdul Kadir Sheikh Fadzir
Domestic Trade and Consumer Affairs	Muhyiddin Yassin
Entrpreneur Development	Mohamed Nazri Abdul Aziz
Housing and Local Government	Ong Ka Ting
Human Resources	Dr Fong Chan Onn
Information	Mohd Khalil Yaakob
Land and Cooperative Development	Kasitah Gaddam
Primary Industries	Dr Lim Keng Yaik

Announced intention to resign on May 22; Source: Prime Ministers Office.

Mahathir and Abdullah's virtual clean sweep of the nominations, despite evidence of rising dissatisfaction with the leadership within UMNO, highlights the inability of the party to reform itself. The Supreme Council clearly maintains a tight grip over party members, who are afraid of defying the leadership for fear of political – and financial – exclusion. The costs of failing to toe the party line were driven home in mid-March, when Malacca Chief Minister Mohamad Ali Rustam blacklisted **Bank Bumiputra Commerce** and **Bank Islam Malaysia** for allegedly supporting the opposition during November's general election by posting confidential financial transactions involving officials and institutions on the internet to suggest wrongdoing. The government is withdrawing MYR40mn (US$10.5mn) in funding from the banks. Mahathir threw his support behind the chief minister, who also terminated the services of 21 doctors, a property valuer, and 20 contractors. Furthermore, he asked state firms, including oil producer **Petronas** and power utility **Tenaga Nasional**, and the Employees Provident Fund to discriminate against businessmen who support the opposition.

The move has been heavily criticised by the opposition, with Democratic Action Party chairman, Lim Kit Siang, accusing the state government of conducting a "witch hunt". Civil rights groups are viewing the development as a test case for the newly established 13-member Malaysian Human Rights Commission and its chairman, former deputy prime minister Musa Hitam. While its establishment was welcomed by activists and legal groups, many doubt the independence of the Commission and argue that it will be restricted by the Human Rights Commission Act's limitation of human rights to those defined by the Malaysian constitution. Local press reports have also suggested that it will be two years before the Commission becomes fully operational.

The Race For The Vice Presidency

To the casual observer, Mahathir and Abdullah's unchallenged positions as head and deputy head of UMNO made for a dull contest in May's party elections. But three vice presidential posts were also up for grabs and, when Mahathir finally relinquishes his role as prime minister, one of the chosen three will more than likely move into the deputy's shoes, putting them in pole position for the premiership. As expected, one of the three coveted spots went to the clear favourite, Defence Minister Najib Tun Razak, who garnered 1,289 out of a total 2,018 votes. Son of Malaysia's second prime minister, Razak Hussain, 46-year old Najib has been a member of the cabinet for 14 years and enjoys strong support among the younger UMNO members despite his narrow 241-vote winning margin in November's general election. He gained 150 nominations for vice president from UMNO's 165

The UMNO vice presidential race was a closely-fought contest. All three winning candidates were members of the Wawasan Team connected to ousted former deputy premier Anwar Ibrahim in the 1993 UMNO elections.

divisions. More surprising, is the reselection of former Selangor chief minister Muhammad Muhd Tajib, despite court appearances on charges of failing to declare cash and assets (he was acquitted). A more obvious choice would have been current Selangor chief minister Abu Hassan Omar, who delivered 42 out of 48 state seats in the general election and is said to be popular with the leadership. And the final place also went to an outsider, Domestic Trade Minister Muhyiddin Yassin. All three candidates were members of the Wawasan Team connected to ousted former deputy premier Anwar Ibrahim in the 1993 UMNO elections, a fact dismissed by Muhammad as mere coincidence. Meanwhile, another key Anwar ally, Ahmad Zahid Hamidi, was elected to the 25-member Supreme Council.

The three new vice presidents faced off tough competition from six other contenders, including second favourite, Abdul Ghani Othman, who secured the second highest number of nominations for the vice-presidency with wide grassroots support. A member of the Supreme Council, Ghani is credited with mobilising Johor's Moslem community in the general election. Another front runner was Sabah chief minister Osu Sukam, the first East Malaysian ever to contest the vice presidency. Osu would have been a useful weapon to woo support from Sarawak residents in the next election.

Abdullah A Shoo-in For Top Job?

While Abdullah, as deputy premier and deputy president of UMNO, is now considered almost a shoo-in for the top job when Mahathir steps down, history warrants a word of caution.

This will not have been Mahathir's preferred vice presidential line-up, and indeed it has been interpreted as a deliberate snub by some observers. But nor will it encourage the premier to listen to his party's dissenters. Rather, he will sit tight until the time is right to step down. When he does, Abdullah, as deputy premier and deputy president of UMNO, is now considered almost a shoo-in for the top job, all the more so following the premier's recent decision to delegate more responsibilities to him. But historical experience warrants a word of caution. Mahathir's fickleness and own particular brand of power politics were highlighted during the election week, when Bank Negara advisor Nor Mohamed Yakcop, a key exponent of capital controls, was appointed as the premier's special economic advisor on matters relating to the National Economic Action Council. Two deputy chiefs for the central bank and a new advisor to the Finance Ministry were also appointed. This effectively dilutes the power of both Finance Minister Daim Zainuddin and newly-appointed Bank Negara governor Zeti Akhtar Aziz. Rumours have been surfacing for some time of a rift between Mahathir and Daim, who replaced Anwar Ibrahim as finance minister in 1998. Issues of contention are said to include banking sector consolidation and the slow pace of corporate restructuring, culminating with Mahathir's decision to block the **Time dotCom/Singtel** deal (*see Foreign Direct Investment*) backed by Daim.

Mahathir denies any fallout, while Daim continues to negate speculation – which has unnerved the markets – that he intends to resign in the near future. Mahathir reappointed Daim as UMNO treasurer on June 5, in a move that may have been intended to quash resignation rumours.

Another unsettling development for market observers came on May 22 with the surprise announcement that Transport Minister and Malaysian Chinese Association (MCA) president Ling Liong Sik intends to quit the cabinet. Ling has not stipulated why he has chosen to leave: Mahathir said the 56-year old wanted to make way for younger MCA members. The MCA is the second biggest party and a key pillar in the ruling *Barisan Nasional* coalition, helping it weather the loss of support among ethnic Malays in last year's general election. Criticism within the party of Ling's failure to capitalise on its strong election showing by translating gains into additional cabinet seats looks to have played a part in the leader's decision. MCA members were particularly riled that the smaller *Gerakan* – also an ethnic Chinese party – gained more government posts after the election. Although it is unlikely to destabilise the coalition, Ling's departure does raise questions over future relations between UMNO and the MCA. Although Mahathir has said that he will not increase the number of MCA members in the cabinet, he may well rethink his position ahead of the next general election in four years time.

Foreign Policy

Malaysia Takes Centre Stage In Hostage Crisis

Malaysia found itself thrust onto the international arena on April 23, when Islamic Abu Sayyaf rebels from the Philippines took 21 hostages at a diving resort off Sipaden Island in Sabah state. The hostages included nine Malaysians, three Germans, two French, two South Africans, two Finns, two Filipinos and one Lebanese, and consequently attracted both widespread international media interest and diplomatic action from a host of countries and the European Union. Malaysia initially stayed out of the negotiations: although the incident occurred in Malaysian territory, the hostages were subsequently moved to Jolo Island in the Philippines. The Filipino authorities – who have never formally renounced a claim over Sabah state – did not invite their neighbours to the negotiating table. Instead, the Malaysian authorities moved to prioritise the establishment of a new naval base at Semporna, near Sipaden, and inflamed Manila by rounding up 1,100 illegal Filipino immigrants from Sabah within two weeks of the kidnappings.

The kidnapping of 21 hostages by Filipino militants in Malaysian territory has strained diplomatic relations between the two neighbours.

Kuala Lumpur subsequently opened bilateral discussions with the captors, which Foreign Minister Syed Albar said had commenced "with the blessings of the Philippine government". But Philippine government chief negotiator Robert Aventajado denied any such blessing, and complained that the move would jeopardise negotiations with the militants. Meeting the rebels has raised the diplomatic stakes for Malaysia. The militants demanded the establishment of a commission to review the status of an estimated 500,000 Filipinos living in Sabah, calling into question Malaysia's claim to the state and questioning its treatment of immigrants. Kuala Lumpur must now weigh up its desire to see its own nine hostages released, against the resultant infringements to its sovereignty and immigration policy. Malaysia – which has considered paying ransom demands – has also left itself open to accusations of favouritism towards its own, Moslem nationals if they are now treated differently from the other hostages. Capitulating to ransom demands would also encourage further kidnappings and jeopardise tourism in the area.

Profile and Recent Developments

The Political System

A Democracy In Name

Malaysia is a constitutional monarchy, with a system of parliamentary democracy based on the British model. It has an independent judiciary and a non-political, professional civil service, army and police. In practice, the Malaysian political structure differs a great deal from the British model, for better and worse. The king is elected: the nine hereditary sultans elect one of their own to be the (largely ceremonial) constitutional monarch, for a period of five years. The country is a federation: there are 13 states, as well as two local territories, including the capital Kuala Lumpur, each with its own head of state, elected assembly and cabinet.

The 69 members of the senate (*Dewan Negara*) are either appointed (43, by the king) or elected (26, two by each local legislature) and serve a six-year term. The 193 members of the House of Representatives (*Dewan Rakyat*) are elected for a five-year term in a single-member constituency system. New general elections must be held within five years of the preceding polls with the next due by November 2005, although it can be held at any time before then.

UMNO And Barisan Nasional Dominate

At a glance, Malaysia's record of parliamentary democracy appears excellent, especially compared with many other countries in the region. Free and reasonably fair elections to the House of Representatives have been held regularly every five years or less. However, since independence in 1957, Malaysia has been ruled by coalitions dominated by the United Malays National Organisation (UMNO). Initially, the Alliance Party combined UMNO with the Malaysian Chinese Association and the Malaysian Indian Congress. The coalition was widened in 1971 to create the *Barisan Nasional* (National Front), which currently includes 14 parties. The absence of regular political change has given Malaysia an enviable degree of stability, which has attracted foreign investment and benefited economic growth. But, the close ties between the business and political elites have also produced favouritism and corruption, willingness to bend the rules, intolerance of criticism and oppression of opposition, which have been highlighted by the economic crisis and the trial of the former deputy prime minister Anwar Ibrahim.

The 14 parties represented in the *Barisan Nasional*, especially UMNO, dominate political life. There are, however, some 40 political parties in Malaysia, most of which are not represented in parliament. The single-member constituency system has produced election results with clear, even two-thirds, majorities for the government, but at the expense of suppressing political diversity. Arguably, some form of proportional representation could create a fairer balance between the three territories of Malaya, Sabah and Sarawak, which make up Malaysia. It is also questionable how relevant the system of government, shaped in the immediate post-independence years, is to the better-educated and wealthier Malaysia of today. Ironically, the economic crisis has led to the return of a more interventionist government, exactly at the moment when calls for change in the political system are increasing.

Political Parties

UMNO - The All Powerful

UMNO, the dominant party in the ruling *Barisan Nasional*, has been at the centre of government since independence in 1957. UMNO has built its support base on the majority *Bumiputra* (ethnic Malay) population and has advanced their economic interests through a long-standing policy of positive discrimination. Under the New Economic Policy, the extensive government holdings in the economy were largely privatised during the 1980s and used to help create a new class of *Bumiputra* entrepreneurs. Many of UMNO's own holdings were transferred to **Renong Bhd**. The Malay business elite has retained close ties with UMNO, although these have been severely tested during the crisis, which highlighted the incompetence of many of the new entrepreneurs.

UMNO's grip on power has rarely been challenged. The most serious attempt was the formation of the breakaway party Semangat 46 in 1987 by Tengku Razaleigh Hamzah, after he almost succeeded in defeating Mahathir as UMNO leader. However, Semangat 46 returned to the fold in 1992. But the November 1999 elections highlighted increasing disaffection with UMNO among ethnic Malays, unhappy with both the treatment of Anwar and the failure of the party to bring in new blood.

The Ethnic Chinese – A Vote For Financial Stability

The two main parties relying on the ethnic Chinese vote are the Democratic Action Party (DAP) and the Malaysian Chinese Association (MCA). The opposition DAP was originally founded in 1966 to promote racial equality and democratic socialism, while the MCA is the second largest in the ruling coalition. The Chinese make up nearly one-third of Malaysia's population and have generally divided their votes between opposition and coalition fairly equally. When the Malays are divided, the Chinese can be swing voters during a general election, as was the case in 1990. In the 1995 general election, some 60% voted for the National Front. Middle-class professionals and younger Chinese tend to be more reform-minded than businessmen and older Chinese. The government has played up the anti-Chinese riots in Indonesia, which invoked memories of Malaysia's own race riots in 1969. Although there is resentment over the pro-Malay affirmative action under the National Development Policy, the Chinese population are primarily interested in stability and continuity and Mahathir benefited from this in the 1999 general election. The ethnic Chinese constituency viewed the Anwar issue as a largely Malay affair and, when the crunch came, was unprepared to back an opposition with no track record of economic management and with links to an Islamic fundamentalist movement.

The MAP won 29 seats in the 1999 election, against the DAP's 10. Opposition and DAP leader Lim Kit Siang, chairman Chen Man Hin and deputy chairman Karpal Singh all lost their constituencies. Lim promptly resigned as party secretary-general, conceding that the party had been sidelined after a "catastrophic defeat". Chinese voters had turned away from the party following its decision to form the *Barisan Alternatif* alliance with the *Parti Islam SeMalaysia* (PAS), *Parti Keadlilan Nasional* and *Part Rakyat Malaysia*. The Pas-led Terengganu government sparked outrage among DAP members just days after the election by announcing its intention to ban gaming and entertainment centres. Arguing that the move had violated the terms of the Alternative Front's election manifesto, the DAP has put in doubt any future co-operation with PAS.

PAS Look To Moderate Fundamentalism

The only significant Malay alternative to UMNO is PAS, which, as an Islamic fundamentalist party, draws its greatest strength in the four northern states of Kedah (Mahathir's home state), Kelantan, Terengganu and Perlis. As a Malay alternative and best-organised opposition party, PAS has benefited from the backlash against Anwar's treatment and made large gains in the 1999 elections, emerging as the largest opposition force. It not only gained 27 seats against eight in the last parliament, but also won the state assemblies of Kelantan and Terangganu and captured eight out of 15 seats in Kelantan. While many observers have focussed on the rise of Islamic forces in PAS's strong showing, they may be missing the point. It was not really a vote for Islamic fundamentalism: it was a vote against UMNO rather than a vote for PAS. Perhaps concerned by the political inexperience of other opposition parties, Malays viewed PAS as the only real alternative. If there was any Islamic dimension to the elections, it was that UMNO had relied on Anwar to enhance the party's religious credentials and once he was sacked, Muslim Malays drifted towards PAS.

Institutions

Mahathir's Iron Grip On Power

Malaysia's democratic institutions have increasingly felt the heavy hand of the government during Mahathir's rule. Although the constitution allows freedom of expression, Mahathir has exercised tight control over the media and has regularly used restrictive legislation – the Internal Security Act (ISA), the Sedition Act and the Printing Presses and Publications Act – to curb freedom of expression and association. The ISA allows police to detain without warrant any person suspected of threatening the national security or economic life of Malaysia for a period up to 60 days. The minister of home affairs can subsequently issue a detention order of up to two years, renewable indefinitely and without reference to the courts.

Political debate is subdued in Malaysia, as the government takes offence easily - the opposition and the news media are quickly sued for defamation and offending editors sacked for printing 'false news'. The judiciary, once independent, has become closely identified with the ruling parties after two decades of attacks by the government. The Anwar trial has drawn attention to the weaknesses of Malaysia's democratic institutions and government abuses. Anwar was arrested without charge under the ISA, and held incommunicado and beaten up while in police custody by the inspector-general of police himself. He was accused of corruption and sexual offences, the details of which were splashed for weeks all over the media. The charges were amended after the defence had discredited the prosecution witnesses and refocused instead on corruption. Anwar's defence, that he was the victim of a conspiracy by powerful personalities, was ruled out as irrelevant. Defence witnesses were made to submit their testimony in advance. The presiding Judge Augustine repeatedly intimidated the defence team and jailed one of the lawyers for three months for contempt of court. Anwar was, not surprisingly, convicted and received a much heavier than expected, six-year jail sentence.

Foreign Policy

Courting Controversy

The sharp edge of Malaysia's confrontational foreign policies has been blunted by signs of an economic recovery. Foreign criticism of Malaysia's economic policies and political protests, as well as the crisis itself, has provoked Mahathir to utter some of his more extreme views - about Jewish plots, foreign racists, speculators out to destroy Malaysia - which have not failed to draw a response from the United States. Singapore, which is frequently at the receiving end of Mahathir's criticisms, has shown remarkable restraint, despite the fact that Singapore's economy, particularly the financial sector, was hurt by Malaysia's decision to impose capital controls. Singapore's politicians have learned that Mahathir thrives on provocation, but US politicians have no such restraint and, as well as feeling rightful indignation about Mahathir's remarks, are inclined to fit criticism of Malaysia into their own private political agenda when convenient. Relations with the US reached a new low after US Vice President Al Gore boosted his own presidential chances by criticising Malaysia's politics at the 1999 Apec conference in Kuala Lumpur. Gore called for *reformasi* in a public speech in the presence of Mahathir and other Apec officials. It was the sort of direct interference in internal affairs which Asian nations avoid, presented in an unusually blunt way. Mahathir's reaction was to use Gore's criticism to stir up nationalism and rally support behind him at a time when there were growing doubts about his policies at home.

BMI feels that any other prime minister would be less confrontational than Mahathir, but would probably also lack his international impact. What is interesting, however, is that Mahathir may have won at least part of the argument about the appropriate response to the crisis, which was also the trigger for the conflict with Anwar. The IMF has admitted that its crisis-management recipe made conditions worse, and there is growing support for currency controls, but **BMI** thinks it unlikely that, given his confrontational policies, Mahathir could turn this into a foreign policy advantage. Malaysian crisis management is not exportable.

Notwithstanding his confrontational style, Mahathir is also a pragmatist who realises the limitations he has to work within while trying to achieve his ideal of turning Malaysia into a developed country. The US is Malaysia's major export destination, and if the US chose to discriminate against its exports, if it thought the bilateral trade surplus was excessive or the ringgit heavily undervalued, this could have a serious impact on the Malaysian economy. Malaysia is protected, to some extent, by the fact that US companies are also the largest inward investors. Malaysia's dream of becoming the Silicon Valley of Asia depends on technology transfer by US high-tech corporations. Some of their top executives have criticised Malaysia's anti-Jewish remarks and treatment of Anwar.

Taking A More Relaxed Approach

Malaysia has territorial disputes with all its neighbours, but they tend to be low level. Potential flashpoints include a dispute with Indonesia over the islands of Sipigan and Ligitan (referred to the International Court of Justice in The Hague) and the dispute with China over the Spratly Islands, where Malaysia is only one of six countries laying claim to the whole or part of the islands. The outstanding issues with Singapore are usually minor and appear to be easy to solve (for instance, moving the customs and immigration facilities, closing a Malaysian-owned railway station on Singapore territory, settling the issue of the blocked Malaysian shares previously quoted on the Singapore over-the-counter market, refunding Malaysian workers' contributions to Singapore's national pension fund), but provoke exaggerated responses on Malaysia's part. Economic recovery is likely to result in the adoption of a more relaxed attitude by the Malayaisan authorities, which will make solving the outstanding issues easier.

The threat to Malaysian security from events in Indonesia and China's claim on the Spratlys has led to Malaysia re-joining regular exercises by the Five Power Defence Arrangements, from which it withdrew in 1998. However, Malaysia has been forced to cut weapons purchases and production and reduce army recruitment this year because of the economic recession.

2 Economic Outlook

Economic Activity

Onwards And Upwards

Real GDP surged 11.7% y-o-y in Q1 00, the fastest growth rate recorded since Q1 96. While coming off a low base – GDP contracted 1.5% in Q1 99 – the magnitude of the rise indicates that the momentum of the economic upturn is gathering pace. GDP – at MYR49.9bn (US$13.1bn) – came in just marginally lower than the preceding quarter (MYR50.3bn). This represents the strongest data ever recorded in the first quarter of the year, which always sees lower output due to peak sales in December followed by both the Chinese New Year and Moslem Hari Raya holiday periods in the first quarter.

The sharp rise reflects the robust performance of the manufacturing sector – representing 33% of GDP – which posted a 27.3% y-o-y rise in the quarter, lifting output above pre-crisis levels. Services – up 6.3% – also supported growth, which broadened out into all sectors of the economy. Even mining managed a 0.8% rise in output, bringing to an end four consecutive quarters of contraction. External demand, particularly for electronics goods, remains buoyant, ensuring a trade surplus for the eleventh consecutive quarter. Meanwhile, domestic demand is also recovering, albeit gradually. **BMI** has consequently revised up its GDP growth outlook to 6.4% in 2000, against the official 5.8% forecast.

A Gradual Consumption Recovery

Doubts have been raised over the strength of the consumption recovery. Imports did not pick up as fast as anticipated in the first quarter – although they climbed a respectable 27.1%, this was off a low base as imports contracted 10.7% a year earlier. Imports of consumption goods rose 22.8% y-o-y in the first quarter, down from 36.2% growth in Q4 99, albeit from a lower base. The rate of growth is comparable to Q3 99, which saw a 22.5% expansion off a similar base. And loan growth remains weak, with total outstanding loans up just 0.4% in March and 1.1% in April.

GDP growth of 11.7% in the first quarter indicates that the momentum of the economic recovery is gathering pace.

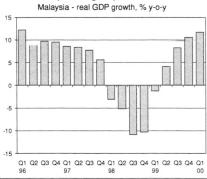

Surpassing Expectations
Malaysia - real GDP growth, % y-o-y

Source: Bank Negara Malaysia.

The domestic demand recovery has so far been slow off the ground, but consumption should pick up in the second quarter.

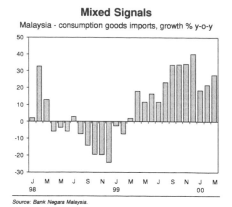

Mixed Signals

Malaysia - consumption goods imports, growth % y-o-y

Source: Bank Negara Malaysia.

Manufacturing output has risen to record levels, underpinned by buoyant electronics and electrical goods exports. The long-awaited recovery in private investment may at last be setting in.

But the latest survey from the Malaysian Institute of Economic Research showed the consumer sentiment index rising to 120.7 points in the first quarter, from 117.7 in Q4 99, indicating that consumption will pick up in the second quarter. Sales tax growth exceeded 50% y-o-y in all four months to March, while consumption credit growth expanded 2.4% y-o-y in March and 4.0% in April, the highest figure recorded since July 1998. While we will not see a dramatic upswing in private consumption, **BMI** expects domestic demand to gather pace in the second half. This will help compensate for a fall off in public consumption as fiscal spending is reigned in. Public expenditure dropped to MYR4,319 in Q1 00, from MYR7,276mn in Q4 99, although this was partly due to seasonally lower disbursements in the first quarter.

Manufacturing Boom

The industrial production index (IPI) rose 17.9% y-o-y to a record 189 in March, bringing growth for the first quarter to 22.1%. The impressive data – the strongest in the region – encouraged analysts to revise up full-year GDP growth expectations, following 23.2% industrial output growth in February. The index contributes 40% of GDP. Manufacturing – up 30.3% in Q1 00 – was the main contributor to the rise in the IPI, driven by strong external demand for electronics, electrical goods, chemical products and telecommunications products. Electronics and electrical machinery and appliances exports reached a record MYR19.9bn (US$5.2bn) in March, from MYR15.4bn a year earlier, accounting for 74% of manufactured goods exports. While strong external demand has underpinned manufacturing output – export-oriented industries climbed 35.8% y-o-y in the first quarter – domestic demand is also supporting the upturn, with growth in domestic-oriented industries up 24.2%. A slowdown in the US economy – accounting for 22% of Malaysia's manufactured exports and 12% of total inward investment – remains the key downside risk to manufacturing output over the forecast period. However, this should be mitigated by a stronger regional and Japanese outlook.

	1992	1993	1994	1995	1996	1997	1998	1999e	2000f	2001f	2002f
GDP, OUTPUT & POPULATION											
Population (mn)	18.76	19.21	19.66	20.11	20.55	21.00	21.39	21.78	22.17	22.56	22.98
Nominal GDP (US$bn)	59.2	66.9	74.5	88.8	100.8	100.2	72.5	78.9	87.0	101.8	115.5
GDP per capita (US$)	3,153.1	3,482.3	3,788.5	4,417.3	4,907.5	4,771.5	3,388.9	3,620.9	3,922.6	4,512.1	5,027.5
Real GDP growth (% y/y)	8.9	9.9	9.2	9.8	10.0	7.5	-7.5	5.4	6.4	6.0	6.5
Industrial output (% y/y)	8.7	9.6	12.4	13.1	11.0	10.6	-7.2	9.0	12.0	8.6	9.0
Unemployment rate (%, an avg)	3.7	3.0	2.9	2.8	2.5	2.5	3.2	3.0	3.0	2.8	2.6

e/f = BMI estimate/forecast; Source: IMF/BNM.

It is still not clear how much new private investment is being generated. Lending to the manufacturing sector has been slow to pick up, rising just 2.6% y-o-y in April despite a 1.4% contraction a year earlier. This compares to 3.8% loan growth to the property sector. But capital goods imports rose 61.8% y-o-y in March. Although this was off a low base – after contracting 22.7% in March 1999 – the strength of the rise suggests that long-awaited private investment may be starting to roll in. And a 27.0% y-o-y rise in intermediate goods imports – against 4.7% growth in March 1999 – gives **BMI** further cause for optimism. Imports of parts and accessories of capital equipment and processed industrial supplies accounted for four-fifths of the increase, largely destined for electronics goods exports.

There is little evidence yet of an expansion in new capacity – gross fixed capital formation rose 12.3% y-o-y in the first quarter, but dropped 3% from Q4 99. Meanwhile, capital goods imports – at MYR9.1bn in Q1 00 – are still some way off pre-crisis levels, averaging MYR14.8bn per quarter in 1997. But existing capacity is being replaced and we expect to see more signs of new capacity coming on stream in the second quarter.

Record Heights
Malaysia - output growth, 3mma % y-o-y

Source: Bank Negara Malaysia.

Balance Of Payments

Wide Surpluses Will Narrow

Malaysia's trade account posted its 11th consecutive surplus in Q1 00, at MYR16.2bn. Although this has narrowed from MYR19.8bn in Q4 99, it is nonetheless sizeable, reflecting favourable conditions in the export sector. Export growth accelerated to 21.9% y-o-y, from 19% in Q4 99, taking volumes above pre-crisis levels at MYR84.4bn. Meanwhile, import growth accelerated to 27.1% y-o-y, on higher demand for inputs into the manufacturing sector and the ongoing domestic demand recovery.

Although Malaysia posted another wide surplus in the first quarter, the latest monthly data indicates that this is starting to narrow as import growth accelerates above exports.

Export growth continues to be driven by electronics and electrical products – up 18.2% and 34.5% respectively, and representing 61% of total exports. Chemicals (up 39.9%), furniture and parts (34.5%), textiles and wearing apparel (20.6%), commodities (29.8%) and petroleum products (146.2%) also performed well. Conversely, agriculture suffered from the weak performance of palm oil – down 25.3% – which has been hit by depressed global prices. The commodity – which accounts for a half of agricultural exports – was responsible for an overall 9% decline in the sector, overshadowing improvements in rubber (up 20.1%), logs (11.1%) and timber (37.4%), which benefited from higher prices and volume. Higher global prices also boosted crude oil and LNG.

Imports Accelerate
Malaysia - merchandise trade growth, 3mma %

Source: Bank Negara Malaysia.

__BMI__ anticipates a gradual narrowing of the trade surplus over the year as investment activity and consumption pick up.

Exports have profited from a weak ringgit and strong external demand in the US and Europe, as well as the regional recovery. The heavy reliance on electronics and electrical products remains a key concern in the longer-term, leaving Malaysia vulnerable to the electronics cycle and the demand conditions of a handful of countries – the US, Japan, Singapore, the Netherlands and Taiwan account for 69.7% of trade in electronics and electrical products. However, downturns in the cycle are typically induced by over supply, in direct contrast to current tight conditions. While some Y2K-related demand will taper off in H2 2000, a components shortage will help ensure that the sector remains buoyant this year and well into next. Nonetheless, the spectacular export growth figures seen in Q1 99 – which benefited from the lagged impact of new US orders – will taper off in Q2 to reach a more sustainable level.

As import growth accelerates faster than export growth, the trade surplus will narrow. But the surplus has not unwound as fast as anticipated in the first quarter, as exports have continued to outperform. The export picture has been distorted by electronics, without which the trade account would be in deficit. Nonetheless, **BMI** does anticipate a gradual narrowing of the surplus over the year as investment activity and consumption pick up. Early signs that this is indeed the case came in April, when the trade surplus narrowed to MYR3.4bn from MYR6.9bn in March, with exports up 11.9% against import growth of 29.5%. Although it is too early to determine a definite trend, we maintain our forecasts of real export growth of 9% in 2000 and 7% in 2001, against import growth of 16% and 12% respectively, with the trade surplus narrowing to US$16.2bn in 2000 and US$13.5bn in 2001. Consequently, the current account surplus will unwind gradually, from an estimated US$12.5bn in 1999 to around US$10bn in 2000.

BALANCE OF PAYMENTS (US$MN)											
	1989	**1990**	**1991**	**1992**	**1993**	**1994**	**1995**	**1996**	**1997**	**1998**	**1999e**
Merchandise exports (fob)	24,776	28,806	33,712	39,823	46,238	56,897	71,767	76,881	77,881	71,845	83,083
Merchandise imports (fob)	20,498	26,280	33,321	36,673	43,201	55,320	71,871	73,055	74,005	54,260	61,101
Trade balance	4,278	2,526	391	3,150	3,037	1,577	-104	3,826	3,876	17,585	21,982
Invisible trade balance	-4,101	-3,498	-4,663	-5,490	-6,315	-6,327	-7,523	-7,494	-7,573	-5692	-7616
Balance on goods and services	177	-972	-4,272	-2,340	-3,278	-4,750	-7,627	-3,668	-3,697	11,893	14,366
Current account balance	315	-870	-4,183	-2,168	-2,990	-4,521	-8,470	-4,596	-4,791	9,376	12,468
Current account (% of GDP)	0.8	-2.0	-8.5	-3.7	-4.5	-6.1	-9.5	-4.6	-4.8	12.9	15.8

e = Bank Negara Malaysia estimate; Source: IMF/BNM.

Foreign Direct Investment

Political Interference

The Malaysian authorities have been seeking to attract more foreign investment after a poor 1999. While net foreign direct investment increased marginally to MYR13.4bn last year, from MYR10.6bn in 1998, foreign investment applications for manufacturing projects contracted 28.4% to MYR9.04bn. Approvals for investment in manufacturing totalled MYR12.3bn, down from MYR13.1bn in 1998. The US remained the number one source of investment applications, amounting to MYR2.5bn for 36 projects, down from MR6.5bn in 1998. Investment applications from Japan increased slightly to MYR1.3bn, as did those from Singapore, at MYR1bn.

Early data suggests that efforts to boost investment may be bearing fruit. Foreign investment applications rose steeply to MYR10.6bn (US$2.8bn) in the first quarter, from MYR3.8bn in Q1 99. Projects approved totalled MYR13.42bn. But **BMI** will be watching closely to see if the collapse in late-April of the sale by **Time Engineering** of a 30% stake in its telecoms arm **Time dotCom** to **Singapore Telecommunications**, will sour investor sentiment. Mahathir halted the deal, uneasy about selling off a stake in such a strategic sector to a Singapore government-controlled company. State-run **Telekom Malaysia** had lobbied hard to block the deal. Now Khazanah Nasional, the Finance Ministry's investment arm, has begun negotiations to buy into debt-laden Time, in what smacks of another government bailout. And there is also speculation that Khazanah will buy into **Naluri**, which holds a 29% stake in heavily indebted flag-carrier **Malaysian Airline Systems**, rather than see an overseas airline get a foot into the sector.

*Foreign investment applications rose sharply in the first quarter, but political interference in the **Time dotCom-Singapore Telecommunications** deal may sour sentiment.*

INVESTMENT IN MANUFACTURING								
	1992	**1993**	**1994**	**1995**	**1996**	**1997**	**1998**	**1999**
Total applications (number of projects)	861	856	1,018	1,116	929	849	726	747
Foreign investment applications (MYRmn)	11,848	7,711	11,856	13,256	17,621	14,383	12,621	9,039
Total approvals (number of projects)	874	686	870	898	782	759	844	708
Foreign investment approvals (MYRmn)	17,772	6,287	11,339	9,144	17,057	11,473	13,063	12,268
Source: Bank Negara Malaysia.								

Monetary Policy

Benign Inflation

An absence of inflationary pressures has allowed the authorities to maintain a low interest rate regime.

Despite the economic upturn, prices have remained subdued in Malaysia, with the consumer price index up just 1.5% y-o-y in the first quarter, against 2.1% in Q4 99 and 4% in Q1 99. This reflects excess capacity in some industries, and consumption below pre-crisis levels. But price pressures will build in the second half as excess capacity unwinds, consumption picks up and the undervalued currency raises import costs and boosts liquidity. **BMI** is forecasting a rise to 3.0% in 2000 and 3.6% in 2001.

Benign inflation has allowed Bank Negara to maintain a low interest rate regime. In late May, new central bank governor Zeti Akhtar Aziz seemed to signal a move towards a tighter monetary stance, stating that, "we hope to see deposit rates edge upwards". Her comments appeared to be made in response to press speculation that real interest rates might turn negative if prices rise. Low deposit rates – three-month fixed deposit rates range from 3.2-3.4% – pose the risk of eroding the country's savings rate, currently around 40%. But Bank Negara will be loathed to raise rates, which could dampen the domestic demand recovery and expose the debt-laden sections of the corporate sector. Loan growth also remains weak, at 1.1% in April. The central bank will be disinclined to hike interest rates until inflation is in the region of 3%, something **BMI** does not foresee happening until the final quarter. We forecast a rise in the intervention rate from the current 5.5% to 6% at end-2000, rising to 7% in 2001.

No Price Pressures Yet

Malaysia - consumer price inflation, % y-o-y

Source: Bank Negara Malaysia.

CONSUMER PRICES											
	1992	1993	1994	1995	1996	1997	1998	1999	2000f	2001f	2002f
CPI (% y/y, eop)	4.89	3.41	5.38	3.21	3.30	2.86	5.29	2.47	3.50	3.60	2.70
CPI (% y/y, period avg)	4.72	3.54	3.76	3.38	3.48	2.71	5.26	2.80	3.00	3.60	2.80
eop = end of period; f = BMI forecast; Source: BNM.											

Interest Rate Differential Will Narrow

In the meantime, the spread between deposit and lending rates will narrow, as banks face increasing competition for market share. A surprise decision by **Maybank** in early May to cut its base lending rate to 6.5% from 6.8% led to similar moves by four other banks. Maybank has traditionally led the market, and more banks were expected to follow its example, but there has been some reluctance to take a hit on profit margins. Maybank's margin between deposits and lending – at 3.9% – is still considerably higher than the 1.6% average spread seen in 1994-96. The average for other commercial banks is around 4.7%. The interbank and intervention rate differential will narrow as inflationary expectations rise and banks seek to maintain profit margins without lowering deposit rates.

Several banks have lowered their base lending rates as they face increasing competition for market share.

Exchange Rate Policy

Unsustainable Peg

The benign inflationary environment has relieved pressure on the authorities to alter the currency peg. The ringgit peg to the US dollar – at MR3.8/US$ – has boosted export competitiveness, while having a limited impact on imported inflation. Wide surpluses on the trade account have increased net demand for ringgit, necessitating the release of ringgit into the system to relieve pressure on the currency. This inflow of funds has yet to have a seriously expansionary impact on money supply, because the central bank has been sterilising the excess currency by borrowing funds from commercial banks. With domestic interest rates so low, and rates rising globally, Bank Negara is currently making a profit from this debt. But this policy is only sustainable so long as commercial banks are willing to lend to the central bank at a low rate of interest, currently around 3%. As inflationary pressures build, and lending rates rise, it will become increasingly expensive to issue sterilisation debt.

As inflationary pressures build, and lending rates rise, it will become increasingly expensive for Bank Negara to issue sterilisation debt.

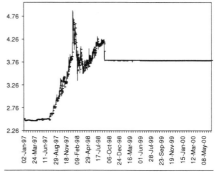

No Pressure To Remove Peg Yet
Malaysia - exchange rate, MYR/US$

Source: Reuters/BMI.

The gradual unwinding of the current account surplus will ease some of the monetary overhang, but at some point Bank Negara must remove the currency peg, which also holds the long-term risk of delaying a move to higher productivity by subsidising inefficient producers. Bank Negara governor Zeti Akhtar Aziz has indicated that the ringgit is undervalued by 6-8%, while other estimates put it as high as 20%. With inflationary pressures expected to build in the second half, leading to an interest rate hike in the fourth quarter, **BMI** expects Malaysia to move towards a managed float of around MYR3.2/US$ towards end-2000 or early 2001. But political considerations may well overshadow economic fundamentals. Mahathir has stated that he will wait until there is global agreement on a new international framework that would prevent speculative attacks on currencies. Re-pegging the ringgit at a stronger level could well lead to increased speculation over future adjustments in the exchange rate.

Global demand conditions will also be taken into consideration, as the currency peg offers Malaysia some protection against a deteriorating external environment. If the downturn in US stock markets becomes more severe and an ensuing slowdown in US growth triggers a fall in the dollar, the weakening ringgit would help alleviate the negative effect on Malaysia's exports. Such a scenario would pose a greater threat to other countries in the region – such as Thailand – whose current account surpluses would risk turning to deficits, not only because of a drop in export volumes, but also because these countries are still in fiscally expansionary mode. As a result, they run the risk of twin deficits, which would exert pressure on liquidity and currencies. In this respect, the peg works in Malaysia's favour.

EXCHANGE RATES											
	1992	1993	1994	1995	1996	1997	1998	1999	2000f	2001f	2002f
MYR/US$ (eop)	2.61	2.70	2.56	2.54	2.53	3.88	3.80	3.80	3.65	3.40	3.40
MYR/US$ (an. avg)	2.55	2.57	2.62	2.50	2.52	2.81	3.92	3.80	3.77	3.53	3.40

eop = end of period; f = BMI forecast; Source: IMF/Reuters.

Surplus Will Narrow

Malaysia - merchandise trade, US$mn

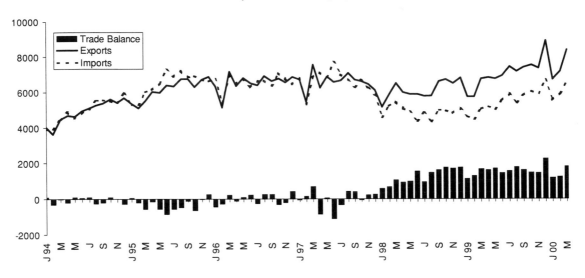

Prospects Look Up

Malaysia - real GDP growth, % y-o-y

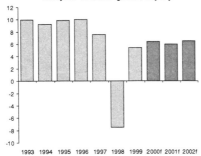

Rising Imports SqueezeSurplus

Malaysia - current account

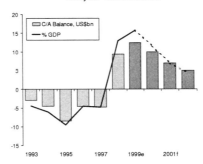

Investment Finally Picking Up?

Malaysia - investment goods imports, % y-o-y

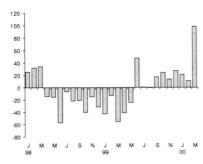

No Room For Further Rate Cuts

Malaysia - interest rates

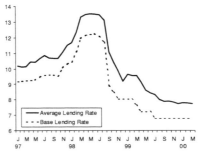

e/f = BMI estimate/forecast; Source: Bank Negara Malaysia; IMF/BMI.

Profile and Recent Developments

Characteristics Of The Economy

Remarkable Progress

Malaysia has been remarkably successful during the past three decades in the way it has managed to maintain a high pace of economic growth, achieve substantial increases in per capita income, raise the standard of living significantly and radically transform the structure of the economy. Viewed from a long-term perspective, Malaysia's economic growth steadily accelerated between the start of the 1970s and the beginning of the Seventh Five Year Plan in 1996. GDP growth averaged 6.7% per annum during the New Economic Policy in the period 1971-1990. The Sixth Plan, 1990-1995, set a target of 8.1% but achieved 8.7%, and the Seventh Plan, 1996-2000, began its first year with an impressive 9.4% and aimed for an average 8.0%. Indeed, **BMI** believes that the underlying cause of the 1998 recession was that the economy had been driven too hard for too long, leading to over-investment and the distortion of investment flows towards property and equities.

The increase in the standard of living has been impressive. Per capita GDP in 1999 was 11 times higher than in 1970. Careful planning has transformed the economy from a structure that relied mainly on the production and export of primary commodities into a modern industrial base. Import substitution and export promotion strategies led to accelerated industrial development under the 1985 Industrial Master Plan (IMP) which broadened the industrial base and raised the level of technological sophistication, and this was further developed under the second IMP. Privatisation since the mid-1980s increased the role of the private sector as an engine of growth. Manufacturing's share of GDP increased from 24.6% in 1990 to 30.1% in real terms in 1999, while the share of the primary sector fell from 25.7% of GDP to 16.6%. The transformation was achieved with remarkably low inflation and Malaysia attained full employment. **BMI** believes it will be more difficult to sustain such economic virtues as the more inflation-prone tertiary sector expands and improves in quality, while the continuing shift from the primary to the secondary sector puts higher demands on the skills and education level of the labour force.

In Search Of Developed Country Status

A mountain of bad debt temporarily impedes economic progress, the planned shift to higher value-added, technology-intensive and knowledge-based goods and services, the raising of the productivity of capital and labour, and improvement of entrepreneurial quality. Malaysia can deal with the debt problem relatively quickly in part because of its extremely high savings rate – at 39.4% of GNP in 1997. Given the country's abundance of natural resources (palm oil, rubber, cocoa, timber, crude oil and natural gas), the share of the primary sector will arguably never drop as low as in the developed countries. In its quest to reach developed nation status by 2020, Malaysia is improving the education levels of its labour force, broadening and deepening its industrial base, developing a resource-based chemical industry and moving to higher value-added production in the electronics and electricals industry, which provides two-thirds of manufactured exports.

Economic Background

Into The Depths

The sharp contraction that hit the Malaysian economy in 1997, following the loss of foreign investor confidence and withdrawal of short-term capital flows from Asia, was partly a consequence of the vulnerability engendered by Mahathir's quest for economic growth. Since 1991, the economy consistently grew above its potential output. Soaring property and equity prices were considered a sign of economic success and not the result of over-stimulation and loose monetary policies. A long period of prosperity made the authorities close their eyes to the possibility that the quality of bank loans was being undermined and the banking system had become susceptible to shocks. Another less obvious sign of trouble was that productivity, as measured by total factor productivity, was slowing significantly by 1996-97. The Malaysian authorities saw this as a positive sign, associated with high capital accumulation and low returns during the transition to a high technology- and knowledge-based economy, while critics considered it a consequence of Utopian dreams and over-ambitious schemes.

The economic contraction became evident towards the end of 1997. The GDP numbers showed a year-on-year decline in all four quarters of 1998, with the steepest decline (9.0% y-o-y) in the third quarter, decelerating to a fall of 8.1% y-o-y by the fourth, after falls of 2.8% and 6.8% in the first two quarters respectively. Industrial production plunged 7.2%, with construction and manufacturing hit especially hard with delinces of 24.5% and 10.2% respectively. By far the most serious damage was to private investment, which more than halved in real terms (down 57.8%), while private consumption contracted by 12.4%, battered by negative wealth effects.

However, essential stability was maintained. Total employment declined by just 3.0% in 1998 (16.9% in the construction sector), with only 84,000 workers made redundant and these were quickly absorbed in sectors where labour shortages continued. The unemployment rate rose from 2.5% in 1997 to 3.2% in 1998. Remarkably, per capita GDP dropped only 1.1% and there was no severe erosion of purchasing power from a surge in imported inflation after the fall of the ringgit. However, measured in dollar terms it looks quite different: Malaysia's per capita GDP slid 29.1% from US$4,772 to US$3,389.

National Economic Recovery Plan

The Malaysian government has shown great determination to halt the decline in the economy. In January 1998, a National Economic Action council was established, which, by the following July, presented a National Economic Recovery Plan (NERP). Of its six objectives, three were financial market related (stabilise the ringgit, restore market confidence, and maintain financial market stability) and three directly concerned economic activity (strengthen economic fundamentals, continue with the equity and socio-economic agenda, and revive adversely affected sectors).

The financial market action points were more urgent and controversial (especially the capital controls) with the establishment of the asset management company Danaharta to take over the bad debts of the banks and the recapitalisation of the banking sector under Danamodal. The restoration of a degree of domestic market confidence was probably the most directly beneficial to activity. The revitalisation of sectors focused in the first place on additional infrastructure spending. The outrage of international investors about the imposition of capital controls has distracted from the systematic way in which the crisis was addressed, even if it took a while to forge a policy consensus.

Outlook Improves In 1999

The strength of the economic recovery witnessed in 1999 was stronger than most analysts' expectations, with real GDP rebounding from a 7.5% contraction in 1998 to 5.4% growth. Exports led the turnaround, reflecting strong US and EU growth, the regional demand recovery and the competitive benefits of an undervalued currency. GDP growth accelerated from 1.5% y-o-y in H1 99 to 9.4% in H2, and broadened out during the course of the year as stimulatory fiscal measures fed into higher domestic consumption. Real aggregate demand grew 1.6% in 1999. By Q2 99, all sectors except mining and construction recorded growth, with construction turning positive in Q3 99. Mining continues to contract as a result of the National Depletion Policy to conserve reserves. Industrial production benefited from the export and domestic demand recovery, recording growth from February 1999, with full-year growth of 8.9% y-o-y.

All this has been achieved against a background of low inflation: consumer price inflation fell to 2.8% from 5.3% in 1998. This has been attributed largely to a stable exchange rate and continued excess capacity in many industries. Meanwhile, the labour market improved, with the unemployment rate moderating to an estimated 3% from 3.2% in 1998.

Exchange Rate Policy

Containing Speculation

Malaysia introduced selective exchange controls on September 1, 1998 with the specific aim of containing speculative capital and, in typical Mahathir manner, blamed the outside world for forcing its hand. Malaysia wanted to shield itself from the instability in regional financial markets, which had turned into a global emerging market financial crisis. It felt it was becoming the victim of foreign speculators and was particularly concerned about the internationalisation of the ringgit an odd concern for a country that has serious plans of becoming an international financial centre. Outflows of ringgit accelerated after April 1998, attracted by interest rates of 20-40% in offshore centres like Singapore and Hong Kong at a time when the Malaysian onshore rate was only 11%. The Malaysian authorities began to feel vulnerable and feared they might have to adjust monetary policy and jeopardise the ongoing reforms. Malaysia regularly and loudly complained about uncontrolled short-term capital and currency flows, but its calls for international controls and reform of the international financial system were largely ignored.

The exchange controls are aimed at eliminating the access of speculators to the ringgit by limiting the currency's supply in the offshore markets, and stabilise short-term capital flows by requiring them to remain in the country for a minimum of one year. In addition, the controls cover ringgit-denominated transactions between non-residents via non-resident external accounts, the import and export of ringgit by travellers, and Malaysian investments abroad. There are no controls on current account transactions (trade and services transactions are to be settled in foreign currencies), repatriation of interest, dividends or fees, and foreign direct investment inflows and outflows, including income and capital gains. On February 4, 1999, the one-year holding rule on portfolio capital was eased to allow foreign investors to repatriate the principal capital and profits, but subject to a 10-30% levy which depends on the time the capital was imported and the duration of the investment. In September 1999, Bank Negara announced a flat 10% tax on foreign capital gains.

A key element of the controls is the fixing of the exchange rate at MYR3.80/US$ on September 2, 1998. After the announcement of selective exchange controls, the ringgit soared by more than 10% against the US dollar. Since then, with the dollar exchange rate stable, the ringgit has gained competitiveness against most regional currencies, which have been appreciating against the dollar as their economies bottomed out. This has helped Malaysian exports to recover. The controls have been effective, although at the expense of the offshore markets. Around MYR4bn of funds flowed back to Malaysia in September 1998 and MYR1.5bn in October, while Bank Negara's external reserves rose from US$19.6bn at the end of August 1998 to US$30.9bn at end-1999. There is no indication that the controls have discouraged foreign direct investment and businesses have, on the whole, liked the predictability of the fixed exchange rate and put up with the extra administration.

3 Key Economic Sectors

Introduction

Record Manufacturing Output

The economic recovery broadened in Q1 00, with all sectors recording positive growth including mining, which edged up 0.8% y-o-y after contracting for four consecutive quarters as crude production rose to meet domestic demand. Manufacturing continued to lead growth, surging 27.3% y-o-y. More impressively, the manufacturing production index rose above pre-crisis levels for the second successive quarter, reaching a record 189. Electronics, chemicals, telecommunications, fabricated metal and petroleum products were key contributors. Strong manufacturing output has fed through into trade-related services, which helped support 6.3% y-o-y growth in services. Restaurants, retail and hotels also performed well. A pick-up in the residential housing market (*see below*) helped boost construction by 1.2% y-o-y. Meanwhile, agriculture grew just 2.9% y-o-y after 6.3% growth in Q4 99, as weak rubber production (*see below*) outweighed the buoyant palm oil sub-sector.

Growth was underpinned by strong external demand – export-oriented industries rose 35.8% y-o-y in Q1 00. Electronics exports (up18.2%) remained robust, but were outpaced by chemicals (39.9%), furniture and parts (34.5%), electrical products (35.4%) and petroleum products (146.2%). Domestic-oriented industries also posted double digit growth, rising 24.2% y-o-y, bolstered by a 12.1% increase in consumer expenditure.

All sectors posted positive growth in the first quarter, led by manufacturing which breached pre-crisis output levels to reach record heights.

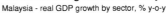

Manufacturing Leads The Way
Malaysia - real GDP growth by sector, % y-o-y

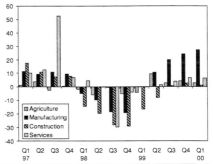

Source: Bank Negara Malaysia.

GDP GROWTH BY SECTOR (% Y-O-Y)										
	1993	1994	1995	1996	1997	1998	1999	2000f	2001f	2002f
Agriculture, Forestry & Fishing	-3.1	-1.9	-2.5	4.5	0.4	-4.5	3.9	2.0	2.5	2.5
Mining & Quarrying	-4.0	6.0	22.9	2.9	2.9	1.8	-4.0	-1.5	1.5	2.5
Manufacturing	14.6	11.4	11.4	18.2	10.4	-13.7	13.5	15.0	12.5	13.0
Construction	10.8	15.1	21.1	16.2	10.6	-23.0	-5.6	2.5	7.0	8.0
Services	14.1	10.1	10.2	8.9	9.9	-0.8	2.9	6.5	8.5	9.0

Source: Bank Negara Malaysia.

Property & Construction

A Segmented Property Market

While residential property is experiencing an upturn, the commercial sector remains hampered by a supply glut that could take up to five years to clear.

After falling precipitously in 1998, Malaysia's property market bottomed out in Q3 99 and has gained momentum this year. This is reflected in rising loans to the property sector, at 36.8% as a proportion of total loans in September 1999 from 35.1% a year earlier. Meanwhile, the national house price index (MHPI), calculated on a half yearly basis, rose 1.2% y-o-y in H2 99, after 18 months of contraction. And property transactions increased 18.6% y-o-y in Q1 00. But the upturn is highly segmented. While low interest rates and fiscal initiatives have boosted residential housing sales, the commercial end of the market remains in the doldrums, and here the medium- to long-term outlook is bleak.

Consumers have been encouraged into the residential property market by the country's low interest rate regime. As savings rates remain depressed, the return to capital on property looks attractive: residential prices have, on average, risen 40% from their lowest point during the downturn, with some prime areas now seeing prices 10% above pre-crisis levels. The ease and cost of borrowing money has also improved, while government incentives – such as a 100% stamp duty exemption on properties valued under MYR75,000 (US$19,737) and 50% under MYR150,000 until end-2001 – have encouraged the less well off into the housing market. Policies have been introduced to rectify imbalances between supply and demand, including instructions to banks from January 5 not to extend funding to new residential and commercial developments costing in excess of MYR250,000 per unit. And banks have been encouraged to loosen credit to facilitate the sale of unsold properties.

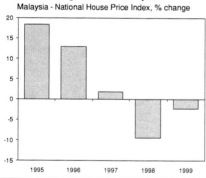

Rising From The Depths
Malaysia - National House Price Index, % change

Source: Bank Negara Malaysia.

Meanwhile, the government has launched three home ownership campaigns to clear unsold stock, offering incentives such as discounts and waivers of stamp duty and low interest mortgages. The first two campaigns were not as successful as hoped, with only 31.5% of properties sold, leading to suggestions that, while beneficial in principal, such initiatives may actually encourage a 'wait and see' attitude in anticipation of more generous government incentives further down the line. But the response from the most recent home ownership campaign, ending May 13, was more encouraging, notching up MYR600mn in its first four days.

During the slowdown, construction was halted or scaled back on many residential projects, reducing stock until an equilibrium was reached between supply and demand. This contrasts with the commercial sector, which is less flexible from a supply point of view, largely because developers must generally build a large number of units together, which all must be completed if any are to be sold. **Benny Chew**, property analyst at **Salomon Smith Barney** in Kuala Lumpur, estimates that it could be five years before this excess supply is cleared. A number of developments will deepen the supply glut: Federal government offices are being relocated from Kuala Lumpur to Putrajaya over the next few years; the banking and other sectors are undergoing a period of rationalisation, and, over the longer-term, technological advances will diminish the need for purpose built offices as increasing numbers choose to work from home. According to a report by the National Property Information Centre (NAPIC), in Q1 00, there were 1,301 purpose built office buildings in Malaysia, or 9.8mn m^2, of which 78% were occupied. The situation varied widely between regions, with Johor suffering from the highest vacancy rate at 45%, against 20% in Penang and 23% in Kuala Lumpur. Retail units had an average occupancy rate of 70% across Malaysia. While it is too late to address this supply/demand imbalance now, the recently-established NAPIC should serve as a valuable warning system to prevent such excessive imbalances in the future.

Construction Could See Mild Turnaround

While the commercial sector offers little joy for the construction industry in the medium term, residential property – accounting for 70% of the market – coupled with public works and infrastructure-related projects in conjunction with the government's fiscal spending programme, could promote a small rebound in construction this year after two years of contraction. The 2000 budget earmarked MYR4.3bn under special funds for low and medium-cost housing programmes and MYR201mn for the construction of 1,592km of rural roads. Meanwhile, work has commenced on a number of new townships (such as Kota Warisan, Bandar Damansara Perdana and Bukit Sentosa in Selangor) and several large-scale infrastructure projects have been resurrected, including the MYR4bn KL Sentral system in Kuala Lumpur. Construction sector output – at MYR6.9bn in 1999 – is still some way off pre-crisis levels of MYR9.5bn in 1997. But the construction sector expanded 1.2% in Q1 00, and cement and concrete production has been trending up since April 1999 after 15 months of contraction, and has been growing at 40%-plus y-o-y since September. Meanwhile, **Rating Agency Malaysia** reported in its sectoral review in May that the construction-related materials index soared 42% in January after climbing 15.1% in 1999.

A more buoyant residential sector and fiscal spending on infrastructure-related projects could revive the construction industry in 2000 after two years of contraction.

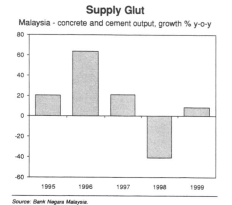

Supply Glut

Malaysia - concrete and cement output, growth % y-o-y

Source: Bank Negara Malaysia.

There is still sufficient excess capacity to prevent overheating.

While this is encouraging, **BMI** cautions against viewing it as evidence of a sharp turnaround in the industry. Cement production still considerably exceeds demand in Malaysia and the government has earmarked several infrastructure projects to reduce this oversupply. Works Minister Samy Vellu has tried to encourage the use of concrete over traditional road methods, arguing that, although it is 25-30% more costly, it requires less maintenance and does not have to be resurfaced after five years. The government has taken a lead role in efforts to revive the construction industry, supporting initiatives such as the Malaysian International Building Exposition (Malbex 2000) planned for September 12-15. Malbex, organised by **Reed Exhibitions**, is said to be more than 90% booked, with expectations for 400 exhibitors from 30 countries.

Low financing costs will encourage a significant increase in residential property development in 2000, with low and medium-cost units and terraced housing – mostly found in Selangor and Johor – in particular demand. In May, property developer **Kumpulan Guthrie** forecast MYR360mn in sales revenues this year, against MYR197mn in 1999. With 50% of the population under the age of 25, Malaysia offers a substantial potential market for developers. Market speculation – which helped create an asset bubble in 1997 – reappeared in the first quarter, but there is still sufficient excess capacity to prevent overheating. Nonetheless, deputy premier Abdullah Badawi has asked for Malaysians to resist the temptation to speculate on the property market, which he blames for encouraging the oversupply of properties. And there have been calls – notably from Mani Usilappan, deputy director general of the Valuation and Property Services Department in the Ministry of Finance – for banks to conduct detailed market research studies before committing funds to property developments. Speaking at a seminar in mid-April, Mani said that a lack of property-based risk analysis had contributed to the asset bubble experienced in the recent downturn.

CONSTRUCTION SECTOR INDICATORS					
	1995	1996	1997	1998	1999
Housing approvals	113,183	115,540	188,400	194,092	183,041
Cement & concrete production (% y-o-y)	20.4	63.7	21.0	-40.8	8.4
Iron and basic steel production (%y-o-y)	12.8	18.6	7.8	-35.6	37.0
Construction-related products production (% y-o-y)	11.8	21.1	11.3	-27.6	14.3
Loans approved for construction (MYRmn)	16,084.5	19,393.5	18,631.9	5,619.8	7,893.7
Import of construction materials & mineral products (MYRmn)	2,491.0	2,511.9	2,547.7	1,651.4	1,785.9
National house price index (% y-o-y)	18.4	12.9	1.9	-9.4	-2.3

Source: Bank Negara Malaysia.

Stockbroking

Stockbrokers Face Rapid Consolidation

Malaysia' Securities Commission (SC) announced plans on April 21 for the merger of the country's 63 stockbrokers into no more than 15 firms by the end of this year. Consolidation in the sector, argued the SC, was " imperative to prepare the industry to face the challenges of liberalisation and globalisation." Under the plans, 15 so-called 'universal brokers' will comprise of no less than four existing companies, with all parties free to choose their preferred partners. The radical shake-up – which follows the consolidation of the banking industry from 54 into 10 institutions – met with resistance from some broking houses, who criticised the short time frame proposed by the SC. Smaller players in particular complained of the difficulties of finding compatible partners and agreeing on pricing within eight months. The plans were subsequently revised in mid-June. The initial merger deadline of December 31, 2000 has been scrapped, but the SC will be monitoring the pace of consolidation with the possibility of review if it is deemed to be too slow. Industry players have indicated that one-to-one mergers by year-end are possible, reducing the number of brokerages to around 30.

A previous condition that barred controlling shareholders of banks from having effective control of brokerages has also (controversially) been lifted, but a new restriction preventing parent stockbroking firms from holding property or construction businesses has been introduced. And under its initial announcement, the SC said that the maximum valuation of a stockbroking company could not exceed 1.5 times its net tangible assets. But after revisions, brokers will be left to choose their own acquisition prices and valuation methods. Each company must have paid-up capital of at least MYR250mn (US$65.8mn), minimum core capital of MYR250mn and a capital adequacy ratio of at least 1.5 times. They must also meet good governance standards and other qualitative standards as laid out by the SC. Merged units will benefit from tax credits and stamp duty and property gains tax exemptions as introduced in the 2000 budget. Universal brokers will be allowed to open an additional branch immediately, and will be permitted to offer the full ranges of capital market services, including corporate finance and derivatives trading: previously companies were required to obtain a separate license to trade in derivatives products under the Futures Industry Act. Foreign equity capital in stockbroking firms is to be maintained at 49%, and foreign equity participation should be through the purchase of new

The Securities Commission announced plans in April for the consolidation of Malaysia's stockbroking industry, reducing the number of brokerages from 63 to 15.

shares and not by buying shares from existing shareholders.

Commission rates will be liberalised in two stages. On September 1, 2000, commission rates for all trades over MYR100,000 will be fully negotiable, and trades under MYR100,000 will be subject to a fixed rate of 0.75%. In Stage 2, on July 1, 2001, commission rates will be fully negotiable for all trades, subject to a cap of 0.7%. The Securities Clearing Automated Network Services clearing fee will be reduced from 0.05% to 0.04% from July 1, 2001, subject to a maximum of MYR200 per contract, while the System on Computerised Order Routing and Execution fee will be reduced in two stages to 0.005% and 0.0025% from September 1, 2000, and July 1, 2001, respectively. And the SC levy will be reduced to 0.015% from 0.02% from July 1, 2001.

Lower Costs Will Boost Industry Competitiveness

Foreign investors are unhappy with some of the modifications – notably the removal of the restriction on banks' having effective control of brokerages – which are viewed as yet one more example of the Malaysian authorities yielding to pressure from vested interests. And while industry players are generally pleased with the SC's revisions, others are still wary of the plans, which do not, as some had expected, name the universal brokers. The fear is that there will be a scramble for anchor status, with the 13 bank-backed brokerages, benefiting from greater financial clout, tussling with non-bank backed but still large brokerages such as **OSK**, **K & N Kenaga**, **Hwang DBS** and **TA**. All four firms saw their share values fall following the SC's announcement. The SC also failed to address what would happen to existing tie-ups between local and foreign brokerages. And futures brokers are facing the threat of new competition, after spending millions on licenses.

But **BMI** believes that the mergers will undoubtedly bring benefits to the industry. While lower commission rates will hit profit margins, this should be offset by an increase in trading volume in a country with one of the highest commission rates in the region added to the 10% exit tax levy. Lower costs will boost competitiveness in time for the opening of the financial services sector in 2003 under membership of the World Trade Organisation. The SC's stipulation that foreign firms must acquire their stakes by purchasing new shares will ensure an injection of fresh capital, enabling industry expansion. And the MYR250mn paid up and core capital requirements will ensure that each universal broker gets off on a healthy footing.

The radical merger plans met with a cautious response from industry players. But lower costs will boost the competitiveness of the industry, ahead of WTO liberalisation in 2003.

Rubber

Arresting The Production Malaise

The Malaysian Rubber Board announced further plans in May to increase rubber production, which has suffered over the past few years as planters have abandoned the industry in favour of more lucrative crops and property development. Production has declined for five consecutive years, dropping to 768,872 tonnes in 1999, from 885,700 in 1998 and 971,100 in 1997. Total planted area is estimated to be 1.5mn ha, haven fallen by an average 20,000-30,000 ha per year over the past few years. Given the long rubber forest plantation gestation period of over 15 years, this does not bode well for future output, and **BMI** forecasts that output will fall below 760,000 in 2000. The latest available data shows output down 30.8% y-o-y in February and 27.4% over the first two months.

Primary Industries Minister Dr Lim Keng Yaik has warned that the rubber industry will die off in 25 years if no new trees are planted to replace those lost to palm oil and property development. He estimates that 50,000 ha per year needs to be replanted to ensure steady rubber supplies, compared to 1,000 ha in 1999. In light of the strategic nature of the sector – feeding into Malaysia's growing rubber-based industry – the government has introduced several measures to boost production. There are plans to replant 80,000 ha of rubber forest this year, of which 30,000 ha will be in Pahang, 18,000 ha in Johor and 8-10,000 ha in Selangor. The remainder will be in Negri Sembilan and Perak. The government has allocated MYR145mn this year for replanting programmes covering 45,000 ha, but only 30% of this is for rubber, with the majority going to palm oil. Further funds will come from the MYR1bn allocated in the 2000 budget for the rubber production industry, some of which can be used for replanting. However, this might still be insufficient to meet the needs of the industry, and the Rubber Smallholders Association has made calls for the government to set up a fund to aid rubber plantation smallholders, proposing that 4% of revenue from rubber production – totalling MYR13bn a year – be put into the fund.

As larger estates switch to palm oil – a hectare of rubber plantation earns in the region of MYR25 per month against MYR175 for palm oil – smallholders now contribute 80-85% of Malaysia's total rubber production. The falling price of rubber has made it difficult to fund replanting. With this in mind, the government has launched a special programme to help smallholders, including a MYR145mn scheme for replanting. And the Malaysian Rubber Board

Rubber production has floundered as planters switch to the more lucrative palm oil sector.

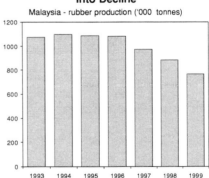

Into Decline
Malaysia - rubber production ('000 tonnes)

Source: Bank Negara Malaysia.

has indicated that the government is laying down plans for a MYR1bn credit facility to finance future replanting to boost the attractiveness of the industry, particularly in areas where the land is unsuitable for other crops. Four ministries – Primary Industries, Agriculture, Rural Development and Land and Cooperative Development – have formed a committee charged with formulating a plan to improve earnings and ensure that the upstream rubber sector is viable.

Inro was formally disbanded in October 1999, following disagreements over pricing levels.

The committee may look at ways to stabilise the price of rubber, which dropped to a 30-year low in 1999. For two decades rubber prices were controlled by the International Natural Rubber Organisation (Inro), which confined prices within a set band. But the organisation was formally disbanded in October 1999, following disagreements over pricing levels. Thailand and Malaysia – the worlds first and third biggest rubber producers respectively – were particularly disgruntled at low prices that favoured consumer country members, at a time when both countries were experiencing an economic downturn. The two nations took it upon themselves to stabilise prices, injecting funds into their state-owned rubber trading agencies to buy up rubber on the market. Some have questioned the viability of the pact between just two countries of limited financial resources. But Indonesia – the world's second largest producer – has also indicated a willingness to co-operate, a development that could just be sufficient to swing prices in the producers' favour. Malaysia disbanded its rubber price intervention programme – the Government Special Purchase Price Scheme – in February this year following a surge in prices, having been in operation for just eight months. Although production costs still far outweighed intervention prices, the government could not raise prices any further for fear of disrupting the open market.

PRODUCTION OF MAJOR AGRICULTURAL AND MINING COMMODITIES							
	1993	1994	1995	1996	1997	1998	1999
Rubber ('000 tonnes)	1,074.3	1,100.6	1,089.0	1,082.0	971.1	885.7	768.9
Crude Palm Oil ('000 tonnes)	7,403.0	7,220.6	7,811.0	8,385.9	9,068.7	8,319.7	10,553.4
Palm Kernel Oil ('000 tonnes)	965.7	978.1	1,036.5	1,107.0	1,164.7	1,110.7	1,338.9
Saw Logs ('000 cubic metres)	37,269.0	35,672.0	31,842.0	30,094.0	31,162.2	21,671.6	21,940.7
Cocoa (tonnes)	200,000.0	177,000.0	131,000.0	120,000.0	106,027.0	90,183.0	83,668.0
Tin (tonnes)	10,384.0	6,458.0	6,403.0	5,174.0	5,065.0	5,756.3	7,336.6
Crude oil & condensates (b/d)	647,605	659,932	705,061	715,710	713,929	725,036	693,491
Natural gas (mmscfd)	2,097	2,362	2,810	3,402	3,926	3,722	3,803

Source: Bank Negara Malaysia.

Given current market conditions, there is an urgent need to raise productivity. **BMI** anticipates some consolidation in the sector, with smaller holdings merging to benefit from economies of scale. Dr Lim estimates that a holding needs to be approximately seven hectares in size to be financially viable, against the country's two hectares average. New, higher yielding tapping methods will also be encouraged.

Profile and Recent Developments

Introduction

Ambitious Plans Set Back

In terms of sectoral growth, the government prioritised manufacturing, services and construction under the Seventh Industrial Plan and Second Industrial Master Plan (1996-2000). The major contribution to growth was expected to come from the electrical machinery and equipment sub-sectors, while increased domestic demand, especially for construction and industrial goods, was expected to boost activity in industrial chemicals and other chemical products, wood and wood products, non-metallic mineral products, transport equipment, and fabricated metal products.

The economic crisis has set back the government's plans by, at the very least two, and more likely six to seven years. The most serious harm has been done to the growth prospects of the two key sectors: manufacturing and construction. The crisis has also cast doubt on the wisdom of over-reliance on the electronics sector, which is vulnerable to a world downturn and subject to intense competition. The crisis has also prompted a rethink about the established priorities, with a determination to broaden the bases of growth and concentrate on resource-based industries as well as electronics and high-technology goods which have a high import content.

Manufacturing

Recovery From Hard Times

The domestic-oriented industries were hardest hit by the economic downturn in 1998. Manufacturing output, measured by the Industrial Output Index (1993=100) fell by 10.2%. Manufacturing value-added fell by 13.7%, led by declines in the construction-related industries, transport equipment and petroleum products. Production by the export-oriented industries held up better, falling 7.2%, largely because of weak demand in East Asia and global oversupply in the electronics sector. Rubber products was the only major category to record an increase.

In 1999, led by stronger external demand, an accelerating recovery started. Overall manufacturing output grew by 12.9% in index terms and by 13.5% in value-added terms. The recovery began in February and accelerated as the year progressed, so that manufacturing value-added rose by 25.2%

y-o-y in the fourth quarter. Both the export and domestic-oriented manufacturing sectors grew in annual terms, by 12.9% and 13.1% respectively, after falls of 7.3% and 13.4% in 1998. Car sales have picked up as consumer confidence improves and the impact of lower interest rates and the fiscal stimulus feeds through. The outlook for manufactured exports is bright, with a rebound in export growth and a pick up in demand for electronic products. Imports of intermediate goods, a leading indicator of manufacturing activity, have firmed.

Lumber And Wood Products

The plywood industry was badly hit in 1998 by a collapse in demand and dumping, which caused severe price falls. Compared with pre-crisis levels of US$420 per m³ for thin plywood and US$400 per m³ for thick plywood, prices dropped to a trough of US$240 and US$180 respectively by May 1998, as the regional economic crisis hit demand for timber and Indonesian manufacturers dumped their stocks on the market. Only vertically-integrated producers, such Sarawak-based **Jaya Tiasa** and **Lingui**, managed to avoid losses.

In 1999, the wood and wood products industry registered a third year of decline, with output falling by 7.3%. Production of plywood and particle board rose as a result of improved external demand, but there was a fall in output of sawn timber because logging was affected by heavy rainfall.

Textiles, Clothing And Footwear

The textile and apparel industry has for many years been a major export earner and employer, but has been declining in importance as manufacturing moves up the value-added ladder. Until the mid-1990s, the industry managed to sustain double-digit export growth. Growing competition, as a result of trade liberalisation under WTO and Asean rules, has made it necessary for the industry to raise productivity by using higher technology and more skilled manpower. It has also tried to gain a larger presence in Asia, reducing its dependence on traditional markets: the US, EU and Canada. Government policy has aimed at strengthening the industry through business mergers, the creation of inter-industry linkages, and emphasis on R&D and an increase in quality. A "Buy Made In Malaysia Products" drive, was intended to create indigenous brands and replace imports. Production of textiles and apparel held up comparatively well in 1998, with a 5.3% drop in output. In 1999 the sector recovered, with output growth of 4%, a result of the continuing effort to enhance quality.

Petroleum Refining And Related Industries

The major oil companies in Malaysia are continuing the aggressive expansion of the chemical side of their business, with companies such as **BP Amoco** and **Shell Malaysia** following the lead of national oil company **Petronas**. The shift of focus away from the simple production of oil and gas for domestic consumption and exports, is the result of a policy to add value to the basic raw materials. The petrochemical industry is capital intensive, technologically driven, has a long gestation period and is cyclical in nature. Petronas has moved far downstream into petrochemicals, well beyond the primary products of ethylene and polyethylene, using best industry technologies in joint ventures with multinationals such as **BP Amoco**, **Union Carbide** and **BASF**. One of the most recent petrochemicals ventures, for a huge low density polyethylene plant in Kertih, is with **Polifin Ltd** of South Africa and **DSM Polyethylenes BV** of the Netherlands, with Petronas providing the industrial infrastructure and 40% of the share capital. Kertih is the location of an Integrated Petrochemical Complex (IPC), one of the cluster-type developments under the Industrial Master Plan. The longer-term outlook of the petrochemicals sector is very positive. New projects worth US$3.6bn, half of which have been funded from foreign direct investment, are due to come on stream, mostly by 2001. Another US$5bn is planned for implementation after 2001.

Petrochemical consumption is closely linked to economic growth, and hence the industry suffered in the downturn from oversupply, low plant utilisation and depressed prices. In an industry that had become used to high growth, the 11.5% drop in production during 1998 came as a shock. In 1999, output declined only slightly, by 0.3%, thanks to a more vibrant world and regional economy. The longer-term outlook remains positive, as Malaysia positions itself as a regional petrochemical centre.

Rubber And Plastic Products

The rubber products sector is unusual in the fact that, unlike almost all other major categories of output, production continued to grow during the economic downturn. As a resource-based industry, the sector has a natural advantage when, as the Seventh Plan stipulates, it moves downstream to produce higher value-added goods, especially given the price weakness of the raw material. Nonetheless, the biggest stimulus to output in 1998-99 came from an export boost due to an artificially weak ringgit. In 1999 growth in output was in fact slower than in 1998 – 3.6% against 7.8%. This reflected intense competition in the rubber gloves sub-sector, so that Malaysian output fell, more than offsetting higher output of tyres and tubes. The persistent weakness of rubber prices makes further specialisation essential, if the industry is to benefit fully from renewed economic growth.

Steel

Output of iron and steel plunged in 1998, as production is closely linked to the construction industry: construction-related business dropped 60%. Strong export growth compensated to some extent for the drop in domestic demand, but also showed that the industry had become competitive at the lower exchange rate.

The sector has also become increasingly export competitive, as policies of import substitution, acquisition of foreign expertise and selective encouragement of foreign investment begin to bear fruit. In galvanised steel products, for instance, Malaysia may soon become a net exporter as a result of a series of eco-friendly plants being set up by the joint venture of Australian **Industrial Galvanisers Corporation** and **Sijas Holdings**.

Nonetheless, the steel industry remains domestically-oriented and driven by construction activity. In the second half of 1999 a still-tentative recovery in the sector boosted demand for construction-related material and iron and steel output rose by 29.5%, after falling by 29.1% in 1998. The large sums earmarked in the government's infrastructure fund for road projects will boost demand for steel. However, even with government stimulation and the onset of a moderate economic recovery, the industry is faced with serious under utilisation of plants this year. **Amsteel** has deferred a 750,000 tonnes a year billet and a 500,000 tonnes a year wire rod plant, while a 360,000 tonnes rolling mill on Sarawak is unlikely to go ahead. While the industry outlook is improving, it is unlikely that economic growth in the next couple of years will be sufficiently strong to wipe out problems of overcapacity.

Electronic And Electrical Products

Electronic and electrical products account for 33% of total industrial production, or 48% of manufacturing, and nearly half of Malaysia's exports. Electrical products is the smaller sector, taking 19% of manufacturing, and includes consumer electrical appliances and industrial electrical apparatus; areas in which there is strong global competition. Malaysia was losing competitiveness in this area before the downturn hit the economy. Growth had turned sluggish in 1996 and production declined by 1.7% in 1997, but the full force of the crisis was not felt until 1998. Production plunged as domestic and Asian demand for electrical goods fell away. Improved demand for office and computing equipment, for consumer durables and air-conditioners in the US and in the Asia region, including Japan, in the second half of 1999, prompted an overall rise of 15.6% in electronics and electrical products in 1999, after a fall on 7.7% in 1998. The competitive benefits of a weaker ringgit are unlikely to help manufacturers much in the longer term, while investment – necessary to move up the value-added scale – is likely to be neglected under the present circumstances.

The electrical and electronic products industry is highly diverse and comprises semiconductors, computers and peripherals, telecommunications equipment, consumer electronics, electrical appliances ('white goods') and industrial electrical equipment. The sector is dominated by foreign multinational companies, which are highly dependent on imported parts and components and export the bulk of their production. It is still primarily an assembly industry, but the availability of cheaper labour in other Asian countries has stimulated a move to a higher, intermediate level of technology, which has also been boosted by a policy of import substitution.

The components made locally are mainly for consumer electronics, specifically in semiconductors. The sector accounts for two-thirds of manufactured exports, 30% of manufactured production and 27% of manufacturing employment. Most of the electronics industry is located on the island of Penang which includes, in addition to global giants such as **Intel**, **Motorola**, **Hewlett-Packard**, **Dell**, **Sony** and **Siemens**, more than 1,000 home-grown companies.

The multinational companies are continuing to outsource production to reduce costs. The new growth in demand is likely to benefit local subcontracting semiconductor businesses like **Unisem**, **Malaysian Pacific Industries** (MPI) and **Globetronics**. Analysts are forecasting 20%-30% growth for the local electronics industry. On the industrial electrical equipment side, **Automotive Industries Corporation** (AIC), contract assembler for **Amtel**, has seen rising orders from the automotive industry. Recovery in the electronics industry will feed through to other parts of manufacturing, such as plastics and rubber.

It is difficult to assess the extent to which the strategy of the Seventh Malaysia Plan to develop a local electronic parts and components industry has been setback by political events and government policy during the past 12 months. Greater reluctance to invest on the part of foreign companies could have more to do with the overall Asian downturn than the Malaysian response to the crisis. Nonetheless, the Multimedia Super Corridor (MSC), Malaysia's version of Silicon Valley, has suffered a loss of momentum at the same time as competition from other centres, such as Singapore and Hong Kong, has increased. Malaysia will have to work harder to overcome foreign scepticism surrounding its ambitions.

Transportation Equipment

Total vehicle sales plunged more than 60% from 405,000 to 164,116 in 1998, and then staged a strong recovery, growing by 75.8%, to 288,547 units, in 1999, as domestic demand revived. To keep matters in perspective, one has to keep in mind that the collapse followed three years of extraordinary boom, during which vehicle sales rose from an annual average of around 185,000, to an all-time high of 405,190 units. The vehicle sector was one of the first to experience the depth of the economic crisis, as customers cut back on purchases of durable goods, especially luxury items such as passenger cars. By comparison with the private sector, the economies made in the commercial sector were even more severe, as spending was curtailed by almost 70% to 21,000 units. The restructuring of the corporate sector is likely to lead to a shake-up of the car industry.

The most important proposal has been the possible sale by highly geared **Hicom** of its crown jewel, national car maker **Proton**, to **Petronas**. The national oil company has also been suggested as a purchaser for distributor **EON**. This deal has yet to be consummated, but is expected to go ahead this year. **UMW** may want to get rid of its stake in **Perodua**, while **Tan Chong** is in the middle of a demerger exercise. Meanwhile, vehicle sales bottomed out in February 1998, with a nine-year low of 5,600 units. The government has cut interest rates and lifted credit restrictions, consumer sentiment has improved a little and there has been a modest revival in demand, from which national car makers Proton and Perodua have benefited in particular. The weak ringgit forced many foreign makers to raise their prices, and the economic crisis has boosted support for the national car brands on patriotic grounds.

As consumer confidence recovers in 2000, there will be a further revival in unit sales of vehicles, but competition will continue to be stiff. The car makers introduced no fewer than seven new models towards the end of 1998, determined to catch the pick-up in demand and – at least for the assembly plants in Malaysia – raise capacity utilisation above break-even point. At the same time, costs are under pressure from the dependence on imported, largely yen-denominated (except for luxury car assembler **C&C Bintang**), parts and components, which ranges from 30% for **Proton**, to as high as 65% for **UMW Toyota**. But there is an encouraging trend for consumers to opt for vehicles with add-on accessories, which will help to boost profits.

In addition, import duties had been raised in 1998 on passenger cars with an engine capacity of 2000cc and higher. It is going to be difficult for manufacturers to recoup their higher costs. The over-capacity in the industry is boosting price competition and the best-selling cars are currently the cheaper models, where margins are low. Price increases are in the pipeline, but it remains to be seen whether they can stick.

Agriculture, Forestry And Fishing

Structural Problems

Production in the agriculture, forestry, livestock and fishery sector rose by 3.9% in 1999, after a fall of 4.5% in 1998, thanks in part to the prolonged dry weather caused by El Niño, as well as the economic downturn. There are also some serious structural problems. Companies are trying to reduce unit costs, which are high relative to regional competitors, especially in palm oil. But average wages in the sector fell by 19.5% in 1999. Malaysia's biggest conglomerate **Sime Darby** is considering combining its plantation and property development activities with **Golden Hope** and **Kumpulan Guthrie**. Together the group would own 300,000 hectares of plantations, and analysts claim it could slash up to MYR380mn per year off costs. The increase in crude palm oil output, as well as logs, fish and livestock, in 1999 was not enough to prevent the sector's share of GDP falling slightly (to 9.3%). Its share of exports and employment also slipped. In 2000 growth in the sector is expected to moderate to 2% overall, mainly because growth in crude palm oil production will ease due to a downturn in the biological yield cycle. Because of the low exchange rate, domestic producers' ringgit revenues from commodity exports have been protected, despite generally poor world prices.

Cash Crops

A prolonged spell of unusually dry weather in 1998 led to significant falls in the production of cocoa (a decline of 15.5%), palm oil (down 8%) and rubber (a drop of 7.3%), while sawn logs production dropped by 15% as a result of the slowdown in the regional construction industry. The declining trend in natural rubber production continued due to global oversupply, weak prices and shortage of labour. However, the weak ringgit also caused a sharp increase in the export prices of some products, such as palm oil, cocoa beans and pepper, and boosted investment in the oil palm sector in particular.

With the return of more normal weather conditions in 1999, there has been a recovery in some sectors. Crude palm oil (CPO) production rose by 26.8%, to 10.6mn tonnes, thanks to increased yields and an expansion in the area of mature plantings. CPO accounted for 32% of the value-added agricultural sector and 52.5% of its export earnings, despite the continuing slump in world prices. Malaysia accounted for 53% of world production of CPO in 1999; eight new mills came into production, bringing the total number in operation to 333 by the end of the year. Natural rubber output fell by 13.5% to 766,549 tonnes in 1999, the industry being affected by continuing low prices, shortages of labour and a reduced area of cultivation. Smallholders – about 400, 000 of them – account for nearly 80% of rubber production, and a government scheme to buy directly from them at above market prices was set up in mid-1999, to support their incomes. Rubber production is expected to remain on a declining trend in 2000, as already low yields fall further in the absence of a strong recovery in prices. Cocoa production has been falling since 1991, as land is converted to oil palm. In 1999 it fell to 83,000 tonnes, a 7.2% decline. Low prices and rising production costs have affected smallholder production in particular and encouraged the conversion of land to other uses. Production was insufficient to meet domestic processing demand, and beans were imported in 1999, chiefly from Indonesia.

Livestock And Fishery

An outbreak of Japanese encephalitis and a Hendra-like virus in pigs, could prove the most serious challenge to livestock rearing in the post-war period, as well as a highly divisive issue. Malaysia's US$400mn a year pig-rearing industry is one of the largest in South East Asia, carried out on small-scale pig farms by the ethnic Chinese population. In April 1999, the US-based Centre for Disease Control and Prevention estimated that 117 people had died since September 1998 from the viral outbreak, while more than 668,000 pigs had been destroyed by the Malaysian authorities, with plans to slaughter a total of 830,000 – about a third of the Malaysian hog population. The social and political harm done by the disease may be more serious than the economic damage. An essential part of the Chinese diet, the pig is reviled by the majority Islamic *bumiputra* population, while the widespread culling of pigs has been carried out by the largely Islamic army. Under mounting public pressure, the Malaysian Health Ministry is currently considering the development of centralised pig farms to ensure standards of hygiene. Demand for chicken has risen by more than 25% since the outbreak, prompting the authorities to import poultry to combat shortages.

Fishery production rose by 5.1% to 1.4mn tonnes in 1999, with both marine fish (90% of production) and aquaculture showing growth, the latter by 28.7%. Exports of fish rose by 1.5% to 152,000 tonnes, mainly to Thailand, Singapore and Japan. Domestic consumption rose to 44kg per head, from 43kg in 1998.

Forestry

Three-quarters of Malaysia is still covered in forest but the production of sawn logs has continued to slide since peaking in 1992 at 43.5mn m³. In 1998, output of sawn logs fell 30.5%, to 21.8mn m³. In 1999 output rose modestly, by 1.5% to 21.9mn m³, as external demand improved. This was entirely the result of higher output in Sarawak, which accounted for 60% of the total. The government points out that the current level of domestic logging is in line with its conservation policy, which has resulted in reforestation, which is intended to ensure sustainable development by 2000. Malaysia is also moving away from basic forestry products to higher value-added production. Demand for saw logs is likely to rise again in 2000, with a 3.3% rise in output forecast.

Mining

Output Rises

Tin production responded to higher prices in 1999, when output rose by 27.6%, to 740,000 tonnes. Three new mines started operations and existing mines increased their output. Natural gas production also rose, by 2.1%, to 3,802mn cf/day as domestic and external demand rose. But the sector as a whole contracted by 4% in value-added terms in 1999 because crude oil output, which accounts for about 80% of sectoral value-added, declined. In 2000, sectoral value-added is projected to rise by 2.1%, mainly thanks to higher gas production, itself based on stronger external demand.

Oil And Gas Extraction

Prospects For Revenue Growth Are Good

Oil production is dominated by the state oil company **Petroliam Nasional Bhd** (Petronas), which produces an average of 630,000b/d of crude oil, of which 400,000b/d are exported. Petroleum export revenues account for around 5% of Malaysia's total exports. Crude oil production (including condensates) fell in 1999, by 4.4%, to 693,200 b/d. This fall was in line with the national depletion policy. Reserves at the beginning of 1999 stood at 3.6bn barrels, enough to sustain production for 15 years.

Export prices for crude oil rose by 25.9% in local currency terms in 1999, after falling by 6.4% in 1998. Thanks to Opec cuts, international prices rose sharply in 1999, with Tapis Blend averaging US$18.6/b, after US$14.2/b in 1998. Crude oil exports rose by 23.9% in local currency terms in 1999 and accounted for 2.9% of total exports. For 2000 the Malaysian government is predicting an average oil price of US$20/b, which may well be an underestimate. In any event, oil export revenues are likely to rise again, with a positive impact on government revenues from royalties. Investment in exploration and development activities increased significantly in 1998-99 as a result of cuts in income tax and export duty on crude oil, and this is likely to boost future production.

Construction

Dawn Of Recovery

After the banks, construction has been the sector worst hit by the economic crisis. Construction sector GDP plummeted by 24.5% in 1998 and it fell again in 1999, this time by 5.6%, as companies slashed investment and developers cut back on the construction of higher-end properties.

During 1999 a tentative recovery set in: construction output in GDP terms rose by 2.7% y-o-y in the fourth quarter. Activity was supported by infrastructure spending under the fiscal package and also by housing. The value and volume of property transactions rose by 23.1% and 21.1% respectively. The Survey of the Construction Sector, conducted annually by Bank Negara, reported an upturn in civil engineering, boosted by infrastructure projects. Commercial property transactions increased with completions of office and retail space adding to an already large overhang.

While most of the construction industry remained depressed in 1999, there was strong demand for residential housing, thanks to a spreading recovery and lower interest rates. Residential property transactions and construction increased, but there was still an overhang of unsold property. Prices tended to fall in 199, because of continuing oversupply, but there were signs of stabilisation in the second half of the year, with strong demand from foreign buyers taking advantage of the low ringgit.

The government is expecting the recovery in construction to be consolidated during 2000, with growth of 5%. This growth is expected to come chiefly from residential construction and civil engineering as domestic demand strengthens further, and pump-priming continues. Commercial construction is expected to remain subdued, partly because banks have been prohibited from financing new hotels, resorts, office buildings, sports and shopping complexes since early 1999.

Utilities

Awaiting Restructuring

The overall economic improvement in 1999 helped to boost services output, which rose by 2.9% after falling by 0.8% in 1998. The recovery in manufacturing helped to stimulate a 4.9% increase in value-added output of utilities. Electricity production was up by 3.9% and water production rose by 2.4%.

Malaysia's dominant power utility **Tenaga Nasional** is in the middle of divesting itself of its power plants and turning itself into a transmission and distribution firm, with equity in power generation. The government has stipulated that Malaysia should restructure its power industry and have a number of power producers of equal size. The subsidiary companies will be active in various fields of the power industry. **TNB Generation** will, for instance, oversee power generation as a whole and provide technical know-how to **Reward Resources** on the operation of **Powertron**'s power plant. Previously such an arrangement would have caused a conflict of interest, when Tenaga was the buyer of the power generated. In December 1998, Tenaga said it planned to sell a 330MW power plant to independent power producer **Powertek,** after selling a 2,000MW plant to **Malakoff** earlier in the year. This process was delayed by the weakness of the stockmarket during 1998-99.

Telecoms

Telecoms Urged To Forge Strategic Alliances

Moves to liberalise Malaysia's fragmented telecommunications industry took at step forward at the end of January 2000, with the Malaysian Communications and Multimedia Commission's (CMC) announcement of new guidelines aimed at stamping out non-competitive practices. These include foreclosure (where the customer is forced to enter into a long-term supply arrangement), refusal to supply goods or services, bundling (whereby goods can only bought in a package), parallel pricing (where there is collusion between rivals to vary prices) and predatory pricing. Unless the uncompetitive conduct is deemed to be in the national interest, a fine of not more than MYR500,000 or imprisonment of not more than five years, or both, will be imposed, plus a further fine for every day the offence continues after conviction. The CMC will also be looking at preventing market domination, and barriers to entry in the industry.

CMC chairman, Syed Hussein Mohamed, has been urging Malaysian telecoms firms to forge strategic foreign alliances to benefit from investment, skills and wider market opportunities. There are currently five main service providers in Malaysia, serving a population of just 22mn. Each of these offers both fixed and mobile services, and has its own lines, satellites and mobile cellular base stations. Three telecoms companies have already forged alliances with foreign providers, following an announcement in April 1998 that foreigners would be allowed to own up to 61% in local telecoms firms, scaling back their equity to 49% after five years. Perhaps the most successful partnership has been **British Telecoms'** purchase of a 33% stake in **Maxis Communications** operated by **Binariang Sdn**, which has successfully widened its market share on the back of aggressive marketing campaigns. Maxis signed a distribution agreement with **Concert** – a joint British Telecom-**AT&T** venture – in January 2000, to provide a range of Concert global network services throughout Malaysia, in a move which Maxis hopes will enable it to maintain 40-60% growth over the next few years. Meanwhile, **Deutsche Telecom** has gained a 21% stake in **Celcom**, operated by **Technology Resources Industries**, and Norway's **Telnor** has a 30% stake in **Digi Swisscom**, operated by **Berjaya Group**.

Faced with tougher competition and burdened with MYR421mn in bad debts, Malaysia's largest telecoms company, **Telekom Malaysia**, is in talks with Japan's **Nippon Telegraph and Telephone Corp** (NTT). Telekom reported lower-than-expected earnings of MYR819.1mn in 1999, against MYR991.1mn in 1998, citing rising debt provisioning and higher labour costs. NTT is looking to acquire up to a 15% stake in the company from **Khazanah Malaysia**. Under the deal, the government's holding in Telekom, through **Khazanah Holdings**, will be reduced to 51.6%: the government is unlikely to relinquish more than this due to the strategic nature of the telecoms industry. The acquisition will allow Telekom to defend its domestic market share through cheaper and better services, while providing it with wider access to foreign markets and the funds to seek further strategic alliances. Telekom has also sold its 40% stake in paging and messaging service **Skytel Systems** to two individuals – Tan Aik Choong and Wah Sze Siang – under a management buyout for a nominal price of MYR1. Telekom said it wanted to concentrate on its core business.

Internet Will Drive Telecoms Growth

BMI expects demand for both fixed line and cellular services to pick up in 2000 as the economy recovers, with wider internet use driving demand. This is something that Celcom hopes to tap into, with plans for a MYR1bn investment in infrastructure over the next two years to be largely channelled into establishing an information technology platform to build into its cellular network. At the same time, however, margins will be squeezed by increased competition, which has already led to aggressive discounting. There are currently estimated to be 4.5mn fixed line and 2.5mn mobile phone subscribers in Malaysia, giving a combined market penetration of 32%. The government will have little difficulty achieving its targeted penetration of 35-40% by 2005, but efforts to open up large, untapped rural areas to telecoms could be hindered by the government-imposed tariff structure, under which cheap local calls are subsidised by expensive long distance and international calls. Industry players, led by Telekom, have called for the tariff regime to be liberalised, arguing that it discourages investment in local loop infrastructure. Instead, the CMC has urged companies to maximise usage of the network, offering value-added services through local networks to increase revenue. But there appeared to be some concessions to the industry in February's Budget, which announced a Wireless in Local Loop system to provide telecommunications facilities in rural areas. The system, costing MYR318mn, will be implemented by Telekom, opening up telecoms services to 120,000 new rural subscribers.

Finance And Insurance

Banks In Trouble

Excessive credit expansion and over-exposure to the property sector finally caught up with Malaysia's banks, when the financial crisis hit in mid-1997. Falling asset prices and a rising level of non-performing loans (NPLs) raised serious doubts about the stability of the whole banking system in an economy where domestic debt was equivalent to 170% of GDP. Although official figures show that the system was strong at the start of the crisis – the level of NPLs was only 3.6% of total loans and the 11.8% risk-weighted capital ratio stood well above the international standard of 8% – the crisis is a stark reminder that banking depends on confidence. This was something that aggressively stimulative and redistributive government policies had undermined, even though the trigger for the crisis came from elsewhere in the region.

The initial response of Bank Negara Malaysia (BNM) in October 1997 – raising interest rates, slowing lending growth and restricting bank lending for construction, property, share financing and consumption – no doubt made the crisis worse. In a controversial change of course at the start of 1998, the authorities returned to more stimulative policies and also adopted a radical new approach to NPLs and bank restructuring. The government set up Danaharta – an asset management company – to purchase, manage and dispose of the bank's NPLs. In addition, it established Danamodal to manage the recapitalisation and reorganisation of the banks, with the aim of establishing a core of strong domestic banks. Debt restructuring was also started under the auspices of the Corporate Debt Restructuring Committee (CDRC).

The imposition of currency controls in September 1998, after the foreign investment community expressed its lack of faith in Malaysia's policies by selling off the ringgit, made it easier to reorganise the banking system by increasing government control and checking speculative capital flows. It also enabled BNM to relax banking rules. The default period for classifying a loan as non-performing was increased from three to six months, bank provisioning would no longer be an automatic 20% of sub-standard loans, but depend on the adequacy of the loan-loss coverage of the individual institution, while restructured or rescheduled NPLs could be reclassified as performing after six, instead of 12 months.

Restructuring And Recapitalisation Progress

By the end of 1999, Danaharta had acquired and was managing NPLs with loan rights of MYR45.5bn (US$12bn). The book value of the loans moved out of the banking system was MYR34bn, about 42% of the NPLs in the banking system. This had reduced the level of NPLs to 6.6% of the total from a peak of 9% at the end of November 1998 (based on a six-month definition of NPLs). As of end-1999 Danaharta had restructured or disposed of MYR17.6bn in loans and assets, with an average recovery rate of 80.2%. It also disposed of foreign currency assets worth US$394.25mn in 1999, by means of restricted open tenders. In its first open tender operation involving foreclosed properties, conducted in December 1999, 24 were disposed of successfully and another 20 were transferred to an asset subsidiary. As of end-1999 the recapitalisation process being undertaken by Danamodal had reduced its capital injections to the first 10 banks which it had targeted to MYR5.3bn, as five banks had made repayments. The RWCR rations of the 10 had improved to 12.3% from 9.9% in September 1998. In terms of corporate restructuring the Corporate Debt Restructuring Committee (CRDC) had completed 19 cases by February 2000, and referred another 10 to Danaharta.

All the 54 financial institutions in Malaysia met the January 31, 2000 deadline to submit merger plans to the central bank. In October the banks were asked to choose their own merger partners and get approval in principal from their directors. Ten anchor banks have been selected to form the core of the restructured banking system: **Malayan Banking**; **Bumputra-Commerce Bank**; **RHB Bank**; **Public Bank**; **Arab Malaysian Bank**; **Hong Leong Bank**; **Perwira Affin Bank**; **Multi-Purpose Bank**; **Southern Bank**, and **EON Bank**. They must now go through due diligence and make sales and purchase agreements. They must each garner shareholders' funds of MYR2bn and an asset base of MYR25bn.

In the 12 months to March 31, 1999, the banking sector made a loss of MYR8.5bn; this turned around from the second quarter of 1999, with a profit of MYR7.4bn in the second-fourth quarters of 1999. Net interest income still fell in 1999, as the value of outstanding loans fell. There was a fall in the total outstanding loans, as loans were sold to Danaharta, written off or converted to other assets, but new loan activity picked up in 1999, to MYR104.8bn from MYR65.1bn in 1998.

Consolidation Has Further To Go

While the new restructured system will be more efficient, benefit from economies of scale and be able to offer a better range of services, it is generally believed than the Malaysian market cannot support the surviving institutions, and that a second wave of restructuring will be necessary within the next few years. There is a risk that excessive stimulation of credit to boost economic growth, together with favouritism as a result of *bumiputra* policies, will once again distort bank lending decisions. Such a risk is clearly present in the tightening of supervision in the new banking rules announced in April 1999. There will be a two-year performance appraisal, and chief executives and bank directors can be sacked if they fail the test. Banks will be monitored, according to the central bank, to see whether they are "playing a dynamic role in restoring economic growth by providing lending to productive industries".

It is generally believed that the government is underestimating the size of the bad loans problem, with foreign analysts generally predicting an NPL peak level of at least 30% (compared with the government's 20-25%) and a minimum of MYR50bn (government: MYR31bn) to reliquify the banking system. Total NPLs, including loans sold to Danaharta, were estimated at 19.1% at the end of 1999.

Insurance

The economic crisis demonstrated the stability of the insurance sector, especially compared with the banks, although the relatively good performance was in part the result of government support. In October 1998, a package of measures gave temporary relief to the insurance industry, by postponing the implementation of higher solvency and capital requirements. The economic downturn hurt the general insurance sector most, especially property and motor insurance, while life assurance was less affected. Shortly before the crisis, the new insurance act came into force, which set new minimum solvency and capital requirements, but also limits on various categories of investment. Consequently, the industry was shielded from the full impact of the crisis and equity investment losses were mitigated. Combined premium income fell by 2.1% in 1998, before recovering to grow by 7.1% in 1999. Life insurers' aggregate premiums rose 12.5% and general insurers' fell 0.9%. Malaysia's insurance industry is relatively under-developed and the potential for new business is large when 'normal' conditions return. Market penetration was only 28.4% in 1998; combined life and general insurance industry premium income accounts for only 4.3% of GDP, while the penetration rate for life business is only 27%. Malaysia has promised the WTO to open up the insurance market to foreign competition by 2003. The industry has started, with government encouragement, to consolidate and rationalise its operations, but the pace is still slow and no official deadline has been set. **Malaysian Assurance Alliance** is restructuring and looking for a local company to take over. Seven insurance mergers involving 14 insurers are being negotiated, of which three were finalised in 1999 and another three are expected to be completed in 2000. A potential threat to the solidity of the industry could be the government's intention to mobilise long-term insurance funds for economic development under the NERP, to underwrite Danaharta and Danamodal bonds.

4 Business Environment

Introduction

Capital Controls Only A Mild Irritant

During 1999 the Malaysian economy began a broad-based recovery from the 1997-98 economic crisis. But the controversial manner in which the crisis has been managed by the Malaysian authorities has left a legacy of doubt about future developments. Prime Minister Mahathir Mohamad has used the crisis to air familiar themes and relaunch broadsides against the Western forces of international capitalism. Such rhetoric is not new; a desire to regulate flows on the capital account and to prevent speculative surges or falls in the exchange rate has been in evidence before. Although the negative effects of the imposition of capital controls on foreign portfolio investment will take some time to reverse – and Malaysia will have to pay a risk premium in order to attract private portfolio capital from abroad – the policy was soon tempered by a large dose of pragmatism and there is no pressing need for foreign portfolio inflows.

The damage to the confidence of foreign direct investors is likely to be far smaller. Foreign investors, like portfolio ones, are accustomed to a divergence between rhetoric and reality in their relations with the Malaysian authorities. The real cost of the economic crisis has been the diversion of government spending towards bailouts and rescues, away from expenditure that could have raised the population's standard of living or improved the business environment. On the other hand, Malaysia's interventionist policies have given local business the kind of protection and active help with restructuring that would be looked at with envy by many other South East Asian countries

In recognition of the improved business climate, the *World Competitiveness Yearbook* 2000 edition has raised Malaysia's ranking by two rungs, to 25th among 47 countries. This ranking reflects a combination of factors based on economic data and surveys. Within Asia, Singapore, Japan and Taiwan ranked higher than Malaysia, while South Korea jumped the furthest, from 38th to 28th in 2000, thanks to the recovery there.

Infrastructure

Priming The Pump

Malaysia has long recognised that an efficient and reliable infrastructure is critical to economic growth. Past government budgets have on average allocated 20% of development spending on infrastructure projects, but the bulk of investment has come from private sources. In the Seventh Malaysia Plan, privatised projects account for three-quarters of the MYR87.5bn forecast spending between 1996 and 2000.

The crisis turned the heavy dependence on private finance, previously considered a strength of the Malaysian system, into a weakness. Many construction companies, property developers and toll road operators have been hit by declining revenues. A prolonged period of excessive loan growth to the building and construction sector peaked in 1997. Many loans to infrastructure projects are now in default, and bank finance for new projects became very difficult to obtain.

The government's initial response to the downturn was to cut infrastructure spending sharply but, aware of its large multiplier effects on the economy, it had a change of heart. Since the start of the crisis, the government has announced two stimulus packages totalling MYR12bn (US$3.2bn), of which MYR7.4bn is for construction related spending. In the 1999 budget, the government established a fund specifically for infrastructure projects that could not be implemented due to difficulties in obtaining bank loans. However, the loans are only for the purchase of land, and are conditional on companies obtaining additional commercial financing. Infrastructure spending is being given priority to stimulate the economy. MYR4.0bn was allocated in 1999 for roads, bridges, rail, ports, civil aviation, sewerage, waste disposal and water supply; 684 projects worth over MYR3bn were approved in the first nine months. The controversial Bakun hydroelectric dam in Sarawak has been revived, but scaled down by two-thirds. The development of the Multimedia Super Corridor, the high technology zone near the capital, and Cyberjaya, intended to be the first 'intelligent' city in Malaysia, has been set back by the economic crisis. Work on the 338km East Coast Highway through Pahang, Terengganu and Kelantan started in November 1999, but the building of the Terengganu sector was suspended soon after the November elections, ostensibly because of PAS's supposed opposition to tolls being imposed in its state. PAS subsequently made it clear that it did not oppose tolls and the federal government undertook in December to restart the project. Work on the Express Rail Link and the People-Mover Rapid Transit System also continued.

In 1999, thanks to counter-cyclical pump-priming, public investment expenditure rose by 10.1% in real terms, against a 19% real fall in the crisis-hit private sector. Public sector funded infrastructure projects and capital spending on capacity expansion by large state-owned enterprises such as **Petronas, Tenaga Nasional Berhad** (TNB) and **Telekom Malaysia Berhad** (Telekom) accounted for most of the additional spending. The 2000 budget envisages continued heavy infrastructure spending, allocating MYR5.33bn for construction and the upgrading and improvement of roads and highways. The projects include the construction of the Simpang Pulai-Lojing-Gua Musang-Kuala Berang Road, Kota Kinabalu-Sulaman Road, upgrading of five interchanges between Kapar-Sabak Bernam and Klang-Banting, Betong-Kayu Malam, as well as improving the Kuala Kangsar-Grik Road. Other priority infrastructure projects – rail, ports and airports – will include the construction of rail links to Pulau Indah Port (MYR27mn) and to Tanjung Pelepas Port (MYR163mn), construction of the Dual Track Sentul-Batu Caves (MYR494mn) and the Rawang-Ipoh Road (MYR458.2mn). Upgrading of air traffic services management, construction of new airports and upgrading and expanding facilities at existing airports will include development projects at Tawau, Kuala Terengganu and Limbang airports as well as the construction of a new terminal in Kota Baru.

Despite the increased government spending, infrastructure has suffered from the effects of the downturn. The construction sector has been hit as a result and construction output fell by 5.6% in 1999, after a fall of 23% in 1998. But there was a recovery in the second half of the year, thanks to public sector infrastructure spending and improved activity in the residential property market. The property overhang fell between the end of June and the end of December, by 26% in value terms, to MYR29.2bn. Capital expenditure in the construction sector fell by 80.2% in 1999. But a recovery is in prospect in 2000, with the exception of the construction of new commercial buildings. The government is forecasting growth of 5% in construction in 2000.

The Domestic Market

The Recovery Begins To Spread

While the economic crisis has not seriously dented the standard of living of the average Malaysian, the impact varies depending on consumption patterns, nature of employment and ownership of wealth. As in other South East Asian economies, the plunge in share and property values hit the urban middle class the hardest, while rural districts have benefited from the ringgitt's weakness, notwithstanding the global decline in the dollar price of agricultural commodities. The Chinese population, which makes up a large proportion of the professional classes and often sends its children abroad to be educated, has been the worst affected, while the rural *bumiputra* population may actually have gained. The Malaysian population is very young, with around 35% in the 0-14 age group and only 4% aged 65 or older. Heavy government spending on education has resulted in a high level of primary school enrolment (96%), a sharp rise in secondary and university student numbers, and a lowering of the pupil/teacher ratio (to 19:1 in primary and 18:6 in secondary education). Key development indicators show improvements in health care coupled with a steady increase in life expectancy. There are still large disparities in income and social welfare standards between the states.

As the process of economic recovery spreads through the domestic market, the behaviour of urban middle class consumers will spur a strong rebound in demand for consumer goods, especially high-end imports. There is considerable scope for recovery from the 1998 trough; an 8% GNP per capita in dollar terms left Malaysia ranking 82nd out of the countries covered by the World Bank's *World Development Report*. Adjusted for purchasing power parity, GNP per head was estimated at US$6,990 in 1998, ranking 79th down from 35th in 1997.

The Labour Market

Labour Market Tightens

The Seventh Malaysia Plan emphasises human resource development in the context of strong economic growth and heavy demand for labour. It calls for the expansion of domestic labour supply and increased labour productivity. As the country moves further towards industrial-based production, the Plan foresees the need to upgrade and expand Malaysia's education and skills base to meet new manpower requirements. It is too early to say how much the 1997-98 downturn has compromised Malaysia's labour force targets. To the extent that it has made the government more determined to provide high quality education and training facilities at home and reduce an excessive reliance on foreign labour, the emergency may produce some benefits. The change in employment structure is also heavily dependent on domestic and especially foreign investment, which will take time to recover to pre-crisis levels.

The economic crisis means, at the very least, a temporary setback for the planned labour market policy. The most obvious change has been the easing of labour shortages which resulted from Malaysia's prolonged period of fast economic growth, despite the import of foreign labour and a rising labour force participation rate. The Seventh Plan predicts average annual employment growth of 2.8%, down from 3.4% in the period 1990-1995. Unemployment was expected to stand at only 2.8% by 2000. Instead, the economic contraction cut employment by 2.5% in 1998, boosting the jobless rate to 3.2% from 2.6% in 1997, despite a highly unusual 1.7% fall in the labour force to 8.88mn, as foreign workers were repatriated.

In 1999 the accelerating recovery in external and domestic demand began to heat the labour market again. The total number employed rose to 8.7mn at the end of 1999, up 1.7%. With the labour force rising to 9mn, unemployment fell from 3.2% to 3%, below the frictional rate of 4%. New job creation was concentrated in assembly and labour-intensive areas of manufacturing. Employment in services overall was stable, but employment in banking fell by 4.5% as consolidation progressed. Employment in construction fell again, by 0.7%, after a 17% fall in 1998, and employment in agriculture continued a long-term decline, falling by 0.9%. The slump in the construction industry has left many foreign workers unemployed, but shortages of workers remain in the plantation sector, and some sub-sectors of the manufacturing and services sectors, especially those at the higher end of the value-added chain.

The number of registered foreign workers, having peaked at 1.2mn in 1997, fell to 697,219 in 1999, down by 10.8%. But the government did allow the intake of 84,150 workers in 1999, as the economy recovered. In agriculture, the number of foreign workers rose by 33.6%, over a third of the registered foreign workforce

Wage Pressures Ease

Despite the economic recovery, pressure on wages remained minimal in 1999; average real wages in manufacturing rose by 2.7%, having fallen by 2.4% in 1998. But overall nominal wages were subdued; Bank Negara data based on three-year collective wage agreements in the private sector showed an overall fall of 8.8% y-o-y. Manufacturing agreements were down 1.1% and only in transport (up 2.1%) and commerce (up 3.1%) were increases recorded. The sharpest falls were in agriculture and mining. The downturn eased wage pressures in 1998; manufacturing wage growth slowed to 6.4% in the first seven months of 1998 to an average MYR1,280 per month. The cost of labour declined to MYR6.36 per MYR100 of sales during the first seven months of 1998, from MYR6.85 during the corresponding period of 1997. There was a recovery in the nominal growth rate of manufacturing wages during the course of 1999, when they rose by 9.4%, but this comparatively modest nominal rise in the ringgit value of wages, combined with the low level of the ringgit:dollar exchange rate, has helped to enhance Malaysia's international competitiveness, at least in the short term.

Education and training remain high on the list of national priorities. A shortage of skills in certain manufacturing and services sectors was long ago identified as a potential barrier to growth. The New Economic Recovery Plan (NERP) sets extra money aside for retraining laid-off workers. Despite the squeeze on government finances, the 1999 budget allocated MYR13.5bn to the provision and upgrading of educational infrastructure and support facilities, as well as for curriculum development. Of this, MYR8bn was for primary and secondary education, and MYR2.85bn was allocated to raising the intake of students into local universities from 77,600 to 84,000 in 1999, as education abroad has become prohibitively expensive for many Malaysians. The 2000 budget takes these concerns further; capital expenditure of MYR3.7bn – 15% of total development spending – has been slated for education and MYR11.9bn has been allocated for operating expenditure, up 5.3% on the 1999 allocation. Efforts are being made to project Malaysia as a regional centre of educational excellence in the hope of attracting students from elsewhere in the region. The drive to encourage education and training among the employed workforce continues, in partnership with the private sector.

Industrial Policy

A Guided Economy

The Malaysian government takes an interventionist role in industrial policy, through which it seeks to meet socio-economic targets as well as driving development. Mahathir's aim of achieving developed country status in terms of key indicators by 2020 remains the overall target, towards which various official development plans strive. Some of the assumptions regarding industrial development, expressed in the Seventh Plan and second 10-year industrial master plan (IMP2), have been overtaken by events. IMP2, which gives a rolling-plan framework for the manufacturing sector, was presented in late-1996, on the eve of the economic crisis. The plan identified eight strategically important sectors, or industrial clusters, (electrical and electronics; textiles and apparel; chemicals; resource-based industries; agro-based and food products industries; transport; materials and machinery) and set as central targets the raising of productivity by an average of 5% per year and achievement of greater technological self-reliance. Assuming average annual growth of 10.7% in manufacturing valued-added, the share of manufacturing in GDP was forecast to increase from 33.1% in 1995 to 37.5% by 2000, and 38.4% by 2005. In 1999, manufacturing recovered, growing by 13.5% and bringing its share of GDP to 30%.

The Malaysian and global assumptions central to IMP2 now appear optimistic. Global growth, for example, was forecast at 3.3% per annum, the value of world merchandise trade forecast to grow by US$200-300bn annually, and FDI flows into developing countries projected to reach US$80bn in real terms by 2000. These assumptions have been set back by the 1997-98 crisis and by persistent sluggishness in the Japanese economy. **BMI** does not doubt that the structural change aimed for will eventually be achieved, but the planned rate of change will have to be revised down.

The crisis has prompted a review of the level of sustainable growth that can be achieved and of the adjustments needed to bring it about. Work on the Eighth Malaysia Plan, the Third Outline Perspective Plan, the Knowledge Economy Master Plan and the Capital Markets Master Plan is proceeding during 2000.

Growth Boosting Measures

In 1998-99, longer-term strategic plans took a back seat to policies aimed at restoring the health of the economy. One positive consequence of the imposition of capital controls, has been a boost to export competitiveness, as the ringgit has been kept at an artificially low MYR3.8/US$ while the currencies of Asian competitors have recovered.

The major taxation change affecting business in the 1999 budget was the waiving of tax on income derived in 1999. This is a result of a move towards tax assessment based on earnings in the current year, rather than the preceding year under the old system, starting in 2000. Of course, corporate income for 1999 was reduced and there was a need to make provisions for bad loans and absorb the higher cost of imported parts and components, but the waiver gave a welcome boost to corporate earnings, while losses incurred in 1999 are also allowed to be carried forward. In addition, the official assessment system will be changed to a self-assessment system for companies starting in 2001. The 2000 budget also contained a number of growth-friendly provisions:

■ Pump-priming capital outlays on physical and social infrastructure;

■ An across-the-board one percentage point fall in personal income tax rates and a rise in the nominal threshold;

■ A generous package for 800,000 civil servants;

■ Import duties on 43 food categories abolished and lowered on 136 others, with tariff cuts on other consumer goods.

Privatisation Derailed

Privatisation has been official policy since 1983 and, as of mid-2000, 457 privatisations had taken place. But the pace of privatisation has been variable and the 1997-98 crisis, with the accompanying falls on the Kuala Lumpur Stock Exchange and the imposition of capital controls, has caused a decline in both domestic and foreign interest. Government revenues from privatisation fell short of their targets in 1998-99. Moreover, it has become clear that many past privatisations have not been successful. Government assets have been given cheap to inept *bumiputra* cronies, who could not cope when business declined, calling on the government for support. A dispute over bailouts given to privatised companies in trouble was one of the reasons why Anwar fell out with Mahathir. The government has admitted that mistakes have been made. Finance Minister Daim Zainuddin said in February 1999 that past privatisations had not been properly assessed and government guarantees had been given too easily. A year later the chief minister of Sabah ordered that all government projects involving privatisation be examined by the state privatisation committee before going ahead. There have been numerous calls for a more transparent privatisation process, which seeks to avoid the creation of monopolies. Among the large government-owned infrastructure enterprises slated for privatisation (sale of more than 50%) in the near future are Bintulu Port and Malayan Railways, the latter delayed from its scheduled 1998 privatisation.

The K-economy

The crisis of 1997-98 highlighted the danger posed to the economy by what is now seen as an excessive reliance on the import-intensive electronics sector. During the 1990s this sector grew very rapidly, contributing to an overall annual average growth rate of 13.9% a year in manufacturing value-added. But the upstream and downstream linkages were weak. Domestic value-added was comparatively low – the 13.9% annual average growth in manufacturing value-added comparing with an annual average growth in gross domestic investment of 18.4% in 1987-97 – and there was a high dependence on imported components, and on a rather narrow export market.

Other structural weaknesses identified before the release of the second Industrial Master Plan (IMP2) included an excessive reliance on imported labour (at both the highly-skilled and unskilled ends of the spectrum) and a dependence on imports of trade-related services.

New worries have been added by the growth of the global information and communications technology-based market. A survey conducted by the Malaysian External Trade Development Corporation in April 1999 found that few had e-commerce strategies and only 24.3% had on-line product catalogues. Only a handful of the country's small- and medium-sized companies (SMEs) had done on-line business as of January 2000. All this is despite efforts by the government to promote IT and its usage, including the Multimedia Super Corridor, set up in 1996 to provide a gateway for Malaysian users to the IT and multimedia spheres.

The government's response has been to call loudly for the development in Malaysia of a knowledge-based economy and manufacturing sector, one in which growth in value-added is driven by the increased application of technology and knowledge rather than the addition of capacity, based on ever-higher levels of fixed investment.

From P to K

The goal, as set out in the most recent Bank Negara Malaysia (BNM) annual report, is to move from a production-based economy (P-economy) to a knowledge-based economy (K-economy). Essentially this entails a leap in the value-added of the manufacturing sector and its close integration with services such as marketing, in a process where the search for sales volume and market share is replaced by a concentration on providing customised products and associated services in market niches. The competitive advantage in such an economy ceases to be based entirely on labour cost and becomes a more complex offering, which needs continuous upgrading.

According to estimates based on 1997 data quoted in the 1999 BNM report, only 10.1% of the Malaysian workforce had the requisite K-skills, compared with about 15% in South Korea and Taiwan, and about 25% in Singapore and Japan. In terms of R&D spend and the K-skill intensity of R&D, Malaysia was identified as lagging even more seriously. A K-economy master plan, due to be published in June 2000, will address these issues and suggest a strategic approach that will have important implications for industrial policy.

Foreign Investment Policy

Maximum Foreign Ownership Share Raised

Despite outbursts of rhetoric against the evils of Western economic imperialism, history has left Malaysia with a large stock of foreign investment, which accounts for about 30% of total equity holding on the Kuala Lumpur Stock Exchange (KLSE). Although the annual inflows are not large by regional standards, the role of the foreign-invested sector in the real economy is important and a supportive policy in reality tempers the periodic anti-Western rhetoric that is driven by domestic political considerations. In recent years, Malaysia has steered investment away from simple assembly operations, towards higher technology, capital-intensive manufacturing and services that make greater use of intellectual capital and produce a higher value-added per employee. To discourage labour-intensive operations, Malaysia requires that new investment in manufacturing meets a minimum capital intensity ratio of MYR55,000 per employee.

The incentives aimed to encourage investment in high-technology industries and stimulate R&D are particularly attractive. For companies involved in new and emerging technologies, these include a 100% tax exemption and a 60% investment tax allowance (ITA) during the first five years. For companies involved in strategic projects, such as heavy capital investment and high technology, with a significant impact on the Malaysian economy, the full tax exemption is extended to 10 years and the ITA raised to 100% for five years. Companies involved in R&D, benefit from either a tax exemption or ITA, or tax deductions on R&D expenditure. There is also a broad range of incentives, including direct grants and long-term low interest rate loans, to encourage the development of electronic chip manufacturing and the Multimedia Super Corridor.

In response to the economic slowdown, in February 1998 Malaysia increased the maximum foreign holding in Malaysian wholesale and retail operations from 30% to 51%, and to 61% in telecommunications companies. In August, it permitted full ownership by foreign investors in new manufacturing projects, without the need to have to meet export conditions, provided the investment was made before 2001. It is expected that this provision may be extended beyond 2001, and a decision on this is anticipated during 2000.

Capital Controls Are Eased, Not Removed

Malaysia partially eased its exchange controls at the start of February 1999 and imposed an exit tax on foreign portfolio investments. The new tax discourages short-term investment and capital flows by imposing a sliding scale from 30% to 0%, depending on the length of the period the funds have been held in Malaysia. Profits on new foreign investment will be taxed at 30% if taken out of the country within one year, and at 10% after one year. Some US$3-6bn of foreign equity investment has been trapped in Malaysia since September 1998, when capital controls were imposed for a period of 12 months. The new tax encourages new foreign investors to keep their money in the country for at least a year, while it also helped to limit portfolio outflows when the temporary ban expired in September 1999. But the new rule also makes it more difficult for Malaysian equities to compete for foreign funds with other regional stock markets, where the return on investment is not taxed at a minimum 10%.

The Malaysian authorities point to the combination of currency and capital controls introduced in 1998 as the prime reason for the rapid return of macroeconomic stability and non-inflationary growth. The IMF has admitted that the measures played a role, while at the same time pointing out that strong external demand was the key to bringing the Asian economies out of recession. The Malaysian government claims that the controls enhanced the foreign investment regime and bolstered confidence by imparting stability: net FDI rose to MYR13.4bn (US$3.5bn) in 1999, which was 4.8% of GNP, up from MYR10.6bn in 1998. As usual, most of the FDI inflows in 1999 went into manufacturing (47%), followed by services (27%) and oil and gas (24%). In the manufacturing sector, MRY12.27bn worth of investment was approved in 1999, down 6.1% on the previous year, with the bulk (82.2%) going to electrical and electronic products, petroleum and petrochemical products and paper, printing and publishing.

Gestures for 2000

The 2000 budget contained moves intended to reassure foreign investors. The ceiling of one year's net profit, or the average of the previous two years' dividends on repatriation of profits imposed in 1998, was lifted. A high level committee was to be established at the ministry of finance to consider the granting of special incentive packages, including a review of the limits on overseas equity in key sectors. This would represent a potential step forward from the temporary lifting of restrictions on manufacturing investments made before 2001, if it led to any dilution of the 30% *bumiputra* ownership rule under the National Development Policy. The committee will sit for six months.

The market index fell by 53% between the end of 1996 and the end of 1998, and then the KLSE Composite Index rose by 39% in 1999. The prospect of a very strong rebound in foreign investor interest remains somewhat muted by currency controls. But the inclusion of Malaysia in the Morgan Stanley Capital International Index, slated for the end of May 2000, was expected to give the market a further fillip (*see Capital Markets*).

Foreign Trade Policy

Mahathir Versus The US

The virulent criticism of Mahathir's policies by Western, especially American, bankers and politicians, may give the impression that the Malaysian government is not committed to free trade, but nothing could be further from the truth. Mahathir's refusal to accept the verdict of freely operating capital markets have not made him an advocate of managed trade. His rejection of the US linkage between free trade in goods with unrestricted capital markets and unfettered international capital flows is increasingly shared in the rest of Asia, where the US belief that free trade inevitably culminates in (US-style) democracy has never been accepted. Malaysia is heavily dependent on foreign trade and has been a strong supporter of trade liberalisation.

Malaysia has given active support to the setting up of regional economic arrangements, but it has tried to exclude the US or limit US participation as much as possible. For this reason, Malaysia's most important trade alliance is the Association of South East Asian Nations (Asean), which consists of Brunei, Indonesia, Laos, Malaysia, Myanmar, the Philippines, Singapore, Vietnam, Thailand and Cambodia. Human rights violations in the participating countries are largely ignored, to the irritation of the US and EU.

Mahathir has been a strong advocate of an Asian counterbalance to the North American Free Trade Association (Nafta) and the European Union (EU) and the perceived American influence in multilateral organisations such as the World Trade Organisation (WTO) and the International Monetary Fund (IMF), but his proposal for an East Asian Economic Caucus (EAEC) never got off the ground. The EAEC consists of Asean together with China, Hong Kong, South Korea and Taiwan, but it excludes the main regional economic power, Japan, which refused to join because it did not want to offend the US. The Asian recession, which forced many countries to ask the IMF for help, weakened any resolve to take collective action. Japan, however, has become more determined to play a regional role, as is evident in the Miyazawa Initiative, and its proposals for an Asian IMF. As tension over excessive Asian trade surpluses with the US grows, Asia may begin to show greater unity of purpose, and Mahathir's criticism of the US may seem less out of place. Proposals to establish and formalise ways in which Asian economies might resist speculative attacks on their currencies, involving swap agreements between central banks, continue to be heard.

Tariffs And Duties Are Cut

In 1992, Asean set up the Asean Free Trade Area (Afta), which is working towards the implementation of a common effective preferential tariff (CEPT) to provide concessional tariffs for intra-Asean trade. The original deadline of 2008 was brought forward to 2000, to which most Asean members are committed on a voluntary basis. Malaysia cut import duties on 2,600 products in 1995 and 1,500 items in 1996, including raw materials, components and equipment. Protectionist tariffs have been reduced, in part because Malaysia's tariff exemptions under the GATT General System of Preferences (GSP) came to an end in January 1997.

While the 1998 budget included few cuts in tariffs and sales taxes, there were some increases in tariffs, for instance on cars and construction materials, to discourage luxury imports or protect critical domestic sectors. The 1999 budget proposed only minor changes in tariffs. But the better economic climate in 1999 led to tariff cuts or abolition of import duties across a wide range of food and non-food consumer goods, including, shoes, textiles and furniture, in the 2000 budget. Malaysia has a (short) list of prohibited imports and protects some products with high tariffs and import licenses, while it restricts access to foreign service providers, especially finance and professional services. Within Afta, however, Malaysia has pushed hard for the opening up of trade in services and the protection of intellectual property rights and it has demonstrated a pragmatic attitude towards foreign access.

Apec Trade Liberalisation Runs Out Of Steam

With the change in the economic climate, Afta's target for CEPT implementation by 2000 looks improbable. Asean's narrow regional basis has become a weakness, because the Afta arrangements do not include two of its major markets, Japan and the US. It was all the more important, therefore, that the Apec meeting of Pacific-rim countries in Kuala Lumpur in late-1998 should not have ended in failure. Apec leaders in 1997 set themselves the target of choosing 15 sectors for trade liberalisation, with the target of establishing free trade by 2010 for advanced economies, and by 2020 for others.

Plans for the first nine sectors got into serious trouble, with the refusal by Japan to open up its politically sensitive fish and forestry sectors. The conference fudged a solution by agreeing to transfer the talks to the WTO, with the aim of including many more countries in a deal by the end of 1999. Growing US dissatisfaction over its huge trade deficit with Asia is an ominous indication that the climate is not right for further trade liberalisation.

Afta On Target

Meanwhile, in the absence of progress on trade liberalisation under the Apec umbrella, and in the wake of the failed WTO meeting in the US in 1999, Malaysia has pressed on with its Afta commitments: as of January 2000 it had included 8,859 products – 96% of its quota – in the list under the CEPT scheme. The Ministry of International Trade and Industry (Miti) claims that Afta is near realising its targets; for the six early members (Brunei, Indonesia, the Philippines, Singapore, Thailand and Malaysia) the average tariff reached 3.52% in January 2000, and was expected to fall to 2.9% the following year, according to Malaysian data. The average for all of Asean was 4.9%. In September 1999 an informal summit agreed to extend the deadline for elimination of import duties to 2010, allowing the four new members (Laos, Cambodia, Vietnam and Myanmar) until 2015.

Bureaucracy And Corruption

Bailout Through The Back Door

There have been many examples of well-connected companies being saved by injections of funds from government institutions, of banks having their arms twisted to continue to lend to businesses with doubtful prospects, of contracts being broken and concessions being rewritten to ensure the survival of companies in need. The government has admitted that the severity of the corporate crisis can at least in part be blamed on lax controls and favouritism during the privatisations of the 1990s, and the *bumiputra* policies, which shifted economic power away from ethnic Chinese to the majority ethnic Malay population. The widespread misallocation of funds was, sooner or later, bound to lead to company failures.

Yet, the early-March 1999 announcement of a new debt restructuring plan for Malaysia's largest conglomerate, **Renong Bhd**, is an indication that cronyism is alive and kicking in Malaysia. The restructuring involves a MYR8.41bn (US$2.2bn) bond issue to repay the debts of both Renong and its associate **United Engineers Bhd** (UEM). Under the plan proposed by Renong and the central bank's Corporate Debt Restructuring Committee, UEM subsidiary, **Projek Lebuhraya Utara-Selatan Bhd** (PLUS), which enjoys a strong cashflow from tolls on the 848km North-South Expressway, would issue the bonds. That PLUS's highway concession was recently extended by 12 years to 2030 and was highlighted, by opposition leader Lim Kit Siang, as evidence that the next generation of Malaysians will be asked to bail out Renong and UEM.

With Renong accounting for around 5% of non-performing loans in Malaysia, there are genuine systemic concerns and, consequently, some hope that alleviating the problems of this "national institution" will produce a virtuous circle of relief for the wider macro and micro environments. Moreover, there was little chance that the politically-connected corporate – formally the business arm of the ruling UMNO Party – would be allowed to go bust. The new deal is better than the original restructuring plan, which involved the government underwriting bond issues worth MYR10.5bn to bail out Renong, but it still amounts to an indirect bailout, albeit a more long-winded one that involves large-scale evergreening as new lenders bail out old lenders. Essentially, Malaysia's financial sector – banks, pension funds and insurance companies – will be arm-twisted into buying the seven-year PLUS bonds, which, even with yields of 10%, look distinctly non-commercial. However, the government is hopeful of attracting some foreign buyers, although these will require a comprehensive set of guarantees. Long term, Renong and UEM will hope that a recovery in asset values averts another crunch.

With the PLUS subsidiary being used as a cash cow, other losers will be UEM shareholders, although it has always been a case of *caveat emptor* when jumping into UEM – those who live by political connections, sometimes choke on them. There is also some concern that, despite the appointment of seven new directors, Renong's old management, led by UMNO insider Abdul

Halim Saad, is still in place and remains largely unaccountable. And, while the waiver of a MYR900mn government loan to Renong over the second Singapore fixed link may be acceptable in the context of an official failure to honour agreed toll rates, the restructuring plan only tackles half of the corporate's problems, with its telecom and hotel units remaining technically insolvent.

Environmental Regulation

Fighting Vested Interests

Malaysia's most serious environmental air pollution was caused by forest fires in Indonesia, which covered many parts of the country in a dense haze from mid-July to early November 1997, harming health, tourism, agriculture and the ecological system. Many fires started up again in 1998 and in 1999, also in Malaysian Borneo, due to the drought caused by El Niño. The pollution has stimulated environmental awareness and regional environmental cooperation, but it is doubtful whether the Asean action plan to prevent haze can achieve much during Asia's economic downturn and Indonesia's political crisis.

Even when times were good, the environment did not come high on the list of Malaysian priorities, although the political sensitivity of pollution issues has increased, as is clear from the passing of new regulations to control vehicle emissions in 1996. Malaysia has drafted a national policy on biological diversity and a national environment policy in recent years, stung possibly by accusations from abroad that it is squandering its natural resources, but change is not easy, given the vested economic and political interests. Part of the problem is that managing forests is often a state responsibility, and logging permits have frequently been connected with the payment of bribes. Malaysia's environmental objectives also include the conservation, not only of the natural but also the cultural heritage, and the achievement of sustainable lifestyles, patterns of production and consumption. The worst examples of aggressive over-exploitation of forest resources and suppression of the native ways of living have been seen in Sarawak. The state recently held a workshop on fire management at which it was revealed that Sarawak currently has about 5,000ha of planted forest, only 0.5% of the amount targeted for planting. The construction slump in Japan and South East Asia will probably do more for conservation than legislation. In April, it was announced that the Environment Quality Act 1974 will be amended to allow the ministry of science, technology and the environment to prevent the development of projects with an adverse impact on the environment.

5 Capital Markets

Equity Markets

Battling Against The Storm

Malaysian equity investors have gone through a protracted period of pain since the KLSE Composite Index (KLSE CI) reached a high of 1271.57 points in April 1997. In the period that followed, the country's economic strengths appeared to unravel, major corporations became virtually bankrupt, a large part of the financial system crashed, the ringgit plunged, Malaysia's sovereign rating was downgraded and its political stability called into question. At the start of September 1998, after the imposition of capital controls (*see below*) and the reversal of tight fiscal and monetary policies, the KLSE CI reached a low of 262.7, a level only one-fifth of the previous peak. New economic policies and restrictions on foreign sellers gave equities a huge boost, while the market largely ignored the growing political protests that followed former deputy premier Anwar Ibrahim's arrest. In the six months that followed the September watershed, share prices more than doubled.

Sentiment improved significantly in Q2 99, when the KLSE CI rose from 527 points on April 1 to pass the key 800-point resistance level on June 24. Investor confidence was boosted by improving industrial production and trade data, coupled with a string of credit rating upgrades and a successful global bond issue. The market capitalisation of the KLSE CI rose by 67% to MYR532bn over the period. The third quarter brought a more bearish period for the market, with the exception of a brief period in August when **Morgan Stanley Capital International** announced that Malaysia would be re-included in the MSCI benchmark indices. Sentiment waned on fears of a US interest rate hike, which dampened confidence elsewhere in the region. Concerns that the end to the 12-month holding period on portfolio flows – which subsequently proved to be overblown – also weighed on the KLSE CI, which ended the quarter on 675.5 points.

The postponement of Malaysia's reinstatement into the Morgan Stanley Capital International indices (from February to May 2000) and political uncertainty surrounding the general election in November, weighed on market sentiment in Q4 99, despite the announcement of a pro-growth budget. But the KLSE CI rose strongly towards the year-end as political uncertainty eased and investors snapped up technology buys. The Composite Index ended the year at 812.33 points, with market capitalisation up 47.6% y-o-y at MYR552.7bn (US$145.4bn).

Capital Controls – The Right Medicine?

In an effort to stem the outflow of capital in the wake of the Asian financial crisis, Malaysia imposed capital controls and pegged its currency in September 1998. A one-year ban on the repatriation of foreign portfolio investment was widely criticised by foreign investors. But Malaysia's stock and bond markets have, apparently, prospered under capital controls. The KLSE CI had gained 123% by the end of December 1999, from a low of 262.7 points reached on September 1 1998. The partial relaxation of capital controls in February 1999 – when the one-year ban was replaced by a graduated foreign capital gains tax ranging from 10-30% – was not followed by large-scale selling, with the capital markets boosted by interest rate cuts. The feared monetisation of the government deficit never took place and the steeply inverted yield curve which characterised the first half of 1998 had reverted to a more normal profile by autumn 1999. In September 1999, Bank Negara announced a flat 10% tax on foreign capital gains. There has been much speculation that this will be removed now that the economy is well along the recovery path, but the central bank reiterated early in 2000 that it had no plans to do so

Clob Share Dispute: Resolution In Sight

Although the KLSE does not appear to have suffered, and indeed arguably has benefited, from the imposition of capital controls, the long-term implications are less clear cut. While strong fundamentals will continue to attract portfolio inflows to Malaysia in the medium-term, the authorities' decision to intervene in the market invariably adds a risk premium to any future investments, particularly if the economy experiences a downturn. In this respect, the resolution of the Central Limit Order Book (Clob) share dispute is welcome. In the region of MYR17bn (US$4.5bn) worth of Clob shares – Malaysian shares previously traded on Singapore's over-the-counter-market – were frozen when Malaysia imposed capital controls in September 1998. Prime Minister Mahathir Mohamad claimed that Singapore-based speculators had deliberately used Clob to drive down the Malaysian Stock Market and currency.

In February, the Malaysian authorities gave the go ahead for **Effective Capital** – established by Singapore businessman Akbar Khan who has close links to Finance Minister Daim Zainuddin – to act as a shelf company for the shares. Investors have been given three options: Either pay a 1.5% transfer commission to Effective Capital to get their shares back over a 13-month period beginning June 31; pay a 1% 'administrative fee' to Malaysia's securities clearing house and wait up to three and a half years to regain control of their shares; or have their shares transferred to the Finance Ministry as unclaimed. Given the poor alternatives, Effective Capital has predicted a 90% take up of its offer, described by the Securities Investors Association of Singapore (SIAS), which represents more than 50,000 Clob investors, as "the best deal under the circumstances." The SIAS had argued for the release of shares over 12 months without penalty, but no previously proposed private sector solution was recognised by the KLSE.

Capital Market Developments

A number of initiatives were introduced in 1999 to improve Malaysia's capital market. On January 1, the Code on Take-overs and Mergers came into effect, to enhance transparency and protect minority interests. This includes provisions to ensure that minority shareholders are given the relevant information to make an informed decision, and the imposition of criminal liability on parties that provide false or misleading information. This was followed on March 25 by a Finance Committee Report on Corporate Governance, containing 70 recommendations to enhance corporate governance standards. An Implementation Project Team has been established to oversee the introduction of the Report's recommendations. And on April 1, restrictions were placed on the number of directorships that may be held by directors of public listed companies (PLCs), to improve corporate governance.

To enhance transparency, from June, 18 companies have been required to present their financial records in accordance with accounting standards issued by the Malaysian Accounting Standards Board. And from July 31, PLCs have been required to file financial statements with the KLSE on a quarterly basis, with the aim of strengthening corporate accountability and disclosure, as well as to aid investors in making informed investment decisions. Capital Adequacy Requirements were introduced on May 28.

To strengthen the financial position of PLCs, revisions were made on April 30 to the requirements for KLSE listings, reverse take-overs and back-door listings. These include more stringent profit track records and higher minimum issued and paid-up capital for companies seeking listing on the KLSE. And in the 2000 budget, tax incentives were introduced to encourage the consolidation of stockbroking companies, including stamp duty and property gains tax exemptions on all mergers completed between October 30 1999 and end-2000.

The Institutional Settlement Service (ISS) was inaugurated on 15 July, allowing custodian banks and institutional investors to participate directly in the clearing and settlement process. An integrated electronic share application system was launched on August 26 to ease the application process.

Options And Futures

At the beginning of 1999, the KLSE completed its acquisition of the Kuala Lumpur Options and Financial Futures Exchange (KLOFFE). The futures exchange is upgrading its trading system with the Eurex software of the German Bourse, which should make it easier for KLOFFE to link up with other international exchanges in the years ahead. KLOFFE, which currently offers KLSE Composite Index futures, may introduce new products, such as options on the KLSE Composite Index and individual stock options. The bond market may also develop into a genuine, broad-based market because of the need to refinance corporate restructuring and create a secondary market for the restructured corporate assets.

Bond Markets

A Liquid Market

Malaysia's bond and money markets rallied strongly in 1999, benefiting from falling interest rates and improved economic fundamentals. Capital controls encouraged the return of funds parked by residents in the Singaporean offshore market to take advantage of higher interest rates. The bond market grew by 28.1% over the year from MYR157.3bn to MYR201.5bn, driven predominantly by the issuance of private debt security (PDS), by the national asset management company Danaharta for corporate debt restructuring, and the purchase of non-performing loans. Bond market liquidity – the ratio of trading volume to amount outstanding – rose from 28.9% in 1998 to 77.4% in 1999. The government raised a 10-year US$1bn bond in May, which was oversubscribed by 300%.

A spate of credit rating upgrades – on improved economic fundamentals, progress on restructuring, the easing of capital controls and greater political stability – served as a further boost to Malaysian bonds in 1999. At the start of April 1999, **Standard & Poor's** upgraded its outlook for the country from negative to stable, to reflect improved foreign sentiment, but affirmed its BBB- long-term foreign currency rating. **Moody's**, by contrast, stuck in mid-March to a negative outlook, which it based on the potentially negative medium-term effects of capital controls and the fixed ringgit exchange rate, such as distortions in capital flows and loss of competitiveness, as well as rising political instability. It warned that political events might make it difficult for the government to return to a more open regime, while a continued rise in problem assets could lead to growing problems in the financial sector and affect liquidity. But in October 1999, it upgraded Malaysia's foreign currency rating to a positive outlook

Standard & Poor's upgraded Malaysia's foreign currency sovereign rating to BBB in November 1999, on the basis of a "stronger-than-anticipated export-led recovery, which will help to reduce fiscal pressure generated by bank and corporate restructuring." Moody's did not follow suit, but in late February 2000 vice president, Stephen Hess, said the credit ratings agency may upgrade Malaysia within the next 18 months, based on the country's increased external liquidity, solid export performance and progress made on corporate and banking sector restructuring. This might not be to pre-crisis levels, however, which would depend on how successful the restructuring process is.

The National Bond Market Committee (NBMC) was established in 1999 to rationalise the regulatory framework for the development of Malaysia's bond market and advise on appropriate strategies to deepen the market. To enhance market development, the 2000 budget saw the introduction of stamp duty and real property gains tax exemptions for asset securitisation, effective from October 30, 1999 until end-2000.

PHILIPPINES 2000

Analyst: Teresa Habitan

Editor: Sara Matchett

Contents

Political Outlook _____ **257**

Domestic Political Outlook 257
Foreign Policy 263

Profile and Recent Developments _____ **264**

The Political System 264
Foreign Policy 268

Economic Outlook _____ **271**

Economic Activity 271
Fiscal Policy 273
Monetary Policy 276
Exchange Rate Policy 277
Balance Of Payments 278
Foreign Direct Investment 280
External Debt 281

Profile and Recent Developments _____ **282**

Characteristics Of The Economy 282
Economic Activity 283

Key Economic Sectors _____ **287**

Introduction 287
Manufacturing 288
Services 292
Transport And Communications 293
Retail Trade 295
Power 296
Financial Services 297
Property 299

Profile and Recent Developments _____ **301**

Introduction 301
Manufacturing 302
Food And Beverages 303
Agriculture, Fishery And Forestry 306
Transport And Communications 307
Finance And Insurance 310
Construction And Property 312

Business Environment _____ **315**

Infrastructure 315
The Domestic Market.. 316
The Labour Market 318
Industrial Policy 319
Foreign Investment Policy 321
Foreign Trade Policy.. 322
Bureaucracy And Corruption 323
Environmental Regulation 324

Capital Markets _____ **327**

Introduction 327
Equity Markets 328
Bond Markets 331

PHILIPPINES: MACROECONOMIC DATA AND FORECASTS

	1993	1994	1995	1996	1997	1998	1999e	2000f	2001f	2002f
Population (mn)	63.7	65.3	67.0	68.6	70.3	71.9	73.5	75.2	76.9	78.6
Nominal GDP (US$bn)	45.4	53.0	54.4	64.1	74.1	83.8	82.2	65.5	76.7	79.3
GDP per capita (US$)	812	934	1,055	1,165	1,118	871	997	1,009	1,058	1,056
Real GDP growth (% y/y)	2.1	4.4	4.7	5.8	5.2	-0.6	3.2	3.5	4.5	5.5
Real GNP growth (% y/y)	1.3	5.3	4.9	7.2	5.3	0.4	3.6	3.8	4.6	5.6
Value of production (% y/y)	17.6	13.8	17.1	9.2	8.8	-2.1	8.5	9.0	10.5	12.0
Annual inflation (% y/y, period avg)	7.0	8.3	8.0	5.1	6.0	9.6	6.8	5.4	5.6	5.0
91-day T-bills (%, eop)	12.4	12.7	11.8	12.3	12.9	15.0	10.0	9.1	10.2	9.8
Deposit Rate (% an. avg)	9.6	10.5	8.4	9.7	10.2	12.1	8.2	10.3	10.8	10.3
Lending Rate (% an. avg)	14.7	15.1	14.7	14.8	16.3	16.8	11.8	12.5	13.0	12.5
PHP/US$ (an. avg)	27.12	26.42	25.71	26.22	29.47	40.89	39.09	41.50	43.00	44.20
PHP/US$ (eop)	27.70	24.42	26.21	26.29	39.98	39.06	40.31	42.00	43.40	44.80
Exports (fob, US$bn)	11.37	13.48	17.45	20.54	25.23	29.50	35.03	38.02	41.92	46.11
Imports (fob, US$bn)	17.60	21.33	26.54	32.43	35.93	29.66	30.73	35.76	40.48	45.34
Trade balance (US$bn)	-6.22	-7.85	-9.09	-11.88	-10.71	-0.16	4.31	2.26	1.44	0.78
Current account (US$bn)	-3.0	-3.0	-2.0	-4.0	-4.3	1.3	7.2	5.8	4.7	3.8
Current account (% GDP)	-5.5	-4.6	-2.7	-4.7	-5.2	2.0	9.4	7.3	5.5	4.4
Foreign reserves (US$bn eop)*	4.7	6.0	6.4	10.0	7.3	9.2	13.2	12.7	12.5	12.4
Import cover (mths)**	3.2	3.4	2.9	3.7	2.4	3.7	5.2	4.2	3.7	3.3
External debt (US$bn)	35.5	38.7	39.4	41.9	45.4	47.8	52.2	54.0	56.1	58.2
External debt (% GDP)	65.4	60.4	53.1	50.0	55.2	73.0	68.1	68.1	65.9	67.0

*e/f = BMI estimate/forecast. * excludes gold, ** no. of months imports covered by FX reserves + gold. Sources: Central Bank/IMF/NSCB/BMI.*

1 Political Outlook

Domestic Political Outlook

Mounting Controversies

Political uncertainty deepened in early 2000, as President Joseph Estrada faced a slew of scandals linking him and his family and friends to an array of misdeeds and misconduct. Alleged coddling of a friend linked to stock market insider trading, the pardon of a particularly vicious convicted killer, and accusations of influence peddling in the use of the state sweepstakes fund were the defining themes of the Estrada administration's first quarter storm. Adding to the heat were a loquacious chief of staff and an eruption of fighting between the army and Muslim seperatist rebels in the island of Mindanao. As the year got underway, the fighting in Mindanao began to acquire increasingly national proportions.

The Estrada presidency is struggling to maintain credibility as a series of scandals and a breakout of hostilities in Mindanao vie for attention.

An Unredeemed Pledge

An insider trading charge against **BW Resources**, owned by Estrada's friend, Dante Tan, almost closed the Philippine Stock Exchange in March. The Securities and Exchange Commission chief, Perfecto Yasay, Jr had disclosed in January that the president had called him on several occasions last year to discuss the involvement of Dante Tan in stock price manipulation. BW is the subject of probes by the stock exchange, the SEC, and the Senate after its stock price rose 5,000% in 1999, and then dropped as quickly.

The BW Resources share price fixing scandal, involving a friend of Estrada, has rocked investor sentiment.

A report by the surveillance and compliance group of the Philippine Stock Exchange (PSE) indicated the presence of enough material to establish *prima facie* evidence of price stock manipulation and insider trading against Tan. The same report also said that at least eight member brokers were liable for complicity, and recommended sanctions against those found to be violating securities laws. In a dramatic twist, the entire surveillance and compliance group later resigned in protest at what they claimed as moves by PSE members to whitewash the results of their investigation. This move prompted Yasay to declare that stock trading would be suspended, unless the group was taken back in by the PSE. Last-minute negotiations by the government's

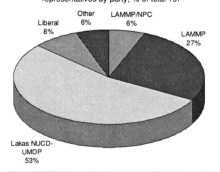

The Good Old Days
Philippines - 1998 election results, seats in the house of representatives by party, % of total 197

Other 6%
Liberal 8%
LAMMP/NPC 6%
LAMMP 27%
Lakas NUCD-UMDP 53%

Source: Philippine Senate and Commission on Elections.

economic managers with the other commissioners of the SEC led to an overturn of Yasay's decision.

While the Philippine stock markets lived to open another day, investor interest remained largely on the sell option. Meanwhile, the president has been making moves to distance himself from the probe and its potential outcome. He has been quoted as saying that, "regardless of who is involved, whether relative or friend, they should face the music. If they are found guilty, they should be meted with the proper punishment". This is an echo of his inaugural speech in 1998, when Estrada pledged that there would be no friend or relative influencing or taking advantage of presidential decisions and authority. Investors, domestic and foreign, are keeping a close eye on how well the president heeds his vow.

THE PHILIPPINES CABINET	
President	**Joseph Estrada**
Vice president & Secretary of Social Welfare & Development	**Gloria Macapagal-Arroyo**
Executive Secretary	Ronaldo Zamora
Secretary of Agrarian Reform	Horacio Morales
Secretary of Agriculture	Edgardo Angara
Secretary of Budget & Management	Benjamin Diokno
Secretary of Education, Culture & Sports	Andrew Gonzalez
Secretary of Energy	Mario Tiaoqui
Secretary of Environment & Natural Resources	Antonio Cerilles
Secretary of Finance	Edgardo Espiritu
Secretary of Foreign Affairs	Domingo Siazon, Jr.
Secretary of Health	Alberto Romualdez, Jr.
Secretary of Interior & Local Government	Ronaldo Puno
Secretary of Justice	Serafin Cuevas
Secretary of Labour & Employment	Bienvenido Laguesma
Secretary of National Defense	Orlando Mercado
Secretary of Public Works & Highways	Gregorio Vigilar
Secretary of Science & Technology	Filemon Uriarte, Jr.
Secretary of Tourism	Gemma Cruz-Araneta
Secretary of Trade & Industry	Jose Pardo
Secretary of Transportation & Communications	Vicente Rivera, Jr.
Director-General, National Economic & Development Authority	Felipe Medalla
Press Secretary	Rodolfo Reyes
Cabinet Secretary	Leonora Vasquez-De Jesus
Source: BMI.	

Cronyism Rears Its Ugly Head

However the controversy which wracked the Philippine Charity Sweepstakes Office (PCSO) again demonstrates the tendency of the president to be quick to the defense of his family, and slow to remember his inaugural pledge. When allegations of inappropriate channeling of PCSO funds were made against the First Lady and the president's eldest son, Jinggoy Estrada, Estrada immediately went to their defense. Unfortunately the accuser, Sister Christine Tan, who was among members of the PCSO board replaced by Estrada in his cabinet revamp and who has worked tirelessly for Manila's impoverished slum dwellers, had too much credibility to be easily disregarded. Shortly after being sacked, Christine Tan wrote to major newspapers and charged that state lottery funds were being used to further the interests of the president and his family, both charitable and uncharitable. The allegations inspired another Senate investigation, in which the First Lady and the president's son were called to testify. The minutes of the PSCO board meetings indicated that some 200 ambulances bought by the PCSO were distributed to different municipalities across the country. While this is normal practice, this time the distribution was carried out by Jinggoy Estrada. The nun also alleged that Jinggoy Estrada had erased the PCSO logos on the ambulances and replaced them with his name.

The First Family has denied any wrongdoing, claiming that none of the requests were illegal. While basically true, the aura of heavy political patronage continues to imbue developments with a heavy stench. In the end, investigations may show that nothing was indeed illegal in the disbursement of state lottery funds. Whether or not these "legal" expenditures are appropriate is an entirely different issue. Local elections in 2001 are not that far off and Jinggoy Estrada has been known to entertain aspirations of running for senator when his third term as local mayor expires next year.

Gunfire In The South And Bomb Scares In Manila

While political scandals wracked Metro Manila, government forces fought gun battles with Muslim separatists in the southern Philippines island of Mindanao. Hundreds of civilians in villages in Maguindanao province were caught as clashes flared between the army and the Moro Islamic Liberation Front (MILF). What started as a pocket sized case of rebel activity earlier this year is fast becoming a nationwide concern, acquiring international notoriety. In March, rebels from the Abu Sayaf, a splinter group, abducted more than 70 students and teachers, including a Catholic priest, on Basilan Island. Even more serious, was the brazen kidnapping by Abu Sayaf of 21 tourists from a Malaysian resort on April 23, 2000. As the Philippines 2000 annual went to press, they were still being held hostage in the jungles of southern

Estrada has been all to quick to jump to the defense of his family, accused of channeling funds from PCSO to further their own interests.

A Regional Concern
Corruption Perception Index

World Ranking	Country	CPI Score*
7	Singapore	9.1
16	Hong Kong	7.8
29	Malaysia	5.3
29	Taiwan	5.3
43	South Korea	4.2
52	China	3.5
55	**Philippines**	**3.3**
61	Thailand	3.0
66	India	2.9
71	Pakistan	2.7
74	Vietnam	2.5
80	Indonesia	2.0

Source: Transparency International; *10 = highly clean; 0 = highly corrupt.

Muslim separatist sentiment in certain provinces of Mindanao is waylaying government plans development the potentially fruitful area.

Confidence Plummets
Philippines - stock exchange, Manila Composite Index

Source: Reuters/BMI.

The Philippine military is ill-equipped to fight a full-blown war with the Muslim separatists in Mindanao.

Mindanao. The hostages included nine Malaysians, three Germans, two French, two South Africans, two Finns, two Filipinos and one Lebanese, and consequently attracted both widespread international media interest and diplomatic action from a host of countries and the European Union. Multinational pressure now bears down on the Estrada administration for a swift and peaceful release of the hostages.

Compounding the seriousness of the situation, is a spate of bombings linked to Muslim rebels of two major shopping malls in Metro Manila. Though just only one life has been lost, the amount of negative international publicity being generated is further burying the country's image in mud.

Mindanao has long been called the Philippines' land of promise. It has rich natural resources and has the potential to become the country's food basket. Intermittent skirmishes with rebellious Muslim groups have left much of that promise unfulfilled. In the years after a peace agreement with the main Muslim group – the Moro National Liberation Front (MNLF) – was reached in 1996, government funds, as well as international donor funds, have poured into the region. In response, trade and development have made progress in many of Mindanao's regions like General Santos, Cagayan de Oro, and Davao. However, the five provinces (Maguindanao, Lanao del Sur, Basilan, Sulu, and Tawitawi) where Muslims are in the majority remain among the poorest. The continuing strong presence of Muslim separatist sentiment in these provinces has waylayed government plans to develop these areas.

Referendum Will Help Decide Mindanao's Future

The present fighting in Mindanao comes just before a scheduled referendum on the island to finally decide its status. An earlier referendum in 1989 enabled the southern provinces to choose between integration and autonomy. Only four opted for the latter, forming the Autonomous Region of Muslim Mindanao (ARMM). Nur Misuari, the head of the MNLF, became governor of ARMM and later headed the Southern Philippine Council for Peace and Development. This body was formed to oversee the 13 provinces in Mindanao. Misuari has since lost popularity and wants the referendum to be postponed. The MNLF rebels want a more drastic solution: an independence vote under UN supervision. But the government does not intend to impose an East Timor solution on the Mindanao province. Despite the spate of recent clashes and the hostage crisis, Mindanao remains generally peaceful and progressive, with only small pockets of unrest in the provinces with a Muslim majority.

The president has indicated that he would be willing to go to an all out war to solve the Mindanao problem. But many are convinced that the situation will not deteriorate to that extent. In any case, it would require a well-armed military with high morale, when the Philippines lacks Budgetary resources have not been sufficient to allow the immediate and comprehensive modernisation of the armed forces. Instead, the Philippine military has had to make do with surplus equipment from the USA.

Wanted: A Credible Presidential Team

It was quite clear from the start of his term in 1998, that Estrada did not have the patience to go through a full weekly cabinet meeting, and he has rarely called for one since he was sworn into office. This management preference has led to perceptions that policies do not undergo sufficient work and analysis before they reach the president. In response, the president created the Economic Coordination Council (ECC) to formulate key development policies. Estrada promised to refer all major contracts to this body and all economic policy decisions are discussed and approved by it. The council combines businessmen and bankers such as Bangko Sentral Pilipinas (BSP) Governor Rafael Buenaventura with sharp academics such as Socio-economic Planning Secretary Felipe Medalla, and Budget Secretary Benjamin Diokno. Jose Pardo – a trusted Estrada advisor who replaced Edgardo Espiruto as finance minister after he resigned from the post in January 2000 – is also a key member of the ECC. As is his replacement at the Department of Trade and Industry, erstwhile House Majority leader, Manuel Roxas II, and Agriculture Secretary Edgardo Angara. The council's Secretary General is Margarito Teves, an economist and well-respected former congressman. The council can invite private sector observers to join their deliberations.

The ECC is seen to represent a line of defense against crony interests and is Estrada's main argument against the perception of policy paralysis in his administration. It helps that most members of the ECC do not have any vested interests and are, on the main, persons of integrity. The Council meets every week, with Pardo generally acting as chairman, and already generates many economic decisions. Its standing as a premier economic body now depends on how much Pardo and the other members can make, or are perceived to make, decisions based on objective economic considerations. Medalla and Diokno are well-known economists, both being former faculty members of the University of the Philippines School of Economics. Pardo is an unknown factor in the field of economics. His main asset so far is the trust that the president puts upon his advice. But he has yet to distinguish himself as the key fiscal manager of the Philippine economy.

Estrada needs a credible management team on his side to turn around his beleaguered presidency.

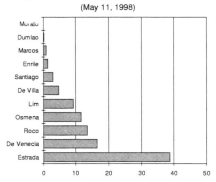

The Way It Was
Philippines - SWS 1998 exit poll - presidential votes, %
(May 11, 1998)

Error margin +/-1.4%; Source: Social Weather Stations.

The president's popularity has steadied as reform bills finally get moving through the legislative process.

No Threat For Now

SWS exit poll - vice presidential votes, 1998 elections, %

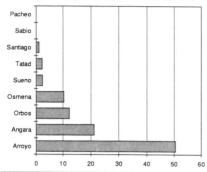

Source: Social Weather Stations.

Estrada Looks Forward And Gets His Act Together

In any case, the creation of the ECC may have already started a positive ripple. After plunging sharply in December, the president's popularity rating remained low but steady in March as reform bills, most of which are pending since the last administration, finally got moving through the legislative process. The Retail Trade Liberalization law was passed and signed into law on March 7, 2000. Following the BW scandal, Congress moved fast to finally pass the Revised Securities Act. The amendments to the General Banking Law have also been approved by both chambers and were signed into law in May 2000. Both the House of Representatives and the Senate also passed their versions of the Omnibus Power Restructuring Bill. With local elections in 2001, it is crucial that all important reform bills be passed this year. No significant legislative activity is expected within the next few months, as members of congress trek back more frequently to their constituents as the May election approaches.

Going forward into 2000, the numerous crisises may bring some positive feedback and political maturity into the governance process. The PCSO scandal reveals the power of an inquisitive media, the backbone of the boisterous Philippine democracy, to translate official ineptitude and corruption into opportunities to instill more openness and transparency into government operations. There is sufficient time for the Estrada administration to take advantage of these benefits in the fours years it has left to govern the country. At the height of all the scandals, there were calls for and from the opposition to take over the reins of government: The vice-president, Gloria Macapagal-Arroyo, who also holds a cabinet position and is titular head of the opposition, has held on to her immense popularity. But, under pressure from leaders of the president's party to disclose her plans, she has stated that she will remain in the president's cabinet for as long as he wishes.

Foreign Policy

Manila & Taiwan: The Bickering Continues

The Philippines and Taiwan remain at loggerheads over an air agreement. Regular flights between the two countries were resumed in February after being cut off since September 1999. In less than a month, the bickering started with the failure of Taiwan air officials to appear in scheduled meetings with their Manila counterparts for a new long-term air agreement. Consequently, direct commercial air links were severed again in March.

Looking forward, the recent election of the opposition Democratic Progressive Party (DPP) in Taiwan, as well as the appointment of Rod Reyes, former Press Secretary, as head of the Manila Economic and Cultural Office (MECO), could favour a resumption of talks along less acrimonious lines. The MECO handles relations with Taiwan for Manila in the absence of formal diplomatic ties. At the least, with both Taiwanese airlines government-owned, a new party in power could mean a fresh viewpoint. Estrada is on record as saying that he wants to end the air row with Taiwan. Barring no new set of aggravations, both sides could come back to the negotiating table very soon.

The Philippines filed yet another diplomatic protest in February against what it terms as an "intrusion" by Chinese fishing vessels in an area claimed by Manila in the South China Sea. The area in question, called the Scarborough Shoal, is also being claimed by China. Diplomatic skirmishes have abounded over the years over this stretch of territory which, including the islands of the Spratlys, are being claimed not just by the Philippines and China, but also by Taiwan, Vietnam, Malaysia, and Brunei. In an attempt to defuse the tension and lower the potential for military maneuverings, the Association of Southeast Asian Nations (Asean) is attempting to bring the disputants, including China, to the diplomatic table. The agenda in a meeting between Asean and China in February was the formulation of a code of conduct over disputed islands in the South China Sea. The code's objective is to persuade rivals to exercise restraint while in the disputed areas. The Philippines supports the crafting of a code of conduct in order to reduce opportunities for military flare-ups in the region.

The election of the opposition Democratic Progressive Party (DPP) in Taiwan could favour a resumption of talks along less acrimonious lines between the two nations.

Profile and Recent Developments

The Political System

Three Branches Of Government

The 1987 constitution provides for three equal branches of government: the executive branch, the legislature and judiciary. The executive branch is headed by the president, the legislative function rests with the congress, made up of the senate (upper house) and the House of Representatives (lower house), and the Supreme Court is the judiciary's highest tribunal. Local governments are established at the provincial, city, municipal and *barangay* (village) levels. These political subdivisions enjoy local autonomy and are entitled to an equitable share of the national wealth.

The president and vice president are elected by direct vote for a term of six years. The president is not eligible for re-election, but the vice president may serve two consecutive terms. Political succession is well defined. The vice president succeeds the president for the remainder of his term should he die, be permanently disabled, removed from office or resign. If the vice president is also disabled, the president of the senate or the speaker of the House of Representatives succeed, in that order, until a new president and vice president are elected.

The current administration under Joseph Estrada may seek to amend the constitution to revise term limits for the presidency and other elective positions. A panel is likely to be assembled to study the question in the first two years of government. Estrada has said that any changes agreed upon will not apply to him, so if the term limit for the presidency is extended to two, rather than the current one six-year term, then it will start with the new president elected in 2004. In this way, Estrada hopes to be able to have debates on vital constitutional issues untainted by personal interest.

Laws are made in the senate, which is composed of 24 members who are elected by direct national vote, while members of the House of Representatives, not to number more than 250, are elected directly by their local constituencies. Senators have a six-year term, while house representatives (congressmen) have three-year terms. The last national and local elections were held on May 11, 1998 for the positions of president, vice president, 12 senators, all congressmen and all local officials (except at the *barangay* level), a total of more than 17,000 positions. The newly elected officials began their terms on June 30, 1998. The next national election will be held in May 2001 for 12 senators and all congressmen, and the next presidential election in May 2004. Judicial power rests with the Supreme Court and lower courts. The Supreme Court is composed of the chief justice and 14 associate justices. All justices and judges of the lower courts are appointed by the president and serve until their retirement.

Political Parties: Lacking Ideologies

Although the Philippines is a multi-party democracy, political parties are not well developed in the sense that there are no well-defined ideologies. Rather parties wax and wane based on the political strength of their leaders, and consequently are easily formed and just as easily change identity. As a result, there is no difficulty with, or stigma attached to, party switching and politicians do this according to their calculations of which top candidates' coat tails are best worth riding on. Among the parties that participated in the 1998 national and local elections, only the Liberal Party has been in existence since the 1950s. But it is a shadow of itself and there is no ideology that can be specifically identified with it. What perhaps marks its members, whose numbers have dwindled sharply over the years, is that most of them are descendants of former Liberal Party leaders. Another formerly powerful party was the Marcos' KBL, which was entrenched during their regime but has been marginalised since their overthrow in 1986. Today, its most prominent members are the Marcos children and allies who have steadfastly maintained their loyalty to the family.

Since 1986, the party that has shown staying power is the Lakas party, to which former presidents Corazon Aquino and Fidel Ramos both belong. First formed as an opposition party to the KBL, it has since grown to include a more diverse group of members as a result of coalitions with other minority parties. Its most prominent member at the moment is Vice President Gloria Macapagal-Arroyo, who became a member via the joining of her Kampi Party with Lakas in a coalition. More than anything, this was seen as a marriage of convenience: it provided Lakas with a popular candidate to buoy the presidential bid of then House Speaker Jose de Venecia, and it gave Macapagal-Arroyo the political machinery with which to transform her high popularity ratings into votes.

If there was no overarching political ideology that bound Kampi to Lakas, as with the other party coalitions Lakas had pursued, equally there was no great ideological divide either. As the Ramos presidency came to a close in 1998, it was widely judged a success, even if the Asian crisis was raging at that point. This was attributed to the political and economic reforms that had begun in the Aquino presidency and continued into the Ramos administration. So widely accepted were, and still are, the fruits of those reforms, that almost no party has since espoused policies very different from them. Indeed, President Joseph Estrada pointedly echoed the deregulation, liberalisation and privatisation thrusts of the Ramos administration during his election campaign. (Although with the twist that these would be specifically focused into uplifting the plight of the poor.)

The ascendancy of Joseph Estrada in 1998 proves the point that one person can make a party in the Philippines. His LAMMP (Laban ng Makabayang Masang Pilipino or Struggle of the Nationalist Filipino Masses) Party did not exist in the 1992 presidential campaign, but was formed prior to the 1998 election to provide a vehicle for his candidacy since his former party, the NPC, had chosen another as its candidate. However, as all surveys repeatedly demonstrated the popularity of Estrada, the NPC formed a coalition with LAMMP, with its presidential candidate agreeing to run instead as Estrada's vice president. Estrada ran on a pro-poor platform and in his inaugural speech he said that no favours would be shown to relatives and friends. It is on these broad promises that his administration will be judged.

Strength Of Democratic Institutions

Since the restoration of democracy in 1986, political institutions and rights have been strengthened. Indeed, this was the first priority of the Aquino presidency, with economic reforms occurring only later in her term. The *Batasang Pambansa*, as the legislature was known during the Marcos regime, served only as a rubber stamp for decisions reached by the executive branch in the person of Ferdinand Marcos. However, this was replaced under the Aquino administration by a truly participatory bicameral legislature, the congress, similar to what had existed before the perversion of the system in the Marcos years. Similarly, the judiciary was also reformed, mainly through the replacement of justices and judges who had been subservient to Marcos. In addition, broadcast and print media were unshackled from the strictures that bound freedom of expression during the dictatorship.

The constitutional changes implemented under Aquino resulted in free and vigorous debate on all issues. The extent of the change may be gauged from the fact that during her term, President Aquino felt compelled to file a libel suit against a newspaper for alleged defamation, which she subsequently lost. Elected and appointed officials have to account for their actions to the public, which comes under constant scrutiny from the press and authorities such as the Office of the Ombudsman. However, despite the strengthening of political institutions and rights, the system is still prone to corruption. Major reasons include the low wage levels that make public officials vulnerable to bribes, and the related problem of not being able to attract the best and the brightest available people into public service. Furthermore, although there has been considerable scope in political reforms, the institutions of government are not yet sufficiently strong to completely withstand corruptive influences. This is true at all branches of government: the executive, legislative and judiciary.

More than the Aquino and Ramos administrations, the Estrada presidency is seen as being prone to cronyism, despite the strong statement made during the inaugural presidential address that no favours would be granted to relatives and friends. Of course, the past two administrations were never entirely free of accusations of graft and corruption, but on the surface this seems to be more widespread and present at higher levels in the present administration. Critics of the president point to the plan to bury former president Marcos at the place known as Heroes Memorial (his widow Imelda Marcos withdrew her presidential candidacy in his favour in 1998) until public sentiment forced him to back out of the offer, the take-over of one of the country's biggest companies **San Miguel Corp** by political partner and financier Eduardo Cojuangco shortly after the election, the prominent association with business tycoon and political backer Lucio Tan who has been the target of a high-profile tax evasion case, and a scandal at the Departments of Education and Budget that apparently involved a relative of President Estrada, but which seems to have been glossed over for now.

In addition, like former president Aquino, Estrada filed a suit against a newspaper for alleged defamation of character. However, the case was never argued in court because it was withdrawn when the owners of the newspaper apologised, allegedly because their other businesses, far bigger than the newspaper, were being placed under pressure by government agencies such as the Bureau of Internal Revenue. Whether the accusations of cronyism against the present administration will eventually be borne out is still unclear, but what is apparent at this time is that allegations made against the government, especially the executive branch, will have to be cleared up satisfactorily if their credibility is to be maintained.

Falling Ratings

Estrada's ratings fell drastically in December 1999, plunging to 44% from 78% in June. While past presidents suffered drops in popularity midway through their terms, Estrada's decline was the steepest during the first six months of office. Behind the drop in the ratings, were real concerns that the administration was adrift, and discontent with Estrada's persistence in seeking to amend the constitution. Rumours of major cabinet infighting were worsened by the perception that Estrada's policymaking was done in an ad hoc fashion, taking the advice of friends over cabinet members.

At the end of the year, Estrada asked for the courtesy resignations of the entire cabinet, in a step seen as an attempt to arrest the decline in his popularity. He has said that this will give him the opportunity to prune his cabinet, get rid of non-performers, and introduce fresh ideas into the administration. He let go two of his more unpopular advisers, in housing and computer education, both of whom had been embroiled in controversies. Still, Estrada promoted his former deputy at the PAOCC to head the country's national police force, a crucial posting. Public reaction has been mixed. Human rights groups have condemned the new police chief due to past records of alleged torture of anti-government protesters and summary executions of captured criminals. However, he has also been credited with the reduction in kidnapping cases, which have bedevilled the country in past years.

Foreign Policy

Supporting Anwar: An Unprecedented Stand

In general, the Estrada administration has trod the same foreign policy path as its predecessor. There has been little or no debate over foreign agreements to be signed or followed, since the priorities of trade liberalisation and the embrace of globalisation efforts are well-known and accepted. However, one of the more notable differences in foreign policy positions taken by the present administration is the support for sacked Malaysian former deputy prime minister Anwar Ibrahim. Estrada regards Anwar as a personal friend and his treatment at the hands of the Mahathir government has prompted vocal support from Estrada. In a speech to the World Economic Forum in 1998, Estrada publicly put his support behind Anwar. This was taken even further during an APEC meeting held in Kuala Lumpur, where Estrada met with Anwar's wife.

Although he had been warned about the possibility of negative consequences that could befall overseas Filipinos living and working in Malaysia and renewed strains over the Philippines' claim to Sabah (which had eased somewhat during the term of Ramos), Estrada has persisted in his position. He has been supported by former president Aquino, who hosted the visit to the Philippines of Anwar's wife during which she was given several chances to air the opposition's view. Because it is uncertain how long it will be before Malaysian Prime Minister Mahathir Mohammad will relinquish his position, the adversarial stance taken by the Philippines with one of its closest neighbours and a co-member in the Asean, which has made domestic non-interference a guiding policy, has unprecedented perils.

Another controversial foreign policy initiative is the ratification of the Visiting Forces Agreement (VFA) with the United States that will allow joint military exercises to be conducted in the Philippines. The Estrada administration favours ratification, but faces opposition from congress. The opposition draws on the same arguments that were used to remove the US bases in 1991. That is, that the Philippines will surrender its sovereignty on important issues such as judicial jurisdiction over possible crimes committed by the American military. As Estrada supported the anti-bases position when he was senator, he has been accused of shifting his loyalties.

However, the Philippine military desperately needs aid to modernise its military forces, especially naval, to deal with the incursions of China into contested Spratly Islands territory that is within the Philippines' 200-mile limit of jurisdiction. China has intruded into the contested area almost with impunity, as the Philippines is incapable of defending the territory against their superior naval forces. To present a credible deterrent, the Philippines needs a strong ally, which it sees in the US, but assistance will only be extended with ratification of the VFA.

Amid tight security, Manila hosted the Asean Summit in November. The Manila summit paves the way for a wider alliance with the bigger economies of China, South Korea, and Japan. Plans to form a broader East Asia forum remained tentative, however, as the Asean economies focused on keeping free trade plans on track amid the backwash of the financial crisis. The Philippines supported the schedule to lift all import tariffs by 2010 for the six founding members of Asean. This is five years ahead of the original schedule.

The Philippines sent a contingent of marines as part of the peacekeeping mission in East Timor. Manila has expressed concern about the reports of massacres and other abuses of the largely Catholic population of East Timor. A number of priests and nuns in east Timor are Filipinos.

Philippine authorities cut direct air links between Manila and Taipei, scrapping a 1996 aviation pact in September 1999. The government accuses Taiwanese airlines of carrying more than their quota of passengers and encroaching on the passenger base of **Philippine Airlines**, the country's flag carrier. By yearend, talks between the two countries' air authorities remained open-ended. with no agreement reached on the issue on onward routing of passengers.

2 Economic Outlook

Economic Activity

Fragile Recovery Dragged Down By Agriculture

GDP grew by a disappointing 3.4% y-o-y in Q1 2000, lower than the official 4.1% estimate. Growth of just 0.04% from Q4 99, suggests that the recovery is running out of steam. Output was tempered by a slowdown in agriculture, which grew by only 0.2% y-o-y, compared to 2.9% in the same period of 1999. The sector, which accounts for one fifth of GDP, has been hit by an upsurge of unrest by Muslim separatists in the important crop-producing area of Mindanao (*see Political Outlook*). The government has subsequently lowered its full-year GDP growth forecast to 4% from the original 5%, but even this looks optimistic. As the troubles in Mindanao take their toll on the economy – and the knock-on affects in terms of reduced consumer spending will be felt hardest from the third quarter – real GDP will struggle to rise by more than 3.5%. The government's forecast relies on a rebound in agriculture from the second quarter. But, despite official reassurance to the contrary, the crisis in Mindanao – an area which accounts for a third of rice and two-thirds of corn output – poses a real threat to the official 3-3.5% farm sector growth target (1999 = 6.49%).

The recovery floundered in Q1 2000, as a weak agricultural sector outweighed manufacturing gains.

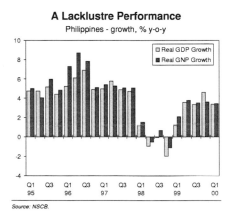

A Lacklustre Performance
Philippines - growth, % y-o-y

Source: NSCB.

Recovery Hinges On Industry

Whether GDP growth does rise above 3.5% will hinge to a great extent on a recovery in manufacturing, which has lagged since the start of the economic crisis. The data so far this year is positive, with total manufacturing output up 5.8% y-o-y in the first quarter. The value of production index (as measured by the Monthly Integrated Survey of Selected Industries) increased by an average of 16.9% y-o-y in the same period, while the volume of production was also significantly higher, climbing 8.1% y-o-y. This compares favourably with contractions of 5.1% and 7.4 % in the value and volume of production indexes respectively in Q1 99. While, the volume of production declined 4% y-o-y in April – with chemicals, basic metals, textiles, electrical machinery, wood and wood products and beverages all posting contractions – net sales were still up, indicating that inventories are

The official 2000 growth estimates hinge on a recovery in the manufacturing sector, which has lagged since the start of the regional financial crisis.

being depleted. **BMI** will therefore be looking closely at imports, which contracted at the height of the Asian crisis and posted only a slight recovery in 1999, as a leading indicator of manufacturing output for the remainder of the year. With many companies in the sector still undergoing restructuring, and Mindanao impacting on investment and consumption in the second half, we do not expect a dramatic upswing. But growth in the value of production of 9% for the full year is feasible.

There are some indications that capacity utilisation rates are also improving. While the average capacity utilisation rate for manufacturing was 81.6% in April, representing a slight fall from 81.7% in April 1999, 11 sub-sectors out of 16 posted higher rates. Only basic metals (68.5%), beverages (80.8%), wood and wood products (73.4%), chemicals (78.8%) and electrical machinery (89.1%) saw declines.

Meanwhile, the outlook for construction is bleak. While, the sector's 0.7% decline in Q1 2000 is a sharp improvement on its deep 12.8% contraction in Q1 99, this has more to do with a low base year effect than any real upturn. Excess supply will ensure that the sector remains in the doldrums this year. Utilities, on the other hand, posted 4.7% growth in Q4 99 and 3% in Q1 2000, and could easily see growth accelerate to 5% in 2000. Services is projected to grow 4.4% this year, following growth of 3.8% y-o-y in Q1. Expansion of the sector is still tempered by the cautious recovery of bank lending: commercial bank lending was up 1.8% in March. But, while still slow compared to pre-crisis years, the rise represents an acceleration from the 0.2% and 1.1% growth rates registered in January and February, respectively. Government services also slowed because of the delay in the passage

Running Down Inventories
Philippines - value of production, 3mma % y-o-y

Source: Monthly Integrated Survey of Selected Industries.

POPULATION & OUTPUT										
	1993	1994	1995	1996	1997	1998	1999e	2000f	2001f	2002f
Population (mn)	63.7	65.3	67.0	68.6	70.3	71.9	73.5	75.2	76.9	78.6
Nominal GDP (US$bn)	45.4	53.0	54.4	64.1	74.1	83.8	82.2	65.5	76.7	79.3
GDP per capita (US$)	812	934	1,055	1,165	1,118	871	997	1,009	1,058	1,056
Real GDP growth (% y/y)	2.12	4.40	4.67	5.85	5.19	-0.59	3.20	3.50	4.50	5.50
Real GNP growth (% y/y)	1.33	5.26	4.87	7.24	5.25	0.40	3.60	3.80	4.60	5.60
Value of production (% y/y)	17.58	13.75	17.09	9.23	8.77	-2.10	8.45	9.00	10.50	12.00

e/f = BMI estimate/forecast. Sources: Bangko Sentral ng Pilipinas/IMF/World Bank/NSCB/BMI/MISSI.

of the 2000 General Appropriations Act.

On the expenditure side, growth will be tempered by a reduction in government spending, in line with efforts to contain the fiscal deficit (see *Fiscal Policy*.) Government consumption dropped 1.9% y-o-y in Q1 2000 after five consecutive quarters of growth. And personal consumption expenditure growth will pick up only gradually, having struggled below 3% in each quarter of 1999 to climb 3.2% in Q1 2000.

The economy's expansion will be tempered in 2001 by the return of the *El Niño* phenomenon, which could pull down agricultural output, although we will not see a repeat of the downturn of 1997. Industry will continue to serve as the key driver of growth, which will range around 4.5%. By 2002, **BMI** expects the economy to pick up more strongly with growth of 5.5%. The recovery will broaden out, with agriculture rising by a forecast 3-4% and a more vigorous manufacturing sector expanding by 6% or more.

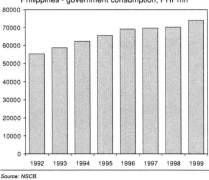

Unsustainable Pump-Priming
Philippines - government consumption, PHPmn

Source: NSCB.

Fiscal Policy

Tightening Up

The government intends to begin the task of fiscal consolidation this year. Investor sentiment has been bearish on anxieties that the government will go on a borrowing binge to finance the wide deficit incurred in 1999. The government's 2000 budget, as approved by Congress, targets a deficit of PHP62.5bn, down from a preliminary PHP111.7bn in 1999. Budget approval was delayed by realignments caused by the weak revenue performance in 1999 of the major revenue generating agencies, in particular the Bureau of Internal Revenue (BIR). An unfortunate combination of weak corporate profits and organisational disarray at the BIR resulted in historically low internal revenue collections. As a consequence, the revenue targets for 2000 had to be revised downwards.

With fiscal managers firm that the budget deficit will be the policy anchor for 2000, they agreed with the Senate on a slashing of disbursements to ensure that the deficit target is met. These cuts have been very deep, and have caused resentment across all sectors.

Fiscal managers have agreed to begin fiscal consolidation in 2000.

Budget Target Likely To Be Missed

The Mindanao crisis will raise expenditure and eat into revenues, putting the official deficit target in jeopardy. Privatisation revenue assumptions are also optimistic.

BMI expects the budget deficit to significantly exceed the target in 2000, breaching the PHP80bn mark. For the first four months of 2000, the deficit was kept below the programme for the period, at PHP13.283bn against the PHP21.331bn target. This compares favourably to the PHP22bn gap incurred in the same period of 1999. The government spent only PHP185.876, against the PHP196.884bn target. But this apparently impressive performance was due less to improved austerity, than to the delayed impact of expenditure incurred later on in the year. The January-May data provide a better indication of fiscal health. The deficit rose to PHP32.546bn in the period, against the PHP34.111bn target, with the deficit for May alone reaching PHP20.828bn – nearly double the programmed deficit for the month. Pardo attributed the poor result to spending on Mindanao, assistance to local government and the release of mid-year public sector bonuses, coupled with shortfalls in tax collection and privatisation proceeds.

The PHP22bn proceeds from privatisation that form part of the revenue assumptions are a key soft spot in the budget. These include big-ticket items like **Manila Electric Company** (Meralco) and Philippine National Bank (PNB). Poor market conditions mean the sale of power distributor Meralco – of which the government owns about 40% – has been postponed to later in the year. The failure of the June bidding for PNB puts in doubt any revenues garnered from privatisation this year. Without the certainty of privatisation proceeds, the budget gap will widen unless budget officials couple certain disbursements with the remittances from the sale of assets. The fiscal programme identifies certain items as linked to the schedule of privatisation proceeds. This is not so difficult to put on paper, but the actual implementation will certainly be challenged strongly, especially with elections looming next year.

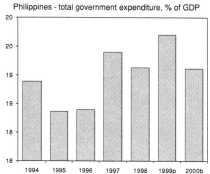

An Optimistic Outlook
Philippines - total government expenditure, % of GDP

p = preliminary, b = budget. Source: Ministry of Finance.

GOVERNMENT FINANCE (PHPBN)								
	1994	1995	1996	1997	1998	1999r	1999p	2000b
Total revenues; of which:	336.2	361.2	410.5	471.9	462.2	490.6	478.5	568.0
Tax revenues	271.3	310.5	367.9	412.2	416.6	441.1	431.7	499.5
Non-tax revenues; of which:	64.9	50.7	42.6	59.7	45.6	49.5	46.8	68.5
Privatisation	29.9	22.8	5.7	9.4	1.7	5.0	4.2	22.0
Economic support fund	0.0	0.0	0.0	0.0	0.0	0.2	0.1	0.2
Foreign grants	0.7	1.0	0.6	1.7	0.4	0.2	0.3	0.2
Total expenditure; of which:	319.9	350.1	404.2	470.3	512.5	576	590.2	629.5
Foreign interest payments	19.3	21.8	17.5	19.6	26.3	30.4	31.3	42.0
Domestic interest payments	59.8	50.8	59.0	58.4	73.5	89.7	75.0	85.0
Budget balance	16.3	11.1	6.3	1.6	-50.3	-85.4	-111.7	-61.5

r = revised budget, p = preliminary, b = budget. Source: Ministry of Finance.

But the real test, especially for the BIR whose target is heavily concentrated in the second half of the year, will come later in 2000. Moreover, the escalation of military attacks by Muslim separatists in Mindanao will raise expenditure, and its adverse impact on the economy will threaten revenue projections as business confidence flounders along with agricultural output. Government planners had projected a cyclical upswing in the corporate sector, after two years in the doldrums, but **BMI** expects flat earnings growth in 2000, as political uncertainty eats further into investor confidence after a moribund performance in the first quarter. And with congressional and local elections within the next few months, pressure will mount against stringent budget controls.

Revenue Collection Must Be Overhauled

In the long run, budget compression may exact a greater negative toll on the economy. The Philippines needs to build better infrastructure nationwide to allow it to compete globally for fickle investor money. The government has programmed a reduction in the fiscal deficit as a percentage of GNP to 1.8% and 1.4% respectively in 2001 and 2002, to be in balance by 2003 at the latest. The only viable way this can be accomplished is via higher revenue generation rather than budget controls. The medium-term framework calls for a return in tax collection revenues to pre-crisis levels of about 15.5% of GNP by 2002, working up to a level of 17.2% by 2004.

Underlying structural reforms include a restructuring of taxes on the financial sector, which the Finance Ministry wants to see legislated no later than 2000. The present levy on banks, or the gross receipts tax (GRT), is set to be replaced by VAT by 2001. Finance officials, as well as the banking sector, are not fully convinced that VAT will be an efficient system for the financial sector, hence an alternative tax system has been proposed by the finance department. The reform package also includes a restructuring of the onerous documentary stamp tax (DST), basically limiting its imposition to primary transactions and reducing the number of rates applicable. The reform bill still has to find a sponsor in Congress, but with firm government commitment, it could pass into law before the present Congress adjourns for election activities next year.

Of concern, however, is the abrupt change since Pardo became Finance Minister in the long-held position of the Ministry of Finance to remove distortions in fiscal incentives. The final phase of the Comprehensive Tax Reform Programme of 1997 would have involved the streamlining of convoluted and overlapping tax incentives, which continue to punch holes into the tax collection system. But with Pardo at the helm of Finance, the

Finance Minister Pardo's support of an amendment which would extend the granting of even longer tax holidays does not augur well for long-term fiscal stability.

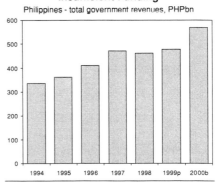

Insufficient Funding
Philippines - total government revenues, PHPbn

p = preliminary, b = budget. Source: Ministry of Finance.

ministry now supports an amendment, which would extend the granting of even longer tax holidays. This about-face in policy does not augur well for long-term fiscal stability.

Monetary Policy

A Balancing Act

The Central Bank has considered adopting inflation targeting, but must balance a concern to contain prices with the need to shore up a currency wracked by political uncertainty and US interest rate hikes.

Bangko Sentral ng Pilipinas (BSP) sets an annual inflation target, but also maintains other objectives, mainly the stability of the peso, as equally important. These dual objectives have often clashed, causing some interest rate policy changes that have confused markets. The action by the BSP in late 1997 to hike interest rates to arrest the decline in the peso has been blamed by critics for an unnecessarily deep contraction in the real sector. Recently, central bank officials have started discussions on adopting a formal inflation target as its sole policy objective. The timetable for the shift is about two years.

No Price Pressures Yet
Phlippines - consumer price inflation, % y-o-y

Source: NSO.

The inflation target for 2000 was originally set at 5.5-6.5%. However, with inflation averaging only 3.6% in Q1 2000 and OPEC policy reversing to higher production levels thereby cooling down oil prices, the BSP has adjusted the inflation target to 5-6%, in line with **BMI**'s own forecast of 5.5%. So far, the impact of higher petroleum prices has yet to filter through to consumer prices. One reason has been that power distributor Meralco has yet to incur any rate hikes. (A petition filed by Meralco with the Energy Regulatory Board on April 14 to increase its basic rate by 30 centavos per kWh, is still pending a hearing after strong protest from consumers.) Most manufacturing firms have also been able to absorb fuel price hikes without pushing up prices, indicating an increase in productivity in Philippine firms.

INFLATION & INTEREST RATES										
	1993	1994	1995	1996	1997	1998	1999e	2000f	2001f	2002f
Annual inflation (% y/y, period avg)	7.0	8.3	8.0	5.1	6.0	9.6	6.8	5.4	5.6	5.0
91-day T-bills (%, eop)	12.4	12.7	11.8	12.3	12.9	15.0	10.0	9.1	10.2	9.8
Deposit rate (% an. avg)	9.6	10.5	8.4	9.7	10.2	12.1	8.2	10.3	10.8	10.3
Lending rate (% an. avg)	14.7	15.1	14.7	14.8	16.3	16.8	11.8	12.5	13.0	12.5
e/f = BMI estimate/forecast. Sources: NSO/IMF/BMI.										

The rice price subsidy introduced in October 1999, has also kept a lid on the food component of the CPI. As of May 2000, inflation had only inched up to 4.1% y-o-y from a 13-year low of 2.6% in January. But the food price subsidy will be unsustainable in light of tighter monetary targets, and lower base years coupled with potential food shortages resulting from the Mindanao crisis will see prices rising gradually through the rest of the year to an average of 5.4% in 2000. El Niño-related commodity price increases will put upward pressure on prices next year, but this will be tempered by falling oil prices.

The central bank aims to keep interest rates low, to avoid a slowdown in the nascent recovery and keep borrowing costs to fund the fiscal gap down. But another hike in US interest rates and further political uncertainty could force Manila to raise rates again to support the peso. The central bank raised overnight rates by a total 125bps in three stages in May – bringing borrowing and lending rates to 10% and 12.25% respectively – following hikes in US rates and a run on the peso in response to the Mindanao crisis. Despite the hikes, the Bankers Association of the Philippines has assured borrowers that banks will maintain their current lending rates for small- and medium-scale lenders and are committed to these levels even if overnight rates are raised again. Wide spreads on these accounts, have enabled banks to contain lending rates.

Under Pressure
Philippines - 3-month interbank rate, %

Source: Reuters/BMI.

Exchange Rate Policy

Political Jitters

Official exchange rate projections put the peso moving to an average of PHP41/US$ this year, but further political uncertainty mid-year may see the peso moving downwards to between PHP41.50-42.00/US$. In May, the Philippine peso reacted to two adverse developments: worries in the Asean region regarding the effects of an increase in interest rates by the US Federal Reserve Bank, and a worsening of the Mindanao problem. The peso breached PHP42.50/US$ in the third week of May following a mall bombing in Metro Manila.

The authorities have tightened monitoring rules for portfolio inflows.

	1993	1994	1995	1996	1997	1998	1999e	2000f	2001f	2002f
EXCHANGE RATES										
PHP/US$ (an. avg)	27.12	26.42	25.71	26.22	29.47	40.89	39.09	41.50	43.00	44.20
PHP/US$ (eop)	27.70	24.42	26.21	26.29	39.98	39.06	40.31	42.00	43.40	44.80

e/f = BMI estimate/forecast. Sources: Reuters/IMF.

The currency remains vulnerable to future hikes in US interest rates – which the authorities will be loathed to match after implementing three interest rate rises already this year. Surpluses on the merchandise and trade accounts will limit the fall, but a long-term trend of a weakening peso against the dollar will continue into 2001, when **BMI** expects a moderate depreciation of about 2.5%. This would bring the peso to a range of PHP43.00-43.50/US$. Moving forward into the medium term, the peso is officially projected to move by 3.0-3.5% to keep the Philippines competitive against its trading counterparts.

In January the BSP issued tighter rules on reporting requirements on dollar inflows and outflows by banks. The move was designed to curb exchange rate volatility and, as central bank officials have stressed, is not meant to be some form of capital control. Rather, the intent is to improve the system for monitoring capital inflows. Portfolio inflows deposited in banks will not be registered unless they are kept in time deposits of at least 90 days. This will quell the tendency of parking funds in short-term deposits for speculative purposes. The new rule will not affect investments in the equity or debt markets. The immediate impact of the regulations, which took effect in February, saw banks with long dollar positions selling their excess dollar holdings. So far, the market seems to have accepted the new rules with grace. The government has always maintained that it upholds a market-oriented exchange rate policy. With the central bank moving towards inflation targeting in the next couple of years, exchange rate policy will become truly more attuned to market considerations.

Balance Of Payments

Trade Surplus Will Narrow

The trade surplus jumped 204.5% to US$871mn in the first four months, from US$286mn a year ago, as exports picked up strongly. But some worrying trends emerged, notably a 4.2% decline in electronics components exports in April to US$1.265bn from US$1.32bn a year ago and US$1.525 in March, despite a weak peso. Electronics components account for 47.4% of total exports. The import of electronics and components – accounting for 22.6% of the total import bill – fell 9% y-o-y in April to US$571.7mn. The fall has been attributed to a drop in confidence in light of the Mindanao crisis and general climate of political uncertainty, with investors and importers choosing to place there orders with competitors. This does not bode well for the long-term future of electronics, as the Philippines already lags behind Singapore, Malaysia and Taiwan in terms of technology and productivity. A

Confidence Wanes
Philippines - exchange rate, PHP/US$

Source: Reuters/BMI.

Political uncertainty has hurt the electronics export sector, but the trade account should remain healthy this year.

slowdown in the US – which accounts for 28.7% of exports – would compound the problem. Two other key export sectors – computer parts and apparel and clothing – also posted contractions in April from March.

Nonetheless, the cyclical upswing in the electronics cycle – downturns in the cycle are typically induced by over supply, in direct contrast to current tight conditions – should ensure that exports sustain growth of around 10% in 2000. With overcapacity lingering in the manufacturing sector, **BMI** does not expect a dramatic upswing in imports this year. But high oil prices and a rise in capital goods and raw materials imports once inventories have been depleted in the second half, will see imports pick up by as much as 12% y-o-y as the year progresses. As import growth accelerates above exports, **BMI** expects the trade surplus to narrow gradually through the forecast period, dropping to US$4.1bn in 2000 from US$4.3bn in 1999. The current account will narrow accordingly to US$5.8bn from US$7.2bn in 1999, falling to US$3.8bn in 2002.

No Dramatic Turnaround
Philippines - marchandise trade growth, % y-o-y

Source: NSO.

BALANCE OF PAYMENTS										
	1993	1994	1995	1996	1997	1998	1999e	2000f	2001f	2002f
Exports (fob, US$bn)	11.37	13.48	17.45	20.54	25.23	29.50	35.03	38.02	41.92	46.11
Imports (fob, US$bn)	17.60	21.33	26.54	32.43	35.93	29.66	30.73	35.76	40.48	45.34
Trade balance (US$bn)	-6.22	-7.85	-9.09	-11.88	-10.71	-0.16	4.31	2.26	1.44	0.78
Current account (US$bn)	-3.02	-2.95	-1.98	-3.95	-4.30	1.29	7.19	5.80	4.70	3.80
Current account (% GDP)	-5.55	-4.60	-2.67	-4.72	-5.23	1.97	9.38	7.31	5.52	4.37

e/f = BMI estimate/forecast. Sources: Bangko Sentral ng Pilipinas/IMF/BMI.

Foreign Direct Investment

Finally Seeing Eye-To-Eye....

Following Pardo's appointment as Finance Minister, a convergence of viewpoints has occurred with reference to the proposed amendments to Executive Order 226 (Investments Code). The strongest opposition against the further extension of income tax holidays as an incentive to foreign investments has been neutralised. Both Pardo and Roxas signed a joint endorsement of the amendments proposed by House Bill 10596, which include a 12-year tax holiday up from the prevailing eight-year tax holiday granted to priority industries.

For this year, the ECC has chosen not to set any investment target. The ECC said that it would wait for the harmonisation of the investment numbers generated by different agencies before coming up with any goals for investment. There are currently at least three government agencies that generate data on investment levels. The Ministry of Trade and Industry provides investment targets and indicators such as public sector investments in build-operate-transfer and similar schemes. The SEC generates investment figures in new and related business, while the BSP figures include portfolio investments. The problem with all these data is that they do not provide a coherent set of information on actual investment inflows.

The ECC designated the Trade and Industry Secretary Roxas to head the task force that will reconcile the numbers of the three agencies. The task force will also develop a mechanism to reflect actual investment inflows and qualify these according to source, nature and purpose. The final objective is to come up with a unified set of investment indicators.

...But Political Uncertainty Will Dampen Sentiment

But any initiatives to attract investors will be wasted if the current climate of political and economic uncertainty lingers – certainly, **BMI** does not expect any pick-up in foreign investment this year as a lack of confidence in Estrada's leadership, interest and exchange rate uncertainty, the Mindanao crisis and now suspected Muslim separatist terrorism in Manila itself, all take their toll. Indeed, poor foreign investor sentiment has in return weakened local investor confidence. Federation of Philippine Industries chairman Raul Concepcion told a press briefing shortly after his return from a trip to the US at end-May 2000 that, "...the image of the Philippines abroad has been badly battered and we are today in a situation similar to [that after] the December

1989 coup attempt". He based his assessment on meetings with the Filipino and American business communities in the USA. The chairman criticised "official foot dragging" in the government over economic policy and its response to Mindanao.

External Debt

Debt Burden Will Rise Too Fund Fiscal Hole

The Philippines debt stock has widened as the government has been forced to fund an ever increasing fiscal deficit. As of end-March, the Philippines' external debt stock stood at US$52.42bn, up from US$52.21bn at end-1999, with longer term borrowings making up 89% of the total. The Philippine's external debt has a maturity profile of 17 years. The government successfully sold US$1.6bn worth of two-tranche bonds in March, of which US$800mn will go to finance the deficit and US$800mn is for National Power.

BMI expects external debt to continue rising gradually, approaching US$54bn by end-year, as the government funds part of its fiscal deficit this year through the international capital markets. Another US$700mn is targeted to be raised, although this may be difficult to achieve. Part of this was supposed to have come from another Euro-denominated issue, planned in April. While the roadshow for investors went on as scheduled, widening spreads on Philippine sovereign issues have forced the government to reconsider the timing of the issue. A faster pace in the passage of the reform bills still pending legislation, especially the Revised Securities Act and the power bill, will restore some investor confidence in the Philippines.

Widening spreads on Philippine sovereign issues have forced the government to reconsider the timing of bond issues.

Funding The Fiscal Gap
Phlippines - external debt, US$mn

f = BMI forecast; Source: BSP.

					DEBT STOCK					
	1993	**1994**	**1995**	**1996**	**1997**	**1998**	**1999e**	**2000f**	**2001f**	**2002f**
External debt (US$bn)	35.54	38.72	39.37	41.88	45.43	47.82	52.21	54.00	56.10	58.20
External debt (% GDP)	65.36	60.41	53.10	49.98	55.25	73.01	68.11	68.05	65.94	66.97

e/f = BMI estimate/forecast. Sources: NSCB/IMF/BMI.

Profile and Recent Developments

Characteristics Of The Economy

A Diverse Economy

The Philippine economy is well represented among the three major sectors. In the primary or extractive industries, it is agriculture, constituting about a fifth of total GDP, which dominates. Crops contribute roughly half of the industry's output, with rice and corn, grown mostly in Luzon and Mindanao respectively, being the major items, while livestock, poultry and fishery make up most of the balance. In 1998, the drought brought by the *El Niño* resulted in a severe contraction of crop output, such that the agricultural sector shrank almost 7%, the worst showing since record-keeping post-World War II. Heavy rains brought by *La Niña* pounded most of the country in 1999 and caused major flooding in Metro Manila. On the whole, the impact of *La Niña* has proven more positive for the economy as agriculture recovered from the drought of 1998. Forestry is part of agriculture but contributes insignificantly to the industry since the felling of trees has been prohibited to stem forest denudation, while commercial forestry is not widely practised. The other extractive industry is mining, but it has assumed lesser importance as global commodity prices have declined through the years and restrictions on foreign investment and environmental safeguards have limited exploration by domestic companies. Of this minor industry, however, gold mining, especially in Northern Luzon and Mindanao, and stone quarrying are by far the most important activities. Although there are crude oil deposits off the island of Palawan, south-west of Luzon, these are small in quantity and the country remains a net crude oil importer.

In the secondary sector, manufacturing, which comprises about a quarter of GDP, takes the lead. In contrast, construction contributes only 6% of GDP and utilities a smaller 3%. With a substantial agricultural sector, food processing is the single biggest component of manufacturing, taking up 35% of production with most of it destined for the domestic market. Petroleum refining, accounting for around 18% of manufacturing production, follows food processing in importance. It is a concentrated industry with three major players, but recent deregulation may lead to the rise of other more prominent participants. Compared to food processing, the fast-growing electronics industry contributes less than 10% of manufacturing output and the bulk of it is exported. Indeed, electronics comprises a growing proportion of total merchandise exports and now accounts for more than 50%. Electronic manufacturing facilities are in export processing zones located all over the country, but most are in the corridor south of Manila in the area called Calabarzon.

The services sector accounts for 45% of GDP, the largest of the three. Furthermore, services proved the most resilient in 1998, posting a respectable 3.5% growth while the two other major sectors contracted. The services sector is also dispersed more uniformly among its constituent industries, although wholesale and retail trade contributes a little more than the others. In 1998, retail trade drew strength from the robust income remittances of overseas workers which compensated for weakness in wholesale trade, thus allowing the overall trade industry to grow, albeit at a slower pace. The problems at **Philippine Airlines** (PAL) affected the transportation industry, but communications grew at double-digit pace as companies rushed to meet regulatory deadlines for installing new capacity. High interest rates and other symptoms of the financial crisis retarded growth in the financial industry. In all, while real GDP contracted a slight 0.5% in 1998, it shrank 21% in nominal US dollar terms to US$65bn as a result of the deep depreciation of the peso.

Economic Activity

Agriculture: Stormy Weather

The *El Niño* and the financial crisis combined to result in a GDP contraction of 0.6% in 1998, following 5.2% growth the previous year. However, it was the drought caused by *El Niño* that had the most impact as agricultural output shrank 6.6%, the sector's worst showing post-World War II. Crop output was severely curtailed; harvests of major commodities such as rice, corn, coconut and sugar cane all suffered double-digit contractions. Only livestock and fishery saw expansions. As the drought was coming to an end at the start of Q4 98, the country was hit by two strong typhoons that inflicted further damage on whatever remained to be harvested, compounding the losses already wrought by *El Niño*. Following this disastrous turn of events, however, the weather improved. With frequent rains from end-Q4 98 onwards, agricultural produce has been bountiful. Rice and corn benefited the most and in Q1 99 grew a phenomenal 34.9% and 61.7% respectively, fuelling the 2.5% expansion in the agricultural sector. In contrast, coconut production suffered from the lagged impact of the drought while other major crops did not benefit from the delayed rainy season and production continued shrinking into Q1 99. Meanwhile, livestock and fishery sustained respectable growth rates. Poultry production declined due to voluntary cutbacks made by industry players as overcapacity continued to be a problem.

Welcome Rains

The adverse impact of *El Niño* on production was completely reversed by the opposite weather phenomenon, *La Niña*. With the rainy weather resulting in bountiful harvests, GDP recovered to post 3.2% growth in 1999. Fourth quarter GDP was strong at 4.6%. Agricultural output expanded by 6.6 % in 1999, with the growth largely coming from harvest of rice and corn. Production of unmilled rice expanded by 38% to 11.8mn tonnes. Corn output hit a 20-year high of 4.6mn tonnes, while sugar production increased by 28.6%, a harvest of 22.3mn tonnes. However, production of coconuts, mango, coffee and tobacco dropped in 1999 as *La Niña* rains came too early in the cropping season.

Manufacturing: Flagging Demand

Manufacturing output fell 1.1% in 1998, mainly due to the depressed states of petroleum refining, construction-related manufacturing and the manufacture of transportation equipment. In contrast to agriculture, which was hit by adverse weather conditions, the manufacturing sector was a victim of the financial crisis. As a result of high interest rates and volatile exchange rates, consumer confidence ebbed and demand weakened. Demand for interest rate-sensitive items was particularly hard hit. These included real estate, and the related building materials industries such as cement and steel, while demand for durable goods such as cars and home appliances also plummeted. Since cement and steel, in particular, are power-intensive industries, petroleum refining also took a hit. On the other hand, the dominant food processing industry and export-based manufacturing, principally electronics and footwear and garments, did well. Food processing, especially of more finished products, benefited from the new-found cost competitiveness of domestic products compared to similar imported items with the peso's steep depreciation. Exports of electronics and footwear and garments enjoyed a lift from the buoyant economies of major trading partners, the US and Europe.

Hopefully Reaching Bottom

With a strong third quarter kick sustained until Q4 99, the manufacturing sector seems to be finally showing signs of recovery. The sector reversed the 1.1% contraction seen in 1998 to post a modest 1.4% growth in 1999. The better performance means economic growth was relatively more broad based than earlier indications. Consolidation and restructuring in the sector, e.g. the closure of the country's only steelmaking firm in November, indicate that the rebound may have already begun. Import volumes have started picking up. Philippine authorities have also remained relatively steadfast in their tariff restructuring plans, providing sufficient incentive for competition and expansion. Six crisis-affected industries registered rebounds in Q499, after more than four consecutive quarters of decline. The tobacco sector registered 17.5% growth, the highest in Q4 99. However, part of the increase in volume could be attributed to stockpiling of cigarette manufacturers ahead of a previously legislated increase in excise tax rates in 2000. Non-metallic firms grew by 6.5% during the quarter. Still to recover are the beverage, chemical, and textile sectors. The overall manufacturing production index expanded by 3.1%, reversing the 11.8% contraction seen in 1998. Transport equipment was the top performer, with a y-o-y growth of 18.3%. The index was also boosted by food manufactures, which grew by 14.9%. Average capacity utilisation in December 99 for manufacturing was 79.4%, up from the 77.2% in 1998.

Services: Bearing Up

The services sector was resilient throughout the difficult conditions in 1998, achieving respectable growth of 3.5%, although this was lower than the 5.4% posted in 1997. Understandably, the finance sector sustained the sharpest decline in activity as growth plummeted from 13% to 4.4%. That the financial industry did not contract may be attributed to the relatively healthy state of the banking sector going into the crisis, enabling it to carry on operations despite an increase in bad loans from 5.4% at end-1997 to 11% at end-1998. Indeed, there was no major bank failure and those that occurred among the smaller banks were, or are in the process of being, rehabilitated without recourse to public funds. A less precipitous decline in transportation and communication is directly attributable to the financial difficulties of flag carrier PAL, as a result of which it cut back on routes and number of trips flown. More stable activity in land and marine transportation, as well as double-digit growth in communications due to deregulation of the telecom sector, partially compensated for PAL's downturn. Wholesale and retail trade went in opposite directions in 1998, with wholesale trade contracting and retail trade expanding. Retail trade activity may have been supported by income remittances of overseas workers, which continued to be robust in 1998.

Service industries bottomed out in Q1 99, and were more robust going into Q4 99. The sector grew by a solid 3.9% in 1999, paced by Q4 growth rate of 4.4%. Transport and communications expanded from a rate of 3.4% in Q1 99 to a hefty 6.1% in Q4, bolstered by intense competition and activity among the companies in the telecommunications sector. The transport sector was relatively stable. Government services was strongest in Q2 99, growing by 5% as the government pursued its fiscal stimulus package. This has, however, slowed to 2.7% in Q4, reaching y-o-y growth of 3.3%. Activity in the housing and real estate sector remained lacklustre with a y-o-y growth of 0.6%. The Q1 contraction of 0.2%, though, has been reversed slowly through 1999 to reach a slight growth of 1.0% in Q4. Wholesale and retail trade remained robust, as prices dropped steadily, and favourable weather assured steady food production and supply. Financial services were sluggish, with quarterly slowdowns, which started in 1998, continuing into 1999. With the pick-up in manufacturing only apparent in Q3, demand for bank loans was still slow for most of 1999. The generally bearish mood in the business sector is putting the brakes on a more solid rebound for financial services.

Spending Squeeze

By expenditure item, the only growth area in 1998 was private consumption. All other major categories contracted: government consumption because of the cuts in spending mandated by the Department of Budget and Management; investments due to high interest rates and weak demand that increased idle capacity, and net exports of goods and services because of the drop in services exports such as insurance, transportation and tourism. However, by Q1 99 public consumption grew sharply as the government's pump-priming programme took effect while private spending maintained a steady 2.5% growth rate. On the other hand, investments and net exports of goods and services were still contracting, albeit by smaller amounts. By the end of 1999, public consumption registered a growth rate of 5.5%. The hefty 7.6% increase in Q1 tapered to only 4.7% in Q4, as the government's fiscal deficit expanded beyond target. The decline was partially offset by an improvement in private consumption growth, which reached 3% in Q4. Investments continued to shrink, though by a smaller amount of 1% in Q4 99. On a y-o-y basis, investment levels were down by 2.1%. Investments failed to perk up, despite an environment of declining interest rates. The market's weak demand is exacting a stronger pull against the reawakening of more bullish investor sentiments. The banking sector's more cautious stance on loans also dampened any possible surge in investments. The paradox of a credit crunch in the midst of ample liquidity characterised much of the credit environment in 1999. As non-performing ratios of banks trended upwards, access to loans of most firms, except perhaps the biggest, tightened. This scenario is likely to have ended with most of the banks now finished with restructuring of accounts, in beefing up reserves and in setting up of provisions.

Employment Woes

Employment trends have been reflective of the direction the real economy has taken. Thus, in 1998, as the economy went into a recession, unemployment climbed to an average 10.1% from 8.7% in 1997. The worst hit sector was agriculture, with 381,000 jobs being lost – a 3% fall – as a result of the *El Niño*. The manufacturing sector also saw a contraction in jobs, but not to the same extent as in agriculture as a decline of only 1% was registered, equivalent to about 15,000 lost jobs. However, the services sector continued to see an increase in employment in 1998, especially in wholesale and retail trade, transportation and community, social and personal services. With the improvement in weather conditions that produced plentiful harvests beginning in Q1 99, the number of farm jobs has climbed. Employment in agriculture improved 3% y-o-y in January and 16% in April. This has since tapered off to 0.6% by October. Again, reflective of trends in GDP, manufacturing employment continued to languish up to April 1999, when it fell 2%. By October, however, employment in manufacturing expanded by 3.4% as firms geared up production for the holiday season. Total employment improved by 2.6%, with services again leading in the number of people employed. People hired in services increased by 4.7%, while those in industry rose by 1.7%.

In spite of the increase in consumer price inflation – the benchmark for wage adjustments – to 9.7% in 1998 from 5.9% the previous year, labour unions passed up on the opportunity to ask for wage increases at the beginning of 1999, the traditional time for pay adjustments. This is a rare occurrence but it was clear from the number of newly distressed companies that additional cost pressures could push them to bankruptcy. The fact that several multinational companies decided to limit their operations, if not entirely close shop, was another factor in labour unions putting a lid on pay demands.

In 1999, inflation slowed to an average of 6.6%, largely due to a more abundant food supply easing the rise in food prices, dampening pressures on wage demands. However, a series of fuel price increases following the advance of international crude oil prices and a hike in its generation tariff rate of state-run **National Power Corp**, the first since 1993, led to slight wage adjustments which took effect in October 1999. The increase in the minimum wage ranged from 1.7% to 4.7% outside and within Metro Manila, respectively. The minimum wage now stands at PHP223.50 in Metro Manila and ranges from PHP117 to PHP200 in areas outside Metro Manila for non-agricultural workers.

3 Key Economic Sectors

Introduction

Manufacturing Drives The Economy

With the exception of agriculture, all sectors of the Philippine economy showed encouraging signs in the first quarter. The manufacturing sector capped four consecutive quarters of expansion with 5.8% growth. The combined transport, communication and storage subsector also performed well, doubling its growth rate to 7% from last year's 3.4%. Communication alone leaped by 9.5%. Meanwhile, financial services grew moderately in the first quarter by 1.5%. This represented a fall from the year ago level of 2.6% and growth of 2.2% in Q4 99, as the lingering effects of the financial crisis and institutional adjustments following the series of big bank mergers in 1999 weighed in. Real estate services grew 1.7% in Q1 2000, up from a contraction of 0.2% in Q1 99. And the 0.7% decline in the construction sector, was a marked improvement on its deep contraction of 12.8% in Q1 99 (albeit due predominantly to the low base year).

Growth was weighed down by poor agricultural output, which rose a much slower-than-anticipated 0.2%. From being the key driver of growth in 1999, **BMI** forecasts a weak outlook for agriculture this year. A high base effect, the onset of El Niño and unrest in the important agricultural region of Mindanao will conspire to contain growth prospects in the sector to around 2%, rising to 3-4.5% in 2001-02.

Growth in the first quarter was dragged down by a poor agricultural performance.

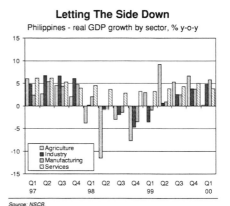

Letting The Side Down
Philippines - real GDP growth by sector, % y-o-y

Source: NSCB.

GDP GROWTH BY SECTOR (% Y/Y)								
	1992	1993	1994	1995	1996	1997	1998	1999
Agriculture	0.4	2.1	2.6	0.8	2.5	4.2	-6.6	6.4
Industry	-0.5	1.6	5.8	7.0	6.4	5.9	-1.9	0.7
Services	1.0	2.5	4.2	4.9	6.5	5.4	3.5	4.1
Source: NSCB.								

Manufacturing

Export Performance: Still Riding High

Expansion in the manufacturing sector will become broader-based and more sustainable.

Of the manufacturing's 20 subsectors, 16 grew in the first quarter, compared to only seven a year ago. The recovery, while early compared to the rest of the countries afflicted with the financial crisis, has been slow to take off. With value of production registering growth of 16.9% in the first quarter and import volumes finally increasing, the probability of manufacturing taking up the slack from agriculture, driving growth momentum forward, is increasing. This favors a more sustainable pattern of growth.

In April 2000, exports posted the biggest rise since December 1999, growing 13.7% y-o-y to US$2.7bn. Higher shipments of disk drives and clothing made up for a decline in electronic exports, indicating that Philippine exports are becoming more broad-based. For the first four months of the year, exports rose by 10.6% y-o-y, reaching US$11.3bn. Government projections put export growth for 2000 at 14.3%, reaching the US$40bn mark. These estimates, however, might have to be reconfigured downwards, if the rift between Taiwan and Manila continues (**BMI** forecasts just 10% growth). Exports to Taiwan – the Philippines' second biggest export destination – have grown 40% in the last two years due to robust demand for semiconductors.

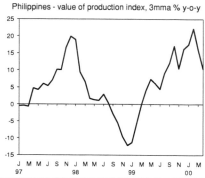

Driving Growth
Philippines - value of production index, 3mma % y-o-y

Source: Monthly Integrated Survey of Selected Industries.

Food & Beverages

The food & beverages sector is undergoing a period of consolidation.

Accounting for 41% of total manufacturing output, food and beverages performed better than most manufacturing sub-sectors in 1999, growing 4.8% y-o-y, despite a 1.2% contraction in beverages. Philippine food and beverage giant **San Miguel Corp** (SMC) netted PHP6bn in 1999, up 82% on 1998 levels. The healthy increase was achieved despite a fall in consolidated net sales to PHP75.6bn from the previous year's PHP78.2bn as a result of a 56% slump in the volume of coconut oil business due to low copra supply. The improvements in operating income are attributed to lower production costs, lower overhead costs and a price increase in beer and liquor products in the second quarter. SMC has also been undergoing organisational restructuring, and is estimated to have saved US$10mn from the relocation of its regional office for international beer operations to Manila from Hong Kong.

All these savings and additional income are adding to coffers already laden with US$1bn in cash from SMC management's divestment of subsidiaries, e.g. **Magnolia** and **Coca-Cola**. With consumption of its flagship product, beer, falling for the sixth consecutive year, San Miguel has been on the lookout for new ventures. In March 2000, it bought **Sugarland**, which dominates four-fifths of the domestic market for ready-to-drink powdered juice. It has likewise expressed interest in investing in **First Dominion**, a large local exporter of canned tuna, and is set to acquire 50.1% of the Australian beer company **J. Boag & Son Ltd**. SMC offered to purchase a majority stake in the Australian brewer for US$52.4mn. The acquisition will allow SMC to penetrate Australia's premium beer market, which is expected to grow by 15% per annum in the medium term. San Miguel will initially produce its Pale Pilsen and Super Dry beer brands, with other products following within the year.

San Miguel's domestic market plans include the establishment of starch plants nationwide to produce fructose, alcohol and biodegradable plastic for its packaging business. The first starch plant will be located in the northern province of Isabela, at an estimated cost of US$10-15mn. The company also has a PHP10bn plan to establish a logistics and distribution hub that will integrate the company's operations from manufacturing and packaging to distribution. This plan has been discussed by company chairman Eduardo Cojuangco in this year's annual stockholders meeting. The proposal is to set the hub up as a 400 ha estate with world-class port facilities and bulk handling capabilities. San Miguel intends to compete for the custom of both domestic and international companies for the distribution of their products nationwide.

San Miguel plans to establish a logistics and distribution hub that will integrate the company's operations.

SMC is also looking at expanding into the franchising business with its flagship product, beer, as the main attraction. For 2000, the company intends to establish 10-20 pubs nationwide. The venture offers three advantages to the food and beverage conglomerate. First, with 84% of the beer market San Miguel pubs can be income generating. They will serve as a showcase not only for beer, but also other San Miguel products. Lastly, the pubs will keep San Miguel informed of emerging consumer habits and preferences.

These possible acquisitions could cost close to the US$1bn that SMC is reported to have as shopping money. There are also moves to resolve the 14-year old government sequestration of 27% of San Miguel Corp. With the government's cash-strapped position, the Estrada administration has been looking for strategic ways to unload these shares and resolve the coconut levy fund issue with minimal political costs. Some analysts have recommended that San Miguel buy back its own shares should the government decide to unload. That would put Coquanco in control of almost 72% of total voting shares in the company.

However, it does not always make good business sense to spend US$80mn just to buy back one's own shares, and San Miguel has looked at other opportunities even apart from its core business. There are talks about a possible purchase of its own gas or petroleum company to take advantage of future trends towards cleaner sources of energy such as natural gas. San Miguel is also casting its eye on the burgeoning market for Internet commerce. With an archipelago-wide distribution system bolstered by 500 independent dealers, who own some 2,000 trucks nationwide, San Miguel can offer a strategic partnership to companies wanting to sell goods through the Internet. San Miguel officials expect Internet sales to account for some 10%-15% of the company's total income in the future.

Pure Foods, the food unit of the **Ayala Group** of companies, is also looking at 2000 as a year of expansion. It intends to invest PHP1.5bn in the pursuit of possible acquisitions, expansion of product lines and wider market penetration. Pure Foods will build up capital through a mix of internal cash generation, bank borrowings, and capital market issues. After investing additional equity in subsidiaries like **Burger King** last year, the company has not yet specified which firms it is targeting for acquisition.

BREAKDOWN OF MANUFACTURING (PHPMN)				
	1998	1999	% of total manufacturing	% change (1999/98)
Food manufactures	78,744	83,049	37.0	5.5
Beverage industries	9,003	8,896	4.0	-1.2
Tobacco manufactures	5,538	5,681	2.5	2.6
Textile manufactures	5,085	4,660	2.1	-8.4
Footwear & wearing apparel	12,699	10,801	4.8	-14.9
Wood & cork products	2,769	2,451	1.1	-11.5
Furniture & fixtures	2,881	2,852	1.3	-1.0
Paper & paper products	2,132	2,033	0.9	-4.6
Publishing & printing	3,093	3,055	1.4	-1.2
Leather & leather products	224	222	0.1	-0.9
Rubber products	1,849	2,065	0.9	11.7
Chemicals & chemical products	14,169	13,868	6.2	-2.1
Products of petroleum & coal	37,472	37,137	16.5	-0.9
Non-metallic mineral products	6,614	5,834	2.6	-11.8
Basic metal industries	4,745	4,206	1.9	-11.4
Metal industries	4,231	4,272	1.9	1.0
Machinery except electrical	3,540	3,555	1.6	0.4
Electrical machinery	19,284	22,277	9.9	15.5
Transport equipment	1,810	1,984	0.9	9.6
Miscellaneous manufactures	5,269	5,769	2.6	9.5
Gross value added in manufacturing	221,151	224,667	100.0	1.6

Source NSCB.

Cosmos Bottling, the beverage subsidiary of food giant **RFM**, is optimistic about future growth prospects despite the continuing poor performance in the soft drinks market. The company's local brands, Sarsi and Pop, offer stiff competition to popular international brands in the provinces. Sales volume grew by 4% last year, despite an industry decline of 14%. Cosmos is competing aggressively in the marketing of its products, fighting for the burgeoning teenage market. The industry should be able to grow modestly this year with the onset of drier weather and with the threat of a possible imposition of a soft drinks tax diminishing as Congress shifts its attention to the elections in 2001.

H.J. Heinz Company, one of the world's leading marketers of branded foods, is signing a joint venture agreement with **Nutri-Asia** of Manila, a major producer of catsup (ketchup) products. H.J. Heinz, Heinz UFC Philippines, Inc., will employ the more than 200 people of Nutri-Asia and existing manufacturing facilities located in Tarlac, Alabang, and Davao will become part of the joint venture. Nutri-Asia brings to the venture a wide distribution coverage in both retail and food service outlets.

Heinz has signed a joint venture agreement with Nutri-Asia of Manila.

Ailing sugar milling and food firm, **Victorias Milling** (VMC) is still in the process of finding its way through a difficult rehabilitation process which has already taken three years. VMC management and the SEC-appointed receiver have been at odds over the direction and scope of the company's rehabilitation plan or whether the company should be finally liquidated. With VMC a major player and employer in the sugar industry, VMC's rehabilitation is being closely watched. The Philippine sugar industry has lagged behind in terms of efficiency and use of modern technology, reducing the competitiveness of Philippine sugar exports.

Electronics And E-Business Software

Electrical machinery performed the best of all manufacturing sub-sector's in 1999, growing 15.5% y-o-y and increasing its share of total manufacturing to 9.9%. Electronics exports fell in April, but the current upswing in the global electronics cycle should ensure that the sector remains buoyant in 2000 and into the first half of 2001, although growth will be tempered by a loss of confidence against a climate of political uncertainty. **Ionics Circuits** secured a strong first quarter performance, posting a net profit of PHP1.69bn, more than 30 times the PHP55.7mn it earned in Q1 99. Ionics manufactures electronics components. The company operates seven production facilities in the Philippines, one in the US, and one in China. It intends to expand production and add new facilities. It is also shifting to full turnkey operations from its old consignment-based operations. The shift is seen as a positive step

The current upswing in the global electronics cycle should ensure that the electronics sector remains buoyant in 2000.

Mixed Fortunes

Philippines - electronics exports, top 10 destinations US$

Country	1999	2000	change, % y-o-y
USA	376.3	311.4	-17.2
Singapore	152.2	166.7	9.5
Netherlands	150.9	150.6	-0.2
Taiwan	118.6	125.5	5.8
Japan	108.8	101.6	-6.6
Malaysia	69.97	86.1	23.6
Hong Kong	69.6	84.8	21.8
Thailand	37.8	47.3	25.2
Great Britain	63.8	42.0	-34.2
South Korea	34.1	41.7	22.3

Source: NSO.

The Philippines has become a major player in the new trend of outsourcing backroom and shared-service centre operations.

from the present assembly-type operations system and is considered by analysts to be a move that will benefit the company and its clients in the long run. The bulk of the gain in net profit came from the PHP1.59bn proceeds derived from the listing of its subsidiary **Ionics EMS Inc** on the Singapore stock exchange. However, earnings of PHP100mn from core operations itself was already impressive, together with a 79% increase in sales volume in Q1 2000 to PHP1.31bn from PHP733mn in Q1 99. One of the main reasons for the turnaround is the improved performance of Ionics subsidiaries, which were debt-laden and operated below capacity last year. Another is the company's expansion into China, which will provide a wider market for its products.

Software A.G., a Germany-based firm, is taking advantage of the pool of Filipino talent in software development by intensifying its three-year operations in the country. It is launching e-business software products to compete in the highly competitive global market. The firm projects that their Philippine operations will be able to compete strongly for the expanding worldwide trend for e-commerce. Software A.G. has also set up the Asia Resource Centre in the Philippines, which has application development capabilities, and provides consultancy service and training.

Services

Outsourcing And Backroom Operations Potential

Already called a jewel in the making by some analysts, is an export alternative that has only lately been attracting attention. Without any overt government support and special fiscal incentives, the Philippines has become a major player in the new trend of outsourcing backroom and shared-service centre operations. Some ten major multinational companies are already utilising the country as an outsource point. These include **America Online**, which employs some 600 Filipinos in the Clark Special Economic Zone, answering e-mails from all over the world. **Andersen Consulting** hires locals to customise and develop software. **Caltex** accountants in Manila process transactions for Southeast Asia and Hong Kong. Animators in Manila produce many of the cartoons watched by children in the USA. Other relocated backroom and shared service functions already operational in the Philippines are call centres, engineering design and review, website design, data entry services, and medical reporting. Aside from AOL, Caltex and Andersen, other firms outsourcing in the country include **Northwest Airlines, UPS, Bechtel, Procter and Gamble, Fluor Daniel, Sea and**

Noble, **Mitsubishi Heavy Industries**, **Sumitomo Corporation**, and **Chiyoda Corporation**.

This new trend highlights an oft-recognised, but least exploited, comparative advantage of the Philippines – the abundance of a cheap, highly skilled, easily trained, creative, and English speaking workforce. These qualities enable the Philippines to beat Hong Kong, Thailand, and Singapore in the provision of outsourcing services.

Transport And Communications

Tan To Sell PAL?

After being in the red for several years, **Philippine Airlines** (PAL) broke even in the fiscal year ending March 2000. However, Lucio Tan seems to have had enough of air turbulence. In April he indicated that he wants to sell PAL. The PAL that he sells will, however, be different from the one he acquired through less than transparent means in 1993. Under Tan's management, PAL has divested itself of several subsidiaries, including lucrative catering and ground handling services firms, in order to acquire cash to concentrate on its core business. These firms are now owned by **Macro Asia**, a holding company also said to be owned indirectly by Tan. PAL could look like a good acquisition for a potential buyer, now that it is leaner, has less employees and hence a weaker union, and has concentrated flights on profitable routes.

Lucio Tan has indicated that he intends to sell off Philippines Airlines, now a much leaner company than the one he acquired in 1993.

Satisfying The Text Generation

Globe Telecom has signed a US$8.6mn purchase deal with telecom equipment maker, **Lucent Technologies**. The deal allows Lucent to supply Globe with different types of communications equipment, including switching, data networking and optical equipment. Globe, on the other hand, is tapping Lucent for the expansion of its international gateway switches to provide additional capacity to its local and international traffic. With PHP14.7bn set aside for expansion, Globe is looking at increasing its market share of the cellular phone market. A merger with **Islacom** in 1999 has added 190,000 new subscribers, increasing the total base to 1.2mn. Globe's GSM system attracted new subscribers due to the popularity of text messaging services. Globe is expected to improve its market share, despite its competition with the slightly more popular **Smart Communications**. The merger with Islacom increased Globe's frequency and will ensure that is has the capacity to expand its subscriber base in the future. Globe pioneered the WAP (wireless

The text generation has bolstered sales of new communications firms.

A settlement of Piltel's financial woes will improve the outlook for PLDT's consolidated income in 2000.

application protocol) and incorporated this into their services much ahead of its closest competitor, Smart. Globe intends to expand WAP use to 50,000 by opening up the service to all subscribers – post-paid, prepaid and roaming. With 70-80% of Globe's subscribers on the prepaid service, it makes good business strategy to include them in the WAP service.

PLDT has formalised its acquisition of cellular firm Smart, and concluded its strategic alliance with **Nippon Telegraph and Telephone**'s (NTT)'s subsidiary, **NTT Communications**. The deal proceeded even as PLDT's beleaguered subsidiary, **Pilipino Telephone** (Piltel) concluded debt agreements with its creditors. A settlement of Piltel's financial woes will improve the outlook for PLDT's consolidated income for 2000. The acquisition of Smart and the NTT partnership are PLDT's major initiatives, alongside a move towards convergence. Venturing into the burgeoning Internet industry, Smart is also offering WAP mail service to its subscribers. The service, offered in partnership with another PLDT company, **Infocom Technologies**, offers GSM subscribers a choice of either accessing email via their Smart WAP cellphones or creating new Smart email addresses for free. Smart is also working on a partnership with Finland's **Sonera Zed**, a mobile Internet leader.

PLDT's expansion is taking the 76-year old company towards the newest ventures in the telecommunications industry – cable and e-commerce. After its purchase of **Philippine Home Cable**, last year, it is now moving aggressively towards further network convergence by acquiring media companies which can provide content. PLDT has formed **Mediaquest** to handle media units and undertake the acquisition of media-related firms, which will include television stations. Mediaquest's acquisitions are to be integrated with the content needs of Smart for its WAP service. **ABS-CBN** is also slowly expanding its Internet services (Skyinet), and its **Skycable network** currently holds the largest market share in the home cable business. The Lopez family-owned firm has enough resources, both financial and political, to provide competition to PLDT in new technology ventures.

TELECOMS				
	1995	1996	1997	1998
Lines	1,877,072	3,352,842	5,775,556	6,641,480
Exchanges	601	741	828	1,050
Source: National Telecommunications Commission.				

Nextel Communications is mulling an additional US$140mn in investment in the Philippines for the installation of its own backbone. It is awaiting the passage of generous incentives for information technology ventures under the proposed amendments to EO 226, or the Omnibus Investments Code. The additional investments will be put into its Philippine subsidiary, **Infocom Communication Network**. Should this materialise, this will be the second US$140mn that Nextel has infused into Infocom. Infocom operates a wireless digital communications network that integrates mobile telephone service, a digital two-way radio service and text/numeric paging into a single phone. The National Telecommunications Commission (NTC) has ordered Infocom to remove its cellular services from its trunk radio operations. The NTC has also asked Nextel to obtain a separate license to operate cellular phone services, in addition to its license to trunk radio operations. Once Nextel has hurdled NTC regulations, it can offer a competitive product and service to both Globe and Smart.

Retail Trade

Foreign Retailers Finally Made Welcome

The much-awaited Retail Trade Liberalisation Law was finally signed by Estrada on March 7, 2000. This law opens up the Philippine market of 75mn people with Westernised tastes and sensibilities to the world's major retailers. It allows full ownership of domestic enterprises by foreigners with a minimum capital infusion of US$7.5mn. Those investing between US$2.5mn and US$7.5mn can own up to 60%, rising to full ownership after two years. The law also requires that 30% of store merchandise be locally made. This could be a sticky point, unless Philippine export purchases by foreign retailers are considered part of the local goods quota.

The Retail Trade Liberalisation Law has been signed at last.

Even before the law was signed, **Casino**, one of France's biggest retailers, acquired the cash-strapped discount retailer, **Uniwide**, for US$100mn. Casino then became the first foreign company in over half a century to get majority control of a retail enterprise in the Philippines. Terms of the agreement had Casino buying a majority stake in a newly-created enterprise, whose assets include 10 Uniwide stores with an average selling area of 10,000m² each, one distribution centre, and five sites for future expansion. Uniwide itself is negotiating to restructure its PHP11bn debt on which it defaulted mainly because of the 1997-98 financial crisis and its unfortunate foray into real property. Casino is expecting sales from the new enterprise to reach PHP12bn in 2001, close to the PHP14.5bn sales of 1997.

The new law is attracting other potential investors such as **Wal-Mart**, **Price Club**, and **Price Smart**. Domestic firms do not seem ready to surrender their market share without a tough fight. The country's top retailer, **Shoemart**, is spending nearly US$200mn over the next three years on five new stores, each covering about 50,000m², and US$7.5mn to upgrade its computer systems. With a population growing at a rapid rate of 2.5% annually, the Philippine market is ready to absorb, and enjoy the benefits of, more open competition in the retail trade sector.

Power

Reenergizing The Power Industry

On the final homestretch before the next Congressional elections in 2001, and after three years of delay, the House of Representatives and the Senate approved the long-awaited bill restructuring the power sector, paving the way for the privatisation of the National Power Corporation (Napocor). This was one of the critical reform bills pending from the start of the current Congress. The Omnibus Power Bill dismantles Napocor's control over the industry and opens it up to new players. A major selling point of the bill is the possibility of lower power costs, which will happen but only over the long-term. To prevent a return of monopolistic control, the bill bans cross-ownership between power generation and electricity distribution firms. Cross-ownership is also banned between distribution utilities and transmission companies.

The Senate has approved its own version of the bill. Both versions will now be discussed and reconciled at a bicameral committee. June 2000 is being talked about as a possible deadline for the ratification of the bill. In the meantime, minor controversy has sprung up with the House approval of the bill. An opposition Congressman has accused House leaders of distributing *payola* (payoff) to ensure passage of the bill. At this point, this seems to be a groundless charge and is not likely to delay its final passage.

After three years of delay, the long-awaited bill restructuring the power sector has been approved, paving the way for the privatisation of the National Power Corporation (Napocor).

Head Above Water

Philippines - gross value added in electricity, gas & water, PHPmn

	1998	1999	% y-o-y	Q1 2000
Electricity & Gas	28,182	28,886	2.5	6,631
Water	2,133	2,373	11.3	729
Total	30,315	31,259	3.1	7,360

Source: NSCB.

Financial Services

General Banking Law Amendments Approved

Following the ratification of the Revised Securities Act, Congress ratified the amendments to the fifty year-old General Banking Act in mid-April. The bill was finally signed into law on May 23, 2000. The amendments open the sector to further foreign participation and strengthen the BSP's supervisory powers. It permits a foreign bank to own up to 100% of only one local bank in the Philippines within a period of seven years from the enactment of the law. Within the same period, a foreign bank that acquires up to 60% equity of a local bank prior to the passage of the law, can raise its stake to up to 100%. However, the Monetary Board must ensure that 70% of the entire banking sector's assets are held by Filipino-controlled banks.

Financial sector consolidation is moving much faster in the Philippines than elsewhere in the region, and the process is, to a large extent, market-driven. Merger fever reached its height in 1999. More banks should continue to merge this year, though for the most part, merged banks will still be adjusting to the fit of their new structures. Some downsides to the banks' marriages of convenience are only now becoming apparent. The investment outlooks for **Metropolitan Bank** and **Trust Company** have been downgraded by **Moody's** and **Standard and Poor's**. The ratings agencies assessed that Metrobank's acquisition of **Solid Banking Corporation** and **Asian Banking Corporation** contributed only marginally to its franchise. **Equitable Bank**'s acquisition of **Philippine Commercial International Bank** (PCIB) was widely applauded but integration has been difficult, with many top officers leaving the merged banking institution. In this case, there seems to be a problem fitting in two different corporate thrusts: PCIB's traditional focus on corporate banking and Equitable's aggressive growth objectives.

BSP Governor Buenaventura expects at least two more major mergers in 2000. After industry consolidation is complete, there could only be about four or five major local banks left. The consolidation process will generally mean some form of foreign ownership in the surviving institutions. The BSP is pushing the merger process in its belief that size matters if banks are to be sufficiently capitalised to undertake extensive technological upgrading. With a moratorium on new branch licenses, even the smaller banks can become attractive targets for acquisitions. Their branch networks create valuable assets for new buyers.

Banking loans are gradually edging up, as banks take time to adjust to last year's frenzy of mergers and consolidation.

Cleaning Up The Books
Philippines - top 10 banks, end-1999

	Tier One Capital, US$mn	Capital Assets Ratio, %	Pre-tax profit, US$mn
Metrobank	1,198	11.96	98
Equitable PCI Bank	1,130	16.81	34
Bank of the Philippine Islands	747	13.03	121
Philippine National Bank	521	9.61	N/A
Far East Bank & Trust Company	480	14.10	13
Development Bank of the Philippines	356	10.36	27
United Coconut Planters Bank	338	12.06	28
Land Bank Philippines	337	6.83	18
Union Bank of the Philippines	280	21.37	25
Allied Banking Corporation	243	10.30	2

Source: The Banker.

The privatisation of Philippine National Bank has been delayed.

Relatively Healthy
non-performing loans - a regional comparison, June 1999

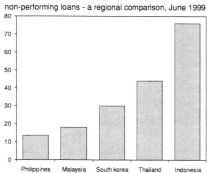

Source: Bangko Sentral Pilipinas.

Rizal Banking Corporation (RCBC), meanwhile, acquired 40% control of **Bankard** from **Equitable-PCI Bank** for approximately PHP1.7bn. Bankard is a publicly listed corporation and was the credit card company of **PCI Bank**. With the merger of Equitable Bank, which also owns **Equitable Cardnetwork** (ECN), and PCIB, Bankard went on the purchase block. RCBC gains a larger presence in the credit card market with its Bankard purchase. Bankard's cardholder base of 308,000 as of Q1 00 accounts for 15% of the market. ECN, which issues Visa and MasterCard credit cards, is the country's leading card issuer with a combined cardholder base of 700,000.

The government formed an agreement with the IMF to have Philippine National Bank (PNB) privatised by June 2000, with the combined shares of the government, Lucio Tan, and Templeton on offer. Two prequalified bidders have emerged. One is RCBC, which had earlier expressed an interest in acquiring other banks as well. The other is a foreign consortium led by **Beatrice Foods**. However, after Beatrice Foods failed to produce a bank partner, it was disqualified and the bidding scheduled for June 9, 2000 was declared a failure. PNB's non-performing loan ratio is among the highest in the industry, but has the benefits of an extensive branch network and residual goodwill from being one of the oldest banks in the country. Good management and insulation from political pressure are necessary ingredients for a comeback for PNB.

The government says that it remains committed to PNB's privatisation. Lucio Tan has also said that he still intends to sell his 46%, if the price is right. Under government rules, a negotiated sale is possible after a second failed bidding. It remains to be seen whether the government can negotiate a fair price, and negotiated bids have the disadvantage of being less transparent. Questions can always be raised over whether government sold at the best price possible. As it now stands, the probability of the government exiting from PNB anytime soon remains murky.

FINANCIAL SERVICES (GROSS VALUE ADDED, PHPMN)			
	1998	1999	Q1 00
Banks	32,804	33,088	8,474
Non-banks	4,211	4,310	1,011
Insurance	8,430	8,913	2,159
Gross value added in finance	45,445	46,311	11,644
Source: NSCB.			

Property

Supply Glut

The property sector is still in the doldrums and is not expected to stage any recovery in 2000. A combination of liquidity problems and a short-term loss of confidence is driving property developers away from investment in the sector. According to the National Real Estate Association, some 40,000 houses nationwide remain unpaid, stemming the flow of funds to developers and stunting the desire to develop more property. Even large property developer, **Ayala Land** ALI has admitted to encountering difficulties in the present property glut. ALI posted lower revenues of PHP8.94mn in 1999, down 14.3% y-o-y. The property firm's income also dipped to PHP645mn in Q1 2000, from PHP650mn a year earlier, due to higher costs and expenses. For 2000, ALI is focused on a major overhaul of its 11ha Greenbelt property in Makati City. Slated to be undertaken within a two-year timeframe, the project will turn the mostly commercial property into a modern retail, residential, hotel and office complex.

Despite the sombre outlook for the sector, there are also some intrepid developers who take a longer-term view. **Greenfield Development**, majority-owned by **United Laboratories**, has expressed plans to develop its 25ha property along EDSA, Metro Manila's major thoroughfare, into a multi-billion peso modern central business district in Mandaluyong City. This is a ten-year plan, which includes the construction of a one-stop-shop, shopping mall, high-rise residential and office towers. The firm intends to take advantage of its strategic location along EDSA and the stations of the Metro Rail Transit. Should this property development take off, it will compete directly with the 16ha Greenhills along Ortigas Avenue in adjacent Pasig City. This property, owned by **Ortigas & Co.**, is also on the offering block. Located in this commercial property is a popular supermarket and the thriving Greenhills shopping mall. ALI has expressed interest in the property, together with other developers like the Gokongwei family-owned **Robinson's Land**, Henry Sy's **SM Group**, and **Metro Pacific**. The property is expected to be valued at PHP25bn.

The property sector is still suffering from excess supply.

Kept Afloat By Government Spending

Philippines - gross value added in construction, PHPmn

	1998	1999	% y-o-y	Q1 2000
Public	42,919	49,335	14.9	13,666
Private	55,912	49,686	-11.1	10,515
Total construction	98,831	99,021	0.2	24,181

Source: NSO.

The government has forecast 2.5- 3.5% growth in the construction sector in 2000, up from 0.2 growth in 1999. The slowdown in Q1 was partly caused by the government's fiscal consolidation and the delayed approval of the 2000 national government budget. This stopped the implementation of even on-going government infrastructure projects. Some pick-up is expected in the next three quarters, especially as 2000 is the eve of the local elections next year. The low end of the growth range for the sector is still achievable if the fiscal position strengthens, allowing for the easier release of appropriations for capital projects. However, **BMI** is not confident that the fiscal deficit target will be met (*see Economic Outook, Fiscal Policy*), and the scope for higher public expenditure on construction in the second half is limited.

Profile and Recent Developments

Introduction

Welcoming Foreign Investment

The regional crisis and the *El Niño* took their toll as the economy went into a mild recession in 1998. High domestic interest rates increased debt burdens, dried up credit and created financial distress for several firms. A significantly depreciated peso drove up prices of imports and made payment on foreign-denominated loans more difficult. Hit hardest, were highly leveraged companies, property and construction-related companies and banks that had lent to them. Meanwhile, the prolonged *El Niño*-induced drought drastically reduced agricultural production, and led to shrinking incomes and increasing unemployment in the farm sector as it underwent the most severe contraction since record keeping began in the 1950s.

To enhance survival, domestic companies welcomed foreign investors. Notably, several global players took significant stakes in local cement companies as the industry reeled from declining demand, falling prices, overcapacity and a surge in debt charges. **Holderbank Financiere Glaris AG** of Switzerland, **Cemex SA** of Mexico, **Blue Circle Industries** of the UK and **Lafarge SA** of France bought up substantial stakes in almost all domestic cement companies, including **Apo Cement, Bacnotan Cement, Davao Union Cement, HI Cement, Alsons Cement, Fortune Cement** and **Southeast Asia Cement**. A change in top management at food and beverage conglomerate **San Miguel Corp** (SMC) allowed Swiss-based **Nestlé** to take over their Philippine operations, in what had up to then been a 45% (SMC) /55% joint venture, as SMC opted to sell assets in order to strengthen its balance sheet. The fall in the stock market, resulting in lower equity prices, prompted a hostile takeover of market leader **Philippine Long Distance Telephone Co** by Hong Kong-based **First Pacific Co Ltd** (FPCL). FPCL took control when it effectively bought a 17% stake.

Manufacturing

The Winners And The Losers

Although manufacturing output shrank 1% in 1998, this was far better than the 7% contraction in agriculture, as the adverse affects of the regional economic crisis did not fall evenly across the sector. Among those that benefited, were domestic producers, which became more cost-competitive with a depreciated peso. As imports became more expensive, consumers turned to cheaper domestically produced products. This was true for food, beverages and paper products. Similarly, exporters enjoyed gains from a weak currency. Manufacturers of electronic products, footwear and wearing apparel and leather products saw an expansion, rather than a contraction, in output. As the country's major markets are the US and Europe, their relatively more robust economies were able to absorb Philippine exports, helping to keep growth rates among the highest in the region. But cheap imports from neighbouring countries, whose currencies had also taken a beating, hurt domestic manufacturers who alleged dumping from countries such as South Korea. This was true of basic metal and metal industries. Meanwhile, flagging demand for non-basic goods such as cars and home appliances kept makers of transport equipment and non-electronic machinery in the doldrums. Weak domestic demand compounded by plummeting oil prices made it difficult for domestic petroleum refiners to keep up with oil traders who simply imported finished products. Consequently, output from the petroleum industry contracted significantly.

In an effort to rationalise costs and streamline operations, multinationals that had long held a presence in the Philippines pulled out to centralise regional operations in other locations, such as Thailand. Among these, are pharmaceutical companies **Novartis**, **Warner-Lambert** and **Abbot Laboratories**, personal care products manufacturers **Colgate-Palmolive Philippines** and **Johnsons & Johnson Philippines** and confectioner **Van Melle**. Counterbalancing the pull-out by multinational companies – which is causing a re-examination of investment and labour policies as well as critical physical infrastructure requirements – is the increased presence of foreign investors in other industries, mostly in joint ventures with domestic companies which see the need for more technological expertise and capital. The food and beverage industry has seen increased participation from the likes of Nestlé, **Unilever** and **Hormel Foods**. The cement industry, formerly almost wholly domestically owned, has undergone significant restructuring to include the newly acquired stakes of foreign players such as **Holderbank**, **Lafarge**, **Cemex** and **Blue Circle**.

The sector ended 1999 slightly upbeat, though still groggy from the combined effects of weak demand, debt restructuring, increasing wage costs, and stiff foreign competition. Accelerating further from growth of 2.4% in Q3, the sector expanded by 3.1% in Q4, allowing it to grow by 1.4% on a full-year basis. This compares to the 1.1% contraction witnessed in manufacturing output in 1998. Export manufacturers continued to enjoy some edge even as the peso has stabilised and strengthened. Electrical machinery and transport equipment producers posted 10.8% and 16.1% gains in Q4. The growth of electronics manufactures has, however, slowed down from the vigorous

45.7% growth it registered in Q3. Food manufactures expanded by 7.4% in Q4, benefiting from improved agricultural production. On the other hand, petroleum refiners managed to squeeze a 0.4% marginal growth in Q4 after six consecutive quarters of decline. The series of domestic oil price increases in the last three months has at least partially mitigated some of the negative impact of the slide in crude oil prices. The unpopularity of domestic oil price increases will, however, keep these price adjustments to a minimum. Tobacco manufactures surged by 17.5% in Q4 after five quarters of successive declines.

Food And Beverages

An Industry In Flux

Accounting for almost 40% of output, the food and beverages industry claims the largest portion of manufacturing activity. It did not fare badly in 1998, as output expanded almost 3% compared to a 1% contraction in overall manufacturing. This was likely due to gains to domestic producers from import substitution by consumers. Despite the better-than-average performance, the industry was in flux as important changes occurred among the big firms. SMC was shaken by a change in management, which passed from the Soriano family – who have been associated with the company almost since it was founded at the turn of the 19th century – to Eduardo Cojuangco, who had served briefly as chairman of SMC in the 1980s. This happened when the Supreme Court allowed Cojuangco to vote the 20% stake he claims and which had been sequestered since 1986 by the government through the Presidential Commission on Good Government. Following this development, erstwhile chairman and CEO, Andres Soriano III, and other directors associated with him resigned, and were replaced by Cojuangco and his associates.

With Cojuangco at the helm, major assets of the company were disposed of in order to strengthen the company's financial position: it was heavily burdened by debt at the time. The first to go was the 25% stake in **Coca Cola Beverages** (CCB), the bottling company responsible for operations in central and eastern Europe. (SMC had acquired a stake in CCB when its 70% holding in **Coca-Cola Bottlers Philippines** was exchanged for a 25% stake in Australian company **Coca Cola Amatil** (CCA), which owned bottling companies operating in central and eastern Europe and in the Asia-Pacific region. CCB was then hived off from CCA.) Proceeds of the sale amounted to US$550mn. Following this, SMC's 45% stake in **Nestlé Philippines** was sold to Swiss-based parent Nestlé, ending a 38-year partnership. Funds raised from the sale amounted to US$700mn.

With a cash hoard amounting to US$1.25bn, SMC is expected to be able to offset debt obligations with interest income. Later on, however, it is anticipated that some strategic acquisitions will be made, although there is no indication as to whether these will be in related businesses only. There have been rumours that non-core businesses may be targets for acquisition, and uncertainty surrounding the disposition of the funds raised from the asset sales has placed a cloud over SMC's future direction.

The expansion of foreign ownership in the food and beverages industry has not been confined to SMC. **RFM Corp**, another food and beverage conglomerate, entered into a joint venture agreement with Anglo-Dutch multinational **Unilever** in ice cream subsidiary **Selecta Dairy Products**. Another joint venture arrangement is expected to be finalised in 1999 in its subsidiary **Swift Foods**, although the identity of the potential partner has not yet been disclosed. **Competitior Pure Foods**, the food subsidiary of **Ayala**, has also forged a joint-venture with long-time partner US-based **Hormel Foods**. The new company is expected to start operations in January 1999 and will provide more independence to Hormel beyond what it could have exercised as an operating division of Pure Foods.

The **Alliance Global Group** created a subsidiary which will consolidate all its interests and assets in the food and beverage business. It has disclosed that the management has obtained its board's imprimatur to tap the international equities market for the expansion of its existing business as well as for the acquisition of companies in food and beverages. The group has also entered into an agreement with **Mckester's USA** for the distribution of the latter's premium product lines in the Philippines and for the local manufacture under license of food products and beverages for the domestic and export markets.

Smaller companies are likely to fall prey to the larger domestic food companies. Some potential targets are candy manufacturers **Goya Philippines** and **Serg's Products**, both of which are labouring under heavy debt burdens and are already in the process of debt restructuring. As smaller companies have succumbed to the financial crisis, those which are financially stronger have taken up their market share. In addition to those mentioned above, another example is **Universal Robina,** which has expanded its presence in branded foods.

Petroleum Refining

Next to the food and beverage industry, petroleum refining accounts for the second largest slice in the manufacturing production pie, with about 17% of total output. In 1997, despite a modest 1% expansion in output, the on-off deregulation of the petroleum industry did not allow the three major oil refiners – **Petron**, **Pilipinas Shell Petroleum** and **Caltex Philippines** – to make timely increases to pump prices as the peso's value fell, leading to substantial losses for all three. Caltex posted an after-tax loss of PHP2.4bn, Shell PHP1.4bn and Petron PHP631mn. In 1998, the problems were declining demand and the impact of greater competition as a result of deregulation. The impact of a shrinking market was felt across-the-board. Sales volume in all fuels declined 6% in 1998 as the economy contracted, and also due to the financial troubles of **Philippine Airlines** that forced it to cut down the frequency of flights and cease operations for a brief period. Refiners responded by contracting output by an equivalent 6%. But because prices were relatively better attuned to market conditions with deregulation in place, losses made in 1997 were reversed.

However, in the future deregulation will have a negative impact on the three major refiners, as market share erosion and thinner profit margins will result from more intense competition. For example, Petron was able to maintain its 42% overall market share in 1998, but in the bunker and diesel fuel segments it was losing out to nimbler importers amid declining fuel prices in the region. Further evidence of the intrusion of other players in the industry, came with the bidding for the fuel requirements of major customer **National Power Corp**: to corner the lion's share of the awards, Petron priced its bid aggressively in the February auction. Deregulation, though, need not presage doom for the entrenched refiners. As long as efficiency is improved, a decline in prices will usually enlarge the market. After deregulation in the less well served areas of Visayas and Mindanao, for example, domestic resellers are finding it profitable to convert consumers who were using firewood and kerosene to liquefied petroleum gas.

Electronic And Electrical Equipment

At 9% of total output, production of electrical machinery accounts for the third largest share in manufacturing. It is also the fastest growing sub-sector, although in 1998 output rose a slower 6% compared to 31% the previous year, as manufacture of electrical home appliances slowed in line with the 32% plunge in sales. On the other hand, high growth was maintained in the production of semi-conductors, micro-circuits and similar items that form the core of the export-based manufacturing sub-sector. In US dollar terms, exports of these electronic products were up 38% in 1998, compared to 35% the previous year, and comprised 52% of all goods exports. Among the leading companies, are multinationals **Texas Instruments**, **Philips Semiconductors**, **Motorola** and **Intel**.

Growth for the sunrise electronics industry is likely to stay healthy with consumers globally shifting to more hi-tech products, continuing investment by the multinational companies, export markets located in the economically stronger areas of the world and a skilled and abundant labour force with competitive wage rates. Indeed, in 1999 **Texas Instruments Philippine**, the country's largest exporter, put US$60mn into expanding production of digital signal processing chips used in cellular phones, modems and disk drives, after having spent US$50mn in investments in 1998. There is also a possibility it will lead the initiative in putting up the country's first wafer fabrication plant. Other companies had proposed setting up such a plant in the Philippines – for instance Philips – but plans had foundered because investment incentives were more attractive elsewhere or market conditions were not right. A wafer fabrication plant would increase the local value-added of domestic electronic exports to 35% from the present 29%.

Global demand for electronics is forecast to remain buoyant at least for the next couple of years. Thus the Philippines can expect to continue to rely on its export sales of electronics products. However, to remain competitive in this business, the Philippines, according to the World Bank, would need to strengthen local content and develop capabilities to adapt to more advanced technologies in the future. It will need to develop capability in producing the more sophisticated types of electronic products. Hence, there is an urgency to the Philippines' quest for a wafer fabrication plant. The prospect of having a wafer fabrication plant is pushing some sectors in the Philippine government to support a bill proposing a 12-year tax holiday targeted specifically for the electronic sector. Certain officials in government hope that this will provide sufficient incentive for a US$2bn project said to be under consideration by Texas Instruments and a Taiwanese investor. The Philippines' Board of Investments has invited eight other foreign firms from the US, Europe and Japan to look into the possibility of establishing a wafer plant in the country.

Agriculture, Fishery And Forestry

Stormy Weather

Agriculture, fishery and forestry, which make up 19% of GDP, suffered a sharp contraction in output and employment in 1998. The devastation on crop production wreaked by the *El Niño* and two strong typhoons that ended the drought in Q4 98, led to a 7% fall in output, the worst since record-keeping started in the 1950s. Almost 400,000 people lost their jobs in January 1998. (By comparison, the next worst hit sector was finance where about 30,000 jobs disappeared.) Major crops suffered the highest damage. Harvests of water-intensive rice and corn crops plummeted 24% and 12% respectively, while sugarcane contracted 14% and coconut 13%. Even poultry was affected by the abnormally hot conditions as chicken mortality rose. The only exceptions to the dismal performance, were fishery and livestock farming.

The succession of *El Niño* with *La Niña* proved to be generally benign to the sector. The more favourable weather conditions allowed the sector to grow by 6.6% in 1999, a dramatic reversal of the deep contraction it suffered in 1998. Palay harvests expanded by 37.8%, ensuring ample supply of rice. Sugarcane crop increased by 22.7%, while corn production grew by 19.9%. Fishery and livestock also expanded by 2.5% and 4.7%, respectively. Poultry partially recovered as rains provided better breeding conditions. On the other hand, coconut production, as well as those of other crops like mangoes, went down by 7.4% and 4.5% respectively. For some of these crops, rains came much too early and too much during the production cycle. The recovery in agriculture resulted in an improvement in labour absorption. Employment in the sector has almost recovered to pre-1998 levels. The bumper harvests of food staples allowed inflation to remain at low, single-digit levels throughout the year, and provided a strong base for economic growth in 1999. However, while better harvests may have increased farmers' income, much of these have gone to paying off debts incurred in the previous year. The improvement in farm income has also been dampened by the PHP2 per kilo reduction in the price of milled rice imposed by the government in October.

Because it employs 40% of the labour force, and thus exerts a considerable multiplier impact on the economy, the government has chosen agriculture as one of the key recipients of increased spending as part of its pump-priming programme. Aside from the regular budgetary allocation, funds for increased expenditure will be sourced from the issuance of five to ten-year ERAP (Economic Recovery through Agricultural Productivity) bonds and loans from Japan's Miyazawa Plan. The government aims to raise PHP50bn in ERAP bonds, which will be used to fund agricultural projects through the government agency National Development Co. The first PHP5bn tranche issued in April 1999 will be used to fund three projects in joint venture with major companies. Tentatively, these are **Dole Philippines**, Nestlé Philippines and **Philippine Long Distance Telephone Co** (PLDT). The joint venture with the latter involves a large-scale rice production project on a 1,000 ha property that PLDT owns in Mindoro. Dole is planning a rice project as well, while Nestlé plans to undertake coffee production for the domestic and export markets.

For its part, the central bank is trying to boost agriculture by implementing the agri-agra law more strictly. The law requires banks to set aside 25% of loanable funds for projects in agricultural or agrarian reform. For lack of viable projects, banks have lent very little for agri-agra projects through the years, preferring instead to place the funds in risk-free government securities. This time, the central bank states it will mete out the statutory penalties for failure to comply more strictly, hoping to encourage lending to this critical sector. However, the private sector has been reluctant to extend credit because of notoriously low productivity. It is here that government projects to improve irrigation, roads, storage facilities and technology will help. It is on these type of projects that the regular budgetary allocation and official development assistance is directed. If successful, it will help improve agricultural productivity, which has long been neglected, and live up to the objectives of the Estrada government, which has made agriculture the centrepiece of its administration.

Transport And Communications

Consolidation

With the deregulation of the telecoms industry, and a deadline to meet for installed capacity requirements imposed by the National Telecommunications Commission, growth in the communications sub-sector accelerated to 18% in 1998, pushing expansion in the transportation and communications sector to 6%. In contrast, transportation dragged down growth, as the financial difficulties of **Philippine Air Lines** (PAL) cut sharply into operations: the sub-sector grew 1%.

Significant changes in the telecommunication industry occurred in 1998, with the change in control of dominant carrier PLDT. Long led by the Cojuangco family – who acquired the company together with other Filipino investors when the founding US investors divested as required by law – management passed to Hong Kong-based **First Pacific Co** (FPCL) when Cojuangco and his allies sold their shares for about US$750mn. Consequently, FPCL chairman Manuel Pangilinan has replaced former CEO, Antonio Cojuangco. Flush with cash raised from selling off assets, FPCL launched what was essentially a hostile takeover of PLDT as it failed in its attempt to acquire San Miguel Corp, with the fall in stock prices making the company an attractive target. FPCL bought a 6% direct stake in PLDT and an 11% indirect stake through **Philippine Telecommunications Investment** for a total 17% stake. Through this, FPCL obtained a voting interest of 27% in PLDT and therefore voting control.

As a result of FPCL's takeover, the telecoms industry has consolidated substantially. FPCL is the parent of local conglomerate **Metro Pacific Corp** and together the two firms own a majority of **Smart Communications**, the leading cellular phone company in the country. On the other hand, PLDT owns the biggest stake in **Pilipino Telephone** (Piltel), which is second to Smart in number of subscribers. Thus, the new PLDT through an operational, if not a legal, merger controls close to 70% of all mobile phone subscribers while at the same time being the dominant fixed-line carrier. As a result, other telecoms companies are actively engaged in forming combinations among themselves to be able to effectively challenge the bigger PLDT telecom conglomerate. **Globe Telecom GMCR** and **Isla Communications** (Islacom) have signed a memorandum of understanding in November which gives preliminary outline of an upcoming merger. The Globe-Islacom tandem will combine equity worth US$2.3bn, and will result in a three-way partnership among **Ayala Corporation, Singapore Telecom**, through wholly owned subsidiary Singapore Telecom International, and **Deutsche Telekom**, through DeTeAsia Holdings. Both Globe and Islacom offer digital cellular service under the European-developed technology global system for mobile communications (GSM). In May last year, Ayala bought the shares of the Delgado company who were the majority owners of Islacom. The merger paves the way for a strong GSM player in the country, with expertise from its foreign partners. On a smaller scale, **South China Resources**, an oil exploration company, entered the telecommunications business by subscribing an additional 3mn shares of the unissued capital stock of **Bell Telecommunication Phil**. In the more basic area of installing landline phones, interconnection agreements are slowly moving forward. **Eastern Telecommunications Phil** signed an interconnection agreement with Bayan Telecommunications despite a dispute over service areas. Both Bayantel and ETPI have been authorised by the Philippines National Telecommunication Commission to provide telephone landline service to Manila. ETPI has earlier signed a similar agreement with PLDT.

However, the new PLDT has its work cut out, as financially distressed Piltel has defaulted on its loans. To bring in more capital and also technological expertise, PLDT is looking for a strategic foreign partner. The best candidate seems to be Japan's **Nippon Telegraph and Telephone**, as it is already a partner in Smart. Meanwhile, an alternative national telecommunications backbone has been completed by rivals of PLDT who have banded into a consortium called **Telecommunications Infrastructure Corp of the Philippines** (Telicphil). The alternative backbone removes the last traces of PLDT's monopoly, as it will allow Telicphil members to route long distance calls without passing through PLDT. But, there are common issues that unite all telecom companies and among the most important are phone metering and affordability of the service. A local metered service had been provisionally approved by the National Telecommunications Commission, but was withdrawn due to populist clamour for the status quo, while the economic crisis has eaten into disposable incomes making some consumers abandon even the relatively scarce telephone service.

The financial plight of PAL has dominated the transportation industry. Labour problems, and an inability to service debt totalling US$2.2bn, forced PAL to shut down briefly last year. During that time, domestic routes were served by Hong Kong's **Cathay Pacific** and it was expected this would give Cathay the upper hand should negotiations with a foreign partner ensue. PAL re-opened when it came to an agreement with its labour unions and Cathay did undertake a due diligence of the company preparatory to a capital infusion. However, negotiations were aborted when Cathay felt it would not have full control of operations. There has since been a change in PAL's management. The management team from Cathay was dismissed in July, with PAL now using an affiliate of Lufthansa as management consultants.

Meanwhile PAL is in the process of rehabilitation with a plan submitted to the Securities and Exchange Commission. Tan is once more at the helm of the PAL board. With his injection of US$200mn in fresh funds, Tan's group now holds 53.7% of the shares. PAL's rehabilitation plan now seems to be meeting with only some muted disagreement from unsecured creditors. Much of the discontent was dissipated with the release of a statement from Estrada that pledged that PAL would not close during his term. Any questions about the transparency of the approval of the rehabilitation plan have, however, remained unanswered. In any case, PAL's fleet now comprises 24 operational aircraft. The return of three Fokker-50s is also being negotiated. The Export-Import Bank of the United States (Eximbank) has withdrawn its threat to seize any of PAL's Boeing planes, which land in the US. Following this decision, the Eximbank formally withdrew its opposition to the rehabilitation plan of PAL, allowing the airline to gain majority creditor support to its recovery plans. Eximbank guarantees nearly 17% of PAL's restructured debt involving the airline's four Boeing 747-400 aircraft, which are used on the busy trans-Pacific routes. PAL's majority creditors, the European export credit agencies which account for 38% of PAL's debts, have earlier given assent to the rehabilitation plan. PAL has slowly started reintegrating itself back into alliances with other foreign airlines in order to expand its route network at minimal cost. The first code-share agreement PAL has established since its rehabilitation is with **Emirates Airlines**. Effective September 1, 1999, PAL gets a seat allocation on each of the Emirates' three non-stop flights between Manila and Dubai. So far, PAL has been hitting its operational targets and ended December 1999 with a PHP240mn profit.

As a result of PAL's lingering financial woes, other domestic airlines, such as **Cebu Pacific** and **Air Philippines**, have been gaining ground. However, their fleets and coverage are minute compared to PAL's. There is also no other domestic airline that can effectively carry the international passenger load of PAL.

Estrada inaugurated Metro Manila's second light rail system. The 10km track runs from the terminus in Quezon City along Edsa, through the Ortigas business district, and ends at the edge of the Makati business district in Buendia. When finished, the full length of the track will reach Roxas Boulevard and intersect with the first light rail system along Taft Avenue. The new system intends to save some 10mn man hours each week that are lost in Metro Manila traffic. The US$655mn first phase will be completed by mid-2000.

Finance And Insurance

Tight Credit

As a result of the economic crisis, growth in the finance sector slowed to 4% in 1998, from 13% the previous year. On account of rising bad loans, the deceleration in output was largest for banks (to 5% from 15%), while non-banks and insurance companies experienced more moderate slowdowns. By December 1998, the level of non-performing loans in the banking system had reached 10.4%, compared to 5% a year earlier, although down from a peak of 12.0% in October. The trend was the same for commercial banks, which contributed 90% of all loans (non-performing loans were a slightly lower 10.4%). As banks increased provisioning for bad loans, especially with the stricter requirements put in place by the central bank in 1997, credit was severely limited. The amount of loans outstanding from commercial banks had contracted 5% at the end of 1998, compared to loan growth of 27% in 1997. Among the credit-starved sectors were manufacturing, agriculture and wholesale and retail trade. Nonetheless, despite substantially higher loss provisions, the banking system remained adequately capitalised with an average capital adequacy ratio in the region of 17% for commercial banks, higher than the 8% international standard and the 10% local requirement.

As the exchange rate has stabilised, and in the expectation of falling inflation, the central bank has been aggressively relaxing monetary policy to relieve some of the stress from the banking system. It accomplished this by reducing its short-term rates and cutting banks' reserve requirements. The BSP kept its borrowing rate at 9% from July to October 1999. (In November, the rate was reduced to 8.8% in anticipation of liquidity demand arising from Y2K concerns.) The overnight lending rate went up to 12% from 11% in July. The reserve requirement has stayed at 12%, 300bps lower than the pre-crisis level. In 1997, this had been raised up to 21% and averaged 17% in 1998. The objective of the central bank is to encourage banks to lend so that economic growth can resume. Thus far, however, the increased liquidity resulting from the loosening of monetary policy has been finding its way into risk-free government securities. For most of 1999, some form of modest loan growth has been tracked. The central bank has hoped to achieve this using moral suasion, some relaxation in prudential requirements (such as the waiver on the 2% general loan loss provision for new loans, and proposals to revise the definition of a non-performing loan to one which is past due 30 days rather than one day) and more stringent implementation of the agri-agra law. While the central bank says it hopes for a 15% rise in loans, the Bankers Association of the Philippines estimates it will be 10%.

To strengthen the banking system, consolidation is being urged by the Bangko Sentral ng Pilipinas. The most prominent example of this is the merger between the **Bank of the Philippine Islands** (BPI) and the **Far East Bank and Trust Co** (FEBTC) announced in October. The merged bank is strengthened by the acquisition of a 7.4% stake by the Development Bank of Singapore (DBS) in FEBTC in November. This would eventually give them a 2.4% share in BPI once both banks merge in 2000. The result is a bank that is second only to market leader **Metropolitan Bank and Trust Co** in terms of assets and deposits based on end-1998 data. **Metrobank** is also on a buying binge, with its subsidiaries acquiring medium-sized banks **Philbank** and **Asianbank Corp**. Metrobank's board has approved its purchase of 51% of the outstanding capital stock of**Solidbank Corp**, which is owned by the Madrigal family. The country's third largest bank was formed with the earlier merger of **Philippine Commercial International Bank** (PCIB) and **Equitable Banking Corp**, with the latter's purchase of 72% of PCIB. In response, universal banks that have been displaced are likely to form combinations with others in order to be able to compete effectively. Adding to this pressure, is the possibility that the central bank may again increase capital requirements beyond those mandated from compliance by 2000. Under the regulations, universal banks need to increase their capitalisation to a minimum PHP5.4bn in 2000, from PHP5.0bn this year. This, in turn, is higher than the minimum capital requirement of PHP4.5bn in 1998. On a smaller scale, two troubled thrifts have been acquired by domestic commercial banks. **ABN-AMRO** bought out **Great Pacific Savings Bank**, **DBS** acquired **Bank of Southeast Asia**, and **United Overseas Bank** bought into **Westmont Bank**. In addition, there is approval for the mergers of**Prudential Banking Corp** with**Pilipinas Bank**, and a memorandum of understanding signed between **Traders Royal Bank** and **Bank of Commerce**. These are medium-sized banks, which are merging in order to fulfil minimum capital requirements. Finally, the government plans to dispose of its 49% stake in **Philippine National Bank** by June 2000. Not only will this raise funds for the government's pump-priming programme, but PNB also needs to be strengthened as it has the highest level of bad loans among universal banks, thus placing its capital adequacy ratio at less than the required 10%.

The Bangko Sentral has offered incentives to promote a viable environment for more mergers and acquisitions in the banking sector. To encourage more mergers, the Bangko Sentral in June 1999 allowed concurrent directorships in cases of mergers or consolidations. It has proposed amendments to existing regulations that would allow the Monetary Board to grant qualified foreign banks 100% ownership of a distressed Philippine bank where local capital is either unavailable or inadequate. BSP circular 172 provide key incentives to nudge banks into more mergers. Among these include allowing the revaluation of fixed assets, temporary waiver of capital adequacy requirements, simultaneous grant of all new licenses for the conversion or upgrading of existing head offices and branches, allowing relocation of branches and offices, allowing additional branches and BSP penalty forgiveness for merging rural banks. Regulators are also exempting foreign banks from the current moratorium on bank branch expansion. This move further tightens competition in the local banking sector and is a strong signal for smaller banks to either expand or sell out.

Construction And Property

Survival Of The Fittest

As the property market collapsed in the face of higher interest rates, the construction industry followed. In 1998, gross value in construction shrank 8%, the biggest plunge by any major sector. As demand weakened, construction on most high-rise buildings (office and residential) and single housing projects stopped, resulting in a 10% contraction in private sector building. Public construction, on the other hand, expanded as infrastructure projects proceeded with funding from soft loans or through long-term BOT arrangements.

Reflecting significantly weaker property demand, property consultant **Jones Lang Wootton** estimates that the vacancy rate in the Makati Central Business District increased to 7.8% at the end of 1998, from 1.7% a year earlier, while the Ortigas area hit 15.6%. As vacancies rose, rental rates and payment terms have become more attractive. In Makati, rental rates have fallen some 14% from their peak in 1997, encouraging tenants, who have renewed or are getting new leases, to upgrade to more desirable premises.

It will take a while for the construction industry to pick up. It finally staged a modest rebound in Q4 99, eking out 0.5% growth after seven consecutive quarters of decline. The sector may have bottomed out while property prices are likely to continue sliding, given the surge in banks' property assets brought about by higher numbers of foreclosures and soft demand. Since land or buildings are the usual collateral put up by developers to obtain credit, the amount available to them will probably take some time to return to pre-crisis levels. During this time, established players such as **Ayala Land Inc** will tend to dominate the market as they have the financial wherewithal to ride out the crisis. Some of the marginal growth in bank lending which has not gone to working capital requirements of top-tier manufacturing firms has been put into the middle-income to high-end housing segments.

One segment of the market that holds more promise, is low-cost housing, though this has received the least priority for bank lending. As part of its pump-priming programme, the government has identified this as a key sector for increased spending. To this end, the trend towards lower interest rates will benefit the sector, especially since there is a substantial amount of unmet demand from end-users. The current backlog in low-cost housing is estimated at 3.7mn units. In an attempt to put housing on top of the government's policy agenda, Estrada created a Presidential Commission on Mass Housing (PCMH). This is a special task force created to fast-track the implementation of mass housing projects for lower income families. The move has triggered a host of mixed reactions from within the cabinet and the private sector. In protest at what appeared to be a subtle sign of presidential dissatisfaction with her performance, Karina David resigned as head of the Housing Urban and Development Council, whose functions are perceived to be duplicated by the PCMH. Her resignation was followed by the resignation of key officials in government agencies in the housing sector, effectively imbuing the issues with a political hue, as well as sowing confusion in an already ailing low-cost housing sector. In less than a month the appointed chief of the PCMH has resigned due to allegations of financial impropriety. Since then, the president has appointed Presidential Management Staff chief, Leonora Vazquez-De Jesus, as head of PCMH.

Aside from political concerns, funding remains the perennial problem in the government's mass housing programme. With a stated objective of constructing 350,000 units of mass housing annually for the next five years, the PCMH needs to obtain sufficient and sustainable funding. Additional funding for low-cost housing will be sourced from bonds to be issued by government housing agency, the Pag-Ibig Fund. Subscription to the bonds is being made more attractive by the government's agreement to guarantee the principal payment and up to 8.5% of the interest rate. Furthermore, the central bank is allowing banks to meet their 25% loan allocation for agricultural/ agrarian reform projects through lending to low-cost housing projects. A proposal has also been put forward that banks' reserve requirements include low-cost housing loans. The president announced the reduction of interest rates to 9% from 16% in October, and the extensions of the amortisation period to 30 years from 25 years.

The government is also supporting an increase in the capitalisation of the Housing Insurance Guarantee Corporation (HIGC) in order to provide a sustainable guarantee system to encourage more bank lending to property developers. Two bills are currently pending in congress, both seeking a substantial increase in the capitalisation of HIGC, which at the moment stands at only PHP2bn. All this government support, if fully realised, means low-cost housing could recover faster than other segments of the property market. The reduction in interest rates, however, while appearing to make mass housing more affordable, may also result in additional budget pressures on government to allow it to support subsidised rates. As with high-rise development, financially strong players, such as **Filinvest Land**, are likely to play a leading role. In comparison, **C&P Homes** has run into financial difficulties and is unlikely to participate as actively as it had prior to the crisis.

4 Business Environment

Infrastructure

Raising Capital

When the crisis struck, one of the first steps taken by the government was to curtail spending in keeping with IMF strictures to tighten fiscal policy. Accordingly, a 25% cutback across almost all sectors was ordered in 1998. However, as the regional crisis deepened, there was acknowledgement that stimulative policies were the more appropriate response and the IMF agreed to allow the government to incur a much larger fiscal deficit later in 1998 and also for 1999. This ensured that projects, especially those without private sector participation, could go forward. Since tax generation was understandably weakened as corporate profits fell victim to shrinking business activity, funds had to be obtained elsewhere. Capital-raising exercises were severely constrained in 1998, and the Russian debt default in September only made matters worse for emerging markets. The Philippine government postponed the issuance of global bonds at that time, as premiums on sovereign risk became prohibitive: it was only in January 1999 that the government was able to approach foreign capital markets. In 1999, the national government successfully floated US$2.5bn to help fund the fiscal deficit of PHP111.7bn (roughly US$2.8bn) in 1999, including a US$368mn Euro issue. Most of this will go towards spending for numerous public projects that aim to improve the country's infrastructure: physical, financial and social. As the government has historically been short of funds, it is concentrating on fully funding smaller projects, which would not usually be considered commercially viable. Such projects include local farm-to-market roads and elementary schools. Larger projects, which are nonetheless regarded as commercially unappealing, are funded jointly with official development assistance.

The bigger, more commercially-viable, infrastructure projects are being constructed almost wholly with private sector participation, on the build-operate-transfer basis that had been so successful in overcoming the power crisis in the early-1990s. In these cases, the government allows an extended concession period, from 10-40 years, during which the project proponent is able to collect fees, allowing a profitable recovery of the project cost before eventual transfer of ownership to the government. Variants of this have been developed (build-lease-transfer, build-operate-own, rehabilitate-operate-maintain, etc.), and are presently used for projects in the capital-intensive power and transportation sectors. Since the projects are commercially viable, these have attracted foreign investors and have also created a more market-oriented economy.

Despite the regional crisis, foreign investors in the BOT projects have persevered. Indeed, even the Indonesian company, **Citra Metro Manila Tollways Corp**, in charge of building the Metro Manila Skyway, has partially completed a portion of the project and has started collecting tolls. However, given the difficult times, the project did not escape controversy when road tolls were increased shortly after partial commercial operations began. Commuters protested against the hefty increases, justified by the operator as a consequence of increased costs due to the financial crisis. The government intervened and ordered a rollback. However, aware that such concessions may undermine the feasibility of other BOT-type projects, a regulatory body that will conduct public hearings is being proposed, so that all sides of an issue may be aired. In the case of power projects, the Energy Regulatory Board already undertakes this function, while the National Telecommunications Commission does the same for the telecoms sector.

In a deregulated sector, such as telecommunications, the government participates only in small rural projects that are not commercially attractive. Otherwise, the private sector is responsible for development, with the government's regulatory role confined to ensuring installation targets are met and pricing guidelines are followed. A sector that may be deregulated in the near future, is the power sector. As a result of the deregulation, it is likely there will be more efficient generation and distribution of power.

The Domestic Market

A Youthful Population

The Philippines is a young nation. In the latest population census, conducted in 1995, almost half of the 69mn population was below 20 years of age, 39% was between 20-49, while only 11% was 50 years and older. This is a result of rapid population growth. The average annual growth estimate from the previous census in 1990 was 2.32%. This compares with 2.35% in 1980-90, 2.71% in 1975-80 and 2.78% in 1970-75.

In terms of geographical distribution, the island of Luzon, the largest in land area, accounts for 56% of the population, the second biggest Mindanao for 24%, and the various islands of the Visayas region for 21%. Metro Manila (in Luzon), also known as the National Capital Region, is notable for its rapid growth and densely packed population. Growth has been fuelled by significant migration as job opportunities in the country's financial, social and cultural capital are perceived to be better than anywhere else.

Migration has also been responsible for the population explosion in Southern Tagalog (Region 4), where the Calabarzon (CAvite, LAguna, Batangas, Rizal and QueZON) provinces are located. Region 4 grew even faster than Metro Manila, as industrial jobs there dispersed into the rapidly increasing industrial estates located in Southern Tagalog, which continue to serve as magnets for new investments because of their superior infrastructure facilities.

It is likely that population growth will continue to slow gradually. The government forecasts that annual growth will average 2.1% to the year 2001, still high, but slightly lower than the 2.32% achieved in 1990-95. While the population will age, more than half will still be below 24 years and there is not expected to be much change in the age brackets above 65.

Income distribution is highly skewed. In the latest survey of family income and expenditure conducted in 1997, with the population divided equally into 10 income classes (income deciles), the top 10% accounted for almost 40% of total income. In contrast, the bottom 50% shared less than 20% of total income. Income distribution changes slowly and the inequitable distribution may be traced to low productivity in the agricultural sector, which employs about 40% of the labour force. A fairer distribution may gradually occur in the years ahead, if the Estrada administration's goal of prioritising agriculture is actively pursued amid an extended period of sustained growth.

Food is the single biggest expense in a family's budget. Although its share has been gradually falling, it still comprised 44% of spending in 1997. Notwithstanding the current economic crisis, the longer-term impact of rising incomes has been to shrink the share of food expenditure in the family budget – as has been the universal trend world wide (although actual spending levels have been increasing as incomes have risen). It is useful to note, though, that a greater desire for convenience has meant that the share of spending on food consumed away from home has risen. A distant second to food, is the 21% share going towards housing expenditure (including housing, household furnishings and equipment and household operations) which, in contrast, has been rising through the years. The combination of strong income remittances from abroad, bank deregulation that forced a broadening of banking services offered and the allocation of more public funds to the government's shelter programmes, all benefited the housing sector.

During the crisis, the most hard-hit consumer items have been durable goods, such as autos and household appliances, which are usually purchased through bank loans. A necessary component then of a revival in demand for these items (distinct from consumer non-durables, where demand has remained robust), is the resumption of bank credit. Falling domestic interest rates, combined with higher employment and continuing inflows of overseas income from contract workers, mean growth in domestic consumption is likely to accelerate.

The Labour Market

Employment Strains

The labour force numbered 32mn in October 1999, increasing by 2.3% over the economically active population in October 1998. Of these, 39% were employed in agriculture, 15.6% in industry and 45% in services. The ill-effects of *El Niño* on agriculture and the financial crisis on the rest of the economy resulted in a rise in unemployment to an average 10.1% in 1998, from 8.7% in 1997. In 1999, the unemployment rate declined to 9.6%. The absolute level of employed workers has stabilised and is now comparable to pre-crisis levels. The increase in employment rate was absorbed mostly by the services sector, specifically among wages and salary and own-account workers. Employment in the services sector increased by 4.7%, y-o-y in October 1999. Employment in agriculture seems to have stabilised, increasing only by 0.6% y-o-y in October. As the economy began to improve, employment in the industrial sector grew by 1.7% for the same period, compared to year ago levels. Among the industrial sector, the manufacturing sector employed an additional 70,000 workers, while those hired by the electricity, gas and water sector increased by 5,000. These higher employment figures were partially offset by decreases in mining (15,000 jobs), and construction (5,000) which still suffered from the crisis.

Minimum wages are set by wage boards in the country's 16 different regions, composed of representatives from government, labour and employers. Thus, there is no one national minimum wage. The highest in the country is in Metro Manila, which is currently set at a basic daily rate of PHP223.50, inclusive of a cost-of-living allowance and a 13th month pay. In regions outside Metro Manila, the equivalent total minimum wage for non-agricultural workers ranges from PHP117-200, and PHP94-175 for agricultural workers. Wages are usually adjusted in January, based on negotiations among the various tripartite wage boards. Normally, a wage increase is phased in two steps, with the first part raise effective in February and the balance in May on Labour Day. A wage settlement became effective in October 1999, with current rates as stated previously. The hikes were slight ranging from 1.7% to 4.7% outside and within Metro Manila, respectively. The adjustments came as a result of the series of fuel price adjustments and transportation costs. While the number of strikes filed increased in 1999, the actual strikes continued to drop compared to the previous year.

The Philippines has a high literacy rate of over 90% and English is widely spoken as a result of an American system of education. Compared to other countries in the region, unemployment in the Philippines has been relatively high over the years, leading to a significant outflow of labour, both skilled and unskilled. The Philippine Overseas Employment Agency estimates that there are 2.45mn documented overseas contract workers, 1.77mn living in other countries as permanent residents and another 1.82mn undocumented workers abroad. The outflow in recent years has consisted of technical (a growing number in information technology), industrial and household workers, with labourers and domestic workers outnumbering white-collar workers. Although the former are not unskilled, they are willing to work at jobs that the more affluent natives are no longer willing to take, but which pay higher wages than those available at home. Historically, a large skilled labour force has made the Philippines an attractive destination for foreign investment, however, since the regional crisis, wages in neighbouring countries have declined. Combined with the regional drop in domestic demand, some high-profile multinational companies have pulled out of the country to centralise regional operations in other locations. This may potentially lead to a cap on wage demands, in an effort to keep the Philippines competitive.

Industrial Policy

New Priorities

The Estrada administration has indicated it will continue the market-oriented policies of its predecessor, but with more emphasis on agriculture consistent with the pro-poor stance of the president's campaign platform. A follow-through on the previous administration's market-oriented policies was evident in the early days of the Estrada presidency in the case of **Philippine Airlines** (PAL). Despite widespread clamour for the government to take over the ailing carrier, it was allowed to close, albeit briefly, and reopened only when a potential private investor took an interest in rehabilitating the company. While the government has stated that PAL will not be the beneficiary of public funds, the president was quoted in May 1999 as saying that the airline would not be allowed "to close on his watch". The statement was made at the height of negotiations between PAL and its creditors on its rehabilitation plan. The airline has been given exclusive use of a new terminal at the Manila airport and there have been reductions in flights of foreign airlines that compete with PAL. Meanwhile, the neglected agricultural sector will receive more attention from the government. To increase credit to the sector, the central bank will now implement more strictly the rule that banks should lend up to 25% of loanable funds for agricultural and/or agrarian reform projects. That is, the central bank will mete the statutory penalties when banks fail to comply with the requirement. In addition, the government has issued Erap bonds, the proceeds of which are intended to be used for bankrolling agricultural projects which will eventually be sold to the private sector. However, not one centavo of the issue has so far been released in the form of equity into any venture.

Privatisation initiatives dwindled in the final months of the Ramos administration, as there are laws that disallow sale of government assets prior to a national election. While the Estrada administration has yet to privatise anything, it has prioritised the sale of some big-ticket items to replenish government coffers that have been depleted during the crisis. Among the easier ones to dispose of, are those that have benefited from past partial privatisation. In this category, are previously wholly state-owned companies **Petron Corp** and **Philippine National Bank**. The latter's privatisation is an integral part of a World Bank loan that aims to reform the banking sector. It is scheduled for completion by June 2000. However, the spectre of cronyism loomed around PNB's privatisation by year-end, as news revealed that Lucio Tan has emerged as a main owner in PNB. Tan now controls 35% of the bank, which is one of PAL's major creditors. PAL's payments on its reported US$70mn debts to PNB have been suspended while restructuring talk continues. Tan's holdings in the bank put him in a strategic position to bid for the government's remaining 30% share of PNB. Tan has resigned as chairman of Allied Bank, which he owns, to become a director of PNB. Tan also brought with him five representatives in the PNB board. Tan's entry into PNB has fuelled talks about a possible merger with **Allied Bank**. In Petron's case, the challenge for the government is to find a strategic investor acceptable to **Saudi Aramco**, which bought a 40% stake in the company when it was first privatised in 1993. The remaining government stake in the **Manila Electric Co** will also probably be relatively easy to dispose of, as the company is publicly listed and its shares are widely traded, as are the two other companies. Difficulties over the handling of sizeable debts in the cases of **Philippine Associated Smelting and Refining Co** and **Philippine Phosphates Fertiliser Corp**, have hindered their sale over the years. Questions of ownership in the cases of **Philippine National Construction Corp** and **Radio Philippines Network** are a stumbling block. A resolution of these issues may be why the Estrada administration says privatisation of the four companies is imminent.

In the meantime, on December 28, 1999, the Philippine Congress passed into law a bill extending the life of the Committee on Privatisation. This gives the Estrada administration greater leeway in pushing through its privatisation initiatives. The extension, however, is for only a year, which means that there will be greater pressure to resolve pending issues blocking the sale of the remaining big-ticket items. Finally, the sale of the **National Power Corp** (NPC) is contingent on the deregulation of the power sector. There are several bills currently being debated in congress that set the parameters of the sector's deregulation, among which is the method of privatising the NPC. The House bill is an omnibus version which encompasses all the different scopes of power industry reform. The senate has unbundled the bill into different coverage, including that of modernising and structuring the power sector, the restructuring and privatisation of NPC, amendment of the charters of the Department of Energy and the Energy Regulatory Board, the creation of transmission companies, and the establishment of a stranded assets and liabilities trust. Among the issues that government will need to clear up is the how to treat these so-called "stranded costs" arising from the take-or-pay contracts with independent power producers. These contractual agreements, entered into mostly at the height of the power crisis in 1992, were instrumental in the solution of the power supply shortage. The government is currently reviewing the options that would provide the most budget-effective solution for the assumption of these stranded liabilities.

The corporate tax rate declined to 33% in 1999 from 34% in 1998, and to 32% in 2000, in line with the provisions of the comprehensive tax reform programme that was legislated in 1997. Alternatively, a company should file a minimum corporate income tax equivalent to 2% of gross income if this is higher. Other relevant tax provisions, are net operating loss carryover (up to three years of operating losses and three years carryover period) and accelerated depreciation.

Foreign Investment Policy

Duplicating Incentives

There are currently several government agencies that offer incentives for foreign direct investment (FDI). Chief among these, is the Board of Investment (BOI): others are the Philippine Economic Zone Authority (PEZA), Clark Development Corporation (CDC), Subic Bay Metropolitan Authority (SBMA), Bases Conversion Development Authority (BCDA) and various regional investment councils. The presence of several government agencies offering multiple investment incentive packages has led to a duplication of efforts, creating conflicts among government agencies and confusion for investors. Also, firms have taken advantage of rent-seeking opportunities. For example, companies nearing the end of their tax holiday period under BOI, can re-establish themselves in an economic zone to avail themselves of PEZA incentives. Or a firm located in, for example, Subic Bay may access incentives from both the SBMA and BOI. In these and other respects, the government is seen as being overly generous, and in the process losing potential tax revenues with no additional FDI inflow.

To remedy these deficiencies, an interagency committee is studying the rationalisation of fiscal incentives so as to optimise tax revenues given desired FDI objectives. The plan is to offer a universal set of fiscal incentives to all investors, which will replace the present ones which include, among others, an income tax holiday and a preferential 5% income tax rate upon expiry of the tax holiday. At the moment, incentives are given to those industries included in the annually renewed Investment Priorities Plan (IPP). However, the World Bank considers this discriminatory and in contravention of commitments to the World Trade Organisation. Instead of an income tax holiday, the universal package of incentives will contain provisions for net operating loss carryover and accelerated depreciation at terms more generous than are currently available. Other incentives planned, are the duty-free import of capital equipment and spare parts, double deduction for training and research and development, tax credits for capital equipment purchased from local suppliers, double deduction for export promotion expenses and tax and duty exemptions on production consumables of firms with bonded warehouses. The grant of incentives will also be subject to "sunset rules" which will limit the duration of incentives to no more than 10 years. The agency's recommendations are intended to plug leakages from an incentive package which weaken the equity and efficiency of the fiscal system. The current system of incentives and use of the IPP is expected to last until 1999. By 2000, the Department of Trade and Industry (DTI) hopes to have the new universal set of incentives legislated by congress.

There is consensus that the present fragmented and uncoordinated approach to the provision of fiscal incentives neither promotes nor enhances the Philippines' attraction to foreign investors. However, while there is general agreement within government that the fiscal incentive system should be simple and more transparent, policy differences abound as to the final version that the fiscal incentives reform bill will take. The DTI, in contrast to the proposals of the interagency committee, still supports the granting of income tax holidays. A 12-year tax holiday is among the perks that it proposes to offer as an incentive to would-be investors in wafer fabrication projects, among others. The DTI-supported bill specifically provides for a 12-year exemption from income taxes to foreign enterprises putting up projects that will manufacture distinctly new products that are primarily meant for exports. The Philippines is angling to become the site of a wafer fabrication plant to be established by US-based Texas Instruments.

Liberalising The Economy

As the Philippines has not been as hard hit by the Asian crisis as its neighbours, and because of ongoing efforts at liberalising the economy, access to industries has not differed significantly from before July 1997. The most visible change is probably in the banking sector, where the central bank is considering up to 100% foreign ownership, but only for ailing banks in order to strengthen the system. (Full foreign ownership is granted to only 14 banks, 10 of which were allowed in when the sector was deregulated in 1994. The other four had been in the country before 1955. Aside from this, foreigners can own up to 60% of a local bank or of a locally incorporated subsidiary.) Increased foreign participation in other sectors of the economy is proceeding as planned even before the crisis broke. Notable, are the deregulation of the retail trade industry and the power sector. Legislation for both had been pending in congress during the Ramos administration, but was overtaken by the 1998 national elections. Consequently, the bills had to be re-submitted to the new congress. In the retail trade industry the sticking point is determining the floor for foreign investment, with legislators worrying that a floor set too low would wipe out local retailers and one set too high would not encourage any foreign entry. In the power sector, there are various versions of the bill, which will have to be reconciled.

Foreign Trade Policy

Courting Controversy

As a signatory to various international trade agreements, the Philippines is bound to specific commitments on tariffs. These commitments have come under fire, as domestic companies have complained about dumping, from countries whose exchange rates have depreciated even more substantially than the peso, and the wider access granted to imports just as domestic manufacturers are being pummelled by the crisis. To alleviate the distress of local firms, the government in January issued Executive Order 63 (EO 63), which increased the level of protection for six industries: iron and steel, garments and textiles, pulp and paper, petrochemicals, batteries and pocket lighters. However, this is effective only for a year, during which time it is hoped the affected industries can recover from the effect of the financial crisis. Nonetheless, there have been comments from the World Trade Organisation (WTO) that EO 63 may be in violation of the international agreement. The government claims no violations were made, as the increase in tariff rates were minimal, were below the committed rates to the WTO (as the Philippines had been liberalising trade faster than required in the WTO) and were time-bound for one year. It says it will wait formal notification from the WTO of any unfair trade practices.

Another trade controversy arose over import control of petrochemicals and plastic products, when the government issued Administrative Order 58 in March. With AO 58, a Petrochemical and Plastics Mobilisation Tax Force will be formed to monitor and regulate the importation of petrochemicals and plastics products. All importers will have to obtain an import clearance from the task force before goods can be released from the Bureau of Customs. The task force is empowered to block the entry of shipments that it believes participate in unfair trade practices. Unlike the temporary tariff increases, this measure is believed, even by other concerned government agencies, to be in violation of the WTO agreement because it imposes import curbs. Furthermore, any trade disputes are supposed to be elevated to WTO for arbitration and settlement: countries should not take unilateral action. Because the processing of AO 58 did not go through the usual government channels, there is a possibility of it being amended, if not revoked.

Bureaucracy And Corruption

Cronyism Creeps Back In

President Estrada came to office with promises to offer no special favours to friends and relatives. Yet within a few days of his inauguration, one of his major financial supporters during the campaign, businessman Eduardo Cojuangco, was able to take control of the giant food and beverage conglomerate **San Miguel Corporation**. This happened after the Supreme Court allowed him to vote his sequestered shares. Shortly thereafter, top management was revamped with Cojuangco becoming the chairman and chief executive officer and his associates placed in key operating positions. In another incident, financial campaign backers of Estrada seem to be reaping the benefits of supporting him. Businessman Lucio Tan, who had been pursued by the previous Ramos administration on tax evasion charges, was apparently given an easier time by the Bureau of Internal Revenue. The tax agency claims the case against him is weak and may not succeed in court, despite more vigorous efforts by the Department of Justice to pursue the case.

While it is true that in both instances the events could arguably be said to have proceeded without political intervention, the timing raises many questions about the value of political connections in the new administration. This is fuelled to a certain extent by the more lenient treatment seemingly given to the Marcos family, who have regained some political presence. The resurgence of political cronyism has been raised by the influential Asia Society and the American Chamber of Commerce as a potential deterrent to foreign investment, especially during a time when increased transparency is the rallying cry of investors hurt by the sharp downturn in the regional economies. This concern is fuelled by the seemingly less than transparent means by which Lucio Tan acquired a controlling stake in the soon-to-be privatised Philippine National Bank. Tan reportedly bought his shares through the stock market and through a rights offering which met with lukewarm interest from other shareholders. The ascendancy of Tan in PNB has sparked fears that other potential investors may shy away from bidding on the government's remaining 30% in PNB.

The government is also perceived to be favouring Tan's PAL because it has been allowed exclusive use of the new terminal in Manila for both its domestic and international flights. The authorities have also taken a strong stand against the resumption of air agreements with Taiwan, which they claim are unfair to PAL. Manila wanted to reduce by half the combined passenger load of Taiwanese airlines from 9,600. It also demanded that these airlines curtail onward routing flights, which eat into PAL's own passenger load. The conflict was not resolved in time before the Christmas holidays when the more than 100,000 Filipino overseas workers in Taiwan were expected to fly home.

Even more controversial, is the pending case of alleged insider trading and price manipulation in BW Resources Corporation (BW), a gaming and leisure company owned by another one of Estrada's friends, Dante Tan (no relation to Lucio Tan). BW was given the licence to operate a nation-wide online bingo operation. Just as the SEC began its investigation of the BW case, Estrada issued an order barring the SEC chief from making statements to the press on issues affecting the equities market. Another of Estrada's cronies, Mark Jimenez, though his son, has acquired a majority stake in the *Manila Times* newspaper. Jimenez' s son bought the shares from *Manila Times*' earlier purported buyers. Media watchers are closely observing any apparent softening of the newspaper's editorial stance on issues involving the president and his friends.

Environmental Regulation

Cleaning Up Its Act

A major environmental initiative, the Clean Air Act, was passed in May 1999. The law proposes a general framework for controlling air pollution levels, which in Metro Manila exceed environmental standards set by the World Health Organisation. Two major provisions of the bill are the limited use or outright ban of incinerators for waste disposal and the limiting or phase-out of certain additives in all types of fuel and fuel-related products. A particular concern to oil companies, is the stipulation that by 2003 unleaded gasoline should contain aromatics not exceeding 40% of total fuel composition, because it would entail the reformulation and replacement of refining capacity. In line with the thrust to clean up the air, a US$300mn soft loan from the Japanese government will be used to finance equipment needed to improve environmental quality controls in Metro Manila. Also, the government is preparing a more stringent motor vehicle inspection system that will promote the use of unleaded gasoline, compulsory use of catalytic converters and closure of obsolete oil-fired power stations.

In a more general action to improve environmental regulation, the Department of Justice (DOJ) and the Supreme Court (SC) are considering the designation of special prosecutors and courts to handle exclusively environmental cases. The DOJ has ordered an inventory of all environmental cases, and designated special prosecutors are expected to handle preliminary investigation and prosecution. More attention will be paid to illegal logging and fishing. The Department of Justice is also seeking the assistance of non-governmental organisations in protecting the environment. Meanwhile, the SC has warned judges against being too ready in the issuance of restraining orders against those who are trying to protect the environment.

325

5 Capital Markets

Introduction

A Modest Recovery

The Asian financial crisis sent the Philippine Stock Exchange composite index (Phisix) from a record high of 3448 in February 1997 to a five-year low of 1533 in January 1998. Renewed turmoil in the financial markets as a result of Russia's debt default, drove the Phisix to an even lower 1082 in September 1998 and a market capitalisation of US$21bn (PHP901bn) – down 76% in US dollar terms and 61% in local currency terms since the record high in February 1997. At the same time, the average daily turnover fell to about US$36mn from US$138mn.

Since then, with the peso appreciating and interest rates declining, the Phisix has recovered, ending 1999 at 2,143, up 8.3% y-o-y. Given the tough financial conditions, the market's price-earnings ratio of 23x is not unduly low. Even after posting a fall in profits of about 31% in 1998, listed companies are not expected to see a V-shaped recovery. Several companies will have to be restructured following the negative fall-out from the crisis and stronger profits growth will have to wait for a more robust economic recovery.

Despite the recent inflow of funds, an indicator that the stock market has not fully recovered is the value of a seat on the exchange. As operations of a number of brokers have ceased, seats have been sold off with the lowest this year placed at PHP12mn, far below the PHP70mn reached during the boom years. The number of initial public offerings (IPOs) dwindled to only two small companies in 1998. In 1999, there were five IPOs. Meanwhile capital raising in the debt market, both domestically and abroad, has largely been confined to sovereign issues as risk premiums have widened and companies remain wary of the possibility of increased interest expenses in a volatile financial environment. However, as capital markets have been calming down and even showing some signs of health, modest recoveries of the equity and debt markets are likely.

Equity Markets

Moderate Prospects

When the Philippine Stock Exchange (PSE) was licensed to operate in March 1994, separate operations of the Manila and Makati Stock Exchanges, established in 1927 and 1963, respectively, ceased. Although two floors (Ayala and Tektite) are maintained, these are electronically linked and one price is posted for each listed issue. As at end-1999 there were 185 members, of which 148 were local and 37 partially foreign owned. The number of listed companies in 1999 reached 226 from 221 in 1998, with five IPOs compared to three the previous year and only one company de-listed. There were three delistings in 1998. The five new listed companies comprise an insurance company, a holding company for a major broadcasting firm with telecommunications tie-ups, a food and beverages concern, a bank and a property development corporation. In addition to the composite index, there are five sub-indices: banking and financial services, commercial and industrial, mining, oil and property. The Phisix is made up of 30 companies and was last revised in March 1998.

In an attempt to boost trading volume, the governors of the Philippine Stock Exchange proposed in September that the Philippines Securities and Exchange Commission allow it to extend trading hours beyond noon. Manila, whose stock exchange is open for trading only from 9:30 am to 12 noon, has the shortest trading hours in Asia. This proposal is currently on hold, as a majority of the membership of the PSE petitioned for its stay. Many brokers do not believe that volume would automatically increase with a longer period of trading.

In the first year of the Asian crisis, the stock market plunged 46% to 1,869 in December 1997 from a record-high of 3,448 earlier in the year as the Philippines followed Thailand in devaluing its currency. High interest rates to defend the peso did not have much of an effect on the currency which grew ever weaker, ending 1997 at PHP40/US$ from PHP26/US$ before the crisis. A weak peso and punishing levels of interest rates took their toll on 1997 corporate profits – earnings per share of listed companies fell around 16% – and there were constant rumours of bank runs such that in early January 1998, the Phisix reached a five-year low of 1,533. An apparent recovery afterwards petered out as external turbulence continued to affect financial conditions. In addition, domestic developments, especially the change in government, following the 1998 presidential election, added to the mood of uncertainty. Bad news, starting with the fall of the Suharto government in Indonesia, economic problems in Brazil and Russia's debt default, caused the Phisix to fall even further in September to 1,082, a seven-year low. By that time, total market capitalisation had shrunk to US$21bn, or PHP901bn, equivalent to a 76% loss in value in US dollar and 61% in local currency terms since the record high in February 1997.

Phoenix From The Ashes

From these lows, the Phisix recovered on news that the US Federal Reserve had cut interest rates by a larger-than-expected amount in the wake of the failure of an American hedge fund and the drying up of credit there. Because this meant there would be less pressure on the peso – which had mirrored the movement of the Phisix, reaching almost PHP44/US$ in September 1998 – the stock market rallied convincingly, rising 82% to end 1998 at 1,969, and up a modest 5% from the end-1997 level.

Earnings per share fell an even steeper 31% in 1998 from 1997 levels of recurring income. On a non-recurring basis, the plunge in earnings was likely to be more precipitous. Contributing to this were the loss provisioning requirements banks have to comply with and contracting loan demand, which eroded their bottom lines. One-time provisions, for a higher amount of doubtful accounts and "soft" assets, pared profits across many sectors including telecoms, food and beverages and among conglomerates. Movement of the Phisix from end-1998 to end-Q1 99 was less dramatic – it inched its way up to 2,028. Mid-1999 saw the return of anxiety to the market. Uncertainties on the political front, volatility in the exchange rate, concerns about Y2K readiness, as well as the seeming inability of government economic managers to control the budget deficit, kept investors to the sidelines until almost the end of the year. The planned cabinet revamp instilled more worry than relief, and the bombing of the office of **Pilipinas Shell Petroleum Corporation** created fears that dissatisfaction in some quarters over the planned fuel price increases of oil companies could take on a more violent nature. A widening probe on alleged price manipulation and insider trading on the stocks of gaming corporation **BW Resources** has also eroded investor confidence in the local bourse. All these factors combined for lacklustre trading going towards year-end.

However, the stock market staged a mild rally in December after hitting its lowest on the back of a technical rebound and favourable investor interest on market heavyweight PLDT following the news of expected favourable 1999 earnings. Selected blue chip stocks hit oversold levels and enticed investors and market players to take advantage of discounts in the hope of immediate profit turnaround and to position for a possible market rebound. Better inflation figures and the government's move to expedite reforms, especially the legislation of the long-awaited retail trade liberalisation law also provided optimism to the equities market. A rally in Wall Street partly influenced local market, as fears of the US Federal Reserve's increasing interest rates waned.

Improving Capital Markets Regulation

The Securities and Exchange Commission (SEC) is in the process of drafting new laws on debt suspensions and bankruptcy that will update existing ones. The issue takes on particular significance in light of the increasing number of firms seeking debt suspension because of the economic crisis. Defaults on debts affect creditors, mostly banks, and unresolved issues regarding distressed firms' obligations to its creditors could have a negative impact on the stability of the banking system. Debt suspension petitions from distressed firms more than doubled to 33 in 1998 from 16 the previous year, while affected assets rose to PHP29.6bn from PHP10.6bn. Part of the plans to update the bankruptcy law is a proposal to set up a special bankruptcy court to hear petitions from distressed companies. This is expected to leave the SEC with more time to regulate and develop the capital market.

In the meantime, the SEC has approved rules on Corporate Recovery on Suspension of Payments. Among these is that any order issued by the Commission is immediately executory. The rules also mandate that upon filing of a petition for debt payment suspension, the SEC shall issue an order that immediately suspends all actions and proceedings to enforce payment of all claims against the petitions for a period of 30 days from the date of the order. The petitioner is likewise ordered to refrain from selling, encumbering, or transferring any of its properties, or from making any payments without approval of the SEC. However, this may answer to short-term concerns, the regulatory role of the SEC can only be institutionalised and enhanced with the passage of the long awaited amendment to the Revised Securities Act.

The 1999 Revised Securities Act has been passed by the senate, but awaits sponsorship in the House of Representatives. Among the salient features of this bill is the shift from merit regulation to a full disclosure regulation. It also strengthens anti-fraud provisions and expands civil liabilities to include fraud in securities transaction, insider trading, and fraud in commodity interest contracts. It will cover new capital market instruments such as asset-backed securities and derivatives, and allows flexibility to adopt modern practices and technologies. The bill authorises exchanges, clearing agencies, stockbrokers and dealers to act as self-regulatory bodies. It will also transform the SEC into a collegial body with flexibility to effect organisational reforms, and empower it to regulate trading in the options and derivatives market. Passage of this bill is crucial for enhancing the regulatory role of the SEC.

The SEC, rather than the central bank, is now in charge of regulating finance companies without quasi-banking functions. These include securities brokers/dealers, lending investors, financing companies, investment houses and mutual fund companies. Regulation will incorporate the listing of non-bank financial institutions in a databank, special examinations akin to bank examinations, regular reports on operations and monitoring of borrowing levels. The SEC assumed jurisdiction over "direct lending" business while bills covering lending investors were in Congress. However, the SEC will furnish the central bank with statements of condition and income statements of the non-bank financial institutions.

Plans to set up a futures exchange have been suspended as the SEC would first like to set up the regulatory framework. The SEC would like to avoid a repetition of the fraud committed at the former Manila International Futures Exchange (MIFE), which eventually caused the SEC to revoke its license in 1997. The MIFE failed to implement reforms that would have made operations more professional. It also did not follow the SEC's requirements that a futures exchange uses the services of a bank for its clearing operations and to develop a programme for surveillance and compliance with SEC rules. At least two applications have been filed for a futures exchange: one from the Philippine Options and Futures Exchange, a subsidiary of the Philippine Stock Exchange, and another from Pilipinas Mercantile Exchange Inc. However, the SEC prefers to have only one futures exchange since the market is still in its infancy. The SEC promulgated the new Rules and Regulations on Futures Trading on July 9, 1999. It directed that the proposed Commodity Futures Exchange shall be a non-profit stock corporation with a PHP200mn capitalisation. Among the financial futures products that the SEC approved to be traded in the proposed futures exchange are currency, interest rates, and indexes. It also gave approval to the request for a study of the futures market in the Philippines to determine its viability.

Bond Markets

A Period Of Stagnation

There are three main issuers of debt in the Philippines: the Bureau of Treasury as fiscal agent of the national government, corporate institutions, which issue mainly short- and long-term commercial paper, and municipal governments, of which there is still only a small number. As the economic crisis caused interest rates to climb to punitive levels, the debt market has stagnated. Even more than usual, it has been dominated by national government issues. Indeed, at the worst of the regional crisis, when sovereign risk premiums on Philippine foreign-denominated bonds reached 1,000bps from the pre-crisis 340bps, even the national government suspended issuance of peso-denominated instruments with longer maturities, such as Treasury bonds and notes. Occasionally, even Treasury bill auctions were suspended. In September 1998, as a result of the turmoil in emerging markets, the national government called off a sovereign bond issue. When sovereign issues were thus penalised, higher risk corporate and municipal issuances suffered even more. However, even at this point, international credit rating agencies such as **Standard & Poor's** never downgraded the Philippines, although the outlook did move to negative and then back to stable. S&P maintained the country's long-term foreign currency rating at BB+, short-term currency rating at B, long-term local currency rating at BBB+ and short-term local currency rating at A-2.

As global capital markets calmed down and sovereign risk premiums narrowed, especially after the US Federal Reserve Bank lowered interest rates three times in succession, the Philippines was able to regain access to the international capital market. In Q1 99, both the national government and the central bank were successful in raising a significant amount of funds. In the case of the former, the US$1.5bn raised was for the financing of the bigger public deficit, because of economic pump-priming and for the latter, it was to refinance maturing short-term obligations which had been taken out at the height of the financial crisis. The success of the international fund-raising can be traced in large part to the Philippines weathering the regional crisis, at that point, better than its neighbours and because the transition to the new Estrada administration went through with no major disruptions.

The Philippine government tapped the international bond markets several times in 1999 to finance the fiscal stimulus budget. In January, the first bond offering under the Estrada administration initially set at US$750mn was increased to US$1bn because of oversubscription and was priced at a spread of 435-475bps. It consisted of a re-opening of the 2008 bond, first offered in 1998, amounting to US$500mn (bringing the total 2008 to US$1bn) and a new US$500mn 20-year bond. The 2008 was priced at 9.123% or 435bps more than comparable US treasuries, while the yield on the 2019 was 10.072% or 475bps more. In comparison, the 2008 offered in April 1998 had a spread of 340bps. In February, the national government floated another US$200mn in 20-year bonds. It re-opened the 2019 bond offered in January so that the issue was increased to US$700mn. Pricing was slightly better than that obtained in January with a yield of 9.787%, compared to 10.072% (coupon of 9.875%) on the earlier offer, and a spread of 436bps versus 475bps. In March, US$300mn in Euro-denominated bonds was floated. The issue had a spread of 425bps relative to German bunds, an 8% coupon rate and will mature in September 2004. The government undertook a Brady Bond exchange programme in October and issued a US$260mn floating rate note (FRN) in November. The three-year FRNs were issued at 185bps over three-month LIBOR, 65bps lower than a previous FRN that the new one is refinancing. Meanwhile, the central bank issued a two-year US$250mn bond with a yield of 8.2% and a 305bps spread over the equivalent US treasuries. In November the central bank raised US$400mn from a five-year syndicated loan facility in which 33 foreign and local banks participated. Proceeds of the loan will be used to refinance a one-year loan with **ING Bank,** which was maturing that month. The loan was priced at 165 points over LIBOR.

Government Securities To Be More Widely Available

In January 1999 the Bureau of the Treasury launched its Small Investor Programme (SIP) for Treasury bills. Five offerings were made throughout the year in six different regions of the country. This ensured a wider availability of government securities. The Treasury reported that among the first investors during the launching were a farmer, a driver, and a bank employee. The government finally realised a long-time plan to issue smaller denominated treasury securities in order to attract savings from the so-called ordinary person on the street. The smallest denomination of the issue is PHP5,000. Total investments in SIP for Treasury bills reached PHP24.5mn in 1999. The second component of the SIP, the Small Denominated Treasury Bonds (SDTB), was launched in two tranches. The first in July 1999 generated PHP11.6bn, while the second in October generated PHP18.6bn through public offerings. Similar to the SIP for Treasury bills, the denomination for the SDTBs went for as low as PHP5,000. The market for the smaller denominated bonds will become more vigorous once the plans to list government securities in the stock exchange pushes through. Listing at the Philippine Stock Exchange will allow secondary trading to take place. The objective is to make government securities available to a wider section of the public in order to encourage savings. Long-term government securities generally carry higher yields than the usual bank savings accounts widely available to the public. For example, the latest offering of 10-year Treasury bonds in December 1999, worth PHP2bn, had a yield of 14.875% compared to average savings deposits of 8-10%. At the moment, only accredited government securities dealers (mostly banks) are allowed to participate in the periodic auctions of Treasury bills, notes and bonds. While theoretically the Treasury bills, notes and bonds could then be repackaged for sale to the public at affordable denominations, this has never taken place on a large scale. Furthermore, there is hardly any secondary trading, with most Treasury instruments held to maturity. At the moment of issue, the smaller denominated Treasury bonds had a yield of 14.25%.

The smaller denominations of Treasury bonds are not expected to be in addition to the present system of periodic auctions of bonds (currently up to maturities of 20 years), and, consequently, the amount of government borrowing should not change. However, it should shift public borrowing to longer-term instruments. Indeed, the Bureau of Treasury has already reduced its weekly auction of Treasury bills to PHP4bn from PHP5bn as funds obtained abroad have been enough to finance current requirements. Thus there should be no impact on the level of domestic interest rates. Instead, there is the probability that a wider pool of potential investors could bid down yields. Finally, secondary trading of long-term government securities should provide a benchmark for long-term obligations. At present, yields at primary auctions of the 91-day Treasury bill serve as the benchmark for loan rates and all sorts of other obligations, whether short or long term. A market-determined long-term rate would be a more appropriate standard. It would also avoid the situation of having no benchmark in certain situations as has happened in the past (such as the Russia debt default) when the government rejects all bids for T-bills at its auction.

Because agriculture is one of the key sectors identified by the government for increased spending, funding for agricultural projects is being increased. Aside from the usual soft loans from multilateral and bilateral agencies and tax revenues, the government is also resorting to the debt market for additional financing. In April the quasi-government agency National Development Co floated PHP5bn five-year ERAP bonds. At their issuance the bonds were almost five times over-subscribed resulting in a favourable 7.875% yield to the issuer. This was the first tranche of a total PHP50bn to be used to finance agricultural projects. Demand was heavy because the bonds are tax-exempt, fully guaranteed by the government and can be used by banks to meet the central bank requirement that 25% of loanable funds be set aside for agricultural and agrarian reform projects, which will be strictly implemented now. The implied yield on the ERAP bonds if it was not tax-exempt is 9.84%, which is significantly lower than the shorter 10 or 91-day Treasury bill which stood 11% when the ERAP bonds were offered.

As interest rates continue to decline, it is likely that companies and higher risk municipalities may feel more confident about accessing the debt markets. At this point, there is still wariness of the risks of increased debt as a result of the tremendous pressure put on balance sheets throughout the financial crisis. However, the national government has already taken the lead in the international capital markets, thus setting a benchmark for corporates to follow. And in the domestic market, the yield curve is once again being lengthened in order to be able to better price longer-term liabilities.

THAILAND 2000

Analyst: Alan Boyd

Editor: Sara Matchett/Georgina Wilde

Contents

Political Outlook _____ **339**

Domestic Political Outlook 339
Foreign policy 344

Profile and Recent Developments _____ **346**

Political System 346
Foreign Policy 352

Economic Outlook _____ **355**

Introduction 355
Economic activity 356
Fiscal Policy 358
Monetary Policy 359
Exchange Rate Policy 360
Balance Of Payments 362
Foreign Direct Investment 364
External Debt 366

Profile and Recent Developments _____ **368**

Characteristics Of The Economy 368
Economic Activity 369
Fiscal Policy 371
Monetary Policy 372
Exchange Rate Policy 373
Balance Of Payments 374

Key Economic Sectors _____ **375**

Introduction 375
Manufacturing 376
Agriculture 379
Services 381
Financial Services 383
Construction 385

Profile and Recent Developments _____ **387**

Introduction 387
Manufacturing 388

Business Environment _____ 393

Introduction 393
Infrastructure Development 394
The Domestic Market 396
The Labour Market 397
Industrial Policy 399
Foreign Investment Policy 401
Foreign Trade Policy 402
Bureaucracy And Corruption 404
Environmental Regulation 406

Capital Markets _____ 407

Introduction 407
The Equity Market 409
The Bond Market 412

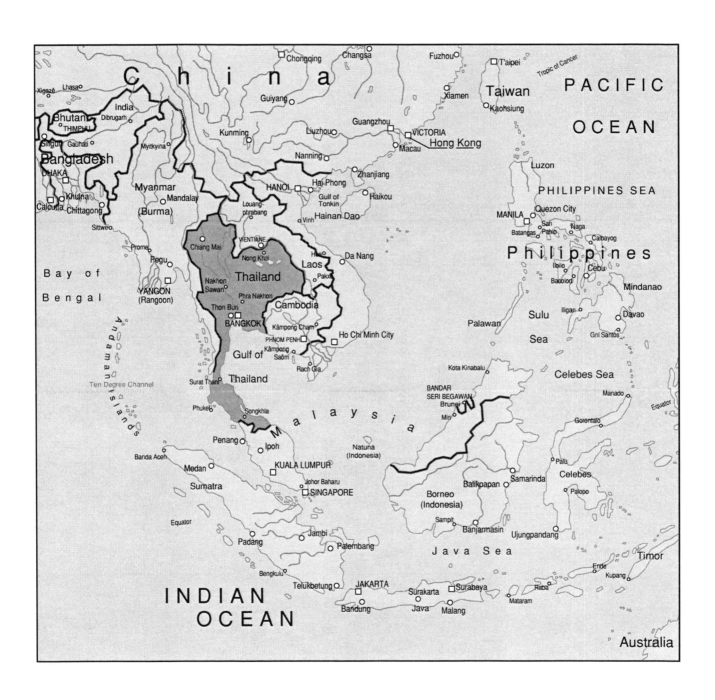

THAILAND: MACROECONOMIC DATA AND FORECASTS

	1993	1994	1995	1996	1997	1998	1999	2000f	2001f	2002f
Population (mn)	58.06	58.70	59.40	60.00	60.60	61.20	62.00	62.80	63.62	64.44
Nominal GDP (US$bn)	125.57	144.52	168.36	185.05	149.07	111.33	127.03	135.79	144.34	144.35
GDP per capita (US$)	2,163	2,462	2,834	3,084	2,460	1,819	2,049	2,162	2,269	2,240
Real GDP growth (% y/y)	8.70	8.62	8.83	5.52	-0.43	-10.18	4.20	4.90	4.20	4.80
Manufacturing production index(% y/y)	10.50	6.40	9.29	8.60	-0.55	-10.65	12.80	8.50	7.50	7.50
Unemployment rate (%)	2.60	2.60	1.70	2.00	1.90	4.40	4.20	4.00	3.80	3.70
CPI (% y/y, an.avg)	3.33	5.16	5.71	5.81	5.62	8.15	0.20	2.44	3.50	3.60
WPI (% y/y, an. avg)	-0.45	3.87	8.33	4.66	4.00	13.80	-6.47	4.47	4.83	3.29
Interbank rate (%, an. avg)	4.5	7.1	10.3	12.1	21.7	2.6	1.2	2.0	2.2	2.3
Discount Rate (%, eop)	9.0	9.5	10.5	10.5	12.5	12.5	4.0	4.0	4.0	4.2
Prime Rate (%, eop)	10.5	11.8	13.8	13.2	15.3	11.5	8.3	8.3	8.3	8.3
Fixed Deposit (1-year, eop)	7.0	8.3	10.3	8.5	10.0	6.0	4.0	3.8	3.8	3.8
THB/US$ (eop)	25.54	25.09	25.19	25.61	47.25	36.69	38.18	38.70	38.80	39.50
THB/US$ (an. avg)	25.32	25.15	24.91	25.34	31.36	41.36	37.84	38.00	38.50	39.00
Merchandise exports (US$bn)	36.96	45.23	56.44	55.72	57.62	54.34	58.51	64.08	68.31	72.15
Merchandise imports (cif, US$bn)	46.07	54.43	70.78	72.32	61.35	42.90	50.40	57.71	62.65	69.49
Trade balance (customs, US$bn)	-9.11	-9.20	-14.34	-16.60	-3.74	11.45	8.11	6.37	5.66	2.67
Current account (US$bn)	-6.36	-8.09	-13.56	-14.69	-3.02	14.05	11.05	8.52	7.26	3.65
Current account (% GDP)	-5.07	-5.59	-8.05	-7.94	-2.03	12.62	8.70	6.27	5.03	2.53
Foreign reserves (US$bn)*	24.47	29.33	35.98	37.73	26.18	28.82	34.06	34.50	33.00	34.00
Import cover (mths)**	5.43	5.41	5.07	5.16	3.99	6.27	6.49	5.78	5.13	4.80
External debt (US$bn)***	52.11	64.87	100.80	108.70	109.30	105.10	95.60	92.00	90.00	88.00
External debt (% GDP)	41.50	44.88	59.87	58.74	73.32	94.41	75.26	67.75	62.35	60.96
External debt (% exports)	105.06	110.54	136.05	144.20	143.52	151.82	129.02	114.84	106.50	99.29

f = BMI forecast. eop = end of period; *excluding gold; ** number of months imports covered by FX reserves, ***break in series in 1995. Sources: BoT/IMF/BMI.

1 Political Outlook

Domestic Political Outlook

Emotions Run High As Poll Countdown Starts...

Tensions have risen in the approach to the pending general election, which will provide a critical test of the constitutional changes that began in 1997-99. Scheduled to be called by mid-November, the poll has evolved into a showdown between the purveyors of old-style money politics and reformists intent on achieving more representative government. **BMI** expects the reformists' momentum to continue, though mixed results from the inaugural Senate poll in March suggest that this transition will not be easy. Widespread fraud forced the Electoral Commission (EC) to nullify voting in 78 seats, and a further 16 were voided in subsequent by-elections. While the unprecedented disqualifications were viewed as a sign of increased political maturity, they nevertheless exposed some shortcomings in the new model of government. In their over-zealous attempts to stamp out vote-buying, the constitution drafters actually encouraged fraudulent acts by declaring a blackout on campaigning, which forced candidates to resort to unethical means to publicise their policy platforms. The EC is likely to amend some of the more glaring inconsistencies to avoid the risk of repeated polls: tainted candidates will probably be banned, and a requirement for the Senate to be totally non-partisan may be lifted.

As the general elections approach, the reformist position is gaining ground. There will be some changes to the electoral arrangements to smooth the process.

...And Electoral Flaws Stall Senate

A failure to fine-tune electoral laws could undermine the general election, as there are similar flaws with the list system that will be used to elect 20% of seats. Evidence of fraud against any individual candidate could force a block disqualification of his party, as seats are to be allocated on a proportional basis through a single national electorate. A discussion meeting held by the EC in mid-June failed to find any remedy. From the government's perspective, the electoral problems could not have come at a worse time. Without a caucus, the upper house cannot be convened until the Senate poll re-runs have been completed, creating a legislative backlog that the ruling Democrat Party (DP) must clear before it can call a general election. Prime Minister

Delays delivering benefits to key constituencies have drawn out the electoral timetable.

Chuan Leekpai has already delayed a dissolution from Q1 because of the slow pace of economic recovery, and is running out of time to create conditions that would favour a DP victory. He wants to woo the crucial middle class vote by completing a programme of business reforms centred on closer regulatory supervision of financial institutions. Grassroots rural constituents were to be courted with packages of agricultural aid and job-creation schemes. But the corporate bills are stuck in the Senate bottleneck, as is some of the farm aid.

Delays in the fiscal 2000/2001 budget bill will also influence the timing of the election, as Chuan is keen to set the agenda for the next government, even if the Democrats do not win. Approved by the cabinet in April, the budget will be vetted by the lower house in July but will probably not reach the Senate until September. Based on these developments, **BMI** expects Chuan to try to delay a dissolution until September, by which time the economy should also be offering a bigger electoral dividend.

Opposition Disarray Lets In Thaksin

However, the risk of the coalition being forced out prematurely has risen as a result of the increasingly desperate antics of the opposition New Aspiration Party (NAP), which orchestrated a walkout by more than 90 MPs in late June in an attempt to galvanise a grassroots uprising. The exodus itself had little impact, as the government still had a quorum. A defiant Chuan vowed to stay until the new budget was in place and the electoral laws had been amended, though it appeared that both sets of bills might be speeded up to allow an earlier dissolution in September. But a bigger threat may come from attempts to exploit the government's delicate situation. The loyalty of minor coalition partners will come into question as the election nears, while more opposition MPs may be lured away.

In this difficult environment, **BMI** believes that Chuan will be forced into a dissolution once the electoral changes have been made, which will probably be in late August. The main beneficiary of the turmoil will be the Thai Rak Thai (TRT) party of businessman Thaksin Shinawatra, who has emerged as Chuan's biggest potential rival. While Thaksin denied that he was behind the opposition stunt, about half of the quitting MPs defected shortly afterwards to the TRT.

Thaksin's enormous wealth has become a magnet for MPs from other parties since he made a comeback last year after an ignominious 1995-96 stint in politics as head of the Palang Dharma Party (PDP) that ended with a crashing defeat by the DP in the PDP's Bangkok stronghold. His own leadership

Chuan faces a new challenged from the re-vived political career of a rival for the middle class vote.

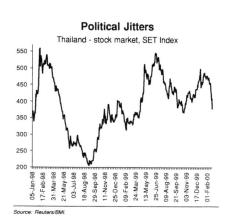

Political Jitters
Thailand - stock market, SET Index

Source: Reuters/BMI.

credentials have been questioned after two uninspiring periods as a cabinet minister, but middle class voters are attracted by Thaksin's pro-business stance. Coalition parties will be judged mostly on their management of the economy, as well as Chuan's commitment to transparent and clean government. Neither is a strong selling point any longer, as corruption and policy miscues have eroded urban support, while rural electorates are unhappy over the neglect of agriculture. Chuan's own standing has suffered from his reluctance to risk internal ruptures by confronting corrupt MPs. Opinion polls indicate that urban voters still prefer him to Thaksin, but he may have fallen behind in the more populous rural constituencies.

THE THAI CABINET		
Post	**Minister**	**Party**
Prime Minister (Also Defence Minister)	**Chuan Leekpai**	**Democrat**
Deputy Prime Ministers		
(Also Interior Minister)	Banyat Bantadtan	Democrat
(Also Commerce Minister)	Supachai Panitchpakdi	Democrat
(Also Public Health Minister)	Korn Dabbaransi	Chart Pattana
	Bhichai Rattakul	Democrat
	Panja Kesornthong	Chart Thai
	Trairong Suwankhiri	Democrat
Ministers:		
Agriculture & Cooperatives	Prapat Pothasuthon	Chart Thai
Education	Somsak Prisananantakul	Chart Thai
Finance	Tarrin Nimmanahaeminda	Democrat
Foreign Affairs	Surin Putsuwan	Democrat
Industry	Suwat Liptapallop	Chart Pattana
Justice	Suthas Ngernmuen	Democrat
Labour & Social Welfare	Pracha Promnoak	Chart Pattana
Science, Technology & Environment	Arthit Urairat	Democrat
Transport & Communications	Suthep Thaugsuban	Democrat
University Affairs	Prachaub Chaiyasarn	Chart Pattana
Ministers attached to the Prime Minister's Office		
	Adisai Bhotaramik	Democrat
	Abhisit Vejjajiva	Democrat
	Jurin Laksanavisit	Democrat
	Savit Bhothiwihok	Democrat
	Supatra Masdit	Democrat
	Somboon Rahong	Rasadorn
	Chaiyos Sasomsap	Solidarity
	Pinyo Niroj	Chart Pattana

Source: Reuters.

Voters in Bangkok will decide the outcome of the election.

Democrats May Claim A Slim Victory....

Voters in the north, the northeast and Bangkok will decide the poll's outcome, as the DP and a handful of small parties already dominate southern and central provinces. The NAP is likely to be eclipsed by a steady stream of defections to the TRT, allowing the DP to increase its presence in the northeast, which returns the biggest number of seats to the House of Representatives. But TRT will probably make some gains in the north at the expense of both the NAP and DP, leaving Bangkok as the decider. Notoriously unpredictable, the capital has switched allegiances between the DP and Palang Dharma at the last two elections, and shows signs of siding with Thaksin this time round. However, Chuan still has one advantage from the constitutional reforms that could give the DP an edge. This poll will be the first fought under a divided electoral system, with 100 of the 500 candidates appearing in party lists. The DP will probably gain the biggest poll dividend because it is one of the few parties that has been operating long enough to establish a national presence. It is also most likely to attract quality candidates with a good chance of winning.

BMI believes that the DP could claim as many as half of the list seats on offer, which would provide a slim margin of victory over the TRT. This scenario could be upset if the multitude of minor parties manage to bury their differences and form an alliance with the sole objective of preventing the DP's return. Most are threatened with extinction during the poll, as they can no longer utilise multi-slate electorates that had returned as many as four MPs from one ballot, and could be dominated from a narrow provincial base. These have been replaced with single-candidacy polls. Few minor parties have the necessary profiles to attract promising candidates for the list system; and most boast disreputable leaders who are out of step with the new era of cleaner politics. Two parties, Chart Thai (CT) and Chart Pattana (CP), are already discussing a re-merger that would reverse a 1992 split, while MPs from Muanchon, Prachakorn Thai, Solidarity Party and Social Action Party have said they will join either the NAP or TRT. Seritham Party is expected to merge with the DP. Based on their current parliamentary strengths, CT and CP would need the support of at least one more party to challenge the DP and TRT. But rival leadership ambitions, especially within the CT and CP, appear likely to block any wholesale consolidation.

... But Will Still Need A Coalition

Another short-lived coalition is in prospect.

Reformists envisage a more settled political environment that would comprise only two or three large groupings, down from the 16 parties that contested the 1996 poll, when nine groupings actually won seats. But there will still be at least seven or eight parties in the next election, and it could be a further decade before the system fully evolves. One stumbling block is the demographic structure, which is heavily polarised on regional lines that reflect the political fabric. Parties are generally coupled together from splinter factions that have little following outside their immediate provinces. On a broader level, factionalism has undermined the stability of government by forcing the larger parties to rely upon coalitions to secure a ruling majority, sparking inevitable rivalries for cabinet posts. This danger will be slightly diminished after the next poll, but the victorious party will need the support of at least one other faction. And although fewer internal squabbles can be expected, the incoming coalition still has only a distant chance of becoming the first government to serve out its full four-year term. This may have to wait for a cult of ideology that can banish the usual preoccupation with self-enrichment and reduce the potential for disruptive power plays.

Assuming it wins the biggest number of seats, the DP will probably seek another coalition with current allies the CP and CT. A linkup with the TRT is unlikely because of personal animosities that date back to Thaksin's political debut in 1995, when he engineered the downfall of Chuan's first government. Whatever the makeup of the coalition, its chances of serving out an entire four year-term term are slender at best. Tensions will probably surface within 12 months because of rival leadership ambitions, as well as the image problems that invariably dog Thai government. It is usual for inter-party relations to become severely frayed within two years, resulting in a dissolution shortly afterwards. On this basis, another election could be expected by mid-2003.

Whatever the makeup of the coalition, its chances of serving out an entire four year-term term are slender at best.

A Democrat government could be expected to maintain most existing policies, but with more of a liberal tone if it had the luxury of a bigger majority. Chuan, almost certainly serving his final stint as DP leader, would strive to leave his imprint on government with a strongly-reformist programme, targeted particularly at encouraging better business practices. Thaksin's plans for government are less clear, though he has promoted himself as a champion of small enterprise and promised speedier resolution of corporate debt problems. Either government would be pro-business and favourable for foreign investment.

Foreign policy

Diplomats Will Help Set Policies

Foreign policy initiatives will focus on economics.

A draft document released in early June has laid down the probable future direction of foreign affairs as part of an continuing reassessment of the way in which Thai commercial interests are advanced abroad. The Foreign Ministry will have an enhanced role in formulating high-level economic strategies, with a specific brief covering international finance, labour and trade. Most promotional activities will be transferred to a proposed new Ministry of International Trade and Industry formed from the industry and trade portfolios, leaving the foreign ministry free to focus on policies. More embassies will be equipped with Team Thailand units, which are now the main spearheads of commercial delegations based in foreign missions. Consisting of foreign service staff drawn from various branches of the civil service, the teams operate under the leadership of Thai ambassadors irrespective of their original service affiliations.

Viewed as the biggest shake-up in foreign affairs for several decades, the new strategy has already produced efficiency gains since it was launched in 1998, through a clearer delineation of responsibilities. Noting that the 1997-99 economic slump had instilled a conviction among political leaders that the way in which foreign policy had been devised in the past left Thailand ill-equipped to adapt to regional or global crises, the document said there was now more co-ordination between the various branches of foreign missions. Moreover few changes are likely at an operational level, as trade and investment policies have loosely matched the regional focus of diplomatic affairs since the end of the cold war in the early 1990s. Jurisdiction for implementing these policies is now being split into four separate geographical regions, but the ministerial document reaffirms the primary importance of Southeast Asia.

Regional Emphasis Will Be Retained

A strong focus on relations with China and with Asean neighbours will continue. Ties with Myanmar will remain difficult.

In one of his few forays into foreign policies, Chuan said in May that greater emphasis within this region would be given to improved relations with Myanmar, Laos, Vietnam and Cambodia, the four newest Asean members. In June he initiated talks in Phnom Penh over outstanding border issues with Cambodia and hinted at a forthcoming trip to Myanmar. The premier has consistently declined invitations from Yangon because of its appalling human rights record, and was instrumental in formulating the harder line that has been taken in recent years towards the ruling junta. A policy statement in March restated Bangkok's objective of having Asean's much-criticised "constructive engagement" relationship with Myanmar replaced with one of selective intervention.

Myanmar has responded since December with a more conciliatory stance on border tensions, including an offer of joint border patrols to stem the inflow of illicit drugs. But there has been no change in Bangkok's belief that Yangon represents the biggest threat to Thai security interests. A government statement in April cited the inconsistency of the junta's policy statements as one cause for concern: the ruling State Peace and Development Council (SPDC) offered in March to host high-level talks on improving mutual ties, but then made this conditional on an end to Bangkok's policy of providing sanctuary for hundreds of thousands of displaced ethnic minorities from Myanmar. Chuan initially supported a repatriation of the refugees under United Nations supervision, but began to backtrack in May following an outcry from human rights organisations.

Lao Frictions Mar Indochina Thrust

Similar obstacles have frustrated efforts to put ties with Laos on an improved footing since a short-lived border conflict in 1987-88 that was triggered by a territorial dispute. Vientiane charged in June that unnamed Thai government officials were behind an orchestrated bombing campaign that has destroyed the tourism industry and driven away investors. In a separate incident in April, a Thai ex-MP was arrested on spying charges while on an apparent business trip to Laos. Bangkok attempted to defuse the row by closing a displaced persons' camp that Laos claimed was being used to shelter Hmong rightwing insurgents opposed to the Communist leadership in Vientiane.

Frictions in the relationship with neighbouring Laos will remain an irritant in Mekong cooperation.

Relations with Indochina and western China will be based increasingly on commercial interests, with investment being channeled into the intra-regional development of the Mekong delta. Thailand supplies more than three-quarters of Laos' national income, mostly through electricity purchases, but direct investment elsewhere has lagged behind other Asean countries. This partly reflects lingering military mistrust of the socialist Indochina states, against which Thailand fought during the cold war. Initial funding under the revamped policy will go to transport upgrades, mirroring government attempts to secure direct access to Chinese markets. Planning budgets were approved in April for a series of Mekong initiatives, including a bridge in northern Thailand that will complete a highway link with Laos, Vietnam and western China.

Profile and Recent Developments

Political System

New Constitution Strives For More Stability

The new constitution was tested for the first time in local elections during 1999. This is the country's 16th constitution since the overthrow of the absolute monarchy in 1932, but arguably the most important. Unlike previous versions, the latest constitution was drafted by a predominantly civilian assembly with the aim of breaking the stranglehold of narrow vested interests that has frustrated efforts to establish a truly representative system of government. Input was taken for the first time from the general public and non-government organisations (NGOs) and the final draft was submitted to a referendum in 1997.

The drafting assembly sought to end the traditional cycles of short-lived, weak coalitions interspersed with military-led regimes by encouraging the emergence of a stronger and more stable party system. While the lower house (of representatives) in the National Assembly was enlarged from 393 seats to 500, multiple-seat constituencies were abolished to make it more difficult for small, localised factions to survive. Voters will in future elect 400 MPs through single-member constituencies, using the first-past-the-post method, and the remaining 100 from a national list system that incorporates an element of proportional representation. Like the single-MP seats, the list system is designed to favour large, well-established parties that are capable of attracting candidates with a national profile.

So far only the key constitutional mechanisms, including a new Electoral Commission (EC), have been put to the test, and with mixed results. The EC sent shockwaves through the political establishment by nullifying the results of a local election in May 1999 after evidence was unearthed of widespread fraud. Although the unprecedented intervention was viewed as a positive step forward, the fraud allegations showed that the political transition still had some way to go. There was also some initial confusion over which electoral agency had overall authority for ordering that the poll be re-run, while reformists were angered by the government's failure to take legal action against any of those implicated in the electoral fraud.

Political power has always rested in the lower house, with the prime minister and speaker of parliament drawn from its ranks. In contrast, the upper house (senate) has long been viewed as a mostly dormant resting place for retired bureaucrats, ex-military officers and businessmen, though this could now change. Previously appointed by the king, the senate will in future be elected for a six-year period (compared with four years at present) and will have 200 seats, down from 270 previously. While it remains politically non-aligned, the chamber is likely to attract a more active breed of politician due to a considerable strengthening of its powers. Senators still cannot vote on bills, but have gained the right to dismiss or appoint any MPs or other public figures if they can gather enough support, submit interpolations and call a debate. Until now they have only been able to screen laws. In a sign of its new assertiveness, the senate delayed a crucial package of economic bills in April 1999 because its business lobby objected to legal amendments that would make it easier for creditors to foreclose on assets after loan repayment defaults.

Centralised Systems Undermine Governance

There has been little change to the other basic structures of the Thai state. Both the administration and legislative systems remain highly centralised, despite the promise of greater autonomy under the new constitution. Provincial and regional councils have no legislative powers and minimal financial autonomy, though some are now allowed to levy their own indirect taxes. Leaders of local governments will also be directly elected in future, and will be given responsibility for welfare, drainage and health services. But most other senior appointments are made from Bangkok, as neither the civil service nor the government is willing to risk a dilution of their political powers. This is despite the fact that rural provinces contain more than 60% of the population and return most MPs to the lower house.

As a consequence, most provincial leaders owe their positions to high-level political benefactors in Bangkok, creating an unhealthy environment of inter-dependency that has inevitably bred corruption and resulted in disjointed development strategies through the misuse of budgets. Institutional authority has been undermined, rendering the police force largely ineffectual and exposing the judiciary to political influence. Rural disenchantment, often aggravated by low prices for agricultural crops and obligatory job migrations, has frequently spilled over into civil unrest, though mostly of a localised nature. Successive governments have sought to correct these imbalances by attracting more investment to remote provinces and devolving some administrative functions. The bureaucracy itself is also being overhauled to improve budget disbursements, which have been a prime cause of funding bottlenecks. However, these initiatives have had a limited impact because of the absence of a strong will by politicians to change a system that works in their favour.

Lingering Resistance May Impede Change

The new constitution is intended to improve transparency of governance in Thailand and strengthen the civil rights of ordinary Thais. Among its provisions are clauses relating to protection from discrimination and abuses of the judicial system, including explicit guarantees against torture. A set of independent bodies with oversight powers has been proposed to protect citizens against maltreatment by the executive arm (ministries and state agencies). There are, however, doubts over the impartiality of some of these new entities, as political leaders have sought to influence the process by installing party sympathisers in key posts.

Politicians of all hues have fought a background struggle against any dilution of executive powers, often in an unlikely alliance with the traditionalists who have the most to lose from the new constitition: conservative businessmen, the military and rural landlords. As a result, the liberal intentions of the constitution's drafters, many of whom were western-influenced academics and activists, have been watered-down during the process of vetting enabling laws for the charter. Conservatives partly succeeded in reducing the independence of supervisory bodies such as the EC, in some cases by threatening to withhold the funds that they needed to operate. Enough safeguards were retained to preserve the original reformist intent, but opponents are likely to continue a rearguard campaign to overturn some of the more unpopular provisions.

A particular bastion of traditionalist power is the Council of State, a body of lawyers which scrutinises all legislation before it becomes law. The Council changed the essence of the draft Human Rights Bill so that its interpretation and administration would be subject to government officials. The 11-member Human Rights Council, designed to oversee executive actions and ensure new legislation is compatible with the law, was originally intended to be independent, reporting directly to the National Assembly. Instead, the government insisted that it answer to the Justice Ministry and mandated that seven of its members be bureaucrats, with only four coming from outside the civil service.

Similar interference in a proposed regulatory framework for the media provoked a confrontation in 1999 with NGOs, journalists and political activists. The government and top bureaucrats were accused of altering the terms of reference so they could dictate appointments to two new bodies that will allocate broadcasting frequencies and licence media outlets. The row was still underway in late 1999 but it appeared that the government would step aside and allow a fully independent system to evolve. Censorship was prevalent in the print media until the early 1990s, and the threat of licensing cancellations is still used as a lever for governments to control radio and TV content.

But in general the Thai media are free from official controls provided it avoids overt criticism of the key institutions of state, such as the royal family and the armed forces. Ownership is so concentrated in the hands of public entities that there will be little scope for campaigning journalism until the regulatory bodies are set up. Five of the six terrestrial TV stations are controlled by branches of the armed forces or government, while the military also operates the biggest radio network. Newspapers are more independent, and have taken advantage of increased access under the new constitution and a Freedom of Information Act to investigate links between politicians, businesses and the civil service. In 1999, leading newspapers brazenly carried reports of bribery allegations against Interior Minister Sanan Kachornprasert, whose own ministry controls the licences of the print media. There was no retaliation.

Parties Have Been Slow To Adapt

Thailand's political parties generally lack an ideological or class base, instead being primarily vehicles for powerful individuals (now usually with a commercial background but also including former senior military officers) and business interests. The prime goal is to use ministerial powers of patronage to reward supporters.

Chart Thai (Thai Nation) was the dominant party for over two decades, but then suffered a serious split in 1996 which has reduced its influence. The main beneficiaries were two parties founded in the 1990s: New Aspiration (NAP) and Chart Pattana (CPP), which also represent combinations of rural and ex-military interests linked to their respective founders. Social Action Party (SAP) and Pachakorn Thai Party (PTP), both breakaways from the Democrat Party (DP), have been the only other durable factions, along with the smaller Muan Chon Party. However, the constitutional changes have forced a process of rationalisation that will probably see only the CT, CPP, NAP and DP survive from the pre-reforms era.

Prachakorn Thai underwent a split in late-1997 when one faction supported the new Democrat-led coalition and the other (which retained control of the party machine and formal title) went into opposition. SAP effectively broke apart following its expulsion from the government in late 1998 over a health graft scandal. And Muan Chun dissolved itself in 1999 and joined the NAP. Further upheaval is likely, as the political reforms are weighted against small, under-funded parties that lack a national profile. The model for most political factions is DP (Thailand's oldest party), whose support for democratic reform has ensured a wide following throughout the country. With seats in both rural and urban electorates, the DP has come closest to securing a national mandate, though is still mostly dependent upon support in Bangkok and the south. Other parties generally supportive of moderate democratic reforms are Seritham and Solidarity.

Immature System Inhibits Innovation

Two attempts during the last decade to establish parties with a distinctive ideological niche each faded after an initially bright start because they were eventually viewed in the same light as other factions. Palang Dharma's strong pro-democracy stance and campaigns against corruption won it considerable support in 1992-95, but the party paid heavily for its misguided decisions to join two coalitions tainted by graft allegations. In late 1999 the party's last MP resigned, leaving Palang Dharma on the verge of collapse. Similarly, former banker Amnuay Virawan managed to attract strong business backing for his Nam Thai Party on a platform of social and economic modernisation, only to precipitate its downfall through an ineffectual participation in the 1995-96 Chart Thai-led government.

Another bid for the educated middle class vote has been made since 1998 by business tycoon Thaksin Shinawatra, a former leader of the ill-fated Palang Dharma Party. But his Thai Rak Thai (Thai Love Thai) Party has already encountered image problems with its efforts to recruit sitting MPs to beef up its campaign strength. The party aims to appeal to business circles and Bangkok residents as an alternative to the Democrats, with a pro-democracy stance on political reform, but a more nationalistic attitude to economic policy. However, it faces a dilemma over the need to meet middle class aspirations of clean government while simultaneously relying upon the support of powerbrokers who might be tainted by corruption allegations.

The Military And Other Political Forces

The military, for long a key player in Thai politics and business, has receded into the background since the 1992 pro-democracy clashes, which severely eroded public confidence in the security forces. A reformist and more youthful leadership has emerged since 1998 with the objective of creating truly professional armed services that will stay out of politics. Significantly, the military resisted the impulse to intervene in the political crisis of late 1997 and played only a supportive role during the subsequent economic downturn. It is slowly divesting itself of significant parts of its business interests, which will also curb its potential political influence. The military's budget (especially for equipment) has been cut sharply – the navy is currently using its new aircraft carrier as a tourist attraction. Recruiting cutbacks are reducing the overall army strength, including the top-heavy officer corps (some 600 generals are currently "inactive"). The risk of armed intervention is now small, though the officer corps still reserves the right to take action in the event of a breakdown of civil order. Internal resistance to the reforms has so far been fairly muted, but they could unravel if a pro-military faction returns to power.

The 'technocratic' elite which runs Thailand's civil service and state enterprises has provided continuity of policy administration, and also a cadre of non-partisan experts (including the top ranks of private firms) to serve in successive governments. Although its competence has been questioned after the failures of economic policy in 1995-97, its influence remains high, especially with a recent trend towards backdoor business links with politicians. A brain drain to the private sector and low morale (mostly caused by poor salaries) have eroded the service's efficiency, but improvements are likely once pending reforms have been completed (*see above*).

Non-governmental organisations (NGOs) began to emerge in the late 1980s as a potent form of activism, especially at a grassroots rural level, and now exert considerable influence on Thailand's political life and business environments. Their presence has mostly been felt in environmental struggles (especially over dam construction), but also in campaigns for constitutional reform and against political corruption. Increasingly, NGOs are forging broad alliances with trade unionists, community groups and liberal political elements to block unpopular measures, often by using direct action such as road blockades. In 1999 they were able to halt work on three coal-fired power stations south of Bangkok by galvanising village opposition.

The labour movement has traditionally been undermined by internal rifts and tough laws against stoppages, with the result that only about 5% of workers have any representation. This decline has been accelerated by the shift away from labour-intensive industries such as textiles and shoes, though white-collar sectors like banking are now becoming unionised for the first time in response to staff cuts. A more militant streak began to appear during the economic downturn, hinting at a revival of labour activism. Public employees have also re-organised following the government's decision in December 1999 to lift an eight-year-old ban on state enterprise trade unions.

The underground economy (which covers both criminal activities and cash-based legal ones) is estimated to be worth as much as 50% of GDP and poses an ongoing threat to the integrity of

Thailand's political institutions. The large money flows generated by "industries" such as gambling, prostitution or drugs, have been a prime cause of the corruption of the police and bureaucracy. Money-laundering legislation was approved in 1999, but political interference has raised doubts over its enforcement.

In contrast, the separatist campaign being waged by a small portion of the Muslim minority in southern Thailand poses a negligible threat to national security. The ineffectual group of militants responsible for sporadic terrorist incidents have little local support and have been largely dispersed since Malaysia agreed to deny their leaders sanctuary in 1998-99. Other minority groups, such as the Laotian-speaking population in the northeast, are primarily seeking greater official recognition of their cultural identity, though this is also feeding demands for further administrative decentralisation.

The monarchy remains a key buttress of Thailand's political system, although the King has no executive responsibility. Respect for the monarch is deeply ingrained in Thai culture and his potential influence is great, though this rests to a large degree upon his personal charisma. King Bhumibol, the present monarch, plays a critical role in unifying the country's five distinct regions and is a key figure in rural development and is immensely popular at all levels of society. He professes a complete disinterest in politics but has used his public mandate to stabilise political crises (most recently during the May 1992 incident). Crown Prince Maha Vajiralonkorn is less well-regarded, but with access to wise counsel should be able to retain the monarchy's prestige and role.

Elections Will Be Called By November 2000

The last parliamentary election was held in November 1996 under the old constitution. The largest party was the NAP, whose leader Chavalit Yongchaiyudh was able to put together a six-party coalition with a comfortable majority in the lower house. His government proved uncertain in its handling of both the financial crisis of 1997 and demands for constitutional reform. Faced with demands from the business community for his resignation, plus widespread street protests which the military was unwilling to suppress, Chavalit was forced to step down in November 1997.

A premature election (clearly undesirable at a time of financial crisis) was averted when the Democrat Party under Chuan Leekpai was able to establish a new coalition. It had only a tiny majority (19 seats) and was reliant on the votes of 12 defectors from the Prachakorn Thai Party, previously allied to the NAP and Chavalit. The prolonged economic slump had undermined the government's popularity by early 1999, but opposition parties were unable to make any impact due to their own blemished management record and a successful divide-and-rule policy by the DP. Chavalit lost his main ally when the Chart Pattana Party (CPP) joined the government in late 1998, replacing the splintered Social Action Party.

This gave the coalition an unassailable majority of more than 120 seats as a shield against the no-confidence motions that are routinely used to force a dissolution. The government survived two censure votes in January and December of 1999, despite the threat of an internal revolt from bickering minor parties that were unhappy with their cabinet allocations. Relations between the DP and CPP have been particularly strained over this issue, and could provoke an early election if a policy paralysis ensues. Chuan is reluctant to cede any additional economic posts for fear of a return to the spending excesses of the past.

An election must be called by mid-November in 2000, but Chuan is likely to hold off as long as possible to reap benefits from the recovering economy. As of early 2000, it appeared that a poll would not be announced until at least July, as the government still had a legislative backlog to clear and was keen to oversee the drafting of the fiscal 2000/2001 budget. Minor parties are also stalling for financial reasons, as the weakness of the economy has eroded corporate sponsorship. The poll appears likely to be a two-party race between the DP and Thaksin Shinawatra's well-funded Thai Rak Thai (TRT) party, with the urban middle classes and voters in the populous north-eastern region likely to decide the outcome. Chavalit's NAP has been wracked by defections to TRT, and is unlikely to succeed in its efforts to forge a broad opposition front against the DP (possibly based around TRT). Prospects for Chart Thai and Chart Pattana are equally grim unless they can engineer a re-merger and pool their diminished resources, as both will be badly affected by the constitutional shift to single-candidacy constituencies.

Foreign Policy

Economic Bias In Diplomatic Ties

Thailand's foreign policy goals have been overhauled under the present government to give a greater emphasis to economic gains, but the underlying strategy has not changed since the early 1990s. Embassies have been told to link bilateral relations more closely to trade and investment, partly to overcome a procedural gap that has seen diplomats and commercial attaches pursue conflicting policies. The tone and direction of foreign relations have not changed, other than a more liberal attitude by the current government towards fringe political movements and human rights issues. Membership of the Association of South East Asian Nations (Asean) lies at the core of foreign policy, as it enhances trade and investment through the Asean Free Trade Area (Afta). Thailand has re-emerged as *de facto* Asean leader following the eclipse of Indonesia's Suharto, and is playing a key role in re-building the bloc's credibility, which was damaged by its ineffectual response to the regional economic crisis.

The reforms have a secondary purpose of improving co-ordination between the 16 agencies (including defence, commerce, agriculture and immigration as well as foreign affairs) that are responsible for staffing the country's overseas missions. This environment has been fertile ground for nepotism and other forms of patronage and corruption. Under the changes now being implemented, Thai ambassadors will be in charge of multi-agency teams tasked with exploiting opportunities for economic linkages. Embassies in Beijing, Manila, Kuala Lumpur, The Hague and

Riyadh began to move over to this arrangement during 1999 and the full process is due to be completed in 2001.

Geopolitical Shifts Have An Impact

Relations with China and Myanmar (Burma) have undergone the biggest transformation in recent years. China's landlocked western provinces have become major trading partners and are keen to develop transport links to deep-sea ports on Thailand's eastern seaboard. The two countries signed an economic co-operation pact (the Greater Mekong Basin scheme) in early 1999 that is expected to lead to joint investment in road and rail projects. However, the relationship is overshadowed by Thai apprehension over Beijing's growing economic and military influence over neighbouring Myanmar, which Bangkok believes is linked to Chinese brinkmanship over the regional security vacuum left by the withdrawal of US troops from South East Asia in the late 1980s.

Any pronounced shift towards China would have adverse long-term implications for Japan (presently Thailand's chief trade and investment partner), and to a lesser extent the US and other western nations, though it appears that Tokyo will retain its leading status due to its massive Thai investments. Japan also won plaudits for its substantial aid programmes during the economic downturn, though its pre-eminence in a regional context may wane unless there is a sustained recovery in the Japanese economy that can boost exports from South East Asia. Relations with the US and the EU countries are of necessity close, because of their economic importance to Thailand, and most of the disagreements that occur are the result of trade-related issued. Apec (which groups together the developed world with the countries of Asean and other East Asian economies) has become an important conduit for Thailand's relations with the US and the rest of the developed world, where its interests coincide with those of its Asean partners, although the response to economic initiatives from Apec has been far less enthusiastic, reflecting Thailand's belief that Asean is the most suitable forum for implementing trade reforms. Like most other Asean members, it regards Apec as a consultative body that can play a useful role in removing structural impediments to trade, such as overlapping customs regulations, but should not set policies. This is partly because of an Asian perception that the US and its western allies in the Pacific are merely interested in using Apec as a counter to European influence in global trade talks. While Bangkok will remain a member of Apec, it is always likely to give more prominence to Asean affairs.

Complicated Relations With Myanmar And China

The closer ties with China have already complicated efforts to ease tensions with Myanmar, which is regarded by Thailand as its only external security threat. Yangon's successful push against ethnic rebels has brought Myanmar troops right on to the border for the first time in half a century, and resulted in a constant series of armed clashes. Relations sank to a new low in October 1999, when Thai authorities freed Myanmar rebels who had briefly occupied Yangon's embassy in Bangkok in a deal to secure the release of several dozen hostages. Myanmar responded by closing all border crossings and cancelling lucrative Thai fishing concessions in its waters.

China has always viewed Thailand as its gateway to improved relations with Asean, but there are signs that a more even-handed relationship might be evolving. Thai leaders have been pointedly cool on Chinese offers of huge infrastructure investment, probably because of security reservations by the armed forces. They have also given closer attention to ties with India and other South Asian states, in what may be an attempt to provide a balance to Chinese ambitions. India is viewed as the central player in an economic linkage through the "Bay of Bengal Forum" that might eventually encompass the Indian Ocean community as far west as Africa. Relations with eastern European countries have also been upgraded because of their economic potential, while the Middle East is a priority because of remittances from labour shipments.

2 Economic Outlook

Introduction

IMF Monitors Withdraw

The IMF completed a three-year financial arrangement with Thailand in mid-June. In its final quarterly economic review, the Fund backed government forecasts of 4-4.5% GDP growth in 2000, noting the strength of external demand, static inflation and the healthy payments position. It called for a continuation of the expansive policies followed since 1998, including fiscal stimulus and low interest rates. But it cautioned that high corporate debt and the weak financial sector could undermine medium-term growth and pointed out that a sharp rise in the level of public debt, to about 55% GDP in 1999, presented a challenge for future fiscal management. Progress on dealing with the restructuring of non-performing loans (NPLs), has been slower than in South Korea or Malaysia, with the NPL ratio still estimated at around 39% at end 1999. This was a point taken up in some detail in the World Bank's *Economic Monitor* for June 2000.

Mounting public debt and the overhang of NPLs could threaten a sustained economic recovery.

The finance minister, Tarrin Nimmanahaeminda, has said that the government will launch a new strategy in July to speed up the restructuring of NPLs. He gave few details, but the package appeared likely to include further tax incentives to banks and changes in bankruptcy legislation to compel debtors to negotiate settlement. Tarrin, the main architect of the government's economic policies, said the recovery strategy was based on a revival of private consumption, which was expected to eventually replace exports as the main growth stimulus. Interest rates would be kept low to encourage increased spending, while the government would also seek to stimulate stronger credit growth.

Confidence in government unity on the policy front was undermined in Q1 by a conflict between the two leading monetary figures over the handling of financial sector debt. Tarrin has been pressing the Bank of Thailand (BoT) governor, MR Chatumongol Sonakul, for access to the BoT's substantial note-backing reserves as an alternative to increases in corporate taxes. However, Chatumongol refused on the grounds that the proposed withdrawal of THB700-800bn (US$18bn) would interfere with the central bank's flexibility in responding to monetary problems. He eventually relented after intervention by the prime minister, but had transferred only THB130bn as of June due to legislative delays. The dispute was triggered by fundamental differences over monetary issues that will not be resolved in the life of the current coalition. Tarrin is expected to retain Chatumongol in his present position to avoid any image problems for the government, but the indecisive handling of the conflict has added to increasing doubts over his own political future. Backbench pressure for Tarrin's resignation will intensify, though it is unlikely that he will be replaced so close to the election.

Economic activity

Growth Surges Despite Rate Fears

Supported by a modest revival in domestic demand, growth will hover at just under 5% in 2000-2002.

Fears of higher interest rates clouded the economic outlook in the first half of 2000, but GDP nonetheless grew by 5.2% y-o-y in Q1 following a surge in exports and a more tentative recovery in domestic demand. The government responded by raising its forecast for the whole year to 5%, at the upper end of previous projections. A possible resurgence in inflation, fuelled by stronger domestic demand and continuing high oil prices, is a source of worry and a number of pre-emptive measures have been taken. The basic wage was frozen for a third consecutive year in May to stem the demand push on prices, more indirect capital controls were imposed and inflation-targeting price monitoring was introduced. Wage negotiations were overshadowed by warnings from business leaders of mass layoffs if the increase of THB18 a day sought by union leaders were granted. Unemployment officially stood at 4.2% in 1999, though independent surveys suggested that the real figure was probably closer to 6%, as the government data did not include seasonal workers such as farmers. Employers, led by the Federation of Thai Industries (FTI), had agreed on a tentative rise of THB20 in the initial round of talks in late 1999, but apparently recanted under pressure from government negotiators. The minimum wage, paid mostly to unskilled construction and factory workers, will stay at THB130-162/month depending on workplace location.

Job security will remain uncertain because of industrial and financial sector restructuring, the impending privatisation of state assets and efficiency

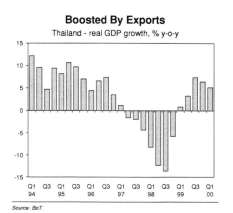

Boosted By Exports
Thailand - real GDP growth, % y-o-y

Source: BoT.

drives resulting from increased foreign competition. However, **BMI** expects unemployment to fall to 4.0% of the workforce in 2000 and 3.7% by 2002, as rising domestic demand and a stronger recovery in industrial output will create more labour opportunities. This will support continued growth in private consumption at around the 5.5% level; hardly a boom but much better than in 1999. **BMI** expects investment prospects to be somewhat dented by a combination of policy drift, leading to slower than expected restructuring and political uncertainty. Growth in gross fixed investment will average 7.8% a year in the three years to 2002, faster than GDP but not fast enough to return investment to its pre-crisis level in constant prices. Private investment is likely to be concentrated in the export sector, especially electronics and information technology, where Thailand's competitive advantage has been enhanced by lower costs.

Exports, meanwhile, having surged by 36.1% y-o-y in Q1 2000, will subside to a healthy annual growth of just under 12% in the forecast period, boosted by strong world trade growth and imports will just outpace them, as stocks are rebuilt and investment recovers. **BMI** is forecasting an overall GDP growth rate of 4.6% in the forecast period, with growth of 4.9% in 2000 falling back a little next year and then entering a period of more sustained recovery from 2002.

On an index basis manufacturing production rose by a moderate 8.8% in Q1, but a surge in imported goods, mostly from larger procurements of raw materials and parts intended for export-based industries, pointed to strong orders. Imports of capital goods alone rose by 21.9%. Over the forecast period, manufacturing will, as usual, lead GDP, growing at about 8% a year, followed by services. Financial services will stage a fairly strong recovery at the end of the forecast period, on the back of restructuring. Agriculture continues to be muted by a lack of investment and poor prices (*see Key Economic Secto*rs)

A Slow Retreat
Thailand - unemployment rate, %

e/f = BMI estimate/forecast. Source: BoT.

POPULATION & OUTPUT										
	1993	1994	1995	1996	1997	1998	1999e	2000f	2001f	2002f
Population (mn)	58.1	58.7	59.4	60.0	60.6	61.2	62.0	62.8	63.6	64.4
Nominal GDP (US$bn)	125.6	144.5	168.4	185.0	149.1	111.3	127.0	135.8	144.3	144.3
GDP per capita (US$)	2,163	2,462	2,834	3,084	2,460	1,819	2,049	2,162	2,269	2,240
Real GDP growth (% y/y)	8.7	8.6	8.8	5.5	-0.4	-10.2	4.2	4.9	4.2	4.8
MPI (% y/y)	10.5	6.4	9.3	8.6	-0.6	-10.6	12.8	8.5	7.5	7.5
Unemployment rate (%)	2.6	2.6	1.7	2.0	1.9	4.4	4.2	4.0	3.8	3.7

e/f = BMI estimate/forecast. MPI = Manufacturing Production Index. Sources: BoT/IMF/BMI.

Fiscal Policy

Funding Lapses Prompt Spending Overhaul

A new system of monitoring spending will help with budgetary management, much needed in view of the sharp rise in public debt.

Weak tax revenues and inefficient disbursements are frustrating fiscal targets, and have prompted a shift to performance-based budgeting. The government's cash balance registered a deficit of THB25.3bn (US$650mn) at the end of April, including a budgeted shortfall of THB24.5bn from expanded public expenditure. Revenues grew by 11% y-o-y, but this was mostly a result of increased trade activity; tax income was down by 1%. In response, the Finance Ministry will monitor spending patterns by two ministries in fiscal 2000/2001 as the first stage in a performance-based overhaul of funding disbursements. Initial aims will be to reduce funding overlaps and gauge whether allocations are being used as intended. Budget laws will also be revamped for the first time in 40 years with the objective of presenting a clearer picture of public finances. According to a policy document released in May, the reforms will include a consolidation of all public debt, a revised management system for support funds, a new approvals structure to improve funding transparency and the decentralisation of budget management. Future budgets may also be prepared on a more frequent basis, instead of the current reliance upon annual disbursements.

These changes are partly a result of 1997-98 constitutional amendments that shifted more administrative responsibility to provincial government bodies. Rural authorities will be allocated total funding of THB30bn under the 2000/2001 budget, a 10-fold increase on the previous fiscal year. City municipalities will get THB40bn, an increase of 25% y-o-y. In all, 20% of total revenues will go to local communities, a share rising to 35% by 2005/2006.

Total expenditures were fixed at THB910bn under the 2000/2001 budget, an increase of THB50bn, or 5.8% y-o-y. The accumulated deficit will remain at THB105bn, reflecting government unease over rising debt repayments, as well as the weak revenues picture. A total of THB224bn, or 24.7% of the

GOVERNMENT FINANCE (THB BN)						
	FY1990	**FY1996**	**FY1997**	**FY1998**	**FY1999**	**FY2000b**
Total revenue	395.0	850.2	844.3	724.7	709.9	805.0
Total expenditure	291.2	750.2	888.5	835.3	822.6	910.0
Budget balance	103.4	104.3	-31.1	-115.0	-133.8	-110.0
% of GDP	4.7	2.3	-0.1	-2.5	-2.9	N/A

fiscal years ending September 30; b = budgeted; Source: Bangkok Bank; Press Reports.

budget, was allocated as development funds and 74.9% as fixed spending, which includes debt servicing of THB12bn. Fixed spending will rise by only 1% y-o-y because of the soaring government debt, which amounted to THB3.26trn, as much as 55% of 1999 GDP as of March 31. About 50% must be repaid within 15 years, but the Finance Ministry expects the burden to peak in 2005, when it will be equivalent to 19.2% of projected spending. Most of the debts represent the accumulated costs of absorbing insolvent banks and finance firms through the Financial Institutions Development Fund (FIDF) lifeboat scheme, as well as the IMF liabilities.

The World Bank has estimated that a primary surplus of around 3% will need to be run in order to lower the debt/GDP ratio to a more sustainable 40%. This is not an immediate priority, but measures to reduce the debt level, and action to boost revenues and cut spending will be needed when recovery is firmly established. This will be an acrimonious feature of budget deliberations in the new parliament.

Monetary Policy

Price Stability Becomes The Central Focus

Inflation-targeting will be used from late July to track price trends and implement monetary policies. Amendments to the Bank of Thailand Act that are expected to be approved by parliament in the third quarter will transfer monetary authority to a new Monetary Policy Board composed of BoT officials and independent economists. Its main function will be to ensure price stability by using a range of indicators, including the consumer price index (CPI) and 14-day repurchase rates. The initial target, which will be used until the end of 2002, is to keep core inflation in a range of 0-3.5%, based on projected GDP growth of 4.5-5.5%. Core inflation is defined as the consumer price index (CPI) exclusive of raw food and energy costs.

With oil prices high and demand stronger, controlling inflation without raising interest rates so high that they snuff out the recovery, will be a delicate task.

INFLATION & INTEREST RATES										
	1993	1994	1995	1996	1997	1998	1999	2000f	2001f	2002f
CPI (% y/y, an.avg)	3.3	5.2	5.7	5.8	5.6	8.1	0.2	2.4	3.5	3.6
Interbank rate (%, an. avg)	4.5	7.1	10.3	12.1	21.7	2.6	1.2	2.0	2.2	2.3
Discount Rate (%, eop)	9.0	9.5	10.5	10.5	12.5	12.5	4.0	4.0	4.0	4.2
Prime Rate (%, eop)	10.5	11.8	13.8	13.2	15.3	11.5	8.3	8.3	8.3	8.3
Fixed Deposit (1-year, eop)	7.0	8.3	10.3	8.5	10.0	6.0	4.0	3.8	3.8	3.8
f = BMI forecast. eop = end of period. Sources: BoT/IMF/BMI.										

Repurchase rates will be maintained at the annualised June level of 1.5%, with closing rates not allowed to depart from the policy rate by more than one-sixteenth of a percentage point. Other repurchase rates will be set according to market conditions.

The low target range reflects government confidence that ample liquidity will shield the economy in 2000 from oil price rises and higher offshore interest rates. Inflation crept up by only 0.9% in Q1 00, largely because weak global grain prices reduced the food index by 1.7%. One-day repurchase rates were quoted in mid-June at a flat 1.125%, with three-month rates at 2.562%. Prime lending rates averaged 8-8.50% in Q1, a decline of 25 basis points from December, though most commercial banks expect an increase of 50 basis points during the second half of the year in response to a further tightening of US monetary policies. This is partly based on expectations that the monetary board will try to counter a further weakening of the baht that could result from the use of the inflation-targeting system. **BMI** expects inflation to exceed official forecasts of 2.5-3% in 2001-02 thanks to stronger domestic demand and a further modest weakening of the baht. But inflation will be well under control.

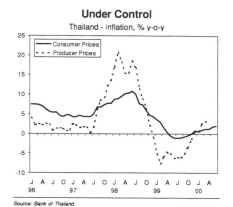

Under Control
Thailand - inflation, % y-o-y

Source: Bank of Thailand.

Exchange Rate Policy

Policy Indecision Over Volatile Baht

In the short term, pressure on the baht will continue, fuelled by politics, but medium term depreciation will be modest.

Renewed currency volatility forced the central bank to intervene frequently on the foreign exchange markets during the first half of the year, and bolstered support for stiffer capital controls. The baht had declined to around THB39.20/US$ by mid-June, losing 4.3% of its December value, amid indications that the BoT had abandoned efforts to preserve its unofficial benchmark of THB38/US$. Senior bank officials indicated that the baht would be allowed to find its own level, despite political concerns over the adverse impact on debt repayments. The BoT is reluctant to raise interest rates. A widening gap of 2-3 percentage points between US and short-term domestic rates triggered net capital outflows of US$4.7bn in the first three months of the year, as offshore investors moved their money back to American markets. About 70% of these funds were withdrawn by portfolio investors, pushing the stock market index down to a 15-month low by mid-June.

In responding to the rate pressures, monetary officials were caught between conflicting demands from the corporate sector, with debtors seeking a stronger baht and exporters a further weakening to around THB40/US$. The compromise rate appeared to be THB39/US$, which was achieved for much of June. However, a lack of consensus over the controls that might be needed to enforce this new benchmark makes it likely that the baht will be given considerable flexibility in responding to offshore movements. The BoT staunchly opposed the adoption of a Malaysian model of currency pegging, preferring instead to rely upon the new inflation-targeting monetary system and other indirect controls to stabilise interest rates.

One tactic is to go right to the source of transactions: banks have been forbidden since early 2000 to conduct daily money transfers exceeding US$50mn. However, Thailand's ambitions to build up a regional presence in financial services have led to some policy contradictions. In April, securities regulators allowed offshore investment for the first time by a range of Thai institutions so they could build up their competitiveness. Yet the BoT rejected an application in the same month from US financial services group GE Capital to issue domestic baht-denominated bonds. Although GEC planned to use the receipts to build up local subsidiaries, the central bank feared that they might be repatriated.

The baht will remain under downward pressure in 2000 due to withdrawals of portfolio capital and accelerated debt repayments, before settling into a more stable range of THB39/US$ in 2001-02. Political jitters could spark bouts of volatility until the elections are well over. However, tighter monetary policies and higher direct foreign investment inflows should reduce volatility and support overall stability from the second half of 2001, as will the continuing, though declining, surplus on the current account.

Under Pressure
Thailand - exchange rate, THB/US$

Source: Reuters/BMI.

EXCHANGE RATES										
	1993	1994	1995	1996	1997	1998	1999	2000f	2001f	2002f
THB/US$ (eop)	25.54	25.09	25.19	25.61	47.25	36.69	38.18	38.70	38.80	39.50
THB/US$ (an. avg)	25.32	25.15	24.91	25.34	31.36	41.36	37.84	38.00	38.50	39.00
f = BMI forecast. Sources: Reuters/IMF.										

Balance Of Payments

Export Revenues Are Buoyant...

Export value grew by 32% y-o-y in baht terms in Q1, with the help of favourable price movements for manufactured goods following the dollar's appreciation. Playing down the impact of higher interest rates, the government raised its year-long forecast for the rise in export values from 7.4% to 12%. The revision came despite an exports slump in April that was attributed to holiday shutdowns. Revenues rose by only 12.1% y-o-y and fell by 13.6% on the previous month, but manufacturers reported that their advance order books were full. Increasing purchases of raw materials for export give some credence to the government's assessment. Most of the 24% y-o-y rise in Q1 import value resulted from shipments of production-based inputs, though there was also a 216% rise in the baht value of oil imports.

Nevertheless, a deeper analysis of the Q1 exports data suggests that the official forecasts are over-optimistic, as the upsurge was recorded against a particularly low base figure for the corresponding period in 1999. The earnings pattern was also noticeably uneven, with a relatively small number of industries contributing the bulk of income: most came from electronic goods, gems and jewellery, integrated circuits, and textiles and garments. All of these are heavily import-dependent and can be expected to lose competitiveness as material costs rise. Shipment revenue from unprocessed agricultural products, which accounts for 10% of export revenues, will remain below 1999 levels due to unattractive prices. The marketing edge from the depreciation of the baht must be balanced against currency declines of a similar scale in other Asian countries, some of which have less to lose from a parallel rise in import costs. Taking price and volume effects into account, **BMI** expects the dollar value of exports to rise by about 7% a year to 2002, when merchandise exports will be worth about US$72bn.

Volume and price effects will combine to reduce the trade surplus, as imports outpace exports.

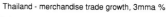

Temporary Hiccup

Thailand - merchandise trade growth, 3mma %

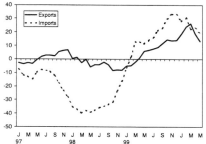

Source: BoT.

	1993	1994	1995	1996	1997	1998	1999	2000f	2001f	2002f
BALANCE OF PAYMENTS										
Merchandise exports (US$bn)	36.96	45.23	56.44	55.72	57.62	54.34	58.51	64.08	68.31	72.15
Merchandise imports (cif, US$bn)	46.07	54.43	70.78	72.32	61.35	42.90	50.40	57.71	62.65	69.49
Trade balance (customs, US$bn)	-9.11	-9.20	-14.34	-16.60	-3.74	11.45	8.11	6.37	5.66	2.67
Current account (US$bn)	-6.36	-8.09	-13.56	-14.69	-3.02	14.05	11.05	8.52	7.26	3.65
Current account (% GDP)	-5.07	-5.59	-8.05	-7.94	-2.03	12.62	8.70	6.27	5.03	2.53

f = BMI forecast. Sources: BoT/IMF/BMI.

...But Will Be Hit By The US Slowdown

Faltering demand in the US and China's impending entry into the WTO are among the potential medium-term threats to exporters. Shipments to the US markets are expected to be down at least 10% this year and 15% in 2001 if growth remains sluggish. In the first indication of what may lie ahead, sales of electronic goods to the US fell in Q1 due to the dollar's appreciation, while orders for consumer electrical products were expected to fall in Q2. Flow-on effects are being felt in some other markets: a weakening of the Euro against the US dollar forced shipment prices down by as much as 30% for some products in western European markets during Q1. Declining access to US markets will be compounded by the steady withdrawal of tariff benefits offered under the American generalised system of preferences (GSP), which cost Thai producers US$740mn in lost export revenues in 1999.

Chinese membership of the WTO will bring longer-term advantages to Thailand through expanded trade and investment market ties. **BMI** expects benefits to become apparent by 2002, when improved transport links through the Mekong delta will hasten the integration of markets in Indochina and western China. However, the immediate impact will be less favourable, as Beijing will be able to use its elevated status to gain access to low-cost grain and manufacturing markets that are contested by Thai producers. Price-cutting is especially likely in low-quality rice shipments and garments, where Thailand has been losing market share since the early 1990s. Surveys by the Federation of Thai Industries have also indicated that as many as one-in-three domestic electronics firms may use China as their exports hub once it joins the WTO. Most expect cost savings and greater marketing opportunities.

The government has said that its key structural challenge is to reduce exporters' dependence upon imported materials, which ranges as high as 100% of shipment content for some electronics industries. Faced with the choice of protecting inefficient local suppliers or improving productivity, policymakers are increasingly siding with exporters. In June, the last local content rules were abolished, liberalising milk products. Similar rules were scrapped in January for the automotive trade. Import content used in exported motor vehicles had fallen in any case to only 10%, from an average of 40% in 1997, because of cost pressures. Food producers, with almost 100% local content, are the least-reliant upon imports. Since efforts to increase domestic value-added will take time to bear fruit, and will anyway run into potential problems in the WTO and Afta arenas, **BMI** expects imports to outpace exports in dollar value and in volume in the forecast period. Although lower oil prices from 2001 will curb the import bill, the

China's impending entry into the WTO will present a new challenge to Thai exporters.

Key Partners
Thailand - exports by destination, THBbn

USA	479.4
Japan	311.8
Singapore	191.0
Hong Kong	112.6
Netherlands	83.1
UK	79.2
Malaysia	80.5
China	70.6
Taiwan	77.3
Germany	55.2

Source: BoT.

terms of trade will generally move against Thailand, so that the merchandise trade surplus will fall back, to under US$2.7bn by 2002, from a projected US$6.4bn this year.

Current Account Heads Down

The current account recorded a surplus of US$4bn in Q1 2000, up from US$2.6bn in Q1 99 and US$1.7bn in Q4 99. But the shrinking trade surplus, coupled with rising services outflows from higher export shipment costs and a return of outward travel and higher outflows of interest, profits and dividends thanks to the growing stock of foreign assets in Thailand are combining to cut the current account surplus.

From a high of 12.6% of GDP in 1998, **BMI** forecasts successive reductions in the current account surplus over the forecast period, taking it to US$3.7bn, or 2.5% of GDP in 2002, from US$8.5bn this year. Thereafter the traditional deficit will reappear, putting a premium on the stabilisation of the debt situation and completion of financial sector and industrial restructuring during the window provided by a period of not needing to import capital in order to finance a savings-investment gap.

The weaker baht will inflate repayment costs on the offshore debt just when sizeable public sector obligations are coming due, adding to outflows on the capital account, which will be dominated by debt repayments. Inflows will be boosted by a combination of a modest revival in foreign direct investment and portfolio investment as markets stabilise.

A declining trade surplus will push the current account towards deficit, but beyond the forecast horizon.

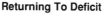

Returning To Deficit
Thailand - balance of payments, US$bn

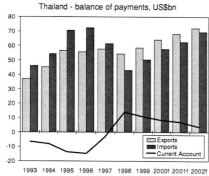

f = BMI forecast; Source: BoT.

Foreign Direct Investment

More Projects, But Stiffer Conditions

Applications for government promotional incentives rose by 60% y-o-y in the five months to the end of May, as manufacturers opened new plant in anticipation of a consumer recovery. The state-run Board of Investment (BoI) reported that 554 investment plans were submitted, with a total value of THB176bn. The monetary value of projects more than doubled on the same period in 1999. Japan remained the biggest source of FDI, followed by firms from Taiwan and the US. About 40% of projects involved joint ventures between Thai and foreign firms and almost 30% were export-oriented. Petrochemicals, food processing and light industries will be among the biggest recipients of the latest capital inflows.

FDI inflows are to be more actively targeted towards key sectors. FDI flows will tread water before the next upsurge, from privatisation, in 2002.

While only about two-thirds of mooted investments usually proceed, the data are encouraging. Total net FDI in 1999 was down by 39%, to THB129.9bn, according to Bank of Thailand data. One positive trend noted by the BOI was that most projects involved support links with existing industries, the market segment that is most needed to reduce Thailand's reliance upon offshore parts and raw materials.

Capitalising on the strong FDI growth this year, the BoI said it would take a more discriminatory approach to the type of businesses approved for government incentives. Under a major policy shakeup announced in late May, the agency announced that from August, five groups of activities would be given top priority: agriculture and agricultural products; environmental protection and/or restoration; direct involvement in technological and human resource development; basic transportation services and infrastructure; and services. A list of targeted industries was submitted, along with those that would be discouraged for reasons of over-supply or unsuitability. Some of the latter were also rejected on environmental grounds.

Most firms will be required to raise their capital bases under the new scheme, with a beneficial impact upon investment inflows. But **BMI** still expects FDI to drop by 10-15% over the entire year, as project figures in the two previous years were distorted by abnormal levels of financial sector recapitalisation. There was also widespread evidence that the Q1 figures were inflated by reports of the imminent shakeup in the incentives scheme, with many firms bringing their plans forward to beat anticipated increases in capital requirements. Individual projects are likely to be smaller in scale this year because of a trend towards supplier relocations that usually involve more compact firms. But at the same time, **BMI** expects a shift to more productive sectors and an increased regional focus ahead of the launch of Asean's free trade area.

The next big wave of FDI is not likely to start until 2002, when the privatisation of state assets will attract high levels of foreign interest. Most capital is expected to go to the telecommunications, energy and transport sectors, through partial sell-offs of the Telephone Organisation of Thailand (TOT), Electricity Generating Authority of Thailand (EGAT), the Petroleum Authority of Thailand (PTT) and Thai Airways International (THAI). Revenues from the disposal of the top 4-5 state enterprises alone had originally been forecast at about THB500bn, but low returns from financial sector asset auctions have forced a downward revision. With most auctions attracting only 20-30% of book prices, the Finance Ministry said in April that declining asset values would diminish the appeal of privatisation, and it was

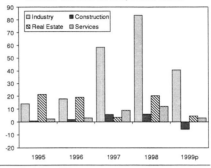

Upsurge Anticipated In 2002
Thailand - net flows of FDI by sector, THBbn

p = provisional; Source: BoT.

Foreign investment figures have been distorted by abnormal levels of financial sector recapitalisation.

prepared to wait until market conditions improved. Share placements are now expected to start in mid-2001, with THAI and TOT going to the market first.

External Debt

Only A Temporary Respite?

External debt figures have been radically upsized, but the outlook is still for a modest fall in the debt to GDP and debt service ratios.

In late June the Bank of Thailand announced that a more comprehensive method of calculation, primarily for non-bank external liabilities, implied a large upwards revision, of the order US$20bn to an estimated US$92.3bn as of the end of March. This compared with US$95.6bn at the end of 1999 and a peak of US$109.3bn at the end 1997, in the midst of the financial crisis. The improvement has mostly been at a corporate level, reflecting changes in the debts composition due to rising government deficits. The private share of liabilities (on unrevised, lower figures) fell to 50% in February, from more than 70% at the onset of the crisis, and this trend is likely to continue until at least the mid-point of the decade. There has also been a continuing improvement in the debt structure, with only 17.1% classed as short term in February, down from almost 40% three years earlier, largely because of a scarcity of financing with a duration of 3-12 months and the restructuring priority given to these loans.

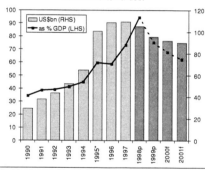

Coming Down
Thailand - external debt

break in series; p = provisional; f = BMI forecast; Source: BoT.

Prospects for a substantial decline in debt levels in 2000-2002 are remote, as export receipts will probably be insufficient to cover the rising cost of the financial sector bailout. Repayments will start in November on loans from the US$17.2bn reserve fund that was set up in 1997 by the IMF, which amounted to US$14.3bn when the government stopped taking withdrawals in June 1999. Instalments are also due on a plethora of relief funds set up by numerous development agencies, while the central bank will start issuing offshore bonds to meet the banks cleanup once it achieves a sovereign credit upgrade. Assuming the upgrade comes through by early 2001, which is by no means a foregone conclusion, especially now that the BoT has discovered so much more debt, the BoT's debt alone is likely to rise from a total of

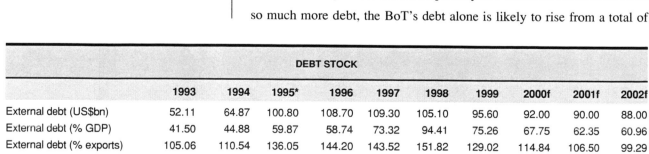

	1993	1994	1995*	1996	1997	1998	1999	2000f	2001f	2002f
				DEBT STOCK						
External debt (US$bn)	52.11	64.87	100.80	108.70	109.30	105.10	95.60	92.00	90.00	88.00
External debt (% GDP)	41.50	44.88	59.87	58.74	73.32	94.41	75.26	67.75	62.35	60.96
External debt (% exports)	105.06	110.54	136.05	144.20	143.52	151.82	129.02	114.84	106.50	99.29

*f = BMI forecast. *Break in series. Sources: BoT/IMF/BMI.*

US$12bn in February to at least US$17bn by 2002. **BMI** expects total foreign debt to fall to about US$88bn by the end of 2002, as IMF repayments reduce the stock of public debt. While the debt burden will impinge on public sector expenditure, there should be little difficulty in servicing repayments. The debt-service ratio peaked at about 19% in 1999 and is set to decline to 17% in 2002, as the stock of debt is reduced. Nevertheless, the government signalled its anxiety over the debt figures by calling in May for a lower foreign borrowing ceiling in fiscal 2000/2001. Currently set at US$5bn, the ceiling is likely to be lowered to about US$$3.5bn.

Profile and Recent Developments

Characteristics Of The Economy

Industry, Services Lead The Way

Thailand is classed among the lower ranks of middle-income countries according to the World Bank, its status having declined sharply in the wake of the 1997-99 economic downturn. In 1998, its nominal GDP per capita fell to US$1819.1, from US$3084.1 in 1996. World Bank data for 1998 show real GNP per capita of US$2,200 (using a three-year moving average exchange rate to dilute the impact of currency movements), down from US$2,800 in 1997. Real GDP declined by 0.4% in 1997 and then by as much as 10.2% in 1998 as the impact of the crisis hit the real economy. Despite the fall in incomes and demand in the 1997-99 economic downturn, Thailand remains a potentially important consumer market and a major player in the global trading economy.

The economy has made a rapid transition since the 1970s from an agrarian base to one that is heavily dependent upon industry. Manufacturing alone provides more than 40% of GDP and 80% of export earnings, while agriculture's share has fallen in each case to 10%. While it still employs more than 60% of the population, the primary sector (especially agriculture and fishing) is now important mainly as a source of inputs for processing industries. But much of Thailand's rich endowment of forests and fishing grounds has been lost through over-exploitation. Services, led by the buoyant tourism sector, contribute about 50% of GDP, though their share has slipped slightly since the early 1990s due to the decline of the financial sector. Financial services peaked in 1993-95, when the government launched an ambitious offshore banking scheme that began the chain of debt leading to the later economic crisis. More than 70 banks and financial firms were closed or forced into equity sales in the subsequent debt clean-up.

From Import-Substitution To High-End Exports

Manufacturing has diversified from import-substitution to a versatile range of industries that parallel the development of the economy. First came basic food processing (sugar, beer), and production of materials (cement), followed by export-oriented industries with a high labour content (textiles, footwear, toys). The third step involved assembling and output of intermediate goods (electrical appliances, computer components, vehicles), as well as heavy investment in capital-intensive upstream industries (steel, petrochemicals) that were aimed at both domestic and export markets. Rising production costs have led to a further shift into value-adding (high-technology, garments), but only hesitant progress has been made due to inadequate labour skills and lack of consistency and drive in industrial policy. The devising and implementation of industrial strategy has been a heavily politicised process, skewed as well by the excessive dominance of the congested metropolitan area in development.

With the exception of the petrochemicals sector and related activities, which are mostly based on the eastern seaboard, manufacturers had tended to base their factories close to the key consumer markets and ports in Bangkok. However, tougher pollution rules in the capital and generous tax incentives have shifted the focus to eastern Rayong and Chon Buri provinces in the past 4-5 years. A shake-up of the government's zoning system in late 1999 is expected to accelerate this trend, as will the upgrading of port facilities in the east

Mining Sector In Decline

Thailand has few mineral resources worth extracting on a sizeable scale, as indicated by the low contribution made to GDP by the mining sector. Tin mining (once a major export) has almost ceased as low prices make Thai deposits uneconomic. Some other metals (including tungsten and zinc) are mined on a small scale, and quarrying of aggregates (for construction) is significant. There have also been recent promising finds of gold and potash, while Thailand has some of the last remaining deposits in Asia of natural gypsum. However, the only minerals important to the wider economy are lignite (brown coal) and natural gas. Soon, the output of gas is likely to exceed demand, despite its increasing use in the power sector and as a fuel and feedstock for industry. But Thailand remains heavily dependent on imports of crude oil and periodically needs to buy refined products as well. Most is used by industry, transport and (increasingly) for power generation. In 1998 imported fuels (predominantly oil) supplied nearly 70% of Thailand's energy needs, down from a peak of 90% in 1992.

Economic Activity

Tentative Recovery Gets Underway

Declining export competitiveness has slowed economic growth since late 1995 and was a key factor in the exchange rate pressures that triggered the 1997 crisis. The stronger dollar boosted input costs in 1996, pushing the trade and current account deficits to unsustainable levels and worsening the debt position of financial institutions. When the first repayment defaults began in early 1997, the monetary authorities resorted to a failed defence of the baht's fixed-exchange mechanism that ultimately exhausted most of the country's foreign reserves. The baht was floated in July 1999 and quickly lost more than half of its value, forcing the government to seek help one month later from the IMF. Under the IMF's austere formula of high interest rates and public spending cutbacks, the economy sank into a deep recession in 1998, shrinking by 10.2%. But a gradual monetary loosening became possible by 1999 as the baht stabilised and lending rates began to fall.

A tentative recovery was underway by Q2 99, but this was largely because of massive injections of public funds that were channelled into rural relief schemes and export funding. Consumption remained low because of job losses and declining purchasing power, as well as a liquidity freeze that resulted from the upheaval in the banking sector (*see below*). Nevertheless, GDP expanded by 4.2% in 1999, well above the initial forecast of about 1.4%. This was partly due to the more stable exchange rate environment, as well as a continuation of the expansive spending policies introduced in the previous year. The baht settled into a new level more than 20% below its mid-1997 value, underwriting a 7.2% increase in export sales and allowing interest rates to ease to record lows. Having fallen by 36.7% in annual average terms between 1998 and 1996 against the dollar, the baht stabilised and has appreciated in 1999, averaging THB37.8/US$1, an 8.4% rise.

Export Manufacturing, Services Rebound

Manufacturing output rebounded by 7.8% in 1999, after a contraction of 9.6% in 1998, despite zero growth in private investment due to high levels of excess plant capacity. Only 60% of total manufacturing capacity was being utilised at the end of 1999, compared with 52% a year earlier, but this ratio was distorted by abnormally low utilisation ratios figures for some depressed industries, such as construction materials. At current absorption rates it is expected to be 3-4 years before utilisation returns to pre-crisis levels, as some industrial segments – notably cement and steelmaking – witnessed extraordinary over-development in the peak investment period of 1993-95. With domestic demand undermined by the weak labour market, export-oriented industries fared the best. Automotive assembly, electronics, petrochemicals and processed foods all rebounded strongly, but construction and real estate activity lagged because of supply gluts. Low global prices and unfavourable weather conditions also adversely affected the agricultural sector, with output rising by a modest 2.6%.

Services did better, registering growth of 5.1% after a sharp contraction of 8.3% in 1998, mostly because of improved tourism and transportation revenues. Retailers reported a 7% increase in sales. But business activity in general was constrained by the liquidity bottlenecks, with retailing/wholesaling, construction and financial services accounting for most of the 6,977 bankruptcies during the year. While this was a 20% improvement on 1998 shutdowns, it nonetheless added to the growing social toll of the crisis. The World Bank estimated that the number of Thais living in poverty (classed as an income of less than US$2 a day) had doubled to 20% between 1997 and 1999, while 60% were in debt. As of December 1999, about 4.2% of the workforce was officially unemployed; however, this was widely viewed as an under-estimation, as it did not include transient and part-time workers. Independent estimates averaged 6.5-7%. Reflecting the soft labour conditions, earnings declined by 12-15%, though some firms revived bonus payments. The minimum wage remained frozen at 1997 levels; however, employers promised to allow a rise of at least 10% during 2000.

Fiscal Policy

Pumping Up The Deficit

Before the 1997 currency and financial sector crises, Thailand did not have a tradition of using fiscal adjustments to influence domestic economic activity. Instead, a balanced budget policy sought to match annual expenditures to projected revenues. In practice, Thailand usually achieved public sector surpluses (averaging around 3% of GDP from FY89 to FY96 – financial years ending September 30), as tax receipts tended to exceed expectations and bureaucratic inertia generally kept spending below planned levels. This comfortable position was eroded in FY97 (deficit of 2.2% recorded), when the weakness in the economy led to revenues falling well below projections, while pre-election commitments pushed up expenditure. These trends illustrated deeper weaknesses in Thai budgetary procedures, which have yet to be cured; in particular, the lack of medium-term planning.

IMF Turns The Screws

Since the first Letter of Intent (LOI) agreed with the IMF (August 1997), the budget process has had to conform to targets agreed with the IMF. Initially, these involved a switch to restrictive policies for FY98, including sharp cuts in expenditure and measures to boost revenues – notably a rise in the VAT rate from 7% to 10%. This was designed to offset the feared inflationary consequences of devaluation and thus bolster confidence in the currency and stabilise private capital flows. In the second LOI, a surplus of 1% of GDP was envisaged but, as it became evident that the fall in output would be greater than expected, this goal was progressively adjusted to take account of the effect on revenues. There was also a deliberate shift to more liberal public spending policies in response to static private consumption, with a resultant impact on budgets. By the end of 1998, the government was running an accumulated deficit equivalent to 2.5% of GDP, excluding the interest cost of liquidity support for the beleaguered financial sector, which amounted to a further 3% of GDP.

Tax and other public revenues fell by 18% in FY98 but recovered by 3.8% in FY99 as corporate earnings picked up and factories placed more orders for production-based imports. The increase would have been far bigger if not for the government's decision in late March to reverse the 3% rise in VAT approved in 1997 (*see above*). Expenditure was boosted by a modest 2.1% to stimulate consumption, helping to contain the budget deficit at about 2.6% of GDP. However, total public sector debt rose to an estimated THB2trn (US$53bn) in 1999, equal to 41% of GDP, prompting unease over the longer-term impact on government finances. Most of this burden was in the form of irrecoverable liquidity injections into ailing financial institutions during 1997. The IMF backed a continuation of deficit budgeting until private investment picked up. With its three-year mandate due to end in August 2000, the agency adopted a more distant monitoring role in the second half of 1999, though it resisted efforts by the Thai authorities for an early release from the programme. A total of US$14bn had been drawn from the IMF's US$17.2bn standby facility by December, but the government said it would not make any further borrowings.

Monetary Policy

From Austerity To Expansion

The monetary policy stance was kept restrictive from late-1995 until the H2 98. Initially this was part of efforts to cool the overheated economy, and later the vain defence of the currency. The IMF assistance programme also required Thailand to maintain high real interest rates in order to restore confidence in the currency in the wake of its depreciation. The Bank of Thailand raised its discount rate by 200 basis points (bps) to 12.5%, in July 1997 and the commercial banks followed suit with similar increases in deposit and lending rates. The reversal of private capital flows added to tightness in credit markets, with inter-bank rates peaking at 22% in mid-1998.

The Bank of Thailand attempted to offset the detrimental impact of this credit squeeze by pumping liquidity into the market and directly to troubled institutions from early-1998. However, these moves had little impact on monetary growth, which slowed alarmingly from mid-1997. Bank credit to the private sector fell by some 0.5% in the first half of 1998 and total domestic credit grew by just over 2%, reflecting increased government borrowing to fund the financial sector rescue packages. Growth in the broad monetary aggregate (M2) slowed to about 2% per quarter, from the 4% average in 1997.

Stable Currency Eases Rates

Some monetary relaxation became possible after the currency stabilised in Q2 98, prompting the central bank to reduce its short-term interest rates from 10% to 5-6% in the second half of the year and boost the money supply. This was partly achieved by imposing a threshold on bank fixed-term deposit rates, which had climbed as high as 16% in H1 98 due to a frantic recapitalisation drive by banks. In the subsequent liquidity bottleneck, commercial bank credit contracted by 9.7% in 1998 and a further 1% in 1999, well below the targets of 4% and 7% growth respectively. Overnight interbank rates fell further to 1-2% by the end of 1999, dragging the prime lending rate down to 8.5%, from an average of 10.5-11% in the previous year. One-year deposit rates dropped to a record low of 4.5%. Ample liquidity acted as a buffer against the upward trend in US rates, leaving additional scope for small rate cuts in 2000. However, some tightening may be needed to counter the inflationary effects of produce shortages and rising oil prices. The consumer price index is expected to rise by 2.5-3% in 2000, compared with 0.3% in 1999.

Exchange Rate Policy

Baht Learns To Swim

The abandonment in July 1997 of the semi-formal regime maintained for over a decade (the baht was effectively pegged to the US dollar at a level around THB25/US$ in the mid 1990s), ushered in a period of confusion for Thailand's exchange rate policy. The initial agreement with the IMF envisaged the currency stabilising quickly as the benefits of the external official funding package and clear policy stance reassured investors. When this failed to happen as fast as had been expected, the authorities' lack of usable foreign exchange reserves prevented them intervening heavily in the volatile markets of late-1997 and early-1998. The reason was the massive use of forward contracts to defend the baht during early-1997, which left the central bank facing large potential losses (estimated at one point to be over US$10bn).

The baht was thus left buffeted in the global storms, sinking to a low of THB55/US$ in January 1998. Its subsequent partial revival (to THB37/US$ at end-1998 and THB38/US$ in December 1999) was due mainly to the restoration of calm to regional financial markets and evidence that the Thai authorities were addressing the country's structural economic problems. Both factors encouraged the resumption of private capital inflows, enabling the authorities to re-build foreign exchange reserves to a level where substantial market intervention would be feasible again.

Further Tinkering Unlikely

The more recent stability in the baht has given Thailand a chance to reconsider its long-term policy towards the exchange rate, but a reversal of the 1997 reforms has been ruled out, despite unease over the disruptive impact of short-term capital inflows. It is more likely that monetary mechanisms will be used to keep the baht in a stable range, including a new inflation-targeting model that was being considered in early 2000. This would allow a wider range of indexes, such as the CPI and prime lending rate, to be used to influence the exchange rate via changes in the monetary stance, without need for direct intervention.

Balance Of Payments

Trade Profile

Thailand's trade structure is evolving in line with its economic development and integration into the global economy. Manufactured products increasingly dominate its exports, with a noticeable shift to products used as inputs in the production process elsewhere (e.g. computer parts, integrated circuits) rather than finished goods. In particular, the low-technology, labour-intensive activities (footwear, garments) which led Thailand's initial push into export-oriented manufacturing have steadily lost ground. In baht terms, the fastest-growing components of exports in recent years have been machinery (especially computers and peripherals) and motor vehicles and parts, which boosted their earnings by 8.7% and 41.2% y-o-y respectively in the first nine months of 1999 – although the automotive sales have risen from a particularly small base. Technology-based goods and processed foods are likely to be the key export earners of the future. On the services side, the tourism industry is the most important source of earnings, accounting for about half of the total in 1998-99.

There have been fewer changes in Thailand's import structure. Oil and other fuels remain important – the drop in their percentage share since 1990 is due mainly to the decline in oil prices. Capital goods and intermediate products used by Thai industries still dominate the import bill. Within the capital goods category the main developments in the last two years have been a switch to electrical machinery rather than mechanical, and imports of intermediate products used in construction and related sectors have fallen sharply because of the depressed real estate industry.

Regional Neighbours' Trade Share Rises

Thailand's regional neighbours have become increasingly important trading partners since the establishment of the Asean Free Trade Area in 1992, though commercial ties fell sharply during the worst of the economic slump, in 1998. Asean became the biggest market for Thai goods in 1995 but fell to third place in 1998 behind the US and EU with 15.3% of total sales. A recovery to around 20% of the total market was expected in 1999. Japan, with an estimated 22% of combined trade in 1999, remains the biggest trading partner, despite a drop in its overall share of Thai trade since 1990 that was partly a result of the weak Japanese economy. The EU and US are Thailand's other major trading partners. The US has increased its share of Thai trade since 1990, mainly at the expense of Japan and the EU.

3 Key Economic Sectors

Introduction

The Recovery Is Still Tentative

Improvements were visible in most economic sectors in Q1, pushing business confidence to a three-year high. Export revenues expanded at the fastest y-o-y rate since 1996, while a sharp increase in imports pointed to renewed demand for production inputs. Private investment rose by an unexpectedly strong 14.6% over Q1 99,though this was partly a seasonal response to stock rundowns. Private consumption remained fragile, with a y-o-y increase of only 5%; but a positive trend was nonetheless evident in the prime indicators, with department store sales increasing by 4.6% y-o-y and value-added tax transactions up by 17.5%. Production has been slowing since Q4 99 because of rising costs in the manufacturing sector and soft agricultural prices, but the industrial outlook is rosy.

Growth prospects through the rest of this year will depend strongly upon manufacturing industries, as farm output is expected to grow by only 2.1%, down from 2.6% in 1999, when rice farmers benefited from regional crop failures. Industry is also struggling with rising costs and excess capacity, but output should steadily rise as debt problems are resolved. The external picture will be clouded by the slowdown in the US economy and China's impending entry into the WTO, and exports appear unlikely to meet public projections. Increased domestic purchasing power will provide a partial remedy, but could be undermined by weak bank lending. Private consumption growth is forecast at a modest 5.8% y-o-y. Credit bottlenecks will not loosen until 2001, while it will be 2002 before income levels begin to return to pre-crisis levels. Taking these factors into account, **BMI** maintains its forecast of 4.5% GDP growth, in the belief that consumption will be undermined by rising prices in the second half of the year, while investment levels will remain inadequate.

Demand constraints will start to ease once interest rates have stabilised in Q4, allowing growth to accelerate after 2001. **BMI** projects GDP to expand by

Growth prospects through the rest of this year will depend strongly upon manufacturing.

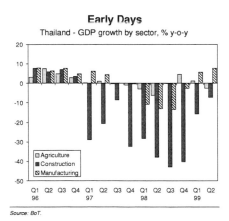

Early Days
Thailand - GDP growth by sector, % y-o-y

Source: BoT.

4.5% in 2001 and 5% in 2002, driven by a return of fixed business investment and renewed consumer confidence. However, competitive pressures on exports will again come to the fore as the baht strengthens towards the end of 2002. Declining duty on imported materials ahead of the start of Asean's free market in 2003 will provide a temporary reprieve, but productivity gains will be needed to prevent another economic downturn towards the middle of the decade. Progress in internal restructuring has so far been inadequate.

Manufacturing

Factories Hampered By Debts, Higher Import Costs

High import costs are undermining growth in the debt-laden industrial sector.

Rising import costs are undermining growth in the industrial sector as it clears a backlog of debts from the chronic over-investment of the early 1990s. Production overheads for export-oriented industries are expected to increase by at least 20% if the baht continues its decline through to the end of the year. Among the worst-hit will be producers of electronics, motor vehicles, steel and petrochemicals, which all rely heavily upon offshore parts and materials. The same industry segments are the most heavily-indebted, accounting for most of the estimated THB1.4trn that was owed by manufacturers to banks at the end of April. This included THB47.9bn in new debt, indicating that industry still has a long way to go before a full recovery.

A delayed impact from oil cost rises will become apparent during the second half of the year, though **BMI** believes that prices will stabilise by Q4, leaving industry relatively unscathed. Domestic consumer goods will bear much of the impact, as 90% of freight is carried by road. Industry accounts for 70% of fuel consumption, but most large factories have stockpiled furnace oils. A slew of human rights and environment regulations affecting export industries has added to cost pressures. Textile factories were forced to cut production in April to comply with stricter limits on working hours demanded by the US in return for market access. Similarly, canned seafood output was reduced after Saudi Arabia and Kuwait banned tuna imports on the grounds that they might contain genetically modified soya bean oil. Saudi Arabia later said it was reviewing its prohibition.

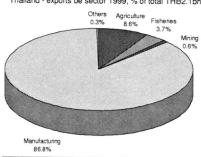

Manufacturing Dominates

Thailand - exports be sector 1999, % of total THB2.1bn

Others 0.3%
Agriculture 8.6%
Fisheries 3.7%
Mining 0.6%
Manufacturing 86.8%

Source: BoT.

Productivity Reforms Make Little Headway...

The Industry Ministry intends to proceed with two further phases of restructuring in 2001-2004.

The government is banking on increased competitiveness to counter rising production costs, but has so far made little headway because of industry reluctance and bureaucratic inefficiency. Only two firms that took part in the first phase of an industry-wide restructuring programme managed to boost their sales, and one of these had to rely upon higher market prices to achieve the target. Some industry groups have blamed poor organisation for the lack of interest: 24 agencies from seven public ministries are involved, and each is pursuing its own agenda. According to the Federation of Thai Industries (FTI), the only real achievement to date has been a machinery replacement scheme in larger factories. Small and medium-sized companies, the key target of the scheme, have shown little interest because they were preoccupied with debt negotiations. The 440,000 SMEs account for 90% of manufacturing output but are also saddled with most bad loans.

Nevertheless, the Industry Ministry intends to proceed with two further phases of restructuring in 2001-2004, focusing on improved production processes, better labour skills, management and marketing overhauls and factory relocations to reduce costs. Participating industries include food processing, textiles, electrical appliances, automotive assembly and parts, steelmaking, petrochemicals and electronic products. The ministry expects to achieve efficiency gains in 50% of all factories nationwide by the end of the scheme, with the textiles industry leading the way. According to the Thai Garment Manufacturers Association, more than half of the ageing machinery in factories has been replaced since 1997 at a total cost of THB5-6bn.

...But Most Industries Are Boosting Output

Most industries are stepping up output in expectation that rising consumer demand will compensate for higher prices, as order books are generally full through to 2001. The finished goods inventory index, which tracks stock accumulations to meet anticipated demand in 10 major industries, rose by 3.6 points to 125.5 points in April, the highest level for six months. Output of automotive vehicles is expected to increase by 35-40% to meet resurgent domestic sales, and advance orders for consumer electronic firms are up by 20%. Steelmakers expect domestic sales to rise by 25% and export sales by 30% because of duty reductions for imported intermediate goods that took

Reforms under Asean's free trade bloc will bring an inrush of cheaper goods from Europe and other parts of Asia.

MANUFACTURING PRODUCTION INDEX (1995=100)						
	1995	1996	1997	1998	1999	% change*
Total	100.0	107.8	107.1	96.5	108.6	2.1
Food	100.0	101.8	103.6	98.1	113.8	3.3
Textiles	100.0	100.5	102.2	105.2	104.0	1.0
Petroleum products	100.0	132.3	153.4	143.5	146.6	10.0
Iron & steel	100.0	106.5	106.4	71.1	81.1	-5.1
Construction materials	100.0	113.8	110.1	67.9	76.4	-6.5
Transport equipment	100.0	104.5	76.8	35.3	63.1	-10.9

Annual average change, 1999/1995. Source: Bank of Thailand.

effect in January, though a prolonged weakness of the baht might trim these forecasts. The Petroleum Authority of Thailand (PTT) announced plans in April for two new intermediate petrochemical projects in anticipation of a 30% rise in demand.

The steel industry, with only 44% of available plant in use as of June, faces an especially difficult adjustment process. Reforms under Asean's free trade bloc will bring an inrush of cheaper goods from Europe and other parts of Asia by 2003, though some upstream producers are expected to secure a reprieve until 2006. Low-cost dumping of intermediate goods has already triggered a series of retaliatory actions by Thai authorities since 1993, mostly against imports from eastern Europe. Over-capacity has prevented the industry from devising a competitive strategy: there are more than 50 steel rolling mills of varying sizes, and half a dozen big upstream manufacturers. Efforts by four key players – **NTS Steel**, **Bangkok Steel Industry**, **Siam Iron and Steel** and **Siam Construction** – to forge a merger have been stalled for two years by the high debt burdens of the first two groups. Another firm, **Nam Heng Steel Group**, withdrew earlier.

Car Assemblers – Revving Up

Automotive vehicle sales rose by 50.8% in the first five months of the year to 98,971 units, putting the year-long target of 260,000 units, based on growth of 19% y-o-y, within reach. While this is still only 40% of pre-crisis demand, the strong recovery has nevertheless reinforced Thailand's claims to Asean hub status. The remaining production volume of 183,000 units will be exported, boosting shipments by a forecast 45.7% over 1999 and confirming the transformation that has taken place since 1997, when less than 20,000 vehicles were being sold abroad. Passenger car market leader **Toyota** will use 60% of capacity this year, an increase of 40%, as part of its first major foray into exports. **General Motors** inaugurated sedan production at its US$750mn plant in May, with the launch of the Chevrolet Zafira compact van. Output will reach 40,000 units in 2001 and the full capacity of 130,000 in 2002.

The strong recovery in the automobile sector has reinforced Thailand's claims to Asean hub status.

A Solid Recovery
Thailand - vehicle production, units

Source: BoT.

AUTOMOBILES ('OOO UNITS)					
	1998	1999	% change	2000f	% change
Output	158.1	327.2	107.0	427.0	30.5
Domestic sales	144.1	218.3	51.5	260.0	19.1
Exports	67.9	125.7	85.1	167.0	32.9
f = BMI forecast; Source: Thai Automotive Industry.					

Agriculture

Weak Prices Deepen Rural Gloom

Falling global prices and adverse weather conditions are likely to reduce farm incomes this year, though output will still surpass that of the last trough, in 1998. Production contracted by 1.6% y-o-y in Q1, while domestic prices slumped by 15.1%, maintaining downward trends that began in Q4 99. Export prices also dropped by 2.8% because of the depreciation of the US dollar, containing shipment earnings growth to 2.6% y-o-y, the worst performance since mid-1999. Little improvement is likely during the remainder of the year, as supply increases from summer harvests generally dampen prices during Q3. Regional export rivals India, Vietnam and Myanmar have all reported bumper grain crops, while improved conditions will also reduce demand from big rice importers like Indonesia.

Shipments of rice, the biggest unprocessed exports revenue-earner, rose by 5% y-o-y in the first five months of the year, but earnings were down by 0.9% due to a 17.5% drop in world prices for quality strains. Domestic prices for first grade paddy fell by 20.7%, despite a rash of government subsidies. While the main growers' association is still confident that the exports target of six million tonnes will be attained, the US Agriculture Department has forecast an 8% drop in global demand this year. Much of the second crop is water-damaged following unseasonal rainfall in early April, and will attract sharply lower prices. Paradoxically, the most popular quality strain, Jasmine, is now viewed in world markets as being too expensive: in June it was trading at US$550 a tonne, compared with only US$160 for comparable Vietnamese quality strains.

Low prices and poor weather conditions will temper agricultural output in 2000.

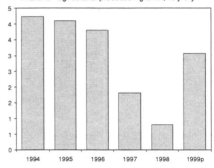

Varied Weather
Thailand - agricultural production growth, % y-o-y

p = provisional; Source: BoT.

AGRICULTURE, MAJOR CROPS (MN TONNES)					
	1995	1996	1997	1998	1999
Paddy					
Output	20.7	22.1	23.3	23.2	23.3
Exports	6.2	5.4	5.6	6.5	6.8
THBbn	48.6	50.7	65.1	86.8	7.1
Rubber					
Output	1.8	1.9	2	2.2	2.2
Exports	1.7	1.9	1.9	2	2
THBbn	61.3	63.4	57.4	55.4	43.9
Maize					
Output	4.1	3.9	3.8	4.7	4.6
Exports ('000 tonnes)	108.2	56.6	61.2	136.9	80.7
THBmn	549	430	536	855	528
Source: Bank of Thailand.					

Some other commodities and processed farm goods also face a difficult year. Domestic prices for cassava roots, the raw material for tapioca, fell by 31.8% y-o-y in Q1 due to an over-supply. Export prices were down by a more modest 3.6%. Frozen chicken export prices slumped to a two-year low due to increased output by South American suppliers, though overall revenues still increased slightly because of bigger volumes. The main exceptions to the prices trend are rubber and maize, which will benefit from reduced global production. Rubber prices rose by 18.5% in domestic markets during Q1, and maize prices increased by 26.4%. Fruit prices are also expected to rise following a drop in global production, but Thai farmers will gain little benefit because of floods damage to crops in the eastern temperate belt of Chanthaburi/ Trat.

Subsidies Hide Structural Flaws

The government has reversed its commitment to the abolition of price subsidies.

Sensitive to the political fallout from reduced farm incomes in an election year, the government has reversed its commitment to the abolition of price supports. Additional subsidies were announced for the sugar, rice, rubber and tapioca industries in Q1, taking the industry closer to the annual limit of THB19bn set during 1996 negotiations with the WTO. An estimated THB17bn was spent last year, mostly through market interventions or the setting of minimum prices. On top of this money, the government usually spends about THB50bn on indirect support programmes, such as development projects and production upgrades. Political leaders argue that subsidies are needed to offset rising farm debt, which amounted to an average of THB30-50,000 for each of the six billion farmers during 1999. However, critics, led by Commerce Minister Dr Supachai Panitchpakdi, who is the designated WTO chief from 2002, have vowed to divert the funds to internal reforms that would concentrate on raising productivity.

A US$600mn restructuring programme was launched with ADB loans in mid-1999, but only six projects had been approved by June due to strict eligibility rules. The response has been much better to a proposed re-zoning of sugarcane, rubber, tapioca and pineapple production that would match output to soil and climatic conditions and impose harvest thresholds. Rice, maize, coffee, oil palm, longans, durians, orchids and black tiger prawns will

AGRICULTURE, DOMESTIC COMMODITY PRICES					
	1996	1997	1998	1999	2000*
Paddy 5% (THB/tonne)	5,084	5,686	6,660	5,436	4,861
Rubber No3 (THB/tonne)	34,321	27,431	26,740	20,858	23,415
Maize (THB/tonne)	5,288	4,703	5,004	4,630	5,222
*Jan-April. Source: Bangkok Bank.					

be added to the scheme if initial trials are successful. However, there are doubts that this approach will work, as it offers little of the political capital that is available from subsidies, while participation will be voluntary. **BMI** believes that output gluts will continue until the middle of the decade, when technological upgrades should bring greater product diversification and improved competitiveness. Global commodity prices are forecast to rise in 2001-2002 due to unsettled weather conditions, but farm incomes are likely to remain static due to the excess supply of key products.

Services

Tourism Boom Underpins Expansion...

Output of services rose by 2.1% y-o-y in Q1, compared with more moderate increases of 1.7% and 1.3% in the two preceding quarters. Strong tourism receipts should underpin growth through the rest of the year, resulting in an overall expansion of 5%. A steady recovery in regional economies boosted inbound travel arrivals by 8.9% in Q1, exceeding the 12-month target of 6.2% growth. Visitor numbers from Taiwan were up by 34.4%, with smaller increases from the US (12%), Japan (6.6%) and China (4.1%). Revenues are expected to reach THB343bn this year, an increase of 18%. Wholesale and retail turnover also grew by 3.2% in Q1, but hotel and restaurant sales were down by 2.9% due to higher costs.

Rising imports and higher shipment costs will progressively trim the services balance, and it is likely to return to a deficit by 2003. Net income is expected to decline to US$1.1bn this year, a drop of US$200mn from 1999. A recovery in outbound travel in 2001 will trim the surplus to about US$500mn, followed by a further drop to US$250mn in 2002. Expenditure on imported services grew by 12.8% in Q1, a rate of increase that will probably be maintained as domestic consumption picks up. Demand has kept pace so far: retailers expect turnover to rise by 15% over the entire year. However, the effects of steeper freight charges, a flow-on effect of the weaker dollar and higher fuel costs will not become apparent until Q4. **Far Eastern Freight Conference**, a shipping cartel operating between Asia and Europe, raised its oil bunker surcharge by 20% in April, and a west-bound US shippers announced a similar rise in May.

Outbound tourism is expected to return to peak 1996 levels this year, though it will probably be a further 12 months before expenditures reach the same level due to greater consumer caution and the depreciation of the baht. The

Strong tourism receipts should underpin growth in services through the rest of the year.

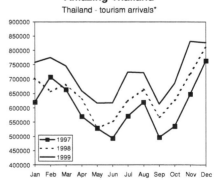

Amazing Thailand
Thailand - tourism arrivals*

excludes overseas Thais. Source: TAT.

Tourism Authority of Thailand (TAT) forecast 1.8mn departures, up from 1.4mn in 1999, but reported that average individual daily spending was only THB3,000 in Q1, from THB5,000 in 1996. The normal length of stay abroad has also fallen from nine days to five because of a shift to closer destinations. Foreign tourists spend an average of THB4,000 a day, and generally stay for 7-8 days. Rising interest in domestic tourism will also ease the impact of the outbound exodus. Receipts rose to THB250bn in 1999, almost matching the income from international arrivals.

...As Globalisation Pressures Intensify

Most industries are unprepared for reforms of services that will take effect from 2006 under Thailand's commitments to the WTO.

Globalisation and reform pressures will threaten services growth in the next 2-3 years, as a neglect of technological advances has left much of business ill-equipped to compete with foreign firms. TAT warned in May that electronic commerce was usurping the traditional role of booking agencies because of low investment in Internet-related services. Hotels and tourism accounted for only 12% of e-com transactions in 1999, compared with 17% for computers, the leading commercial sector. Total transaction value is forecast to rise by 70% y-o-y to US$50mn this year, but only 1.5% of Thais have access to the internet and a mere 6% of websites offer interactive services.

Independent studies have found that most industries are equally unprepared for reforms of services that will take effect from 2006 under Thailand's commitments to the WTO. Investment access to seven sectors – air transport, business services, construction, financial services, maritime transport, telecommunications and tourism – is also being negotiated separately through Asean. Most remaining ownership restrictions on service occupations were removed under 1999 changes to the Foreign Business Law. However, reforms of telecommunications, rail transport and aviation are 18 months behind schedule because of legislative delays.

TOURISM ARRIVALS						
	1997	1998	1999	2000f	2001f	2002f
Arrivals ('000)	7,190	7,760	8,580	9,438	10,476	11,701
% change	0.4	7.5	10.5	10.0	11.0	11.7
f = BMI forecast. Source: Bangkok Bank.						

Financial Services

Banks Held Back By Bad Loans

Output of financial services rose by a muted 4.3% y-o-y in Q1 due to the corrosive effects of debt and recapitalisation demands. Even though this was still a big improvement on the Q4 99 contraction of 21.4%, the plodding progress in restructuring non-performing loans points to a painfully slow recovery period. Bad loans totalled THB1.95trn at the end of April, or 36.47% of total credit, a gain of only 2.4% since the end of 1999 and 28.6% since the peak of THB2.73trn that was reached in May 1999. About THB1trn of NPLs were under negotiation as of June, but creditors complained that many debtors were stalling in expectation that improving economic conditions would ease their repayment burrden. Legislative changes were pending in June that would tighten loopholes in foreclosure laws that are being exploited by debtors to avoid a resettlement, including a vague definition of bankruptcy status. Adding to the banking industry's woes is the high level of recurring NPLs, which was estimated at 10-15%. This is partly a result of banks taking the soft option of resheduling bad loans rather than undertaking costly and lengthy foreclosure procedures.

Monetary authorities plan to introduce new measures in July that are intended to slash NPLs to as little as THB268bn, or 7.4% of credit, by the end of the year. Some of the initiatives are expected to be tax-based, but most will revolve around the central bank's efforts to shift the emphasis of financial sector restructuring to asset management companies (AMCs) and loan-loss provisions. Most banks plan to use AMCs to write off irrecoverable loans, while "doubtful and bad loans" can be removed from balance sheets once they have set aside full provisions. Doubtful loans are classed as those on which servicing of principal has stopped, but periodic interest repayments are still being made. The deadline for meeting 100% loan-loss provisions is December 31, with an 85% compliance rate achieved as of June. At the worst, the BoT expects NPLs to decline to THB1.16trn on December 31, or 25.67% of total loans, if tax disincentives block banks from setting up AMCs. Only two were operational in June, but some of the tax problems are expected to be resolved by the pending government package.

The snail pace progress in restructuring non-performing loans points to a painfully slow recovery period for the banking sector.

Weighed Down
Thailand - top six banks, US$mn

	Tier one capital	% change	Total assets	% change
Krung Thai Bank	2,548	13	26,458	-6.6
Siam Commercial Bank	1,295	36.6	18,369	-3.8
Thai Farmers Bank	1,199	-8.4	19,539	4.1
Bank of Ayudhya	932	36.5	11,873	7.4
Bangkok Bank	810	-66.7	31,495	-6.9
Thai Military Bank	487	-8.4	8,974	-5.3

Source: The Banker.

Credit Is Still Contracting

Repercussions from the debts problem have been felt at several levels of the economy. Lending activity has stalled due to the massive recapitalisation needed to meet higher debt provisions, interest rates have not fallen as low as desired by business, and portfolio investors have pulled out because of the dampening effects of low bank profitability. Bank credits declined by 4.7% in April and 5.2% in Q1, putting the government's year-long target of 4% growth beyond reach. While the BoT issued a revised forecast of 2-3% lending growth in June, most commercial banks expect a maximum expansion of 1%. A rise of 3% is needed to meet the new GDP growth projection of 5%. The Q1 decline was partly a result of banks switching to higher-yielding debenture issues due to low interest rates, a trend that will put further strains on credit availability in the second half of the year.

Production sectors, including manufacturing, have fared the best during the credit squeeze, taking 37% of total loans in Q1. Trade and services absorbed 25% of loans, real estate 18% and consumption 4%. However, overall lending for production still fell by 7.3% y-o-y, trade credits were down by 14.5%, real estate by 15.4% and consumption by 5.3%. The declines in trade credits and consumption loans raise particular concern, as these two sectors will be the main drivers for the economy in 2001-2002. One official explanation is that more borrowers are turning to equity and bond markets; debenture issues rose sharply to THB53.3bn between January and April, but only THB4.6bn was raised through stock exchange shares issues.

Improving financial sector profitability offers some hope for an easing of credit bottlenecks. Combined Q1 losses by listed banks fell to THB18.6bn, from THB31bn in Q1 99, while most firms made operating profits. Finance and securities firms lost only THB422mn, compared with a loss of THB7bn in the same quarter a year earlier. Continuing losses were generally credited to provisioning requirements, which had already exceeded THB900mn as of June. Most institutions are now likely to return to full profitability in Q1 01 if there is no further deterioration in loan quality. However, the recovery could be put back to 2002 if a growth slowdown forces a further round of provisioning to cover expected increases in bad debts.

CREDIT GROWTH, COMMERCIAL BANKS						
	1997	1998	1999	2000f	2001f	2002f
Credit (THBbn, end year)	6,061	5,423	5,428	5,482	5,647	5,929
% change	23.4	-9.7	-4.1	1.0	3.0	5.0
f = BMI forecast. Source: Bangkok Bank.						

Construction

The Worst May Be Over

A 1.1% rise in output during Q1 raised hopes that the worst might be over for the depressed construction industry, which is the only major production sector still to recover from the economic downturn. Results of listed stocks appear to confirm this trend, with combined losses falling by 70% y-o-y to THB2bn in Q1. Materials firms saw a profit of THB2.8bn, against a loss of THB3.7bn in the same quarter in 1999. But the number of construction firms actually making a profit halved to only nine, indicating that debts restructuring costs are taking a heavy toll. Ten materials producers were in the black, up from seven in the previous year. Contracting market leader Italian-Thai Development, which posted a net loss of THB237.5mn, compared with a profit of THB347.5 in Q1 99, said its revenues from construction services had fallen by 40% y-o-y. **Christiani and Nielsen (Thai)** and **Sino-Thai Engineering** and Construction were among the other construction firms that suffered reversals.

The bad news for contractors is that the window of opportunity for consolidating recent gains is rapidly closing due to concerns over the rising public debt. Government planners recommended in May that a dozen big-budget infrastructure projects worth THB250bn be scrapped due to liquidity problems, signalling a reversal of the liberal spending policies pursued since the middle of 1998. Among the projects that would be affected are the second phase of Bangkok's subway system and several urban expressways. Expected to be approved, the scaledown will reduce public expenditure on infrastructure to THB768bn in 2000-2006, compared with THB887bn in 1997-99 alone. About 80% of this investment will come from government agencies and the remainder from private concessions.

In making the cutbacks, the government will merely be returning to pre-crisis levels of public spending, as investment on infrastructure amounted to a more restrained THB1.54trn in the 15 years to 1996. Spending was stepped up sharply in 1997 as a substitute for depleted private project financing, but was only intended as a short-term solution to liquidity bottlenecks. Nevertheless, the move was viewed as premature by construction contractors, which

A reduction in public spending on infrastructure will hurt the fragile construction recovery.

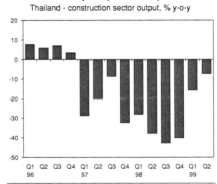

No Speedy Recovery
Thailand - construction sector output, % y-o-y

Source: BoT.

The construction sector will continue to struggle until at least 2004.

have been relying upon public projects for 80-90% of their revenues since the onset of the economic crisis. With project financing still mostly moribund due to bank debt problems, few big private schemes are being implemented. Most operators are also being squeezed by the continuing slump in real estate, which is not expected to ease for at least a further two years. The wider growth impact of the cutbacks will be less severe, as investment in infrastructure only accounts for 5-6% of GDP.

Real Estate Shows Signs Of Life

Property development, the biggest focus of construction activity in the early 1990s, is expected to increase by 15% in 2000 and 20% in 2001, but transaction values are generally 40-50% below 1996 levels. Only 50,000 housing units are expected to be sold, compared with 170,000 in 1996, the last year of strong growth. At least 200,000 empty units are on the market. Real estate firms still owed an estimated THB500bn to banks in June, a figure that has not changed greatly since 1997 due to a low repayment capacity. Banks have responded by severing credit lines, making a recovery even more difficult: lending contracted by 5.4% y-o-y in Q1, compared with a 2.4% drop in the same quarter in 1999. Consequently, only about 3,000 new units were released on to the market in 1997-99, though at least 2,000 are expected to be completed this year. Thailand Real Estate Association calculated in May that there was already THB800bn worth of unsold real estate, despite historically-low mortgage rates of 5-6% and an extension in repayment periods.

With interest rates likely to rise in 2001 and the public role in infrastructure diminishing, **BMI** believes that the construction sector will continue to struggle until at least 2004, when improving real estate sales will offer a lifeline. Total sector growth of 5-7% y-o-y can be expected in 2000 and a maximum of 15% in 2001-2002, with all improvements occurring from low bases. Even then, activity will mostly be limited to selected market segments tied to resurgent private investment in manufacturing, such as commercial real estate and rural roads. Development of industrial estates and retail facilities will see the biggest growth, with office projects returning once vacancy levels have been absorbed in 2002. Domestic banks are unlikely to re-enter project financing markets until 2004 or 2005, leaving offshore development banks as the main independent sources of infrastructural funding.

Profile and Recent Developments

Introduction

Picking Up The Pieces

Thailand's economic structures have altered considerably even in the last decade as its transformation into a modern industrial society continues. The agricultural sector's share of total output has declined further (to below 10% in 1999), although its contribution to exports (directly and through processed foods) and employment is far greater. The decline has been most marked in the fishing and forestry sub-sectors. The latter has been hit by the depletion of native woodlands and the former by the exhaustion of Thai coastal waters. For much of the 1990s, increases in agricultural output lagged behind overall GDP, and only periodic rises in global prices (most notably in 1998) kept the sector afloat.

The mining industry also fared badly in the early-1990s, owing to the collapse of tin extraction in the late-1980s. But the exploitation of natural gas fields has reversed the decline in its share of GDP, and it is becoming important as a replacement for costly imported fuels and as a feedstock for new industries.

The manufacturing sector has become the dynamo of the economy. It provides about 40% of GDP and 80% of export receipts, and (until the recession) was among the fastest growing sources of employment. Thailand has an effective presence in a broad range of industries. In addition to those analysed below, other significant activities include textiles, footwear and toys. These are largely relatively low-technology and labour-intensive activities, dating from the early days of Thailand's export-oriented industrialisation. Thai firms are making heavy weather of moving into the higher technology areas needed to sustain progress.

The construction sector enjoyed a long boom up to 1996, in a period of over-investment fuelled by easy credit. In this period, it recorded near double-digit annual increases in output, which raised its share of GDP by over a quarter from 1986. However, the devastation wrecked by the economic downturn had a severe impact and 90% of developers were insolvent by the end of 1999.

The utilities industries (gas, water and electricity) experienced steady growth in demand during the boom, at rates faster (on average) than the economy as a whole. Whilst contributing only a small fraction of total output, their importance lies mainly in sustaining the ability of industry and commerce to operate. The boom stretched their capacity to near bursting point, and the slowdown will provide only temporary relief. The transport and communications sector experienced similar trends, for the same reasons, with the telecommunications industry being the most buoyant.

The financial services industry expanded rapidly (if over-enthusiastically) after its liberalisation in the early-1990s. At one point, Thailand had pretensions of being a regional hub for financial services, but the recession exposed weak management practices. Other services have generally performed in line with overall economic trends. The distributive trades are important employers, but the most significant activity is tourism (and related leisure trades), which is the most important source of export earnings.

Manufacturing

Motor Industry Sputtering Back

Thailand has become a regional hub for the motor vehicle industry since the early 1990s, both for vehicle assembly and components. In addition, it has a long-standing motorcycle industry, based on Japanese technology. Foreign assemblers were initially attracted by a series of tariff reductions on kits and parts in 1992-93 and improved access to the sizeable domestic market, while the extensive support industry has more recently attracted investors. Thailand is now viewed increasingly as an export base for Asean and elsewhere in Asia. Production built up rapidly in the early-1990s, with growth averaging 10% per annum in 1991-96, to a peak of nearly 560,000 vehicles (plus nearly 1.5mn motorcycles).

The recession and subsequent credit squeeze (the finance companies, which provided most loans for car purchase, were largely shut) devastated the industry. Vehicle production fell by 36% in 1997 and a further 56% in 1998, to only 158,130 – back to the level of a decade earlier. There was a cumulative drop of 60% in production of motorcycles over the same two years. At end-1998, capacity utilisation was just 25%, making it the worst afflicted manufacturing industry. Several expansion or investment plans were postponed or scaled down in response to the slump.

A modest recovery began in 1999, with vehicle output rising to 327,233 units, though this was mostly due to a sharp increase in export orders. Motorcycle production rose to 725,425 units. As of December 1999, most of the 15 assembly plants had re-opened in anticipation of stronger demand, and investment in support industries had started to pick up. Hire purchase and leasing contracts were at their highest levels for three years. Nevertheless, the Federation of Thai Industries forecast that it would be a further 2-3 years before plant was fully utilised: only 37.8% of combined capacity was in use in December. Domestic sales of motor vehicles in 1999 were 51% above 1998 levels, but still only 25% of the 1996 peak. Some assemblers have shifted more of their marketing focus to export sales, but have encountered stiff competition from other regional producers. Shipment value of motor vehicles and parts rose by 80.2% to THB60.1bn (US$1.6bn) in 1999, including 125,720 vehicles worth THB50.2bn. However, **Mitsubishi Sittipol**'s one-tonne light truck accounted for over 80% of vehicle exports, and markets are still largely undeveloped. **Isuzu** (motor parts) and **Honda** (motorcycles) were also significant exporters.

The abolition of local content rules in late 1999 is expected to act as a catalyst for further investment, as it had been regarded by some prospective European and US assemblers as a key obstacle to the establishment of domestic plants. **BMW**, **Daimler-Chrysler**, **Porsche**, **Fiat** and **Renault** were among the firms that announced tentative investment plans following the withdrawal of the rules. Thailand mostly competes against the Philippines for assembly operations, but has an edge in terms of numbers of suppliers and other support industries. Its main disadvantage is a shortage of technical, engineering and design skills, which has hampered technology transfers. Most output is still at the assembly level and it is expected to be as long as a decade before a design capability emerges.

Electronics – Growth Segment

The electronics sub-sector has been one of Thailand's main growth industries and one whose development is encouraged by the full panoply of official investment incentives. Products range from low-tech consumer goods (TV tubes and computer monitors) to advanced microchips. In the field of disk drives, **Fujitsu**, **Seagate** and **IBM** alone employ a combined 45,000 and generate more than US$4bn in exports. However, the sector relies heavily on foreign technology (either from direct investment or under licence) and suffers from shortages of experienced professional and scientific staff.

Output was not greatly affected by the economic downturn, as it is mostly exported. But some intermediate products, such as hard disk drives, suffered from global surpluses and higher costs of imported materials due to the weaker currency. Overall production rose by 10% in 1999, compared with a pre-crisis average of 15-20%. Integrated circuits (one of the key computer component segments) recorded a 31.8% in output, largely because of a 20.1% in US dollar export sales that resulted from higher world prices. Overall, electronics sector exports rose by 13.2% to THB791.6bn (US$21.4bn) in 1999.

Higher domestic demand for consumer goods, coupled with an increase in operating margins, created an improved operating environment in 1999. Component producer **Delta Electronics** saw net profits rise by 65.8% to THB2.7bn, largely due to a 15.6% rise in margins and lower exchange losses. **KCE Electronics** (a producer of printed circuit boards) recorded a 136.2% increase in earnings because of smaller debt provisions and an extraordinary write-off of a THB1bn stake in a failed US disk-drive venture in 1998. Hard disk components producer **KR Precision Instruments** saw a reduced loss of THB17.7mn but still suffered a 22% drop in revenues due to a decline in export orders.

Some low-cost assembly operations have started to move out of Thailand because of rising production overheads, but their place is being taken by high-technology plants. The government said in late 1999 that it was discussing several investment options for a proposed US$1bn silicon wafer fabrication plant that would probably replace a stalled scheme that was devised by the ailing Alphatec Group in the mid-1990s. Japan's **Minebea,** a manufacturer of precision instruments, announced plans in early 2000 for a THB4bn project that will produce advanced fluid dynamic bearings for hard disk-drives for disk assembler **Seagate Technology.** In the consumer electronics segment, **Sony** announced plans for a 30% production increase in response to rising export orders for TVs, audio equipment and semi-conductors. And **Matsushita Electric** said it would spend another THB728mn on assembly lines for National Panasonic audio goods.

Food Processing – Taking Off

Among Thailand's initial manufacturing activities (and for long a poor relation to more glamorous sectors), the food and beverages industries are now seen as a development priority with substantial export potential. Emphasis has shifted in recent years from basic refining processes such as sugar refining, flour milling, beers and soft drinks to value-adding, though much of the industry is still geared to the domestic market. Ready-to-eat meals are one of the biggest growth segments, along with processed seafoods and snacks. Staple foods generally fared well during the recession, but "luxury" items such as beer, soft drinks and fast foods recorded annual sales declines of 7-15%. Beer is the only basic segment with an export potential, though this has barely been tapped. The brewing sector has been liberalised since 1994 with the entry of foreign firms like **Heineken** and **Carlsberg**, but domestic producer **Boonrawd Brewery** still leads the mass market with its Singha brand.

Canned foods are the main processed food export earners, also benefiting from substantial domestic sales. The main products are canned fruits, vegetables and seafood. Exports of canned goods rose by 6.8% in 1999 compared with 1998, but sales of fishery products were down by 11.6% due to intense competition from other producer countries. Important companies in the canning industry include **Thai Union Frozen Products** (the largest canned seafood producer and exporter), which saw its net profit rise by 45.9% in 1999, and **Malee Samprun** (204.3%).

The food processing industry is in a transitional stage that should produce a wider diversity of product lines and secure a global image for Thai goods. Leading the way is **Malee Sampran**, which aims to establish a brand identity for its products by 2003. Existing items like sweet corn will initially be given wider marketing treatment, but new product lines are also being studied. Multinational groups such as **Nestles** are developing additional capacity in readiness for the full start of Asean's free trade bloc. The Swiss firm is investing THB600-800mn a year in its eight plants, which cover the full range of product categories from ice-cream and chocolate to mineral water, instant coffee and seasonings. Thailand is already the Asian base for output of Coffeemate non-dairy cream. **Kellogg**, the US cereal maker, uses Thailand as its regional base for sourcing raw materials (especially rice) and for the production of ready-to-eat cereals. **Uni President (Thailand)**, a subsidiary of Taiwan's **President Group**, is expanding production of its branded fruit and vegetable health drinks, and will market them throughout East Asia, the Middle East and Europe. It is also introducing a new range of fruit teas and coffees.

Among the marketing niches being explored is the canning of traditional Thai dishes such as *tom yam kung* and *paad Thai* in a ready-to-eat form. Two rice dishes, *khaolam* (a rice dessert baked in bamboo trunks) and *krayasart*, a stick rice dessert, are already being sold in Asian markets such as Japan and China. To encourage such innovations, the ministries of agriculture and industry are promoting the establishment of industrial estates devoted to agro-processing activities, usually located near the prime raw material supplies. Sweet corn, spices, fish, pork and soybeans are seen as having the main potential for processing into higher value-added products. The production of *halal* food, for the regional Islamic market, is another potential niche.

Petrochemicals: On The Rise

Thailand's natural gas is being used as the raw material for an ambitious programme to develop a world-class petrochemicals industry. Central to this scheme is the investment in three giant olefins complexes in the Eastern Seaboard Development Zone, to provide inputs for the production of numerous derivatives.

Petrochemicals output has been affected much less severely by the downturn than other manufacturing sub-sectors, with higher export demand pushing output up by 2.1% in 1999. A decline of 6.7% was recorded in 1998. Capacity utilisation slipped to 72.4% in December 1999, from a crisis peak of 87% in 1998, but it has consistently been the highest of any industry sector. On the downside, petrochemical firms accumulated massive debts during the mid-1990s manufacturing build-up and some key firms have suffered badly from the financial squeeze of the past three years. **Thai Petrochemicals Industries** (TPI), the largest single corporate debtor in Thailand, was declared insolvent in early 2000 after ceasing payments on outstanding loans of US$4.4bn. Creditors are expected to take control of the olefins producer.

Refiners have sustained the biggest losses due to their reliance upon the depressed oil retailing sector. Industry leader **Thai Oil**, owned jointly by the government and international firms **Caltex** and **Shell**, negotiated a restructuring agreement on debts of US$2.29bn in early 2000 that will see the state-owned **Petroleum Authority of Thailand** (PTT) become the biggest shareholder in exchange for a capital injection. **PTT** had wanted to merge Thai Oil with its own subsidiary **PTT Oil**, but it appears that the two will remain separate entities. Some consolidation is taking place in the refining business, however, with the operational merger of two refineries controlled (as majority shareholders) by Caltex and Shell. **Bangchak Petroleum**, another state-owned refiner, is also expected to merge some of its operations with other players once the next phase of privatisation has been completed. The government agreed in early 2000 to offer a 38% stake to the public, mostly from public shareholdings held through PTT and **Krung Thai Bank**.

Foreign investment is accelerating as the debt picture begins to clear. Germany's **Phenolchemie** announced plans in late 1999 for a cumene plant that will provide feedstock for a phenol facility that is likely to be set up with PTT. Together with promotional incentives, the total investment is estimated at THB10.7bn. **Chevron** is investing US$14mn in an aromatics facility at Map Ta Phut, to become operational in mid-2000. A similar project by **Exxon**, located at its refinery in Chonburi, is expected to start production in early 2000. **Montell**, **Bayer** and **Chemical International** are other firms with major projects underway.

4 Business Environment

Introduction

Corporate Tightrope

The unprecedented scale and depth of the economic downturn produced a sea-change in the environment facing companies operating in Thailand. The profitability of operations in most sectors in 1998-99 was at best poor, and mostly negative – the combined losses of listed firms (including numerous joint ventures with foreign entities) was THB333.2bn (US$8.8bn) in the first nine months of 1999, a 108% increase on losses recorded in the same period of 1998. A better performance is expected in 2000, but some sectors will continue to lag for a further 2-3 years due to high debt levels and surplus capacity. The five most unprofitable listed sectors between January and September were banking and finance, chemicals and plastics, building and furnishing materials, communications and property development. By contrast, the outlook is bright for agribusinesses, food and beverage firms, electronic components, insurance and energy, which reported combined profits of THB15.2bn in the nine months to September. Business sentiment as a whole will improve once structural reforms have shown more progress.

Expected improvements include:

■ Improved foreign investment access is likely through changes in ownership laws, including the amended Foreign Business Law and more lenient rules on real estate purchases.

■ Deregulation of key service sectors such as telecommunications, transport and banking, through the divestment of state-owned enterprises (SOEs) and market liberalisation.

Against this are potential or ongoing negative influences:

■ The high debt burden will erode investor confidence and disrupt liquidity flows, at least until banks have met their full reserve provisions in late 2000.

■ Political uncertainties will dampen investment through much of 2000, as an unfavourable election result (especially a return of the unpopular New Aspiration Party) could provoke capital outflows. Private investment is too low to sustain a strong recovery. Government funding will probably begin to dry up by the end of 2000 due to concern over high public debt levels.

Deeper Reforms Needed

The key short-term requirements to improve the business environment are progress on bank recapitalisation and corporate debt restructuring – to allow new capital to flow to companies and improve consumer confidence. Here the prognosis is on balance favourable, though additional public aid will be required for some banks.

The long-term outlook will depend on government commitments to complete the deeper structural reforms that were promised in the initial letters of intent to the IMF, but have made only hesitant progress. Heading the list are crucial changes in production methods, including the introduction of new technology that can prevent a further loss of export competitiveness. Productivity improvements are needed by both industry and agriculture, while the capital and debt markets badly need an overhaul to boost corporate financing options. The authorities will also need to give priority to improving "soft infrastructure" features if Thailand is to sustain its attractiveness to investors. While official and social attitudes are fundamentally favourable to private enterprise, business remains hampered by skills shortages, corruption, bureaucratic inertia and weak contract laws.

Infrastructure Development

Planners Take A New Route

The current Five Year Development Plan (1997-2001), Thailand's eighth since 1961, gives a lower priority to infrastructure that reflects disenchantment with the top-down planning policies that were viewed as partly responsible for the 1997-98 debts cycle. An initial version of the plan, released just before the economic storm hit, had shifted most of the spending emphasis to correcting structural defects, headed by poor labour skills and environmental neglect. A hasty revision was conducted after the onset of the crisis to restore much of the deducted infrastructure funding, but the final plan retained its overall focus on social flaws and resource allocations, with rigid targets for boosting education standards and narrowing income inequities.

As it stands, the plan involves a total investment of US$78bn that is included in annual budgets but often funded independently through development loans, SOE reserves and borrowings and private sector participation. The latter range from Build-Operate-Transfer type (BoT) contracts for the construction of expressways and Mass Rapid Transfer (MRT) systems in Bangkok, to the installation under contract of telephone lines and the construction of privately-owned and operated power generating plants.

Even before the recession led to the revaluation of both long-term needs (especially in power generation) and available finance, the Thai authorities had experienced problems with the detailed administration of contracts, notably for transport links in Bangkok. These included disputes with the foreign builders and potential operators of toll roads, and the long and sorry saga of delays to the three Bangkok MRT schemes caused by changes to contract specifications, financing difficulties and obstruction by some elements in the bureaucracy (e.g. on land-use approvals). The trend since 1993 has been for governments to handle major projects themselves whenever possible, while relying upon low-interest financing from development agencies.

Some Progress Can Be Seen

The immediate effect of the economic downturn was felt at a funding level. The state share of infrastructure financing doubled to more than 80% in 1998-99 as a substitute for virtually dormant private-sector participation, while overall investment fell by 16% and 12% respectively in these two years. Political expediency ensured that rural road allocations – a prime source of kickbacks for politicians – remained almost untouched, but this was mostly at the expense of urban expressways and big-budget mass transit projects. Among the biggest casualties was the **Hopewell** elevated road and rail mass transit system in Bangkok, which was cancelled in early 1999 after the Hong Kong-based contractor missed a succession of stage deadlines. Only 12% complete after eight years, the project was dogged by repeated disputes over land clearance and Hopewell's failure to raise sufficient funding. Rail authorities commissioned a consultancy study in late 1999 on possible adaptations of the scheme, which would probably be built and operated on a concession basis. A China-based consortium that includes shareholders of the rival Bangkok Transit System Corp (BTSC) project is among the front-runners to land the construction contract.

BTSC, led by property developer **Tanayong**, succeeded in opening Bangkok's first rail mass transit network two years late in early December, after overcoming its own financing problems and an 11th-hour take-over bid by creditors. The elevated light railway is still likely to change hands, as passenger numbers in the first four months of operation were well below the break-even level for investors. City councillors approved a three-route extension of the BTS in early 2000 that is expected to improve its financial viability. Similar teething problems were encountered by Bangkok's underground railway, which had to be rescued by Japanese development aid after central government funds dried up. It was 40% complete by December, and expected to open on time in 2002 despite a contractural row over fare structures.

Further disruption to Thailand's infrastructure programme can be expected during 2000, as delayed mega-projects like Bangkok's second international airport will absorb a bigger share of short-term funding. However, political leaders have returned to the big-budget thinking of the early 1990s in their search for a growth stimulus, and overall funding is likely to match pre-crisis levels under the next national plan, which starts in 2001. Among the projects already approved is a national highways programme that could cost as much as THB800bn (US$21bn). Less likely to win approval are revived plans to build a land bridge across the southern Kra Isthmus as a shortened shipping route between the Indian and Pacific Oceans. It would cost at least THB600bn, but feasibility studies have so far shown little economic benefit and funds are unlikely to be approved. One possibility is that it might be scaled down to only an oil pipeline crossing.

The Domestic Market

Uneven Distribution

Thailand's population at end-1999 is estimated at 62.08mn, putting it behind only Indonesia and Vietnam in regional terms. A successful campaign to promote birth control has led to a significant fall in the population's growth rate, from 2-3% per annum two decades ago to around 1% per annum in the 1990s. Thailand's population is largely youthful (nearly 60% below the age of 30) and only 5% above 65, which will stimulate continued steady growth in both the total population and labour force.

Bangkok is the sole large conurbation; the population of its core city is officially recorded at 5.8mn. However, this is only based on household registrations and does not take account of the city's 2mn shanty-town dwellers and transient workers. The population of the greater metropolitan area is estimated at about 12-14mn. Thailand remains predominantly rural, with the overall proportion of the population living in urban areas (30%), still below the norm of 40-60% for middle-income countries. Provincial capitals Nakhon Ratchasima (300,000), Songhkla (260,000) and Nonthaburi (250,000) are the other main urban communities.

There are substantial regional inequalities. Average household incomes in Bangkok are nearly two and a half times the national average, and over four times those in the poorest region. Moreover, Thailand has a relatively high incidence of (absolute) poverty for a country with its per capita GDP and a concentration of wealth in the top 10% which, although not exceptional in South East Asia, is towards the top end of the range for middle-income countries. These factors perhaps explain Thailand's weak performance on a range of social and development indicators, such as access to safe water, infant mortality, or telephone lines per thousand people, despite its rapid economic growth in the past three decades.

The Labour Market

Low Skills Undermine Effectiveness

Thailand's labour market has been a source of both strength and weakness for employers over the past decade. Positive features include the light regulatory burden. Thai labour laws on employment security, mandatory benefits and working conditions are in line with those elsewhere in the region and enforcement is not over-rigorous. In the past, the high birth rate had led to continued growth in the labour force. Migration from the rural provinces has also been an important growth factor, though its impact has been reduced by a trend in recent years for Thailand to make large labour exports to East Asia and the Middle East. The widespread availability of primary education has created near-universal literacy and basic skills, while social mores have helped keep Thai workers disciplined and hard-working. With the notable exception of textiles, trade union power has been in decline since the early 1990s due to falling membership and a shift away from labour-intensive industries.

However, since the mid-1990s, other adverse factors have weighed more heavily on employers. Most pressing is the severe shortage of workers qualified to fill skilled technical and professional posts, resulting from flaws in Thailand's system of higher education. Colleges, technical institutes and universities have long suffered from inadequate secondary enrolment rates (the lowest among the six more advanced Asean countries) and faulty curriculum targeting. Only 15% of students are enrolled in scientific or technical subjects, partly because of a traditional bias towards public-sector employment. The National Science and Technology Agency estimates that the country needs some 35,000 additional technicians each year, while the requirement for graduate scientists and engineers is put at 27,000 a year. Only about 10,000 technicians and 20,000 scientists and engineers graduate annually.

One outcome of the tight labour market has been increased wage pressures, with some white-collar salaries (especially for banking and financial services) multiplying by 40-50% a year during the early 1990s. Above-inflation rises in the minimum wage also made sunset industries like textiles, footwear and toys uncompetitive, hastening their relocation to China, Laos and Vietnam. A slowdown in the growth of the labour force since 1995 has created shortages of workers in some unpopular industries like fishing and stevedoring; these were filled by illegal workers (mostly from Myanmar) until late 1999, when the government began expelling thousands of foreigners to create more jobs for unemployed Thais. Another initial repercussion from the tight labour market was a rise in trade union militancy, though this mostly dissipated as jobs disappeared during the economic downturn. Tough laws on industrial action, including a requirement for most workers at a plant to give their support, and mandatory arbitration hearings, limit the risk of full-blown strikes, though work stoppages are fairly common. Most grievances are over unpaid benefits and unsafe working conditions rather than wages. Foreign firms invariably include labour problems at the top of their list of investment drawbacks, and an increasing number are convinced that

Thailand will experience difficulty in moving to the next level of technology-enhanced production.

Employers Benefit

The economic slump brought changes to both the policy environment and labour market balance, mostly to the benefit of employers:

■ A two-year freeze in the minimum wage eased production costs, while mass layoffs in the ravaged services sector ended the salaries free-for-all.

■ Pending revisions in the collective bargaining system will further weaken the power of trade unions, as provincial bodies will be permitted to set their own localised rates. Union power is weak outside the cities.

■ Funding allocations for job-relief schemes and industry have shifted the employment focus to retraining, enhancing the overall level of skills.

On the other hand, the government took advantage of the weaker market to push through tighter laws on working conditions, including improved holiday and retirement benefits. But in general, the recession worked in favour of employers by easing recruitment bottlenecks, making it easier to retain staff and bringing substantial cuts in unit labour costs in most industrial sectors. Less certain is how long this situation will remain, as the economic crisis also had the less beneficial effect of diverting attention away from longer-term remedies. Plans to introduce 12 years of compulsory education fell by the wayside because of spending cutbacks, while a dismantling of state controls over universities was delayed. Investors have already concluded that the private sector will have to carry the main burden of improving workplace skills and are setting up their own training programmes. The government has also recognised that this formula offers the easiest route forward: since 1995 it has been offering tax incentives for investment in technical colleges and international universities, and now requires foreign firms to make technology transfers as part of their initial investment approvals.

Industrial Policy

The State Slowly Withdraws

Thailand has never had a formal industrial strategy, tending to rely instead on *ad-hoc* development policies to set national priorities. These have mainly been aimed at spreading industry to rural provinces and encouraging a transition to higher value-added manufacturing activities. These ambitions satisfy both the Thai elite and their political masters – who are mostly from rural provinces – and are therefore not at risk from political changes. The vast majority of agricultural, industrial and commercial activities are in the hands of the private sector, and the state's role is being reduced. Direct price controls have gradually been reduced since 1996 but the Commerce Ministry still maintains a list of 20-22 key sectors (such as cement and bottled drinking water) that are subject to specific monitoring under the 1999 Price Maintenance on Goods and Services Act. Unfair trading practices are controlled through another 1999 law, the Business Competition Act, which is intended to prevent market monopolies at the supply, pricing or selling levels.

Investment in certain industries (e.g. petrochemicals, motor vehicles/components, steel and electronics-related products) qualifies for various tax and other promotional incentives. These are administered via the Board of Investment (BOI), which is also the main promotional agency for attracting new industry. Tax privileges are used to regulate the pattern of preferred investments and to decide where they will be located. Hence, additional incentives are available for investment in transport projects, R&D work and environmental conservation, while the best privileges are offered for factories set up in rural provinces that are distant from Bangkok. Similarly, congested Bangkok offers the lowest privileges to deter potential newcomers.

But Privatisation Push Stutters

The economic slump and its impact on tax receipts gave a new impetus to the privatisation of Thailand's numerous and influential SOEs, but entrenched interests have succeeded in pushing the timetable well behind schedule. SEOs have the dominant role in most areas of communications, transport, power generation, energy (oil and gas exploration, extraction and supply) and water supplies, while they also influence scores of industries through the use of quotas and other market instruments. Successive administrations have seen privatisation and deregulation as a means to improve service standards and reduce SOEs' dependence upon central budgets, but their lacklustre efforts have been hampered by opposition from both management and workers. The number of SOEs has declined from a peak of 61 in 1995 due to the closure of some inactive smaller agencies, but none of the bigger SOEs has given any ground. As of December 1999, only about 50 SOEs were still classed as operational, down from 53 a year earlier.

As part of the economic reform programme agreed with the IMF, the Chuan government prepared an ambitious timetable for the restructuring of 10 large enterprises. This is designed to raise

THB600bn (US$1.6bn), much of which will be used to fund financial sector restructuring. By the year 2002, it is proposed to dismantle all state monopolies and strip existing regulatory functions from any remaining operating entities. Entities being "corporatised" will be turned into companies in which government ministries hold shares, allowing them to be listed on the stock exchange in advance of eventual sales to public investors. This formula was followed successfully in 1994-96, through the partial listing of subsidiaries of the **Electricity Generating Authority of Thailand** (EGAT) and the **Provincial Waterworks Authority** (PWA) and a minority shares offer in **Thai Airways International**(THAI). In late 1999, EGAT also offloaded another subsidiary, Ratchaburi power station. However, the deadline of mid-1999 for putting the 10 key parent agencies on sale was missed due to legislative delays, pushing the schedule back to late-2000. THAI is expected to be the first SOE offered to the market, followed by the **Petroleum Authority of Thailand** (PTT) and the **Airports Authority of Thailand** (AAT). The latter manages more than a dozen airports that will also be offered on a concession basis.

Labour resistance poses the biggest potential obstacle, especially in the militant telecommunication and energy SOEs, as trade unions stand to lose substantial benefits from contract kickbacks and other backdoor payments. Most agencies hope to circumvent this problem by granting equity to employees. Another difficulty is timing: top civil servants and government ministers are reluctant to sell equity at depressed market prices, making it possible that the 2000 deadline will also be missed.

The deregulation programme accompanying the privatisation process is likely to have a more far-reaching impact on the Thai business scene. The previous gradual opening up of utilities sectors to private participation, through the contracting out of specified activities (e.g. the IPP scheme in electrical power generation and the fixed-line telecommunications installation contracts), brought only marginal benefits to the wider business community. However, more radical measures approved for the natural gas industry are expected to be followed by the further liberalisation of the telecommunications and power generation sectors, to the benefit of both new entrants and business customers.

Downturn Delays Corporate Tax Shake-up

The present effective rate of taxation on companies operating in Thailand is 33.5% – the combination of the standard rate of corporate income tax (30%) and the withholding tax on dividends. This is in the middle bracket of taxes for South East Asia, but higher than the rates levied by investment rivals like Malaysia and Singapore. The Finance Ministry intends eventually to shift the tax burden to consumption and is working towards a cut in standard corporate tax to 27%. But this is not likely to happen until the full VAT rate has been restored in 2001 and other sources of revenue have been found. In late 1999 the government said it would review the issue again during 2000, but did not expect any early reduction in corporate tax. Instead, the focus shifted in 1999 to import tariffs, which the government is obliged to reduce to a range of 0-5% by 2003 to meet the Afta schedule. Revenue shortfalls are also being addressed through efficiency drives that have improved collection procedures, closed loopholes and reduced tax evasion.

Foreign Investment Policy

Reforms Gain Impetus

Investment regulations have been under a periodic review since 1996 due to **World Trade Organisation** opposition to the system of tax incentives, coupled with a political perception that they were not proving effective. The economic crisis forced the issue to the top of the agenda, as debt pressures underscored the classic conflict between the targeted benefits (providing capital, technology and "know-how") and a fear of foreign domination as cheap assets came up for sale. Legislation dating back to military rule has kept foreign investors out of certain business sectors since the early 1970s – usually for security reasons – but the overriding need for capital has chipped away some of these barriers since 1997 (*see below*). A small number of occupations is still reserved for Thai nationals on cultural or security grounds, while there are continuing restrictions on ownership of land and housing and curbs on the use of foreign staff. Some exemptions are available from the real estate ban, for firms promoted by the BOI.

Since late 1997, a succession of reforms have been approved to stimulate foreign investment:

■ The 1972 Foreign Business Law was overhauled in 1999 to allow access to most service and professional sectors, including architecture, building, advertising and law. Farming is the main occupation still reserved for Thais.

■ Most limits on the purchasing of banks, finance firms and securities companies were removed in 1997, followed by further liberalisation of the insurance industry in 1998 and 1999.

■ Since 1998, investors who bring in a designated amount of capital have been permitted to buy a limited amount of residential land. The amount that could be bought was initially fixed at THB25bn, but raised to THB40bn in 1999. Longer leases are also now available and permitted foreign stakes in residential condominiums have been increased.

■ Ownership restrictions for retailing were lifted entirely in January 1999, following partial increases in 1997. The relaxation took full effect after the adoption of the new Foreign Business Law.

The New Foreign Business Law

The changes in the Foreign Business Law will have the greatest investment impact. Not only will the amendments open dozens of industries to outside ownership, but they will simultaneously close long-standing loopholes that have been used by foreign firms to control their investments without having direct voting rights. Investment is grouped in three categories under the new system, with two carrying equity restrictions. The first category of 14 businesses (including advertising, publishing and transport) still requires prior cabinet approval because of their importance to national security, cultural interest and the environment, and an equity limit of 60% applies. A special licence is needed to invest in the second category of 17 professions and businesses, which include engineering, accounting and legal services. There are no restrictions for the final category. All three lists will be reviewed every two years to determine whether any additional industries require protection. One minor improvement is the removal of an irritating requirement for foreign businessmen to register at 90-day intervals with the authorities.

Openness Rules – For Now, At Least

Because of these reforms, most of Thailand's economy will become accessible once the privatisation process is completed in 2002, though it will be a further four years before some service sectors (notably telecommunications) are fully liberalised. The business climate in general has been improved through more effective bankruptcy and foreclosure laws that have made it easier to implement corporate takeovers or mergers. One cloud on the horizon is the pending introduction of a new zoning system by the BOI that reduces the appeal of tax incentives for firms that are unwilling to move to the more remote rural provinces. Due to take effect in April 2000, the revised scheme restricts the full range of benefits to investors setting up in only 18 border provinces that have low per capita incomes. Most have severely limited infrastructure and are inaccessible to overseas markets. However, it is unlikely that many investments will be scrapped, as improvements in other areas – notably the tariff regime – will more than compensate for reduced BOI benefits.

Foreign Trade Policy

Import Barriers Are Falling

Thailand has a generally liberal approach to foreign trade and is a committed member of both the World Trade Organisation (WTO) and regional trade forums. Its overall policy on imports is in line with WTO requirements. Most local-content rules were phased out in January 2000 and replaced with a restructured tariffs system.

Similarly, import bans, quotas and licensing requirements that apply to some commodities, basic manufactures and "luxuries" are progressively being abolished, along with export subsidies and other price supports. It appears likely that some goods, especially in the agricultural sector, will continue to be protected because of their political sensitivity. However, the current government has generally taken a tougher line than its predecessors, with steelmaking and petrochemicals among several "strategic" industries that were exposed to more competition during 1998 and 1999. Restrictions on the import of six agricultural products (including rice and palm oil) were also loosened. Subsidies for a range of crop prices were maintained in a 1999 review, but for the first time in several years were not increased. The WTO will also eventually require Thailand to phase out the various subsidies and tariff exemptions available to promote exports. Separately, a revised anti-dumping law took effect in 1999 after it had been amended to meet WTO concerns.

The current general import tariff schedule is relatively simple, featuring three standard rates of duty: 5% (on capital goods and raw materials), 10% (on intermediate products) and zero on most finished goods. Special rates (0%, 1% or 30%) apply in cases where it is thought essential to provide Thai products with either cheap inputs or greater protection – import duties on raw materials and intermediate products used by the steel industry were cut sharply in late 1998. Customs procedures have been overhauled to eliminate burdensome procedures, but the system remains overly complex. Faster processing is likely following the adoption of an electronic data interchange system in 1999, but compliance by shipment agencies has been slow for cost reasons.

Asean Leads The Way On Reform

The Asean Free Trade Area (Afta), initiated by Thailand in 1992, continues to be the key trade priority. As amended in 1998, the Afta accord sets a two-track schedule for compliance with a common effective preferential tariff rate (CEPT) for most industrial imports. Goods on a fast-track list will join the scheme in early 2001, with those on the standard list complying by 2003. Duty is to be reduced to a range of 0-5%, with the average set at less than 3%. However, the scheme is voluntary and exemptions are permitted for products that might be unduly affected by increased competition. Tariffs affecting more than 10,000 items have been reduced as part of Afta since 1994, including a new schedule for 1,900 finished and intermediate goods that took effect on January 1, 2000. Duty on a further 153 products was also lowered under a separate information technology agreement with the WTO.

With its versatile export profile, Thailand is expected to gain the most benefit from the Asean liberalisation. Industries that will gain particularly from increased market opportunities as Afta comes into full effect include gems and jewellery, ceramics, the motor vehicle sector, domestic electrical appliances, pharmaceuticals and some sectors of the chemicals industries. Industries potentially at risk from increased competition include palm and vegetable oils, plastic pellets, glass, fertilisers, soaps, pulp and the nascent petrochemicals industry.

Progress has been less pronounced in other trade sectors. Tentative Afta agreements have been secured for raw agricultural goods and services, but prospects for full compliance are not high. Thailand, like Malaysia and Indonesia, is keen to protect its farm sector, while most of Asean is reluctant to allow unrestricted entry to Singapore's more efficient service industries. Similarly, there has been limited progress in developing industrial linkages that were intended to serve as the main instrument of production integration by encouraging foreign manufacturers to treat Afta as one unified market. Thai-based firms had secured approval for only a handful of projects as of early 2000, mostly in the motor vehicle industry. Intra-regional investment rivalries have been the main hindrance to a wider use of this scheme. Nevertheless, closer integration (on the pre-EMU EU model) is seen as inevitable, and the Thai government has responded with a package of promotional incentives aimed at attracting more regional operations.

As noted above (*see Foreign Policy*) Thailand is not overly enthusiastic about the trade-promoting initiatives that have come from Apec, because Thailand believes that Asean is the most suitable forum for implementing trade reforms. Like most other Asean members, it regards Apec as a consultative body that can play a useful role in removing structural impediments to trade, such as overlapping customs regulations, but should not set policies.

Copyright Enforcement Improves

Until the mid-1990s, Thailand had been considered among the worst offenders against Intellectual Property Rights (IPR), because of a combination of inadequate laws and lax enforcement. Its poor record served as an obstacle in trade relations with most of the developed world, and led to the imposition of punitive trade sanctions by the US and EU. This strained situation began to ease in 1995, however, with the approval of an amended version of the 1978 Copyright Act, followed by changes in patent laws later in the decade. Further patent amendments are due to be implemented in 2000. Enforcement has also improved since an intellectual property court began operation in late 1997; one side-effect has been to help firms reach out-of-court settlements with offenders.

Washington responded by dropping Thailand from a Special 301 priority watchlist for serious offenders, though it remains on a more routine monitoring list because of doubts over enforcement measures. US Generalised System of Preferences (GSP) benefits were restored for some goods in recognition of this progress. The EU also maintains a monitoring stance, as it regards the current legal framework as incomplete. Outstanding areas of US disagreement mostly concern the 1992 Patent Act, which provides only limited "pipeline" protection for pharmaceuticals and offers different TRIPs (Trade-Related Aspects of Intellectual Property Rights) treatment to foreign and domestic firms. The EU wants more effective action against counterfeit CDs. In addition, foreign businesses are concerned at the inadequate patent cover for computer software copying. Changes in the patent act are expected to win approval in mid-2000, but these are unlikely to fully address the foreign complaints. A specialised economic crime unit has been beefed up to tackle the CDs problem.

Bureaucracy And Corruption

Cracks In The Civil Service

Originally established around a British model in the early part of the 20th century, the centralised civil service has failed to keep pace with rapid changes in the economy and is now barely able to cope. Designed to reward patronage rather than ability, the service has always been a paternalistic presence at planning levels and was a strength during the early phases of industrial development. However, it was ill-equipped for the transition to a predominantly private operating environment, lacking the experience and regulatory framework for the market liberalisation that began in 1989-90. Consequently, complex issues such as infrastructure contracts were mishandled, while inadequate monitoring safeguards were installed in the financial sector. In the most blatant example of this growing ineffectiveness, the tradition-clad Bank of Thailand was able to squander most of the nation's foreign reserves after the onset of the currency crisis in 1997 because no system existed for outside scrutiny of its actions. In part, the failings of the civil service have been linked to frequent changes of government and consequent constant re-negotiation of lucrative contracts to suit party patrons, at times to the detriment of foreign investors and Thailand's reputation, e.g. the saga of the various transport projects in Bangkok.

Poor co-ordination between different arms of government has caused difficulties for businesses in fields such as the licensing of foreign investments, which involves several agencies. But even when dealing with only one ministry, procedures can be slow and cumbersome, though improvements have been achieved in such areas as expatriate work permits through the establishment of one-stop processing offices. Slow VAT refunds (mostly a result of heightened fraud checks) were a frequent source of complaints in 1998, but the backlog cleared considerably during 1999.

An overhaul of the civil service that was started in 1998 with World Bank funding has made some progress, despite internal conflicts over management restructuring and the sensitive issue of staffing levels. The main aims are to improve overall levels of public service, speed up funds disbursements and re-train staff to deal with the demands of economic liberalisation. In the meantime, one way of cutting through much of the red tape is to rely upon the Board of Investment (BOI), which handles most approvals for promoted firms. But even the BOI application procedures can take an unduly long time, while some of its rules (such as preventing companies in the same industrial estate from trading with each other) are restrictive. The Industry Ministry, Immigration Department and Commerce Ministry also offer various forms of one-stop service, covering such areas as work visas, factory permits, VAT refunds and entry permits

Service With A Kick

Corruption is institutionalised in Thailand, to a point where non-compliance can effectively force a company out of business. Kickbacks are routinely paid for state contracts, procurements, faster import clearance and to avoid excessive regulatory scrutiny. The most enduring problem is with petty bribery among officials in regulatory agencies, the police and SOEs. Dockers at Bangkok's port went on strike in early 1999 to protest against attempts to stamp out their taking payment to speed up cargo-handling. Nevertheless, investor perceptions of the extent of corruption have noticeably improved since the early 1990s, with most business groupings convinced that the government is making an effort to improve the country's image. Thailand was ranked 68th of 90 countries surveyed by **Transparency International** (TI) in 1999, putting it ahead of Indonesia but behind Malaysia and Singapore. However, in terms of the incidence of bribe-taking, Thailand was ahead of Malaysia.

Environmental Regulation

Laws Adequate, But Compliance Patchy

Thailand's environmental protection laws date from the early-1990s and stem from a belated recognition of the damage wrought by decades of poorly-regulated industrialisation. Strict rules now apply for all forms of factory and motor vehicle emissions, zoning prohibitions are used to force dirty industries out of urban areas and the polluter-pays principle has been established to pay for treatment of commercial waste. Firms setting up in environmentally-sensitive sites are required to commission impact studies and install full treatment facilities.

But in practice, enforcement is lax due to overlapping regulatory jurisdictions, while penalties are too low to act as a viable deterrence. Pollution control officers lack the authority to initiate criminal charges, usually having to rely upon un-cooperative police units to take action. Consequently, controls are widely flouted at a factory level, especially on industrial discharges. Economic difficulties have worsened the problem since 1997: one casualty was the polluter-pays principle, which had still not been implemented at the end of 1999 because of its political sensitivity. Tighter vehicle emission standards for lorries and motor-cycles were also delayed under industry pressure.

Legal amendments that were pending in 1999 are expected to give more teeth to existing legislation, but deeper improvements will probably have to wait until environmental awareness climbs up the list of political priorities. Public concern is rising but economic conditions still take precedence over pollution. Nevertheless, some government agencies have indicated a greater willingness to take direct action against projects in response to environmental objections, resulting in delays and design alterations. Protests over the location of a station near a school were partly responsible for a two-year delay in the completion of the elevated Bangkok Transit System railway (coupled with financial difficulties), while public opposition has forced the relocation of several toxic waste treatment projects. Local residents succeeded in blocking the planned construction of three lignite-fuelled power stations south of Bangkok in 1999 after NGOs revealed that requirements for an environmental impact study had not been met.

5 Capital Markets

Introduction

Capital Reforms Fuel Boom... And Bust

A consistent policy of successive Thai governments has been to encourage the growth of domestic capital markets. Their motives included broadening the sources of finance available to Thai companies (to stimulate the investment needed to upgrade Thailand's industrial base), and encouraging greater household savings by extending the range of financial instruments on offer. The most recent key moves were the launch of an offshore banking sector in 1993 and the completion of a reform white paper in 1995. At a regulatory level, the establishment in 1992 of the Securities and Exchange Commission (SEC) brought greater supervision of capital markets (equity and debt), with powers to set rules on disclosure requirements, take over procedures and other aspects of investor protection.

The Stock Exchange of Thailand (SET) has acted as the main non-banking source of capital since the late 1970s and became the prime gateway for foreign portfolio investment in the peak growth period of 1993-95. As of December 1999, a total of 450 securities were listed on the market, a figure that has been virtually static since the start of the economic downturn. The top year for new entrants was 1993, with 82 listings, but subsequent years have seen a decline in interest due to bearish trading conditions. The fastest area of growth is in corporate bond listings, which have seen spectacular returns since their inception in 1992, though they are still dwarfed by equities in overall market terms.

Much of the SET's peak growth between 1993 and 1996 was a result of the easier access to capital that ensued after the launch of offshore banking. The SET index rose by more than 300% in this period, only to crash just as quickly once the capital pool was withdrawn. One reason was the speculative nature of many investments, with big-capitalisation real estate and financial stocks attracting the bulk of support purely because of their ability to move the market index higher. The government had intended that the fund inflows would be used for improvements in industrial technology and operating methods, and this misuse of resources was a key factor in the debts cycle that enveloped financial markets in 1997.

Despite its meteoric rise, the SET has remained a relatively minor source of company funds compared to loans from Thai banks and global capital markets, partly because it is not truly representative of the corporate elite (*see below*). Investors have also become disillusioned by the poor earnings record of many sectors: in 1999, about half of listed stocks were effectively insolvent, though market regulators have taken a more relaxed view of trading targets until economic conditions improve. A total of 26 firms were de-listed in 1999, up from 14 in the previous year, leaving a total of 392 stocks. Daily trading volumes on both the securities and bonds markets fell to record lows in 1998 because of interest rate uncertainties and the bleak economic outlook, but made a partial recovery during 1999. Brokerage firms suffered a severe impact, with a number closing down. The SET responded by speeding up pending moves to lift the remaining restrictions on foreign ownership of securities houses/brokerage businesses, resulting in increased offshore investment.

Regulators Act To Improve Market Appeal

The monetary authorities responded with numerous measures to bolster confidence in the markets and improve their functioning. Most are detailed below under the individual market to which they apply. Among those of broader significance for the future are the government's decision in late 1999 to set up a national equity fund to stimulate the small venture capital market and the establishment in June 1999 of a new trading exchange for small and medium-sized companies, which have suffered most from the banks' reluctance to make new loans. The equity fund will invest in Thai corporates that have restructured their debts but lack an adequate equity base to expand operations, while the Market for Alternative Investment (MAI) replaces the moribund Bangkok Stock Dealing Centre, which was originally intended to perform a similar role as an OTC market. There are also plans to introduce index options based on the benchmark SET-50 index, as well as exchange and interest rate instruments. Asset management firms are being encouraged to launch new specialist firms dedicated to high-risk investments ("junk" bonds or small companies' equities).

At a monitoring level, the government will implement a new regulatory structure for capital markets in 2000 that is expected to remove ambiguity between the respective roles of the SEC and SET board. Based partly on a financial sector white paper that was prepared in 1995 but never introduced (due to the government's premature collapse), the framework will beef up the SEC's powers and enable it to enforce better corporate governance and improved accounting procedures and disclosure standards. The SEC is already taking a more interventionist role: 118 fines or other penalties were imposed in 1999 for trading violations, while 15 reports of insider trading were investigated.

The Equity Market

Trading Systems Have Been Tightened

The SET is now a relatively mature market, after significant changes to its supervision and trading practices in the early-1990s. Its traditional investor base is local Thai retail investors, who retain the largest share of outstanding securities on the SET and account for 70-80% of trades. Foreign shareholdings accounted for 25% of the market's capitalisation at end-1999 and trading on the Alien Board (see below) accounted for 30% of total turnover in 1999 and 35% in 1998. Local investment institutions (mutual funds and unit trusts) have grown in importance. Contractual savings vehicles (pension funds, insurance companies, social security funds) have been relatively small players in local capital markets, but will take on a larger role in coming years due to plans for mandatory corporate pension and social security covers.

Trading and settlement procedures are generally satisfactory. Trading is computerised (stocks are generally traded in lots of 100) with foreign investors restricted to trading on the Alien Board. This is due to the restrictions imposed by the Foreign Business Law (*see Business Environment*) on foreign shareholdings in Thai companies. The SET has limits on the permitted daily movement of both individual stocks and the overall market, which are progressively revised. Settlement is managed relatively efficiently either manually or on a net basis through the exchange or the Thai Securities Depository Company, with settlement on the basis of T+3. Securities are registered and mostly held in physical form, with separate registers for domestic and foreign holders of equities.

Foreigners Kept On Fringes

The benchmark index remains the Bangkok SET index, based on April 1975=100. This is calculated on an inclusive basis, i.e. it covers all the companies listed on the exchange. These, however, are not fully representative of Thailand's corporate sector. It was calculated in 1999 that only about 25% of the 500 top Thai firms had SET listings, partly because of tough disclosure rules that undermine the traditional family management style and invite attention from tax authorities. Listed firms may have a substantial proportion of their equity held by strategic partners (Thai or foreign), reducing the shares actively traded. Export-oriented companies are notably under-represented in the Index, as most prefer to rely upon low-interest shipment financing. In contrast, banks and other financial institutions accounted for almost half of the SET's capitalisation at the end of 1999 (above their contribution to the economy), reflecting the speculative nature of most retail investment. The SET-50, an index introduced in 1996, tracks the performance of the top 50 companies on the SET by capitalisation. It is also dominated by the financial sector.

Shares on the Alien Board often trade at a premium to the prices paid by domestic investors, a distortion due to the restrictions on holding a foreign stake in a Thai company. This acts as a trading disincentive, as do the limited selection of quality stocks, and the tendency for shares to come on the market only at irregular intervals. Unlike domestic investors, most foreign traders deal only with firms that have established track records and solid fundamentals. One alternative is the Thai futures index that began trading on the Singapore International Monetary Exchange in late 1998, and enables foreigners to avoid the premium.

Relaxed Rules Ease Listing Pressures

Listing and trading rules have been overhauled since the onset of the economic crisis in an effort to restore liquidity and provide an alternative to scarce bank loans:

- The product range was broadened in 1999 to include new classes of equities, debt and hybrid-debt instruments and hybrid unit trusts. Privatised state enterprises and basic infrastructure projects gained easier access due to relaxed listing requirements.

- Listing rules were relaxed during 1999 to provide struggling stocks with a breathing space and reverse a steady decline in the number of securities. Applicants are now allowed to have a smaller capital base and lower profits.

- Tax concessions, including exemptions from corporate income tax on dividends received from listed companies and on personal tax on capital gains, have been offered since 1998.

- The introduction of a net settlement rule in 1998 (requiring clients to pay only the difference between their purchase and sales on the day of trade) helped cut trading costs and is thought to have helped boost trading volumes.

- Short-selling was regularised in 1997 to improve liquidity and trading volumes.

Troughs And Peaks

A succession of shocks to investor confidence from mid-1996 generated a steep decline in Thai share prices over the following three years. The trend was not uniformly bad; the period saw several sharp rallies, such as the "bounce" in the immediate post-devaluation period and another in early-1998 after the successful restructuring of Korean banks' external short-term debt. However, these all proved to be "false dawns", each being followed eventually by a renewed slide to deeper lows. Triggers for these falls varied from domestic influences (slow realisation of the scale of the financial sector's problems, ever-more pessimistic output trends, or the slow pace of reform) to the succession of crises which affected global investor sentiment towards emerging markets in general – Korea, Indonesia, Russia and Brazil. In 1998, the latter influences were probably the predominant factor behind each decline, as the domestic environment (though hardly favourable) did not see many sudden shocks.

It is noteworthy that foreign investor sentiment was, on the whole, supportive of the market in this period, with significant net purchases being made in both 1997 and parts of 1998. These may have been concentrated in periods when it looked as if a final turning point had been achieved or when the implementation of structural reforms boosted the long-term attractiveness of Thai equities. For

Thai investors (especially retail ones), factors such as tight liquidity conditions in domestic money markets may have been as much a reason for dis-investing as the admittedly dire picture for corporate earnings and dividend payments since late-1997. The high risk of corporate failures will also have been a deterrent, while from mid-1998 the auctions of public bonds gave investors an attractive alternative to equities.

From a 10-year low (340) in early January 1998, the SET index rose 65% to 559 in mid-February and remained relatively strong for a few weeks. From early March, however, a series of further slumps, punctuated by only brief pauses and slight rallies, took it to a new low of only 204 on September 4, a decline of almost 65%. At this point, the SET index stood at a level under an eighth of its all-time high reached at the start of 1994 and in real terms was less than that at its opening in April 1975. In these months, both local and (unusually) foreign investors were reported as heavy sellers, a suggestion supported by the heavy volume of trading. Between January and August a total of 30bn shares were traded, more than in the whole of each of the previous three years.

The Worst May Be Over

From this nadir, the market staged another strong rebound, which saw it rise by two-thirds to 352 at end-December 1998. The recovery was sustained until mid-1999, with the index breaching the 500-point market for the first time in 15 months on a wave of optimism that was mostly sparked by the enactment of new bankruptcy and foreclosure legislation. Daily turnover rose from THB3.44bn (US$92mn) in March to THB7.35bn in April and THB13.75bn in June, pushing the index up by 40% between January and June. However, a spate of poor bank earnings quickly brought the market back down to earth and the index again settled into the 400-point range through the rest of the year. Market sentiment was undermined by concern over the rising cost of financial restructuring, slow debt negotiations and political uncertainties.

Falling interest rates and improved consumer demand should translate into better earnings by mid-2000, with flow-on benefits in equities trading. Mutual funds are gaining deposits at the expense of banks, while more medium-sized firms are turning to domestic baht-bonds as an alternative to finance firms. However, the SET invariably takes its lead from foreign traders, and offshore interest is not likely to pick up until banks have resolved their capital deficiencies and accelerated the pace of debt restructuring. Foreign institutions also want to see more tangible progress in structural reforms of the economy. None of these will happen until the second half of the year. In the meantime, trading is expected to be fairly subdued, with any recovery in turnover probably being short lived. The main uncertainty is movements in US interest rates, though liquidity was still adequate in early 2000 to absorb modest increases.

The Bond Market

Becalmed After Rapid Expansion

The Thai bond market was both small and illiquid until the early-1990s, when official efforts to encourage companies to tap it as a source of capital began to bear modest fruit. The most significant move was the relaxation in 1992 of restrictions on the issuance of corporate debentures, which was followed by regulatory changes to encourage purchases and trading in corporate bonds. The Bond Dealers Club (BDC) was established in November 1994 to regulate the nascent debt market, but trading continued to be done via the SET's BONDNET system. In 1998, the BDC was renamed the Thailand Bond Dealing Centre and licensed through the SET.

The stock of corporate bonds outstanding rose substantially from 1993 and at the end of 1996 it was approximately 20% of the SET's market capitalisation – some THB500bn (US$13.5bn). In addition to debentures, there was widespread trading in short-term bills of exchange, largely issued by finance companies – many of which were closed in 1997. But the bond market almost collapsed in the wake of the 1997 currency crisis, which saw scores of debenture issues go into default. Trading volume declined from the 1996 peak of about THB1bn to less than THB100mn in early 1998, far below the levels needed to sustain a viable market. This was despite regulatory changes, which encouraged the pooling of loans into bonds or other tradeable securities.

Public Issues Lead The Revival

Declining interest rates began to revive trading in the second half of 1998, but most activity centred around a spate of public bonds that were issued to pay for financial sector restructuring. Government and SOE bonds accounted for 80% of turnover by the end of 1998, with corporate issues only returning in strength during 1999, when banks began to return to the debts market. Most government paper was issued via the Bank of Thailand and the Financial Institutions Development Fund (FIDF), a lifeboat fund for the financial sector. Bonds worth more than THB500bn were sold at auction in 1998-99, though the FIDF ended up buying a large portion back for its own portfolio. The FIDF also issued a further THB200bn to financial institutions in private placements, often as part of recapitalisation exercises.

These issues contributed to a renewed expansion in the total stock of bonds traded on the market, to an estimated THB800bn in 1998 and THB1.5trn (US$40.5bn) at the end of 1999. In addition to the government paper, there were also sizeable issues in 1998 from state-owned entities (SOEs, such as **Bangchak Petroleum** and **PTT**), corporates (notably **Shinawatra Satellite** and **Siam Cement Group**) and banks, to boost their capital base. **Siam Commercial Bank** and **Bank of Ayudha** issued subordinated debentures (in the former case convertible into equity).

Banks were also responsible for much of the 1999 turnaround, with **Thai Farmers Bank** and **Bangkok Bank** both launching so-called SLIPS issues, which coupled preference shares with subordinated debentures. Other notable issuers included **National Petrochemical, Charoen Pokphand Feedmill** and **Advanced Info Service**, while the government continued its regular auctions of 8-10 year bonds. In March, SOE **Expressway and Rapid Transit Authority of Thailand** announced an issue of THB1.3bn nine-year bonds, carrying an attractive coupon (8.1%) to refinance previous loans for one project. **The Electricity Generating Authority of Thailand** (EGAT) launched its second US$300mn issue within 12 months. In the corporate sector, **Siam Cement** increased a batch of debentures from THB10bn to THB24bn, after earlier completing a THB35bn package. However, there were reports in early 2000 that it might be withdrawn.

Reflecting the increased issuing activity, volume has picked up markedly since mid-1998, when falling interest rates cut funding costs. This was partly in response to the volatile economic conditions, which persuaded many investors that government paper would be a "safe haven" for funds at a time when rates were declining. Average daily turnover reached THB850mn in late 1998, double the level of only a few months earlier, and rose again to THB2bn (US$54mn) in early 2000, or about 40% of SET volumes. But the vast majority of trades (85%) were in government bonds, with a further 12% being accounted for by SOEs, and it was not until the third quarter of the year that private bonds re-emerged. By December, corporate issues accounted for slightly more than half of market value, and turnover averaged THB1.7-1.9bn, just above the peak recorded in 1996.

Low Rates Favour A New Boom

A number of factors point to a continuation of the stronger trading performance that was recorded in the second half of 1999. The availability of bank financing is likely to remain low, especially for small and medium-sized firms (which account for more than 90% of business output but are also the most heavily indebted). Bank deposit rates are expected to remain around the 3% mark for a further 12 months, channelling the savings of millions of low-income earners into mutual funds. Offshore borrowings are beyond the reach of almost all Thai companies due to unfavourable credit ratings and global interest-rate uncertainties. And equities will not offer good returns until the wider economic picture clears. Perhaps the biggest factor of all is the low level of domestic interest rates, which has substantially reduced issuing costs.

On the downside, much of the recent bond activity has taken place outside the formal market structure, raising questions over the regulatory situation. Most of the THB135bn (US$3.6bn) of capital securities issued during 1999 was placed privately with prime bank customers, depriving the market of a benchmark and shutting out individual investors. Similarly, **Siam Commercial Bank**'s THB35bn issue was traded through banks directly to investors. The SEC is keen for the debts market to be grouped together on the new MAI secondary market, as it has no authority over price movements in informal trading. With the objective of protecting investors, the commission ordered in 1999 that bonds traded on the MAI must be rated and fully comply with SET disclosure regulations.

The Bank of Thailand has made debt markets a cornerstone of its financial services development plans, and intends eventually that the value of bond trading will surpass that of equities, as is the norm in most advanced countries. But some other obstacles to the market's growth remain. Foreign investors have yet to become major players, accounting for at most 2-3% of turnover – far below their participation in the equity market. This reflects concerns over the potential for further defaults, coupled with doubts over the solvency of some issuing firms. There is a greater tendency now by foreign investors to fully research the fundamentals of companies, whereas in the past they might have been satisfied with reading their trading records. Efforts to extend mandatory credit ratings to all fixed-income instruments are likely to bolster the market's image. Thai Ratings and Information Service (TRIS, established in 1993) also wants to rate all institutions that accept investment funds from the public (including mutual funds and insurance companies).

VIETNAM 2000

Analyst: Martin Gainsborough

Editor: Sara Matchett/Georgina Wilde

Contents

Political Outlook _____ **419**

    Domestic Political Outlook 419
    Foreign Policy 424

    Profile and Recent Developments _____ **426**

    Political Background 426
    Foreign Policy 429

Economic Outlook _____ **431**

    Introduction 431
    Economic Activity 432
    Fiscal Policy 433
    Monetary Policy 435
    Exchange Rate Policy 436
    Balance Of Payments 438
    Foreign Direct Investment 439
    External Debt 441

    Profile and Recent Developments _____ **443**

    Economic Background 443
    Fiscal Policy 445
    Monetary Policy 446
    Exchange Rate Policy 447
    External Trade 448
    Foreign Direct Investment 448

Key Economic Sectors _____ **451**

    Introduction 451
    Textiles And Garments 452
    Footwear 453
    Food And Beverages 454
    Electronics 455
    Automobiles 455
    Motorcycles 456
    Plastics 457
    Agriculture 458
    Oil & Gas 460
    Construction 461
    Power Generation 462
    Telecoms 463
    Banking 463
    Tourism 465

Profile and Recent Developments _____ **467**

    Introduction 467
    Manufacturing 467
    Agriculture, Forestry And Fisheries 470
    Energy 471
    Construction And Property 472
    Utilities 473
    Telecoms 473
    Finance 474
    Tourism 475

Business Environment _____ **477**

    Introduction 477
    Infrastructure 477
    The Domestic Market 478
    The Labour Market 479
    Industrial Policy 480
    Foreign Investment Policy 482
    Foreign Trade Policy 483
    Bureaucracy And Corruption 484
    Environmental Regulation 485

Capital Markets _____ **487**

    Equity Markets 487
    Bond Markets 489

VIETNAM: MACROECONOMIC DATA AND FORECASTS

	1994	1995	1996	1997	1998	1999	2000f	2001f	2002f
Nominal GDP (US$bn)	15.5	20.3	23.4	25.3	25.5	26.4	28.7	30.7	34.5
Population (mn)	72.5	74.0	75.4	76.7	78.1	79.5	80.9	82.4	83.9
GDP per capita (US$)	214.2	273.9	311.1	329.5	327.1	331.8	354.3	372.8	411.1
Real GDP growth (% y/y)	8.8	9.5	9.3	8.8	5.8	4.8	5.8	5.5	6.5
Industrial production (% y/y)	13.7	14.0	13.8	13.8	12.1	10.8	11.5	11.2	11.8
CPI (% y/y, period avg)	9.6	16.4	5.9	3.1	8.8	4.3	5.0	7.0	8.0
CPI (% y/y, eop)	14.5	12.7	4.5	3.6	9.5	0.1	5.0	7.5	9.0
VND/US$ (an. avg)	10,960	11,000	11,031	11,700	13,267	14,100	14,132	14,646	15,153
VND/US$ (eop)	10,955	11,016	11,085	12,297	13,892	14,016	14,288	15,003	15,303
Exports (fob, US$bn)	4.1	5.2	7.3	9.1	9.4	11.5	14.5	16.7	20.5
Imports (fob, US$bn)	5.3	7.5	10.5	10.5	10.4	11.6	16.0	19.2	22.6
Trade balance (US$bn)	-1.2	-2.3	-3.2	-1.4	-1.0	-0.1	-1.5	-2.5	-2.1
Current account (US$bn)	-1.2	-1.9	-2.4	-1.7	-1.1	-1.0	-1.2	-1.3	-1.2
Current account (% GDP)	-7.6	-9.5	-10.4	-6.7	-4.2	-3.8	-4.2	-4.2	-3.5
Foreign reserves (US$bn)*	0.9	1.0	1.3	1.8	1.3	1.5	2.6	3.2	3.5
Import cover (mths)**	2.0	1.6	1.5	2.1	1.5	1.6	2.0	2.0	1.9
External debt (US$bn)***	5.4	6.5	8.3	9.6	10.8	11.1	13.5	14.7	15.5
External debt (% GDP)	35.0	31.8	35.3	37.9	42.1	42.2	46.9	47.9	45.0

f = BMI forecast; *excluding gold; ** number of months imports covered by FX reserves; ***convertible; Sources: Ho Chi Minh City Statistical Yearbook/World Bank/BMI.

1 Political Outlook

Domestic Political Outlook

Political Jockeying Before Party Congress

Vietnam is approaching its five-yearly Ninth Party Congress. This important event sets out the broad policy agenda for the next five years and changes the line-up on the top-level Party bodies – the Politburo and Central Committee. An earlier campaign launched to root out corruption in the party, which was to run as a kind of party-cleansing exercise before the Congress, had implied that the meeting would occur in May 2001. But more recent press comment now suggests it may be held in "early 2001". It is normal for the political atmosphere to thicken in the run-up to a Congress, as senior and junior ranks jockey for position and try to secure or retain Politburo or Central Committee positions. The main Congress document, the Political Report, is drafted at this time. However, the jockeying is less about what goes in the report than who rises and who falls.

The political jockeying in the first half is within normal limits, but it has helped to delay the US trade accord and deter foreign investment.

The approach to the Ninth Congress has been no different from previous ones, although it looks as thought the jockeying began earlier than usual because of the concurrent anti-corruption campaign. An early high-level casualty was the deputy prime minister, Ngo Xuan Loc, who in late 1999 was implicated in a corrupt land deal related to a private sector water park project and as a result lost his job. In early 2000 the political temperature in Hanoi rose sharply as other ministers and officials feared for their positions. In April the planning and investment minister, Tran Xuan Gia, was reprimanded by the party for his apparent involvement in, and mishandling of, the water park project, although he retained his government position.

These events cannot be seen as part of a struggle between conservatives and reformers, but rather simply reflects fairly machiavellian contests for power in which both so-called 'reformers' and 'conservatives' are equally likely to be found exploiting their public position for private gain. Furthermore, reinforcing the idea that politics in Vietnam is very often not all that it seems, Loc appeared to make a comeback in April when he was made an advisor to the prime minister, Phan Van Khai. This is especially puzzling because Loc has always been linked to the former party general secretary, Do Muoi, who is usually regarded as a conservative, while Khai is very much identified with the other major political group led by the former prime minister and reformer Vo Van Kiet. Both Kiet and Do Muoi, although formally retired with the positions of party advisers, continue to wield a great deal of influence. One possible interpretation is that Khai is seeking to protect himself from his critics by appointing someone from a rival camp as an adviser. In April there were reports that Khai was under political pressure.

Personnel Changes Show Some Winners

A reshuffle of important local party roles in the three main cities is suggestive about future rising stars.

The run-up to the Congress was also marked in early 2000 with a reshuffle involving a number of key party and government posts. This saw the appointment in January of both a new foreign minister and a new trade minister. The new trade minister, former deputy foreign minister Vu Khoan, was seen as being brought in partly to inject new life into the relationship with the US after the government had backed off from signing the bilateral trade accord. The appointment of a new foreign minister, Nguyen Dy Nien – a politician with broad international experience – marked the retirement of the long-standing holder of the post, Nguyen Manh Cam, who now also looks likely to relinquish his Politburo seat at the Ninth Congress.

A simultaneous reshuffle involved four key party positions. The party secretary in Ho Chi Minh City, Truong Tan Sang, was made head of the party's Economic Commission in Hanoi. Sang was replaced as party secretary in Ho Chi Minh City by Nguyen Minh Triet, who until his appointment was the head of the party's Mass Mobilisation Commission in Hanoi. Triet, meanwhile, was replaced by the former party secretary in the central city of Danang, Truong Quang Duoc. Completing the reshuffle, the former head of the Economic Commission, Phan Dien – whose former job went to Sang – was made party secretary in Danang. Four of those affected are members of the Politburo. They are all likely to retain their seats at the

THE POLITBURO (IN ORDER OF RANK)			
1	Le Kha Phieu*	10	Nguyen Thi Xuan My
2	Tran Duc Luong*	11	Phan Van Tra
3	Phan Van Khai*	12	Le Minh Huong
4	Nong Duc Manh*	13	Le Xuan Tung
5	Nguyen Van An	14	Truong Tan Sang
6	Nguyen Tan Dung	15	Pham Thanh Ngan
7	Nguyen Manh Cam	16	Nguyen Minh Triet
8	Nguyen Duc Binh	17	Phan Dien
9	Pham The Duyet*	18	Nguyen Phu Trong

Denotes member of Politburo Standing Board. Source: BMI

Congress. The one who is not, Truong Quang Duoc, looks a strong candidate for Politburo promotion in 2001.

Ruling Troika Will Stay Until 2002

BMI expects that the ruling troika, who currently hold the top three Politburo seats – the party general-secretary, Le Kha Phieu, the president, Tran Duc Luong, and the prime minister, Phan Van Khai – will retain their party positions at the Congress. Phieu has only held the general secretary post since 1997 and all three – being in their 60s – are relatively young by the standards of recent Vietnamese leaders. Furthermore, if it is true that the former top leaders Do Muoi and Vo Van Kiet continue to wield a large amount of power, there is a certain logic to their keeping Phieu and Khai – historically rather weak leaders – in power. The least politically secure leader is probably Khai, but it appears he has recently taken steps to shore up his support. Beyond this there are around six currently serving Politburo members who look like possibly being replaced at next year's Congress. However, this would be in keeping with normal turnover rates. In 2002 Vietnam will hold its National Assembly elections. This also marks the end of the present government's five-year term, which is another point at which Khai, or indeed Luong, could be replaced. Assuming Phieu stays on as general-secretary at the Congress, he is most unlikely to be replaced in the remainder of the forecast period.

The ruling threesome is likely to stay in place until 2002.

Reform Will Progress, But Slowly

The jockeying for position earlier this year and the political uncertainty associated with the run-up to the Congress in general have not been good for reform. The government's unwillingness to sign the bilateral trade accord with the US after having earlier signed an agreement in principle was first and foremost a consequence of this climate of uncertainty, which meant senior leaders became reluctant to stick their necks out on an issue which is potentially controversial. This is not to say that the top leadership fear the consequences of the economic liberalisation required by the accord and objected to signing on these grounds. The delay is fundamentally a matter of politics, namely that any politician too closely associated with opening up to the US could find it used against them even if there is not in reality any great ideological divide on the issue.

A combination of state business interests and a deep-rooted contol reflex in the bureaucracy are the main constraints on reform. They can only be overcome gradually.

Recent political uncertainty has also had an adverse effect on a number of large foreign investment projects, notably the Nam Con Son natural gas project backed by **BP/Amoco** and some large infrastructure deals. In particular, the political difficulties faced by the planning and investment minister, Tran Xuan Gia, have meant he has been less able to act decisively in this area. Moreover, his problems do not seem necessarily to be over. In June, he received a grilling from National Assembly delegates concerned that the government was in danger of giving in too much to foreign investors.

The Political Report, which will accompany the Ninth Party Congress, is unlikely to contain any big surprises in terms of broad policy goals. There is, for example, unlikely to be any relaxation of current restrictions on foreign share ownership in equitising state companies, nor a greater commitment to increased foreign participation in the stock market, which is due to be launched on a preliminary basis in July. The Political Report is likely to contain bold words on eliminating political support for surviving state enterprises and creating a level playing field for the private sector. However, progress in these areas will continue to be slow over the forecast period thanks to the combined blocking effect of a combination of powerful interests within state companies and the tendency of the bureaucracy to over-regulate.

The government's administrative reform programme and its ongoing abolition of large numbers of business licenses are designed to tackle some of these problems but actually changing the prevailing political culture, which lies at the root of many of the country's problems, will take a lot longer. Despite these difficulties, **BMI** believes that a number of the currently stalled foreign investment projects are likely to move forward during 2000-02 with the need to boost foreign investment inflows acting as a powerful incentive. Equally, the government is likely to sign the bilateral trade accord with the US either in late 2000 or perhaps more likely after the Ninth Congress in the first or second quarter of 2001. In June there were signs that both sides were preparing to resume discussions on the trade accord.

Political Stability Is Likely To Be Maintained...

Vietnam will remain politically stable both before and after the party Congress and until the end of the forecast period. This is in strong contrast with neighbouring Laos, where the ruling Communist party has recently faced an attempted pro-democracy demonstration and a series of bomb attacks by those opposed to its rule. In many of the areas where Laos looks weak, Vietnam looks comparatively strong: the Vietnamese government's nationalist credentials are stronger than Laos because it defeated France and the US largely by its own efforts; Vietnam is ethnically homogenous where Laos is not; and as a large country with a strong national identity Vietnam looks far less vulnerable to potentially transforming outside influences compared with Laos, which is small, landlocked and economically and culturally heavily influenced by Thailand. Political opposition to the party

A Key Concern

Corruption Perception Index - a regional comparison

World Ranking	Country	CPI Score*
7	Singapore	9.1
16	Hong Kong	7.8
29	Malaysia	5.3
29	Taiwan	5.3
43	South Korea	4.2
52	China	3.5
55	Philippines	3.3
61	Thailand	3.0
66	India	2.9
71	Pakistan	2.7
74	**Vietnam**	**2.5**
80	Indonesia	2.0

*10 = highly clean; 0 = highly corrupt; Source: Transparency International.

The greatest threat to political stability comes from public disillusionment at corruption or conflict among the ruling elite. Neither looks likely to reach a critical point in 2000-02.

in Vietnam exists but the security apparatus in Vietnam is still pervasive enough to make organisation difficult. It is also striking that party membership is rising: in 1999 114,000 people joined the party, up 7.25% on the previous year making it the largest single annual increase since 1986. Party membership, although not the passport to status and career success it once was, is still widely regarded by many as an important part of getting on. Furthermore, to succeed in business requires good political connections. As a result the tendency to date has been for successful companies to cultivate close ties with the government rather than to emerge as a force at loggerheads with the system, pushing for more radical change.

While the cohesive political culture heralds continued political stability, there are downsides. Like Vietnam's relative impermeability to outside influences compared with Laos, the emergence of a new business elite deeply wedded to the existing political system has negative consequences in terms of reform and the emergence of either a law-based, rules-based economy or a meritocratic society.

...But There Are Risks

Vietnam has witnessed an increase in rural unrest during the 1990s. This primarily reflects discontent precipitated by corruption and elite abuse of power. To date, unrest has mainly occurred in fairly remote provinces where there is little foreign business involvement. However, there have occasionally been problems in some of the wealthier southern provinces close to Ho Chi Minh City where foreign investment is much more common. Whenever unrest occurs, the party launches an investigation designed to address the underlying causes of discontent but there are serious doubts whether in cases like this the party is really capable of reforming itself given that the problems are often systemic. Corruption risks causing widespread popular disillusion with the party, which if unchecked could ultimately lead to its downfall. To some extent, disillusion exists already – particularly in certain parts of the south where support for the party has never run deep – but it has not reached a critical stage yet.

There are sporadic outbursts of discontent and corruption is a long-term threat.

The other principal danger as far as political stability is concerned relates to the possibility of conflict within the ruling elite. Compared with other Communist countries Vietnam does not particularly have a history of internecine warfare within the party. However, there is a danger that as Vietnam increasingly comes face to face with key economic and political choices in a situation where the potential goalposts are ever widening, senior party figures will attempt to take the country in new more radical directions. The risk in this respect is presently quite small but it is there. Opposition to the government from disaffected intellectuals, certain religious groups and overseas Vietnamese tends to receive a lot of attention in the media, but it in **BMI**'s view the greater threat to stability comes from unchecked corruption and conflict among the ruling elite.

Foreign Policy

No Major External Threats

In the forecast period, Vietnam's foreign relations will continue to be characterised by gradually improving ties with the USA, closer economic integration with the Association of Southeast Asian Nations (Asean) and largely stable relations with China despite historic rivalry between the two neighbours. The visit of the US defence secretary, William Cohen, to Vietnam in March 2000 at a time when the government had balked at signing the bilateral trade accord, indicated both how far US-Vietnam relations have come and how far they still have to go. Cohen's was the first visit to Vietnam by a US defence secretary since the end of the Vietnam War. However, Cohen's comment that visits by US naval ships were not an immediate prospect, illustrates that a certain level of mistrust still remains. Visits by European naval ships are routine.

Renewed negotiation with the US will begin in July 2000 and it is probable that the pact will be agreed by early 2001, although the Vietnamese may delay until after the party Congress before signing. This will mark an important milestone in US-Vietnam relations. However, it is unlikely to result in a problem-free relationship thereafter. It is quite probable that the award of most favoured nation (MFN) trading status, which is expected to follow the signing of the trade accord, will be followed by the imposition of quota restrictions on Vietnamese textile and garment exports. Moreover, there are likely to be periodic differences between the two countries over politics and human rights. Nevertheless, better relations with the US will remain important, both as a counterbalance to China, and for their own sake.

In December 1999 China and Vietnam signed an agreement settling the demarcation of their 1,200km land border. They have also pledged to resolve their territorial differences in the Tonkin Gulf in 2000. While this is likely to be realised, there will be no settlement of their territorial dispute over islands in the South China Sea during the forecast period. However, as relations between the two countries are on a much firmer footing compared with the early 1990s, the likelihood of a military clash is small. Relations

Ties with Asean neighbours will grow closer, as will relations with the US and China.

Key Partners

Vietnam - investment to date by country, % of total US$35.96bn (as of April 18, 2000)

Singapore 19%
Taiwan 14%
Hong Kong 7%
France 5%
B.V. Islands 3.4%
UK 3%
Others 19%
U.S. 3%
Russia 4%
Japan 11%
South Korea 10%

Source: Vietnam Investment Review.

have warmed considerably in recent years, with numerous high-level exchanges. Vietnam's economy suffers from an inflow of cheap Chinese imports, many of which are smuggled. However, it is unlikely that this will effect wider political relations. Meanwhile, Vietnam keeps a close eye on the progress of the Chinese economy and does not always like what it sees. China has gone far further along the path of reform and dismantling of the command economy apparatus and has achieved much faster growth, but the attendant social disruption has complicated the task of maintaining stability. In June, in a surprising twist to Vietnam's traditional 'younger brother' relationship with China, 16 senior Vietnamese went to China to attend a seminar on economic reform without loss of party control and China announced a grant of US$55mn to modernise two Chinese-built steel and fertiliser plants.

Economic integration with Asean will proceed as Vietnam continues to lower tariff barriers as part of its commitment to the creation of the Asean Free Trade Area (AFTA). Relations with the more politically pluralist Asean states, such as Thailand and the Philippines, could periodically be strained during 2000-02 by differences over the position to adopt towards Myanmar and Cambodia. Instability in Cambodia and Laos could have some commercial fallout for Vietnam, but political relations are likely to remain close.

In May the Canadian government announced a suspension of all ministerial exchanges with Vietnam and the postponement of its support for Vietnam's bid to join the World Trade Organisation (WTO). This followed the Vietnamese government's execution of an Overseas Vietnamese woman with Canadian citizenship who had been found guilty in a Vietnamese court of drug smuggling. The Canadian government believes the conviction was in doubt. The incident is revealing insofar as it shows how the Vietnamese government's activities can periodically lead it into quite serious diplomatic conflict with Western nations. This kind of incident could occur again during 2000-02 with potential commercial damage. Meanwhile membership of the WTO will not be pursued as a matter of urgency; when Vietnam joins the WTO, which is not likely within the forecast period, it will be as a developing country, so the terms of entry are not likely to be onerous or contentious.

Profile and Recent Developments

Political Background

The Politburo Sits At The Political Apex

Vietnam is one of five remaining Communist Party states in the world. The Communist Party is still the only political party in the country. According to the constitution, the party is "the force leading the state and society". Thus, the government, the National Assembly and the military are all formally junior to it. The highest policy-making body of the party is the Politburo, which currently has 18 members (it had 19 members but one died in 1999). There is also a much larger Central Committee. Since 1996, there has been a five-member Politburo Standing Board – sometimes referred to as the "super-Politburo". While those who sit on the standing board are usually senior Politburo members, they are not necessarily more influential than the rest of the Politburo. Moreover, the formal position is that the board handles affairs on a day-to-day basis on behalf of the Politburo and does not make decisions. However, its formation is also viewed in some quarters as an attempt by the Communist Party to increase control over the government.

Every five years, the Communist Party convenes its National Congress – the last one was the Eighth Congress held in 1996. The congress sets out the broad policy focus for the next five years, contained in its Political Report, while it is also an occasion for the election of a new Central Committee, with invited party delegates electing the new one. The Central Committee, in turn, elects the Politburo. In reality, both the Central Committee and Politburo line-up is selected in advance of the congress. Precisely how this happens is poorly understood, but it is likely to be the task of the outgoing Politburo, taking into account a range of other interests. However, changes to the Politburo line-up are sometimes made at times other than the five-yearly party congresses.

The Ruling Troika Have Been In Office Since December 1997

The highest position on the Politburo is that of party general secretary, currently held by the 68-year old Le Kha Phieu. The other positions are ranked in order of seniority. The president, 62-year old Tran Duc Luong, ranks second while the prime minister, Phan Van Khai, who is 66, is third. These three individuals make up what is widely referred to as the ruling troika. At the time of his appointment in December 1997, Phieu was a bit of an unknown quantity. As a career soldier, however, who headed the army's Political Department prior to his appointment, he was widely judged to be a conservative. In fact, he has turned out to be more progressive than anticipated. A range of backgrounds and affiliations are represented on the Politburo. Overall, it is appropriate to view the Politburo as pro-reform, but with a heavy dose of caution rooted in the leadership's desire to ensure that change is achieved without a loss of political or social stability. However, it is true to say that the Politburo is only one factor among many affecting the momentum of change in the country.

The last changes to the Politburo were made in December 1997, when the current general secretary was chosen. At the same time, four new Politburo appointments were made, namely Major-general Pham Thanh Ngan, Nguyen Phu Trong, Phan Dien and Nguyen Minh Triet. General Ngan is an associate of Le Kha Phieu, having worked under him at the army's Political Department. Nguyen Phu Trong and Phan Dien are party secretaries in Hanoi and Danang respectively, posts they have both taken up in 2000. Nguyen Minh Triet is the party secretary in Ho Chi Minh City, a position taken up in January 2000. The former Ho Chi Minh City party secretary, Truong Tan Sang, is now the head of the party's Economic Commission in Hanoi. Another prominent figure on the Politburo is Nguyen Tan Dung, who is also deputy prime minister. At 50 years old, his rise has been meteoric.

The incoming Politburo members were appointed as three older members – the ruling troika of Do Muoi, Le Duc Anh and Vo Van Kiet retired. They have all been maintained as party advisers. Do Muoi and Kiet remain active and are still influential – possibly to the extent of limiting the freedom of manoeuvre of their successors. Le Duc Anh has been less active since suffering a stroke while still in office.

Although the post of general secretary is the most senior position in the party, the party emphasises a tradition of collective leadership. This is designed to prevent the emergence of personality cults that have been commonplace in other communist countries. What precisely it means in practice is unclear. It is often felt that it has merely resulted in indecision and an unwillingness to take decisive action. However, it is likely that such problems exist for other reasons, and are not just a feature of the collective leadership. In recent years, some have begun to regard the role of the general secretary as that of 'balancer' between different interests.

The Central Committee comprises some 170 members. This includes representatives from the centre and the provinces, the military and security apparatus, state enterprises and other economic and social institutions. The Central Committee meets twice a year when it convenes plenum meetings. These usually revolve around a particular theme – at least in terms of their public presentation. Recent themes have included the economy, including the bilateral trade accord with the USA, corruption and political reform.

Political "Reform" Means Making The Existing System Better

Beyond the Politburo and Central Committee, the party extends down to the grassroots. Thus, there are party committees at the provincial and city level, continuing down to the district, quarter and commune level. Party representation actually continues further down still, so that at the bottom of the chain, there will be a party chapter grouping of no more than a few families. The party operates a system of democratic centralism, whereby the decisions of higher levels are binding, at least in theory. There are also party cells in companies – notably state enterprises – and other government and social organisations. In 1998, the party had a membership of about 2.3mn people nationwide, representing a big jump compared with previous years, with 106,000 new members.

A key thrust of the reforms articulated at the Sixth Congress in 1986 was that changes were needed to the way in which the political system operated. This did not represent a questioning of the system of one-party rule itself, but it did embody recognition that the existing set-up was not working as it should be. Central to the critique was that the party had come to "control the whole show", stifling the function of the government and the National Assembly. Thus, from 1986, there emerged a desire to strengthen these institutions and distinguish more clearly between the role of the party and the government. Formally, it was stated that the party "leads", providing broad parameters, while the government "manages", being responsible for the more practical aspects of implementation. Part of the shift in thinking also included a desire to turn Vietnam into a state under the rule of law rather than party fiat. This has arguably led to a stronger National Assembly, which seriously debates issues and amends legislation. However, the National Assembly is also emerging as a forum where different party interests battle it out.

However, the extent of these changes should not be exaggerated. Firstly, the reining in of the party, as called for by the 1986 critique, has not been pursued consistently. Indeed, it has been reversed in some areas, with party cells being re-established in government ministries, for instance, after they had been disbanded earlier. Secondly, where such changes have been pursued, they have encountered resistance. Moreover, distinguishing between the party and the government is in some ways rather meaningless, given the way in which the party is represented in all government institutions and the National Assembly. More appropriate is to conceive of alliances and struggles between different institutions, some from the party and some from outside, but all with at least some party interests represented therein.

Where Does Real Power Lie?

In Vietnam, the reality is often far removed from the formal depiction of how the political system operates. One political scientist writing in 1997, has captured something of the complexity of Vietnamese politics a decade into reform, viewing "the party as consisting of clusters of interests" reflecting the increasing organisational complexity of the party apparatus itself. The author also seeks to get away from the idea that policy-making is "concentrated in the hands of a small number of top leaders", or in a monolithic party. Instead, the author emphasises the importance of "vertical relationships between different tiers of party members and connections between party members and their constituencies outside the party apparatus" in influencing the policy-making process.

A major difficulty, which renders risk analysis on the part of businesses operating in Vietnam that much more problematic, is the closed nature of the political system. The result is that it is very difficult to decipher which interests are likely to predominate in a given situation. As a basic rule of thumb, it is wise to view power as generally being scattered between a myriad of different political and economic institutions, which tend to defend their 'patch' strongly. Both the military and police have more influence than their formal position suggests. Interests associated with the state economic sector, which often embody party interests, tend to wield above average influence. Provincial, city party and government interests will often resent interference from the centre, but will not always be able to avoid it. Similarly, district level authorities frequently do not work well with their city counterparts while rivalry between government institutions at the same level is commonplace. The result is a high degree of unpredictability for all involved – whether in positions of authority, international and local businesses, or the population at large. The political culture is also highly nepotistic, although there are moves to make it more meritocratic. This unpredictability and nepotism have spawned a system of political "umbrellas", whereby people in senior positions offer support, protection and career advancement to those in junior positions.

Most of the time, therefore, power is scattered, with all the problems that this brings. However, in certain situations, the political centre does clamp down to reassert order. In the past, this has included such things as excessive property speculation or black market trading. Clamp downs also occur as part of an orchestrated campaign – smuggling being a good example. In these circumstances, the centre or local party-state can show itself to be quite powerful. However, its ability – or as is often the case, its desire – to maintain such a 'hard line' is usually limited.

Foreign Policy

Strengthening Relations With The USA

Relations with the USA have been on a gradually improving trend since the establishment of diplomatic relations in 1995. A high point was the visit to Vietnam of the US defence secretary, William Cohen, in March 2000 – the first such visit since the end of the Vietnam War in 1975. However, still outstanding is a bilateral trade accord which will clear the way for the USA to award Vietnam normal trade relations (NTR). The trade accord was signed in principle in July 1999 but the government then balked at taking the next step. The delay is thought to relate more to domestic political manoeuvring rather than specific problems with the accord, although there are those in Hanoi who believe that Washington has been overly severe in forcing concessions. Beyond trade issues, relations with the USA have been troubled periodically by differences over human rights – notably over the arrest or imprisonment of Vietnamese dissidents.

Integration With Asean

The development of relations with the Association of South East Asian Nations (Asean) – like improved ties with the USA – provides one of the firmest guarantees of stability in Vietnam's external environment over the next few years. For Vietnam, relations both with the USA and Asean are viewed as providing at least a measure of protection against a potentially overbearing China. The holding of the annual Asean summit meeting in Hanoi in December 1998 was viewed as a major diplomatic triumph in Vietnam, providing a stark illustration of just how much the situation has changed from the 1980s, when Vietnam was a pariah nation in South East Asia. It was a disappointment for the Vietnamese government that Cambodia's membership of Asean was not cemented at the summit. However, a ceremony was held in April 1999 in Hanoi when Cambodia was formally admitted.

Better If Mistrustful Relations With China

There are a number of more overt tensions in Vietnam's foreign relations. The principal one concerns the territorial dispute with China over the Spratly Islands in the South China Sea. There has been a long-standing history of mistrust, and Vietnam and China's rival claims to sovereignty over the Spratly Islands in the South China Sea periodically lead to sharp diplomatic exchanges. However, in general, relations with China are on a much firmer footing compared with the early 1990s, driven by commercial ties and a sense of shared challenges as surviving communist parties in a post-communist world. During a visit to China in 1999, Vietnam's general secretary, Le Kha Phieu, emphasised the need for China and Vietnam to "compare notes and share experiences" as reforming socialist countries. Moreover, the two countries signed an agreement settling the demarcation of their 1,200km land border in December 1999 and have pledged to resolve outstanding territorial differences in the Tonkin Gulf in 2000.

Cambodian Instability

The other potential trouble spot in Vietnam's foreign policy environment involves relations with Cambodia. During 1999, the country was more stable, but problems in recent years have included border disputes, disagreements over shipping rights on the Mekong river and anti-Vietnamese sentiment in Cambodia, including attacks on ethnic Vietnamese living there. However, the government in Phnom Penh is dominated by the pro-Vietnamese Cambodian People's Party and this has made managing relations easier. Vietnam's invasion and occupation of Cambodia in the late 1970s and 1980s proved very costly and there is no desire to repeat the experience.

2 Economic Outlook

Introduction

Growth Curbed By Slow Reform

Preliminary data for H1 2000 show a recovery after the sharp slowdown that followed the Asian economic crisis. Most striking has been the rapid acceleration in private sector industrial growth. The private sector has long been discriminated against and although such problems have not disappeared there have recently been improvements. Equally, export growth has bounced back as regional economic demand has recovered. However, not all the data are so promising. Serious problems remain in the agricultural sector, which are curbing growth.

Foreign investment, both in terms of approvals and disbursals, is still dramatically down on historical levels. Moreover, although the government has not been wholly idle in the aftermath of the Asian crisis in terms of tackling the structural problems that are holding the economy back, progress is often painfully slow. A key constraint – possibly the most serious one – is weak state capacity. This means that reforms continually run up against – and can often founder on – the hidden agendas and vested interests of different levels of the party, government and bureaucracy. Enhanced state capacity will only emerge very gradually. Political manoeuvring in early 2000 has delayed the signing of a bilateral trade accord with the US, with economic repercussions well into the forecast period. While the accord remains unsigned, the US market will remain largely closed to Vietnamese manufactured exports, with an associated drag on foreign investment inflows.

The high hopes of the early 1990s have evaporated. Without faster progress on reform, growth will remain below the peaks of the last decade.

Economic Activity

A Slower Growth Trajectory

Economic data for H1 2000, suggest a recovery. Preliminary H1 GDP growth is put at 6.2%, after only 4.8% growth in 1999. Most promising is the performance of the industrial sector. According to government data, industrial output growth in the January-June period was 14.5% y-o-y, the highest since 1997 after 10.8% in 1999. The turnaround has been sharpest in the non-state or private sector, which registered output growth of 18.5% in H1. This appears in part to reflect official measures introduced with the Enterprise Law in January 2000 that have cut red tape and resulted in a surge in new industrial start-ups. Growth of state industry has bounced back into double digits (12% y-o-y in H1) after managing no more than 4% growth last year.

The official figures almost certainly exaggerate the true picture but nevertheless suggest a positive trend. Given sluggish domestic demand, the recovery appears predominantly to be export-led, reflecting higher regional demand as Vietnam's neighbours overcome the worst effects of the Asian crisis. The government has sought to stimulate the economy by increasing capital expenditure. However, with revenue growth lagging it is far from clear that expenditure targets will be met. Reports in early 2000 suggest that domestic investment is continuing to lag as a result of unresolved problems in the banking sector. Foreign investment in the first four months of the year fell 43% in terms of approvals.

Leaner Years

Vietnam - real GDP growth, % y-o-y

e/f = BMI estimate/forecast; Source: Ho Chi Minh City Statistical Yearbook/BMI.

GDP, OUTPUT & POPULATION								
	1994	1995	1996	1997	1998	1999e	2000f	2001f	2002f
Nominal GDP (US$bn)	15.5	20.3	23.4	25.3	25.5	26.4	28.7	30.7	34.5
Population (mn)	72.5	74.0	75.4	76.7	78.1	79.5	80.9	82.4	83.9
GDP per capita (US$)	214.2	273.9	311.1	329.5	327.1	331.8	354.3	372.8	411.1
Real GDP growth (% y/y)	8.8	9.5	9.3	8.8	5.8	4.8	5.8	5.5	6.5
Industrial production (% y/y)	13.7	14.0	13.8	13.8	12.1	10.8	11.5	11.2	11.8

e/f = BMI estimate/forecast; Sources: Ho Chi Minh City Statistical Yearbook/World Bank/BMI.

Against this rather mixed backdrop, **BMI** is forecasting GDP growth of 5.8% in 2000, up from an official figure of 4.8% in 1999. Industrial output growth in 2000 is likely to be 11.5% y-o-y compared with 10.8% in 1999. Looking further ahead, we expect GDP growth to slow slightly in 2001, easing to 5.5% as regional demand eases off, oil prices fall and in the absence of strong measures to boost investment. But it will recover in 2002, possibly reaching as much as 6.5%, if the trade accord with the US is signed in time to boost investment and export prospects in that year.

During 2000-02 the government will make limited progress in dealing with banking sector problems, which is likely to hinder credit growth. Moreover, Vietnam's reputation as a difficult and over-priced investment destination coupled with the delay in signing the bilateral trade accord with the US will combine to prevent anything but a gradual recovery in foreign investment inflows until 2002.

Unemployment Rate Will Remain High

Job creation in the industrial sector will only have a limited impact on current unemployment levels with a labour force growth of about 1mn a year. Urban unemployment is likely to hover at a rather high 8% during the forecast period, falling slightly below this level in 2002. The total labour force is estimated to be around 40mn, of which about two thirds are employed in agriculture. Along with more modest economic growth compared with the mid-1990s, this will limit upward pressure on wages. However, pressure for wage increase is likely to increase towards the end of the forecast period as inflation begins to rise.

Fiscal Policy

Fiscal Deficit Rising

In the wake of the economic slowdown the government has sought to apply fiscal stimulus to encourage growth. However, it has been only partially successful since it was forced to cut back on planned capital expenditure in 1999 when revenue collection fell below target and disbursement of overseas development aid slowed. Capital expenditure has hovered at about 5.5% of GDP in recent years. During 2000-02, the tax take is likely to recover in nominal terms on the back of the strengthening economy. Incomplete fiscal data for the first quarter suggests revenue receipts were below target in some areas: reduced revenue from businesses licenses following cuts in licensing with the business law, for example. However, overall, we are forecasting an

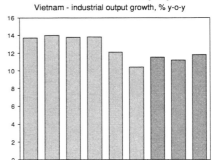

No Return To The Heydays
Vietnam - industrial output growth, % y-o-y

e/f = BMI estimate/forecast; Source: Ho Chi Minh City Statistical Yearbook/BMI.

Unemployment will remain the most serious issue and the chief focus of policy.

Government revenue targets will be missed and expenditure will have to be curbed if the deficit is to be held to the level agreed with the National Assembly.

increase in revenue in absolute terms in 2000 with gains coming from both the acceleration in external trade and stronger growth in the state sector. Aid disbursals are also running strongly, suggesting that capital expenditure will meet its targets. Over the forecast period, the government is committed to lowering import tariffs in line with its membership of the Association of Southeast Asian Nation (Asean) and its associated Asean Free Trade Area (AFTA). Cuts in import tariffs are being made annually with a view to reducing tariffs to below 5% on a wide range of products by 2006. This will result in a fall-off in revenue from this source during 2000-02, although it will be offset by increased revenue from the private sector and from VAT, which the government introduced in January 1999. The introduction of VAT has not gone smoothly. However, changes are likely to be made during the forecast period, which will result in a more effective tax system and ultimately higher revenue.

During the next three years, there are also likely to be efforts to levy personal income tax on Vietnamese citizens, although it will remain a minor source of revenue. Despite the expected rise in nominal revenue, the tax take is likely to fall in GDP terms in 2000 before stabilising in 2001-02 at around 18% of GDP. This is still significantly down on levels reached in the early 1990s.

During 2000-02 the government will again attempt to raise capital expenditure in a bid to stimulate growth. Increased spending is likely to be targeted at infrastructure, notably rural infrastructure. However, the government's now well-demonstrated determination to keep the fiscal deficit within prudent limits will once more oblige it to put projects on hold if revenue is lower than targeted or there are problems in aid disbursement. In 2000, we expect the budget deficit to rise to 5% of GDP – the maximum permitted level agreed last year with the National Assembly – before falling back to 4.5% and 4.0% in 2001 and 2002 respectively. The government will finance the deficit by non-inflationary means, namely foreign borrowing and grants along with domestic bond issues. The higher deficit means it is now much more reliant on foreign capital sources than in previous years. However, this dependence will ease from 2001.

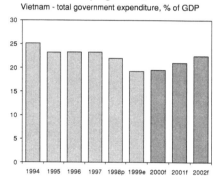

Pumping Growth
Vietnam - total government expenditure, % of GDP

p = preliminary, e = official estimate, f = BMI forecast; Source: World Bank.

Monetary Policy

Cautious Monetary Policy Loosening Is Possible

The government has not relaxed monetary policy despite the economic slowdown. This reflects its deep-seated concern about fuelling inflation despite the fact that it is at historical lows. Nominal interest rates on dong loans have been repeatedly lowered. In May 2000, they stood at 0.85% per month. Lending rates have been at this level since end-1999. However, rates have fallen more slowly than inflation with the result that real lending rates are in fact higher than a year ago. There have been some hints of disagreement between the State Bank of Vietnam and the finance ministry on monetary policy with the finance ministry favouring greater loosening than the State Bank. Monetary policy may be relaxed a little in the early part of the forecast period, but it will be tightened again at the first sign of a pickup in inflation. The government has said it is aiming for domestic credit growth of just over 20% per annum during 2000-01. This compares with around 14% in 1999, suggesting some loosening of monetary policy is likely.

The repeated lowering of lending rates has caused difficulties for the banks, which have become reluctant to lend. This is naturally harming credit expansion. Such problems should ease somewhat during 2000-01, both as problems in the banking system are gradually addressed and as rates rise with higher inflation later in the forecast period. The government has recently been talking about allowing interest rates to be more market determined. However, this has not been matched by concrete actions and its plans currently appear to be on hold. By the end of the forecast period, administrative controls on interest rates are likely to have been reduced but moves in this direction will be cautious

Government targets suggest it is planning a slight loosening of monetary policy in 2000-01. However, the State Bank is likely to urge caution.

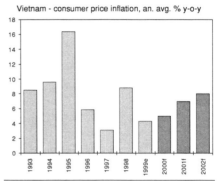

Inflation No Concern Yet
Vietnam - consumer price inflation, an. avg. % y-o-y

e/f = BMI estimate/forecast; Source: General Statistical Office/BMI.

CONSUMER PRICES									
	1994	1995	1996	1997	1998	1999e	2000f	2001f	2002f
CPI (% y/y, period avg)	9.6	16.4	5.9	3.1	8.8	4.3	5.0	7.0	8.0
CPI (% y/y, eop)	14.5	12.7	4.5	3.6	9.5	0.1	5.0	7.5	9.0
e/f = BMI estimate/forecast; eop = end of period; Sources: Ho Chi Minh City Statistical Yearbook/World Bank/BMI.									

Inflation Will Remain In Single Digits

In 1999 annual inflation was 4.3%, down from 8.8% in 1998. In March, April and May 2000, the economy saw a return to month-on-month deflation, reflecting the fact that domestic demand remains weak even though the economy is beginning to recover. Even in the run-up to the Tet Lunar New Year holiday – usually a time of sharp price rises – inflation rose very little. In May 2000, prices fell 2.3% y-o-y and dropped 0.6% on the month. During 2000-02, we expect inflation to pick up as the economic recovery becomes more entrenched. However, it is likely to remain in single digits throughout the forecast period. This reflects the fact that growth is not likely to return to the highs of the mid-1990s. The slight depreciation in the dong expected over the next three years is likely to contribute to slightly higher inflation. The running of a larger budget deficit in 2000-01 will not be inflationary because it will not be financed by printing money.

Exchange Rate Policy

Dong Will Depreciate Gradually

The government has long favoured a policy of allowing the dong to depreciate very gradually. This reflects its desire to build confidence in the local currency, and not fuel inflation or aggravate the debt payment burden of state-owned enterprises. During the Asian financial crisis it was unable to sustain this position, but it has successfully resumed it since Q4 98.

During 1999 and in the first half of 2000 the dong has been very stable against leading currencies. Since February 1999 the authorities have run a 'managed float' exchange rate. In Vietnam's case this means that the currency can fluctuate daily within a narrow 1% band either side of the previous day's interbank market rate. Given market belief that the dong is overvalued – it is in fact no longer so overvalued against regional currencies – it might have been expected to fall by the maximum amount each day. However, the depreciation has been much slower than this, reflecting the fact that the authorities are tending to intervene at the end of each day's trading to skew the average interbank rate.

In Q2 2000, a small differential (VND100-200) opened up between the interbank and black market exchange rate, the result of higher demand for dollars as imports have risen with the economic recovery. This pattern may well reoccur throughout the forecast period and if shortages of foreign exchange become acute the authorities could be forced to devalue the

With Vietnam on a lower growth trajectory, the danger of overheating in 2000-02 is much reduced.

Foreign exchange shortages could force the government to devalue, but downward adjustments of more than 5% are unlikely.

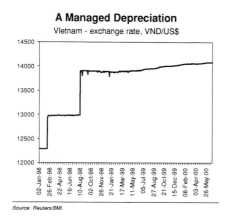

A Managed Depreciation
Vietnam - exchange rate, VND/US$

Source: Reuters/BMI.

currency at a faster rate than they prefer. During 2000-02 we expect a fall in the dong of around 9%. This incorporates a larger devaluation of around 5% later in the forecast period, which we have factored in for 2001.

Dong Convertibility Is Still Some Years Off

The government says it is still committed to making the dong fully convertible on the current account, although it has not set a target date for this. Progress will to a large extent depend on the speed at which exports develop and reserves grow. **BMI** would be surprised if current account convertibility was achieved during the forecast period. One tactic the authorities may adopt during the next three years is to widen the band within which the dong can fluctuate. This would at least make the currency more market determined. The size of the reserves is not routinely released since they are considered a state secret. However, a leaked figure in June 1999 suggested they were worth US$2.2bn, which is equivalent to around 10 weeks imports. We are forecasting a gradual strengthening of reserves during 2000-02.

The government imposes strict capital controls both on the inflow and outflow of currency. Capital controls were tightened during the Asian financial crisis and have not yet been relaxed. In 2000 only US$500 could be taken out of the country without declaration, down from US$7,000 a few years ago. Although this figure is likely to be increased during the forecast period, strict capital controls will remain in place.

Although current account convertibility is a goal, it is still some time away.

EXCHANGE RATE									
	1994	**1995**	**1996**	**1997**	**1998**	**1999**	**2000f**	**2001f**	**2002f**
VND/US$ (an. avg)	10960	11000	11031	11700	13267	14100	14132	14646	15153
VND/US$ (eop)	10955	11016	11085	12297	13892	14016	14288	15003	15303
e/f = BMI estimate/forecast; eop = end of period; Source: Reuters.									

Balance Of Payments

A widening current account deficit will not rival the pre-Asian crisis highs or present serious financing problems.

Trade Deficit Set To Widen Again

Galvanised by the downturn in the external sector that followed the Asian financial crisis, the government has taken steps to stimulate exports. These have mainly focused on cutting red tape but have also included the abolition of restrictions that forbade private companies from exporting directly. Although it is taking time for companies to reap the dividends – especially in terms of private companies breaking into export markets hitherto dominated by state firms – the benefits are gradually beginning to show and further gains are likely to become evident over the forecast period. In recent years, Vietnamese exporters have made great strides in terms of increasing garments and footwear exports and this, along with the development of other light manufactured exports, is likely to continue in 2000-02.

After bouncing back in 1999, export growth has been even faster in 2000. During the first six months of the year, exports were up 26.2% y-o-y in dollar value. Higher oil prices accounted for half the increment, but sales of commodities (excluding rice and coffee) were well up and exports of textiles and garments rose 5.2%. We are forecasting annual average export growth of around 20% in dollar terms over the next three years, reflecting continued strong demand in Asia and the EU as well as the beginnings of the benefit which will accrue from access to the US market following the award of most favoured nation (MFN) trading status. This depends on the government signing the bilateral trade accord with the US, which we expect in early 2001, with the effects showing through in 2002. Breaking into the US market will not be easy given stiff competition from other producers, but inroads are likely to be made. The award of MFN may also be followed quite quickly by the imposition of quota restrictions on Vietnamese garment and footwear exporters, but there will still be plenty of scope for growth. The exchange rate, which will be gradually depreciating over the forecast period, will not have a constraining effect on exporters.

Bouncing Back
Vietnam - merchandise trade growth, % y-o-y

f = BMI forecast; Source: World Bank/BMI.

BALANCE OF PAYMENTS (US$BN)								
	1994	**1995**	**1996**	**1997**	**1998**	**1999e**	**2000f**	**2001f**	**2002f**
Exports (fob)	4.05	5.20	7.33	9.15	9.37	11.50	14.50	16.70	20.50
Imports (fob)	5.25	7.54	10.48	10.46	10.35	11.60	16.00	19.20	22.60
Trade balance	-1.20	-2.35	-3.15	-1.36	-1.03	-0.10	-1.50	-2.50	-2.10
Current account	-1.19	-1.93	-2.44	-1.70	-1.07	-1.00	-1.20	-1.30	-1.20
Current account (% GDP)	-7.63	-9.52	-10.42	-6.71	-4.20	-3.79	-4.19	-4.23	-3.48

e/f = BMI estimate/forecast; Sources: Ho Chi Minh City Statistical Yearbook/World Bank/BMI.

Imports have bounced back strongly in H1 2000, rising 32.9% y-o-y and taking the trade deficit to US$677mn, up from only US$232mn in H1 99. The import bill has been boosted by higher prices for oil products, although it also reflects moves by domestic firms to resume importing amid signs of an upturn in demand: imports of steel for example rose 43% y-o-y in value. This is likely to continue, with a small deceleration possible in 2001 as growth dips. We are consequently forecasting nearly 25% annual average import growth in 2000-02. The trade deficit will rise as a result, although it will stay below the highs of the mid-1990s.

The services deficit is expected to increase in 2000-01, reflecting higher trade turnover although it is likely to level off in 2002. However, this will be partly offset by strong growth in tourism. On the capital account, an increase in repatriated profits over the next three years is likely to be roughly matched by transfers into the country by overseas Vietnamese and improved disbursement of aid. The larger trade and services deficit will swell the current-account deficit but it will moderate by historical standards and will be relatively easily financed by a mixture of overseas aid and to a lesser extent foreign investment.

Imports Boosted By Oil Price Surge
Vietnam - merchandise trade deficit, US$bn

f = BMI forecast; Source: World Bank/BMI.

Foreign Direct Investment

Foreign Investment Unlikely To Recover Fast

In 1999 foreign direct investment fell to its lowest level since the early 1990s, both in terms of projects approved and actual investment. In 2000 approved investment is likely to fall further. In the first five months, the government approved 90 projects worth just US$252mn, down 43% on the same period last year. Actual investment in 2000 is likely to increase very slightly on the previous year's low, reflecting improving balance sheets amongst regional investors and the fact that there are still many projects that have been licensed but were put on hold either because of the Asian financial crisis or for other reasons. So far this year most of the approved investment has come from Taiwan, Australia and Japan. Both approved and actual investment is likely to pick up in 2001-02 although the rate of increase will at first be sluggish and the level of investment will not return to the highs of the mid-1990s. There are a number of large infrastructure projects in the pipeline, notably in power generation, while there is also the US$1.5bn **BP-Amoco** Nam Con Son gas project. If these are approved, they would push the foreign investment figures higher than the levels we are currently forecasting.

The government faces major problems wooing a jaded foreign investor community. The US trade accord and will help, as will unblocking some large projects.

In June 2000 the National Assembly passed amendments to the Law on Foreign Investment. The changes focus on land issues, the transfer of business ownership and the legal framework for infrastructure projects and dispute resolution – all of which were greatly needed. However, what was actually passed was considerably less liberal than the revisions originally put forward. Indeed the debate in the National Assembly symbolised much that is still wrong with the foreign investment regime in Vietnam. Some delegates, it appears, continue to view foreign companies primarily as a source of tax revenue, something which the Minister of Planning and Investment, Tran Xuan Gia, was at pains to correct. It is unlikely that amendments to the foreign investment law will have a major impact on investment flows during 2000-02.

More likely to propel a gradual recovery in investment, is access to the US market later in the forecast period, following the signing of the stalled bilateral trade accord. Also on the horizon is the planned phasing out by 2001 of the dual pricing system, where foreigners pay more than local for utility and other services. This would also represent an important step forward. Progress in this area is likely to be made but we suspect there could be some slippage in terms of timing.

Ongoing government moves to reduce red tape along with its more flexible attitude on allowing companies to form 100% foreign-owned entities should also result in a gradual improvement in the level of foreign capital inflows. Part of the problem at the moment is that whatever the government does it continues to receive bad press because the large gap between expectations and reality in the mid- and late-1990s has made investors cynical. While the investment environment in Vietnam in the next three years will neither be easy nor as cheap as its low cost labour label suggests, it is likely to become more price competitive and somewhat less weighed down by red tape.

Waning Interest

Vietnam capital investment by country to date, US$mn

Source: Vietnam Investment Review.

	1995	1996	1997	1998	1999e	2000f	2001f	2002f
			FOREIGN DIRECT INVESTMENT (US$BN)					
Approvals	6.6	8.5	4.5	1.8	1.3	0.8	1.0	1.4
Actual	1.8	2.3	2.4	0.6	0.7	0.7	0.8	0.9

e/f = BMI estimate/forecast; Ministry of Planning & Investment; World Bank.

Equitisation Will Remain Limited

The government continues to pursue a policy of selling shares in state-owned enterprises, known locally as equitisation. A handful of foreign companies have successfully bought shares in Vietnamese firms. However, identifying good prospects and getting permission to invest is both difficult and time-consuming. Foreign companies are also limited to owning a maximum 30% stake in a local company. Over the forecast period opportunities for foreign investors in this area are likely to remain limited.

Opportunities to buy into domestic companies will be limited by the quality of companies available.

External Debt

Rising Debt Stock But Lower Debt Service Ratio

The World Bank classifies Vietnam as a severely indebted country, qualifying for relief measure under the heavily-indebted poor country (HIPC) initiative. Excluding the non-convertible debt owed mainly to Russia, the World Bank estimated Vietnam's debt stock at US$11.14bn at the end of 1999, or around 40% of GDP. Two-thirds of this is public or publicly guaranteed. Around half the debt is concessional. Vietnam's non-concessional debt is mainly linked to foreign investment projects. By 2002, total debt stock is forecast to rise to over US$15bn. Most of the increase will come from official creditors on concessional terms. Access to commercial borrowing will remain limited, with very few entities able to contemplate such borrowing. Certainly amongst senior officials there is recognition of the dangers to macroeconomic stability of drawing on non-concessional sources.

Talks have taken place on and off for years with Russia on the non-convertible debt. However, the two sides have been unable to agree on a rouble exchange rate. Vietnam has successfully concluded debt agreements with other former Eastern bloc countries and we expect an agreement will be reached with Russia during the forecast period. This is expected to take the form of a part write-off and part rescheduling of the debt. We have factored this in for our forecast for 2001, which lies behind the quite large increase in total debt stock that year. However, the impact on the debt service ratio will be limited, given rising exports of goods and services.

A rescheduling of the rouble debt owed to Russia will increase the total debt stock during the forecast period. While it can borrow from official sources, the government will avoid incurring commercial debt.

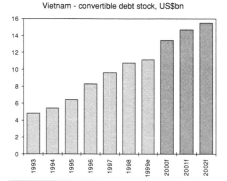

A Rising Burden
Vietnam - convertible debt stock, US$bn

e = World Bank estimate; f = BMI forecast; Source: World Bank.

DEBT STOCK									
	1994	1995	1996	1997	1998	1999e	2000f	2001f	2002f
External debt (US$bn)*	5.43	6.45	8.28	9.59	10.76	11.14	13.46	13.82	14.38
External debt (% GDP)	34.95	31.84	35.32	37.95	42.13	42.23	46.95	47.86	44.95

*e/f = BMI estimate/forecast; *convertible; Sources: Ho Chi Minh City Statistical Yearbook/World Bank/BMI.*

The debt service ratio has declined since the early-1990s. This partly reflects debt agreements with both the Paris and London Clubs in 1992 and 1998 respectively. In 1999 the World Bank estimated the debt service ratio at 15.3%. It is forecast to fall to below 11% by 2002.

Profile and Recent Developments

Economic Background

Characteristics Of The Economy

Although Vietnam has a large population, its economy is small in comparison to its regional neighbours. In 1999, GDP stood at US$26.4bn, up from US$23.4bn in 1996. This translates into annual income per capita at a very low US$332. GDP per capita is growing at a slower pace than nominal GDP: in 1995-99, it rose by an annual average of 5.5%, compared with growth in nominal GDP of 7.7%. Per capita income growth has slowed significantly since 1998, reflecting both slower economic growth and the fact that annual population growth has been averaging a relatively high 1.9%. There is, however, considerable regional variation in terms of annual income. Annual average per capita income is around US$1,000 in Ho Chi Minh City, while income levels in a number of other larger cities are also considerably above the national average. In 1999, Vietnam's population was estimated to be around 79.5mn.

Industry And Services Contribution To Total Output Has Risen

The economy remains predominantly rural in terms of the percentage of the population living and working in the countryside. However, the reform years have been characterised by a fall in the contribution of agriculture to GDP. In 1998, agriculture, forestry and fisheries contributed 23.5% to total output, down from 26.3% in 1995. The decline in the importance of the agricultural sector in GDP terms has been matched by steady growth in industry and construction as a percentage of total output. Industry and construction accounted for 34.0% of GDP in 1998, compared with 29.9% in 1995. Services, although contributing the largest share to GDP, has been static in terms of its contribution to total output since 1995. Another change during the 1990s has been the emergence of new industrial sectors, such as textiles and garments, food processing, electronics and plastics. Much of this has been on the back of foreign direct investment (FDI), despite total inflows into Vietnam having declined since 1996. The commanding heights of industry are still dominated by state companies. In services, the private sector has a greater role, although state firms often predominate in peak distribution.

The emergence of new light industrial sectors has had an impact on the structure of exports. Garments, shoes and sandals in particular are now significant export earners. However, on the whole, Vietnam's exports are still dominated by primary products, such as rice and various other agricultural products, reflecting the relatively undeveloped nature of its industrial sector. Vietnam also exports all but a fraction of its crude oil output, although it is a small producer in global terms. Apart from oil, the country's resource endowment includes significant quantities of natural gas, coal, iron ore, manganese, gold and bauxite. The agriculture, fisheries and forestry sectors also represent an important resource base, although there are problems with the latter relating to its unsustainable exploitation.

The Economy Shifts To A Slower Growth Trajectory

During 1996-99, real GDP growth averaged 7.2% per annum. However, in the period 1998-99, growth had slowed to 5.3%. The beginnings of an economic slowdown first became perceptible in 1996 before the Asian financial crisis struck, with a slight drop in growth that year. This reflected slower growth in services and in agriculture rather than industry, which according to revised government figures saw a higher growth rate in 1996 compared to 1995. Signs of a slowdown became more evident in 1997, although it was as much rooted in domestic economic circumstances as the impact of the Asian financial crisis. Industrial growth slowed sharply in 1997 as companies reined in production, faced with rising stockpiles in the light of weak consumption. The slowdown reflected a range of others factors, too. Overall business sentiment had suffered a knock in the wake of the bursting of the property bubble from 1995 and a downturn in foreign investor sentiment. There were also serious problems in the banking sector, which curbed the availability of credit, including foreign exchange. Furthermore, strict administrative restrictions on imports in 1996 may have reduced the availability of essential inputs needed for industrial production, with consequences in 1997.

The extent of the economic downturn was much more dramatic in 1998 and 1999, when growth fell to 5.8% and 4.8% respectively, according to government estimates. The World Bank and the IMF dispute these figures, suggesting that growth in these years was no more than 3-4%. Whatever the actual GDP figures, the sharp fall in growth relative to earlier years reflected the impact of the Asian crisis, which led to a fall in export demand – notably in neighbouring Asean countries – and lower investment. This, in turn, had knock-on effects for both domestic demand and local investment.

Industrial growth averaged 11.3% in 1998-99, compared with a trend rate of 13.6% for the previous three years. The real laggard in the industrial sector in 1999 was state-owned industry, which for the first time grew more slowly than the non-state sector, which showed unprecedented buoyancy in the second half of the year. Slower economic growth in 1999 paradoxically occurred despite a partial recovery in export demand and, by some accounts, a slight strengthening of domestic consumption. However, the slowdown almost certainly reflects the delayed impact of lower levels of approved foreign investment since 1997. Slower services growth in 1998-99 followed a downturn in tourism, financial services and the real estate market.

Slower growth in 1998-99, particularly in 1999 when regional economies were strengthening, also reflects limited progress on key structural reforms. This includes state enterprise and banking reform, moves towards dong convertibility on the current account, and the ironing out of obstacles in the foreign investment and trade environment, which are restraining business activity, and hence the potential for economic growth. Nevertheless, some progress was made during these years. The procedures for establishing a private company were greatly simplified in 1999 with the introduction of a new Business Law, while changes were also introduced in the area of foreign exchange liberalisation, partially reversing the backward steps introduced in the face of exchange rate turbulence in 1998. Moreover, state enterprise and banking reform remained on the agenda. That said, results continued to fall short of intentions so that administrative and political obstacles to business activity remained a problem. In such a climate, a rather bruised foreign business community remained deeply sceptical.

Unemployment Is High

Reliable nationwide employment data is sparse. However, the picture is of a rapidly growing labour force given that the population is a young one. **BMI** estimates the labour force numbered around 40mn in 1999. During the late-1980s and early-1990s, unemployment rose substantially in the face of layoffs from the state sector and demobilisation following the military withdrawal from Cambodia. Employment creation was rapid during the 1992-96 period, although there was little change in unemployment levels owing to the continued sharp rise in new entrants to the labour force. The economic downturn, especially in 1998-99, has resulted in substantial job losses and a rise in urban unemployment levels. According to figures released by the Ministry of Labour, War Invalids and Social Affairs, urban unemployment in 1998 was six times higher than the previous year. In Hanoi, 9.1% of the labour force were unemployed in 1998 compared with 7.7% in 1997. In Ho Chi Minh City, unemployment was 6.8% in 1998, although no corresponding figure for 1997 is available. These figures may well be an underestimate, especially if one includes the large numbers of rural migrants who come to the city in the hope of finding work.

Fiscal Policy

Smaller Budget Deficits

During the 1990s, fiscal management improved, resulting in smaller budget deficits compared with the previous decade. In 1996-99, the budget deficit averaged around 3.7% of GDP. The government has consistently shown itself willing to postpone capital expenditure if revenue targets are not met. Financing the budget deficit has not been a major problem given the availability of foreign aid and loans. The deficit has also been financed by domestic bond issues. Nevertheless, tax evasion in all sectors of society, including the state and private sector and in the area of personal income tax, remains a major problem that is curbing further revenue gains.

Slower economic growth in the face of domestic and regional difficulties has led to a more difficult fiscal situation since 1997, with the result that revenue and expenditure, although increasing in nominal terms, have fallen as a percentage of GDP. The bulk of revenue (around 40%) comes from taxes on state-owned enterprises (SOEs) and trade tariffs (around 25%). However, the importance of SOEs in terms of revenue collection is declining. As recently as 1993, their contribution was as high as 50%. The introduction of a value-added tax (VAT) in 1999 was designed to compensate for the loss of customs revenue anticipated as tariff barriers are brought down, although the early application of the tax left a lot to be desired. Both the non-state sector and foreign-invested enterprises contribute more to total revenue compared with earlier in the 1990s.

Monetary Policy

Consistently Tight Monetary Policy

In terms of both domestic credit growth and total liquidity (M2), the 1996-99 period has seen the government maintain a considerably tighter monetary policy compared with earlier in the decade. This has been maintained during 1998-99 despite the economic slowdown, reflecting government concerns about fuelling inflation even at a time when it was at a historical low. According to the State Bank of Vietnam, domestic credit growth in 1999 was 14.2% y-o-y compared with 20.1% in 1998. Total liquidity growth was also slower in 1999 at 24% y-o-y compared with 26% in 1998. This tightening of monetary policy has largely been achieved via direct central bank controls on credit expansion, notably credit ceilings on bank lending. Interest rates are still relatively ineffective at regulating monetary growth.

Trends in interest rates reflect the classic tussle between wanting to push credit out to enterprises and farmers – necessitating low lending rates – while at the same time seeking to improve domestic capital mobilisation via the banking system, requiring positive real interest rates. The government still imposes ceilings on maximum permitted lending rates, which in turn results in commercial banks offering low deposit rates to protect margins. Nominal interest rates were lowered repeatedly in 1998 and 1999. However, rates have fallen more slowly than inflation, resulting in a significant upward shift in real interest rates in 1999 relative to 1998.

Exchange Rate Policy

The Currency Escaped The Worst Of The Asian Crisis

Vietnam's currency has fallen much less sharply than many of its regional neighbours since the onset of the Asian financial crisis in July 1997, reflecting the fact that the exchange rate is still tightly controlled. However, the country has experienced its own mini version of currency instability, the impact of which has been severe even if the margins by which the dong has fallen have been relatively small. After some years of stability, downward pressure on the dong first became evident in 1996, amid a perception that the currency was overvalued and as foreign investment began to slow. In the aftermath of the Asian crisis, the dong was devalued three times – in October 1997, February 1998 and August 1998 – resulting in a total depreciation of 18.5%. Much of 1997-98 was characterised by intense shortages of foreign exchange, reflected in liquidity shortages on the interbank market and heightened black market trading. In 1997, banks heavily over-issued deferred payment Letters of Credit (LCs), which, as they came due, resulted in strong demand for foreign exchange, causing repayment difficulties. During 1999, the foreign exchange shortages witnessed in the previous two years eased considerably, reflecting the contraction in imports. As a result, the dong was largely stable in 1999, depreciating by less than 1%.

The exchange rate turbulence of 1997-98 led to the introduction of tighter foreign exchange controls. In September 1998, the government introduced Decree 173, whereby all domestic firms and foreign companies with State Bank foreign exchange guarantees were required to sell 80% of their surplus foreign exchange holdings to banks within 15 days. This was later changed to immediate sale after companies used the 15-day period to evade the restriction. In addition, the government lowered the amount of capital that can be taken out of the country without declaration from US$7,000 to US$3,000 and then to US$500. In 1999, as the exchange rate stabilised, the authorities moved to loosen the restrictions, with the relaxing of Decree 173. Moreover, it also stopped announcing a daily official exchange rate and instead shifted to a "crawling peg" system, whereby the exchange rate is calculated on the basis of the average interbank market exchange rate of the previous day. While the new system has the potential to be more market-oriented, the exchange rate is currently unable to move more than 0.1% either side of the interbank rate each day. The restrictions on taking capital out of the country remain in force.

External Trade

Not As Buoyant As In Past Times

During 1996-99, exports averaged annual growth of 21.0% and import growth at 10.3%. There has been, however, wide variation from year to year. In 1996, both exports and imports grew in excess of 30%, while in 1998 export and import growth was very small. In 1997, the first effects of the Asian financial crisis began to be felt, although the slowdown in exports was quite small, suggesting it may have had more to do with the cyclical downturn in the Vietnamese economy. Import growth fell sharply in 1997, but this was more the result of administrative curbs on imports imposed by the government after the trade deficit ballooned to US$3.9bn in 1996. In 1998, the impact of the Asian crisis was unmistakable. Export growth was just 0.9%, while imports fell 3%, reflecting a reduction in demand both in Vietnam's main export markets and in the slowing domestic economy. Moreover, it was a loss of demand rather than the relative stability of the dong, compared with regional economies, which was the main cause of the export slowdown. The poor export showing also reflected lower prices for many key export commodities, including crude oil. In volume terms, some sectors saw quite respectable export growth in 1998. During 1999, exports bounced back in terms of dollar earnings growth. This was mainly the result of a sharp rise in the oil price, although there were also some strong volume gains for both primary products and some light manufactures. Imports, meanwhile, grew by just 0.9%, indicating continued weak domestic demand.

Foreign Direct Investment

Foreign Investors Face Red Tape and High Costs

During the first half of the 1990s, Vietnam was one of the most popular foreign direct investment (FDI) destinations in the world, as measured in terms of foreign capital as a percentage of GDP. This began to change around 1996. In statistical terms, approvals peaked in 1996, while disbursements continued rising until 1997. However, a downward trend in foreign investment approvals was perceptible from 1996, although the final year's figures were boosted by two very large investment projects, hastily approved in the final days of the year (one of which has since collapsed). The downturn reflected a realisation among investors that Vietnam was a much more difficult market in which to operate successfully than had been originally thought. Initial expectations, it is now realised, were far too optimistic. Such a change in sentiment came about as hoped-for liberalisation of certain sectors did not happen, or happened much more slowly than had been forecast. It also reflected the fact that as much as the government tinkered with the foreign investment regime, problems of excess bureaucracy and red tape did not disappear. In addition, Vietnam turned out to be more expensive than its low-cost labour label suggested, because of a dual pricing system whereby foreigners paid more for land rents, utility bills and domestic airfares. In

1999, the government announced a timetable to phase out the dual pricing system although it has yet to have much impact on investors.

It is against this backdrop that the impact of the Asian financial crisis must be seen. The regional downturn has greatly exacerbated the slowdown in foreign investment in Vietnam, but it is by no means the only factor. Nevertheless, reflecting the impact of the crisis, foreign investment plummeted in both 1998 and 1999 when approvals fell by 60% respectively. According to the government, disbursements were down 22% at US$1.52bn although this is disputed by the multilateral institutions, which estimate disbursements at US$600mn in 1998. If correct, this would be the lowest level of actual foreign investment since 1992.

Vietnam has historically depended on regional investors for a large proportion of FDI. The top five investors are Singapore, Taiwan, Japan, Hong Kong and South Korea, contributing some 60% of total FDI. As can be seen, ethnic Chinese investors are heavily represented among the top five investors by country. Smaller amounts of ethnic Chinese investment also come from mainland Malaysia, Indonesia and mainland China. A not insignificant amount of ethnic Chinese investment is conducted on an informal basis and does not show up in the statistics. As the Asian crisis struck, and regional currencies were devalued by much larger amounts than in Vietnam, the heavily dollarised nature of the Vietnamese economy became an added disincentive for these investors. Labour costs, land rents and many other business costs, which are all denominated in dollars, became much more expensive, especially for labour intensive operations. Other leading investors come from France, the USA and Australia. However, US investment has been constrained, at least to some extent, by the absence of normal trading relations (NTR).

In the early-1990s, there was a bias in FDI towards hotels and tourism and the oil and gas industry. However, their importance in terms of the sectoral destination of foreign capital has now declined, although hotel and tourism still account for around 22% of total investment. The largest share of investment (33%) has been directed at industry, with heavy industry receiving more than light industry. Popular industrial sectors include steel, cement, plastics, textiles and garments and electronics, although many of these are now suffering from overcapacity. Communications, including telecoms, has received some 9% of the total. Investment in agriculture and forestry has been quite low, at 3% of the total despite government efforts to attract it.

3 Key Economic Sectors

Introduction

A More Subdued Performance

Compared with the 1990s, output growth is likely to be lower in most sectors during 2000-02. On the back of strengthening external and domestic demand, some of the best performers will be in light industry including textiles and garments, shoes, food processing and plastics, even though there are problems with competition and product quality in most of these areas. The award of most favoured nation trading (MFN) status by the USA later in the forecast period will particularly aid garments and shoes. A more promising performance is also forecast in tourism and to some extent in the auto sector.

Formerly rapid growth sectors such as construction, oil and gas, banking and telecoms are likely to be more subdued over the next three years. The recent amendments to the foreign investment law are unlikely to have much impact on investment inflows in the short term, although there is likely to be a slow but gradual pick-up in both domestic and foreign investment during 2001-02. One of the main constraints on the Vietnamese economy – high transaction costs caused by too many licenses, bureaucratic inefficiency and corruption – will continue to exert a drag across the board. However, recent government efforts to cut down on unnecessary red-tape will start to have a positive effect later in the forecast period.

No sector will repeat the growth of the 1990s, but stronger demand, MFN and progress at cutting red tape will aid recovery.

The Lucky Few
Vietnam - capital expenditure to date by sector (as of April 2000)

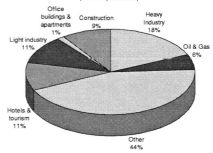

Source: Vietnam Investment Review.

Textiles And Garments

The US Market And Lower Costs Are Key

Growth is likely to pick-up following MFN, but breaking into the US market will not be easy.

In response to higher overseas demand, textiles and garments are likely to achieve higher output growth in 2000-02 compared with the previous three years. Initially increased demand is expected to come from the EU and Japan. Together these markets account for about 80% of Vietnam's textile and garment exports. In April 2000, the government negotiated a 27% increase in the size of its EU quota, effective until end-2001. From 2002, the sector should begin to benefit from access to the US market. However, there will be no export surge reflecting the fact that it will take time for Vietnamese exporters to establish themselves in the US market. Moreover, the experience of other countries is that exporters are likely to quickly encounter quota restrictions following the award of MFN. During 2000-02, **BMI** is forecasting average annual export growth in the sector of about 21%, accelerating slightly later in the forecast period. By 2002, we expect export earnings from textiles and garments will be worth just over US$3bn, compared with US$1.7bn in 1999.

Apart from a lack of access to the US market, the principal constraint on the sector's expansion will be its tendency towards high production costs, particularly compared with Chinese and South Asian manufacturers. This reflects its reliance on imported material and higher labour and domestic transport costs. All will remain a feature of the environment to a greater or lesser extent during 2000-02. Investment, notably from foreign sources that propelled the sector's expansion in the first half of the 1990s but has since declined, is likely to recover later in the forecast period.

Low Value-Added

Vietnam - main goods exports

Export	Unit	1997	1998
Shelled Ground Nut	1,000 tonnes	83	87
Rubber	"	195	185
Coffee	"	389	379
Tea	"	32	34
Rice	"	3,550	3,800
Crude Oil	"	9,613	12,122
Coal	"	3,450	3,163
Marine Products	US$mn	781	850
Garments	"	1,349	1,350
Shoes & Sandals	"	965	960

Source: Ho Chi Minh City Statistical Yearbook.

TEXTILES AND GARMENTS EXPORTS					
	1996	1997	1998	1999	2002f
value (US$mn)	1,150	1,349	1,350	1,747	3,000
% of total exports	15.7	15.1	14.5	15.2	14.6

f = BMI forecast; Sources: World Bank, UNDP, BMI.

Footwear

Shoe Companies Struggle Against Cheap Imports

Growth in the footwear industry in 2000-02 will be driven by improved access to EU markets along with strengthening Asian demand. In the absence of a bilateral trade accord with the US, the sector has made little impression on the American market. This should begin to change from 2002. However, progress is likely to be slow since competition will be strong, notably from China. Investment, which has eased off in recent years, will recover later in the forecast period as companies look to increase production in order to export to the US. **BMI** is forecasting annual average export growth from footwear of around 16% in 2000-02, with faster growth towards the end of the period. By 2002, export earnings from the sector are likely to be worth around US$2.1bn compared with US$1.4bn in 1999. Output growth amongst the many domestic subcontractors that supply the industry is generally considerably lower than the sector's export growth rate, reflecting the fact that many firms are struggling to compete in the face of cheaper imports. This will continue to be a problem over the next three years.

Notwithstanding the price pressures imposed by cheaper imports, higher demand initially in Asia and the EU and later in the US will fuel a partial recovery in the sector

FOOTWEAR EXPORTS					
	1996	1997	1998	1999	2002f
value (US$mn)	530	965	1,001	1,350	2,100
% of total exports	7.2	10.6	10.7	11.7	12.6
f = BMI forecast; Sources: World Bank, BMI.					

Local companies are starting to produce higher quality products for the domestic and overseas market.

Food And Beverages

Local Raw Material Sources Problematic

Growth in the food processing industry, including fruit, vegetables, meat products and seafood, is likely to pick up slightly during 2000-02 driven by higher demand and increased foreign investment. Improving consumer confidence as the economy recovers is likely to lead to increased domestic demand, including growing demand for products that traditionally have not had much of a niche. Some of the new locally produced products (e.g. fruit juice) are very price competitive on the domestic market compared with foreign imports.

Since 1999, overseas demand has been increasing and this is likely to continue over the next three years. A major market is Japan, where economic recovery is gradually taking root while demand is also expected to come from China, the EU and the US. Processed food exports to the US are not affected in the same way as textiles and garments. Recently the sector's growth has been constrained by a lack of investment. However, as rising demand shows signs of becoming entrenched, we expect investment to pick up. Difficulties in the food-processing sector relate to an inability to source local raw materials reliably despite the country's rich resource base as well as production processes, which often do not meet international hygiene and other standards. New investment will go some way to improving processing techniques over the forecast period although sourcing problems will persist.

KEY CONSUMER PRODUCTS			
	1990	1995	1998	% change 1998/1995
Glass ('000 tonnes)	39	77	67	-4.5
Porcelain (mn pieces)	140	187	190	0.5
Salt ('000 tonnes)	593	689	717	1.3
Sugar ('000 tonnes)	323	517	657	8.3
Beer (mn litres)	100	465	656	12.2
Cigarettes (mn packs)	1,249	2,174	2,178	0.1
Tea ('000 tonnes)	24	24	49	26.9
Fish sauce (mn litres)	131	149	180	6.5
Textile fibres ('000 tonnes)	58	59	71	6.4
Cotton (mn metres)	318	263	317	6.4
Soap ('000 tonnes)	55	129	216	18.7
Source: General Statistical Office.			

Electronics

Low Purchasing Power And Market Saturation

After experiencing very rapid growth in the first half of the 1990s, the electronics industry has suffered from a combination of market saturation in the main urban centres and low demand outside of them. However, as the economy recovers over the forecast period, demand will pick up in both quarters. In Ho Chi Minh City and Hanoi, where market saturation is greatest, improving consumer confidence during 2000-02 should lead to a rise in the numbers of people looking to upgrade to the latest model, which should aid the sector's recovery.

Growth in electronics will recover, averaging just under 10% annually.

The more buoyant regional economy will also lead to increased opportunities for the export of electronic goods and this is also likely to fuel growth in the sector. Higher demand can be expected to lead to a recovery in investment by both foreign and domestic companies over the next three years, although all the normal caveats regarding constraints on investment growth apply. That we are not forecasting faster growth in the electronics industry during 2000-02 reflects still low purchasing power outside the main cities along with other problems which have plagued the sector such as smuggling and the high tax rate on imported components. Progress towards developing a domestic components industry will continue to be slow. The government's original target that 60% of parts in electronic products be manufactured locally by 2000 has not been reached, and it probably will not be achieved by 2002.

Automobiles

Rising Sales With Modest Profits

Low demand and excess capacity have resulted in poor sales and losses for the eleven companies assembling cars, buses and trucks in Vietnam. However, while profitability remains a major issue, the outlook for the sector is somewhat more promising. In 1999, sales by local auto producers rose 38.4% y-o-y to 6,882 units. Q1 2000 sales have also been very strong, with 2,585 units sold representing a 101.3% increase on the same period last year. During 2000-02, **BMI** expects demand to continue rising on the back of a strengthening economy. Demand is also strengthening in the face of increased vehicle purchases by the private sector and this is likely to

The increases in demand witnessed in the first half of 2000 will be sustained; the private sector is a new source of growth.

continue. In addition, auto firms have recently been more successfully in targeting the market with niche models (e.g. low end of the range 'family' cars and light trucks). Nevertheless, the Vietnamese auto market is a small one and is likely to remain so for the duration of the forecast period. **BMI** believes combined sales by local auto companies are unlikely to be much higher than 11,000 units annually by 2002.

Auto companies are continuing to suffer from the government's changing import policy. In late 1999 the authorities announced imports of between 7,000-10,000 mini-vans with 15 or more seats. This caused consternation within the industry, which favours greater protectionism. Smuggling is also a problem. The upshot is that local producers supply only about 20% of the market in any one year. Greater consistency and transparency in import policy during the next three years is unlikely. It is by no means out of the question that some car companies will shut down during the forecast period.

Motorcycles

Competition Points To Modest Growth In 2000-02

By 2002 total output is likely to be in excess of 445,000 units. Congestion is unlikely to curb continued expansion in the medium term.

Output by Vietnam's four motorbike joint ventures fell nearly 9% y-o-y in 1999, in response to slack demand in light of the depressed local economy. In early 2000, demand continued to be rather slow although it showed signs of rebounding in the second quarter. After last year's fall in production, local manufacturers are all targeting an increase in output in 2000 although not an especially large one at around 6% y-o-y. During 2000-02 **BMI** expects the number of units produced to increase at an annual average of just under 8% reflecting stronger growth later in the forecast period as consumer confidence strengthens.

The government is taking steps to try and persuade people to use public transport to reduce motorbike congestion, but this is going to have very little impact on demand for motorbikes which are set to continue rising over the forecast period. The problem for Vietnam's motorbike producers is that competition for sales is stiff. This is the case both at the top end of the market – where the desire to own the latest model appears to be unceasing – and at the lower end where imported Korean and Chinese bikes are selling more cheaply than locally assembled models. In response, local firms have been forced to lower prices and offer other incentives to lure customers companies. This is necessarily cutting into margins. Illustrative of the problem, there have been reports of price dumping by motorbike sales agents.

Motorbike producers are under pressure from the government to source parts locally. Progress is being made: **Yamaha**'s latest 100cc Sirius model sources 30% of its parts in Vietnam and this is set to rise to over 70% by 2003.

Plastics

Lower Import Taxes Spur Growth

The prospect of faster growth in plastics follows the government's decision in late 1999 to reduce the import tax on PVC (polyvinyl chloride) resin from 10% to 5% after strong lobbying from domestic plastic companies. The higher tariff had increased the cost of locally produced plastic products, making them less competitive both in domestic and overseas markets. As a result, firms cut production. Some companies that rely on imported PVC resin are suggesting they could achieve annual growth rates in excess of 20%. This seems optimistic and we are forecasting an annual average growth rate of just over 13.5% in 2000-02.

*After a sharp slowdown in 1999, **BMI** is forecasting double-digit growth in plastics in 2000-02.*

Despite lower import tariffs, regional competition is likely to remain strong. This is a problem for local plastic firms both domestically in the face of cheap imports and overseas where Vietnamese firms are in competition with companies from Thailand and China for a share of the Cambodian and Lao markets. Nevertheless, demand for plastic products both at home and abroad is likely to strengthen during the forecast period in tandem with the wider domestic and regional economic recovery. There is slightly less certainty over demand in Laos during 2000-02 given economic problems there, although any fall-off should be partly offset by stronger growth in Cambodia.

The unpredictable nature of the government's policy on import tariffs is likely to act as a deterrent to some foreign companies considering investing in the petrochemicals industry. The lowering of the import tax was strongly condemned by a Japanese joint venture, **Mitsui Vina**, which produces PVC resin and which had earlier successfully lobbied for the tax to be increased. It says it may now have to close, although there are also reports that its relations with its joint venture partner are difficult. However, foreign investment in the sector is unlikely to dry up completely.

Despite the general slowdown in foreign private capital inflow, new investment in the sector was forthcoming in 2000 and more is likely in 2001-02, not least on the back of generous tax incentives for foreign companies investing in the sector. Local plastic companies looking to increase capacity during 2000-02 may struggle to secure the necessary capital given weaknesses in the domestic banking sector, although some of the stronger firms are likely to find that capital is forthcoming from foreign sources.

Agriculture

Better Prices Will Provide Some Relief

BMI is forecasting annual average agriculture growth of just over 4.0% in 2000-02. This is lower than in the previous three years, when the sector recorded annual growth of 4.4%. The forecast reflects both short-term difficulties caused by low commodity prices and more deeply rooted structural problems in the sector. In the first five months of 2000, coffee producers have been particularly badly hit by low world prices having seen robusta coffee prices fall some 40% since the end of 1999. Rice prices are also substantially down.

One of the consequences of lower commodity prices is a reluctance among farmers to expand production and particularly to diversify from rice production to commercial crops, such as tea, coffee, rubber and cotton. Nevertheless, commodity prices are expected to recover over the next three years. Prices are not expected to bounce back to the highs of the 1990s but they will pick up sufficiently to enable a slight recovery in the sector.

With the government seeking to encourage farmers to diversify production away from an over-reliance on rice, commercial crop production is also likely to be the more buoyant component of the agricultural sector during 2000-02. There are, however, a number of longstanding problems in agriculture, which explain why we are not forecasting a more robust pick-up in growth:

Taking growth above 4.0% will require radical structural reforms. This is not going to happen in the short term.

A Structural Shift
agriculture - a regional comparison

	% of GDP		Average annual % growth	
	1980	1998	1980-90	1990-98
Vietnam	-	26	4.3	4.9
India	38	29	3.1	3.8
Philippines	25	17	1.0	1.5
China	30	18	5.9	4.4
Indonesia	24	20	3.4	2.6
Malaysia	22	13	3.8	1.3
Thailand	23	11	3.9	2.6

Source: World Bank.

AGRICULTURAL EXPORTS					
	1995	1996	1997	1998	1999
Rice (US$mn)	549	855	870	1,024	1,025
Rice ('000 tonnes)	2,052	3,003	3,553	3,749	4,508
Rubber (US$mn)	181	163	191	127	125
Rubber ('000 tonnes)	130	122	195	191	212
Coffee (US$mn)	495	337	491	594	592
Coffee ('000 tonnes)	200	239	389	382	N/A

Sources: World Bank; UNDP; press reports.

First, there is still a bias in the sector to small-scale household farming, which is making it difficult to improve productivity beyond the gains achieved with the move away from collective farming in the late 1980s. There are exceptions to this pattern of small-scale agriculture, particularly in the south where larger landholdings are more common. However, the government still officially imposes limits on how much land an individual can own the rights to. This is also acting as a constraint on foreign investment in the sector, although again exceptions have been made to allow foreign companies to develop large-scale acreage. Foreign investment is particularly needed in the sector to improve crop quality and to create a reliable raw material base for the processing sector. During 2000-02 we do not expect any formal move away from restrictions on land ownership.

Second, growth in agriculture is constrained by the existence of monopoly state purchasing and trading networks. By squeezing farm-gate prices, these also work to discourage farmers from increasing or diversifying production. At a national level, there is recognition that this is a serious problem but local state business interests are powerful and cannot be dislodged easily. Recent government measures, which have seen the easing of restrictions on who can engage in rice exporting, are part of a move by central government against these interests. However, changes expected in this area over the forecast period are only likely to have a gradual effect on the sector.

AGRICULTURAL PRODUCTION ('000 TONNES)			
	1990	1995	1998	% change 1998/1990
Paddy	21,488	27,571	31,854	14.0
Paddy (kg/head)	323	373	408	8.1
Cotton	3.1	12.8	20.7	88.3
Soybeans	86.6	125.5	141.0	17.6
Tea	32.2	40.2	51.0	16.6
Coffee	92	218	409.3	64.5
Rubber	58	123	1,318	183.4
Source: General Statistical Office.			

Oil & Gas

Amended Petroleum Law Unlikely To Woo Investors

Lower tax rates for companies exploring in difficult deep-water blocks will not lure investors to return in large numbers.

BMI is forecasting slower growth in the oil and gas sector during the forecast period, at just over 14% annual average growth. In the short term, the sector will benefit from the higher oil price but this will not last for the duration of the forecast period. **BMI** expects oil prices to fall back sharply in 2001-02, to US$18/b in the latter year from US$23.5 on average in 2000. Moreover, foreign investors are likely to hang back from investing in the sector. There have been two foreign investment projects in H2 2000 worth US$22.5mn and US$10.5mn respectively. However, in general, foreign investors are not enamoured of the operating environment affecting the sector.

In May 2000, the National Assembly passed amendments to the Petroleum Law, which the government claims will result in increased investment. However, this is doubtful. Although both royalty and corporate tax rates have been lowered, they have been done so selectively and overall the tax package remains uncompetitive. It is consequently unlikely to lure investors to explore the geologically difficult deep-water blocks as the government is hoping. There are also a number of unresolved issues relating to the need for harmonisation between the Law on Foreign Investment and the Petroleum Law and on licensing.

Without a pick-up in foreign investment growth rates in the oil and gas sector are unlikely to return either to the levels recorded in the previous three years or to those earlier in the 1990s. We are, however, expecting some pick-up in growth in the oil and gas sector during the forecast period. This reflects our expectation of further increases in demand in the already buoyant liquefied petroleum gas market, along with progress on the foreign-invested Nam Con Son gas project and the Dung Quat oil refinery.

	OIL				
	1995	1996	1997	1998	1999
Oil exports (US$mn)	1,024	1,346	1,413	1,232	2,092
Oil exports (% of total exports)	19.6	18.3	15.4	13.1	18.1
Sources: World Bank; UNDP.					

Construction

Infrastructure And Houses Will Fuel Recovery

After recording growth of just 2.4% in 1999, the construction industry started to recover in Q1 2000. Reflecting this, cement output rose 15.0% y-o-y, while steel production increased by 19.5%. Both sectors have been saddled with large stockpiles as a result of the economic downturn. During 2000-02 we expect the construction industry will continue to recover, with growth averaging 9.8% for the period. This is only slightly higher than the average for the previous three years although this was boosted by a strong performance in 1997 reflecting the tail end of the property market boom. In 2002, construction growth is forecast to be 11.0% – not as high as 1997 but not far off it. There is no shortage of potential demand in the sector given the poor quality of Vietnam's infrastructure. During 2000-02, growth will in large part derive from aid-funded infrastructure projects, notably road and bridge building.

Another source of growth is likely to come from demand for residential housing, which is in short supply. The government is, as a result, planning a major programme of house building. Demand for commercial property and hotels is unlikely to pick up until later in the forecast period owing to the fact that very rapid growth in this section of the market in the mid-1990s has led to a situation of oversupply which is unlikely to ease off until 2001-02. However, there are many unfinished building projects, which investors put on hold in the aftermath of the Asian economic crisis and some of these are likely to be revived as economic growth picks up. In the short term, the construction industry should see some additional demand from rebuilding work in central provinces necessitated by flooding in November 1999.

The main constraint on the sector is likely to be inadequate levels of investment. In seeking to stimulate growth in the economy more generally, the government pledged to increase capital expenditure in 2000, much of which would have indirectly benefited the construction industry. However, poor revenue collection looks likely to result in expenditure having to be reined in. There should be some improvement in public finances in 2001-02 but not a great deal. The other constraint relates to private investment. Much potential overseas investment in infrastructure is being held up by continued problems with the regulatory framework (e.g. governing build-operate-transfer projects). Again, such difficulties are likely to be ironed out gradually during 2000-02. This in part underpins our expectation of faster

An oversupply in the commercial sector will curb growth in 2000-02, but there will be a recovery in the latter year.

construction growth in 2002. There are still problems regarding competitiveness and product quality affecting domestically produced cement and steel as well as other building materials. As Vietnam further integrates in the world economy, protecting inefficient producers will become more difficult, pointing to the fact that companies will ultimately either have to become more competitive or close. However, these issues will not be fully resolved in the next three years.

Power Generation

Regulatory Problems Remain

Growth in electricity demand will remain high. The need to build new generating capacity will push the government to encourage private investment.

Growth in generated electricity capacity is forecast to average 11.7% during 2000-02. This reflects the fact that a number of new power stations are likely to come on stream during the forecast period, including the Phu My I, Ialy and the Hinh River plants. By 2002, generated capacity is expected to be 33bn kWh. More rapid progress in building new capacity will continue to elude the sector for most of the forecast period as outstanding problems with the regulatory framework affecting private sector investment continue to be ironed out. But there should be some progress in this area over the forecast period, which ought to allow some of the stalled build-operate-transfer (BOT) power projects to move forward by 2002.

Electricity demand is forecast to pick up over the next three years, averaging 11.3% annual growth. This is well below the highs of the last decade, reflecting less rapid industrial growth. One new area of growth in demand relates to the government's target of bringing electricity to 80% of rural households by 2005, compared with around 25% now. This is unlikely to be achieved on schedule, but it will result in higher household demand during 2000-02 compensating to some extent for lower industrial growth. Despite new capacity and lower growth in demand, there will continue to be periodic power cuts and brown outs in the forecast period, particularly in the faster growing south during the dry season.

Telecoms

The Problems Of The 1990s Will Receive Attention

Growth in the telecoms sector is forecast to recover in 2000-02, averaging around 15.5%. However, this is well below the trend rate of the previous three years, which is itself a steep reduction on earlier expansion rates. Problems in the sector include high costs, with prices set by the General Department for Posts and Telecommunications, a lack of competition, and foreign investor dissatisfaction with the business cooperation contract (BCC) vehicle by which companies are required to invest in the sector.

Our forecast of slightly higher growth over the next three years is based on the expected recovery in the domestic economy which will boost demand for both fixed lines and cellular. If the government's target of four fixed lines per 100 people in 2000 is not achieved on schedule, it is likely to be met soon after. Furthermore, after the problems with the BCC, we expect the contract to be revised in order to attract investment in the sector, which is urgently required. The entry of new operators in the telecom sector, namely **Vietell** and **Saigon Postel**, will also aid growth even though the companies are both government controlled.

Telecoms will gain momentum in 2000-02 as the domestic economy strengthens. The government is likely to address investor dissatisfaction.

Market Potential

telecoms subscriptions - a regional comparison

Countries	Population (mn)	Subscribers (mn)	Density (per 100)
India	929	21.9	2.36
Bangladesh	120	0.4	0.37
Taiwan	40	21.5	46.6
South Korea	45	19.6	43.26
Vietnam	**76**	**2.5**	**3.20**

Source: Vietnam Investment Review.

Banking

A Stronger Banking Sector Is Still Years Away

In the aftermath of the Asian economic crisis, the multilateral lending institutions have reminded the government of the importance of pressing ahead with financial sector reform. How much progress is made will be crucial to the performance of the country's banks during 2000-02. The other key issue is the extent to which the government moves to allow an element of foreign competition. Overall, change is likely to be gradual rather than dramatic.

The fragility of the domestic banks and the lack of a level playing field for foreign banks will constrain growth during 2000-02, despite some improvements.

BMI is forecasting growth in the sector to be about the same in the forecast period as the previous three years at around 11.5% annually. Both the state-owned commercial banks and many of the joint stock banks are fragile. No one knows precisely the extent of non-performing or overdue loans since such data are not routinely released. However, figures were published in the press in early 2000 suggesting bad loans were worth VND9,920bn

(US$706.2mn) or 7% of total lending. However, based on other data and off-the record comments by State Bank officials, many believe the true figure may be nearer to VND35bn or around 25%. The government has mooted plans to recapitalise the state-owned banks but this has yet to progress. Moreover, it has pledged to close the weaker joint stock banks or merge them with stronger banks. This has begun to happen but progress is slow reflecting the difficulty of reconciling competing interests within the banks. Over the next three years, rationalisation of the joint stock banks will continue, although difficulties will by no means be entirely solved either here or at the state-owned banks.

Underpinning bank weakness is the fact that loan applications are often not properly scrutinised while banks are often subject to political pressure to lend. As a result, bad loan problems are likely to recur. Against this backdrop, both the public and smaller companies will retain their deep-seated mistrust of the banks, thereby curbing the scope for growth in bank deposit bases. Weak deposit bases will in turn impose limits on bank lending, which is also constrained by distortions in the interest rate structure. In order to stimulate lending following the economic downturn, the government has repeatedly lowered ceiling interest rates, which has had the effect of squeezing bank margins. In such circumstances, many banks complain that interest rates do not cover the risk of lending and hence are unwilling to do so. Such problems will also curb banking sector growth during 2000-02. The government has announced plans for a shift to more market-determined interest rates, but the timetable is not clear. In all likelihood, interest rate distortions will remain at the end of the forecast period.

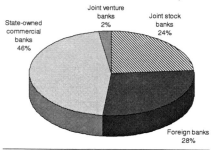

Foreign Banks Grab Larger Share
Vietnam - market share in Ho Chi Minh City

State-owned commercial banks 46%
Joint venture banks 2%
Joint stock banks 24%
Foreign banks 28%

Source: Vietnam Investment Review.

SELECTION OF COMMERCIAL BANKS		
State-owned Banks	Vietcombank	Incombank
	Agribank	Vietindebank
Joint Stock Banks	Asia Commer	Oricom Bank
	East Asia Ban	Exim Bank
	Maritime Bank	Que Do Bank
	Saigon Bank	Sacombank
	Viet Hoa Bank	VP Bank
Joint Venture Banks	FirstVina Ban	Indovina Bank
	Vid Public Bank	
Foreign Banks	ANZ Bank	Citibank
	Deutsche Ban	Hongkong Bank
	Chinfon Bank	Bank of Tokyo Mitsubishi

Source: BMI.

The absence of a level playing field for the foreign banks reflects a wish to protect local banks. Over the next three years, some progress will be made in reducing discrimination, not least under pressure from the USA and other partners, but it will not be particularly fast. The two most likely areas for change are an easing of current restrictions on the percentage of dong deposits foreign banks can hold, and granting foreign banks the right to lend in hard currency to exporters. However, the foreign banks will still be disadvantaged in relation to their domestic counterparts in 2002.

Tourism

'Frontier' Image Will Continue To Fuel Tourism

During 2000-02 foreign tourist arrivals are forecast to average 12.7% annual growth compared with 2.6% growth in the previous three years. The much higher forecast growth rate is explained by the fact that the number of arrivals fell sharply in 1998 in the wake of the Asian economic crisis. However, our forecast for the sector is in line with growth in 1999 and in Q1 2000 when arrivals increased 14.2% y-o-y to 530,000. The sector should continue to benefit from greater buoyancy in regional economies, which are an important source of tourists.

By 2002, Vietnam is likely to receive in the region of 2.4mn visitors compared with 1.7mn in 1999. In the mid-1990s, growth in tourist arrivals was much faster than it is now. We do not expect a return to such growth in 2000-02. The sector's performance correlates to some extent with international business sentiment. Given that business sentiment towards Vietnam is likely to remain cautious over the next few years, there is unlikely to be a surge in tourist visitors either.

There is no denying that Vietnam has great potential as a tourism destination. Not only does it have a long coastline, but also an interesting ancient and modern history. The scope for battlefield tours is clearly there but has yet to be properly exploited. Equally, the country has great potential in terms of ecotourism, such as trekking or wildlife spotting. Again, development is at an embryonic stage. To date, Vietnam's tourism sector has demonstrated a fixation with hotels. In the recent past, Vietnam did lack international standard accommodation – something which has largely been put right – but it is widely recognised that attention needs to be focused elsewhere for the sector to develop.

Tourism is undergoing a mini-boom as regional countries recover from the Asian crisis. However, further improvements to infrastructure and a greater range of tourist facilities are needed to attract a wider clientele.

Lagging Behind
selected tourism indicators - a regional comparison

	Inbound Tourists ('000)		International Tourism Receipts (US$mn)		International Tourism Receipts (% of exports)	
	1980	1998	1980	1998	1980	1998
Vietnam	N/A	1520	N/A	86	N/A	0.7
Indonesia	527	4606	246	4045	1.2	7.4
India	1194	2359	1150	3124	10.2	6.6
Thailand	1859	7843	867	5934	10.9	9.0
Malaysia	2105	5551	265	2456	1.9	3.4
Philippines	1008	2149	320	2413	4.4	6.5
Singapore	2562	5631	1433	5162	5.9	4.0

Source: World Bank.

Beyond hotels, entertainment and other facilities are limited. Museums are generally not user friendly. Moreover, connecting infrastructure between places of interest, or to some of the beach resorts that have recently sprung up, is generally poor. Often the only option is to travel on a badly made-up road. Other common complaints of foreign tourists focus on the government's requirement that all visitors must obtain a visa, and the dual pricing system whereby foreigners pay more than Vietnamese for hotels, domestic flights, tours etc. Some improvement in the areas where the sector is deficient is likely during 2000-02. There are plans to phase out the dual pricing system, although Vietnam is likely to remain rather expensive for quality of service. Visas are likely to continue to be required, although there may be a shift to being able to obtain them on arrival, which is currently only available for those arriving on a state-approved organised tour.

The government has recently coined the slogan "Vietnam: A Destination for the New Millennium" – and various associated events are planned – in a bid to attract more visitors and there is generally a greater awareness of the importance of overseas marketing if numbers are to increase. Foreign investment in the sector in areas such as hotels, resorts, and recreational and other facilities will continue to be welcomed, although the activities of foreign tour operators are likely to remain restricted.

Profile and Recent Developments

Introduction

Slower Growth In Most Sectors

The general pattern is one of a slowdown in most sectors during 1997-99. This was greatly influenced by the onset of the Asian financial crisis, as demand for exports slowed and the country became less competitive following the large regional currency devaluations relative to the dong. However, growth began to slow in a number of sectors before the crisis, illustrating clearly that many of the difficulties are systemic and unique to Vietnam. A large part of the problem relates to the difficult operating environment encountered by both domestic and foreign investors. This includes too much regulation and bureaucracy in some areas, although not enough in others. Foreign companies are restricted in terms of the activities they can engage in, often reflecting the persistence of powerful lobbying on the part of domestic companies seeking protection from foreign competitors. The introduction of VAT in 1999 proved very disruptive to business.

The economic downturn and the fall-off in foreign direct investment has led to increased efforts on the part of the government to cut back on red tape and discriminatory business practices and improve incentives, notably during 1998-99. This saw the authorities respond in part, or in full, to long-standing foreign investor complaints about the dual pricing system, dollar-denominated wages and punitive personal income tax rates. However, implementation has generally been disappointing.

Manufacturing

Food processing

Food and beverages production, including food processing, is the largest single contributor to manufacturing output. Annual average growth was in the region of 15% during 1995-98. This is slightly higher than manufacturing growth overall, but lower than some other sectors such as garments. The processing sector has great potential given the country's rich agricultural and seafood base. Moreover, the government has recognised this, designating processing as one of a number of sectors where foreign investment is "especially encouraged", which carries accompanying incentives.

To date, foreign investment in food processing has been far below its potential. The principal constraint relates to the fact that it is still difficult to consistently procure sufficient quantities of raw materials to the required quality standards. This in turn is a feature of the way in which the agricultural sector is geared towards small-scale production and notably small land holdings. It is possible in theory to obtain the large land holdings necessary for industrial-scale agricultural production and a number of foreign companies have done so, although in practice this can be quite difficult. A further problem is that farmers will often prefer to sell their produce for direct export, rather than sell it to companies wishing to process it locally, since the former generally yields a higher price. In addition, in order to be near the raw material base, companies wishing to invest in processing are often required to operate in areas of the country less familiar with international business practices. Indicative of the problems in procuring raw materials locally, a number of prominent local companies such as **Vinamilk** and **Vocarimex**, which specialise in dairy products and vegetable oil production, source a significant percentage of their materials overseas.

Local processing companies are grouped in conglomerates such as **Vinatea**, **Vinacafe** and the **Vietnam Vegetable and Fruit Company**. In Ho Chi Minh City, prominent food processing companies include **Vissan** and the **International Beverages Company**. A number of foreign companies are operating successfully in the food processing industry. To date, seafood processing has been more popular than fruit and vegetable, notably with Asian investors. In general, companies have found that developing a good relationship with local producers is crucial to success.

Textiles, Garments And Footwear

The potential of textiles, garments and footwear first became apparent in 1994, when textiles and garments emerged as the second largest export earner after crude oil. Earlier in the decade, the sector was recording annual growth rates in the region of 30-40%. Foreign, largely Asian, investment have played a major role in the sector's emergence. With the onset of the Asian crisis, growth has slowed substantially to around 9% in the case of textiles and 13% for garments in 1998. However, textiles and garments have retained their position as the second largest export earner, while footwear exports now rank third. Footwear output also appears to have been less affected by the regional economic downturn than textiles and garments.

The fall in overseas market demand hit the garment sector very badly in 1998 although the situation improved in 1999. Purchases from Japan, which is the industry's largest non-quota market, have plummeted. Demand from the European Union has been maintained, but here the problem is one of market access, namely that producers are capable of producing more than current quota levels permit. A major constraint on the sector's development during the second half of the 1990s has been its lack of access to the US market in the absence of NTR. Textile and garment exports recorded zero growth in 1998. The sector has also become less price competitive since the large size of regional currency devaluations relative to the dong during 1997-98. Another long-standing weakness in the textile and garment sector, is its reliance on imported cotton. Plans are underway to increase local production, but it remains to be seen whether it will be price competitive.

There are two state conglomerates in the sector: the **National Textile and Garment Corporation** (Vinatex) and **Vietnam Leather and Footwear Corporation**. Prominent garment firms include **Viet Tien, Garment Company Number 10**, and **Huy Hoang**, which although a private firm, is closely connected to the political establishment. The leading local shoe company is Sino-Vietnamese company, **Bitis**. Many of the state companies in the sector are due to undergo equitisation but progress has been slow.

Electronics And Electrical Equipment And Components

Earlier in the 1990s, the electronics industry was averaging growth rates in excess of 30-40% y-o-y. Since 1997, growth has slowed, although it remained in double-digits during 1998-99. Some companies, however, have coped much less well with the economic downturn and a number have shut assembly lines. Export demand fell sharply during 1997-98 and this has also affected the sector. A further problem in the industry is that the key markets of Hanoi and Ho Chi Minh City have become saturated for products such as television sets and videos. Demand outside the main urban centres is rising, but purchasing power is still low. The industry is also vulnerable to the presence on the market of cheaper, smuggled items. This continues to be a problem even after a major electronics smuggling ring was uncovered in 1998. In addition, taxes on imported components, on which the industry still relies, are high.

Development of the domestic components industry has been slow, and capacity remains weak. On the whole, domestic firms are producing low end products such as voltage stabilisers and transformers, rather than moving up-market to higher technology products. Government plans to increase the share of locally manufactured components have yet to proceed as anticipated. Foreign investment has played a key role in the electronic sector's development, accounting for over 90% of total investment to date.

Motor Vehicles

The car industry in Vietnam has so far been a great disappointment. Moreover, many would argue that the decision to invest on the part of 14 foreign companies were poorly thought through, and made in a climate of over-optimism about the Vietnamese market in the mid-1990s. The car market is a small one and likely to remain so for many years to come. Vietnam is probably not an investor's first choice as a manufacturing base for exports given the lack of a domestic parts industry. Sales of locally assembled vehicles peaked in 1996 at 11,500 before falling sharply in 1997-99. In 1998 only around 4,500 units were sold, compared with a combined annual capacity of 130,000 units of the 11 operational car companies. Total market demand is only for around 25-35,000 vehicles per year. Around 80% of this is satisfied by imports of new and second-hand models, many of which are smuggled. In 1999, the government responded to protectionist calls from the industry and announced a ban on the import of all new and second-hand vehicles with less than 12 seats. Foreign companies operational in Vietnam, include **Toyota, Ford, Mercedes Benz, Isuzu, Daihatsu** and **Daewoo Motors**. They have all formed joint ventures although a number have been trying to shed their local partner.

Motorbike production has proven a better investment than car production. Motorbikes are the preferred means of transport. Moreover, the wealthier urban middle classes are desirous of owning the latest model. There are six companies licensed to assemble motorbikes. **Honda** has the dominant share of the market, followed by **Suzuki** and the Taiwan-invested **VMEP**. **Suzuki** began exporting bikes in 1999.

Petrochemicals And Plastics

Average growth in petrochemicals and plastics has been above that of overall industrial growth during 1996-99. However, growth slowed during 1997-99 in the face of the Asian crisis and the domestic economic downturn. In particular, the sector suffered as a result of competition from cheap imports, which have entered the country following the large currency devaluations in neighbouring countries. This resulted in calls from domestic producers for the government to raise tariffs on imported products, notably PVC (polyvinyl chloride). However, the possibility of increased import tariffs on PVC products has been heard before without effect. More widespread development of the petrochemicals industry is being constrained by slow progress in developing a local oil refining capacity and a number of key gas projects.

Existing capacity is heavily concentrated in Ho Chi Minh City, with around 70% of production coming from the private sector. Local Sino-Vietnamese dominate the industry. Leading local companies include **Tan Tien Plastics** Packaging Company and **Tan Dai Hung Plastic Company**. There is also a state **Vietnam Plastics Company** (Vinaplast), grouping some 14 firms. Foreign investment has come from a wide range of countries, including Japan, South Korea, the US and France.

Agriculture, Forestry And Fisheries

Agricultural Sector Performs Below Potential

Although eclipsed by industry and services in terms of its contribution to GDP, the agriculture, forestry and fisheries sector still contributed some 23.5% of price constant GDP in 1998. This makes it more significant in output terms than any single industrial or services sub-sector. Agricultural produce and seafood are also key exports, accounting for in excess of 30% of total dollar earnings annually. Vietnam is the world's third largest rice exporter, the fourth largest coffee exporter and the second largest cashew nuts exporter. Furthermore, the agriculture and fisheries sector is seen as representing a crucial resource base for the development of light industry, notably processing.

During 1996-99, the sector averaged 4.4% growth. This is significantly below growth rates in industry and services, although this is to be expected. However, a number of areas have seen more rapid expansion, notably industrial crops such as coffee, tea and rubber. The Ministry of Agriculture and Rural Development spoke in 1998 in terms of an expansion of land under cultivation and output for nearly all areas over the next few years. While this is certainly the intention, its comments came against the backdrop of a politically driven campaign to stress the importance of agricultural development. Higher levels of public investment in agriculture have been promised, although it is questionable whether this will be followed through.

There are some quite serious systemic problems in the agricultural sector, which are constraining its development. Limits on land holdings, poor infrastructure and limited access to credit are part of the problem, although at its root is the existence of monopoly purchasing and trading interests dominated by central and local state enterprises. This is putting downward pressure on farm gate prices, and is having an adverse impact on farmers' decisions to expand or diversify production in some cases. At the national level, it is said repeatedly that the aim is to eliminate such obstacles – including allowing private rice exporters, for instance – but progress is in practice likely to be slow.

Key agricultural commodities are represented by state corporations, such as the **Vietnam General Rubber Company**, **Vinacafe**, **Vinatea**, and **Vietnam Tobacco Corporation**. The two leading rice exporters, out of around 40, are **Vinafood I and II**.

Energy

Foreign Investors Face Hurdles

During 1995-98, oil production has risen by an average 22% annually, while gas has increased by 152% (admittedly from a virtually non-existent base). Foreign investment has played a key role. Since 1988, 35 production sharing contracts have been signed between foreign companies and the state-owned **PetroVietnam**, with investment of US$3.1bn. Nearly all of Vietnam's crude is exported because, apart from a very small plant outside Ho Chi Minh City, the country lacks a refining capacity. Vietnam's gas output is piped onshore to two power stations.

For foreign oil companies, Vietnam has not been an easy operating environment. Much of the optimism towards the industry in the early-1990s dissipated in the second half of the decade in the face of a difficult regulatory framework, protracted negotiations and a steep fiscal regime. The drawn-out negotiations between the Vietnamese government and the **BP** Amoco-led consortium on the US$1.5bn Nam Con Son basin gas project, which were still ongoing in 1999, epitomise some of the difficulties faced by investors in the industry. The project is to build a 390km pipeline to bring gas ashore to Vung Tau in the south for use in a power and fertiliser plant. In 1999, the Malaysian oil company, **Petronas**, withdrew from the Dai Hung oil field saying that it was no longer commercially viable. The extent of the reserves in the Dai Hung field had been repeatedly downgraded. The participation of foreign companies in distribution is still heavily restricted.

The less bullish sentiment towards Vietnam's oil industry also relates to the fact that its oil reserves are probably much smaller than originally thought – maybe about one-third of Indonesia's. The outlook for the gas industry is more promising. Proven gas reserves are estimated at 200-300bn m³, with prospective reserves estimated at around 1700bn m³.

Construction And Property

Slow Growth In The Construction And Property Sector

Growth in the construction sector has slowed considerably since the first half of the 1990s. The construction boom had its origins in the relative freeing up of the land market earlier in the decade which, in combination with the opening up of the country to foreign investment, led to a surge in private house building and high rise office construction. This saw a surge in demand for cement, steel, glass, ceramics and sanitary ware. Government measures to cool the overheated property market in 1995 were followed, in turn, by a downturn in business sentiment towards Vietnam in general, and the Asian financial crisis, resulting in much slower construction sector growth. Both the cement and the steel industry suffered from serious problems of over capacity during 1998-99, resulting in workers being laid off.

The fortunes of the construction industry are inextricably tied up with the property market, which during 1998-99 was itself in a situation of oversupply. Combined with the economic slowdown, this saw price falls in excess of 50% compared with the US$45 per square metre rental rates charged in 1997. In 1997-98, there was no new investment in office and apartment construction.

Many of the leading construction and property companies are state owned. In 1998, the government approved the establishment of the **Saigon Real Estate Company**, grouping 20 property and construction companies. Another prominent local property company is **Fimexco**, which belongs to the People's Committee in Ho Chi Minh City's District 1. Foreign construction companies include Australia's **Transfield** and the UK's **John Laing**, as well as a number of Asian firms. However, most foreign firms are scaling back operations to sit out the downturn.

Utilities

Delays In Project Implementation

Rapid economic growth in recent years has highlighted the need for a major expansion of the country's power generation and distribution network. Slower economic growth during 1997-99 resulted in lower demand but has not altered this fact. Growth in electricity output has averaged around 15% annually since 1995, although it slowed to around 12-13% in 1997-99. Despite ambitious plans to increase generating capacity, project implementation has been slow, reflecting difficulties with the disbursement of official financing as well as problems with the regulatory environment for private sector financing. As a result, power demand has frequently been ahead of supply, leading to power cuts.

During 1998-99, the government said it wished to move away from an emphasis on hydroelectric power, relying more on gas and coal as a source of power. A particularly serious drought in 1998 led to a sharp fall in reservoir levels, forcing power plants to operate at below capacity during the dry season. The government is concerned that this may be setting a pattern for the future. Hydroelectric power was responsible for generating around 67% of total capacity in 1998. The government also wishes to develop a nuclear power generating capacity although this is essentially a long term goal. Another area of focus during 1996-99 was improving the electricity distribution system, which is weak in a number of respects.

Although the government is keen to attract foreign private capital to the power sector, the domestic state company, **Electricity Corporation of Vietnam** (EVN) holds a monopoly position in the sector. The government has come under international pressure to dismantle this.

Telecoms

Expansion Of Telecoms Sector Has Slowed In Recent Years

Expansion of the telecoms sector has slowed from the 30% annual growth achieved in the early-1990s. However, it was still expanding at a rate of around 18% during 1998-99. Despite improvements, the telephone penetration rate is still low and there is a need to upgrade and modernise systems and equipment across the board. There has been substantial foreign investment in the sector – some US$3.2bn approved to date. Leading foreign companies in the sector include: **Telstra, France Telecom, Cable and Wireless** and **Nippon Telegraph and Telephone Company.** Foreign firms have been involved in the upgrading of international switch boards, the installation of optical fibre cable systems, satellite station construction as well as internet and mobile phone projects. The country has three mobile phone networks serving some 200,000 subscribers. All foreign-invested projects to date have been in the form of revenue-sharing

Business Cooperation Contracts (BCCs) with the state-owned **Vietnam Posts and Telecommunications** (VNPT), since 100% foreign investment is not permitted. Foreign companies operating in the industry are seeking to move away from BCCs, although this has yet to receive official approval. Since 1995, there have been moves to dismantle VNPT's monopoly position in the sector. This began with the establishment of two new state companies, namely the military's **Vietel** and **Saigon Postel**. However, in 1999 they had yet to establish their own networks.

Finance

Activities Of Foreign Banks Heavily Restricted

The banking sector contributes just over 2% of GDP, reflecting the undeveloped nature of the banking system. The country is still very much a cash economy even a decade after reform began. Beyond the corporate sector, very few people have bank accounts. Since the early-1990s, there has been a rapid increase in the number of banks operating in Vietnam, with the formation of domestic shareholding joint stock banks and the entry of foreign and joint venture banks. Around 40% of bank lending derives from the four state banks, with 30% coming respectively from the joint stock and foreign and joint venture banks. The development of the domestic banking sector has been problematic, and on the whole the joint stock banks are very weak. Overdue loans in the banking sector have been conservatively estimated at 12-13% of total credit, but the figure is nearer 25% in the case of the joint stock banks. Falling land prices in particular left a number of the joint stock banks badly exposed in 1995-97. Some of them are in line to be merged with stronger banks or closed down, and some progress was made in this respect during 1998-99. In an attempt to improve regulation, the State Bank placed four joint stock banks under "special control" in 1998, namely **Viet Hoa Bank**, **Que Do Bank**, **Ficombank** and **Nam Do Bank**. However, few, if any, of the new domestic banks can be regarded as commercially safe. Aside from a lack of experience in assessing lending risk, difficulties faced by the domestic banks include political interference in lending, including for the joint stock banks, many of which have state shareholders and problems in foreclosing on bad debts.

Foreign banks have begun to carve out a niche for themselves in what is a rather narrow market. The majority reported profits in 1998, although less so in 1999. Competition between the foreign banks is intense, given that there are only a limited number of companies – almost entirely from the state sector – which they feel confident to lend to. There are also restrictions on the activities of foreign banks in terms of the types of collateral they can accept. Foreign banks are still not permitted to take security over land and the regulations governing taking fixed assets as security are burdensome. Foreign banks are also restricted in the amount of dong deposits they can accept.

Tourism

Slowing In Growth In Recent Times

Growth in the tourism sector has averaged around 17% annually since 1995 in terms of foreign arrivals. However, up until 1996 the sector was growing much faster. The number of arrivals fell in 1998, before increasing by a modest amount in 1999. The result has been low hotel occupancy rates and falling prices, which is making it difficult for smaller hotels to keep operating. The root cause of the slowdown can part be laid at the door of the Asian crisis, since some 60% of visitors are from Asia and they have been travelling less. Moreover, the relative stability of the dong has made tourism in Vietnam less competitive in the face of large devaluations in the region. However, there has also been a fall-off in sentiment towards tourism in Vietnam, reflecting problems in the sector. These largely relate to poor infrastructure, particularly linking the main cities with beach resorts, poor service and bureaucracy, for example when obtaining a visa.

Vietnam has also gained a reputation for being expensive. This relates to the dual pricing system, whereby foreigners pay more for accommodation, transport and entry tickets. The government has pledged to phase this out although the practice of charging foreigners more remained commonplace in 1999. The key cities now all have top class hotels. However, leisure and entertainment facilities are quite limited compared with competitor tourist destinations. The availability of high standard hotels reflects heavy foreign investment in the sector – a total of US$8.1bn, or 22%, of total approved investment to date. However, the rate of foreign investment in hotels and tourism declined during 1995-99, partly reflecting the fact that the sector has reached saturation levels and partly reflecting increased government restrictions.

In 1999, the government announced the formation of a tourism steering committee chaired by the foreign minister and deputy prime minister, Nguyen Manh Cam. The committee is overseeing a promotional campaign entitled: "Vietnam 2000 – A Destination". The leading tourism companies are **Saigon Tourist**, **Ben Thanh Tourist** and **Sinh Café**, which aims at the large, backpacker market. The industry is managed by the Vietnam National Tourism Administration.

4 Business Environment

Introduction

Investors Tire Of Difficult Business Environment

Compared with the mid-1990s, investor enthusiasm for Vietnam has reached quite a low point. Much of the initial optimism about Vietnam's future as an investment location and market, has evaporated in the face of too many promises and not enough actual change. The government has been working hard to respond to investor concerns, particularly since the Asian financial crisis struck, causing already slowing foreign investment inflows and exports to plummet.

However, implementation remains poor in the face of political vested interests and bureaucratic weakness. There is still a residue of goodwill among existing businesses in Vietnam, but head offices and potential investors are less convinced. Progress in a range of areas is urgently needed if investment is to recover. Key areas include foreign exchange, high personal income tax rates, deficiencies with build-operate-transfer (BOT) financing and red tape.

Infrastructure

Infrastructure Remains Very Underdeveloped

Vietnam's infrastructure is very poor by regional standards. Its road network is generally in a state of disrepair, making road travel slow. Power generation is struggling to keep up with rising demand, resulting in frequent brown outs and power cuts. Many of the industrial zones (IZs) do not yet have the necessary infrastructure. Other areas are less of a problem. Internal air travel is satisfactory, as is telecom provision, although both are currently expensive for foreigners who are charged more than locals. Internet access is adequate if rather slow.

The country's seaports, which have seen a rapid increase in traffic during the 1990s, need improvement, although infrastructure provision is less of a problem than red tape in customs procedures. Furthermore, some areas are improving. Highway One, which is the main north-south trunk road, has benefited from multilateral donor funding and is in much better shape than a few years ago.

Project Finance Regulatory Environment Remains Weak

Financing infrastructure remains problematic. The main problems relate to the fact that pledged capital or approved projects are often held up by an unsatisfactory regulatory regime and other disbursement problems. A particular weakness is BOT. Delays in creating a satisfactory BOT framework especially run the risk of aggravating the country's power shortages, since a total of nine power generation projects are due to be financed by BOT arrangements.

In January 1999, the government issued Decree 2 amending several articles contained in Decree 62, which covers BOT financing and was passed in 1998. The new Decree responded to a number of issues raised by investors, notably on dispute resolution. However, it does not satisfactorily address all investor concerns, with problems remaining in relation to state guarantees, foreign exchange and security. Although more work needs to be done – some of which might be settled on a case-by-case basis – BOT projects are likely to get underway over the next few years. Problems still exist in relation to the disbursement of donor funding. The amount disbursed has risen in most years since 1993, but bottlenecks still occur and there is anxiety on the part of some lenders as to whether all money is reaching the intended recipients.

The Domestic Market

Urban Purchasing Power Is Well Above That In Rural Areas

Vietnam's population is estimated to have reached nearly 79.5mn in 1999, up 1.9% on the previous year. This makes it a large population both regionally and globally. However, it is also a poor one, curbing its attractiveness in the short and medium term as a global market. Annual per capita income is just US$302, although it is significantly higher in urban areas which are proving attractive, if rather small, markets. In Ho Chi Minh City, which is the richest city in the country, average per capita income is a little over US$1000 annually. The per capita figures are somewhat misleading, since a lot of business activity takes place informally and hence does not show up in the statistics. Moreover, informal, often family-based, saving and lending mechanisms mean that seemingly poor families manage to obtain relatively expensive consumer products, such as motorbikes, electrical and white goods. Even taking into account the Asian financial crisis, and slow progress on reform, growth in Vietnam is likely to be above average compared with more developed markets, pointing to rising purchasing power in the years to come. Ho Chi Minh City is home to a large ethnic Chinese community, making up around 10% of its population. Economically it is more significant, holding connections with Chinese networks in the region.

Some 78% of the population lives in the countryside. This is gradually falling as urbanisation takes place. The main cities, notably Hanoi and Ho Chi Minh City, are swelled by rural migrants. Ho Chi Minh City's formal population is measured at 5mn, but it is thought to be nearer 7.5mn. The population is a young one, with around 36% under the age of 14. The balance between men and women is now statistically normal, despite wartime casualties.

The Labour Market

Labour Not As Cheap As The Minimum Wage Implies

Vietnam's labour force is typically described as being well-educated and low cost, making it one of the most attractive aspects of the country's business environment. This is not untrue based on minimum wage levels and a comparison between Vietnam and similar income level countries in terms of literacy or mean schooling years. However, the day-to-day reality is inevitably more complicated. Until recently, wage contracts for Vietnamese employees of foreign-invested enterprises were required by law to be denominated in US dollars, which resulted in a loss of labour price competitiveness as a result of the large falls in regional currencies against the dollar relative to the dong. Since July 1999, the government has allowed wages to be denominated in dong. However, foreign representative offices, banks and law firms are excluded from the change. Moreover, the government has inserted a clause in the decree that whenever prices rise 10%, there will be an automatic wage adjustment to compensate, which is of continuing concern to investors. The minimum wage currently stands at US$45 per month in Hanoi and Ho Chi Minh City and US$35-40 in other areas.

The cost of employing professional Vietnamese is punitively high for foreign-invested enterprises, owing to a very high income tax rate. A Vietnamese employee earning just US$10,000 a year is taxed at a rate of 60% along with a surtax of 30% on after-tax income in excess of VND8mn a month. In Vietnam, most of the cost of the high income tax rate is borne by the foreign investor. To pay a local employee US$2,000 a month, a company must spend over US$9,000 a month, or US$108,000 a year. As the environment currently exists, it is often cheaper to employ an expatriate. The tax regime, therefore, works directly against the government's stated policy of encouraging foreign companies to train local staff to take over expatriate positions ("localisation"). A further consequence is that the technology transfer process breaks down as foreign expatriates rather than Vietnamese fill key managerial or technical positions. The government has talked for some time about lowering tax rates for professional Vietnamese but as yet has not done so.

Complying With Labour Regulations is a Time-Consuming Process

There has been some tightening up of the regulations governing the employment of foreign expatriates. Since 1997, expatriates employed in Vietnam have been required to have a work permit in addition to a visa. Obtaining this can be rather bureaucratic although companies are finding ways around this. Work permits are valid for five years but in practice are likely to be renewable. A scare in late 1998 that the government was moving to enforce an earlier requirement that foreign companies must recruit via official agencies, has proven no more than this.

Skilled Labour Is In Short Supply

Notwithstanding Vietnam's high literacy rate, the quality of labour varies. There is no shortage of unskilled labour, but it often requires close supervision to ensure consistent results. Culturally different approaches to management have led to incidents, and sometimes strikes, especially in Korean and Taiwanese firms. However, such problems are relatively rare. The fact that they have been rising, reflects greater investment activity of recent years rather than the emergence of a more militant labour environment. The Vietnamese authorities are often sensitive to layoffs. Nevertheless, foreign companies are generally able to dismiss workers when necessary.

Shortages of skilled labour are a present-day reality. The authorities are focusing on this issue, but the bottom line is that educational and technical training programmes are insufficient to meet the requirements of the labour market, with the exception of some areas such as information technology. Such problems are likely to persist for the foreseeable future, particularly in light of government fiscal weakness. Basic labour regulations are contained in Vietnam's Labour Code passed in 1995, although there has been a vast amount of supplementary legislation since then.

Industrial Policy

Consistency Lacking In Industrial Policy

Policy shifts introduced with economic reform resulted in greater emphasis being placed on export-oriented, labour intensive light industry. However, there are so many competing goals in terms of industrial policy that it is hard to speak of a coherent focus. The government also seeks to promote areas of heavy industry, which it regards as strategically important, while there are still strong instincts towards import substitution. Furthermore, even if the government does seek to 'pick winners', its industrial policy goals are too broad for limited public resources to make a difference. Moreover, state investment tends to be disbursed according to political criteria rather than coherent well-thought out industrial policy ones.

A major issue in industrial policy is the degree to which private companies continue to be disadvantaged in relation to their state counterparts. The corporate private sector – as opposed to private household businesses – is still very small in Vietnam, with less than 3% of total industrial output coming from private corporates as recently as 1997. Typically, SOEs have received preferential access in terms of credit, land and various types of licenses. Moreover, SOEs often hold monopolistic or protected positions in the market. None of this is official policy. Indeed, senior leaders frequently emphasise – and are serious about – the need for a level playing field between different types of capital, and the removal of monopolies and other anti-competitive practices. However, implementation comes up against political obstacles so that the reality changes more slowly. In addition, there are contradictions between stated goals and policy in some areas. The formation of general corporations (*tong cong ty*), which were established from 1994 by grouping state enterprises operating in similar areas under a single umbrella, risks squeezing out private sector participation, although the government insists this is not the intention. In 1999, general corporations came up for review because some of them have not been working very well. The upshot was to make adjustments not dismantle them.

It is possible to exaggerate the state-private sector issue in Vietnam, even though the bias is a real one. Not all SOEs receive preferential treatment, whether it be access to public investment capital or foreign exchange, particularly in a climate of shortage. Moreover, some private companies manage very well. It is more important, therefore, to look at the origin of capital. Well-connected private companies, with party or state shareholders, may also receive preferential treatment.

Privatisation

While the government has made clear that it sees the state sector continuing to play a central part in the economy for the foreseeable future, it also recognises the need to create a leaner, more efficient state sector. In late-1997, the World Bank estimated total SOE debts at US$7.3bn, with some 60% of firms unprofitable. The number of SOEs has been cut in half since the late-1980s through a system of mergers and closures, especially at the local level. There are now some 6,000 SOEs, but this number is expected to fall considerably over the next few years as the government has decided that many SOEs do not need to remain in state hands.

A central plank of the government's strategy is its partial privatisation programme, known as equitisation. This has been official policy since 1992, although to date progress has been very slow. The speed picked up greatly in 1998 and there were some 140 companies undergoing equitisation by the end of the year. The target for 1999 was to commence proceedings for another 500 SOEs, but in the end only an additional 100 firms commenced equitisation. While welcome, the sudden acceleration reported by the government is also cause for some concern insofar as it is very unclear what exactly is going on, i.e. who is buying the shares, what changes to management practices, employment levels and so on are taking place. Some of this will probably become clearer over the next year or two as companies complete formalities. However, it remains to be seen whether equitisation – as is taking place – will create a more efficient state enterprise sector. Furthermore, it is possible that the apparent quickening of the pace of change will get bogged down since it is far from clear that the long-standing obstacles to equitisation have actually been overcome. These, in part, have to do with complicated procedures and difficulties in evaluating company assets. However, it is often a question of politics. In practice, real ownership of state assets contained in SOEs has frequently shifted into private hands insofar as the operators of the enterprise are conducting activities for personal gain. Equitisation potentially threatens these interests and hence is resisted.

The government has stated publicly that it is prepared to accept large layoffs from SOEs in order to push ahead with reform, but again such decisions have to be agreed at the level of the enterprise where different interests are frequently at play. Nevertheless, some SOEs are opting for equitisation with enthusiasm. Foreign investors are permitted to buy up to 30% stakes in equitising companies and a handful of small SOEs have sold shares to foreigners. There have been suggestions that the government may increase the 30% limit for foreign investors although this looks unlikely in the short term. New legislation on corporate tax came into effect in 1999. Many companies are now eligible for a corporate tax rate of 25%, although it can rise to as high as 45%.

Foreign Investment Policy

Renewed Efforts To Attract Foreign Investment

The sharp fall in FDI, notably since the Asian financial crisis struck, has prompted major efforts by the government to improve the foreign investment regime. A number of important changes were introduced with Decree 10, which was issued in January 1998, although not all of these are being implemented as stated. The Law On Foreign Investment is also in the process of being amended.

Overall, the government remains pro-foreign investment. Indeed, given limited domestic resources, it is essential that the country continues to attract foreign capital inflows. The government particularly encourages foreign investment in labour-intensive export-oriented sectors, with special emphasis on primary products processing, manufacturing and environmental protection. Decree 10 contained details of new tax incentives for foreign investors, notably those investing in areas encouraged by the government. This included profit tax exemption for four years from the first profit-making year, followed by a 50% reduction for the following four years. Investors are also able to import a wider range of products for use in production duty free than previously. Furthermore, land rents have been lowered.

There are a number of areas where the government restricts foreign investment. This can be in terms of requiring that an investor forms a joint venture with a local company or insisting that a product is exported. The government also limits investment in some areas of infrastructure on national security grounds. Restrictions on foreign investment also stem from a tendency of the authorities to bend to pressure from local producers to protect their market.

Many Problems Still Remain

Despite recent government efforts, dissatisfaction with the government's policy towards foreign investment remains widespread amongst investors. This relates to various issues, such as uncertain access to foreign exchange and high personal income tax levels (especially for Vietnamese professionals). Foreigners tend to pay more than Vietnamese for utility costs including electricity, water, telecommunications, domestic air travel and land rent. Other issues include the requirement that wages of Vietnamese employees at some foreign companies be denominated in dollars as well as limits on 100% foreign-owned investments and excessive amounts of red tape, despite improvements in the speed at which the initial licence is issued.

The government has been moving to address many of these concerns. The dual pricing system is being phased out and it is now only at foreign representative offices, banks and law firms that the salaries of Vietnamese employees must be denominated in dollars. The government has also been relaxing earlier requirements that foreign investors enter joint ventures, allowing a number of foreign businesses to buy out their local partner. This represents a significant advance since for many investors the joint venture experience has not been a happy one.

Notwithstanding these improvements, the investment environment in Vietnam continues to be difficult. While the senior leadership understand the difficulties faced by foreign investors well – and is doing its utmost to solve the problems – investors will continue to encounter obstacles caused by less enlightened, and often blatantly obstructive, lower level officials. Changing this type of mentality will take a long time. Meanwhile, such obstacles will push up business costs.

Foreign Trade Policy

Domestic Politicking Hits Trade Accord With US

Tariff barriers are scheduled to be reduced in line with Vietnam's commitments as a member of Asean's Free Trade Area (Afta). Vietnam has been given a slightly longer time to cut barriers than the more developed Asean members but slightly less than Cambodia, Laos and Myanmar. By 2006, tariffs on a wide range of products must be reduced to below 5%. Membership of the Apec forum, which Vietnam joined in November 1998, and its application to join the World Trade Organisation (WTO), will also require pursuit of trade liberalising policies.

In July 1999, Vietnam signed in principle a bilateral trade agreement with the USA. However, the accord then got caught up in domestic political manoeuvring in Vietnam which has prevented the agreement being confirmed. This has also held up the award of normal trade relations (NTR, formerly most favoured nation trade status) to Vietnam since Washington is insistent that the trade accord must be in place first. The Vietnamese government has also suggested that it is unhappy with aspects of the accord, but the US government has insisted that there is no scope for re-negotiation.

The regional financial crisis, which has been accompanied by slower export growth, has prompted intensified government efforts to remove administrative constraints on exports. This has focused on cutting down licensing requirements and red tape at customs, although implementation has been rather poor. The government has pledged to ease barriers to entry into the export sector which currently exist. This has included permitting a number of private companies to break into the rice export market, although the hold of a handful of key state firms is likely to remain intact for some years. There has also been talk of establishing some sort of export credit fund, but progress has been delayed by debate over the precise institutional form it should take.

Protectionism Is Still A Factor

Despite trends towards greater trade liberalisation, countervailing protectionist sentiment exists too. Protectionist measures are seen as a way to limit the size of the trade deficit. They also stem from a desire to protect revenue sources as well as pressure from domestic producers. The government regularly announces lists of banned goods and those governed by export quotas and import licenses. Export quotas only exist for rice as far as the Vietnamese regulations are concerned, although garment exports to the EU and other markets are licensed by quotas imposed in Brussels or elsewhere.

Intellectual property protection is poor despite the government's stated determination to clamp down on abuse and the signing of an intellectual property accord with the USA. A few test cases involving Vietnamese musicians whose work had been plagiarised have recently taken place, but the much larger areas, such as the production of fake Compact Disks and videos where vested interests are much stronger, have yet to be seriously tackled.

No Current or Capital Account Convertibility

The regional financial crisis proved very disruptive in terms of the availability of foreign exchange, with frequent shortages in 1997-98. This prompted the government to take a number of retrogressive steps in terms of foreign exchange reforms, including the introduction of a decree in September 1998, requiring companies to sell 80% of their surplus foreign currency holdings to banks within 15 days (Decree 173; later changed to immediately), and lowering the amount of capital that can be taken out of the country without declaration from US$7,000 to US$500.

The government has pledged that it remains committed to moving towards eventual full dong convertibility. In September 1999, the restrictions embodied in Decree 173 were eased. Nevertheless, until foreign investment and exports pick up, bold reform steps are unlikely. Furthermore, even if the government was to respond to calls from foreign investors to grant all businesses conversion rights – rather than on the selective basis which currently exists – doubts would remain over whether the authorities could always honour their commitments. Current account convertibility is unlikely in the next two or three years, while the lifting of restrictions on the capital account remains more remote still.

Bureaucracy And Corruption

Red Tape And Corruption Remain A Problem

Administrative procedures in Vietnam are generally unwieldy and confusing. Obtaining the correct documents or the necessary government stamp is often a time-consuming and frustrating process. This is the case for both domestic and foreign investors. In the case of foreign investors, the problems rest less with obtaining the initial investment licence, which although the process is still unnecessarily bureaucratic now happens quite quickly, than with post-approval procedures. Thus, if a company wants to change some aspect of its operations, it must seek official approval rather than just reporting the changes to the relevant agency. Procedures involving land, customs and tax are commonly the most onerous for foreign investors, although difficulties can sometimes be eased with the help of a good local partner.

The highly regulated business environment in Vietnam creates an ideal climate for corruption to flourish. The fact that state officials are paid so little clearly fuels corrupt practices such as bribe-taking, which are commonplace. Different companies take different views on the matter, with some saying that they get by adequately without ever paying bribes. Others are quite open, and regard corruption as just another business cost and a manageable one at that. Corruption is less of a day-to-day concern for foreign investors than tortuous administrative procedures. It is sometimes suggested that US companies are disadvantaged in terms of bidding for contracts because of very strict anti-corruption legislation in their home country which specifies that they can be prosecuted for their actions abroad.

Environmental Regulation

Enforcement Of Environmental Regulations Is Poor

In recent years, the government has become more active in the area of environmental protection in response to the pressures caused by industrialisation and urbanisation. This has involved creating a legal framework governing environmental regulation. There is now a Law on the Environment, which was passed in 1993. In addition, steps have been taken to establish the necessary institutional mechanisms to enforce regulations. Responsibility for enforcement, and formulation of, environmental policies, rests with the Ministry of Science, Technology and the Environment (MOSTE), which was set up in 1992. It is represented at the provincial and city level. The government is receiving technical and financial assistance from the Swedish International Development Agency (SIDA) on environmental matters.

Foreign companies wishing to invest in Vietnam are required to carry out an Environmental Impact Assessment (EIA), which must be approved by MOSTE as a pre-condition before an operating licence is issued. This has not, however, prevented increasing pollution, which reflects the fact that EIAs are not properly scrutinised and that many domestic companies are still not properly regulated. In addition, the authorities are overseeing a programme of relocating industries away from residential urban areas, but this is progressing very slowly, often because of unresolved issues over who will pay.

Scrutiny of the EIA, and the standards it must adhere to, are expected to get tougher. Industrial zones (IZs) and companies operating in them are likely to face close regulation. In this regard, the government has recently issued new regulations governing the management of environmental issues in IZs. Companies found to be polluting the environment can expect to be fined. There has been talk in the past of the government introducing an environmental tax on pre-tax profits, although the legislation on this is not progressing very fast.

5 Capital Markets

Equity Markets

Undeveloped Capital Markets

Vietnam's formal capital market is at an embryonic stage of development, although there is an extensive informal market. The country still lacks a stock market and a secondary market for bonds and bills. As a result, the burden has fallen heavily on the banking sector as a provider of capital. However, the banking sector is weak and not working effectively in this respect. A stock market, where bonds and bills will also be traded, will probably get off the ground in 2000 but only on an experimental basis. Problems in the banking sector will take longer to fix, although the vision needed to tackle weaknesses is gradually being articulated more clearly by the country's leaders.

The Delayed Launch

The planned launch date of Vietnam's stock market has been repeatedly put back. The idea of establishing such a market was first aired in the early 1990s. However, the plans got caught up in a combination of ideological objections – doubts about whether such a mechanism could be sufficiently controlled and fear of the consequences if it could not – and bureaucratic weakness. Foreign capital flight from regional stock markets, which accompanied the Asian financial crisis, did not encourage those in the leadership who were already uneasy. However, the Asian crisis has not led to a rejection of the idea of opening a bourse altogether.

There were small signs of progress towards establishing a stock market in 2000. The State Securities Commission (SSC), which is responsible for preparing for the eventual launch, announced in February 2000 that it was planning to test a trial stock trading system in Ho Chi Minh City in April, ahead of a formal launch before the end of the year. This followed the go-ahead being given to test the trial system by the deputy prime minister and Politburo member, Nguyen Tan Dung. The stock trading system has emerged as a preferred 'intermediate step' to a fully fledged stock market, which is still some years away. The initial exchange is expected to operate like an over-the-counter market, with both stocks and bonds being traded. In January, the prime minister, Phan Van Khai, approved a US$13.7mn plan to upgrade the building in Ho Chi Minh City expected to house the bourse. The SSC has also said that tenders for the purchase of equipment needed for a full trading floor are due to be held in June or July. As ever, these dates could still slip.

Clues as to the likely structure of the future stock market can be seen in Decree 48/1998/ND-CP, issued on July 11, 1998. Decree 48 covers organisations issuing securities, securities companies providing brokerage and trading services, as well as underwriting, investment portfolio management and consultancy work. It also covers the role of investment funds, custodial service organisations and public investors. The Decree deals in general principles but is due to be followed by a raft of implementing regulations which will provide more details.

According to Decree 48, securities companies must be limited liability or joint stock companies. Banks and insurance companies wishing to participate in securities trading must form independent securities companies. Securities companies must meet minimum legal capital requirements as follows: brokerage, VND3bn; trading, VND12bn; investment portfolio management, VND3bn; underwriting, VND22bn; and Securities Investment Consultancy, VND3bn. Securities companies and banks will provide custodial services as long as they meet legal capital requirements and are technically qualified as specified by SSC. To date, some seven local organisations have applied to establish securities companies. They are mainly banks, including the state owned **Vietcombank** and two joint stock banks, **Asia Commercial Bank** and **Phuong Nam Bank**. The state owned **Ho Chi Minh City Investment Fund For Urban Development** (HIFU) has also applied to set up a securities firm. The SSC has said there needs to be at least 6-10 securities firms for the market to work properly.

Few Companies Meet Listing Requirements

There is still uncertainty as to how many companies will be listed at the outset. Decree 48 has set tight listing requirements. Companies wishing to list must have minimum legal capital of VND10bn. They must also have operated profitably for the past two years while a minimum 15-20% of the issued shares must be sold to over 100 investors outside the issuing organisation. The founders of the issuing company must hold at least 20% of the organisation's shares for at least three years from when they are issued. Where the value of the shares issued exceed VND10bn, it is necessary that the issue be guaranteed by another organisation. There are still very few companies in Vietnam which meet these requirements, particularly in terms of company size and profitability. SSC chairman Le Van Chau said in an interview in early 2000, that his organisation is in the process of selecting suitably qualified companies to list from the ranks of former state firms which have completed equitisation (partial privatisation) procedures. However, he said that out of the 240 firms which have been equitised, it has identified just seven or eight which meet the listing requirement. Of greater concern, in terms of listings on the future stock market, is the rather unclear way in which the equitisation process is proceeding. This is unlikely to be conducive to the smooth running of a bourse.

At various times, it has been suggested that 'private' joint stock companies will be able to list – as opposed to just equitised former SOEs – which if confirmed will boost the numbers which are eligible. The government has also said that bonds and one-year maturity bills, issued by the Finance Ministry, commercial banks and SOEs, will be traded. In particular, the SSC has been pushing for blue chip Vietnamese corporations such as **Vietnam Airlines, PetroVietnam, Electricity of Vietnam** and **Vietnam Posts and Telecommunications** to be able to issue bonds for trading on the forthcoming stock market. While it is still unclear what exactly will be traded once the market is up and running, the bottom line is that the number of listed companies will be small and trading light initially and for the foreseeable future. Shares are expected to have a primary minimum offer value of VND10,000 and bonds of VND100,000.

Limitations On Foreign Participation

The participation of foreign investors in Vietnam's stock market will be restricted in the early years. It had long been assumed that a foreign institutional investor would be limited to a 30% share in a listed company's equity, in line with the 30% stake it is currently permitted in an equitised company. However, the SSC issued new regulations in January 2000 stating that the maximum permitted foreign share in a listed company's equity would be 20%. A single institutional investor is not permitted to hold more than 7%, falling to 3% for an individual. The SSC's announcement has been met with dismay by foreign investors, many of whom believe that healthy foreign participation is important to enliven interest in the stock market. The implication of the new regulation is that the foreign stake in an equitised company would have to be reduced before the firm could list on the bourse, if it was at the maximum 30%. However, this has yet to be spelt out. Proposed changes to the foreign investment law currently under consideration have suggested allowing joint venture companies with foreign investment to list on the stock market although there is no guarantee that this will be approved. Earlier regulations have stated that 100% foreign-owned securities companies will not be permitted to operate on the bourse, although foreign companies can form a joint venture with a Vietnamese organisation.

A mock stock market in Hanoi has been used to train brokers and other staff since 1997. In the absence of a formal stock market, a small grey market in company shares has emerged. This has mainly involved the management of equitised companies buying out workers' shares.

Bond Markets

Regular Bond Sales But No Secondary Market

The State Treasury has been issuing bills and bonds for many years. However, the first treasury bill auction only took place in June 1995. Since early-1996, auctions have been held every two weeks, mainly of one-year bills. The most frequent buyers have been domestic commercial banks and insurance companies. Foreign banks have occasionally participated, but not recently. The attractiveness of the auctions has often been limited by a low annual coupon. Bidders have also been nervous of committing too many resources denominated in dong, in case of a devaluation, although such concerns eased in 1999 as the currency lost only 1% of its value. In the absence of a secondary market, most of the bills have been held by the original purchasers, although they can be sold to the public. The plan is to allow treasury bills to be traded on the stock market once it gets underway.

During 1999, the government announced a number of bond issues. This included the sale of foreign currency bonds to assist in financing infrastructure projects. The bonds, which were worth a total of US$300mn, were issued through commercial banks, finance companies and other agents, to assist in financing infrastructure projects. In addition, the Ministry of Finance sold VND4,000bn (US$288mn) worth of five-year bonds to fund rural infrastructure and other agricultural projects. The bonds were issued in Vietnamese dong in 11 denominations from VND20,000 to VND50mn, with an annual coupon of 1.5% plus inflation. In the end, the VND4,000 target was met, but not without pressure being put on the population, especially public sector employees. The largest buyers were state institutions. The government has sought to reassure potential buyers of the bonds that there are clear financial benefits, including a pledge to make up any shortfall, if the bond interest rate falls below the bank rate. The bonds can also be sold at any time to commercial banks as well as inherited, according to the Ministry of Finance.

Corporate bond issues have been few and far between in Vietnam to date, although they are likely to become more common. A landmark issue took place in 1996, when the Ho Chi Minh City-based **Refrigerator Engineering Company** issued two-year convertible bonds worth US$4.5mn on an experimental basis, which included foreign participation. The original idea was that the bonds would be converted into shares which could be traded on the stock market. There are plans for a number of large state enterprises to issue bonds to be traded on the stock market when it is up and running.

Limited Activity In International Capital Markets

Vietnam made its first foray into the international capital markets in March 1998. This involved the issuing of US$234.5mn of par bonds, US$25.3mn of discount bonds and US$293.9mn of past due interest, as part of the rescheduling agreement covering its London Club commercial debt. Rescheduling of the London Club debt, clears the way for Vietnam to borrow further on the international capital markets. For a period, there was talk of a US$100mn Eurobond issue, but this appears to have been put on the back burner. This followed comments from the World Bank that it would be unnecessary and expensive, particularly since Vietnam has access to relatively cheap loans from the international donor community. In 1999, there were suggestions that PetroVietnam was planning an international bond issue to mobilise capital for oil and gas projects although as yet nothing has come of this.

An international bond issue would also be expensive, following a downgrading of Vietnam's debt rating by **Moody's Investor Services**. Vietnam originally had a Ba3 rating, which was lowered to B1 in 1998. In 1999, Moodys changed its outlook to negative for Vietnam's B1 foreign-currency ceiling for bonds and notes, stating that a lack of progress in structural reforms and difficulties in the domestic and regional trade environment had increased risks to the balance of payments.

EMERGING EUROPE

HUNGARY 2000

Editors: Anthony Cooke/Ann-Louise Hagger

Contents

Political Outlook _____ **497**

    Domestic Political Outlook 497

    Profile and Recent Developments _____ **503**

    Introduction 503
    The Political System 504
    The Political Parties 505
    Recent Developments 507
    Foreign Policy 509

Economic Outlook _____ **511**

    Overview 511
    Economic Activity 512
    Fiscal Policy 513
    Monetary Policy 514
    Exchange Rate Policy 515
    Balance Of Payments 517
    The European Union 518

    Profile and Recent Developments _____ **521**

    Characteristics Of The Economy 521
    Economic Activity 521
    Fiscal Policy 523
    Monetary Policy 524
    Exchange Rate Policy 525
    Balance of Payments 527
    Foreign Direct Investment 528
    External Debt 530

Key Economic Sectors _____ **531**

    Introduction 531
    Petroleum And Related Industries 533
    Electricity 534
    Telecommunications 535
    Pharmaceuticals 537
    Automotive Industry 538
    Tourism 539
    Construction 539

Profile and Recent Developments _____ **541**

Introduction 541
Agriculture 542
Construction 543
Manufacturing 544
Energy Sector 545
Communications 547
Retail Trade 549
Banking Sector 550

Business Environment _____ 553

Introduction 553
Infrastructure 554
The Domestic Market 555
The Labour Market 556
Taxation Policy 557
Industrial Policy 559
Foreign Trade Policy 560
Bureaucracy And Corruption 562
Intellectual Property Rights 562
Environmental Regulation 563

Capital Markets _____ 565

Introduction 565
Equity Market 565
Recent Performance 567
Bond Market 568

HUNGARY: MACROECONOMIC DATA AND FORECASTS

	1993	1994	1995	1996	1997	1998	1999	2000f	2001f	2002f
Population (mn)	10.310	10.277	10.246	10.212	10.174	10.100	10.027	9.954	9.881	9.809
Nominal GDP (HUFbn)	3,548.3	4,364.8	5,561.9	6,823.3	8,461.6	10,087.0	11,498.0	13,126.1	14,703.4	16,394.2
Nominal GDP (US$bn)	38.60	41.51	44.25	44.70	45.30	47.05	48.48	49.07	57.24	63.14
Real GDP growth, % y-o-y	-0.8	2.9	1.5	1.3	4.6	4.9	4.5	5.5	4.5	4.8
GDP per capita (US$)	3744	4039	4319	4377	4453	4658	4836	4929	5793	6437
Industrial production (% y-o-y, period average)	4.0	9.6	4.6	3.4	11.1	12.5	10.2	14.3	8.0	6.5
Unemployment rate (%, end period)	12.6	10.9	10.9	9.9	8.7	7.8	7.0	6.4	6.9	6.7
Central budget (HUFbn)	-199.7	-277.2	-307.1	-132.4	-342.1	-553.9	-331.6	-389.0	-456.0	-443.0
Central budget (% of GDP)	-5.6	-6.4	-5.5	-1.9	-4.0	-5.5	-2.9	-3.0	-3.1	-2.7
Consumer prices (% y-o-y, end period)	21.1	21.2	28.3	19.8	18.5	10.3	11.2	8.3	7.2	6.5
Consumer prices (% y-o-y, period average)	22.5	18.9	28.3	23.5	18.3	14.2	10.0	8.7	7.5	6.7
Producer prices (% y-o-y, end period)	-	-	30.2	20.1	19.5	7.1	6.5	5.5	4.5	4.0
Producer prices (% y-o-y, period average)	10.8	11.3	28.9	21.8	20.4	11.3	7.3	6.1	4.9	4.3
Exchange rate (HUF/US$, end period)	100.7	110.69	139.47	164.93	203.50	219.03	252.52	262.60	252.00	266.10
Exchange rate (HUF/US$, period average)	91.93	105.16	125.68	152.65	186.79	214.40	237.15	267.52	256.86	259.64
Lending rate (% per annum, end period)	-	29.7	32.2	24	20.8	18.8	15.4	13.6	13.7	12.7
Deposit rate (% per annum, end period)	-	23.6	26.1	20.1	16.8	14.3	11.7	9.2	9.5	8.7
90 day t-bill rate (% per annum, end period)	-	-	30.54	22.24	19.28	16.29	14.5	10.5	11.0	10.0
Money supply, M3 (HUFbn, end period)	2016.5	2279.1	2736.4	3350.9	4011.0	4619.7	5356.1	6132.0	6870.0	7560.0
Money supply, M3 (% y-o-y, end period)	15.3	13.0	20.1	22.5	19.7	15.2	15.9	14.5	12.0	10.0
Merchandise exports (fob, US$bn)	8.09	7.61	12.81	14.18	19.64	20.75	21.84	23.80	25.00	26.40
Merchandise imports (fob, US$bn)	11.34	11.25	15.25	16.83	21.37	22.87	24.02	25.70	26.80	28.00
Merchandise trade balance (fob-fob, US$bn)	-3.25	-3.63	-2.44	-2.64	-1.73	-2.12	-2.18	-1.90	-1.80	-1.60
Current account balance (US$bn)*	-3.45	-3.91	-2.48	-1.68	-0.98	-2.30	-2.08	-2.13	-2.28	-2.03
Current account (% of GDP)	-8.9	-9.4	-5.6	-3.8	-2.2	-4.9	-4.3	-4.3	-4.0	-3.2
Foreign debt stock (US$bn, end period)	24.56	28.52	31.66	27.55	23.75	26.75	26.38	27.00	27.70	28.30
Foreign debt stock (% of GDP, end period)	63.6	68.7	71.5	61.6	52.4	56.9	54.4	55.0	48.4	44.8
Foreign debt stock (% of exports, end period)	-	-	-	-	91.7	99.9	92.9	87.5	85.8	83.5
Foreign exchange reserves (US$bn)	6.70	6.74	11.97	9.72	8.41	9.32	10.95	11.50	11.00	11.00
Import cover (months)	5.9	5.7	7.7	6.6	3.6	3.7	4.8	4.7	4.3	4.7

f = BMI forecast. Source: Hungarian Central Statistical Office, National Bank of Hungary, IMF.

1 Political Outlook

Domestic Political Outlook

Coalition Set For Full Term Despite Tensions

With a clear parliamentary majority, a reasonably harmonious working relationship and an opinion poll rating that has yet to reflect its relative economic success, the coalition of Fidesz-Hungarian Civic Party (Fidesz-MPP) and the Independent Smallholders' Party (FKGP) is on course to serve out its four-year term. Economic growth will remain sufficiently strong to supply the extra budgetary resources for rural development and employment creation, which has been the main source of contention between the two coalition partners. With the Hungarian Democratic Forum (MDF – the first post-communist ruling party) also backing the coalition and holding a token seat in cabinet, Viktor Orban's government should be able to withstand the well-coordinated opposition of the Hungarian Socialist Party (MSzP), while keeping its distance from more extreme anti-socialist groups such as the controversial Hungarian Justice and Life Party (MIEP).

With a shared interest in staying in power until the economic upturn starts to win back voters, the ruling coalition is unlikely to let disagreements drag it down before the scheduled 2002 parliamentary election.

The coalition's cohesion was tested in H1 00 as its members disagreed over the choice of presidential candidate, but tensions were largely defused when FKGP leader Jozsef Torgyan agreed not to seek nomination. Parliament's subsequent vote in favour of compromise candidate Ferenc Madl was less convincing than usual for the coalition (in Hungary it is parliament which decides who will fill the largely ceremonial post of president). This suggests that not all Torgyan's supporters were happy to see him out of the race, but Torgyan took his "very difficult" decision to avert a possible split in the coalition, and subsequently entered talks with Fidesz president Laszlo Kover on a "long-term" cooperation pact. The primary political force immediately after World War 2, the FKGP has been in long-term decline, its support remaining inescapably rooted in the slowly depopulating rural areas. Unless allied to a party with a strong urban following, it has little chance of playing a role in national politics. As long as he retains the agriculture portfolio and is seen winning additional funds and price support for the sector, Torgyan is therefore very unlikely to push any arguments to the point of his party leaving the coalition.

From National To European Battleground

The next parliamentary election, due to be held by May 2002, will be fought on substantially different and, in general, more forward-looking policy issues than the last. In 1998 it was still possible for Fidesz – which was formed and run by politicians who had opposed communist rule or were too young to have been politically engaged with it – to tilt opinion against the MSzP by recalling its command-economy roots. However, the MSzP's leadership has passed to a new generation and its policies now more formally embrace the social-market approach forced on it while in power in 1994-98, with the result that the MSzP can now battle Fidesz on the competence rather than the contents of its economic policy. Its campaign is likely to centre on charges that the present government has been too slow in narrowing the budget deficit, completing the privatisation process and following it up with regulatory reform designed to maximise inward investment to utilities and energy, and extending economic freedom to the media and migrant labour. Politically, the MSzP will adopt a more internationalist stance, arguing that Fidesz's frequent criticism of the European Union (EU) hesitation over enlargement, and periodic rekindling of the debate over Hungarian communities in neighbouring countries, have slowed the rebuilding of regional relations.

Indeed, the agenda for the next election will largely be set – as has most economic policy for the past five years – by the EU accession process. Officially, all political sides expect and wish Hungary to qualify for membership by 2003. There is a general consensus that accession would confer both economic and political benefits, and that Hungary should not be kept waiting if other Central European applicants fall behind in the convergence process, even if Brussels would prefer them to enter as a group. However, the slow pace of pre-enlargement policy reform within the EU, and its recent diplomatic signals suggest that accession for Hungary (or any of the other "first wave" applicants) is unlikely to occur before 2005, even if the Hungarians meet the conditions substantially earlier. So the government elected in 2002 is likely to be judged on the success of its final preparations for EU membership, as much as on the formal achievement of membership, which may well have to wait until after another parliamentary election.

Relations With The EU Becoming Strained

The EU's economic and social policy demands are ostensibly easier for Fidesz than for the MSzP and other opposition parties to conform to. Fidesz has long been sympathetic to the policies of industry and utility privatisation

With communist-era policies and personalities fast fading among the major parties, the next parliamentary election will be fought on more forward-looking issues than the last. The main battle will be over competence in guiding the economy and spreading the benefits of growth between populist anti-communists and reconstructed ex-communists whose programmes, both shaped by EU entry requirements, now overlap extensively.

Both major parties have important differences with the EU, mainly over the extent of short-term state backing and protection from free trade pressures for infant and vulnerable industries.

and deregulation, free trade and open capital markets which the EU now espouses, and which the Hungarians will need to adopt before accession can occur. Fidesz's leaders generally lean towards Western Europe or North America, in contrast to the more regionally-based or Russian-oriented focus of the MSzP's past upper ranks, and its vote is concentrated among those who stand to gain from reductions in public expenditure and tax cuts. Sensitive to its support-base in the more educated and pro-Western sections of society, Fidesz has found more resources for higher education, defence and small business support even as it scales down social spending in other areas and moves to eliminate subsidies to older industries.

However, the present coalition's relations with the EU are subject to a number of strains, and these are likely to worsen as the next election approaches. They arise principally from the political priorities of the Small-holders, who have already supported additional subsidies and import tariffs for agriculture which run counter to the moves required for integration to the EU's Common Agricultural Policy (CAP). The EU has also been critical of the coalition's handling of Phare pre-accession aid and its retention of control over broadcasting appointments and sections of the press. The extent to which Fidesz can uphold an EU-friendly free-market agenda is limited by its own populist wing, which sees faster economic growth, active job-creation measures, trade protection for sensitive sectors and a still-generous welfare state as the only ways for the party to win the next election.

From Bureaucrats To Technocrats

Although the Young Democrats' original upper age limit of 35 has been scrapped, and MPP has been appended to their title, the leading figures in Hungary's current ruling coalition represent a new phase in post-communist politics. The politics of Orban and his followers were not forged within the former communist party, as were those of the technocrats who rose to power in Poland and Slovakia in the mid- and late-1990s, nor were they formed in opposition to it, as is the case with the present ruling parties in Poland and the Czech Republic. Instead, Fidesz won power on the strength of its more meritocratic and technocratic image, strong anti-corruption stance, and promises of better economic management leading to faster output and income growth. This enabled it to appeal to both the expanding group of entrepreneurs and private-sector professionals who have made strong economic gains since the fall of communism, and the (generally older) victims of the change, who are now looking for the restoration of their old jobs, living standards and welfare entitlements.

In practice, many of the key policies pursued by the current coalition –

Youthful energy, lavish promises and a presidential leadership style have ensured a rapid ascent for the present ruling party, but its reforming zeal is constrained by a coalition partner still sensitive to traditional economic lobbies, and its efforts to by-pass bureaucracy have lost public trust without noticeably speeding up the decision-making process.

including privatisation, EU harmonisation, pension reform, Nato membership and improved regional relations – were set in train by its MSzP predecessors, who also laid the groundwork for the economic acceleration enjoyed by Fidesz in its first two years. The coalition has also not been immune to some of the MSzP's less benign tactics, maintaining a strong official grip over press and broadcast media, appointing close supporters to some public agency and enterprise boards, and applying tactical pressure to certain central bank decisions. However, it has escaped involvement in the most serious of the corruption cases that have come to light since 1998, most of which relate to the collapse of state-owned **Postabank** after various lending irregularities during the MSzP's term in office.

Fidesz has strengthened its reputation for decisive expert-driven action through the significant strengthening of the Prime Minister's office, which now has its own minister without portfolio and in the first two years took direct control of a number of problem areas including the handling of telecoms privatisation/regulation and the Postabank affair. Orban's more presidential style of government has been effective at acting on certain issues which had stalled under the previous coalition's more consensual approach, and also shows signs of enforcing the interdepartmental coordination needed to accelerate work on the more contentious elements of EU harmonisation. However, the remit of the Prime Minister's office has been incomplete because of the Smallholders' reluctance to cede authority over their three portfolios (agriculture, defence and Phare administration), and is in danger of ranging too widely to maintain adequate oversight of all areas, despite Orban's undoubted intellectual and physical energy and the quality of advisers on tap. The extension of prime ministerial powers has also caused resentment among opposition parties, which hold it responsible for making some key areas of decision-making less accountable to parliament. The additional control afforded by the office will be too tempting for other future prime ministers to forgo, but it has left the overall quality of government more dependent than before on the individual qualities of the premier. A strong prime ministerial hand proved valuable when the government had to take rapid decisions over the Kosovo crisis within days of joining Nato in 1999, and will be especially useful in the closing stages of the EU accession talks. However, it raises the danger of inadequate ministerial input and parliamentary scrutiny being given to certain less urgent and equally complex measures, especially given the absence of a second parliamentary chamber.

2002 Election: Continuity Despite Likely Socialist Win

The MSzP's strong mid-term opinion poll lead is expected to narrow as the next election approaches, with the coalition recapturing some protest votes as faster economic growth and direct tax reductions leave average households feeling better off. However, Fidesz will still disappoint the expectations it raised during the last election campaign – of GDP growth reaching 7%, inflation slowing further, and early EU entry being secured – and this will limit the swing back towards it. While the new economy minister, Gyorgy Matolcsy, continues to hint at approaching the 7% growth target during the present parliament, the 6.8% expansion achieved in Q1 00 is likely to have been a one-off peak. Instead, the coalition will have to let the economy slow again in 2001 (by reducing the fiscal deficit and letting real interest rates rise slightly) to avoid inflation and the current account deficit worsening again. Abandoning the Smallholder link might help the recovery of Fidesz's core urban vote, but could also force early elections, which the party is unlikely to want to risk. The MSzP, under new post-communist era leadership and able to claim that it both set in train and could better sustain the current economic acceleration, is likely to emerge with a small majority, albeit insufficient to form a government on its own.

If the MSzP wins, its most likely option would be to seek coalition with the Alliance of Free Democrats (SzDSz) as it did in 1994 despite then commanding an absolute parliamentary majority. The SzDSz lost ground at the 1998 election, but is likely to benefit (along with most other smaller parties) from greater disaffection with both major parties next time round. Although either of the smaller parties in the present coalition might conceivably ally with the MSzP, neither the FKGP nor the MDF leadership is likely to pursue this, given their policy differences with the Socialists and the likely electoral backlash from such a move. While the chances of a smaller party making the breakthrough into three-figure parliamentary representation, as Fidesz did in 1998 are small, formal amalgamations between them also seem remote at this stage. Unless there is a major economic reversal (which **BMI** views as unlikely), the total vote for the present and previous coalition groupings should rise, further isolating the MIEP, if not actually forcing it below the 5% threshold for parliamentary representation.

EU Question To Test Parties

A "grand coalition" of Fidesz and the MSzP, should neither be able to easily assemble a parliamentary majority, might make sense if urgent EU-related legislation were otherwise at risk of stalling. But past ideological differences are likely to set the leaderships of both major parties against this, even though the campaign will confirm an even closer overlap between their principal

Present opinion poll evidence and economic trends suggest a swing back towards the Socialists at the next election, with the danger of an inconclusive result if smaller parties benefit from an expanded protest vote. Provided one or other of the existing major parties can assemble a stable coalition, present reform momentum should be maintained, with looming EU accession shaping much of their agenda.

The major parties are unlikely to pool their efforts formally, even if a hung parliament makes this the best way to speed up necessary reforms. This leaves a small but recognisable danger that final EU accession measures could be delayed as infighting among the parties in favour opens the door for blocking tactics by those still against.

economic and social policies than in 1998. Although neither party will wish to be seen delaying EU qualification for political reasons, both will be hoping to be in power when the accession date finally arrives, and will therefore want to ensure that entry occurs on terms they fully approve. This could lead to the Socialists making a stand in favour of more generous industrial and social policy spending than EU structural fund allocations and budget deficit guidelines would currently allow. Fidesz, especially if it were still counting on Smallholder support, could seek an agricultural deal that better shelters Hungary from any income supports or export subsidies still being paid out within the EU.

The risks involved in a politically ineffective minority or loose coalition government after the next election will be greater than that of an economically appropriate government with a strong mandate. Coalitions led by either the MSzP, Fidesz or a resurgent centrist party will not differ significantly in their commitment to EU economic and Nato defence integration, and to pro-business tax and regulatory policy at home, provided they are not seriously constrained by more lobby-prone coalition partners. However, despite the likely swing towards smaller parties as some voters who deserted the MSzP in 1998 grow equally disaffected with Fidesz, a two-party system appears well enough established to keep the risk of a hung parliament low. Competition among pro-EU parties to be credited with securing accession and last-ditch attempts by anti-EU elements (likely to cluster around the MIEP) to derail the process, will raise the chances of rifts even among nominal friends in the next parliament. But EU guidelines and deadlines will also provide both an incentive to avoid excessive divisiveness and an expedient to de-politicise contentious decisions. Indeed, enough of a bipartisan approach to international issues should survive to keep Hungary at the head of the "first wave", provided expectations of a relatively benign economic situation are realised.

Profile and Recent Developments

Introduction

An Early Proponent Of Reform

While the first post-war election, held in November 1945, resulted in the Smallholders' Party (FKGP) winning a majority, the outcome of a second poll two years later proved to be very different, and had a significant influence on the country's political and economic system for the next four decades. In the election of 1947, the Communist Party won the most votes. It nationalised most private property over the next year, and eventually eliminated all other political parties. A communist constitution was introduced in 1949, resulting in the introduction of Stalinist policies that dominated Hungary until 1953. The uprising of October 23 1956, which began in Budapest, was short-lived. Soviet troops moved in on November 4, and by mid-December all resistance had been crushed. The Soviet Union ensured that Hungary returned to the Warsaw Pact and that the Communist Party was once again in firm control.

The early 1960s brought some moderation, both politically and economically, with the 1956 revolutionaries finally granted amnesty in March 1963. The re-styled Hungarian Socialist Workers' Party (MSzWP) introduced an economic reform package in 1968, which resulted in a boom in both agricultural and consumer goods production. However, supporters of the reforms came under attack from hardliners and trade union leaders, as they increased income inequality. The combined effect of the mid-1970s oil shock and the worsening trade balance caused Hungary's foreign debt to rise to over US$11bn by the early 1980s. While the focus of economic reform shifted to small-scale private production, the failure of the MSzWP to agree upon substantial policy changes at its 13th congress in 1985, caused unrest to rise both inside and outside the party. Reformists finally gained control of the party in 1989, with then prime minister Miklos Nemeth starting the process of political liberalisation. In October 1989, the reformists in the MSzWP joined opposition groups in negotiations and formed a new political party. This transformed the MSzWP into the Hungarian Socialist Party (MSzP).

The MSzP lost the 1989 and 1990 elections, which resulted in it losing control of the reform process. The opposition Hungarian Democratic Forum (MDF) emerged as the most popular party in the March 1990 parliamentary elections, and formed a coalition government with the FKGP and the Christian Democratic People's Party (CDPP). The liberal opposition included the Alliance of Free Democrats (SzDSz), the Alliance of Young Democrats (Fidesz) and the MSzP. The MDF's four-year term was one of strong ideological disputes between the government and opposition parties.

The MDF's downfall came from its undisciplined spending programme, which led to the 1994/95 crisis and the devaluation of the forint. The MSzP was returned to power in May 1994, by forming a coalition with the SzDSz. The austerity programme following the March 1995 election initially caused a fall in economic growth and real wages, but was yielding impressive results by 1997. However, in the May 1998 election, voters punished the MSzP-led government for the early years of hardship, with the Federation of Young Democratic-Hungarian Civic Party (Fidesz-HCP) winning 148 seats, against 134 for the MSzP. Fidesz leader Viktor Orban became the new prime minister and formed a coalition government that took office in July 1998.

The Political System

A Complex Political Structure

The present constitution is a radically amended version of its communist-era counterpart. It now guarantees Hungary's multi-party system, as well as defining the electoral process and the role of the president and judiciary. Presidential elections are held every five years, and decided by a parliamentary vote. The position is largely symbolic with very few powers, and includes nominating candidates for certain posts that are usually ceremonial. The constitution allows an individual to stand for only two terms in office. The independent judicial system has three tiers: local, county and high courts. In addition, a 1997 amendment to the constitution added a Court of Appeal, which hears appeals submitted from the lower courts. There is also a very active and forceful Constitutional Court, which has the power to review and abolish parliamentary acts.

The electoral process defined in the constitution is relatively complex and unique. The unicameral National Assembly (parliament) has 386 seats and is elected for a four-year term. Deputies are elected in one of three ways: either directly from an individual constituency, from regional party lists or from national party lists. An election consists of two rounds, with voters casting two votes in each. The first is for an individual candidate in their respective constituency and the second is for one of the regional party lists. This second vote is used as a party endorsement rather than for a specific candidate. There are 176 single-member constituencies. The first step in the election process requires a candidate to collect at least 750 nomination petitions to enter the ballot. To win the seat directly, he/she must receive over 50% of the valid votes cast, from a turnout of at least 50% of the constituency. In the May 1998 election, only one of the 176 candidates qualified in the first round of voting. If no candidate is successful in the first round, a second ballot is held on a first past the post basis.

The regional lists provide candidates with the second method of gaining a seat in the parliament. A party can announce regional lists in all counties and in Budapest, provided it has fielded candidates in at least 25% of the regional electoral wards, and has at least two candidates standing in individual constituencies. The party must also receive at least 5% of the national vote to gain representation – this is also a requirement to qualify for the national lists. In the last three elections – 1990, 1994 and 1998 – the regional list system has acted as a filter against extremists, with only eight of the 32 registered parties able to put up a list in Hungary's 19 counties and Budapest. The last route into parliament is through the national list. Here parties win seats in proportion to the total number of votes they have received. Under this method voters do not cast a direct vote.

The Political Parties

Federation Of Young Democrats-Hungarian Civic Party

The Federation of Young Democrats-Hungarian Civic Party (Fidesz-HCP) was formed in 1988 by law students in Budapest. While in opposition in 1990-94, it espoused a liberal ideology and often cooperated with the Alliance of Free Democrats (SzDSz) against the conservative government. In order to win wider support, Fidesz dropped its maximum age limit of 35 in 1993 and has gradually distanced itself from its more liberal policies. It lost a number of its leaders to the SzDSz after the 1994 election, when the MSzP-SzDSz coalition government was formed. Fidesz added the Hungarian Civic Party to its name in 1995, in an effort to broaden its appeal beyond the youth vote. Since then the Fidesz-HCP has become increasingly populist and conservative, and formed an electoral alliance with the Hungarian Democratic Forum (MDF) before the May 1998 parliamentary election.

Smallholders' Party

The Smallholders' Party (FKGP) is an attempt to recreate the popular party of the same name that won the first post-war election. Its improved performance in the 1998 election was the key to the formation of the current coalition. While in opposition, the party focused on one issue: the re-privatisation of land. Its influence can be seen in the complicated land compensation programme that worked to maintain small land-holdings. The party has strong support from the older rural population. It has also been critical of Western investors and is still opposed to foreign ownership of land.

Hungarian Democratic Forum

Formed in 1988, the Hungarian Democratic Forum (MDF) was once a leading force in government, gaining the largest percentage of votes in the 1990 election. Since then, its fortunes have waned and it is currently a minor partner in the Fidesz-led government. Its downfall is directly attributed to moves away from its populist roots towards a more conservative and Christian Democratic approach. This resulted in a bitter split within the party contributing to its defeat in the 1994 general election. The party failed to recover from this setback and it is believed to have gained most of the 17 seats it won in last year's election mainly on the strength of its alliance with Fidesz.

Hungarian Socialist Party

The Hungarian Socialist Party (MSzP) came into being in October 1989 when the old HSWP congress voted to change both the party's name and orientation. The MSzP changed direction, as it modelled itself on a Western European-style socialist party, and has a diverse constituency, including liberals, social democrats, trade unionists and mid- and low-level civil servants. Despite its successful handling of the economy in the 1994-95 crisis, it was voted out of office in the last election. Under its new leader, Laszlo Kovacs, foreign minister during 1994-98, the MSzP is the main opposition party.

Other Parties

The Alliance of Free Democrats (SzDSz) first came into being in the 1980s, when it organised underground protests against the former communist system, and was prominent in the political transformation of 1988-89. The SzDSz presents itself as a liberal democratic party and draws its main support from younger, urban voters. Traditionally, it also has had the best contacts with the West. The last of the opposition parties, the Hungarian Justice and Life Party (MIEP), is an offshoot of the MDF. It was formed in 1993, when radical populist Istvan Csurka and his supporters were expelled from the party. It is one of the few political parties that opposed Hungary's Nato membership. The MIEP received enough votes in 1994 to pass the 5% threshold for parliamentary representation, although the other conservative parties have tended to distance themselves from its policies.

Administrative Changes

In line with the promises in its manifesto, the Orban government has implemented several administrative changes, as it moved the government structure in the direction of a chancellorship. As part of this restructuring, two new units have been established in the Prime Minister's Office: the strategic planning group and the ministry liaison unit. The strategic planning group is responsible for longer-term planning and studies, primarily covering the balance of the government's term in office. It also provides comprehensive analysis of current issues. The main responsibility of the ministry liaison unit is to ensure that the government's day-to-day operations run smoothly. Its two main functions are to provide a direct link between the Prime Minister's Office and the ministries, and to monitor their activities. The primary objective of the unit is to reduce internal conflicts and ensure that the government's policy initiatives are being implemented.

The coalition has also increased the number of ministries to 14, compared to 12 under the former administration. These changes were based on the premise that the ministries should be structured to fulfil the tasks they are assigned. While no super-ministries exist, and all are theoretically equal in legal terms, several ministries, such as the Ministry of Economic Affairs, have had their responsibilities increased. In restructuring government machinery, EU requirements were taken into account to ensure that by the end of the present parliament there would be no major differences from the structure stipulated under EU accession criteria.

Recent Developments

Orban Consolidates Power

The first task undertaken by Prime Minister Viktor Orban after taking office was a radical overhaul of the structure of government. The central part of this plan was to strengthen the role of the Prime Minister's Office (PMO). The head of the PMO was given ministerial rank, in line with Germany's chancellor model. The new structure gives the prime minister more direct control over the government's activities. The PMO has also taken over supervision of the privatisation process, following the elimination of the Privatisation Ministry, a move that has prompted criticism from the opposition. Istvan Stumpf, the PMO minister, has been given the task of developing the office's role, including coordinating legislation, acting as a link between ministries and ensuring that government policies are implemented.

A second major change in the cabinet's structure was the creation of the new Ministry of Economic Affairs, which consolidated the work of the Industry, Trade and Tourism Ministry and the Labour Ministry, both of which were abolished. The government's economic policies and long-term strategy will now be developed jointly by the Finance Ministry and Economic Affairs Ministry. While the latter will be responsible for almost every aspect of economic policy, the former now has its powers limited to monetary and fiscal policies, as well as the management of the state debt.

Mixed Success For Anti-Corruption Campaign

Fidesz's promise of strong legislation against corruption, including passing a law to ensure that political appointees declare any conflict of interest that may occur as a result of their business affairs, ran into trouble fairly quickly after the party took office. In early August 1998, a local newspaper printed allegations that members of the Fidesz government had been involved in illegal privatisation practices. A police investigation was set up, and charges of forgery, deception and misappropriation were filed. The head of the State Privatisation and Holding Company denied any wrongdoing. Despite strong condemnations of their predecessors' propensity for political appointments to state-owned companies and agencies, the new ruling parties were forced early on to withdraw two corporate board nominations given to relatives of Smallholders' Party leader Jozsef Torgyan.

In June 1999 it was revealed that politicians of several parties, senior public servants and various politically-connected celebrities had received preferential loans and deposit facilities from Postabank, the state-owned savings bank which the previous government had bailed out at an eventual cost of more than US$1bn. Because no senior Fidesz or Smallholder officials were caught up in the 'VIP list' scandal, the episode appeared to vindicate their high-level inquiry into Postabank's collapse and general anti-corruption stance. But it also confirmed that Hungary had not been immune to the political use of commercial power during and after the privatisation process and, with even trade unionists and journalists named on the list, dealt a further blow to public faith in the transparency and accountability of new democratic institutions.

Media Freedom Remains Controversial

A media law passed by the previous Socialist government allows political parties to nominate supervisory board members for state-owned television and radio in proportion to their parliamentary representation. However, in March 2000 state radio posts were assigned exclusively to government-backed candidates, after opposition groups withdrew from the process alleging under-representation. Although subsequent public protests were mainly against the exclusion of opposition representatives, the whole principle of political representation has come under fire from allied governments and free-press campaigners. The EU singled out the broadcasting board bias for criticism in its 1999 progress report, but two government-suggested compromises – each party making one nomination to the eight-member boards, or transferring media oversight to the parliamentary culture committee – have so far been rejected by the opposition.

Fidesz has also been studying plans to create a more sympathetic daily newspaper to counter the privately-owned, but still opposition-identified *Nepszabadsag*, whose circulation of almost 800,000 is more than 10 times the nearest pro-government equivalent. However, this effort has also incurred EU criticism. Ministerial sensitivity to the bringers of bad news was highlighted when the director of the state-funded Institute for Economic Analysis was suspended in June 1999 for critical comments about the government's fiscal strategy. Politicians are likely to be forced eventually to distance themselves from media control through fear of destroying the prize they are fighting over: the arrival of new private TV stations. These have already reduced the main state channel, MTV, to an average audience share of less than 15%, and failure to dispel the impression of political control could put the whole future of public-service broadcasting at risk.

Foreign Policy

Shifting Towards The West

Under communist rule, Hungary was a member of the Warsaw Pact (1955) and the Council for Mutual Economic Assistance (CMEA, or Comecon, 1949). Both of these alliances formerly ended in 1991 and Soviet troops were withdrawn in 1992. Nonetheless, during this period Hungary joined several Western-style organisations, such as the IMF and the World Bank (both in 1982); it is also a member of the World Trade Organisation (WTO) and was a founding member of the European Bank for Reconstruction and Development (EBRD). To replace Comecon, Hungary, Poland and the then Czechoslovakia formed the Central European Free-Trade Agreement (CEFTA). The OECD extended membership to Hungary in March 1996. This was viewed as an important step towards its integration with the West.

EU Membership: Edging Towards A Target Date

Hungary applied for EU membership in 1994, was admitted to the five-member 'fast-track' list in 1997, and began formal accession negotiations in November 1998. Its early move towards EU-style commercial laws and institutional structures, recent rapid progress in economic expansion and restructuring, and complementarity to the existing EU economies have made it (alongside Slovenia) the country expected to enter the Union first. The official target entry date of 2003 is ambitious, but cannot be ruled out; the EU Commission has promised that a firm accession timetable will be set out during 2000. The move to a fixed exchange rate, planned for early 2001, is intended as the first step towards qualifying for the EU's economic and monetary union within 2-3 years of accession. The EU Commission's 1999 enlargement progress report recognised that Hungary was on course to meet the competitive challenged of the single market, concentrating its criticisms on slow progress towards meeting EU environmental standards, eliminating corruption, and ensuring press freedom and minority (especially Roma) rights. Hungary, proportionally, is by far the largest recipient of inward investment from the EU, and is already well integrated into its industrial supply chains. Commercial pressure for early entry will mount steadily over the next two years even if political opinion, both in the EU and in Hungary, remains more cautious about the economic and social risks.

A number of obstacles to early entry mean that 2003 is still the best-case scenario, and that actual accession could be delayed for up to three years beyond this. The path to monetary convergence with the EU may not be smooth, with particular risks to the stability of interest and exchange rates and the reduction of inflation. Hungary's lack of 'real' convergence, particularly its substantially lower per capita GDP, high unemployment rate and comparatively high levels of taxation and welfare spending, could force it to delay entry to avoid premature exposure to the full force of free intra-EU trade and capital movement. The competitiveness – with or without state subsidy – of some of its industries could lead some EU members to seek a delay, even though most studies show Hungary's export potential to be too small to do serious damage to 'sensitive' sectors in any other member-state. Agricultural subsidies, which the Smallholders' Party is committed to defending, were singled out for criticism in the EU's 1999 progress report. The EU's slowness to switch its own agricultural support from euro-standardised price guarantees to income support that could be varied at member-state level could be another cause of delay. But Hungary is less vulnerable to this than most other East European applicants, and in October 1999 took another important step towards full single market privileges with the signing of an agreement on mutual recognition of safety standards. This removes destination-country checks on around 70% of Hungary's industrial exports, including pharmaceuticals, electrical goods, machinery and medical equipment.

Nato Membership: Calm After The Storm

Within weeks of its formal admission to Nato on March 12 1999, Hungary was offering rhetorical and some logistical support to the alliance's air campaign and threatened land war against Serbia-Montenegro over Kosovo. The month-long campaign, though cautiously supported by the government, raised fears that Serbia's estimated 300,000 ethnic Hungarians (concentrated in its Vojvodina region in the north) might become the next target for the Milosevic regime and a settlement-ground for Serbs fleeing Kosovo. Nato membership also means pressure for increased defence spending (which had been cut to little more than half the Nato average of 2.8% of GDP), and loss of strategic independence. The price is generally reckoned to be worth paying in return for Nato's security umbrella, and membership was supported by 85% of those who voted in the November 1997 referendum. Nato will help to cover the cost of military upgrades, some of which (including a much-delayed US$1.5bn fighter aircraft purchase) would have been necessary in any case. Membership is also consistent with longstanding government plans to professionalise the army and set up a rapid deployment force for use in regional emergencies. Hungarian defence contractors believe that access to the Nato market could help rebuild their order book, though only to a modest US$400mn per year.

Regional Relations Continue To Improve

The Fidesz-led government has pursued a policy of improving relations with its neighbours, as well as increasing support to ethnic Hungarians living outside its immediate borders. Relations with Slovakia improved following the election of a pro-Western government in September 1998. The new Slovak coalition government, which includes the main ethnic Hungarian party, has pledged to improve relations with Hungary and signed a new agreement to this effect in November 1998. As part of the protocol, the Hungarian government has agreed to support Slovakia's bid for Nato and EU membership, while the Bratislava government confirmed its commitment to pass legislation on minority rights. The two governments are also moving ahead with plans to rebuild a bridge link over the Danube, as well as resume talks about a disputed dam project. Relations with Romania have also improved as the two governments have had several discussions on issues from ethnic rights to improving transport links, and Hungarian support for Romanian membership to Nato and other Western organisations. Here again Orban has decided to follow an aggressive policy, as he attempts to serve as a bridge between Eastern and Western Europe.

2 Economic Outlook

Overview

Brakes Off, At Last

Shrugging off the setback to growth and inflation-control in the aftermath of the 1998 Russian crisis, Hungary's economic performance since mid-1999 has been its strongest since the end of communism and one of the strongest in the region. Real y-o-y GDP growth rose to 6.8% in Q1 00, driven by an export expansion rate which has stayed at or above that of imports despite rising investment expenditure and continued real appreciation of the exchange rate. The stronger forint and subdued real wage growth had helped bring inflation back down to around 9% by mid-year, despite strong rises in food and imported oil prices. Improving productivity has prevented the production recovery from substantially reducing unemployment, but this had nonetheless dropped to a regionally creditable 6.7% in the first four months of 2000. With strong activity boosting tax revenue, and inflation staying above official projections, the public sector budget deficit was well within target at mid-year.

The current economic recovery is substantially more secure than the last significant upturn of 1993-95. The latter ended with excessive consumption growth, an unsustainable current account deficit, and forced devaluation. This in turn triggered a painful two years of wage restraint, job losses, public expenditure cuts and rapid privatisation. This time, the current account deficit is shrinking as a proportion of GDP as exports continue to drive economic growth, and long-term capital inflows remain sufficient to finance the external deficit without a resort to dangerous short-term borrowing. Indeed, the National Bank of Hungary (NBH) has been working to discourage short-term inflows, mainly by substantially reducing domestic interest rates since late 1999. Real wage growth also remains subdued in comparison to the industrial productivity trend, and while consumer expenditure has been growing faster as a result of rising household borrowing, the main increase has been on a narrow range of durable items which, in contrast to the mid-90s, are now largely domestically produced. Public finances are also

The economy has bounced back strongly from setbacks to trade expansion and capital inflows in 1999. Concern has now shifted to the possibility of overheating. Although the government has revived its 7% GDP growth promises, expansion is set to slow in 2000-01 as the price of keeping inflation and the external deficit under adequate control.

Slower Growth To Come
Quarterly GDP growth, % y-o-y

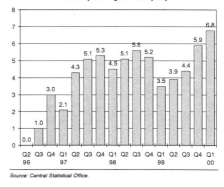

Source: Central Statistical Office.

benefiting from a cyclical upturn in revenue and downturn in obligatory spending (notably on social security), preventing a recurrence of the "twin deficit" problem which eventually caused foreign investors to abandon the country in 1995.

Economic Activity

Concern Turns To Overheating

The government is under mounting pressure to tighten finances after the NBH's change of monetary policy direction to keep the exchange rate fairly valued.

While the strong economic start to 2000 encouraged ministers to recall their more ambitious election pledges – including a substantial fall in unemployment powered by GDP growth of up to 7% – some slowdown in growth is inevitable. **BMI** expects a relatively soft landing in 2000-01, with GDP growth still strong, inflation slowing and the trade deficit continuing to moderate as the forint appreciates only modestly against the euro in real terms (its sharper rebound against the dollar mainly reflecting the forecast euro recovery). Unexpectedly fast interest rate reductions in Q4 99 and Q1 00, primarily designed to arrest the forint's rise against the euro, has raised the danger of excessive consumer-driven economic expansion in 2000 forcing monetary policy tightening and a harder landing in 2001. But the NBH appears justified in arguing that interest rates have done little more than follow medium-term inflation expectations downwards; that fiscal consolidation is proceeding fast enough to justify a modicum of monetary relaxation; that lower interest rates will sustain the export stimulus to growth by preventing the exchange rate from strengthening further as it approaches full flotation expected in early 2001; and that cheaper credit shows no signs of setting off an unsustainable growth in consumer expenditure, or in speculative investment activity.

External Demand Lifts Output
Industrial output growth

Source: Central Statistical Office.

Threats to the attainment of an orderly slowdown in economic growth are as much political as economic. With elections due by June 2002, the government will be looking to keep GDP growth above 5%, even though the economy's current strength is deterring it (and private industry) from some

NOMINAL AND REAL GDP						
	1997	1998	1999	2000f	2001f	2002f
Nominal GDP (US$bn)	45.30	47.05	48.48	49.07	57.24	63.14
GDP per capita (US$)	4,453	4,658	4,836	4,929	5,793	6,437
Real GDP growth, % y-o-y	4.6	4.9	4.5	5.5	4.5	4.8
f = BMI forecast. Source: Central Statistical Office/BMI						

of the structural changes needed to make such a rate sustainable. In particular, ministers will be reluctant during the remainder of their current term to implement reforms that would substantially reduce the state healthcare fund deficit, even though they are keen to deliver further business and personal tax cuts. Although faster economic growth improves the conditions for doing so, they will also be wary of withdrawing the remaining producer subsidies keeping jobs alive in agriculture and unprofitable (and largely state-owned) heavy industries, and the consumer subsidies still holding down the prices of domestic energy and prescription drugs.

Fiscal Policy

A Stubborn But Sustainable Deficit

Although budget deficit reduction in 1999-00 was due more to cyclical recovery than structural change, public finances are on an improving trend despite a number of economic growth-promoting revenue sacrifices. These include a substantial reduction in standard corporate tax, which has helped maintain post-privatisation fixed investment inflows, and a diversion of payroll taxes into private pension funds, with employers' social charges set to fall further as employees move more heavily into private provision. The central government's primary budget (ie before obligatory payments on public debt) is already in surplus, and the overall public sector deficit is small in comparison with both Hungary's recent past and other governments in the region.

Despite this impressive record, further deficit reduction is expected to be slow. Additional scope for social and corporate welfare cuts is limited, especially ahead of the next general election, and some discretionary expenditures – especially on infrastructure, defence and environmental improvement – will have to increase to satisfy EU and Nato entry conditions. On the revenue side, corporate and personal income tax rates must fall further if the recent downward trend elsewhere in the OECD is to be followed, and there will be insufficient compensation from higher indirect tax flows if consumption stays as moderate as sustainable economic growth requires.

A relatively unambitious 2000 fiscal deficit target will be met largely due to the cyclical upturn, with scope for further reduction limited by the government's postponement of radical health reform, and corporate tax cuts already agreed.

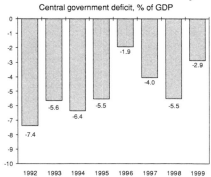

Further Deficit Reductions Unlikely
Central government deficit, % of GDP

Source: Central Statistical Office.

CENTRAL GOVERNMENT BUDGET						
	1997	1998	1999	2000f	2001f	2002f
Balance (HUFbn)	-342.1	-553.9	-331.6	-389.0	-456.0	-443.0
Balance (% of GDP)	-4.0	-5.5	-2.9	-3.0	-3.1	-2.7
f = BMI forecast. Source: Central Statistical Office/BMI						

The pension reform launched in 1998, and the part-privatisation of healthcare funding which must eventually follow it, involve a loss of revenues which must result in temporarily higher deficits and public borrowing if the cost of switching is to be spread across its future beneficiaries rather than imposed on one transitional employee cohort. Recurrence of other one-off costs, such as the bank recapitalisation, which pushed the 1998 budget deficit to almost three times its target, cannot be ruled out as the government continues to pursue a reform agenda which will sometimes impose adjustment costs that need to be cushioned at public expense.

Monetary Policy

Relaxed, But Not So Easy

Sharp interest rate cuts in H1 00 represented a departure from previous NBH caution over monetary policy relaxation, and were mainly designed to avert a currency overvaluation by deterring short-term portfolio capital inflows. Although the reductions could be justified by the expectation of slower inflation and the fall in long-term interest rates as convergence with (and eventual entry to) the euro-zone moves onto the horizon, there are a number of reasons for anticipating a modest rise in real short-term interest rates in late 2000 and early 2001, before the gentle downwards course of recent years is resumed. Consumer price inflation is set to end 2000 above the government's 7% upper-range target, mainly because world oil prices have failed to fall as assumed in the budget and, indeed, had gone above US$30/b by the time of Opec's mid-year meeting. Consumer expenditure, fuelled by borrowing for certain durable items, is likely to show greater strength in H2.

This year's steep fall in real interest rates has done little to dispel upward pressure on the forint, and leaves the NBH contemplating a gradual re-tightening of monetary policy – holding rates while inflation falls – until the government moves more decisively to tighten the budget.

Oil Makes Prices Sticky
Consumer price inflation

Source: Central Statistical Office.

The central bank is pressing for an early fixing of the forint's central band against the euro, although ministers are resisting this through fear of impeding the export-led recovery. Although this is likely to be accompanied by wider fluctuation bands, which will on balance increase the NBH's monetary policy discretion, it will also tie Hungarian rate-setting more closely to that of its major trading partners. Already it is difficult for the NBH to withstand for long periods tighter monetary policy trends in the euro-zone and the US, both of which returned to raising interest rates as their economic growth picked up in 2000.

Euro Fix To Ease Pressure On Interest Rates

The HUF's euro peg, expected during 2001, is intended to begin a phase of exchange rate stability against the EU single currency, keeping open the option of Hungary joining the economic and monetary union (EMU) relatively soon after its accession to the EU. This sort of currency targeting traditionally limits a country's discretion over interest rates, requiring rates to rise if a worsening external deficit, or general pull-back of portfolio flows from emerging economies, brings the currency under selling pressure. However, after initial uncertainty surrounding the planned change of exchange rate regime next year, the opposite pressure is expected to prevail. Increased long-term portfolio inflows attracted by prospects for local currency asset appreciation as financial markets converge with those of the EU, continued foreign direct investment (FDI) strength, and the retreat from direct short-term capital controls under pressure from the OECD, are likely to return the NBH to its early 2000 situation of reducing real interest rates.

Interest rate volatility is likely to increase after the proposed move to a fixed central exchange rate in January 2001.

Exchange Rate Policy

Avoiding An Unhealthy Fixation

The adoption of a fixed monthly depreciation for the forint against a dollar/euro basket (and more recently against the euro alone) made a vital contribution to the economic recovery since 1995. The crawling peg helped stabilise and, through successive reductions in the crawl (to 0.3% from April 1 2000), gradually reduce inflation expectations, so defusing the wage-price spiral. But by leaving room for continued nominal depreciation, the system insulated trade-exposed sectors of the economy from the loss of competitiveness due to domestic costs and prices rising faster than those of trading partners. Real exchange rate appreciation was held below the rate of productivity growth in most sectors, avoiding the choice that would otherwise have had to be made between squeezing profit margins to stay competitive, or steadily sacrificing international market share.

Next year's anticipated move to a fixed central exchange rate is expected to be accompanied by a widening of the HUF's trading bands, deterring speculative short-term capital inflows and allowing the NBH to continue respecting domestic conditions in the setting of interest rates. International developments, with the euro regaining strength against the dollar, should be favourable for retaining export competitiveness while keeping the exchange rate as an anchor against inflation, especially from higher imported commodity prices.

INFLATION AND EXCHANGE RATE						
	1997	1998	1999	2000f	2001f	2002f
Consumer prices (% y-o-y, end period)	18.5	10.3	11.2	8.3	7.2	6.5
Consumer prices (% y-o-y, period average)	18.3	14.2	10.0	8.7	7.5	6.7
Exchange rate (HUF/US$, end period)	203.50	219.03	252.52	262.60	252.00	266.10
Exchange rate (HUF/US$, period average)	186.79	214.40	237.15	267.52	256.86	259.64
f = BMI forecast. Source: NBH/BMI						

The planned transition to a fixed central forint:euro parity from the start of 2001 is a logical extension of policy to date. With inflation still stuck at close to 9% y-o-y in mid-2000, it will restore a domestic price discipline which has been lost in recent months as present – largely cyclical – efficiency gains move into line with the rate of competitiveness loss. The expected recovery of the euro against the dollar in 2000-01 will add to this discipline for those trading with the dollar zone. But since most trade is with the euro-zone, pegging to a rising euro will mean reducing the cost of commodity imports and dollar-denominated debt service with little loss of competitiveness for processed exports, a favourable realignment which will go some way towards reversing the disadvantages of linking to a euro that weakened against the dollar in its first 18 months. If, as is expected, the end of the pre-announced crawl is accompanied by a widening of the fluctuation bands from their current +/-2.25%, there will also be an increase in the downside risk for short-term portfolio investors sufficient to ease the inflow of hot money to domestic currency and asset markets which kept the forint on the strong side of its central rate for most of the year to mid-2000.

Although a smooth switch from crawling to stationary peg will be further helped by the strong international reputation and healthy reserves position of the NBH, it may not prove a problem-free route towards convergence and eventual entry to the EU's single currency system. Fixing the exchange rate deprives the government of currency depreciation as a way to restore competitiveness after a phase of domestic unit cost growth, which could still happen if Hungary's productivity growth slows or trade-sector real wages accelerate. While it will add to the country's attractions as a destination for foreign investment, it will also provide domestic borrowers with greater scope for sidestepping monetary restraint by borrowing at lower cost abroad. Hungary's investment-grade sovereign credit rating and low eurobond spreads against EU equivalents already encourages this, and while a repeat of their experience is unlikely, a fixed forint will put Hungary on the same path as the high-growth East Asian economies before their 1997-98 exchange rate crises. The adoption of strong currencies supported by high domestic real interest rates encouraged these countries' larger firms to borrow cheaply abroad on the promise of exchange rate stability. Central banks then postponed a necessary devaluation because of the damage it would do to private debtors with foreign-currency exposure, instead spending official reserves and letting the overvaluation worsen until violently corrected by a foreign capital pullout.

Hungary will be shielded from a similar experience by present reserves strength, single-figure and subsiding inflation, short-term capital controls,

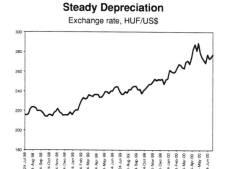

Steady Depreciation
Exchange rate, HUF/US$

Source: Reuters

and a banking system now strong enough to withstand sharp increases in short-term interest rates if these prove necessary to defend the forint. But it shares the East Asians' pre-crisis situation of strong capital inflows which tend to keep the market exchange rate even stronger than its appreciating central rate, and lacks the balanced central budget and high private sector savings rate which helped the "tiger" economies recover quickly from their devaluation crises. With inflation still well above the EU rate, wage growth below trend and output growth still vulnerable to renewed current account deterioration, and with the EU single currency set to reverse its early depreciation, Hungary may still have to adjust its euro peg downwards at least once before it can stabilise at a realistic parity for entering the euro-zone. When capital controls are removed, as they will have to be under EU and OECD rules, such realignments are always hazardous, leading in the worst case to an overshoot which punishes foreign borrowers including the government, fuels inflation and forces a phase of high short-term interest rates which can severely damage investment plans and stock market performance.

Balance Of Payments

Current Account: Financing Easier Than Closing

For its first post-communist decade, Hungary's return to economic growth was associated with worsening trade and current account deficits as firms looked abroad for new capital equipment and households chose imported brands over mistrusted locally-made generic goods. The first recovery in 1993-95 was choked off because the resultant external deficit proved impossible to finance. The second, which began in 1996, owed its survival to the one-off financing raised by the privatisation of strategic state assets mainly to foreign buyers. The tailing-off of privatisation receipts since early 1999 has not, however, re-imposed the balance of payments constraint that frustrated the earlier dash for economic growth. This is because post-privatisation restructuring and new greenfield opportunities have continued

Exports are showing enough resilience to the appreciating real exchange rate to keep the current account deficit stable in relation to GDP, allowing the external debt load to continue to lighten as effective interest rates fall. Although relatively high at around 4% of GDP this year and next, the current account deficit is financeable through long-term capital inflows, most of which carry the seeds of their own repayment through export generation.

BALANCE OF PAYMENTS						
	1997	1998	1999	2000f	2001f	2002f
Merchandise exports (fob, US$bn)	19.64	20.75	21.84	23.80	25.00	26.40
Merchandise imports (fob, US$bn)	21.37	22.87	24.02	25.70	26.80	28.00
Merchandise trade balance (fob-fob, US$bn)	-1.73	-2.12	-2.18	-1.90	-1.80	-1.60
Current account balance (US$bn)	-0.98	-2.30	-2.08	-2.13	-2.28	-2.03
Current account (% of GDP)	-2.2	-4.9	-4.3	-4.3	-4.0	-3.2
f = BMI forecast. Source: NBH/BMI						

to draw in substantial long-term investment to cover the current account deficit, and because that deficit is itself shrinking in relation to GDP as exports continue to outpace imports in defiance of the rising real exchange rate.

In absolute euro terms, the current account deficit is set to worsen in the next two to three years as the growth differential over the EU continues to draw in capital goods and intermediate inputs from the euro-zone faster than it generates exports to them. This widening will look more serious in dollar terms because of the euro's forecast appreciation against the US$. However, the growth differential will prevent any worsening of the deficit in relative terms; and at a forecast 4% of GDP in 2001 the current account deficit should remain well within the financing limit set by present FDI flows and long-term credit opportunities. Although it must continue to borrow abroad to finance part of the external gap and to roll over foreign debt, the NBH should be able to keep external debt well within the 60% of GDP which the EU has set as a limit for economic and monetary union (EMU) qualification, and debt repayment obligations well within the comfort zone implied by export revenues. Having refused to reschedule its debt in the early 1990s, Hungary does not face the sharp increases in debt obligations early on this decade for which other transition economies must prepare as their grace periods run out. Conversely, a resumed downtrend in the interest rate premium Hungary must pay over EU governments for its new foreign borrowing will allow the cost of servicing the present debt to continue to fall through the forecast period, even though the completion of large-scale privatisation slows the rate at which the total debt can be reduced.

The European Union

Single-Minded For The Single Market

Hungary's application and preparations for EU membership have already brought substantial benefits for medium-term growth. Much of the FDI inflow during and after privatisation has aimed to build up export capacity in preparation for full access to the EU single market (this has already been substantially secured for manufactures through the association agreement with the EU). Fiscal and monetary policy tightening, aimed at the reduction of inflation, interest rates and "twin deficits", have been maintained – in the face of much political protest – largely to meet the goal of monetary convergence with the EU. The equally painful structural changes caused by the withdrawal of industrial and social subsidies have similarly been endured

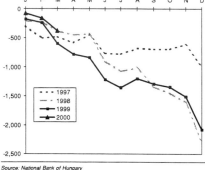

Export Growth Keeps Deficit Stable
Cumulative current account, US$mn

- - - 1997
—— 1998
—●— 1999
—▲— 2000

Source: National Bank of Hungary

The EU will continue to play a central role as setter of economic priorities for all future governments, and as scapegoat for the less popular social measures needed to meet EU-specified macroeconomic and structural reform targets. A likely delay in EU accession, to at least 2005, will not seriously disrupt FDI inflows predicated on single market access, and will improve Hungary's chances of qualifying for single currency adoption within three to four years of accession.

largely to meet EU fiscal and harmonisation requirements.

With around three-quarters of Hungarian exports now going to the EU – a substantially higher proportion than for most existing member-states – early EU entry will remain a priority for all mainstream parties, since current free-trade arrangements do not gain complete access for Hungary either to the single market or to the regional and social programmes designed to cushion its adverse local effects. Since currency risk will continue to hinder operations in the single market and investments designed to promote them, policy will remain geared to securing euro-zone entry two to three years after joining the EU. Even if public opinion turns against EU membership – a growing danger as Brussels tightens its preconditions in what is widely seen as an attempt to avoid setting firm accession dates – businesses which have positioned themselves for EU entry will remain a powerful lobbying force. The substantial presence in Hungary of EU-based multinationals already makes it difficult for the EU to invoke anti-dumping or other *ad hoc* trade barriers against it, and will make it increasingly difficult for Brussels to avoid setting a 2003-05 entry date if there is no serious reversal to convergence.

EU accession will impose a number of economic changes tougher still than those involved in membership preparation. The free-trade agenda will move on from manufactured products, where Hungary has been able to exploit its relative efficiency under the asymmetrical tariff reductions specified in the association agreement, to traded services and agricultural products. Trade friction over agriculture, already recurrent within the Central European Free Trade Area (Cefta) and between Cefta and the EU, will worsen as governments increasingly resort to import taxes or bans using allegations of dumping, possible risks to human health, or animal welfare as a pretext. The EU's slow progress in removing its price supports, and its planned retention of direct income support for farmers after pricing returns to the market, presents a continued danger that it will offload its own overproduction onto other markets, including those of Eastern Europe, and maintain the right to put extra tariffs on imports it considers too cheap. Cefta nations' political difficulty in removing restrictions on foreign ownership of farmland and enforcing hygiene rules and labelling requirements on their smaller producers, will make it hard for them to object to such protectionism. With its rural distribution and marketing arrangements also lagging the growth of foreign-owned retail distribution chains in its towns, Hungary therefore risks moving into a wider external deficit in raw and processed agricultural products, even though many of its farms are close enough to EU productivity levels to be operating subsidy-free.

Trade in services has taken longer than goods to liberalise within the EU, and in this case resistance to the extension of the single market to Hungary is likely to come from domestic sources. Financial and business services, neglected under communism, remain comparatively underdeveloped, and there is a strong "infant industry" case for giving domestic providers some time to build up skills, scale and a customer base before facing the full force of international competition. However, this is likely to be outweighed by government concerns to give businesses and itself access to the best available services, and to implement EU service directives fast enough to avoid any accession delays. The pace at which open entry to, and foreign ownership of, the finance and energy sectors has been set in train suggests that other components of the single services market may extend to Hungary almost as soon as they are adopted within the EU. This will enable foreign providers to exploit their knowledge and resource advantages in fast-growing areas such as accountancy, consultancy, fund management and waste management. But it will also limit the opportunities for large domestic players to develop, most Hungarian firms being forced – as is already evident in financial services – to enter alliances with EU- and US-based multinational companies (MNCs) or occupy relatively small niches in which local expertise is of particular advantage.

EU membership will also put an end to preferential bilateral trade arrangements with non-EU countries, a requirement which could impede Hungary's re-expansion of trade and investment links with the former Soviet Union and those countries to its east still on the slower EU accession track. The trade volume affected by this is comparatively small, however, and not especially sensitive to tariff barriers, so that the advantages of easier EU market access should outweigh any impediment to trade relations on its periphery.

Profile and Recent Developments

Characteristics Of The Economy

Building On Early Market Reforms

Hungary has graduated from being a transition economy to one that is progressing relatively quickly, and with limited pain, along the European Union (EU) convergence path. That it heads the list of potential EU members is directly attributable to the fact that it already had the foundations of a market economy in place before political reforms started at the beginning of the 1990s. While economic reform and privatisation have been top priorities for all of the post-communist governments, Hungary's basic economic composition and its traditional direction of trade favoured a quick transformation. In spite of government changes, the ongoing commitment to economic reform, and a willingness to take difficult decisions, have been key contributors to the economy's success. Moreover, the authorities recognised that, given its 10mn population and geographic location at the heart of Central Europe, foreign investment and ownership was necessary to fully exploit Hungary's competitive advantage, even if it meant foreign control of key industries and sectors.

Despite strong inward capital flows, a financing crisis and forced devaluation necessitated austerity policies, which severely slowed the economy in 1994-96. Only in 1998 did strong industrial expansion push growth above the 5% rate that government economists judged attainable on the basis of investment and productivity trends – and necessary if the income gap with the EU is to close within an acceptable timescale.

Economic Activity

Russia And Serbia 'Shocks' Shrugged Off

Growth slowed again in the first half of 1999 as war in Yugoslavia dampened investment and consumption spending (especially from tourism), slow EU growth and the Russian downturn arrested the rise in exports, and a portfolio capital outflow (sparked mainly by unease over Russia) forced tighter monetary policy and some public spending cuts. However, the swift reversal of these concerns produced a strong rebound in H2, with Q4 GDP growth of 5.9% y-o-y (and double-digit industrial output growth) restoring full-year growth to 4.5%, Central Europe's highest rate.

Growth in 1999 was generally balanced across GDP components, with private consumption rising by 4.6%, gross investment by 6.4% and exports by 13% y-o-y in real terms. Rising investment contrasts with the mid-1990s situation, when market-driven reallocation of capital allowed growth to resume while investment was still stagnant or falling, and the new trend confirms Hungary's convergence to a growth pattern more characteristic of OECD economies.

The continued strong rise in exports (up 13% in 1999 after 16.7% growth in 1998) and their crossover with imports (12.3% higher in 1999 after 22.8% in 1998) contrasts with other countries in the region, which saw both flows decline in the first half of 1999 and then imports recover at least as strongly as exports. This is another signal of Hungary's relatively early progression to quality-competitive processed imports which are relatively insensitive to slowdown in main trading partners. As EU growth gathered speed in the second half of 1999, exports steadily outgrew imports despite being made relatively more expensive by the forint's real appreciation against the euro, with exports in Q4 19% higher than a year before, compared with import growth of under 17%. Quick recovery in tourism, whose net revenues fell only slightly for the full year as visitors returned quickly after the Kosovo conflict ended, also helped limit the damage to external accounts.

Overheating Fears Allayed In 1999

The strong end to 1999 growth was helped by monetary policy relaxation, as the National Bank of Hungary (NBH) overcame earlier fears of a consumption boom and overly relaxed fiscal policy. Previous accelerations of growth had been characterised, and ultimately undermined, by a strong upturn in real wages and household consumption, which fed quickly through into imports, producing an external deficit that could only be financed through large-scale privatisations which, by 1999, were mostly complete. Lower inflation and the arrival of Western-style retail banking (hastened by privatisation) also threatened to fuel consumption out of expanding consumer credit, even if real wages did not bounce back strongly from the cuts imposed in 1995-97. New car sales – the main target for consumer borrowing – rose by 24.8% in 1999.

However, real retail sales growth was held to a more modest 7% in 1999, as average real wages rose just 2.5%, well within what most employers could finance through productivity growth. The jump in domestic auto sales was undramatic in a sector more than 80% of whose output had gone to exports the year before. High unemployment, job insecurity and weaker bargaining as workplaces grow more dispersed and less unionised, have kept wage growth in check in most areas, with only higher-skill groups in main growth centres (especially around Budapest) receiving, borrowing and spending significantly more. With the public sector also finishing within its deficit targets in 1999, and the familiar shortfall on state pensions and healthcare being partly ascribable to the transitional costs of partial pension privatisation, the NBH was sufficiently confident in supply-side strength matching demand-side recovery to reduce interest rates sharply in Q4 99, turning its attention to preventing an overvalued exchange rate arresting the trade balance recovery.

Fiscal Policy

An Improving Balance

Finance Minister Zsigmond Jarai resisted calls for fiscal tightening when inflation ticked upwards and growth slowed in the first half of 1999, and was rewarded with a strong second-half recovery which kept the public-sector deficit within target at 3.9% of GDP. The government had briefly cut the target to 3.5% of GDP in February, but put it back to 4% in March, allowing it to escape with only token spending cuts even when the Q1 99 deficit surged to 68% of the annual target, after welfare spending overruns and heavy debt servicing. Defying the consensus among economists, Jarai correctly anticipated that full-year growth would stay above 4%, allowing indirect tax receipts to recover fast enough to redeem the deficit target. Above-target inflation also helped to bring revenues back on track, while spending obligations were substantially lower in the second half. The general budget recorded a primary surplus (before payments on external debt) of close to 2% in 1999, as capital inflows remained more than adequate to finance the current-account deficit without additional borrowing. The 1999 outturn was a substantial improvement on 1998 (when the public-sector deficit reached 4.6% of GDP), rising to 6.8% after special allocations to rescue two banks: **Postabank**, and **Magyar Fejlesztesi Bank**.

The present medium-term target for fiscal policy, to a general deficit below 3% of GDP by 2002, mainly reflects the cyclical improvement suggested by official growth forecasts. Although the government has commitments to structural reform – reaffirmed in the joint policy assessment signed with the EU in April 2000 – which will eventually reduce public welfare costs, these will do little to ease budgetary pressures in the forecast period. Indeed, the pension reform launched in January 1998 has temporarily increased the budgetary demand from the state pension fund, which lost more payroll tax revenue than expected as take-up of private second pensions exceeded official forecasts. Partly for this reason, the government has postponed any follow-up launch of private healthcare arrangements. A new cost-cutting plan involving some privatisation of medical practices was presented for cabinet discussion in December 1999, after the EU warned that more reform would be needed before accession; but an improving economy will absolve the government from taking radical action before the next election, and it is likely to concentrate on forcing down costs (especially of pharmaceuticals and other supplies) rather than boosting non-state purchasing power through the expansion of private funds or managed-care organisations.

Even after a one-off boost from asset sales, the state pension and health funds together comprised almost 20% of the public-sector deficit in 1999. The social funds' HUF41bn deficit target for 2000 is likely again to be overshot. Although above-target health spending growth is now the main problem, the funds' recurrent overruns were first exacerbated by the 1998 pension reform. Widespread voluntary take-up of private second pensions, on top of the compulsory enrolment for younger workers, has caused a significantly larger revenue loss for the state pension fund than was built into its medium-term budget allocations. There is also a concern that inappropriate switching to private funds by some lower-income households will prevent a matching reduction in its future obligations. However, Hungary's pioneering move into three-tier pension reform has been widely praised by the EU, multilateral creditors and credit rating agencies. The recognition that such reforms must (to be socially just) involve some run-up in public debt has made such organisations tolerant of additional social fund overruns, leading to relatively slow public deficit reductions, in the early stages of welfare privatisation.

Monetary Policy

National Bank's Tight Policy Pays Off

As in the case of exchange rate policy, the National Bank of Hungary (NBH) has complete independence in setting monetary policy. Since 1995, following the devaluation of the forint, the central bank's prime objective has been to reduce inflation, while maintaining a stable currency. In its pursuit of this goal, it has maintained a tight monetary policy stance by keeping short-term interest rates relatively high. This policy has proved extremely successful in meeting the twin objectives. The decline in both producer and consumer prices during 1998, allowed the central bank to steadily reduce its benchmark rate several times, while maintaining relative exchange rate stability. The NBH did have to raise short-term rates 100bps in September 1998, moving its benchmark rate to 18%, to support the forint, which had fallen to the bottom of its trading band at the height of the Russian-related turmoil. Nonetheless, it was able to reverse this move in November 1998, and as the currency recovered, foreign investors returned to the domestic bond market and inflation headed towards target. Since then, the continued improvement in inflation has been the main influence in allowing the NBH to ease interest rates further.

Fears of stronger consumption growth and possible fiscal overshoot kept monetary policy on a cautious setting through the first half of 1999, when currency weakness following post-Russia-crisis capital flight and higher food prices also pushed consumer-price inflation back above 10%. In late 1999, however, the NBH softened its stance and embarked on a series of short-term interest rate cuts. With public finances back within target, portfolio capital inflows recovering strongly and inflation slowing (to less than 10% again by Q1 00), central bank concern shifted to the effect of previous bouts of monetary tightening on the exchange rate. To stop the forint breaking through the stronger end of its fluctuation bands and endangering the export-led recovery, the NBH reduced main money-market rates by more than 3% between mid-December 1999 and April 2000. The bank also reaffirmed restrictions designed to deter foreign investors from speculating in the domestic treasury-bill market, and banks from extending loans from the resultant volatile foreign reserves.

This sudden relaxation was forced on the NBH by its commitment to retaining narrow (+/-2.25%) fluctuation bands for the currency, and to keeping its central rate on a steady downward path (depreciating 0.3% per month from April 2000) before the planned fix against the euro in early

2001. It was encouraged by confidence that inflation would fall sharply from April 2000, as the previous year's sharp fuel and food price rises dropped out of the index. However, the rate-cutting exercise was in sharp contrast both to previous NBH policy and to regional partners' approach to similar currency appreciation problems, where monetary tightening was still preferred because of its assumed anti-inflationary effects. Scope for continuing the Q1 00's rate cuts was limited by the possibility of a sudden downward movement in the forint should lower domestic yields, unfavourable trade figures or an external shock caused foreign portfolios to pull back. In March 2000 the NBH moved to stabilise short-term rates after endorsing finance ministry comments that these had dropped "unrealistically low." Exports resilience to persistent currency strength, and the long-term need to raise household savings rates to finance investment with less reliance on imported capital, were also reviving the more cautious NBH stance of a year before.

Exchange Rate Policy

Adjustable Peg: A Job Well Done

After being forced to devalue the forint by 20% in 1995 to correct an unsustainable external payments deficit, the NBH adopted a 'crawling peg' under which the currency was kept within pre-announced fluctuation bands around a central rate which depreciated by a specified amount each month. This was a calculated compromise between a fixed exchange rate and a floating rate. The former imparts a strong disinflationary impulse but makes domestic monetary expansion reliant on capital inflows exceeding the current-account deficit. The latter retains domestic monetary independence but invites price and currency instability that can deter foreign and domestic investment. The new currency regime resulted in Hungary making substantially slower progress against inflation than the Czechs (with an informally fixed exchange rate) and Baltic Republics (with formally fixed rates). But it helped the economy to avoid outright recession during the austerity measures of 1995-7, and to end the decade with growth accelerating, inflation slowing and the external accounts well within their financing limits.

The new currency regime also allowed Hungary to keep to its IMF/OECD-agreed timetable for liberalising the capital account: the forint became fully convertible for current-account transactions on January 1 1996, and restrictions were subsequently removed on all long-term inward capital movements. Only short-term flows remain subject to NBH regulation. Here, a number of restrictions have been kept, with multilateral approval, to prevent speculators exploiting, and possibly undermining, the crawling-peg arrangement. But with the remaining curbs due to be dropped in time for EU and EMU membership, full convertibility is expected by 2002.

The forint's central rate was initially pegged against a currency basket of 70% ecu/euro and 30% US dollars, reflecting the balance of foreign revenues (exports by 2000 being more than 80% directed at the euro zone) and payments (more weighted towards dollars because commodity imports and debt obligations were mainly denominated in it). On January 1 2000 the peg was changed to one entirely against the euro, reflecting the shift towards it as a means of settlement, especially through the rolling-over of external debt into new euro issues. However, this change came too late to save Hungary from a double blow from the adverse effects of the euro's (unexpectedly) strong depreciation against the dollar during 1999: processors sustained increases in their (dollar-priced) commodity imports which they could not pass on to (euro-priced) EU exports except by sacrificing volume, and external borrowers (including the government) faced a rise in dollar debt costs.

Crawling To A Halt In 2001

The monthly forint depreciation rate began at 1.9% in March 1999 and has been successively lowered as domestic inflation slows, to 0.3% from April 1 2000. A further cut is expected in H2 00, before the currency becomes fully fixed against the euro – a move expected early in 2001. Except in the six months following the Russian devaluation crisis of August 1998, when heavy investment-income withdrawal forced intervention to strengthen it, the forint has been kept at the top end of its fluctuation band by strong capital inflows. In early 2000, concerned that intervention to stop further appreciation would cause an inflationary growth in foreign reserves (which form part of the domestic monetary base determining credit expansion), the NBH and government announced more direct curbs on short-term capital inflows, including an increase to 50% in banks' reserve requirement against foreign loans of less than one year.

The proposed fixing of the exchange rate against the euro, without an adjustment from the end-year central rate as determined by the current crawl, is a gamble in several respects. Since Hungarian inflation will still be at least 5% above the euro-zone average, even if the best official forecasts are met, trade-sector producers will have to maintain a comparable productivity growth differential, or keep a tight rein on real wages, if they are to keep sales expanding and still earn sufficient profit to fund investment plans. The removal of downside currency risk for foreign investors in Hungarian equity and bonds means that the new regime could exacerbate the usual early-year surge of portfolio inflows, against which remaining short-term capital controls are unlikely to be sufficient protection. The fixing of the rate is likely to be accompanied, or quickly followed, by a widening of the fluctuation bands, to increase the currency risk; the NBH may even concede such a band-widening before the end of 2000, if its early-year interest-rate cuts prove insufficient to defuse upward currency pressure.

Balance of Payments

Trade Flows Shift Towards EU

Given the fact that it is a small country with poor natural resources, Hungary's economy has historically been geared towards foreign trade. Even when it was under communist rule and a member of the Council for Mutual Economic Assistance (CMEA, or Comecon) its trade was evenly divided between the East and West. The fact that many domestic firms had experience of producing goods that satisfied Western consumer standards made it easier for Hungary to make inroads into these markets after the collapse of communism in the early 1990s. The EU now accounts for over 70% of Hungary's total exports, and is the source of over 63% of its imports. Germany is by far its most important trading partner, purchasing 37% of Hungary's exports and accounting for 30% of its imports. While it ran a trade surplus of US$245mn with the EU in 1998, the US$1.1bn bilateral trade surplus with Germany was the main reason for this. Four out of five of its largest trading partners, in terms of both exports and imports, are EU members. While this helped to limit the impact of the August 1998 rouble collapse on most Hungarian firms, it makes the local economy very susceptible to any economic slowdown within the EU, particularly Germany.

Since 1995, the average annual export growth rate has been an impressive 20.5%. This is directly attributable to a diversification in the type of products that Hungary produces. While agricultural and processed food products remain important sectors, apparel, clothing accessories, auto parts, and machinery equipment are also becoming significant. Machinery and transport exports as a percentage of total exports rose to 52% in 1998, up from 11.3% in 1995. Hungary's success in attracting significant amounts of foreign direct investment has been key to the transformation of the export sector. The five industries that experienced the largest increase in exports from 1993-98 had foreign participation of more than 80%. In this regard, the auto industry stands out, with foreign firms such as **Opel**, **Ford** and **Audi** taking advantage of the government's customs-free zone programme to set up assembly plants that re-export their products to the EU.

Steady growth of exports ahead of imports since mid-1999, despite the appreciating real exchange rate, is gradually winning economic opinion over to the government's view that trade sectors have been sufficiently upgraded (with the help of earlier inward investment) to stay competitive with the euro-zone, despite steadily losing their initial labour-cost advantage. Indeed, the faster real appreciation expected after the nominal exchange rate is fixed against the euro early in 2001 could even enhance export competitiveness, through faster suppression of domestic inflation (especially by making energy and raw material imports cheaper). Despite Hungary's faster growth and real appreciation against the euro-zone in 1999, its trade deficit deteriorated only slightly, to US$2.18bn. An improved service balance helped to narrow the current-account deficit in dollar terms despite a larger income deficit, as foreign investors stepped up their repatriation of interest and profit; and consensus forecasts of a wider deficit in 2000 are consistent with projected faster growth.

The trade balance is still at risk of sharper deterioration if consumption growth accelerates, or the forint becomes substantially overvalued; and deterioration in the income balance is likely to continue as foreign investors continue to take their payoff from several years of heavy investment in Hungary's export base. The medium-term growth rate that can be sustained within external financing limits thus remains some way below the 7% rate referred to by the government in its election pronouncements and recent economy ministry statements. **BMI**'s more cautious (but still bright) growth outlook reflects a continued reduction in the trade and current-account deficits (in proportion to GDP), assisted in 2000-02 by faster EU growth.

Hungary was a co-founding member of the Central European Free Trade Agreement (Cefta), the region's replacement for Comecon. As part of the original agreement and the group's Protocol V, tariffs on 90% of Hungary's industrial goods within the group have already been removed. The removal of remaining tariffs is scheduled for completion by 2002. Hungary's trade flow with Cefta continued to grow in 1998, and recorded a US$245mn surplus as demand for agricultural and engineering products helped the region maintain its share of Hungary's total trade. The only major drop in trade, as would be expected due to their dependence on Russia, was from the Commonwealth of Independent States (CIS), which was a major factor behind the drop in Hungary's fourth quarter trade levels.

Foreign Direct Investment

Foreign Flows Fuel Growth

Since 1989, Hungary has received over twice as much foreign direct investment (FDI) in per capita terms as the Czech Republic, and over nine times more than Poland. In addition to its geographic location at the centre of Europe, which makes it an ideal regional hub for multinationals, Hungary has several key Western-style characteristics that attract investors. These include a stable political system and a legal framework that has a tradition of protecting private ownership rights. In addition, Hungary benefits from a relatively cheap and well-educated workforce, and the government's programme of customs-free zones has also been a major factor in pulling in investment. The customs-free zones were initially established close to Hungary's western border, and provided international companies with easy access to EU markets by allowing them to import raw materials and components for duty-free assembly, under condition that the finished product was then re-exported. However, the government is now attempting to redirect more of this "greenfield" investment to the north-east of the country, in order to redress the regional imbalance of industrial development caused by investment flows. While most foreign operations initially used their traditional network of suppliers, the rapid development of the small and medium-sized enterprise (SME) sector, partly encouraged by government programmes, has started to break into their extensive feeder network. This trend is expected to continue as the SMEs attract strategic foreign investors, and government support helps them to develop the skills and products to service foreign operations.

The ownership structure of Hungary's industrial sector has undergone a dramatic change since 1990. While the government's extensive privatisation programme has been a major factor, the flow of FDI into the economy has also played a major part. At the end of 1998 there were over 25,000 companies with at least some type of foreign participation. Their production accounted for 32% of GDP, and they employed one quarter of the private sector workforce and produced 45% of the manufacturing sector's value-added. In the past two years, the largest sources of FDI were Germany, France, Austria, the US, the UK and the Netherlands. There is little doubt that the US$19.2bn of FDI that Hungary has attracted since 1990 has become a driving force in the economy. The fact that one-third of total exports are produced by foreign firms operating within the customs-free zones highlights the dependence on both foreign investment and the zones.

The distribution of foreign investment by sector is relatively even. The main exception is agriculture, as currently the law prohibits foreign ownership of land. The electronics sector was one of the first to benefit from FDI flows, with large multinationals such as **IBM**, **Sony** and **TDK** establishing hard-disk and consumer electronics manufacturing facilities. The major Western automotive firms were quick to follow. **General Motors' Opel** division, and **Ford**, **Audi** and **Suzuki**, have all set up production and assembly operations. A majority of both the retail and banking sectors are either foreign-controlled or have some degree of foreign participation. The focus of FDI has been moving up-market, in line with Hungary's shift of locational advantage from low-cost towards higher-quality and knowledge-intensive production. These new motives for establishing and expanding Hungarian operations helped double FDI to US$1bn in 1999, almost all of it going into new production and research facilities.

External Debt

Debt Structure Continues To Change

Over the past four years, the government has successfully pursued a policy of extending the average maturity of its debt portfolio, while reducing its dependence on floating rate and foreign debt. Improved liquidity and growing foreign interest in the domestic government bond market, along with a rising sovereign credit rating, has assisted the government in this policy. Since 1995, it has increasingly replaced maturing foreign debt with forint-denominated paper, and in 1998 it started financing the interest payments on its foreign currency debt with forint issues. The net effect was a 2% drop in foreign debt as a proportion of total debt to 39% by the end of 1998. In addition, as part of a plan to extend the average maturity of the debt portfolio, which was 1.4 years at the end of 1998, the government has started issuing longer maturities, in both forint and foreign currency debt. This is expected to have a significant impact in the next three years, given the large number of maturities that will fall due during 2001.

The pricing of Hungary's euro debt issues in 1999 (EUR500mn eurobonds of 10-year maturity in January, 7-year in April, 5-year in June, and a EUR300mn syndicated loan in July) marked a retreat from previous records, as the threat of Balkan insecurity and rising US interest rates temporarily dampened investor optimism for emerging Europe in general. However, this was compensated in H2 99 by a substantial reduction in domestic funding costs, as a surge in demand for forint-denominated bonds allowed the NBH to make substantial interest-rate cuts on issues of up to 10 years. The finance ministry announced in March 2000 that the year's foreign debt repayments – estimated at around US$1.6bn, split evenly between principal and interest – could be met entirely through domestic debt issues, leaving the NBH free to time its next foreign borrowing to catch the best market conditions. The continued reduction in foreign and domestic debt costs was further assisted by credit-rating upgrades during 1999, which leave Hungary's sovereign rating with main agencies just one grade below region-leading Slovenia and the Czech Republic – a substantial achievement for a country which inherited significantly larger communist-era debts. The expectation of a further upgrade guaranteed a return to high demand and competitive pricing of euro issues once optimism on regional stability and growth prospects returned towards the end of 1999. Hungary is the first East European EU applicant to issue eurobonds in a full range of maturities, perceived default risks on which further receded when it moved to a euro-only currency basket at the start of 2000.

3 Key Economic Sectors

Introduction

From Processing To Outsourcing

The strong acceleration in industrial production growth under way since mid-1999 – which saw annualised rates topping 20% in March and April 2000 – has been driven by sectors which were negligible or non-existent when the economy was formally disengaged from communism a decade ago. Hungary is being transformed into a production centre for relatively capital-intensive, technologically sophisticated goods and services dependent on skilled management and labour and high-quality communications and transport infrastructure. Low labour costs are still an attraction to Western multinational companies (MNCs), especially those with facilities located not far inside the EU's current eastern border.

But with the real exchange rate strengthening against the euro, and real wage growth beginning to catch up with labour productivity growth in the traded-goods sectors, the continued competitiveness of Hungarian industry increasingly rests on accelerating innovation, improving inventory management, and greater integration into international supply chains. Hungarian industry's relative success in doing this is indicated by the continued inflow of long-term investment into industrial projects, and by the increasing research and development (R&D) activity of both internationally-partnered and larger domestic firms.

The main vehicle for this transformation continues to be foreign direct investment (FDI). Hungary's end-1999 per capita FDI was 22% above the Czech Republic's at US$1,764, and more than three times that of Poland. The virtual completion of privatisation, with even the country's utilities, energy companies, financial services and infrastructure programmes extensively transferred to multinational ownership and management, has slowed the FDI inflow but shows no sign of halting it. Follow-up investment in the modernisation and expansion of privatised operations, foreign participation in initial public offerings by newly formed or spun-off companies, and the develop-

Hungary has transformed rapidly from a processor of imported primary inputs to a supplier of intermediate and final products, many of them destined for Western markets. FDI has driven the country's integration into EU-based production and service networks.

ment of industrial finance by largely foreign-owned banks and venture capital firms, have filled much of the gap left by sales of equity in former state enterprises. In 1999 HUF70.5bn (US$325mn) flowed in from competitive bidding for Hungary's third national mobile phone licence, confirming the power of fast income growth to outweigh the disadvantage of small national size in promoting Hungary's benefits to MNCs, as a market as well as a supply source for new technology goods and services.

The present administration has established an accommodating approach to FDI. There will be greater emphasis on attracting FDI into goods and services whose inputs can be extensively sourced locally, and whose outputs can generate exports or substitute imports in areas of fast-growing demand. Electronics, computer hardware and software, pharmaceuticals, motor vehicles, light engineering and upmarket tourism are among the leading sectors in which MNCs, as owners or strategic partners, have accelerated the modernisation of communist-era companies whose expansion and innovation have created opportunities for new local enterprise.

Although inward investment has accelerated the stabilisation and restructuring of Hungary's economy, there are dangers in the current reliance on MNCs to determine sectors' relative development and generate their exports. Any decline in demand for the goods and services whose production has been outsourced to Hungary, or in the country's competitiveness as a location compared with other transition and emerging economies, could prompt MNCs to begin repatriating profits rather than reinvesting them, leading to the running-down and eventual closure of their facilities. The obverse of strong positive linkages to the domestic economy when input-intensive MNC production expands is a serious downward impact on local producers if the MNC unit downsizes or disinvests. MNCs have also tended to treat their Hungarian subsidiaries and partners mainly as production centres, keeping R&D, design, marketing and other strategic decision-making closer to home. This increases Hungarian units' vulnerability to

SHARE OF INDUSTRIAL PRODUCTION (%)				
	1997	1998	1999	Jan-Apr 2000
Mining	1.0	0.7	0.6	0.4
Manufacturing	85.8	87.7	89.1	90.4
of which:				
Food, beverages and tobacco	18.2	16.3	15.1	12.9
Chemicals	18.3	16.6	13.9	6.9
Machinery and equipment	26.6	33.3	40.3	25.7
Electricity, gas and water supply	13.2	11.6	10.3	9.2
Source: Central Statistical Office				

being treated as branch plants to be closed rather than upgraded if their market becomes unviable, and tends to generate price competition which forces domestic rivals to adopt a similar low-cost, low-R&D strategy (a response especially evident in the pharmaceutical, auto, electronics and software industries).

Petroleum And Related Industries

An Energy Hub?

As an integrated oil and gas company with international interests (through its partnerships with Croatia's **INA** and Slovakia's **Slovnaft**), **MOL** has the potential to become a leading player in the region. Its scaling-down of exploration activity in favour of increased production investment, with new ventures in Russia and Croatia under study, will reduce earnings risks without noticeably affecting returns. Furthermore, recent acquisitions greatly strengthen its involvement in downstream oil and gas processing and refining. However, EU membership preparations require competition to be introduced into the import and sale of gas, and the company has already reorganised into separate distribution, transport and storage operations in preparation for possible break-up. The liberalisation of electricity generation will add to medium-term competitive pressures, as power plants look for cheaper gas sources. MOL's call for a 'big bang' deregulation of the sector from January 1st 2002 does not entirely demonstrate its commitment to a free market, or confidence of prospering in one. The initial effect of liberalising prices would be to let them rise, increasing profitability, and making room for a pricing strategy to deter new rivals from entering. The government, concerned to create enough sector competition to limit the rise in prices when they are eventually freed, is expected to follow a slower deregulation path, not designed to be completed before the target date for EU accession.

The profitability of MOL's wholesale gas business has been undermined for several years by price controls, which are expected to persist throughout the forecast period. The government restricted the July 1 2000 wholesale gas price increase to 12%, less than half the year-on-year rise in MOL's import cost, and has made it clear that the 2001 increase will be limited to 5% – another real reduction – to help contain consumer-price inflation and cushion the impact on lower-income households. Ministers' refusal to review the rise (which the company calculates will impose a gas-trade loss of up to HUF100bn), or to approve a price formula that supports its investment plans,

Although inflation concerns have delayed the final phase of gas and petrol price liberalisation, Hungary's early start in implementing energy deregulation along EU lines has cushioned the effect on industrial costs of removing past energy subsidies, while retaining the incentive for heavy post-privatisation investment in the downstream energy sector.

prompted the resignation in July of chairman Janos Csak after only a year in the post. MOL's petrol price rises have also come under government fire, although an attempt to reverse them was abandoned after the company threatened legal action. The government argues that MOL has used its monopoly power to pursue excessive price rises under the guise of adjusting to world levels, and to let its costs remain unnecessarily high. The electoral costs of such actions outweigh the fiscal benefits now that the state stake has been reduced to 25%.

However, despite hints from the company that it might abandon gas trade, the government's offer to buy back the wholesale business is unlikely to be taken up. MOL's wholesale trade complements its upstream activities, and should return to profit once the price curbs are removed, as they have to be before EU accession. Strongly rising demand and limited world supply are expected to ensure greater price strength and margin resilience after 2010. Return of the gas business to state ownership would also damage Hungary's investor-friendly reputation, by setting a dangerous precedent of using profit-restraining policies to devalue assets before renationalising them. With the possibility of price regulation continuing after the target liberalisation date in 2002, MOL is expected to remain under pressure to cut costs, continuing a programme which saw the payroll reduced by around 7% during Csak's short chairmanship. However, the company's recent spate of acquisitive growth is likely to slow after the Slovnaft takeover is completed in late 2002, recent purchases having take it close to the self-imposed 40% debt-equity ratio.

Electricity

EU Accession Fatigue Interrupts Liberalisation

The pace of electricity supply liberalisation has slowed, benefiting regional distributors at the expense of end-users.

As with gas, the present government is dragging its feet on the final stages of power-market liberalisation. With parliament not due to debate the new electricity act until Q3 00, the January 1 2001 date for the first (heaviest) industrial users to start choosing their supplier will almost certainly be delayed, along with new electricity trading arrangements. Later extensions of the free market, to lighter industrial users and households, are also expected to be delayed, as the government resigns itself to slippage from the target 2003 EU entry date. In contrast to gas, these delays improve the profitability outlook for power distributors, which can expect to see prices driven down once the competition for business users gets under way. However, wholesale electricity competition will take several years to reduce prices significantly. This is because: there is insufficient domestic capacity for extensive shopping-around (which could remain confined to the largest users for at least two years); electricity imports remain under the control of grid operator **MVM**; and many generators are still supplying distributors on long-term contracts (whose benefits to the coal sector blunt the political incentive to truncate them).

Generators are, however, already preparing for tougher supply deals when the present contracts are renegotiated, increased competition from large industrial users acquiring their own plants, and a delay before they are allowed to integrate forward into retail supply. Gains in energy efficiency mean that rapid industrial growth over the forecast period will convert into only moderate electricity demand growth, with household demand actually falling in some regions as the end of subsidies deters usage. Coordination among the six regional distributors is therefore expected to increase, even if regulators rule out consolidation, with shared foreign ownership already providing scope for this in the case of **Emasz** and **Elmu**.

Although geology has deprived it of substantial raw energy resources, geography could allow Hungary to become an important player in the unified European energy market on the strength of these early reforms. Already a likely host for expanded FSU gas and oil flows into Germany and the EU pipeline network, it could soon acquire a similar position in the widening EU electricity network, and become a significant exporter of power and oil products as generation and refining expand with the help of foreign invest-ment. The announcement in early 2000 of a German-Hungarian consortium to develop telecoms transmission through long-distance powerlines re-vealed another possibility for capturing international traffic through existing energy assets. Even if the Czech Republic (which has greater electricity export potential) or Poland (which boasts the region's first electricity spot market, opened in mid-2000) beat it to becoming the region's main energy *entrepôt*, significant opportunities should develop in Hungary for providers of goods and services related to the expanding international energy trade.

Telecommunications

Addressing Communications Problems

Rapid demand growth, especially for data services, and a strong foothold in 'converging' cable television, mobile phone and internet businesses, mean a continued bright profit outlook for main provider **Matav**. However, this

The post-communist telecoms deficit has been addressed by rapid expansion of both fixed and mobile networks, leaving a supportive base for the development of manufacturing and services dependent on fast and reliable data transmission.

reflects the difficulty in establishing competition in the sector, despite the early start to deregulation in 1992. The final stages of deregulation have yet to be put to parliament, and it is likely that the government will continue to use regulation rather than competition to keep prices down and services expanding, not implementing the full EU free-market prescription until shortly before its EU accession date. In principle, Matav will lose the last of its monopolies (on the voice traffic 'local loop') on January 1st 2002. In practice, it has retained a strong grip on fixed-line voice and data traffic where these have already been exposed to competition, while building up substantial market shares in mobile telephony and cable broadcasting. Matav's strength in these areas could be especially problematic for opening-up the local loop, without which rival networks cannot be completed. Regulatory treatment of the former monopolist's market power has been relatively light because of Matav's heavy investment in upgrading the main network, which is now of comparable reliability and density to those of the EU. Around two-thirds of the company's revenues still come from areas sheltered from competition. The transfer in 2000 of telecoms regulation to the prime minister's office can only be a transitional arrangement – an independent regulator being required from 2002 – and is not expected to change the regulatory climate in the interim.

Even if full deregulation is delayed, sector competition is expected to intensify over the forecast period as new technologies and demand sources help rival operators compete more directly with Matav, over its network and their own. Hungary is set to leap-frog to many of the latest data-transmission-based technologies, including business-to-business exchanges, internet banking, internet telephony, multi-media mobile telephony and video-on-demand. A strong domestic software and information-technology sector will support swift exploitation of new technologies, especially those aimed at business-to-business dealings. This will, in turn, ensure the continued fast growth of Hungary's telecoms hardware production, with significant export potential as the rest of the region pursues network expansion from a generally lower base.

Rising demand will ensure several years during which the more responsive operators will be able to offset lower margins against higher volume. Mobile services, with a subscription base still less than one-third of that in most EU countries, are set for especially rapid growth, helped by the price war that continued through 2000 as **Vodafone**, **Pannon** and Matav's **Westel** vied to sign up new subscribers. In the longer term, however, 'commoditisation' of basic transmission services will tip the advantage towards companies that have moved into the provision of information and entertainment services.

The downside of last year's lucrative HUF70.5bn auction of the latest mobile franchise is that it ensured the award went to an existing large player (Vodafone Airtouch/**RWE**). With **Deutsche Telekom** taking full control of the consortium that controls Matav, Hungary's telecoms networks are being integrated into those of the wider Europe in a way which is potentially beneficial for investment levels and interconnectivity, but raises long-term questions about the extent of competition.

Pharmaceuticals

Medicine Chest To Run Low?

Whereas most of its industrial chemical production is of fairly standardised products that compete on price, Hungary's main drug makers retain a foothold in the higher-margin proprietary and branded-generic areas. **Richter Gedeon** and **Egis** continue to research new compounds and delivery systems, funded through the profits from manufacturing generic products of their own and licensed from other OECD manufacturers. However, while the sector's profitability has recovered strongly from the temporary arrest of Russian sales in 1998-99, it will remain under medium-term pressure from government policy. Prescription drug prices remain heavily capped as part of efforts to cut the costs of state healthcare, and Richter's sales actually fell 4% in Q1 00 as domestic demand shifted more heavily on to generics.

Drug makers' profits and scope for proprietary research are being undermined by price caps and health providers' increased use of generic products.

In June 2000 the Competition Office launched a major investigation into the industry's proposed 8.5% rise in prices of drugs qualifying for state subsidy. With health providers forced to prescribe generic products wherever possible, and source them abroad if cheaper, the scope for funding proprietary research is steadily diminishing. The future even of Hungary's largest groups is likely to be as high-quality production branches and specialist research centres within alliances built round the main US- and EU-based multinationals, which are now the only ones able to fund the systematic research needed to identify and screen new compounds for commercial use. Acquisition in March 2000 of **Novopharm** by Israel's **Teva**, which itself has links to US research-based companies, confirmed that smaller players' futures are mainly as links in international networks, a future which even Richter will find hard to avoid in the longer term.

Automotive Industry

Meeting The Demand For Public Transport

The auto sector is benefiting from rising demand for luxury cars and buses.

Despite its small domestic market, Hungary has attracted substantial multinational investment into auto production, which (with related industries) now comprises more than one-third of total engineering output. The quality of production labour and of locally sourced components have made it the first eastern European country to embrace luxury car production, with **Audi** already producing up-market (TT) models, and **BMW** investigating new model possibilities following its withdrawal from UK production. A BMW deal moved closer after the government approved a package of tax concessions for a new plant near the German border, which could create an additional 1,500 jobs and secure a share of BMW's R&D operations.

Although inward investment has been concentrated on greenfield ventures, longer-established vehicle manufacturers have recently been staging a revival after several years of depressed orders and cost problems following subsidy withdrawal. **Ikarus** is now winning a steady flow of export orders for its buses, and North America-based counterpart **NABI** marked its re-emergence as an international player with the takeover of Britain's **Optare** early in 2000. Needing to raise its margins after record sales converted to reduced profits in 1999, NABI is expected to use its acquisition to reproduce in the EU its North American formula of exporting components for local assembly. These once embattled firms now stand to gain from renewed worldwide interest in small, low-cost buses suitable for the rapid expansion of public transport, especially now that they are adapting to lower-emission engine systems. Their stabilisation brightens the outlook for component maker **Raba**, which has also had some success in developing its export and outsourcing business.

Tourism

Moving Upmarket

Tourist numbers are levelling off, after several years of growth, as Budapest and the main Lake Balaton resorts reach the limit that can be served without damaging their attractions. However, tourism revenue is set to continue to grow as the government and private sector work together to attract higher-spending visitors for longer stays. Gross annual revenue from foreign tourists is now approaching US$3bn, making a significant contribution to offsetting the continued visible trade deficit. The government anticipates US$1bn of infrastructure investment in the next 3-5 years to sustain the sector's growth, although it will look to private sources for most of this. The high rate of hotel renovation and construction after the sector's privatisation augurs well for this, although there remains a danger of temporary over-expansion depressing initial returns on investment. A state-sponsored marketing effort helped rapidly restore visitor confidence after the outbreak of war in neighbouring Kosovo in 1999, so that tourists' numbers and average spend were slightly higher year-on-year in H1 00 despite the forint's real appreciation against the euro. Parallel efforts to cleanup the environment, improve transport and communications and cut down on urban crime will also work to the advantage of tourism, especially in the high-margin areas of culture, health and sport.

A strategy of targeting wealthier travellers has ensured the quick recovery of tourism revenues from the Kosovo setback, with post-privatisation investments helping to divert upmarket visitors from costlier EU resorts.

Construction

Road And Rail: Desperately Seeking Investment

Although its passenger and freight rail services emerged from communism in relatively good shape, Hungary was relatively under-equipped for the substantial growth of road and air travel that has accompanied transition. In 1998 it had 83km of railway per thousand square kilometres of land, compared with an EU average of 48km, but this represented a relative disadvantage after taking account of the low quality of track and rolling-stock on many of these lines, and the quantity of goods and people they had to carry which in EU countries has generally been transferred to roads. Motorways, by contrast, covered just under 5km per thousand square metres, compared with almost 15km in the EU. Difficulties in turning rail monopoly **MAV** and national air carrier Malev to profit and finding private sector partners capable of supplying their investment needs, have delayed the

Deficiencies in physical communications are proving slow to remedy, with delays already experienced and cost overruns on the horizon in the road upgrading programme, and fast railway investment constrained by the existing network's unprofitability.

development of high-speed passenger rail services of the type now familiar within the EU, and allowed foreign airlines to capture much of the traffic growth between Budapest and other main European cities.

High-speed road coverage is proving even harder to extend, despite government commitments of HUF60bn in 1999 and HUF27bn in 2000 (on top of a basic road maintenance budget of HUF87bn) to speed up motorway construction. The latest plan aims to add 600km of motorway over the next five years, and completion of 80km in 1998 showed this to be a realistic aim. But slowness in selecting private sector contractors and approving their designs have raised the danger of serious delays, while rising land and labour costs add to the difficulty of delivering this volume of expansion within budget. Strong competition among contractors has so far allowed the government to assign construction tenders at relatively low rates, but this has left the viability of some of the project partners in doubt, and the labour-intensity of road and rail building (the M7 Budapest-Balaton upgrade could provide employment for up to 200,000 workers in some capacity) means that costs could rise sharply if continued economic growth achieves the hoped-for sharp reduction in unemployment. Scope for self-financing the new developments by raising MAV fares and raising road tolls is limited by the dependence of many lower-income households and firms on the currently subsidised networks for basic transport services. The EU will provide additional funding for those schemes which complement its designated 'trans-European networks', but Hungary is destined for some time to pay the price of the neglect of its international transport links under communism.

Profile and Recent Developments

Introduction

Foreign Investment And Privatisation Key To Growth

Hungary's economy has been exposed to two major shocks since the early 1990s. The first shock was the collapse of Comecon, the Eastern Europe trade body that tied the command economies together and guaranteed large state-owned industries a protected market. In Hungary, economic liberalisation preceded political reform, as many firms set their sights on rapid integration into Western European markets. What followed was one of the most successful privatisation programmes seen in the region, with Hungary attracting over US$19bn in foreign direct investment since 1991. The manufacturing, telecommunications, oil and gas, and utility sectors have been the leaders in the liberalisation process. Manufacturing slightly increased its contribution to the overall economy, despite an initial high proportion of ageing factories and industrial sites. While the transition to private ownership resulted in some pain, it has helped produce several well-managed firms that are able to compete with their EU and Western counterparts. It should be noted that several sectors that have not been opened to foreign/private ownership, particularly agriculture, have seen their contribution to GDP slide. Some others that have been privatised, such as many firms in the construction industry, have suffered from slow sector growth. The dramatic change in ownership structure that began in 1991-92 resulted in foreign investors controlling over 50% of the engineering industry by 1996. This high level of total investment is a direct result of Hungary's legal framework, protection of private investment and political stability.

The second shock was the collapse of the Russian economy during the second half of 1998. This tested the viability of individual firms within several sectors. Key sectors, such as telecommunications, utilities and retail, which mainly rely on the domestic market, were indirectly affected as economic growth slowed. The greatest impact has been felt in sectors where exports to Russia account for a significant proportion of sales, such as auto parts and production, food processing, chemicals and pharmaceuticals.

The information technology (IT) sub-sector is worth highlighting, given its strong growth potential. While its overall contribution to GDP is currently low and it has a large number of small firms, it should experience significant growth during the forecast period. Hungary could potentially become the "Silicon Valley" of Eastern Europe, with a highly skilled workforce and low operating costs providing incentives to foreign investors. **Nokia** has made Budapest its largest software development centre outside its headquarters in Finland, while local firms have been able, and will continue, to attract foreign investor interest. A case in point is the software design firm, **Graphisoft**, which floated on Frankfurt's Neuer Markt in 1998. While the company suffered a slight setback, due to a drop in sales in Asia, it is the world's third largest producer of computer design software used by architects. Other firms have pursued a different route. **Cygron Kft** agreed to be purchased by **Mindmaker Inc** of the US, providing the Hungarian company with the necessary sales and marketing expertise needed for expansion. With further liberalisation, as Hungary continues to implement the reforms needed to enter the EU, the service sector is expected to increase as a share of GDP.

Agriculture

A Difficult Transition To Date

Historically, agriculture and farming have played an important role in Hungary's economy, and despite the dramatic drop in the sector's contribution to GDP, from 7.8% in 1991 to 5.2% in 1997, it still plays an important role, particularly as a source of employment. Hungary is virtually self-sufficient in almost all agricultural products. During the communist era, it exported about one-third of its total output, mainly to its Eastern bloc neighbours. In 1956, the collective farm structure was enforced nationwide when the Communists came to power. The combined effects of dismantling this system in 1992-93, along with the drought that occurred during this period, saw agricultural output fall by 16.6% in 1992 and 7.9% the following year, on a value-added basis. The structural adjustment from collective farms to the current system of small/medium holdings and cooperative ownership has proved difficult for the entire sector. The government used a coupon auction system, which by 1994 saw that all of the collective farms were in private ownership. While it is far from ideal, the current ownership structure will remain in place, for at least the medium term, since there are limitations on the transition from cooperatives into joint-stock companies, as well as a number of constraints on land sales and leases. In addition, foreigners are not allowed to purchase farmland, a regulation that the government will have to amend in order to conform to EU laws. No change in this law is expected until a more definite timetable has been established for Hungary's EU entry. Members of the current government have started to lobby for additional support for small and medium-sized farmers, and clearly oppose changes to the foreign ownership restrictions.

Direct government farm subsidies and price supports are relatively low, particularly when compared to the current EU average. According to a recent report on Hungarian farm policies by the World Trade Organisation (WTO), Hungarian farmers receive roughly a quarter the level of EU farm support. The WTO has warned that Hungary's policies will become more protective when it joins the EU, since regulations will have to be amended to adhere to the EU's policies. With the exception of restrictions on foreign ownership of agricultural land, Hungary's farmers are more market-oriented than their EU counterparts, and will face less problems concerning competition from existing EU members than other aspirant members. The government's main support is in the form of export and credit subsidies. In 1999, the level of farm subsidies increased to HUF143.2bn, with HUF123.5bn coming directly from the government's budget versus HUF100bn in 1998. In keeping with its criticism of the previous government, the highest subsidy rates will be paid to small and medium-sized farmers.

Construction

Looking For A Public Spending Boost

Since 1992, when construction accounted for 5.2% of GDP, the construction sector's importance to the economy has steadily declined, and accounted for just 3.4% of GDP in 1997 – a drop of over one-third. As was the case for most industries, the transition of the early 1990s was destabilising. In theory, the sector should have been better protected; many aspects of the construction sector, particularly private developments and housing, were not a top priority under communist rule, and investment largely came from private sources. The extent of the decline is partly attributable to the combined effect of high interest rates and the drop in personal income, which put pressure on the housing market. While residential construction increased by 18% in 1995 and 15% in 1996, on average it has been basically flat for the past three years. The sector received a boost from the government's decision to reimburse VAT for housing projects with permits granted after January 1 1999.

House building has also been promoted through increasing state assistance to residential purchase and improvement to HUF71bn in 2000. Although new house completions fell another 5% to 19,300 in 1999, additional state spending may add fuel to the fire ignited by faster income growth, falling interest rates and a growing domestic mortgage market. Whereas most cities (including Budapest) still report adequate commercial building supply following a building boom in the mid-90s, there are signs of housing shortage as more families acquire the means to escape traditional high-rise living, with issuance of house construction permits up 30% in 1999. In the wake of a run-up in residential property-related shares, leading tile maker **Zalakeramia** unveiled plans for a HUF500mn plus capital increase in March 2000 in a confirmation that financing conditions on the sector's supply side are also starting to ease.

Road building is at the centre of new public infrastructure projects announced in March 2000, with HUF27bn to be spent in the first year of a five-year programme to extend the motorway network by 600km. The transport ministry aims to supplement this with up to EUR175mn of EU funds for international road and rail upgrades. This increased state commitment recognises the slow progress made in raising private funds for new motorways, the initial stretches of which have failed to generate sufficient traffic to hit their toll-revenue targets.

Manufacturing

Food And Beverages

The food processing subsector, which includes meat, fruit and vegetable processing/canning along with beverages, has much in common with its main source, the agricultural sector. Both have experienced a dramatic change in ownership structure since 1990, and are strongly export-oriented sub-sectors of the economy. Due to the relatively low-cost base, the sector as a whole is highly competitive on international markets. Unlike the farming sector, where foreign ownership is currently not allowed, the food processing subsector has benefited significantly from inflows of foreign investment, and foreign ownership rose from 20% of the industry's capital in 1992 to 52% in 1997. Some of the world's largest food processing companies, such as **H. J. Heinz**, **CPC International** and **Unilever**, have established production and distribution operations in Hungary, many of which are used as a central base to supply the rest of the region.

While drought and transition-related shocks in the agricultural sector during the early 1990s caused supply problems for Hungary's food processing companies, and forced many to import raw materials, the collapse of the Russian export market in the second half of 1998 had an equally serious effect. Hungary's food processing industry relies heavily on Russia compared to the economy as a whole, with 18% of total food exports destined for Russian markets, compared to only 5% of total exports.

The two beverage firms that are listed on the Budapest Stock Exchange have a dominant position in their respective markets. **Zwack Unicum Rt**, the liqueur manufacturer and drinks distributor, enjoys a 40% share (including the black market) of the HUF67.4bn spirits market. Despite a decline in overall spirit sales in 1998, Zwack saw sales revenue rise by 27.8% to HUF11.5bn that year, due to its strategy of focusing on high quality brands, and reduced the proportion of unbranded liqueurs from 70% to 30%. Zwack was privatised in 1992, but only 24% of its shares are traded on the stock exchange, with **UDV** and the **Underberg Group** owning 26% and 50% (plus one vote) stakes, respectively. **Brau Union Hungaria**, which is involved in the brewing, marketing and distribution of beer, is considered to be Hungary's premier brewer. Austria's **Brau Union AG** holds a 73.1% stake in the company, while the balance is traded on the local stock market. The company's focus on strong brand recognition and marketing enabled it to increase sales revenue by 19% in 1998, despite an overall drop in total beer sales of 6.7%. Both Zwack Unicum and Brau Union Hungaria are expected to remain dominant players in the domestic market, even after EU membership.

Chemicals And Pharmaceuticals

The chemicals and pharmaceuticals industry was the third largest industrial sector and the second largest earner of industrial exports in 1997 and 1998. Unfortunately, the combined effect of the drop in chemical prices, along with the collapse in the key export markets of the CIS, and Russia in particular, put an end to the recovery that started in 1997. Petrochemicals and plastics account for two-thirds of the sector's total exports, while pharmaceuticals, the third largest sub-sector, produces 25% of exports. The financial results for Hungary's two largest chemical producers, **TVK** and **BorsodChem**, were affected by the worldwide fall in the price of bulk chemicals during 1998.

Energy Sector

Petroleum And Related Industries

Despite a relatively high level of foreign ownership, Hungary's oil and gas sector remains tightly regulated, causing a number of problems. In particular, the gas sector, the larger of the two sub-sectors, has a two-tier structure. The first tier is made up of **MOL**, effectively the monopoly wholesaler controlling gas exploration and imports. MOL also controls the national gas distribution system. The second tier consists of six regional gas distributors and two marketers/distributors of liquefied petroleum gas (LPG). This structure was set up in 1991, when the government split up the **National Oil and Gas Trust** (OKGT), which controlled the entire sector under the communist regime. The state's approval of a privatisation resolution in May 1995 required it to retain a 25% plus one share interest in MOL, but allowed the APV to sell the remaining shares to the public. The sale programme took place in three tranches: January 1996, May 1997 and March 1998. The six regional gas distributors were privatised at the beginning of 1996. Initially foreign investors were only allowed to purchase 50% plus one share, but several have significantly increased their stake. Market share is not divided evenly among the six distributors, with the two largest, **Fogaz** and **Tigaz,** supplying 60-65% of the total gas delivered.

As part of the sales agreement and pricing control mechanism, which is regulated by the Ministry of Economy and the Hungarian Energy Office (HEO), the government has agreed to a pricing formula that should insure an 8% pre-tax return on equity for the distributors. However, under the 1995 pricing formula, only Tigaz attained this level of return in 1997, and the pricing policy is currently under attack from the six regional distributors, which have taken the government to court after an application for MOL to cut its prices was rejected in early-1999.

Despite the strong showing of its gas division, which saw 1998 profits rise to HUF15.2bn compared to a loss of HUF8.7bn in 1997, MOL also experienced internal problems last year. In February 1999, dissatisfied investors forced the resignation of its chairman, as well as five of the six members of its supervisory board and eight of its 11 directors. New chairman, Janos Csak, pledged to push through cost reductions and a refinery modernisation programme, allowing MOL to capitalise on wider margins due to the decline in oil and European gas prices, and relatively strong domestic growth. He also planned to prepare the company for Hungary's entry into the EU and to take advantage of increased offshore joint ventures and possible acquisitions. The company's move into LPG distribution is also seen as a move to capitalise on its dominant position as the country's main supplier in the non-regulated market. MOL diversified further by agreeing to acquire chemicals group TVK in 1999 and 36% of Slovak oil refiner **Slovnaft** in April 2000, while also moving closer to an international merger (with Croatia's **INA** the front-running partner). Its core gas importing and wholesaling business appears set for at least another year of loss, as the government in early 2000 again failed to deliver a pricing formula that would ensure domestic sales cover procurement costs, approving a 12% mid-year price rise which was less than half what MOL claimed was needed to restore investor confidence.

Electricity Sector

Though Hungary's electricity sector is currently the most liberalised sector in Eastern Europe, further deregulation is necessary to conform with EU directives. The sector has a three-tiered system, which consists of generators, a national transmission grid (**MVM**) and six regional distributors. At present, a single-buyer model is applied to the transmission and distribution side, based on the "least-marginal-cost" model. MVM, the sole operator of the national grid, invites the electricity generators to provide services in the order of the lowest cost first, which insures overall cost efficiency. It then sells the electricity to the six regional distributors, which provide it to their customers.

The privatisation process began in 1995, when small holdings in the regional distributors were sold to employees. The process sped up dramatically in 1996, with foreign investors allowed to purchase stakes of up to 49%, with an option to increase their holding to majority ownership. The net result is that all six distributors are at least half foreign-owned. While all of the generators and the MVM were also offered to foreign investors, only two of the largest power plants were successfully sold at that time. Two more plants were sold in late-1996, but the remaining three plants attracted little interest due to their age and integration with inefficient and over-staffed mines. Meanwhile, MVM's ownership of the Paks nuclear plant is seen as a major stumbling block in attracting foreign investors. The sector's current capacity is divided between nuclear (24%), coal (26%) and oil/gas (49%), with hydro-energy producing just 1%. In contrast, the production structure is heavily skewed in favour of nuclear (40%), at the expense of oil/gas (32%), while coal (27%) provides a level similar to its capacity component.

The industry's regulatory system is comprised of three bodies. The Electric Energy Act, which defines the conditions for the three tiers, as well as listing the responsibilities of the other two regulators. The HEO is the main executive body, and submits proposals for tariff changes to the Ministry of Industry based on changes in production costs. The HEO also prepares the basis for all energy-related laws. The Ministry of Economy, the main regulatory body for the system, fixes the official price of electricity based on proposals from the HEO. It also awards licences for new power plants, as well as regulating all imports and exports. Prices are currently regulated for all three levels of the system. As part of the privatisation agreement, the government promised foreign shareholders that prices would be adjusted to allow companies to achieve a pre-tax return on equity (ROE) of 8%. While the return for each level is calculated separately, it is based upon a total segment return, rather than on an individual basis. Therefore, the spread between the most and least efficient can vary significantly, as can be seen from the 1998 results for the six distributors, which shows that **Demasz** had an ROE of 12%, while **Titasz** achieved just 5%. The regulators also limit a company's maximum return, since it stipulates that if a company's ROE exceeds 12%, it must share 50% of its extra profits with its customers in the coming year. In February 1999 the government announced the first major step to full liberalisation, scheduled to start in 2001.

Electricity supply is to be liberalised in stages. The heaviest (100-plus gigawatts/year) industrial users will be able to choose their supplier from January 1 2001, to be followed by lighter industrial users and households once the new arrangements have been perfected. Urgency has been added to the process by the need to have a free electricity market before entering the EU, and by threats by large users to start building their own dedicated generators if a clearer route to cheaper, reliable supplies were not spelt out. However, the economy ministry has warned that competition among suppliers may take longer to establish in the highest-consuming regions, including the industrial north-east. It also remains unclear whether an exchange for the spot-trading of electricity will be operational in time for the start of 2001, and whether generators will be able to enter the free market by supplying end-users directly.

Communications

Deregulation Is The Key To A Dynamic Sector

Matav, Hungary's largest company, was created in January 1990 when it was spun off from **Hungarian Post**, signalling the end of the state's telecommunications monopoly. Further deregulation and the establishment of a framework for the current structure took place when the Telecommunications Act was introduced in the summer of 1993, effectively dividing services into two classifications. The first group, containing the traditional public and national fixed-line and mobile services, was placed in the more regulated sector, where concessions to service the 54 telephone regions were eventually granted. All other services, such as data transmission, were classified in the competitive sector.

Hungary has one the most advanced telecommunications sectors in Eastern Europe and in many aspects, such as privatisation and pricing, is ahead of several EU countries. Fixed telephone lines increased by 11% y-o-y in 1998 to 2.7mn, representing a 35.4% penetration rate. This puts Hungary just behind Portugal, which has a 39% penetration rate, and well ahead of its larger regional EU aspirant Poland, with a penetration rate of just over 20%. While Hungary does not yet have an independent regulatory authority, it is considered to be one of the region's most competitive telecommunications sectors, and Matav not only meets EU directives but will profit from further integration.

Matav In A Strong Position

Matav benefits from strong foreign investor ownership by **Magyar Com**, a 50:50 consortium of **Deutsche Telekom** and **Ameritech**, which first took a 30% stake in December 1993 and increased its interest to 59.6% two years later. Shares were later offered to the public in October 1997, and are now traded on both the Budapest and New York stock exchanges. Matav has a monopoly on fixed-line services in 36 out of the 54 local telephone regions, accounting for over 80% of the population, including the fast-growing Budapest region. It also has a monopoly on domestic long distance and international services. While these monopolies are not due to expire until December 31 2001, the government has expressed an interest in negotiating an earlier end. Matav also occupies a strong position in the non-regulated sector, such as data transmission. It achieved a network digitalisation rate of 75.7% at the end of 1998, and the growth of two mobile businesses, jointly-owned with **US West**, will remain strong following a 50.7% y-o-y increase in the number of subscribers to its digital system during 1998. About 1mn people, or 10% of the population, currently use mobile phones, but this number is forecast to rise to 30% by 2005. Therefore, when compared with other regional and EU telecoms firms, Matav's strong position will see it outperform both its peers and the local BUX index. The company's 1999 results bear this out. Consolidated net income rose 35% to HUF78.6bn on the strength of rapid volume growth, especially in data transmission and mobile services, where **Westel900**, in which it holds a 51% stake, accounts for more than half the GSM market.

Record Demand For Latest Mobile Licence

Westel900's main rival, **Pannon**, moved into profit in 1999 after a 25% operating revenue gain, confirming the rapid market growth which led to exceptional demand for the third GSM licence, auctioned in June 1999. **Primatel**, a consortium of **RWE** and **Vodafone Airtouch**, reportedly paid HUF70.5bn (US$325mn) for the new franchise, which will enable it to offer DCS-1800 services. Despite its unexpectedly large payment for the franchise, the new operator launched its service in December 1999 with prices claimed to be around 10% below those of its rivals, setting a first-year market share target of 10% and ensuring the competition needed to maintain rapid market growth. Hungary's total cellular subscription, at around 10% of the population in mid-1999, was still only half the EU average, which has continued to rise steeply as prices fall and new data services become available.

Retail Trade

Foreign Firms Dominate Changing Retail Sector

Since 1990, Hungary's wholesale distribution system and retail sector has changed dramatically, as many traditional businesses have disappeared and new ones emerged, including the development of shopping malls and chain stores. The concept of direct marketing has also been introduced by Western firms, which have used the information technology revolution (including bar codes and computerised inventories) to target specific consumer groups, particularly young urban professionals. As the presence of these large European and US retailers becomes more prominent, the vertical integration within the supply chain between wholesalers and retailers will increase. The transformation from state-owned distributors to Western-style retailers has orientated the market more towards the customer. As consumers are no longer seen as a single entity, the concept of marketing has been introduced and competition has increased significantly.

The recent success of US consumer products along with the proliferation of Western European supermarket and hypermarket chains has resulted in a dramatic decrease in the Hungarian share of the sector. Furthermore, the decrease in retail trade in real terms during 1990-97, as the population adjusted to the transition to a market economy, was an extra squeeze on the sector. Despite this, several large retail chains have remained in local hands, although most have received funds from offshore investors. In 1998, the trend in spending patterns was reversed and, with personal incomes expected to grow and inflation to continue on a low trend, the retail sector will be a major contributor to economic growth.

The consolidation that has taken place in recent years has seen 10-12 companies and groups gain control of 20% of the retail market. Food sales represent 40% of total retail trade, and it is here that competition is tightest. The majority of the large chains operating in the retail food sector are foreign, with Austrian-controlled **Alfa Trading Plc**, France's **Cora** and **Auchan**, Swiss-owned **Metro Holding Kft** and Britain's **Tesco** all present. Austria's **Julius Meinl Gruppe** also controls the Hungarian supermarket chain **Csemege**, which it acquired in 1990. The net result of this foreign-controlled market share has been a dramatic rise in competition and significant upgrading of stores and the services they provide to consumers.

The other parts of the Hungarian retail sector are mainly dominated by small, family-owned outlets, which were sold off during the 'pre-privatisation' programme in 1990. Until 1998, **Centrum Plc** was Hungary's largest department store chain, when it was acquired by **Skala-Coop Holding**, a majority-owned subsidiary of Germany's **Tengelmann Group**. Centrum operates 23 department stores nationwide, selling a full range of products. **Fortex Holding** is one of the few publicly-traded retail groups, which operates several chains, each selling different goods such as appliances, electronic equipment, optical and audio goods and furniture. It was started after a local entrepreneur received financing from a US venture capital group. **AFEOSZ** is a Hungarian-owned chain operating general consumer stores in smaller towns and cities.

Foreign investors have also been involved in the development of shopping malls. The first, **Duna Park**, is a Hungarian-Israeli joint venture with 114 tenants and is located in a suburb of Budapest. The others, such as **Polar Centre** (Hungarian-Canadian investors) and **Europark** (owned by a German company's subsidiary **Spar Magyarorszag**), also combine a large number of retail outlets along with leisure activities, such as cinemas. All three groups are reported to be planning several additional developments across Hungary.

Banking Sector

Encouraging Foreign Participation

The primary regulator of Hungary's banking sector is the Ministry of Finance, which works closely with the NBH in making key decisions on credit institutions' activities and the setting of mandatory domestic and international reserve requirements. Once a specific policy is approved by parliament, the responsibility for monitoring, investigating and enforcement is passed to the State Financial and Capital Markets Supervisor (APTF), the same body that supervises the stock exchange. Over the past several years the government has actively encouraged the development of the banking sector through privatisation. In doing so, it has also encouraged the entry of foreign banks into the Hungarian market. Foreign financial firms have been able to open branches in Hungary since January 1 1998. There are 44 banks, four building societies, two mortgage banks, 249 savings cooperatives and eight loan co-operatives currently operating in Hungary. Of the top 10 banks, only **OTP Bank**, the country's largest, is listed on the BSE. In commercial banking services, OTP is the only domestic bank that directly competes with the foreign-controlled banks, which include a number of domestic banks that were recently privatised and now have majority foreign ownership. At the end of September 1998, 56.5% of total banking assets were controlled by foreign banks, which had a majority ownership in 30 of the country's 44 banks.

Direct state-ownership in the banking sector had fallen to 16.5% of total assets as of September 1998. The regulatory pattern affecting banking over the past two years, along with the government's policy of encouraging foreign ownership, has been shaped by the regulator's attempt to modernise the industry, as well as harmonising financial regulations with those of the EU and the Organisation of Economic Cooperation and Development (OECD). Increasing competition among the top banks has led to a significant improvement in, and modernisation of, banking services across the board. The most noticeable improvement has been in corporate lending, although retail services have also been upgraded. However, both areas still lag far behind Western standards.

One reason for the heavy reliance on imported capital in the first 10 years of Hungary's transition was the very limited availability of domestic finance for investment in industry and services. The socialist system bequeathed a limited domestic savings base – soon to shrink further as output collapsed in the wake of the Soviet bloc's fragmentation – and no institutional means to channel household savings into commercial investment. Although banks had been effective at concentrating and mobilising savings, their tendency before 1989 was to direct them, for political reasons, towards a narrow range of increasingly inefficient traditional industries, and for several years afterwards to focus on investment in government debt, which carried by far the highest and safest return. Runaway inflation in the early 1990s reduced the incentive to keep savings in domestic currency or in banks, and the fragile state of the banks – several of which collapsed under the weight of bad debt despite an expensive government rescue effort – remained a deterrent into the late 1990s.

Bank lending to industry is set to expand in the medium term as lower interest rates and improved credit analysis lift its earnings potential, while also reducing the relative attractiveness of government debt. Borrowers will benefit from the high degree of multinational involvement in Hungarian banking, which makes it likely that most of the banks now operating in the country will continue to compete for custom rather than going in for widespread mergers and acquisitions. The revival of industrial bank lending, on more market-led terms, will be especially helpful to the development of small and medium-sized enterprises in relatively familiar expanding sectors, for whom bond and equity finance is not a viable option.

4 Business Environment

Introduction

Early Reforms Yield Benefits

The fact that Hungary will be one of the first members of the old Soviet bloc to take part in the expansion of the EU is attributable to the introduction of economic reforms before the installation of a democratic government in 1990. It was in the early 1980s that Hungary's socialist government initiated the "new economic mechanism", which allowed it to become a member of the World Bank in 1982. This permitted Hungary to draw on the bank's financial assistance in the mid-1980s, when it started its privatisation programme, industrial and banking sector restructuring, and public finance reforms. The privatisation programme, which saw the largest sale of state enterprises in the early 1990s, is considered to be one of the most successful in the region. As a result of these early reforms, the private sector's share of GDP reached 80% in mid-1998, according to an EBRD study, placing Hungary well ahead of other regional EU aspirants, such as Poland and the Czech Republic.

There are several other factors that have made Hungary the initial choice for investment inflows to the region by foreign companies. These include its location, which is viewed as a natural bridge between Western and Eastern Europe; relatively sound infrastructure; a well-educated and skilled workforce; a Western-style tax structure and a functioning legal system. Furthermore, consecutive stable and reform-minded governments have also inspired investor confidence.

Small Business Boost To Tackle 'Dual Economy'

The extensive foreign ownership of Hungary's main manufacturing, financial service and utility industries following privatisation has long been a source of economic and political concern. Although an estimated 800,000 small businesses sprang up in the immediate post-communist period, many were wiped out by the subsequent recession, inflation and credit squeeze. Many of the survivors have failed to achieve sustained growth or the level of productivity needed for survival in the EU single market. In 1997-99 a small number of foreign multinational companies (MNCs) accounted for most of Hungary's fixed investment, exports and productivity growth, as domestic firms' generally lower profit margins and higher capital costs left them unable to invest in new capacity, skills and distribution networks on the same scale. A 1999 Budapest Chamber of Commerce survey reported 80% of local SMEs lacking the funds to expand production or make the investment needed to become MNC suppliers.

Successive governments have set out plans to promote domestic small and medium-sized enterprises (SMEs), but the 'Szechenyi Plan', unveiled by the present coalition in 1999, is the most ambitious to date. With neither the ambition nor the resources to promote 'national champions' capable of matching the MNCs in the near future, the government's main aim is instead to promote domestic SMEs as local suppliers and niche exporters. In pursuit of an EU-recommended target of 50% domestic sourcing by processing MNCs, small businesses are to be offered preferential long-term loan facilities, special tax reliefs and regulatory exemptions. In addition, SMEs are to be the main beneficiaries of future business tax cuts, starting with the reduction of standard social-security payroll tax to 33% from 39% in 1999. Some signs that the reviving economy was giving a relative boost to SME performance emerged from official production data released in April 2000, which showed gross national income (which excludes the net exports still dominated by MNCs) closing the growth differential with GDP in 1998.

Infrastructure

Transport And Communication Links Need Upgrading

Both past and present governments have viewed infrastructure improvements as an important part of economic development and a key factor in helping to narrow regional disparities and encourage job creation. To take advantage of Hungary's central location, which makes it a logical East/West base for trade and commerce, the government has adopted a programme of working closely with international organisations, such as the EU and EBRD, as well as the private sector, to improve its transport and communication links.

By Eastern European standards, Hungary's communications system is relatively well developed. Deregulation and foreign investment have been key to the transformation that has seen the number of telephone lines increase by two-thirds, from 1.8mn in 1989 to just over 3mn at the end of 1997. In the early 1990s, the government sold off a controlling interest in **Matav**, the state telephone monopoly, to a joint venture of **Deutsche Telekom** and **Ameritech**. The success of the foreign investors can be seen from the improvement in services and in the continued increase in the number of lines. The combined result of foreign expertise and deregulation, with private competitors bidding to provide regional services, has helped Hungary develop a communications network that is moving closer to Western standards. While the household telephone line penetration rate was only 40% at end-1998, well below the lowest levels seen in the EU, if current projections of reaching 50% by mid-2005 are attained, Hungary could enter the EU at a similar level as Greece and Portugal.

Improving the highway network was the initial priority during the early 1990s. EBRD funds supported the expansion and widening of the Vienna to Budapest M1 road. There are eight national highways that converge on Budapest, but since most of the 381km motorway network is located in the westernmost region of the country, the government is now looking at upgrading the main eastern link, the M3, and the southbound M5 and M7 motorways. Road and rail network improvements are being part-funded by the introduction of tolls and a nationwide tagging system, which is consistent with EU proposals. This policy is also aimed at addressing the switch to road use that has taken place since 1989, a direct result of the road improvement programme.

As part of its policy to reduce traffic pollution, the government plans to make public transport more attractive. It has started pursuing a policy of upgrading the railway network in line with EU guidelines. While the 7,711km of railway track is only a fraction of the 30,000-plus kilometre road network, the government has undertaken to supplement the high speed Vienna rail link by introducing similar services to eastern destinations, particularly with the construction of the new Hungary-Slovenia line.

Despite being landlocked, shipping also provides an important means of transport. With 1,373km of navigable waterways, the Hungarian sector of the Danube is expected to become an integral part of the European river system. The government is currently working with the EU to ensure that the shipping network conforms to European regulations and standards. With access to ports on both the North Sea, via the Rhine-Danube canal, and the Black Sea, water transport is seen as a key contributor to both growth and investment.

The Domestic Market

Population Decline Continues

Hungary is a relatively small country, with a land area of 93,000km², just 1% of Europe's land mass, and a population of 10.09mn at the end of 1998. The Central Statistical Office reported that 1998 saw the largest drop in population for 18 years. While the domestic birth rate has been falling almost continuously since World War II, the accelerated fall in births is attributed to the decline in living standards following the collapse of communism. This has also pushed Hungary's life expectancy down to 65 years for men and 74 years for women, the lowest of the 28 OECD countries.

Hungary's population is unusually homogeneous. Over 96% are ethnic Hungarians, with the remainder mainly German, Romany, Croatian and Slovak minorities. Budapest, the capital, is by far the largest city with a population of 1.89mn. Overall, the population is fairly heavily urbanised, with 65% reported to be living in urban centres, although the next three largest cities – Debrecan (0.21mn), Miskolc (0.18mn) and Szeged (0.17mn) – are significantly smaller than Budapest. While per capita income has been increased steadily since 1990, standing at US$4,836 in 1999, the gap between the highest and lowest incomes, and the regional differential, have both widened. Although the real value of social transfers to the lowest income groups increased considerably in 1998, the gap moved beyond 1995's spread of 7.5 times. The income gap between the Transdanubia (A Dunantul) and Budapest over the eastern half of the country, which includes the Great Plain (Az

Alfold) and the Northern Highlands (Az Eszaki Hegyvidek), has more than doubled in the past eight years, reflecting the fact that most foreign investment has been confined to the western regions. However, as more entrepreneurial zones are established, the eastern regions are expected to start to close the gap.

The Labour Market

Labour Reforms: An Untouched Area

The highest level of spending on education in Eastern Europe is another factor that has attracted many major multinationals to invest in Hungary. While education's share of GDP has dropped from a high of 7% in 1990 to 5% in 1998, education and skills levels remain the highest in the region. This has helped to attract several large auto makers to set up plants in Hungary, including **General Motors' (GM) Opel** plant in Szentgotthard, where 53% of the workers have a high school, college or university education, a level significantly higher than that found in GM's German plants. School attendance is compulsory from the ages of six to 16, and in 1998 the completion rate was 97.1%. This provides the economy with a high adult literacy rate: approximately 98.5% of the population at end-1998. The Fidesz-led government's decision to abolish its predecessor's introduction of fees for second- and third-level schools is expected to cause a further rise in enrolment ratios. Despite the introduction of such fees, the enrolment ratio for 18-22 year olds in higher education has already risen steadily from 10.4% in 1990 to 16.1% in 1996. While the level of education and skills are acknowledged to be lower in the north-east and eastern regions, the government has an incentive programme that provides funding for part of the training costs.

Nevertheless, Hungary's labour code is relatively inflexible. While it has been largely ignored by most major firms, it is viewed by many as a possible stumbling block to the successful development of new and alternative forms of employment. This could prove problematic in the future as the government looks to attract additional investment to develop the lagging north-east and eastern regions. The basic labour law is modelled on EU precedent and practice, and while social protection and charges are lower than the EU average, they are still considered too high given Hungary's level of development.

Total union membership is estimated at two-thirds of the total workforce, in line with the current EU average. Unions are arranged along industry lines but the overall level of organisation and effectiveness is poor compared to Western standards. A 1996 labour survey reported that 46% of individual union organisations claimed to be on good terms with their respective management counterparts and saw "their relationship with employers, as one of cooperation and partnership". These results are high for the region. In contract negotiations, collective bargaining is held at the enterprise level, and in the past decade strikes have been infrequent and short. Labour contracts are the norm and workers' councils are mandatory in all workplaces employing 50 or more people. These councils are based on the German *Betriebsrat* model.

The labour code sets out the basic minimum wage in monthly terms for all types of work, as well as the regulations concerning working hours. Higher rates may apply depending upon the type of work, skill level, industry and level of responsibility. The basic working week is set at 40 hours, and a 15% premium is required for night work. Overtime commands a 50% wage premium and is limited to eight hours per four-day period. In practice, this time limitation is widely ignored by agreements between management and individual workers.

Taxation Policy

Compliance And Enforcement On The Rise

Hungary had a comprehensive tax system, geared to accommodate its relatively large private sector, well before the transition to a market economy began. However, the tax laws have been subject to significant and frequent changes since 1989. This has caused difficulties in maintaining a consistent interpretation of the tax laws, which has created uncertainty for both taxpayers and tax collectors.

The system uses a self-assessment basis, with relatively early filing deadlines. While a limited amount of information is required when filing, the authorities carry out periodic detailed audits. Late payments are subject to both interest and penalties, which may be significant. Historically, tax compliance and enforcement have been relatively poor when compared to Western standards. While recent governments have taken steps to address this, it will be some time before the tax system reaches the effectiveness and efficiency of its EU neighbours. The two main problems have been the lack of experience with practical treaty issues and the tax treatment of foreign nationals working in Hungary.

Corporate Tax

The basic corporate tax rate of 18%, which applies to the taxable profits of a company, is well below those of the rest of the region, as well as most of those found in the EU. There is also a 20% dividend withholding tax payable on any profit distributed to shareholders. This replaced the 23% tax on distributed profits abolished on January 1 1997. The dividend tax must be withheld and remitted to the authorities by dividend payers. A dividend tax rebate is available if the recipient of the dividend is a resident of a country that has a tax treaty with Hungary. The dividend tax does not apply to distributions to Hungarian entities. Since partnerships are not financially transparent under local law, they are subject to both the corporate and dividend withholding taxes, as if they were incorporated associations, such as Kft.s and Rt.s.

Corporations may carry losses forward for up to five years. The law also allows for any losses incurred during the first three years after incorporation to be carried forward indefinitely. Only certain agricultural companies are allowed to carry losses back, and then only for a maximum of two years. The tax code also uses the straight-line method of depreciation of tangible assets. There are also several tax incentives for both domestic and foreign-owned companies that are available as part of the government's industrial policy.

Payroll Taxes

The low corporate income tax rate has traditionally been offset by relatively high employer social security contributions, which in 1998 amounted to 44.5% of the gross wage bill. Reducing this contribution (spread across the state pension, healthcare, unemployment and training funds) has become a priority, as the government responds to similar cuts made during 1999 by other Cefta countries even though its pension and health reforms have yet to deliver any significant social-fund savings. The 1999 budget reduced employers' standard payroll tax for the pension and health funds to 33% from 39%. This was mostly clawed back by the introduction of employee contributions, but ministers appear committed to using the eventual fruits of welfare reform to keep payroll taxes among the lowest in Central Europe. Employees are also required to make healthcare and pension contributions equal to 3% and 7% (rising to 9% in 2000), respectively, of their gross annual salary, up to HUF156,585. Since January 1998, workers may choose to place up to 6% of their pension contributions in a private fund. They must also pay 1.5% of their salary in unemployment contributions.

Value-Added Tax

The general turnover tax is, in fact, a conventional value-added tax (VAT), as defined by EU directives. It is, in effect, a consumption tax charged by all entities providing goods and services on a regular basis within the domestic economy. It is collected in advance, and businesses may credit input payments against output receipts, or recover them from the tax authorities. The normal VAT rate is 25% for most goods and services. A reduced rate of 12% applies to public utilities, publishing, raw materials for (and products of) the food industry, and certain healthcare products. All exports and certain medical and dental pharmaceuticals are exempt from VAT. Similarly, financial services, insurance and communication services are not subject to VAT. However, all imports are subject to VAT based on a sum of their customs value, including duties and fees. Companies can apply for free zone status, if they meet the requirement that all goods imported into the zone are used exclusively in the production of exports. Hungary maintains a VAT rebate agreement with most EU members and its framework is consistent with EU policies. The government has signalled its intention to raise the preferential rate to 14%, offset by a reduction in the standard rate to 20%. This would bring it closer to EU norms, but the likely revenue loss from such a move and its short-term inflationary impact means that direct-tax changes are likely to take priority.

Personal Income Tax

Income tax is currently administered according to four marginal rate bands, and collected directly from employers on a pay-as-you-earn basis. Reform plans published early in 1999 envisage a reduction to two bands, 25% and 40%, with further administrative savings from restricting compulsory tax returns to those on salaries of more than HUF3mn. Given its need to reduce the fiscal deficit, however, the government is expected to make detailed calculations on the revenue impact of such a change before agreeing its implementation, which may also be phased.

Industrial Policy

A Targeted Industrial Policy

In its effort to conform to EU policies, the Hungarian government has pursued an industrial and investment policy that applies to both foreign and domestic investors. Therefore, there are no longer any tax incentives available specifically to foreign investors. The incentives on offer are geared towards fulfilling the government's twin goals of employment creation and economic modernisation. A main concern of the current Fidesz-led government is the disparity between the western and eastern regions of the country. The Hungarian government and international organisations – including the EBRD, EU and several foreign governments – have introduced programmes to help regions with high unemployment, such as the north-east. These regions receive preferential treatment by being designated as 'entrepreneurial zones' (defined separately by law), as in Zahony and its surrounding area, or by being a region of high priority with an unemployment rate of over 15%.

The government's main programmes are applied through tax incentives. Enterprises can receive a 100% tax holiday of up to 10 years, for any new investment of HUF10bn or more, in a manufacturing project started after December 31 1996. To qualify for the tax incentive the project must employ at least 500 additional people and result in an annual increase in sales of 5% of the value of the investment, or achieve a similar revenue increase. For those projects which are located in entrepreneurial zones and priority regions, the minimum initial investment is HUF3bn and the number of new employment positions to be generated falls to 100, provided the project meets the annual sales increase of 5% of the investment. A 50% tax credit is available to new projects that involve a lower initial investment of HUF1bn, provided the 5% sales target is met.

Companies also receive tax credits for hiring the long-term unemployed by charging the social insurance contributions (currently 39% of base salary) for every new job given to a worker unemployed for over a year against the corporate tax bill for the first 12 months. Corporate taxpayers who participate in school-type vocational training are allowed to charge up to HUF6,000 per month for each trainee. In addition, the government's Labour Market Fund (which had a budget of HUF130bn in 1998) subsidises the cost of training workers who are currently employed and expected to work for the firm for at least one year.

The Ministry of Economic Affairs also manages the government-sponsored Target Allocation for Economic Development programme aimed at manufacturing and infrastructure ventures. This is more of an industry-specific programme, which provides interest free loans of up to 25% of the project's value for five years. It also provides loans to small and medium-sized companies that invest in targeted sectors or export production. Interested companies can also establish a free zone, if their production is geared towards the export market. Such a move allows the company to claim a full rebate on VAT and qualify for export loans at preferential rates. It should be noted that these zones are likely to be abolished under EU trade rules when Hungary becomes a member.

Privatisation: Ending On A High Note

With 80% of GDP now originating from the private sector, Hungary is the 'transition' economy furthest advanced with large-scale privatisation, and has in fact gone further towards this than a number of EU member-states. The state shareholdings still up for sale are mainly minority stakes in energy, utility, media, and older manufacturing companies. These are likely to be disposed before 2003, in readiness for EU accession officially targeted for that year. The largest single sale of 1999 comprised HUF70.5bn (US$325mn) paid by the winners of the latest national mobile phone franchise.

Foreign Trade Policy

Forint's Crawling Peg Successful To Date

The Foreign Exchange Act took effect on January 1 1996. It was part of the stabilisation package of the previous year, that included a one-off 9% devaluation of the forint aimed at arresting the widening trade deficit. The Act gave the National Bank of Hungary (NBH) full jurisdiction over all foreign exchange matters and regulations, including individual transaction approvals, and introduced the current crawling-peg regime. This allows the forint's mid-rate value to devalue monthly against a currency basket, while setting a narrow band as its trading limits. The success of this policy is seen from the fact that the monthly devaluation rate has been reduced from 1.8% when the regime was established, to 0.6% on January 1 1999. The forint's basket was also modified at the beginning of 1999, when the euro replaced the deutschemark. The euro now accounts for 70% of the basket, with the balance made up by the US dollar. The 1996 act also removed or liberalised many restrictions on financial activities applying mainly to businesses and, to a lesser extent, individuals. Since January 1996 the forint has been fully convertible for all current account transactions. However, while all in-bound long-term capital account transactions are basically unrestricted, restrictions still apply to some outbound capital account transactions and all short-term flows. The restrictions on outbound flows are being systematically phased out as part of the requirements of Hungary's OECD membership, and as it continues to move closer to EU regulations. NBH policy is directed at the earliest possible qualification for EU monetary union, the next significant step towards which will be the fixing of the forint's central rate against the euro at the start of 2001.

EU Agreement Helps Trade Policy

Hungary's Association Agreement (AA) with the EU in 1991 helped it redirect trade towards the West, in the aftermath of the collapse of the Council for Mutual Economic Assistance (CMEA, or Comecon as it was better known). The AA removed tariffs on most non-agricultural Hungarian exports to the EU, boosting the proportion of exports bound for the EU to 71.2% of total exports in 1997, compared to an even division of exports between Comecon and the West prior to 1991. The EU has also become the main source of imports, accounting for 62.6% in 1997. Germany is now its largest single trading partner.

The redirection of Hungary's trade since 1991 has been accompanied by a change in export composition, with mechanical and electrical engineering raising their contribution sharply, while traditional clothing, textiles and industrial machinery have fallen away. The decline in exports of semi-processed materials and intermediate components such as auto parts, indicates the rising extent to which these now feed into domestic production of higher-value-added exports. Food and agricultural products remain significant contributors to exports, but there is again an ongoing shift to greater domestic processing. The transformation of trade, whose improving balance despite real exchange-rate appreciation during H2 99 signalled a new quality-competitiveness that augurs well for future production growth, has relied heavily on foreign direct investment: the five industries which expanded their exports fastest in the mid-1990s had foreign participation of more than 80%.

Trade Liberalisation Is Lagging

While Hungary was initially considered a leader among transition countries in trade liberalisation, the growing trade imbalance has caused it to lag behind. World Bank sources estimate that its average tariff of 14.4% in 1997 was relatively high, and the average weighted tariff declined to only 10.9% in 1997 compared to 12.3% in 1991. Despite this, the government has continued to pursue full harmonisation with EU policies. The Customs Law and Customs Tariff Act of April 1996 brought 70% of Hungary's customs regulations into line with the EU by 1999, and the target for full tariff compliance is 2001. Last year also saw the establishment of a complete free-trade area, (with the exception of agricultural products), as part of the AA. The June 30 1997 Protocol of Adaptation to Hungary's AA, defined the framework for agricultural trade between the EU and Hungary, and while it is not officially in force, both sides have agreed to be governed by its terms. This limits two-way trade between both sides until 2005.

Hungary was a founding member of the Central European Free Trade Agreement (Cefta) and as part of the original agreement and Protocol V, tariffs on approximately 90% of industrial trade with the group (75% with Romania) have been removed. In March 1993, Hungary signed a free trade pact with the Euro-Free Trade Agreement (Efta), which allows it to open markets to Efta countries at a slower pace than EU members through to 2000. Hungary is also a member of the World Trade Organisation (WTO), which in its most recent evaluation commended Hungary's commitment to the liberalisation process. In particular, it highlighted the January 1996 decision to eliminate most quotas and attempts to make the tariff structure more transparent and compliant with WTO policy.

The present government, largely for the purposes of improving its international relations, signed a number of new bilateral free-trade deals in 1998 and 1999, including a pact on industrial trade with Croatia, and on farm trade with Israel. Under pressure from the EU, which regards such deals as obstructive to Hungary's eventual admission to its own single market, the government has now pledged to end these deals (or at least restrict their concessions to those offered to EU member-states) before accession, which it officially hopes to secure in 2003.

Bureaucracy And Corruption

Reforms Aimed At Meeting EU Practices

All aspects of Hungary's commercial law, including contracts, have been reformed at least once since the fall of communism in 1989. At present the judicial system operates adequately in accordance with its legal statutes and guidelines, which have a strong resemblance to German statutory laws. Any further reforms are geared towards further harmonisation with EU practices. At present, the court system can be slow, since it is overburdened. Depending on the subject matter of a contractual dispute a final decree can take up to a year or more. Thus, out of court settlements are becoming more common, increasing the cost of business in certain sectors. While the civil service has a relatively low level of corruption by regional standards, its poor pay scales compared to the private sector have encouraged many of the most qualified employees to leave. Therefore, while corruption is not unknown, its occurrence is on par with that seen in the EU itself, and delays in approvals and applications are more likely to be caused by "red tape" bureaucracy, rather than demands for bribes.

Intellectual Property Rights

Enforcement Is Still A Problem

All internationally-registered patents, trademarks, copyrights, industrial designs and models are legally recognised and protected from infringement under existing Hungarian law. But while the current legislation covering intellectual property rights is now equivalent to that found in Western Europe, there are certain areas, such as software piracy, branded apparel and some pharmaceutical patents, where enforcement has reportedly been a problem. The new Fidesz government has started to tighten enforcement, since it is considered to be a key requirement to EU membership. The 1995 Protection of Inventions by Patents Act conforms to all current EU legislation, as it provides patent protection for 20 years and includes detailed provisions against infringement. An amendment to the 1995 Act has extended the availability of temporary restraining orders to intellectual property matters. This is a key issue that will bring domestic enforcement closer to current EU practices.

Environmental Regulation

Environmental Protection: EU Forces The Pace

While in the early post-communist years, environmental concerns, and in turn legislation, took a back seat to economic modernisation programmes geared towards improving living standards and raising incomes, the government is now keen on applying, and adhering to, EU norms as quickly as possible. This can be seen from the recent increase in cooperative programmes and the closer working relationship between the Ministry of Environmental Protection and the EU on further legislative harmonisation. In addition, as incomes have risen, particularly in the wealthier western half of the country, so have quality of life and environmental concerns.

The 1995 Environment Act was based upon an EU white paper and contains the three main principles of Hungary's environmental protection policy. These are: that polluters should pay for all damage caused to the environment; the environment should be protected and all damage reversed at the source of the pollution; and that protective action should be taken, even without proof. The government now requires an environmental impact assessment to be performed for all investments that are considered to be potential polluters. In addition, local authorities must issue a permit for all projects that are associated with any type of dangerous waste or toxic substance. This latter regulation is seen as increasing the cost of the potential investment, since it both slows down the process and can include a significant fee

Originally proposed by the previous government, pollution fees were brought back onto the agenda in 1999, with a view to imposing them from 2001. The new fees will be aimed at upstream producers, in the hope of minimising their inflationary impact, and revenue will be earmarked for subsidies to environmental projects. The new proposals would also impose much stiffer fines on companies breaching emissions regulations and a requirement to submit environmental reports alongside annual financial reports. Although reluctant to introduce measures that could raise industrial costs and reduce Hungary's attractiveness to investors, the government is being forced to act by the risk that EU member-states could block Hungarian exports on 'environmental dumping' grounds – and even delay its accession – if it does not move closer to EU environmental norms over the next three years. The EU currently pays around EUR500mn per year for environmental improvement, but estimates that Hungary must spend more than EUR15bn over 12 years to come into line with its requirements. Public concern over environmental damage, already aroused by serious air pollution in Budapest and other main cities, was further aroused in 1999 when Hungarian sections of the Danube and Tisza rivers were seriously polluted by a cyanide spill from a Romanian gold mine. There is a strong domestic environmental lobby, whose campaigning has already been a significant factor in compelling Hungary's withdrawal from the Nagymaros (Gabcikovo) Danube dam project drawn up with Slovakia before the iron curtain fell.

5 Capital Markets

Introduction

After the general downturn in market sentiment caused by the August 1998 Russian crisis and prolonged by the extended buildup to the April 1999 Nato intervention in Yugoslavia, equity and debt markets rebounded strongly in the second half of 1999. Budapest shares, which virtually halved in value in August-September 1998 as Hungarian export industries were identified as among those most at risk from sudden collapse in Russian purchasing, had mostly returned to pre-crisis levels by the time investors began pulling back from the market for the extended 'Y2K' break. A strong ascent resumed in early 2000, with most analysts forecasting a sharp rise in the Budapest Stock Index (BUX) for the year. Banks, now almost entirely in foreign partnership or control, recorded generally improved performances in 1999, with no repeat of the previous year's confidence-sapping collapses.

Equity Market

Budapest Stock Exchange

Hungary's stock exchange was established in 1864 by royal decree. By the turn of the century it had enjoyed significant growth and took an active role in the region's economy. In line with other world markets, it also suffered a major decline in the early 1930s. It was officially closed down following the communist take-over after World War II, but was revived by a group of 41 members on June 21 1990. In its nine years, the exchange has become internationally recognised for its advanced regulatory and technical framework, as well as becoming the major focal point of the country's capital markets. The exchange currently has 58 members, most of whom are owned by Hungarian and foreign banks. Hungarian financial markets watchdog, APTF, regulates the exchange and also supervises the country's banks and brokerage firms. The clearing of stock exchange transactions is done on a T+5 day basis. In 1993, the Budapest Stock Exchange (BSE) along with the National Bank of Hungary (NBH) and the Budapest Commodity Exchange (BCE) jointly established the Central Clearing House and Depository Ltd (KELER Rt). This is one of the safest financial institutions in the country, and its function is to secure and clear every transaction made on the exchanges. KELER Rt, has share capital of HUF500mn, with the BSE and BCE each holding a 25% stake.

While over half of the exchange's turnover, on a market value basis, is generated by government security transactions, the value of equity transactions between 1996 and 1998 grew by over 1,650%, slightly above the exchange's total growth figure of 1,500%. International investors play an important role on the BSE, generating an estimated 65-70% of its total turnover in 1998. While there were 54 companies and one investment fund listed on the BSE at the end of 1998, most of its trading volume was attributable to a select group of large companies, such as energy company **MOL**, telecommunications group **Matav**, and **OTP**, Hungary's leading bank. The BSE now operates on a three-tiered system, with the introduction of Category C shares in February 1999. The key factors that determine a company's category are its size (asset value), the percentage of shares publicly traded, total number of shareholders and the frequency it reports its financial statements. Category B and C firms are smaller and less liquid shares.

In an effort to improve its technical support and meet the steady increase in trading volume, the BSE introduced a new computerised trading system at the end of 1998. The system allows brokers to execute transactions from their offices, no longer requiring them to have a physical presence on the trading floor. The system is also used by the Hungarian Debt Management Agency, which now uses the MMTS system to hold primary auctions of government securities. The new system has improved efficiency on the execution of orders, will provide the necessary support for the introduction of options trading by the exchange, and allow trading hours to be extended. The introduction of electronic trading is key to the BSE's plans to expand its cooperation with the region's other exchanges, which it is already working with in adapting to EU regulations. Recognising the trend towards financial-market integration across the EU area, and the likelihood that some of its larger companies will choose Western markets for future equity and debt issuances, the BSE is deepening its links with both Cefta and EU counterparts, and signed a cooperation agreement with the London Stock Exchange in 1999.

Budapest Stock Index

The Budapest Stock Index (BUX) is a capitalisation-weighted total return index that reflects the price movement of 20 stocks. The index's base date is January 2 1990, and its base value was 1,000, but it did not become the BSE's official index until January 1995. A company must meet at least three of the following requirements to be included in the index: a minimum face value requirement; a defined minimum price; a minimum number of transactions and a cumulated minimum turnover of 10% of the registered capital during the six months preceding the revision of the index. The index is updated biannually on March 31 and September 30.

Recent Performance

Caught By The Tech Stocks Wave

In the aftermath of the economic woes and forint devaluation of 1995, the BUX share index enjoyed a dramatic rise of 479% from January 1996 to April 23 1998, when it reached an all-time high of 9,016.36. This represented an impressive average annual return of over 200%. The rise was helped by the government's economic reforms and privatisation programme, which attracted both domestic and international investors. In contrast, the remainder of 1998 was a period of high volatility and losses, as investor confidence was shaken by concerns over the election of a Fidesz-led government in May and the Russian collapse in August. At the height of the Russia crisis, the index hit a low of 3,775 in late-September, a drop of 54.5% from its post-election high. The recovery that took place in Q4 98 was again a result of the worldwide fall in interest rates and investor realisation that the impact of Russia's economic woes would have a limited effect, and would only cause major problems for the most inefficient companies. Nevertheless, the BUX ended 1998 down 24.4% for the year as a whole, and over 30% down from its all-time high.

By mid-April 2000 the BUX had recovered to just under 9,700, a year-to-date rise of almost 11%, with analyst polls suggesting that a further 15-20% rise was possible by year-end. The sharpest gains were generally in companies whose prices had suffered most during the Russia crisis, especially pharmaceuticals, civil and mechanical engineering. However, telecoms, electronics, software and computer companies also caught the international wave of enthusiasm for technology stocks, and there were gains for energy-related companies as industrial demand picked up and clarification emerged of the timetable for electricity deregulation.

Budapest Commodity Exchange

The Budapest Commodity Exchange (BCE), was started in 1989 as a private commodity exchange modelled on its successful American counterparts. The first futures contracts were based on agricultural commodities. The exchange's second and most successful section opened in March 1993, with the introduction of financial futures, the first being currency contracts for the deutschemark and dollar. These were soon joined by contracts for the euro, Swiss franc and sterling. In 1994, a 90-day BUBOR interest future was introduced, which was soon followed by a 30-day contract. However, on a trading volume basis, these instruments were overtaken by 3-month and 12-month t-bill futures. In March 1995, a standardised contract on the BUX index was introduced, and this became the most traded contract on the BCE in turnover value terms, accounting for 71% and 65% of the exchange's total turnover in 1997 and 1998 respectively. While the BUX contract was initially viewed as a competitor to the BSE, the two are now working closely together, as can be seen from their joint interest in their common clearing house, KELER Rt. In addition to the BUX contract, the BCE also trades futures on three of the BSE's largest companies: **Matav**, **MOL** and **TVK**.

Private Pensions

While legislation governing voluntary private pensions was approved in 1993, partial privatisation and reform of the mandatory system did not take effect until 1998. Under the 1997 Private Pensions Fund Law, the government undertook to reform the existing state system by allowing people to elect to place some money into privately-run funds, which in turn were allowed to invest a portion offshore. On January 1 1998, reforms were put in place that required channelling one-third of mandatory contributions for all new workers into a private pension, while those currently working and aged under 47 could voluntarily join a private fund. These funds became operational as of July 1998. The government's original forecast, that 1.5-2mn people would elect to be part of these private funds by 2000, proved to be an underestimate. By the end of 1998, 1.4mn workers had joined a private scheme, bringing with them assets totalling HUF29bn. The net result of this was a larger than expected deficit at the National Pension Fund, which pays benefits to current retirees, and increased pressure on the government's overall budget deficit. The deficit appears to have narrowed during 1999, with the health fund taking over as the principal cause of state welfare overruns, although the plugging of part of the gap through asset sales makes the underlying trend less clear. The possibility was discussed during 1999 of restricting access to private pensions for workers for whom they are not compulsory, but the long-term gains anticipated from wider opting-out are likely to prevent this.

The investment guidelines for these funds are strict. The regulations define four asset classes, each with its own limit: cash, which has a minimum 10% holding requirement; bonds and property, both of which have a 30% investment limit; and equities, with a 60% investment limit. The potential growth of these funds is expected to give the BUX a boost as they start to diversify their holdings.

Bond Market

Government Bonds

The government debt market is modelled along the lines of its US counterpart. The National Bank of Hungary (NBH) issues both short-term debt, in the form of treasury bills (t-bills), and longer maturing treasury bonds (t-bonds), through the government's Debt Management Agency (AKK). The AKK first issued t-bills in 1991, while the first bonds were auctioned in 1993. Both bills and bonds are traded on the BSE, as well as on an over-the-counter (OTC) basis. At the end of 1998, there were a total of 75 outstanding t-bill issues, with a total value of HUF838bn. The AKK holds a weekly auction on Wednesdays for 3-month t-bills, while auctions for 6-month and 12-month bills are held fortnightly on Thursdays and Fridays respectively. However, foreign investors are not allowed to participate in these auctions due to current regulations forbidding them from purchasing government debt instruments with a maturity of less than one year. All three maturities are sold on a discounted basis.

The t-bond market is open to foreign investors, with around 55 government issues available on the market. There are several different types, including both floating and fixed coupon bonds, as well as a CPI-linked instrument issued in 1995. The most liquid issues are the two- to five-year maturities. Average daily turnover is between HUF10-14bn, with the average sized deal HUF300-400mn. Foreign traders are active in the secondary market, accounting for over 20% of the domestic bond market. Liquidity has improved since the primary dealer system was put in place in 1996. There are currently 24 primary dealers in the market, who have exclusive access to each bond auction. In contrast, t-bill auctions are open to local banks and brokerages. Government securities can be settled either on the BSE, with a T+2 settlement period, or through KELER Rt, the central clearing house, where the settlement period is negotiated between the counterparties.

After climbing to almost 20% at the height of the Russian crisis in late 1998, short-term interest rates declined sharply during 1999. An improved fiscal position and a heightened concern to stop 'hot money' inflows overvaluing the forint helped to drive down bill and bond yields, especially at the shorter end. Issuance has remained strong during 2000, with the NBH raising its domestic financing plans 18% to HUF3.1bn to cope with rising repayments, reflecting the still short-term nature of most public borrowing in the late 1990s. However, rising foreign enthusiasm for the market, as currency risks fade, ensured a strong reception for new issues in H1 00, and allowed the process of lengthening maturities to continue: the proportion of gross financing raised through issues of two years or over is planned to increase this year to 31%.

Other Bond Markets

In addition to its first 10-year domestic bond, Hungary also went to the eurobond market for the first time with a EUR500mn 10-year issue in February 1999. It was also the first time that a bond was issued in the name of the Republic of Hungary, rather the NBH. It was issued with a 4.375% fixed annual coupon, 87bps above comparable bunds, and 51bps over EURIBOR. To date, the corporate bond market has been restricted to a few well-known names. However, this is changing as more Hungarian corporates become internationally recognised and look to reduce their heavy reliance on bank credits.

Hungary's Debt Rating

The latest round of long-term sovereign credit rating upgrades – to Baa1 from Baa2 by **Moody's** in June 1999 (with a positive outlook added in April 2000), and BBB+ from BBB by **Standard & Poor's** in January 2000 (Fitch-IBCA making the same move in October 1999) – moved Hungary more firmly into investment-grade territory, and to within one grade of the region's best-rated economies (Slovenia and the Czech Republic, both A). Domestic debt is already rated A by S&P, reflecting confidence in long-term fiscal stability and the narrow-band exchange rate regime that limits foreign investors' downside risk. The latest upgrades reflect Hungary's relatively light escape from the 1998 Russian crisis, costly but effective bank-sector clean-up, and satisfactory progress towards EU accession requirements.

POLAND 2000

Analyst: Anthony Cooke

Editor: Ann-Louise Hagger

Contents

Political Outlook _____ **575**

Domestic Political Outlook 575

Profile and Recent Developments _____ **581**

The Political System 581
The Main Political Parties 582
Recent Developments 584
Foreign Policy 588

Economic Outlook _____ **591**

Economic Activity 591
Monetary Policy 592
Fiscal Policy 594
Exchange Rate Policy 597
Balance of Payments 600

Profile and Recent Developments _____ **602**

Characteristics Of The Economy 602
Economic Activity 603
Fiscal Policy 604
Monetary Policy 607
Exchange Rate Policy 609
Balance Of Payments 610
Foreign Direct Investment 611
External Debt 612

Key Economic Sectors _____ **615**

Introduction 615
Information Technology 616
Telecommunications 619
Automotive Industry 621

Profile and Recent Developments _____ 625

Introduction 625
Agriculture 626
Manufacturing 627
Energy 629
Construction 631
Banking And Insurance 633

Business Environment _____ 635

Introduction 635
Infrastructure 636
The Domestic Market... 637
The Labour Market 638
Corporate Taxation 639
European Union Membership 640
Industrial Policy 642
Foreign Investment Policy 643
Foreign Trade Policy.. 644
Bureaucracy And Corruption 645
Intellectual Property Rights.. 646
Environmental Regulation 646

Capital Markets _____ 649

Introduction 649
Equity Markets 650
Derivatives 653
Bonds.. 654

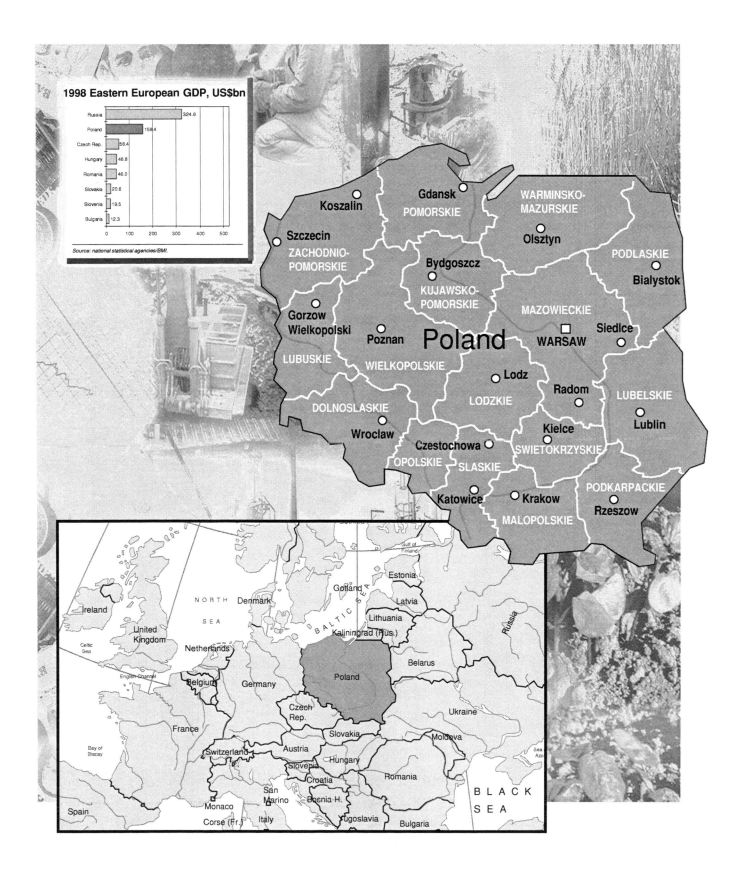

1998 Eastern European GDP, US$bn

Russia	324.6
Poland	158.4
Czech Rep.	56.4
Hungary	46.8
Romania	46.0
Slovakia	20.6
Slovenia	19.5
Bulgaria	12.3

Source: national statistical agencies/BMI.

POLAND: MACROECONOMIC DATA AND FORECASTS

	1993	1994	1995	1996	1997	1998	1999	2000f	2001f	2002f
Population (mn)	38.46	38.54	38.59	38.62	38.66	38.67	38.66	38.65	38.65	38.64
Nominal GDP (PLNbn)	155.78	210.41	301.35	382.55	469.37	551.11	617.00	705.48	782.38	853.50
Nominal GDP (US$bn)	86.00	92.60	124.27	141.89	143.13	158.57	155.53	163.31	178.08	190.57
Real GDP growth, % y-o-y	3.8	5.2	7.0	6.0	6.8	4.8	4.1	4.9	4.5	5.0
GDP per capita (US$)	2236	2402	3220	3674	3703	4101	4023	4225	4608	4932
Industrial production (% y-o-y, period average)	6.4	12.0	9.6	8.3	10.8	6.2	4.8	6.9	5.6	6.2
Unemployment rate (%, end period)	16.4	16.0	14.9	13.2	10.3	10.4	13.0	13.7	13.8	13.5
Wages in the enterprise sector (PLN/month, annual average)	-	-	-	957	1162	1349	1835	2398	2830	3269
Wages in the enterprise sector (% y-o-y, annual average)	-	-	-	-	21.4	16.1	36.1	30.7	18.0	15.5
State budget (PLNbn)	-4.34	-5.74	-7.45	-9.17	-5.90	-13.19	-12.6	-14.9	-14.2	-13.5
State budget (% of GDP)	-2.8	-2.7	-2.5	-2.4	-1.3	-2.4	-2.1	-2.1	-1.8	-1.6
Consumer prices (% y-o-y, end period)	37.5	29.5	22.0	18.8	13.2	8.5	9.8	7.5	5.8	4.5
Consumer prices (% y-o-y, period average)	36.8	33.3	26.8	20.2	15.9	11.7	7.3	9.4	6.4	5.5
Producer prices (% y-o-y, end period)	35.9	27.9	18.6	10.7	11.5	4.8	6.7	6.6	4.6	4.2
Producer prices (% y-o-y, period average)	32.2	30.2	25.5	13.2	12.2	7.2	5.3	6.7	5.4	4.5
Exchange rate (PLN/US$, end period)	2.134	2.437	2.468	2.876	3.518	3.504	4.148	4.350	4.430	4.520
Exchange rate (PLN/US$, period average)	1.812	2.272	2.425	2.696	3.279	3.480	3.970	4.320	4.390	4.480
Rediscount rate (% per annum, end period)	29.0	28.0	25.0	22.0	24.5	18.3	19.0	20.0	18.5	16.5
3-month t-bill rate (% per annum, end period)	33.70	27.00	24.18	18.81	23.78	13.54	15.50	16.53	15.50	13.90
Money supply, M2 (PLNbn, end period)	55.9	77.3	104.3	136.7	176.4	220.8	263.5	304.3	355.0	408.3
Money supply, M2 (% y-o-y, end period)	36.0	38.3	34.9	31.1	29.1	25.1	19.3	15.5	15.1	15.0
Merchandise exports (fob, US$bn)	13.59	16.95	22.88	24.42	27.23	30.25	26.36	29.50	33.10	36.10
Merchandise imports (fob, US$bn)	15.88	17.79	24.70	32.57	38.50	43.91	40.88	44.00	47.50	50.35
Merchandise trade balance (fob-fob, US$bn)	-2.29	-0.84	-1.83	-8.15	-11.27	-13.67	-14.53	-14.50	-14.40	-14.25
Current account balance (US$bn)*	-2.33	-0.94	-2.30	-1.35	-4.27	-6.81	-11.67	-11.90	-12.55	-11.90
Current account (% of GDP)	-2.7	-1.0	-1.9	-1.0	-3.0	-4.3	-7.5	-7.3	-7.0	-6.2
Foreign debt stock (US$bn, end period)	47.25	42.17	43.96	40.56	40.50	42.00	42.50	43.00	44.00	45.00
Foreign debt stock (% of GDP, end period)	54.9	45.5	35.4	28.6	28.3	26.5	27.3	26.3	24.7	23.8
Foreign debt stock (% of exports, end period)	295.8	215.8	162.3	138.5	125.1	114.1	129.7	119.1	108.4	-
Foreign exchange reserves (US$mn)	4,092	5,842	14,774	17,844	20,407	26,432	24,535	26,030	24,410	24,000
Import cover (months)	2.3	3.1	6.0	5.6	5.6	6.2	6.2	6.3	6.0	5.9

f = BMI forecast; * Up to 1995 old methodology. Source: IMF, Central Statistical Office (GUS), National Bank of Poland

1 Political Outlook

Domestic Political Outlook

AWS In Government, But Not In Power

Intra- and inter-party tensions had been part and parcel of Solidarity Electoral Action (AWS) and the Freedom Union's (UW) two-and-a-half-year-old coalition. Despite having made significant reforms in the key areas of local government, health, pensions and education, the leadership of the two parties had substantial disagreements over fiscal policy and the pace, method and scope of privatisation. Party management and coalition policy negotiations were complicated by the parties' various factions – most notably those of the AWS – each often holding conflicting opinions and with different vested interests to satisfy. But who would have thought that Prime Minister Jerzy Buzek's interference in the running of Gmina Centrum – one of Warsaw's 11 boroughs – in mid-May would prove the final straw for UW leader, Leszek Balcerowicz, and mark the beginning of the end of the AWS-UW coalition.

In brief, the post-communist Democratic Left Alliance (SLD) and the UW formed a coalition to run the central Warsaw council, and in early April elected a UW mayor for the city and an SLD-aligned councillor to lead the Centrum borough. The AWS subsequently refused to participate in council proceedings and the latter appointment was vetoed by the head of the province that covers Warsaw. In a move interpreted – depending on one's political persuasion – either as an effort to break a political gridlock, or an attempt to get AWS hands on the levers of local power, and amidst accusations of corrupt practices in public procurement, Buzek appointed an AWS-backed emergency administrator to run the borough. But the prime minister's decision was reportedly contrary to what he had told Balcerowicz in private, and left the then finance minister feeling, once again, that he could not trust Buzek.

Balcerowicz had grown increasingly frustrated at Buzek's inability to discipline AWS dissidents who seemed intent on undermining attempts at

For UW leader Leszek Balcerowicz, the majority coalition government behaved, de facto, as a minority government. But leaving the government is a high-risk strategy for the UW, and one the leader did not necessarily intend.

fiscal and structural reform, with electoral considerations weighing ever heavier ahead of October's presidential and autumn-2001's parliamentary elections. In May, for example, just before the UW left the coalition, 26 AWS backbenchers in the *Sejm* sided with the opposition SLD to introduce a zero rate of VAT on agricultural products, supplanting the government's proposed 3% rate. (The original measure has since received the Senate's support but may still be rejected when it returns to the *Sejm*).

However, the decision to actually quit the government has not been satisfactorily explained, suggesting that the members of the UW's executive board did not all have the same end game in mind when they proposed, on May 22, that their ministers resign.

Balcerowicz and his supporters within the party were perhaps engaging in high-level brinkmanship aimed at replacing the prime minister and changing key elements of policy ahead of next year's parliamentary elections. Hence, Balcerowicz suggesting that Buzek not accept the resignations of the UW's eight ministers, tendered on May 29, and instead complete a fortnight's negotiations aimed at salvaging the coalition – Balcerowicz hoping, additionally, that the prospect of a UW withdrawal, and near certain electoral defeat for the AWS, would serve as a restraining influence on Solidarity's rebels.

However, others in the UW may have viewed the events preceding May 22 as providing ample justification for exiting a politically sinking ship, and the 10 months or so before a general election could realistically be held as providing enough time to build a new platform from which to fight. It is this grouping that may seek to replace Balcerowicz before the next general election and, so as to avoid being consigned to the political wilderness, attempt to forge greater links with the SLD. But this is a high-risk strategy, for if the SLD wins a landslide victory, it will not need the UW's support.

In any event, Buzek was willing to stand down if agreement could be reached on his replacement. Names in the frame included Monetary Policy Council (RPP) member Boguslaw Grabowski, *Sejm* speaker Maciej Plazynski, and Marian Krzklewski – AWS chairman and leader of the Solidarity trade union. Grabowski was felt to lack the political clout to steer bills through parliament – a factor he himself accepted. A number of UW politicians instead favoured Plazynski, a more liberal AWS member, but Krzklewski, fearing the prospect of Plazynski consolidating power on the political right, would probably have blocked his candidacy. Presidential candidate Krzklewski is the AWS's chief power-broker who effectively plucked

United They Stand, Divided They Fall
Parliamentary seats by party, May 2000

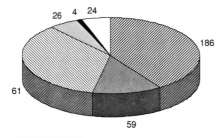

☒ AWS - Solidarity Electoral Action
▣ UW - Freedom Union
▨ SLD - Alliance of Democratic Left
☐ PSL - Polish Peasants' Party
■ ROP - Movement for the Reconstruction of Poland
☐ Other

Source: Sejm/BMI

Buzek from political obscurity in 1997 to make him prime minister – leading to Buzek being caricatured as his puppet.

Government Unlikely To Go The Distance

The AWS and UW failed to reach agreement on a candidate for the premiership or on a policy agenda and talks broke down on June 6 with the AWS subsequently forming a minority government with 186 of the lower house's 460 seats. With opinion poll ratings of only 14% in May, compared with the SLD's 36%, the AWS wants to stave off early elections in the hope that its popularity rises before the life of the current parliament expires next autumn. Survival will require the leadership to placate its own factions as well as offering some concessions to appease the opposition. Both the UW and the SLD have said they will support policies in line with EU accession, and the (presently embattled) Treasury Minister Emil Wasacz has confirmed that this year's privatisation programme will remain unchanged. But with a burgeoning current account deficit undermining investor confidence, market participants will watch the government's fiscal plans closely.

New Finance Minister Jaroslaw Bauc will no doubt attempt to keep a tight grip on the public purse, but his fiscal conservatism is unlikely to rub off on Solidarity's rebels, and Krzaklewski said recently that the forthcoming budget must cater for social and economic needs. This has been interpreted as being supportive of populist measures and inconsistent with Balcerowicz's aim of bringing the 2001 consolidated budget deficit down to 1.5% of GDP from this year's planned 2.7%, and to the enactment of complementary tax reforms. Bauc's task is made harder given that the mantle of deputy prime minister, typically bestowed on finance ministers, has passed instead to Economy Minister Janusz Steinhoff, who is seen as more likely to push for

Opposition parties now have the opportunity to thwart the government's agenda by tabling no confidence motions against individual ministers, and the UW has a pivotal position in determining the fate of ministers and deciding whether the government topples over the 2001 budget.

KEY CABINET MEMBERS*	
Name	**Position**
Jerzy Buzek	Prime Minister
Longin Komolowski	Deputy Prime Minister, Minister of Labour and Social Policy
Janusz Steinhoff	Deputy Prime Minister, Minister of Economy
Jaroslaw Bauc	Minister of Finance
Marek Biernacki	Minister of Internal Affairs
Artur Balazs	Minister of Agriculture
Tomasz Szyszko	Minister of Communications
Emil Wasacz	Minister of the Treasury
Wladyslaw Bartoszewski	Minister of Foreign Affairs
Franciszka Cegielska	Minister of Health
Andrzej Wiszniewski	Minister of Science

* Appointed on 20 June 2000. Source: Government Information Centre

pump-priming aimed at boosting growth and job creation. Bauc's proposals, published as we went to press, attempt to steer a path between these competing views. However, it is not clear, given the definitional changes that have been made to produce a new deficit measure, whether any real tightening is to be undertaken (*see Fiscal Policy*). The Council of Ministers will now consider, and perhaps amend, the proposals before presenting them to parliament. Central bank president, Hanna Gronkiewicz-Waltz has indicated that interest rates will remain high as long as the political and fiscal outlook is uncertain.

Budget Blow To Knock-Out Government?

For reasons explained below, it is difficult to remove the government under the new constitution, but votes of no confidence against individual ministers simply require the tabling of a motion by at least 69 deputies, and these may be used to greater effect than previously. First in the firing line is Treasury Minister Emil Wasacz, who managed to dodge the no confidence bullets in January. The Polish Peasants' Party (PSL) was threatening, at the end of June, to table such a motion, claiming that the minister had planned to sell the state insurance company **PZU** to **Eureko** without a public tender and below the company's real value. The *Sejm*'s privatisation and treasury committee was equally damning of Wasacz's proposal, putting pressure on the prime minister to sack him. Irrespective of the outcome, the incident serves to highlight how the swing in the balance of power towards the opposition parties could cause major disruptions to the government's legislative timetable.

Although the government may be rocked by votes of no confidence against individual ministers, the passage of the 2001 budget is the event most widely tipped to trigger the government's eventual collapse. Under the constitution, a draft budget must be presented to the *Sejm* by October 1, and if it is not approved within four months (that is, by end-January), parliament may be dissolved within two weeks, and a general election held within the next 45 days. Some Solidarity members favour a deficit for 2001 above 2% of GDP, which would be unlikely to meet with UW approval. Bauc has proposed 1.7% in terms of the old consolidated budget measure, and 1.6% under the new measure to be targeted – the economic deficit. Balcerowicz has been critical of the proposal (*see Fiscal Policy*), which suggests that the UW is likely to oppose the bill, reinforced by an election-hungry SLD. Balcerowicz indicated previously that he favours a spring election since it would negate the fulfilment of any pre-election spending splurges.

The government could fall before next year, but the main circumstances in

Parliamentary opposition to the 2001 draft budget is widely expected to lead to parliament's early dissolution, and a general election in spring 2001.

which this could happen appear unlikely to occur. For example, managing the competing demands of AWS factions could finally take its toll on Buzek, leading to his resignation. The president would have to appoint a new prime minister and cabinet within two weeks, the government-elect would then have to present a policy manifesto to the *Sejm*, and secure the support of an absolute majority of deputies in a vote of confidence. Alternatively, a constructive motion of no confidence – that is, one that proposes an alternative premier – could be tabled by at least 46 deputies. However, winning such a vote would require agreement between the SLD, UW and at least 11 other deputies, which is highly unlikely.

The constitutional difficulty of removing Buzek, in theory, affords him the opportunity to obviate Krzaklewski's grip on power. However, though Krzaklewski's control of the party is weakening he probably has more clout than the prime minister. The political scene is therefore set for a lame-duck government to carry on until early next year, with sluggish progress towards further structural reforms confirming that while the AWS may be in government, it is not governing.

As the year progresses, attention will turn to the implications for economic policy of a Democratic Left Alliance (SLD) government. Under its leader Leszek Miller the party has done much to shed its communist past, embracing parliamentary democracy and the market economy. Details of the SLD's policies are sketchy, but as a pro-EU party that held power competently between 1993-97, and whose finance minister, Marek Belka, was respected by the markets, **BMI** would expect it to pursue structural reform and macroeconomic stability. The SLD shows more "solidarity" than the AWS, which may make for more decisive government. But, given the composition of the SLD's rank-and-file, concerns remain as to it's appetite to restructure heavy industry, reform the agricultural sector, and pursue other structural reforms. Although opposition politics is a different game to that of being in power, the SLD's failure to support some tax reforms and opposition in some quarters of the party to foreign ownership of Polish companies may impart a degree of wariness to investors. However, precisely the same could be said of elements of the AWS.

The presidential race is little more than a sideshow. The president has few real powers and Aleksander Kwasniewski should be comfortably re-elected.

Kwasniewski A Shoo-In For President

The coalition's breakdown overshadowed President Aleksander Kwasniewski's announcement that he will seek re-election on October 8, the date first-round voting for the presidency is to take place. SLD-backed (but not controlled) Kwasniewski is a shoo-in to win. In an opinion survey published in early July, the president polled 62%. Marian Krzaklewski, the AWS-nominated candidate, mustered a mere 7%, and concerns remain as to whether he will attempt to persuade the government to spend on populist measures to boost his popularity. Before recent events, Krzaklewski would probably have attempted to woo UW supporters whose party has failed to provide an official candidate. Former finance and foreign minister Andrzej Olechowski, who may have filled that vacancy but for internal party wrangling, is instead likely to gather the UW vote, and July's poll placed him above Krzaklewski with 11%.

The main contenders to Kwasniewski can only hope to make up enough ground before October to prevent the president winning over 50% of the vote in the first round, thereby sending the contest into a second round. Kwasniewski has chosen to campaign on his track record as president. Krzaklewski is emphasising investment in job-creating sectors of the economy, and fighting crime. However, the simple fact is that the president has only limited powers under the constitution. Substantive policy proposals are likely to come to nothing without the prime minister's support. Although Kwasniewski would generally comply with the wishes of a government headed by Leszek Miller, he has shown himself to have an independent streak and has not shied away from criticising the SLD leader in the past.

Profile and Recent Developments

The Political System

Power Rests With Parliament

Poland has a bicameral parliamentary system based on parties. The legislature is the *Sejm*, the 460-seat lower house, while the upper house, the 100-seat Senate, acts as the revising chamber. Elections for both chambers are held every four years, with thresholds of 5% for parties and 8% for party alliances in order to be represented. The last *Sejm* and Senate elections were held in September 1997, and are due next in September 2001.

The president, as head of state, is elected separately for a five-year term, with the top two candidates from the first round of voting proceeding to a run-off if no-one secures an absolute majority. In the last presidential election in November 1995, Aleksander Kwasniewski, a former communist minister and founder of the Democratic Left Alliance (SLD), beat the incumbent Lech Walesa. Kwasniewski subsequently resigned from the SLD. The next presidential election is due in October 2000.

A new constitution approved in May 1997 enshrines representative democracy, defines the relationship between parliament, government and president, and provides for an independent judiciary. It guarantees essential elements of a free market economy (including private property rights and free trade) while stressing the need to respect social needs. It establishes the *Sejm* as the supreme political authority, while the president's powers are limited to appointing the prime minister, vetoing key ministerial and judicial appointments and legislation, and representing the country abroad. The *Sejm* requires a 60% majority to overturn a presidential veto and two-thirds to change the constitution. Although Solidarity and other Catholic groups opposed the constitution because it failed to outlaw abortion, its own version did not receive sufficient parliamentary support to be presented as an alternative in the referendum. Constitutional revision is not on the present government's agenda.

The Main Political Parties

Solidarity Electoral Action

Solidarity Electoral Action (AWS) was founded in 1996 by Marian Krzaklewski as an umbrella party to encompass disparate Polish anti-communist groups and present a cohesive opposition to the post-communist Democratic Left Alliance (SLD). It comprises around 40 political parties, unions, foundations, youth movements and other groups. Union members affiliated to NSZZ "Solidarity" form the largest core. Other important groups are the Centre Alliance (PC), the Christian National Union (ZChN), Conservative Peoples' Party (SKL), Polish Federation of Catholic Families, the neo-liberal Ruch (Movement) 100, the Lech Walesa Institute and numerous green, Christian-Democrat, farming, patriotic and youth groups. The AWS won the largest number of seats in the 1997 elections, although not enough to form a majority. Its continued cohesiveness requires that the prime minister satisfy the demands of the various factions for portfolios and policies, and so remains vulnerable to defections. The AWS registered itself as a formal Christian Democrat-style party, Solidarity Electoral Action Social Movement (RS AWS), shortly after the elections. Former president Lech Walesa has also registered a group with similar aims: the Christian Democratic Party of the Third Polish Republic, which technically supports the AWS. In September 1998, in a further move to separate the Solidarity trade union from the political party, union leaders were barred from holding posts in the political party. Prime Minister Jerzy Buzek was elected head of the RS AWS in January 1999, while Krzaklewski remains head of the Solidarity trade union and chairman of the AWS.

Democratic Left Alliance

The Democratic Left Alliance (SLD) was established in 1991 as an umbrella organisation for 15 post-communist political and union groupings, with Aleksander Kwasniewski as head of the parliamentary caucus. Since then it has grown to encompass more than 30 factions and bodies. Numerically the largest factions are Social Democracy (SdRP) and the leftist OPZZ union. SLD's roots in the former Communist Party make it the best organised party, especially at grass roots level, and the best disciplined, with little public in-fighting. In the 1993 elections it gained a commanding majority in the *Sejm,* largely by presenting a model of order against the chaos raging in the right and centre-right. In the absence of a non-communist left it has a large constituency of those social groups which lost out from economic reforms. At the same time, it presents itself as a Western-style social democratic party, thereby appealing to younger voters. In the 1993-97 government its approach to the budget was tougher than that of its centre-right predecessors and it made some progress on privatisation, but complacency and indifference towards the damage caused by catastrophic floods lost it the 1997 election. In opposition, the SLD's main task has been to provoke the AWS to self-destruct so that it can emerge unopposed as the largest cohesive party. In April 1999 the SLD registered as a political party, while the SdRP disbanded two months later.

Freedom Union

Freedom Union (UW) was formed from a merger of the Democratic Union and the Congress of Liberals, two of the original post-Solidarity parties. It contains many of the movement's leading intellectuals, including Leszek Balcerowicz, UW party leader and former finance minister, Tadeusz Mazowiecki, Poland's first prime minister after communism ended, former premier and justice minister Hanna Suchocka, former foreign minister Bronislaw Geremek and Jacek Kuron, founder of the KOR dissident movement in the 1970s. Its weakness as a party has been its inability to broaden its support beyond the intellectual centres of the larger cities, and it has also lost many ultra-Catholic voters who consider it too secular. As Poland's largest economically liberal party, its support is growing alongside that of the Polish middle-class, but it remains destined to be a third party for some time to come.

Polish Peasants' Party

The Polish Peasants' Party (PSL) predates World War II. It was co-opted by the communist administration as a puppet party for the peasant class, re-emerging after 1989 as a conservative, Catholic group for the large rural constituency. The party governed in coalition with the SLD over the 1993-97 period, but lost credibility through its inability to exert much influence on its larger partner or obtain any of the senior economic portfolios, and the tendency by some of its members to initiate no-confidence votes in the government. In the 1997 elections it dropped from second to fourth place with only 26 seats. Since the elections it has attempted to reinvent itself as a party for all Poles, not just a particular social class. Former agriculture minister Roman Jagielinski defected from the party in late-1997 and formed the Peasant Democratic Party (PLD). His party represents larger farming interests which believe they have a future in the EU.

Reconstruction of Poland

The Movement for the Reconstruction of Poland (ROP) is a conservative, nationalist and Catholic Solidarity offshoot formed by Jan Olszewski, a former human rights lawyer, adviser to Lech Walesa and briefly prime minister. Olszewski founded the movement essentially to initiate lustration, the exposure of former communist collaborators in public life. As prime minister, Olszewski's preoccupation with lustration threatened to ensnare a large part of the Solidarity movement, including the saintly Lech Walesa, who promptly dismissed him. The party remains a one-man band, refusing to be subsumed into the AWS and destined for smallness. Two of its six deputies defected to the AWS after the 1997 elections.

Recent Developments

A Semblance Of Party Unity

The primary challenge for the AWS since winning the 1997 elections has been to keep the various factions united. The prime minister could keep most of the camp happy through a judicious allocation of portfolios, but running policies that suited them all was never possible, and inevitably there have been defections. The earliest group to rebel was the Confederation for an Independent Poland-Patriotic Camp (KPN-OP) faction, which accused the AWS of subsuming its policies to those of the UW. In June 1998, two deputies from the group were expelled from the AWS for voting against the administrative reforms, and were joined by six other faction members who resigned in protest. In July 1998, a faction known as the "Radio Maryja Gang" because of its close association with the influential Catholic radio station, left after a series of disagreements with the AWS to form Our Circle (NK). The faction objected to the AWS's lack of commitment to pro-family policies and its subservience to the UW, and EU policy orientations. The final straw was the government's decision to allow the Gdansk Shipyard to be sold to the rival Gdynia Shipyard. Also in July 1998, Ryszard Czarnecki, head of the influential ZChN wing of the AWS, was dismissed as head of the European Integration Committee, after the EU docked Ecu24mn from Poland's Phare programme for wasting the money on spurious projects. However, with a shrinking majority, the government could not risk the ZChN decamping to one of the rightist camps, and retained Czarnecki as minister without portfolio. A shrinking majority also made the AWS more dependent on the UW.

Ambitious Reforms Are Set In Train

The AWS's 1997 electoral manifesto centred on a series of structural reforms, some of which were initiated by the previous government. The four main areas were local government, pensions, health care and education.

Decentralisation: So Far So Good

The local government reforms were aimed at devolving more powers (but not tax-raising powers) and financial resources to local governments, and rooting out bureaucratic corruption. Based on Poland's pre-war system, the reforms streamlined the 49 former *voivodships* (provinces) into 16, each with their own locally elected parliaments and governments responsible for environmental issues, health, education, transport and security. A new middle layer of 373 *powiats* (counties) handles secondary education, large hospitals, fire and police services. The third tier consists of 2,489 *gminas*, or local councils, responsible for community services and elementary schools. Local protests, although exploited to the full by the opposition, were confined to those areas with a strong identity such as Czestochowa, which did not want to merge into a larger province and eventually obtained its own *voivodship*. The only major concession that the government eventually made was to increase the number of provinces from 12 to 16, after President Kwasniewski vetoed the first parliamentary bill. While the administrative changes prompted a small defection of deputies from the AWS, who voted against the first bill, they have proved to be the least controversial of the four major reforms.

With local government structures now more directly answerable to the electorate and holding greater budgetary powers, subsequent elections should start differentiating between the competent, the incompetent and the corrupt, regardless of party affiliation. Concerns remain, however, about lack of effective checks on local governments' ability to borrow. The IMF, for example, has suggested that central government transfers to local government be reduced when the latter exceed prescribed borrowing limits.

Pension Reform Has Been Uncontroversial So Far...

Pension reform is designed to defuse a potential demographic time-bomb, constituted by an ageing population being financed by a shrinking active workforce. Furthermore, higher savings – public and private – are essential for current account sustainability in the medium- to long-term. Poles under 30 are now required to take out a personal pension with one of the 21 private funds, while those over that age may choose to remain within the pay-as-you-go system. Although the pension reforms have gone to great lengths to ensure that beneficiaries are not short-changed by funds underperforming or overcharging, the ultimate success of this programme depends on strong local capital market performance and continued economic growth. The only political clash so far concerned the miners, who objected to waiting until the age of 65 years to receive their benefits, as stipulated under the national pension law. Following some protest actions they obtained a special parliamentary bill entitling them to pensions after 25 years' service.

...Not So The Health Reforms

Health workers were the first to confront the government, which in October 1998 faced an anaesthetist's hunger strike over pay and contractual obligations. With the pay of medical professionals below the national average, and traditionally supplemented by patient "gratuities", health workers regularly resort to industrial action, and protested vociferously against the health reforms that came into force on January 1, 1999. Under the new set-up, 17 regional health funds are financed by compulsory contributions of 7.5% of taxable income, with employee's income tax bills being reduced by a corresponding amount. Contributors and their families are entitled to most health services free-of-charge, and can choose their clinics, hospitals and doctors. Unfortunately, non-contributors such as pensioners have lost out and there is a widespread public perception that the reforms are not working. Those who have not opted for private primary care have been frustrated by the long waiting times for treatment. Though health care functions have been formally split between providers (general practitioner clinics and hospitals) and purchasers (the health funds), many of the details covering payment and contractual arrangements necessary for the market system to work effectively are missing, and require additional legislation.

Education Reforms Have Been Badly Handled

Although there is general agreement that Poland's education system – with its overemphasis on increasingly obsolete vocational skills and its failure to extend its much-vaunted national literacy and numeracy skills beyond the larger towns – is in serious need of overhaul, the government's plans have succeeded in alienating teachers, parents and local communities without much prompting from the opposition. The most disruptive element of this reform, which extends compulsory education from age 14 to 16, is that each school is now designated according to a specific age-band – such as primary, secondary, etc – and cannot cater for children outside that band. Parents are thus being forced to find new schools earlier than they expected. In less densely populated rural areas, where schools have traditionally catered for wider age brackets, villages will have to bus pupils out to the appropriate establishment, and this has caused uproar.

Farmers: A Potent Political Force

Farming protests have proved the biggest headache for the government. The first wave of demonstrations to confront the AWS-UW government started in June 1998 and was directed at cheap grain imports, primarily from Hungary and Slovakia. The protest organisers included the Solidarity Private Farmers' Union and the left-wing National Union of Farmers' Circles and Organisations, but the violence was largely due to *Samoobrona* (Self-Defence), a far-right organisation which believes that imports are undermining Polish self-sufficiency in food. Its leader, and candidate in the 2000 presidential elections, Andrzej Lepper, has a long history of confrontation with Polish governments. The government removed proposals to levy value-added tax and a tax on farm incomes planned for 1999, and the demonstrations petered out in September after the government imposed import duties on grain and raised its own purchases.

In December 1998, action restarted as cheap meat imports flooded into Poland from countries diverting their exports after Russia's financial collapse in August closed off one of the world's largest markets. Spearheaded once again by Self-Defence, the protesters repeated their demands for a ban on imports as well as Leszek Balcerowicz's resignation. The meat demonstrations were more extensive than the earlier grain protests, and more violent.

The EU had earlier halved subsidies but refused to cut them altogether. At the same time, Poland could not block the imports because of WTO obligations. The government was instead forced to amend the budget to allow the State Agency for the Agricultural Market, the state procurement agency, to make intervention purchases. Although the final roadblocks disappeared in February and the government thought the issue was settled, protests resumed in March, including a march on the capital. The major agricultural lobbies, including the PSL, demanded government subsidies and a ban on imports. The government, consequently, has seen its credibility dented. On the one hand it was forced to cave in to violent protests. On the other hand, the farmers attracted massive public support – around 80-90% depending on the opinion poll, and far more than the miners, teachers, railway workers and doctors – as a result of the strong rural roots of even the most urbanised Poles.

Coalition Members Agreed To Differ

Until recently, the AWS and the UW managed to keep their nerves intact, if not their policies. But fiscal policy, and the privatisation process in particular, exposed the ideological differences separating the two coalition members. During deliberations over the 1999 budget, AWS factions pressed for pro-family measures, including tax exemptions for larger families, while Leszek Balcerowicz pushed for a flat tax rate. Eventually, the larger party scored a victory when Balcerowicz's plans were postponed while some family tax concessions went through.

Similarly, disagreement, at the end of 1999, between Leszek Balcerowicz and Solidarity's left-wing over the then finance minister's ambitious tax and deficit reduction plans, brought the minister to the brink of resignation. In the event, it was a veto from President Kwasniewski that sunk key elements of Balcerowicz's plans, including reductions in personal income tax rates. The privatisation programme also caused heated debated. In general terms, the UW's intention to sell to the highest foreign bidder was at odds with AWS election pledges to use privatisation for "popular enfranchisement" via domestically-held investment funds. The commercialisation and privatisation bill that entered parliament this year represents something of a compromise between the AWS and UW in this respect. Nevertheless, some AWS factions argue in favour of safeguarding jobs and keeping some of the country's strategic "crown jewels" in Polish hands.

Another area of contention has concerned the power of the unions, with the UW arguing that trade unions play too great a role in government policy. In November 1998, the UW's Eugeniusz Morawski resigned as transport minister in frustration after the government yielded to union demands to amend his plans for restructuring **PKP**, the state railway company. Buzek countered that the government would be incapable of carrying out any major industrial restructuring without securing the workforce's cooperation.

The Prime Minister Fights For Peace

In early-1999, the cabinet faced open warfare, with Balcerowicz publicly criticising the government for slow economic reforms and privatisation, while a large section of the public held the finance minister responsible for the increasing chaos. The prime minister diffused the crisis with a series of compromises, including postponement of the enfranchisement programme. Meanwhile, the government's approval rating sunk from 43% in November 1998 to 29% by the following February. By spring, Buzek was facing calls to replace those ministers responsible for the controversial reforms, as well as pressure from his own party to rebalance the cabinet with more AWS members, and stave off accusations of the tail wagging the dog. The agriculture minister, Jacek Janiszewski, was forced to resign in March following disclosures of nepotism in an earlier job as head of the Szczecin branch of the Agricultural Property Agency. A government reshuffle later that month also replaced the telecommunications and health ministers, as well as the culture minister – the only UW post sacrificed to the AWS. Since the UW retained the finance, foreign affairs, defence, justice and transport portfolios, Buzek went out of his way to keep the junior party on board. A further cabinet reshuffle failed to materialise in late-1999/early-2000, despite rumours that one was on the cards.

Relations With The President Have Been Civilised

President Aleksander Kwasniewski was initially lukewarm about the AWS-UW government's programme, but relations between the two branches of power have generally been smooth. In foreign policy there was an early agreement between the president and foreign minister to coordinate strategy on Nato and EU entry. The architect of the SLD's return to government in 1993-97, Kwasniewski has successfully distanced himself from all parties since becoming president in 1995. Although the AWS-UW government lacked a sufficient majority to overrule presidential vetoes, he has used his powers sparingly. He did veto bills banning compulsory sex education, cutting army and public service pension increases, and lowering personal income tax. But Kwasniewski was wrong-footed over his attempt to veto a bill allowing access to police files compiled during the communist era, when the AWS mustered the support of the PSL, ROP and all non-SLD deputies to provide the necessary majority to override him. At the same time he signed the Concordat with the Vatican against the wishes of the SLD – the only party to vote against it – and agreed with the government and against the SLD to postpone local elections for the lowest tier of local government until October 1998.

Foreign Policy

Nato Membership Is Secured...

Poland was formally invited to join Nato, along with the Czech Republic and Hungary, in 1997, and officially became a member on March 12, 1999, in a low-key ceremony designed not to appear triumphalist to Moscow. From the Polish perspective, membership of the alliance secures its eastern borders. Unlike the Czech Republic and Hungary, Polish defence expenditure has increased in real terms, accounting for 2.4% of GDP in 1998 (the Nato minimum is 2.0%, the average is 2.8%). The government provided unqualified support for Nato's bombardment of Yugoslavia in spring 1999, dispatched units to Albania, and offered ground troops. Parliamentary opposition to Nato's action was confined to the political fringes. Membership of the alliance will strain the budget if Poland wants to bring its armed forces up to scratch and play an active role in the alliance.

...But The EU Will Take Longer

Although EU membership remains the principal foreign policy goal, the possible entry date is getting pushed further into the future. The government's target date of 2003 for joining the Union will almost certainly be missed, and entry is unlikely until at least 2005-06, partly because of EU internal wrangling over institutional and budgetary reforms, and partly because Poland will have to engage in difficult negotiations over environmental protection and agriculture. Indeed, with a younger generation of leaders taking over in Western Europe, the EU's own enthusiasm for eastward expansion is waning as economic considerations take precedence over issues such as European stability, which underpinned the EU's original conception. Austria and Germany, facing high unemployment at home, are now voicing concerns about an influx of Polish workers. Gerhard Schröder's election as Germany's chancellor received a muted welcome in Poland, as hc has yet to demonstrate the same commitment to eastward expansion as his predecessor, Helmut Kohl. Poland's bilateral relations with Germany have been complicated by a Bundestag resolution in

May 1998, which demanded resettlement rights for Germans expelled from Poland (and the Czech Republic) after the World War II, and by Germany's refusal to increase compensation to Poles incarcerated in concentration and prison camps, or forced to work as slave labourers. Relations with France have a long historical pedigree and former Polish foreign minister Bronislaw Geremek, who once taught at the Sorbonne, was subsequently awarded the French Legion of Honour. Locally, interest in the Union is slipping. Public support for EU membership has fallen steadily from opinion poll highs of 80% in 1996, to just over 50% in early-2000. However, entry is still backed by the main political parties and outright public opposition to entry rarely breaches the 25% mark.

Poland's progress in adopting the *acquis communautaire* – the EU's bible – has been mixed. As of May 2000, of the 31 chapters requiring negotiation, nine have been provisionally closed, 14 remain open and negotiations over the others are pending. Agriculture remains the key issue and in meetings with EU officials in April, the prime minister reiterated the government's position that the Commission should extend compensation under the Common Agricultural Policy (CAP) to farmers upon accession. Buzek also argued that EU regulations should be amended to permit the saving of funds earmarked for the enlargement process, but not used from 2002 onwards. The ring-fenced funds would provide part of the funding solution for new members. The EU has previously ruled out making direct income support payments to aspirant countries' farmers, but an alternative mechanism has yet to be devised, and no timetable exits for when a decision will be made. The question of payments is unlikely to be addressed until late-2000 at the earliest. Farm Commissioner Franz Fischler is said to be considering the phasing-in of direct aid payments, conditional on wide-ranging sectoral reform and acceptance of CAP's system of supply controls, such as land "set aside". Proposals along these lines are likely to meet with little resistance from Poland's 250,000 or so farms, out of an estimated 2mn, that produce significant quantities and would find their incomes boosted if such a policy were introduced. But the majority of farms are subsistence operations and would thus be ineligible for EU support. With their livelihoods under threat, those farmers will remain a potent political force. Farmers' protestations caused the government to raise tariffs last year, thereby incurring the wrath of EU officials (and the Monetary Policy Council). Such actions are in direct conflict with the Commission's proposed "double zero" programme, which envisages the phased reduction of tariffs and subsidies for applicant states, starting (fortunately for Poland) with produce they do not supply.

Eastern Relations Have Been Redefined

Accession to Nato has major implications for Poland's relations with its eastern neighbours: Russia, Lithuania, Ukraine and Belarus. Poland's border with Russia is along Kaliningrad, a region separated from the rest of the federation by Lithuania and Belarus. Russia remains an important trading partner as well as an unstable large neighbour. Moscow growled about Nato's eastward expansion, but in reality presented few obstacles since the alliance confined itself to three countries outside the former Soviet Union. However, the Baltic states are also keen to join, and Poland is championing Lithuania's membership. For its own strategic reasons, Poland does not wish to remain Nato's eastern frontline state.

Ukraine is strategically important because it is integral to any potential restoration of the Soviet Union. Since independence in 1991, it has remained neutral and its president, Leonid Kuchma, has refrained from any reunification discussions, despite the nostalgia that the former Soviet Union still holds for a sizeable portion of the population in the eastern half of the country. Poland has invested a lot of diplomatic effort in Ukraine, with Kuchma and Kwasniewski holding regular meetings.

Poland's most difficult relations are with Belarus, whose eccentric president, Alyaksandar Lukashenko, has rewritten the constitution to his own liking, extended his term of office, replaced the previous parliament with one of his own choosing and reinstated a Soviet-style command economy. Lukashenko is also in the throes of forging a union with Russia, supposedly on the basis of a confederation of two equal states. Should this happen Poland's border with Russia lengthens dramatically. A number of opponents shelter in Poland, which is the base for opposition broadcasts to Belarus, while Minsk regularly accuses Warsaw of spying and hatching coups. Poland's membership of Nato raised the diplomatic temperature as it enabled Belarus to start questioning the logic of adopting neutrality and nuclear-free status in its constitution, and backtracking on its commitment to reduce its armed forces under the Conventional Forces in Europe Treaty. With a population of between 300,000 and 400,000 Poles in Belarus, Poland has to tread carefully. It did not take part in a visa ban on Belarusian officials in 1998 after Lukashenko evicted the foreign diplomatic corp in Minsk from their compound and took over the property for his own use.

In practical terms, the most serious effects on eastern relations have come from EU-led initiatives rather than Nato membership. In early-1998, Poland imposed visa restrictions on Russians and Belarusians as part of an agreement to tighten border restrictions against smuggling and illegal immigration from the east. It paid a heavy economic price as small traders, whose economic existence depended on mutual if unregistered trade, saw business collapse. A visa-free regime with Ukraine was maintained because it, unlike Russia and Belarus, was willing to accept illegal immigrants turned back from Poland, although the EU is unhappy about this arrangement and is exerting pressure on Warsaw to include Ukraine in the arrangement.

2 Economic Outlook

Economic Activity

Signs Of Slowdown, But Net Export Growth Returns

Contrary to many analysts' early-year expectations, real GDP growth slowed marginally in Q1 00 to 6.0% y-o-y from 6.2% in Q4 99. However, the slowdown in domestic activity may be more marked than suggested by the headline figure as Q1 growth benefited from a particularly favourable base of comparison: real GDP grew a sluggish 1.6% y-o-y in Q1 99. Significantly, GDP growth in Q1 00 outpaced domestic demand (as it did in Q4 99) suggesting that net export growth has indeed resumed.

After strong growth at the beginning of the year, industrial output turned soft in March and April but rebounded in May, growing by a better-than-expected 12.3% y-o-y. Manufacturing output leapt 10% on the previous month and 13.3% y-o-y, though the data have yet to be adjusted for the extra working days in May. Considering that domestic demand slowed to 5.1% y-o-y in Q1 00 from 5.6% y-o-y in Q4 99, and with few signs that it has taken an upward path in Q2 00, this would seem to imply rising external demand for Polish exports. An alternative explanation might be that firms have involuntarily built up stocks as a result of weaker-than-expected domestic and external demand and, as a consequence, an inventory correction may lead to falling output over the course of H2 00. But on balance, **BMI** does not believe this to be the correct story for the economy.

There is mounting evidence that the domestic economy is slowing under the weight of monetary and fiscal tightening. There are also signs that net exports have embarked on the comeback trail.

To Slow In H2 00
Quarterly GDP growth, % y-o-y

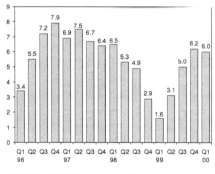

Source: GUS

		GDP, OUTPUT & POPULATION				
	1997	**1998**	**1999**	**2000f**	**2001f**	**2002f**
Population (mn)	38.66	38.46	38.66	38.59	38.65	38.64
Nominal GDP (US$bn)	143.13	158.57	155.53	163.31	178.08	190.57
GDP per capita (US$)	3703	4101	4023	4225	4608	4932
Real GDP growth, % y-o-y	6.8	4.8	4.1	4.9	4.5	5.0
Industrial output (% y-o-y, period average)	10.8	6.2	4.8	6.9	5.6	6.2
Unemployment rate (%, end period)	10.3	10.4	13.0	13.7	13.8	13.5
f = BMI forecast; Source:GUS/BMI						

That domestic demand is starting to moderate under the weight of previous bouts of monetary and fiscal tightening is evidenced by less rapid growth in retail sales and car sales falling 11% y-o-y in the January-May period. The growth in private consumption decelerated to 4.6% y-o-y in Q1 00 from 5.6% y-o-y in Q4 99 and will continue to be checked by high real interest rates, slower real wage growth and stubbornly high unemployment. Although unemployment dipped slightly to 13.5% in May, having fallen in April for the first time in almost a year, this was largely due to seasonal factors. The wealth effect is unlikely to be strong in Poland, but recent NASQAQ-related volatility in the local stock market may still have served to undermine consumer confidence. In addition, uncertainty over future economic policy and the prospects for EU entry in the medium term may cause consumers to adjust downwards their expectations of future income, thereby dampening current consumption.

With the National Bank of Poland (NBP) having abandoned the policy of managing the exchange rate, and free to pursue direct inflation targeting, the real economy risks being squeezed in a monetary straitjacket made that much tighter by the growing uncertainty about the future path of fiscal policy. Not only did the rate of private consumption growth slow in Q1 00, so too did investment: gross fixed capital formation dropped to 5.5% y-o-y, a growth rate below that of any quarter in 1999.

BMI's prognosis remains for a modest pick-up in exports to contribute to real GDP growth of 4.9% in 2000. The real economy has yet to yield fully under the NBP's restrictive monetary stance, which is now likely to remain tight for longer than needed – hence our below-consensus forecasts for 2000 and 2001.

Monetary Policy

Rate Of Disinflation To Be Slow...

Unconstrained by exchange rate considerations, in theory at least, now that the zloty is freely floating, the central bank's Monetary Policy Council (RPP) can gear monetary policy more effectively towards the pursuit of end-year inflation targets – 2000's being 5.4-6.8% y-o-y, falling in stages to 4% by 2003.

Cumulative monetary tightening of 450bps since September 1999 finally appears to be affecting the domestic economy with negative real money

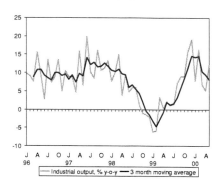

Producing To Export?
Industrial output growth

Source: GUS.

Credit growth is proving resilient despite the squeeze. But inflation expectations are coming down, slowly.

supply growth – partly due to tighter fiscal policy – and rising real interest rates signalling the beginning of a domestically-generated disinflationary impulse that should impact more in H2 00. GDP data for Q1 00 shows both private consumption and investment slowing from Q4 99 (*see Economic Activity*), and there are indications that the pace of consumer demand is waning with retail sales slowing and new car sales falling.

The extent of this demand dampening is still uncertain. Household borrowing appears to be growing more slowly — but it is still growing. Furthermore, high interest rates have not yet had the desired effect on personal savings: the ratio of personal borrowing to deposits has been around the 28% mark all year and was 29% on June 10 – some 10% higher than the equivalent ratio for Hungary. However, having disappointed in April, average real wage growth fell back in May to 1.2% y-o-y (12% y-o-y in nominal terms but this figure includes social security contributions). **BMI** believes it is too early to say that inflation expectations have been quashed, although there is little evidence to suggest that a wage-price spiral may be triggered in the coming months.

...For Supply More Than Monetary Reasons...

Consumer price inflation in March, at 10.3% y-o-y, was lower than that recorded in the previous month for the first time since July 1999. The movement continued in April with inflation dipping below 10% but was arrested in May when the annual rate rose to 10%. With domestic demand exerting less upward pressure on prices, inflation's stickiness may be attributed to unfavourable base effects over the early part of the year and largely exogenous factors such as the persistence of high global oil prices. The base of comparison has now moved into more favourable territory and should assist the headline rate's decline over H2 00. However it is these supply shocks that are likely to ensure the disinflationary path is anything but a steep descent. Inflation's upward tick in May was attributed to higher energy prices with petrol prices up 4.6% m-o-m as local fuel processors and distributors passed on the costs of earlier oil price hikes, and electricity prices up 4.7% m-o-m.

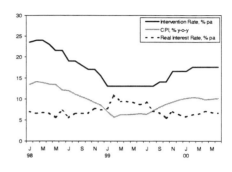

Real Interest Rate To Rise In Q4
Real interest rate and inflation

Source: National Bank of Poland, GUS and BMI

The short- to medium-term outlook for inflation is more favourable than the near-term, which is dominated by adverse supply shocks feeding into higher oil and food prices.

CONSUMER & PRODUCER PRICES						
	1997	1998	1999	2000f	2001f	2002f
Consumer prices (% y-o-y, end period)	13.2	8.5	9.8	7.5	5.8	4.5
Consumer prices (% y-o-y, period average)	15.9	11.7	7.3	9.4	6.4	5.5
Producer prices (% y-o-y, end period)	11.5	4.8	6.7	6.6	4.6	4.2
Producer prices (% y-o-y, period average)	12.2	7.2	5.3	6.7	5.4	4.5
f = BMI forecast; Source:GUS/BMI						

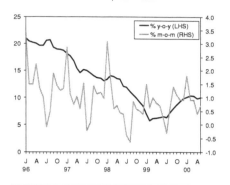

Supply Shocks Offset Monetary Squeeze
Consumer price inflation

Source: GUS

Despite signs of a slowdown in domestic activity, the end-year inflation target will be overshot, partly due to exogenous factors outside of the RPP's control. Interest rates are likely to remain unchanged this year.

Fiscal tightening has been set in train for 2000, and with higher than anticipated inflation boosting the revenue side of the balance, the government should achieve its targets. But the proceeds from surprise inflation may be used for electioneering purposes.

Energy prices will continue to have an uncertain effect on the CPI over the remainder of the year. The consensus view is that oil prices will fall or at least stabilise, putting downward pressure on the index. However, upside risks to the oil price still remain. The RPP notes that the liberalisation of domestic electricity prices will also have an uncertain effect. Food prices also present an upside risk to inflation in Q3 00 with the rise in the wholesale price of grain due to the recent drought expected to filter through to final prices. The Finance Ministry maintains that the stocks of the Polish Farm Market Agency (ARR) and the recent relaxation of import controls are sufficient to keep a lid on prices. However, the ARR has now been granted a duty-free grain import quota sparking fears that its intervention stocks have been depleted with clear implications for prices in local markets.

Finally, the zloty's recent slide against the dollar on the back of euro weakness and a souring of investor sentiment (*see Exchange Rate Policy*) runs the risk of imported inflation offsetting the disinflationary benefits of monetary tightening. NBP President Hanna Gronkiewicz-Waltz has indicated that the RPP will maintain its "policy tightening bias" while the political and fiscal outlook is uncertain, and has implied that interest rates may be raised again should fiscal policy be loosened or uncertainty spark a marked weakening of the currency.

...Suggesting Interest Rates Will Not Be Raised

The balance of inflation risks has shifted to the upside and **BMI** has revised upwards its inflation forecasts for 2000 with the upper bound of the NBP's inflation target likely to be overshot by 0.7%. The Finance Ministry reportedly expects the headline rate of inflation to remain around 10% y-o-y until September. The probability of a cut in interest rates before end-2000 has now diminished, although we do not rule out the chance of a 50bps cut in Q4 00. However, while this may be warranted by a slowdown in domestic activity and improving external balances, the RPP may maintain a cautious stance given the uncertain economic implications of the political situation.

Fiscal Policy

Tighter In 2000, Hard To Cut Further In 2001

Current account dynamics continue to be driven by an imbalance between gross domestic investment and savings as a proportion of GDP. With a low propensity to save on the part of households due to consumption smoothing and developments in the banking system, the onus is on lower public dissaving to contain the gap, a view shared by the RPP, Finance Minister Jaroslaw Bauc and his predecessor Leszek Balcerowicz.

The government has targeted a fair degree of fiscal tightening for 2000. The consolidated deficit is planned to contract to 2.7% of expected GDP from 3.4% last year, while the state (central government) deficit is due to fall to 2.2% of GDP from 2.4% in 1999. The decline in the state deficit is modest as more central government expenditure – amounting to around 1% of GDP – is being used to subsidise the pension system. This amount relates to the cost of people switching from state to private pensions and is arguably not really part of the fiscal thrust. Adjusting for this measure means that the fiscal stance is in fact tighter than that implied by the headline figure. Strictly speaking, a further adjustment should be made in the other direction to allow for the off-budget compensation to individuals for earlier high inflation.

According to the AWS-UW government's long-term fiscal strategy produced last year, the consolidated deficit is due to fall to 1.9% of GDP in 2001 and former finance minister Balcerowicz was reported recently to favour a deficit nearer the 1.5% mark. But fiscal restraint is now widely expected to be rejected by Jerzy Buzek's minority government as the electoral cycle approaches its peak (*see Political Outlook*). Some Solidarity members favour a deficit above 2% of GDP (the psychologically important figure for the markets) for 2001, which is unlikely to meet with UW approval, but which would still be below this year's target.

The AWS is well aware of the favoured scenario that parliament will be dissolved if a budget unpalatable to the UW is proposed (and of the disciplining force of the market should it engage in profligacy). Finance Minister Bauc and some RPP members have pointed out that getting spending down to even lower levels in 2001 will be constrained by additional mandatory expenditure on public sector wages and state pensions to compensate for an inflation outturn which is expected to be above that assumed in the 2000 budget. In addition, unemployment and rising debt service payments will keep upward pressure on the expenditure side of the balance in 2001.

The state deficit grew to 65% of the plan for 2000 in the January-May period, but should be tempered in H2 00 when revenues are traditionally higher, boosted this year by higher than anticipated inflation. But the risk has also risen that these additional revenues will work their way into a pre-election spending splurge.

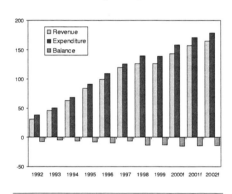

State Deficit Under Control
State budget deficit, PLNbn

f = BMI forecast. Source: GUS/BMI

Finance Minister Bauc's 2001 budget proposals fall somewhere between the competing demands of UW leader Balcerowicz and those of his Solidarity colleagues. Built on dubious assumptions, the plans involve little, if any, additional tightening on 2000. However, substantial tightening may not in fact be needed as the economy slows and exports improve. But the chances of an early election have risen.

Proposals Flawed, But Not Profligate

As we went to press, the Finance Ministry unveiled its budget proposals for 2001. The plans may be revised by the Council of Ministers before being presented to parliament. Under the proposals, the state deficit is to be reduced to 1.4% of GDP in 2001, while the consolidated deficit is to fall to 1.7% of GDP. However, not is all as it seems, for the ministry has decided to change the measure of the fiscal deficit it targets. The new measure – the economic deficit – is to be adopted from 2001, and incorporates the adjustments referred to above. Transfers to pension funds will therefore be subtracted from the expenditure side of the consolidated balance (which also includes spending on central and local government), but compensation payments added. The economic deficit is expected to be 2% of GDP in 2000, and 1.6% in 2001 – roughly in the region already priced in by the markets.

However, a number of initial concerns have been raised. The head of the Finance Ministry's financial policy department, Witold Skrok, resigned his position following the plan's release, arguing that the economic deficit for 2000 had been artificially inflated to allow for a favourable comparison with next year's plans. It is interesting to note in this respect that comparable adjustments to the 2000 budget plans made by the IMF in its staff report produced earlier this year, yielded an economic deficit of 1.7% of GDP. This would seem to suggest that, if 2% of GDP has been pencilled in for 2000, the government intends to increase spending in H2 00. Bauc has also been criticised for including in next year's budget revenue forecasts expected proceeds (totalling PLN7bn in 2001) from the sale of third generation UMTS mobile phone licences , rather than treating them as a below the line item.

Crucially, Balcerowicz described the proposals as an "adept pre-election budget", and implied that items on both sides of the balance had been exaggerated. The former finance minister is reported as saying that a clause

MINISTRY OF FINANCE 2001 BUDGET PROPOSALS & MACROECONOMIC ASSUMPTIONS			
	2000	**2001**	**2002**
State Budget (% of GDP)	-2.2	-1.4	-
Consolidated Budget (% of GDP)	-2.7	-1.7	-
Economic Deficit (% of GDP)	-2.0	-1.6	-
Privatisation Revenues (% of GDP)	3.7	2.3	-
Real GDP Growth (% y-o-y)	5.3	5.7	5.6
Consumer Prices (% y-o-y, period average)	9.1	6.1	4.9
Current Account Balance (% of GDP)	-7.7	-7.1	-6.5
Exchange Rate (PLN/US$, period average)	4.32	4.42	4.46
Exchange Rate (PLN/EUR, period average)	4.12	4.37	4.74
Source: Ministry of Finance			

should be added to the budget bill to ensure that any shortfalls in spending against that planned be earmarked for specific purposes so as to safeguard against funds being used for pre-election hand-outs. As the UW and SLD appear unlikely to support the proposals, the probability of the failed budget/ spring elections scenario being played out has risen.

The lack of clarity (so far) in the new plans adds to existing problems in keeping tabs on fiscal policy. Although the finance minister should be able to keep the state finances in order, he has less control over expenditures by local government and the health sector as well as other numerous extra-budgetary funds – giving some scope for politically-motivated spending. In addition, Solidarity may attempt to "buy" votes, not necessarily by boosting government expenditure, but through quasi-fiscal channels – for example, by softening the budget constraints faced by state-owned firms.

The debate about the extent to which policy has been tightened, if at all, will rumble on for some time. However, if the government falls, the plans will guide policy only until a new government takes office towards the middle of 2001. Although fiscal policy needs to be kept in check, substantial tightening was, arguably, never politically feasible in 2001, and **BMI** expects the arguments for such tightening to be defused by end-2000 as slowing domestic demand and export growth arrest the rise in the current account-GDP ratio.

Exchange Rate Policy

Capital Controls To Go Now Zloty Is Floating

The timing of the decision to float the zloty from April 12 took most market participants by surprise and flew in the face of IMF advice that exiting the crawling peg regime should be delayed until the current account deficit had fallen from its present high level. In fact, NBP President Hanna Gronkiewicz-Waltz voted against the move.

Floating the currency is seen as a way of improving the effectiveness of monetary policy and deterring short-term speculative inflows.

The decision followed a period of rapid zloty appreciation triggered by favourable yield differentials, with domestic interest rates in April some 1,400bps over euro-zone rates and 600bps over Hungary's. This proved something of a policy headache for the authorities with the currency's strength having the potential to hurt exporters, and the economy vulnerable to a sudden reversal of short-term speculative inflows. As well as permitting

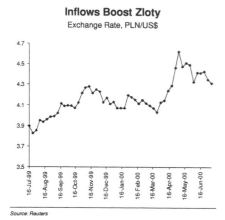

Inflows Boost Zloty
Exchange Rate, PLN/US$

Source: Reuters

Prior to the coalition's collapse, changing sentiment towards Poland was arguably driven not by a trend deterioration in economic fundamentals, but by inconclusive evidence that they were actually improving. This was compounded, crucially, by rising risk aversion in light of a changing global macroeconomic backdrop.

the RPP – unconstrained by exchange rate considerations – to embed direct inflation targeting as the economy's nominal anchor, freeing the zloty was seen as a way of increasing currency risk, thereby tempering undesirable inflows.

Furthermore, the remaining controls on short-term capital flows have been kept to limit the economy's vulnerability to currency and capital flow volatility. At present, non-residents are required to obtain a permit from the NBP to trade derivatives or purchase zloty deposits of less than three months duration, and Polish companies must have authorisation before opening currency accounts abroad. The government is committed to fully liberalising the capital account before the end of 2002, and finance minister Jaroslaw Bauc hinted recently that the controls might be lifted at the beginning of 2001.

Zloty To Track The Euro

The liberated zloty had a shaky start, diving to a record low of PLN4.74/US$ in early May as investor sentiment turned sour in response to poor current account figures for March. Although the authorities hoped to deter some "hot money" flows, the extent of the zloty's depreciation – 11.5% between 12 April and 8 May – was somewhat surprising, for although March's current account deficit, at US$1.4bn (8.3% of estimated GDP), was above market expectations, the data did not convey any new information about the fundamental state of the economy. In fact, the deviation between expectations and outturn was attributable almost entirely to a one-off foreign debt payment of US$340mn.

The fall suggests investors are making more realistic assessments of the balance between risk (the external deficit and potential political instability) and reward (higher yields). In this respect, the zloty's free fall and subsequent partial recovery to PLN4.53/US$ by May 19 may be interpreted as a correction relative to the earlier steep appreciation.

The currency's slide may also be attributed to the euro's weakness. Under the

EXCHANGE & INTEREST RATES						
	1997	1998	1999	2000f	2001f	2002f
Exchange rate (PLN/US$, end period)	3.518	3.504	4.148	4.350	4.430	4.520
Exchange rate (PLN/US$, period average)	3.279	3.480	3.970	4.320	4.390	4.480
Rediscount rate (% per annum, end period)	24.5	18.3	19.0	20.0	18.50	16.50
3-month t-bill rate (% per annum, end period)	23.78	13.54	15.50	16.53	15.50	13.90

f = BMI forecast; Source:NBP/BMI

crawling peg regime, the zloty's central parity was linked to a 55% euro, 45% dollar basket. This meant that the dollar's strength against the euro boosted the zloty for purely technical reasons. However, now that the zloty is floating, its fortunes will be tied more closely to those of the euro, since Poland's main trading partners are in the euro-zone. Indeed, around 55% of trade is denominated in euros and 35% in dollars. It is therefore easy to understand why the authorities were so concerned about the implications for price competitiveness of the zloty's sustained strengthening against the euro over the first four months of 2000.

FDI Inflows To Ensure End-Year Appreciation

In H2 00 the currency's evolution will again depend largely on the perceived balance between risk and reward with the former dominated by the economic implications of recent political developments. The markets reacted calmly to the AWS-UW coalition's collapse, suggesting that a large degree of political risk has already been priced in for this year. In fact the zloty has appreciated in nominal terms since early May though its ascent has been volatile. Moreover, the markets were already geared to a general election next year – one that the AWS-UW was not expected to win – so recent events merely bring forward that eventuality. The variable in the hands of the politicians that could engender a wave of selling is agreement on a budget deficit above 2% of GDP – which has fast become the psychologically important mark. A deterioration in export performance could have a similar effect, although **BMI** remains optimistic about export growth.

On the reward side, increased currency risk reduces the carry trade from the interest differential. However, investors may be enticed back into zloty assets in Q3 00 given the RPP's tightening bias and the expectation that the council may limit the currency's downside or otherwise risk further endangering the inflation target. The RPP retains the power to intervene in the foreign exchange market under the terms of the agreement struck between the government and the central bank.

Strong FDI flows and export growth should also provide support for the currency over the remainder of the year. The effect on the currency, especially of privatisation inflows, will depend upon the extent to which funds are channelled into the foreign exchange account held by the Finance Ministry at the NBP rather than exchanged for zlotys on the local market. It is not inconceivable that the ministry could use the account to actively smooth the exchange rate. **BMI** expects the zloty to strengthen against the dollar by end-2000. However, its y-o-y trend over the forecast period will be to depreciate in nominal terms against both the dollar and the euro.

The currency's long-term trend will remain a nominal depreciation although volatility will be higher around that path as expectations about monetary variables play a stronger role in the absence of a central parity marker.

Balance of Payments

Exports To Allay Twin Deficits Fear

A sustained recovery in exports is expected to allay fears about the external balance and defuse the argument for tightening the fiscal thumbscrews much further.

The current account has been the most widely watched indicator this year, and it is concern about the size of the deficit that has effectively determined both fiscal and monetary policy. Having disappointed throughout the year, May's figures, released on July 3, came at just the right time for the government. Export growth in May outpaced import growth on both a m-o-m and y-o-y basis, contributing to a narrowing of the monthly current account deficit to US$376mn – the lowest level since August 1998. On the NBP's payments-based data, exports declined 3.4% y-o-y in the January-May period while imports grew at the same rate over the period, pushing the five-month trade deficit up nearly US$1bn to US$5.8bn. Import growth continues to reflect higher world commodity prices and the zloty's trend depreciation against the dollar over the past year.

The evidence is mounting that export performance has reached a turning point and, although the usual *caveat* about not reading too much into one month's figures applies, the NBP's data at last appear to be confirming the rosier picture painted by the Central Statistical Office (GUS). Indeed, the GUS' customs-based data are fast becoming considered more reliable than the central bank's payments-based data. The discrepancy between the two is large. In the January-April period, GUS data show exports growing 11.5% y-o-y, while the NBP's show an 8.4% drop over the same period. Why the difference? A small part may be due to the time lag between goods entering Poland (counted by customs) and companies being paid for those goods (reflected in bank transactions). A more significant factor relates to the methodological changes made in 1999 by the NBP that allow firms to report only net trade.

Solid industrial output at a time of moderating domestic demand suggests that firms are producing for overseas markets (*see Economic Activity*), and

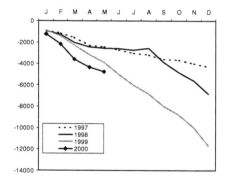

Large, But Manageable
Cumulative current account, US$mn

Source: National Bank of Poland

	CURRENT ACCOUNT					
	1997	1998	1999	2000f	2001f	2002f
Merchandise exports (fob, US$bn)	27.23	30.25	26.36	29.50	33.10	36.10
Merchandise imports (fob, US$bn)	38.50	43.91	40.88	44.00	47.50	50.35
Merchandise trade balance (fob-fob, US$bn)	-11.27	-13.67	-14.53	-14.50	-14.40	-14.25
Current account balance (US$bn)*	-4.27	-6.81	-11.67	-11.90	-12.55	-11.90
Current account (% of GDP)	-3.0	-4.3	-7.5	-7.3	-7.0	-6.2

f = BMI forecast; Source:NBP/BMI

BMI maintains its view of a mild recovery in exports over the year. Some of the steam should be taken out of import growth by the anticipated slowdown in private consumption (*see Economic Activity*), but not enough to narrow the trade gap. Therefore, although we believe export performance to be better than balance of payments data suggest, we do not foresee any substantial narrowing of the current account deficit. In fact, **BMI** does not see this necessarily as a problem in 2000 or over the remainder of the forecast period. In the midst of the zloty's turmoil in May, **Standard and Poor's** upgraded Poland's credit ratings one notch, arguing – correctly in our opinion – that the current account deficit, "mainly reflects the economy's maturing transition stage," and is sustainable as long as fiscal consolidation and structural reforms continue. That said, we remain concerned that greater political turbulence as the elections approach will cause progress in reforming the more sensitive sectors to wane.

Over the forecast period, the majority of the current account deficit should be financed by FDI inflows. Net FDI, at US$2.3bn, was up 31% in the first five months of 2000 compared with the same period of 1999. And according to the Treasury, up to US$4bn is expected in Q3 00 from the sale of telecoms giant **TPSA** to **France Telecom**.

Profile and Recent Developments

Characteristics Of The Economy

Industry Still Dominates

Poland remains primarily an industrial-based economy with industry accounting for around one-quarter of GDP. Since 1990, manufacturing has accounted for around 85% of industrial sales, with food production by far the biggest sector at 18-19%. Growth industries, geared to both the domestic market and exports, have included cars and machinery, the latter providing basic inputs into German production. There have been three distinct stages of industrial restructuring since the transition process began. The first occurred in the wake of the economic collapse that followed the political changeover in 1989, when many heavy industries closed as their traditional markets disappeared. The second stage started in the early-1990s as foreign investment and privatisation gathered momentum, with the private sector accounting for some 65% of industrial production by 1997. The third stage started in late-1998 as the government squared-up to the realities of changing world markets and EU demands, and started tackling labour-intensive sectors such as coal and steel. Heavy industries, such as steel, have been scattered throughout the country without any particular regard for proximity of resources, although the heaviest concentration is in the Silesian coal belt. The textiles industry has traditionally centred around Lodz in central Poland, while shipping and oil refining are located on the northern Baltic coast.

Western Poland has benefited from its proximity to, and good transport links with, Germany, which has generated a services-led boom in Poznan and Wroclaw. Warsaw, as the capital, remains the natural financial centre. However, the Polish policy which initially created a number of strong regional banks from the central bank's commercial operations, has enabled cities such as Gdansk, Poznan, Katowice and Krakow to develop significant financial services in their own right.

Eastern Poland has traditionally been more depressed, relying in post-communist times on close but informal trading links with Russia, Lithuania, Belarus and Ukraine. The region has enormous tourist potential, particularly in the Bialowieza forest straddling Belarus. Outside Warsaw and Krakow the major tourist centres are in Zakopane, in the mountainous south, and the lake resorts in the north.

Poland's main mineral resources are coal and copper, both have suffered from weak world commodity prices and cheaper production costs elsewhere. Other significant resources include sulphur and zinc. Proven oil reserves are insignificant and, until recently, there has been no incentive to explore potential reserves since most electricity generation is geared to coal. Crude oil imports, mainly from Russia, service a large refining industry. Poland does, however, produce enough natural gas to service 30% of its domestic requirements, as well as coal methane deposits.

Agriculture has contributed little more than 6% of GDP for several years (4.2% in 1998), in part because many of the estimated two million farms are family subsistence operations. It is, nevertheless, a significant employer, an important sector in social terms, and has at least kept an already high unemployment rate from soaring higher. Poland's market services sector has, on paper, stabilised at around 37% of GDP. Accounting for many self-employed, it is not fully captured in official statistics. Anecdotal evidence would suggest that in the cities at least, with the growth of catering, computing, repair and other services, it is a rapidly growing sector.

Economic Activity

External Shocks Hinder Growth

In 1992, Poland was the first former communist country to stage an economic recovery, and in 1996 became the first to nurse GDP back to 1989 levels. The economy grew at an average of 5.8% per year over the 1993-97 period. Manufacturing has been the main engine of growth, enhanced by FDI and trade reorientation toward the EU. To some extent this rapid growth was achieved at the expense of an inflation rate higher than its peers in the region, which enabled the banking and corporate sectors to deflate domestic debt costs. Although the National Bank of Poland has often missed its annual inflation rate target, there has been an implicit agreement between the central bank and finance ministry that economic growth was a priority, and that deflationary policy would be avoided as long as inflation was reduced each year.

By late-1997, there were serious concerns that the economy was overheating, and high real interest rates succeeded in dampening some of the consumer-driven momentum. GDP growth in Q2 98 fell to 5.3% y-o-y from 7.5% in 1997, and to 5.0% in Q3, compared with 6.7% the previous year. With hindsight, the monetary authorities probably overreacted as growth had peaked by summer 1997 in response to an economic slowdown in the EU and a lack of restructuring within Polish industry. The Russian crisis in August 1998 changed the outlook markedly, as GDP growth in Q4 98 slumped to 2.9%, and a mere 1.5% in Q1 99. Russia's collapse hit not only primary exporters (such as food producers) and service exporters (such as construction and shipping), but the banking sector, which had lent to companies doing business in Russia as well as speculating in GKOs (Russian treasury bills). While the informal economy, including the many traders in eastern Poland who relied on business with Russia, as well as Lithuania, Belarus and Ukraine, suffered the most, there was also a psychological effect on consumer confidence throughout the country.

Industrial output growth peaked in June 1997, before slowing in response to lower world demand.

The slowdown became more profound after the Russian crisis, and by October 1998 output from the sector was declining in annual terms. A large proportion of Poland's exports to Germany consists of industrial inputs, and with German manufacturing experiencing a 2% y-o-y contraction in Q4 98, a reciprocal downturn in Polish output followed as a matter of course. After five months of continual decline there was a 3.3% rebound in March, although production in Q1 99 was still down by 2.6%.

A V-shaped recovery was completed in Q4 99. GDP grew by 6.2% y-o-y in the final quarter, boosted by high industrial output and accentuated by a favourable base of comparison. Q4's strong performance lifted the annual real growth rate to 4.1% y-o-y, higher than most commentators' expectations earlier in the year.

The recovery has been mainly domestic-driven. Fixed investment remains the strongest component of GDP, although its growth rate halved last year to 6.9%, while net exports started to drag on growth. Domestic demand has also been lifted by private consumption, which grew 5% y-o-y, buoyed by real wage growth and the rising popularity and availability of consumer credit. Consumer borrowing grew over 50% last year and credit card issuance doubled to 6.5mn. The availability of finance facilitated a 23% rise in new car sales. Domestic credit expansion has also contributed to a worsening trade gap, and called into question the sustainability of the recovery. But the real problem is on the export side. Though private consumption has been rising, its growth rate is not out of line with the average over the past four years.

Fiscal Policy

Shrinking Deficit Is A Priority

Between 1993 and 1997, Poland managed to lower the state budget deficit progressively. Keeping the deficit below the 3% Maastricht criterion for EMU is regarded as proof of fiscal responsibility to both the EU and the financial markets, which determine the cost of Polish borrowing. Moreover, with monetary policy constrained in the fight against inflation by the fear of fostering an uncompetitive exchange rate, fiscal policy is the one weapon the authorities possess which, through its impact on domestic demand, can both reinforce the inflation battle and help plug the trade gap. Moreover, higher savings (public and private) are required in the medium term to ensure external sustainability after privatisation-related inflows begin to wane.

Though the state (central government) deficit came in PLN211mn below plan at PLN12.6bn (2.4% of GDP) in 1999, the broader, consolidated deficit widened to 3.4% of GDP as welfare and health reforms absorbed additional government spending. In particular, public finances deteriorated because of the deficit run-up by the Social Insurance Office (ZUS) following substantial revenue losses related to the introduction of the new pension system. The planned state deficit for 2000, at PLN15.4bn (2.3% of expected GDP), is broader because more central government expenditure is to be used to subsidise the pension system. To compensate ZUS for revenue losses as people switch to the funded pension scheme, an additional subsidy amounting to 1.2% of GDP (PLN8.3bn) is included. However, ZUS's impact on public dissaving is less of a stimulus than it at first appears, since it is partially offset by higher private saving.

Furthermore, although not counted as current spending by the government, provision is also made for compensatory payments of PLN3.5bn this year (with another PLN10bn to be paid out over the 2001-2004 period) to state employees and pensioners for the high inflation at the beginning of the 1990s.

The consolidated deficit is planned to fall to PLN18.5bn (2.7% of GDP) as the budgets of ZUS, local government and the health sector are all trimmed, though managing this in a pre-election period may prove challenging. As the fiscal deficit is now wider than the government first planned, because of the size of the pension fund shortfall, the target for privatisation revenue has been upped from PLN11.7bn to PLN20.1bn, in order to avoid a large increase in public debt.

The provisions of the tax reform legislation passed in tandem with the 2000 budget should also help to boost tax revenues. VAT and excise taxes are being altered to comply, at least partially, with the EU Sixth Council Directive, which relates to the harmonisation of indirect taxes. The corporate tax rate is to be lowered to 30% this year from 34% in 1999, and under the new law is to be reduced in stages to 22% in 2004.

Plans to reduce personal income tax have been more contentious and nearly led to Balcerowicz resigning last year. The measure was eventually vetoed by the president, but is due to be reintroduced in 2000. The dispute between the finance minister and members of Solidarity – with the latter preferring slower tax and spending reductions – reinforced the NBP's view that fiscal slippage was a distinct possibility this year and next as the electoral cycle kicks-in. The RPP's hawkish stance and "tightening bias" adopted in early-2000, may be interpreted as insurance against possible fiscal laxity

Tackling Social Security

Social security and pension payments account for the largest share of central government expenditure, at over 30% of the total, but this proportion is expected to shrink gradually as the 1999 pensions law takes effect. The law transforms pensions from a pay-as-you-go system administered by Zaklad Ubezpieczen Spolecznych (ZUS) to a three-pillar system comprised of: a mandatory scheme administered by ZUS, compulsory privately managed schemes, and voluntary plans. People over the age of 50 years remain with the first pillar, while those aged 30 years and under must join a second-pillar scheme as well as pay ZUS contributions. Those between can choose to join a second pillar plan or rely entirely on the state-funded system. One of the budgetary side-benefits of the reforms is that it makes life in the shadow economy less attractive, as the ultimate pension will depend on a lifetime's contributions, not the final salary. For the same reason, workers will have less incentive to opt for early retirement. The average retirement age in Poland is 59 years for men and 55 years for women, against the official ages of 65 years and 60 years respectively.

Under the old system, ZUS was funded by employers' contributions, equivalent to around 45% of an employee's income, with the state making up the deficit. Under the new scheme, ZUS still collects the compulsory premiums but transfers 7% to the private schemes, with the government financing the shortfalls from privatisation revenues. Like all social security systems, the scheme is prone to abuse, either by employers delaying their contributions or employees milking the sickness benefit schemes.

Long-Term Strategy To Aid External Sustainability

In early-1999, Poland's economic committee considered three fiscal strategies for 2000-2010, and in April 1999 adopted one aimed at realising an optimistic or "pro-active" scenario. This assumes average GDP growth over the period of 7-8%, with growth of 5-6.2% in 2000. The key elements of the strategy, which is to form the basis of future budget decisions, are:

- a reduction in the public sector deficit to zero by 2003, with a budget surplus thereafter being used to pay off foreign debt. Public debt as a proportion of GDP would fall from 48% in 1999 to below 20% by 2010;

- a reduction in direct taxes to boost investment through increased savings. The plan assumes that savings as a percentage of GDP will rise from 19% in 1998-99 to 28% by 2009-10, boosting foreign direct investment by a further 1-2% of GDP;

- a reduction in real government spending growth over the 2001-03 period to 3%. This would entail a 25% cut in subsidies, as well as a shift in government spending to infrastructure investment. The optimistic scenario envisages that public spending as a percentage of GDP falls from 43.5% in 1998-99 to 39% by 2003 and 35% by 2010;

- an acceptance that unemployment will rise, from 11.9% in Q1 99 to above 12% in 2002-2004, falling thereafter to 7.7% by 2010.

Monetary Policy

Inflation Is Now The Target...

Monetary policy was highly politicised over the 1994-96 period. Despite high real interest rates, inflation remained higher than targeted, with the central bank accusing the government of failing to restructure the economy and liberalise prices, while the finance ministry blamed the central bank's high rate policy of inflating the money supply by attracting speculative capital. Sole responsibility for monetary policy has shifted from the central bank (in consultation with the finance ministry) to the Monetary Policy Council (RPP) which is chaired by central bank governor Hanna Gronkiewicz-Waltz, and started operating at the beginning of 1998. The *Sejm*, Senate and president each appoint three of the nine members. Although initially viewed as a threat to the independence of the central bank, its decisions have generally proved apolitical, if not unanimous. The Polish constitution in any case enshrines the central bank's powers and has removed parliament's right to change monetary policy guidelines.

The central bank maintained high real interest rates from mid-1997 to dampen consumer demand, by making household credits expensive. By the time the RPP took over in 1998, inflation was falling sufficiently to warrant rate cuts, a policy reinforced by trade and current account deficits, which until the Russian crisis in August were also improving. Through a series of four cuts the Lombard rate, which acts as the reference for household and small business credits, came down from 27% to 20%, and the rediscount rate from 24.5% to 18.25%. The key intervention rate, the floor for one-month Wibor (Warsaw Interbank Offered Rate), fell from 24% to 15.5% as a result of six cuts. The penultimate cut of the year, in October, was the RPP's reward to the government for agreeing to a fiscally austere budget.

Although the RPP promised greater transparency, to some extent its policy frameworks have been overtaken by external events. In October 1998, the RPP announced that under its medium-term strategy it would adopt direct inflation targets, which would fall in stages to 4% by 2003. On January 20 1999, the RPP slashed 250 basis points off the intervention rate to 13%, 300 basis points off the Lombard rate to 17% and 275 basis points off the rediscount rate to 15.5%. Despite the new policy, the cut was not targeted at inflation, but addressed the Russian-induced economic slowdown – including the news that industrial output in Q4 98 had fallen – and a deterioration in the trade and current account deficits after August. Although the size of the cut took the markets by surprise, the council reasoned that the risks of refuelling consumer demand were more than outweighed by the benefits of stimulating an economy in danger of stagnating.

...But The Targets Are Proving Hard To Hit

Last year saw a U-turn on the disinflation path traversed since transition as Polish producers hiked fuel prices in response to rising world oil prices, protectionist measures pushed up food prices, and the zloty depreciated. In addition, households, perhaps anticipating higher permanent incomes ahead of EU entry, displayed an increasing eagerness to consume. The growth in personal bank deposits fell, and personal borrowing rose 53%, facilitated by lower nominal interest rates in H1 99, and a softening of collateral requirements for loans. Corporate credit growth at 21.9% was somewhat lower, reflecting weaker demand for Polish products. Rising consumption sucked in imports and contributed to a widening trade deficit. For these reasons, the RPP raised interest rates 350bps in total in September and November, in the hope that curbing credit and money growth would offset rising food and fuel prices. It is worth noting that although consumer credit has grown rapidly, it has done so from a low base. As bank debt as a proportion of GDP is relatively low in Poland, large rate increases are deemed necessary to alter behaviour.

The end-1999 target was for CPI growth of 6.6-7.8%, against December's headline rate of 9.8% y-o-y. The inflation target for 2000 has been lowered but the range widened to 5.4-6.8% y-o-y, by the year's end. A wider range reflects the uncertainty of the relationship between policy instruments, principally interest rates, and inflation. In addition the bank has cited the twin deficits on the current account and fiscal budget, and the expectation of uncertain changes in raw material and food prices (which have a 30% weighting in the CPI index) as factors that will make attaining the target more difficult in 2000.

The same forces were at play in Q1 00. The CPI rose 10.1% y-o-y in January on the back of higher food prices, which were in turn boosted by the introduction of VAT and a base effect. February's index was similarly affected with food prices rising 1% on January, contributing to CPI inflation of 10.4% y-o-y. Furthermore, broad money fell 3.1% m-o-m in January and consumer credit slowed to 0.8% (versus an increase of 4.7% in December), though as NBP President Hanna Gronkiewicz-Waltz rightly pointed out, this was due more to seasonal factors than November's monetary tightening. In fact, January's inflation rate was marginally below market expectations. Hence the surprise that greeted the Council's decision on February 23 to increase its three interest rates (lombard, discount and intervention) by 100bps. The then deputy finance minister Jaroslaw Bauc described the decision as "slightly hasty".

The RPP blamed the increase on resurgent inflationary expectations that could threaten this year's target (though no doubt took into account the deteriorating external balance) and announced that it was adopting a "policy tightening bias" for future decisions. With the effects of previous measures beginning to filter through, rates were kept on hold in H1 00.

Exchange Rate Policy

A Stage-Managed Performance

As well as holding sole responsibility for monetary policy, the RPP also determines exchange rate policy in conjunction with the finance ministry. It continued with the Polish established practice of using real exchange rate appreciation as a means of bringing about controlled disinflation, but in a more aggressive manner. The RPP's first decision, in February 1998, was to reduce the zloty's monthly crawl from 1.0% to 0.8%, and to widen the fluctuation band around parity from 7% to 10%. The crawl was further reduced to 0.65% in July, 0.5% in September and 0.3% in March 1999, while the fluctuation band widened to 12.5% in October 1998 and 15% in March 1999. While the wider band minimised the effect of the exchange rate on inflation, it reduced the need to draw on reserves to support the currency.

The NBP has also edged itself out of the official foreign exchange market. In December 1998, it introduced spreads on deals transacted at its daily fixings, which were themselves abolished in June 1999. Along with widening the band, the disappearance of the fixing sessions was a further move towards permitting the currency to float freely.

As the euro made its debut at the beginning of 1999, Poland followed suit by redenominating its basket. On January 4 1999, it moved from a basket comprising 35% deutschemarks, 10% pounds sterling, 5% French francs and 5% Swiss francs to a 55:45 euro/dollar basket. Although EU countries account for around two-thirds of Polish exports, a high dollar weighting was maintained to reflect the large percentage of trade which remains dollar denominated irrespective of origin or destination. In addition, more than half of Poland's US$40bn of foreign debt is denominated in dollars. Ultimately, the objective is to join the ERM2 mechanism.

Volatility Seen As Speculator Deterrent

The central bank has never welcomed short-term capital inflows, because of their destabilising effect on the zloty, and has to some extent encouraged exchange rate volatility, for example, by maintaining a relatively wide fluctuation band to deter speculation. The side-effect of such a policy is that Polish exporters and importers have had to second-guess exchange rate fluctuations to get the best rate for their receipt conversions, while the high volatility has made foreign exchange options expensive. The zloty, nevertheless, tended to trade well above parity.

The main external events that temporarily impacted on the zloty's value were the Asian crisis in 1997, the August 1998 devaluation of the Russian rouble, concerns about Brazil in January 1999, and news that the Czech recession was set to continue through 1999. Domestic events included poor external deficits and other bad economic news. Overall, the zloty weakened during 1999 but strengthened rapidly towards the end of the year as favourable yield differentials between Polish and euro-zone securities attracted interest-sensitive inflows.

Balance Of Payments

EU's Importance Continues To Grow

Export growth has been a key factor driving economic recovery over the past few years. There has been a significant reorientation of trade since the early-1990s. The EU's share of Polish exports has grown from 44.0% in 1990 to 73.6% by 1998; the share of imports rose from 63.8% to 65.6%. Germany, Poland's biggest trading partner before World War II, has regained this position. In 1998, it accounted for 25.8% of imports and 36.3% of exports, with no other country even in double figures. Russia, Poland's second largest export market in 1997, slipped to third place in 1998, overtaken by Italy, which was also Poland's second-largest importer.

Since the early-1990s, Poland's trade pattern has been dictated by membership of the main trading blocs. Under the association agreement with the EU signed in 1992, Poland has been obliged to dismantle its industrial tariffs progressively. These were originally set to disappear by 1999, but Poland has stalled on sensitive sectors such as steel. WTO membership, which was ratified in 1995, also demands a dismantling of industrial tariffs. Poland was a founder member of the Central European Free Trade Agreement (Cefta) in 1992. The bloc was initially expected to instil trade bloc discipline among member countries, all of whom aspired to join the EU, but has diminished in importance.

The Russian Effect

The collapse of the Russian economy in August 1998 was initially greeted with complacency by the Polish authorities and other Central European countries, which had likewise reoriented their trade westward. Although Russia accounted for only 8.4% of Polish exports in 1997, prior to the economic crisis, the effects proved more profound than initially expected. The food sector was hit because of Russia's importance as a market for all European producers. The last quarter of the year is traditionally the strongest season for exports, but in 1998 they were down by 1.4% q-o-q and 0.8% on Q4 97.

Current Account Deficit: A Cause For Concern

No indicator is more keenly watched than the current account. Poland's current account deficit is structural, reflecting the tendency of a restructuring and growing economy to suck in investment goods. The deficit ballooned in 1999 to US$11.67bn, from US$6.81bn in 1998, and was pushed up by larger trade and services deficits and a lower balance on unclassified transactions (suitcase trade). At 7.6% of GDP, last year's deficit was worryingly large, though the majority of it was covered by foreign direct investment.

The trade balance was affected, particularly in H1 99, by a loss of export markets (primarily food products) following the Russia crisis and its spillover effects on other CIS markets. Sluggish demand from German consumers (Germany takes around 37% of Polish exports) also prised the gap wider while the import bill was inflated by rising world oil prices, which by December 1999 had leapt 155% y-o-y. Lower demand from German and CIS consumers also caused a sharp drop in "suitcase" or "shuttle" trade – the former deterred by higher excise taxes at the border, the latter because of the loss of favourable relative prices following the rouble's devaluation.

As the OECD pointed out in its most recent survey of Poland, the current account deficit has mirrored the stream of net FDI. Net FDI of US$6.6bn covered 57% of last year's deficit. The 2000 budget anticipates US$4.9bn in privatisation proceeds, which the government believes could be surpassed as the stock market's ascent has boosted the valuations of state assets such as the telecommunications monopoly TPSA, 25-35% of which is slated for sale in 2000. At current prices this sale alone could raise just under US$4bn (although it is likely to be sold at a discount if the share price bubble continues). Portfolio investment – a more contentious form of financing – topped US$1bn last year, and is set to climb higher in 2000.

Foreign Direct Investment

The Money Pours In

In the early post-communist years Poland developed a reputation for political instability on top of Western perceptions of a country bedevilled with smokestack industries, a large peasantry and uncomfortably powerful trade unions. Foreign investment remained subdued until 1995-96, when it rapidly accelerated as a result of stronger growth, the retail market potential of its sizeable population, and increasing Western familiarity with the region as a whole. Poland's acceptance into the "fast-track" group of countries eligible for early EU accession talks is an important factor for manufacturing investors, who needed the assurance of access to the larger market. The country is also benefiting from the trend of eastward sourcing employed by some conglomerates, which are shifting production from Western Europe to the take advantage of lower wages.

Two sets of figures are produced for foreign investment inflows. Those compiled by the Polish Foreign Investment Agency (PAIZ) include commitments and are generally believed to over-estimate of the true figure. The National Bank of Poland's cash-based data excludes in-kind investments and reinvested profits, and therefore under-estimates the true amount. According to PAIZ, foreign investment in 1998 totalled US$10.1bn, while NPB figures put inflows at a much lower US$6.3bn, with the true figure somewhere in-between, closer to the accrued data which the NPB compiles about two years after the event. The cumulative total since 1989 ranges from US$15.07bn according to the EBRD, to US$30.7bn according to PAIZ, which uses data based on NBP figures.

Although the rate of FDI inflows has increased impressively by either measure, the amount of FDI per head, US$389 at the end of 1998 according to the EBRD, is less than a quarter of that in Hungary and lower than the Czech Republic, Slovenia and the three Baltic states. However, given the relatively recent increase in inflows, FDI has yet to make its full impact on employment, export generation and other elements of the economy. The trend remains encouraging because, in addition to the two standard sources of FDI – privatisation and greenfield investment – there is the relatively new development of foreign takeovers, friendly as well as hostile, of established Polish private and privatised companies.

External Debt

Prudence Is A Virtue

During the communist era, Poland embarked on a borrowing spree, with the lending community mistakenly assuming that fear of Moscow acted as the ultimate sovereign guarantee. Poland regained its financial respectability only after rescheduling its Paris Club (sovereign) debt, by 50%, in 1991 and its London Club (international banking) debts in 1994. The bank debts were reduced by US$6.5bn and rescheduled over 30 years. The 1994 Brady Plan involved US$8bn of bonds, of which nearly US$3bn had been bought back by March 1999. Poland's relatively low investment grade ratings in relation to its economy reflect the earlier communist-era defaults.

Since the debt rescheduling, Poland has been prudent in its external borrowing. Despite extremely favourable conditions for Eastern European borrowers over 1995-97, it issued only three eurobonds and one Yankee – US$790mn in total. Issuing was done as much to establish a presence and develop a yield curve as to take advantage of lower rates. Principal repayment on the first of these, for US$250mn, is due in 2000, the second, for DEM250mn, in 2001. A US$300mn Yankee repayment falls due in 2004, with a further US$100mn in 2017. Unlike debt issued by other transition countries, none of Poland's euromarket borrowing was used to finance the budget deficit or service energy debts. Although investors remain risk-averse, there is still an appetite for better rated credits with stronger underlying fundamentals. Poland was set to take advantage of its favourable credit ratings in 1999 with a euro-denominated eurobond, but cancelled the floatation as privatisation proceeds exceeded expectations.

The ratio of foreign debt in convertible currency to GDP has fallen from around 55% in 1993 to 40% in 1999, well within the 60% Maastricht criteria. However, according to IMF projections, medium-and long-term debt service is to rise from around US$5bn in 1999 to US$14bn in 2004. Furthermore, Paris Club amortisations are expected to rise steeply over 2004-09, peaking at US$5.3bn in 2005. The intention to have the budget deficit in surplus from 2004 onwards is driven in part by the need to build a cushion to service these debts. Although a new government may well be in place after the 2001 parliamentary elections, future spending plans will be constrained by the need to avoid a repetition of the traumatic and internationally embarrassing communist-era default, particularly if Poland is to have any chance of joining the EU in the near future. The looming debt repayments will also ensure that Poland keeps its future euromarket forays to a minimum. Domestically, conditions for rolling over debt have become progressively easier and cheaper for the finance ministry. Polish banks have been attracted back into the local treasury bond market by falling inflation and interest rates, and the bruising experience some received from speculating further afield in higher yielding Russian and Ukrainian securities. The newly established second-pillar private pensions funds, which have investment constraints on all assets bar Polish treasuries, are a captive market and will inevitably drive down yields. They will also enable the state to extend the maturity of its bonds. In the past, the euromarkets were the only opportunity for Eastern European countries to issue medium- and long-term debt, but the finance ministry issued the first fixed-rate 10-year domestic bonds in 1999.

3 Key Economic Sectors

Introduction

Money Too Tight For Business?

The economy grew robustly in H1 00, driven by both domestic and external demand. The benefits of growth appear to be broad-based, with sectors from construction to financial services all experiencing a pick-up in activity. The net profit of the banking sector, for example, grew by 22% y-o-y in Q1 00. With the stock market booming early in the year, brokerages saw their revenues more than double in Q1. However, early-year optimism is starting to wane as high real interest rates dampen consumer demand and hinder companies' investment plans. Business climate indices dipped downwards in June, and revealed a souring of confidence in the manufacturing and retail sectors.

Consumers and firms should feel the effects of tight money in H2 00, leading to a moderate slowdown in activity.

BMI expects the economy to slow in H2 00 but the tradable sector should benefit from an upturn in demand from the EU and Russia. Furthermore, although the political situation is likely to cause the pace of structural reform to slow over the next 12 months, several privatisations are still on track, and the sale of a number of energy companies should be completed in H2 00.

GDP & GROWTH OF VALUE-ADDED BY SECTOR (%)					
	1996	1997	1998	1999	2000f
GDP	6.0	6.8	4.8	4.1	4.9
of which:					
Private Consumption	8.3	6.9	4.7	5.1	4.9
Gross Fixed Investment	19.7	21.7	14.2	6.9	7.7
Gross value-added	5.3	6.5	4.7	3.9	4.5
of which:					
Agriculture:	2.4	1.1	6.1	-	-
Industry	7.6	10.3	4.3	4.6	5.4
Construction	2.8	13.6	9.1	3.7	4.5
Services	5.3	4.4	4.8	4.9	5.2
f = BMI forecast. Source: GUS					

Information Technology

Bridging The Digital Divide

Information technology (IT) expenditure in Poland – a paltry 1.4% of GDP in 1999 – is expected to grow rapidly over the next 5-10 years as the economy experiences fairly robust real GDP growth, industry continues to restructure and the service sector expands. In general terms, IT companies can adopt a business-to-consumer (B2C) model and/or a business-to-business (B2B) model, with the Internet facilitating both. It was B2C that caught the imagination of investors around the world in 1998/1999 as vast sums of money were poured into e-tail and portal initial public offerings (IPOs).

The Polish Internet market is undeveloped but growing quickly. Internet penetration, at 4% of the population in 1999, was one of the lowest rates in Western and Central Europe. Telecoms giant **TPSA** remains the dominant Internet service provider (ISP), with at least 85% of all access lines. **Netia** and **Softbank** are smaller ISPs. Unlike many other countries, Poland's ISPs have been traditionally independent of portals. However, TPSA and **Elektrim** have both expressed an interest in capturing users at their entry point to the web, either by developing their own portals or acquiring existing ones. New entrants will, of course, slow the growth of incumbent portals. The country's leading horizontal portal (that is, one which provides news, directories, chat rooms etc) is **Onet**, which has successfully exploited its first-mover advantage since the mid-1990s to maintain its hold on the market. Onet is a subsidiary of **Optimus**, a PC assembly and systems integration company. Local portals are also under threat from the entry of international portals such as **Yahoo!**, which was ranked third, behind Onet and **Wirtualna Polska** (owned by **Prokom**), in a recent survey of portal popularity.

Optimus is currently up for sale and it would appear to make strategic sense for one of the ISPs to acquire it in order to exploit Onet, which at present has over 400,000 registered users, with the number expected to grow by nearly 50% by end-2000. The other parts of the company could be divided up and sold-off. **Lockheed Martin**, for example, which partly owns the systems integration division, may wish to own it outright. However, a buyer for Optimus has yet to come forward suggesting that portals are not as attractive as they once, very recently, seemed. The portals' profitability depends upon gaining and retaining a critical mass of users. But the necessary scale is difficult to achieve, since the barriers to entry for potential competitors are relatively low (especially since online charges are set to fall as telecom

After driving the stock market to record highs earlier in the year, investors turned bearish on Poland's technology, media and telecom (TMT) stocks in the aftermath of NASDAQ's crash in March. Although investors are right to question the value of such companies, the long-term outlook for the technology sector is positive.

Lagging Behind, But Raring To Go
Internet penetration, 1999 (% of population)

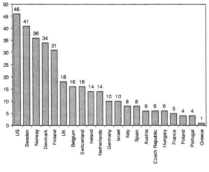

Source: International Telecommunications Union.

services are liberalised), and building a loyal customer base entails high marketing costs. Avoiding short-term financial losses is something that portals would like to, but seldom achieve.

Profiting through B2C in Poland is made harder since consumption patterns differ from those in the US and EU. **BMI** forecasts GDP per capita of US$4,888 in 2002 – low compared to the main industrial nations. As real income rises over the 2000-02 period, it is unlikely that households will purchase the same goods and services as wealthier and more sophisticated consumers in Western markets.

Continued Restructuring To Boost Demand For IT...

Investors have started to evaluate companies following B2C type strategies more carefully, not because B2C will fail to generate significant future revenues, but because of the difficulty any single firm will face in winning a large slice of those revenues. By contrast, B2B has become accepted as the sector in which firms are likely to have the greatest potential. As Poland emerges from its transition stage, the pressure of greater competition will drive companies to restructure and seek efficiency gains. The Internet offers businesses the scope to reduce procurement and distribution costs. IT companies operating in this space may, for example, operate auction-type commercial portals. In addition, the adoption of Internet-based IT solutions makes it possible for firms to save money by outsourcing financial and information management systems. It is IT companies servicing these needs, and particularly those involved in e-finance and application service provision (ASP), that are widely perceived to have the greatest growth potential in the IT sector.

The potential for companies providing systems integration services and Internet-based IT solutions is great, as the corporate sector restructures and the public sector modernises.

The leading Polish companies providing IT solutions include Prokom and Softbank. Through its ownership of Wirtualna Polska, Prokom has already invested heavily in B2C. However, the company's software division has carved out a niche for itself to supply IT services to the public sector. For example, the company has contracts with the social insurance agency (ZUS), state insurer **PZU** and TPSA, with which it agreed a US$47mn deal in May to develop an accounting system. Softbank, on the other hand, has gained a foothold as a systems integrator and provider of IT solutions to the banking sector. The company is currently seeking a strategic investor but has not ruled out merging with a domestic software firm.

The company most highly regarded by analysts is **ComputerLand**. The company has a broader client base than either Prokom or Softbank, operating in the financial, telecoms and public sectors, in addition to industry in general. This diversity offers protection against a downturn in any one sector. ComputerLand has gradually moved away from its roots as a distributor of hardware, towards systems and network integration. More recently it has taken a step further and engaged in business process outsourcing (BPO). **Millennium Bank**, for example, has outsourced its telephone system to the company to reduce costs. Competing in this market has led ComputerLand to explore innovative ways of pricing its services. Rather than simply using cost-plus pricing, for contracts such as that with Millennium, it is seeking a share of any savings it helps to generate. ComputerLand is also looking in 2000 to develop business billing systems, and may eventually move towards application service provision (ASP).

...But IT Infrastructure Remains Poor

The IT sector's potential is clearly large. However, anecdotal evidence suggests that systems integration work grew sluggishly in H1 00 with relatively few contracts offered for competitive tender. Part of the problem is that demand for IT services is confined largely to those sectors that most need to invest in information systems to survive in the marketplace, namely financial institutions and telecoms companies. Many of these companies, however, are still in the early stages of adapting and integrating their systems so there should be a steady trickle of new contracts over the next few years, picking up as e-finance catches on.

The small- and medium-sized enterprises (SMEs) that are essential to Poland's long-term growth prospects have been slow to embrace IT. As the necessary infrastructure is still lacking – a recent academic study ranked Poland second-to-last among OECD and CEFTA countries in terms of IT infrastructure – the days of the hardware market are far from numbered. Indeed, ComputerLand still generates around a quarter of its revenue from reselling hardware. SMEs' demand for software solutions over the next few years should follow on from their greater investment in hardware. Furthermore, IT expenditure in Poland's public administration is set to rise as the government travels along the path to EU accession. Forthcoming contracts in H2 00 are expected to include the post office and the central registrar of vehicles and drivers.

A further wave of demand for IT services should come over the next few years as smaller private-sector firms invest more in hardware and software.

Telecommunications

Competition Increases In The Fixed-Line Sector

The **Telekomunikacja Polska SA** (TPSA) privatisation saga should finally draw to a close early in Q3 00 with the consortium of **France Telecom** and Poland's privately-owned **Kulczyk Holding** set to acquire a 35% stake in the state-owned operator for an expected US$3.5-4bn. The consortium will be permitted to raise its stake to a majority holding by September 2001. Kulczyk Holding's role in the sale is something of a mystery. Founder, Jan Kulczyk, is said to have strong political connections, particularly with the Democratic Left Alliance (SLD), which is likely to form the next government in spring 2001. Several analysts have suggested that the company performed a useful lobbying function for France Telecom. Furthermore, it is still not clear what the company's share of TPSA will be, or what role it will play after the sale.

Poland is a laggard in fixed-line telephony, with a penetration rate of a mere 26% at end-1999. However, the sector is growing and competition is increasing. The new telecoms bill, which lays out the regulatory framework that is to underpin the sector's liberalisation, is due to be signed into law in Q3 00. But many of its provisions are unlikely to take effect until H2 01, and some even later. The legislation provides for a cost-based formula for interconnection payments between TPSA and other operators, in effect determining the degree of competition TPSA will face in the fixed-line market. Importantly, the bill provides for a price cap for tariffs, but no formula is given. And although an independent regulator is to be appointed, this will not happen until 2002, so the Communications Ministry will remain in charge until then.

The cosy duopolistic structure that has existed in the local calls market since 1996 was upset in July when **Netia** – the country's second largest provider of fixed-line services behind TPSA – was awarded a licence to operate services in the Warsaw region. This was much to the dismay of **El-Net**, the telecom subsidiary of **Elektrim**, which claimed that the Communications Ministry had given an assurance that it would be TPSA's sole competitor in the city until the local call market is fully liberalised after January 1, 2002. Netia, meanwhile, has been busy raising finance through a mixture of equity and eurobond issues to invest in its fibre-optic network and expand service provision. The company debuted on the Warsaw stock exchange in July, and is already listed on NASDAQ.

TPSA is at last facing a modicum of competition in some segments of the fixed line market, but it will be some time yet before its dominance is eroded.

End-users should also benefit from the granting in May of domestic long distance licences to three consortia – **Netia 1**, **National Grid Koleje Telekomunikacja** (**NKGT**) and **Niezalezny Operator Miedzystrefowy** (**NOM**). TPSA is likely to make a pre-emptive strike against the new competitiors in H2 00 by cutting domestic long-distance tariffs by as much as 30-40%.

Despite Netia's ambitions, and a rise in competition, it will take some time before TPSA's dominance is eroded. At end-1999, TPSA had around 10 million fixed-line subscribers compared with Netia's 300,000. Furthermore, TPSA was also busy fund-raising in H1 00, and has started to modernise its network to allow faster Internet access and data and video transmission. More importantly, the local and domestic long-distance market is not to be fully opened up to competition until 2002, with the international segment to follow after January 1, 2003.

Asking Price For UMTS Licences May Be Too High

The mobile sector is growing rapidly from a low base. Competition is limited on the GSM network, but 3G licences are now up for grabs.

The poor provision of fixed lines in Poland has been a godsend for mobile telephony, which is a cheaper service for operators to provide. While the number of fixed-line subscribers is expected to top 11mn by end-2000, the number of mobile users is estimated to reach 6.5mn, from around 4mn at end-1999. In fact, the number of subscribers is estimated to have grown nearly 100% in 1999. Three companies dominate the market – **PTC Era** (owned by Elektrim and **Deutsche Telekom**), **Centertel** (TPSA/France Telecom) and **Polkomtel**. All operate on the popular GSM network and should be able to entrench their place in the market since the Communications Ministry has said that no new GSM 900 licences will be issued until after January 2002.

However, UMTS or third generation (3G) wireless licences are to be awarded in 2001, and a notice to tender should be issued by end-2000. 3G technology brings Internet capabilities to mobile phones, and some analysts believe it will be the way that the majority of people access the Internet in the medium term. The Communications Ministry has yet to decide whether four or five licences will be offered, and if they will be auctioned or awarded through a "beauty contest". TPSA is likely to be excluded from the competitive tender and granted one of the licences automatically. But the ministry must decide soon because the Finance Ministry's 2001 budget proposals hinge, crucially and controversially, on PLN14bn in proceeds being raised over the 2001-02 period from the sale. Ratings agency **Moody's Investor Services** warned in June that the high costs of purchasing licences and investing in UMTS networks in Europe could lead to a deterioration in the credit quality of some firms. Given the investment costs and the fact that mobile penetration in Poland is a mere 10%, it is questionable whether local companies would be willing to spend up to US$800mn acquiring a licence.

Automotive Industry

New Car Sales Boomed In 1999...

New car sales surged 24% in 1999 to 640,000 units, facilitated by cheaper and readily available consumer credit, according to Samar, the agency monitoring the Polish automotive industry. The rise exceeded early year expectations, which were formed in the light of 1998's relatively poor performance when new car sales rose by 7.8% – poor, that is, compared with a 41% increase in 1996 and 28% in 1997. The earlier rises reflected decades of limited supply, waiting lists and low consumer spending power. Last year's revival meant Poland ranked as Europe's seventh largest automobile market.

Fiat Auto Poland is the largest foreign investor in Poland's automotive industry. According to the Polish Agency for Foreign Investment (PAIZ), Fiat's cumulative investment in the sector topped US$1.3bn by end-H1 99, just ahead of **Daewoo-FSO**, which has ploughed US$1.24bn into its Polish operation. The investments appear to have paid off. Last year, Fiat Auto Poland maintained poll position in a market where total sales revenue for the 16 leading companies amounted to PLN22.4bn (US$5.6bn). Fiat's profits totalled PLN124.9mn (US$32mn), with the *Seicento* by far the company's most popular model with 83,291 sold last year. Daewoo retained the number two spot.

However, these are worrying times for the carmakers. Neither firm is watching their market share grow on the back of their investments. Rather, more recent entrants into the market are loosening the companies' grip. Fiat, for example, has seen its market share eroded from 45% in 1996 to 29% in 1998 and 27% in 1999. Daewoo, by contrast, built up its share from 17% in 1996 to 27% in 1998. But the company struggled in 1999 – its market share edge downwards and sales revenues dropped 11% on the previous year.

...But Are Reversing In 2000 As Prices Rise

The car market appears to have entered the doldrums in 2000. In the January-May period, sales of new passenger cars fell 11% compared with the same period in 1999. The sharpest drop occurred in May when sales plummeted 26% y-o-y – a fall due largely to stronger sales prior to an excise duty increase

As real incomes have risen over the past few years, so demand for new passenger cars has grown. The major players can still profit from the local market, but not necessarily by producing there.

Higher excise duties, fuel prices and financing costs have dampened demand in H1 00.

in April. Daewoo-FSO has suffered particularly badly with car sales falling 27% in the first five months. Part of Daewoo's problems is firm specific. The parent company is soon to be taken over. The winner of the tender is due to be announced in September and **Ford** is widely tipped to be the victor. Troubles in Korea have had repercussions for the subsidiary's sales in Poland. Concerns about Daewoo's future presence in the local marketplace, and the availability of parts and servicing have all weighed heavily on consumer demand. The company has tried to allay those fears through promotional campaigns, enticing potential buyers with a three-year after-sales service package.

However, several other factors are behind the general downturn in the passenger car market. At the turn of the year, excise duty rose to 4% from 2% for cars with engine capacity up to two litres, and to 15% from 10% for cars with larger-sized engines. In April, the duty on the smaller engine cars rose again to 6% putting further upward pressure on final prices. In addition, the high international oil price has gradually found its way into higher petrol prices at the pumps. Insurance premiums have also risen this year, and with interest rates still high, financing has become more costly. As a consequence, car sales are likely to end 2000 around 15-20% down on 1999's level.

Production Hit By Elimination Of Customs Duty

Higher car and associated prices have not had a uniform impact on consumer demand. Although total sales fell 11% in the January-May period, sales of cars produced in Poland dropped a sharper 23% (to 147,148), while those manufactured abroad rose 22% (to 83,485). As imported cars tend to be destined for the more expensive and luxury end of the market, this suggests that those higher up the income distribution are largely unaffected by price and petrol rises and more interested in quality and brand status. Indeed, carmakers such as **BMW**, **DaimlerChrysler**, **Peugeot-Citroen**, and **Renault** are all benefiting from sales growth.

In terms of sales growth, the domestically produced/imported balance is tilting more towards the latter for another reason – the closing down of car assembly plants in Poland. The battle for market share has been conducted against a background of high customs duties and special tax breaks for individual investors. **General Motors** (GM), for example, obtained extensive tax concessions, including 100% relief on its corporate tax for 10 years, by locating its assembly plant in a special economic zone. Customs duties and the zones are both being phased out, but it is the effect of the former on production decisions that has more far-reaching consequences.

Lower customs duties and larger quotas are reducing the financial viability of EU carmakers' earlier decisions to locate in Poland. Assembly plants are being closed as a result, and imports will plug the supply gap.

High import tariffs on EU and non-EU sourced cars were designed to protect local manufacturing. From the mid-1990s, companies found that the only way to escape the 30% plus duties was to construct plants within Poland from which cars could be assembled from knocked down kits – an additional cost advantage being that the parts could be imported duty-free. Car assembly rules were changed in 1998 after EU complaints that widespread loopholes encouraged abuse, and protests by some established manufacturers that certain companies were assembling cars from imported components without investing in any production facilities. As of January 1998, companies wishing to import parts for assembling cars require licences and proof that the components will be used for completely-knocked-down (CKD) rather than semi-knocked-down (SKD) assembly.

However, as part of its EU accession efforts, the government is reducing customs duties for cars manufactured in and imported from the EU from 15% in 1999 to 10% in 2000, and to 5% in 2001 before eliminating them in 2002. In addition, the duty-free quota of cars imported from the EU has risen in 2000 to 43,750 vehicles from 42,000 in 1999. Meanwhile, cars manufactured outside of the EU, CEFTA and EFTA will face an increasingly uneven playing field: the customs duty applied to them will remain at 35%.

The upshot is firms such as Fiat, Ford and GM-owned **Opel** shutting many of their assembly plants and importing cars from plants located elsewhere in Europe where they benefit from various economies of scale. Utilising their main factories is also to the carmakers' advantage since "Made in Poland" unfortunately does not carry the right cachet in the broader European marketplace – or indeed with a growing number of Poles. And there is no suggestion that Polish demand for cars will fall in the longer term. On the contrary, the demand for cars is expected to continue to grow – even if it tails off in 2000 – given the expectation of robust GDP growth over the next few years and a passenger car per-capita ratio half that of Western Europe.

From Kits To Components

All is not lost. Cars produced from semi-knocked-down kits amounted to under 10% of the total number of cars produced in Poland last year. And most of the major firms will continue to use Poland to produce lower range cars for the Emerging Europe market. Moreover, as business activity expands, so the demand for trucks and vans is set to grow, and many of these will be manufactured locally. Daewoo, for example, has invested PLN1.5bn in a project to manufacture upwards of 30,000 trucks per year in Lublin from 2001. Indeed, while the number of passenger cars produced fell 3% y-o-y in the January to May period, the production of vehicles with a passenger load

Many firms will continue to supply the Central and East European market from Poland, and component manufacturers will benefit from broader automotive sector activity.

of ten or more grew over 50% y-o-y. Finally, though recent developments are likely to stunt the local production of passenger cars, this has not deterred firms further down the supply chain such as component companies from investing in Poland. Several companies have been busy locating in the special economic zones before the concessions such zones offer are phased out. **Delphi Delco Electronics Systems**, producer of audio systems and engine controls, is opening a factory in Katowice, and **Faurecia Bertrand Fure** intends to produce seat adjustment mechanisms and frames from end-2001 in Walbrzych. As well as supplying the major car manufacturers locally, such producers often tend to manufacture sub-assembly components for their factories in other parts of the world. The brakes may be on, but Poland's automotive industry is far from slamming to a halt.

Profile and Recent Developments

Introduction

Industry Dominates Production

Traditionally an agricultural country, Poland was subjected to massive industrialisation after World War II, with the emphasis on heavy industry such as coal mining and steel production. All major cities were required to have their own heavy industrial plants, regardless of the proximity of raw materials. Since the collapse of communism in 1989, industry has remained the main sector of the economy, accounting for 54% of GDP in 1998, but there has been a shift away from heavy industrial production towards consumer goods. Food production accounted for 21.2% of all industrial sales in 1998, by far the biggest share, and had an above-average industrial growth rate of 7.5% that year. Like food, the best performing sectors in Polish manufacturing have been those capturing an upturn in domestic demand, such as radio, television and communications equipment, vehicles manufacture (as well as plastics and rubber, a large part of which services the automobile manufacturing industry), and printing and publishing, which has also given a boost to the paper industry. In contrast, those sectors competing in oversupplied global markets have fared poorly. Sales of petroleum, other hydrocarbon derivatives and mining fell by 13.1%, and base metals by 5.7%.

In terms of the overall U$27.3bn of capital invested by the end of 1998, food processing had attracted the largest share, with 16.4%, followed by transport equipment (including cars), at 13.3%. In contrast, agriculture had attracted a tiny proportion at 1.1%, and is unlikely to significantly improve on this amount in the future. More than 90% of agricultural output remains in private hands, so the government can do little through the privatisation process, and the sector's role in Poland's EU accession talks is uncertain.

Poland's weaker sectors have exposed the country's vulnerability to global events. The 1997 Asian crisis further weakened the prices of commodities such as oil and metals, while the collapse of the Russian market dented exporting sectors, including food processing, and a number of investment banks that should have anticipated the crisis. These events also highlighted the difficulties faced by countries that are not part of powerful trading blocs such as the EU.

Agriculture

Trouble Looming Over EU Entry

Poland is a significant producer by world standards, ranking as one of Europe's largest producers of soft fruit, potatoes, cabbages and rye, and is the world's largest exporter of apple concentrate. In economic terms, the sector has underperformed the rest of the economy, with output increasing by 2.2% in 1998, compared with 4.8% for the whole of GDP. Since 1995, output has increased by only 0.5%. Although there has been some foreign capital inflow into the sector, such as **Farm Frites** of the Netherlands, which is investing in potato cultivation, agriculture had only attracted US$24mn in foreign direct investment by the end of 1998.

The agriculture sector is the biggest obstacle to early EU membership and one which is starting to make many Poles question the wisdom of entry. Agriculture employs around a quarter of the population but generates under 5% of GDP. Poland escaped both the land consolidation that occurred as a result of the industrial revolution in Western Europe, and the enforced collectivisation of the Soviet era. It has an (unreliably) estimated 2mn farms, compared with 7.5mn in the whole of the EU, but of these 56.3% were smaller than five hectares in 1997. A large proportion of holdings classed as farms are barely self-sufficient, let alone selling produce into the market. Nevertheless, they qualify for a range of benefits and tax exemptions. Although producer associations are being established, the small scale of many enterprises prevents them from penetrating highly standardised markets such as the EU, which demands products machine-graded by size. There has also been no concerted move to target growth markets such as organic produce, where the smaller scale of the local farms would actually work to Poland's advantage. Larger, successful farmers argue that Polish agricultural support is so diluted as to be worthless for the bigger concerns trying to compete in the EU and global markets. As the EU share of Polish agricultural exports fell, Polish farmers reoriented their sales to Russia where their produce commanded a premium, boosting the Russian share of food exports to 44% in 1997. Russia's economic collapse the following year closed off the market, and while all European food producers were affected to a greater or lesser extent, the EU had the muscle to redirect its surplus produce, notably pork, into countries such as Poland. Polish farmers responded with widespread protests and blockades in early-1999, and though the government eventually cleared the roads by intervention buying, it acquired a 150,000 tonne meat mountain in the process.

The government has drafted proposals for reforming the sector, including: pensions benefits for older farmers who sell their land to larger neighbouring concerns; the creation of non-farm jobs in the countryside through infrastructure projects; introducing market pricing mechanisms for produce through a network of commodity exchanges; and the imposition of stricter veterinary controls on larger farms, mainly as a result of the EU banning Polish dairy imports in late-1997 due to poor hygiene. A new Veterinary Act came into effect in 1998.

Manufacturing

Food Processing: FDI Pours In

Due to the large domestic consumer market, the food processing sector has been highly successful in attracting foreign investment, with **Coca-Cola**, **Nestlé**, **PepsiCo**, **Mars**, **Unilever** and **Cadbury Schweppes** ranking among Poland's 50 largest investors. Of the US$15.9bn that flowed into Polish industry by the end of 1998, 28% was invested in foods, drinks and tobacco. Alongside the novelty of foreign brands, which initially captured consumer interest in the early-1990s, foreign companies have been able to strengthen their grip on the Polish consumer market by means of their purchasing power in the advertising market. In the confectionery industry, foreign brands control more than 80% of the local market. However, established Polish brands have also survived, even under foreign ownership. For example, PepsiCo, which bought **E.Wedel**, Poland's leading confectionery company in 1991, maintained and expanded the Polish company's chocolate products, before eventually selling the chocolate division to Cadbury Schweppes, and the biscuits subsidiary to **Danone**.

The domestic industry has had to fight for its own market share while trying to carve out new export markets. In the EU, Polish processed products have traditionally had a specialist market amongst the large émigré community, but have not succeeded in broadening their appeal to a wider audience, either through marketing or adjusting the products to Western tastes. However, Eastern markets proved more successful: in Russia, Ukraine and the CIS region, Polish fruit juices, jams and other goods were sold as higher quality, but nevertheless affordable brands, until the collapse of the Russian market in 1998.

The Polish food processing industry is burdened by overcapacity. Up to 40% of the hundreds of small firms are expected to disappear in the next five years, as bigger companies, such as **Animex**, itself 73.4% owned by **Smithfield Foods** of the US, which holds around 12% of total market share, and **Sokolow**, with 7%, snap up the smaller ones. Of the three leading companies, **Agros** and **Rolimpex** are former trading companies, while **Hortex** is a former fruit and vegetables processor, with the leading share in local fruit juice and frozen vegetables. Agros has been the most assertive in marketing and developing new product lines, such as frozen ready-made meals. Both Agros and Rolimpex have also diversified into agricultural production. This diversification has allowed the big three fruit and vegetable-based producers to entrench their positions in the Polish market by establishing brands. The main question is how long Polish food companies intend to remain independent. In April 1999, Agros sold 74.1% of its voting shares to **Pernod Ricard** of France for an undisclosed sum. The French company is set to back its new Polish partner in bidding for the **Polmos** vodka distilleries being privatised by the government. Meanwhile, the meat sector is facing a much tougher time, although the leading producers have, at least, recognised that one of the keys to successfully entering Western markets is to reduce the fat content of Polish processed meat from the unacceptably high 55%.

Chemicals And Pharmaceuticals: Acqulsitions In The Air

The Polish chemicals, pharmaceuticals and associated industries are fragmented, with no conglomerates to capitalise on economies of scale or invest sufficiently in research and development. Consumer chemicals, such as detergents and cosmetics, was one of the earliest sectors to be privatised, largely to foreign buyers such as **Benckiser** and **Henkel**. Meanwhile, the paints industry attempted to survive by consolidation, with **Polifarb Cieszyn** and **Polifarb Wroclaw** merging in 1998 to form **Polifarb Cieszyn-Wroclaw**, the country's largest paint manufacturer. However, competition from the multinationals forced the company to cut prices at the expense of profitability, and with its stock price languishing, the new entity became the first to suffer a hostile takeover on the Warsaw Stock Exchange, being taken over in early-1999 by **Kalon** of the UK.

In pharmaceuticals, Poland lagged behind as Hungary became the region's designated "medicine chest". The industry is falling to foreign buyers, including **Polfa Poznan**, which was acquired by **Glaxo Wellcome,** and is being turned into the British company's regional centre for Central and Eastern Europe. **Polfa Krakow** was bought by Croatia's **Pliva**, and **Polfa Rzeszow** is now majority owned by **ICN**. **Jelfa** and **Polfa Kutno** are the two leading Polish-owned companies, both quoted on the local stock exchange. While Poland has still to pass a medicines act, drug prices, currently 70% subsidised, are being liberalised, increasing the profitability of over-the-counter medications for the major firms. In January 1999, a new health act modelled on the German system came into effect. The new system will be administered by 16 health insurance funds, with employers financing the cover for employees and their dependants. It is expected to introduce competition in the health provision market.

Iron and Steel: Burdened By Overcapacity

The iron and steel industry has been a source of continual dispute in Poland's accession talks with the EU. In 1998, Poland once again succeeded in watering down its import tariffs to 4% instead of 3%. With final abolition due by 2000, the government has been warned that it can have no further extensions. The Polish steel industry suffers from overcapacity and low productivity, with an output of 119 tonnes per year per worker compared, with the EU average of 483 tonnes. Two plants – Huta Katowice and Huta Sendzimira – account for 60% of total production. In return for tariff concessions Poland has agreed to restructure the sector, including privatising the remaining state-owned plants, and reducing the workforce from 87,000 to 47,000 by 2001.

Plans to privatise the two big mills collapsed in early-1999. Huta Katowice, which specialises in processed and rolled steel, came close to being bought by **British Steel**. A consortium of the Netherlands' **Hoogovens** and Austria's **Voest-Alpine Stahl** was the front runner during the sell-off of Huta Sendzimira, which produces mainly raw product, but also wanted the other mill and pulled out when the government refused to sell the two together. The government's revised plan has now paired off Huta Sendzimira with one of its customers, **Huta Florian**, while Huta Katowice will be sold with **Huta Cedler**.

Copper Loses Its Lustre

With proven reserves of 33.5mn tonnes of copper, Poland ranks as the world's sixth-largest producer. **KGHM Polska Miedz**, the mining company privatised in 1997, produced 450,000 tonnes of cooper in 1998, as well 1,032 tonnes of silver. Like producers elsewhere, KGHM was hit by plunging copper prices caused by oversupply and weak Asian demand. Copper prices started tumbling after the Asian crisis, from an average US$2,276 per tonne in 1997 to US$1,652 the following year. KGHM's profits fell in tandem, from PLN501mn in 1997 to PLN200mn in 1998. Although the company cut copper production costs to US$1,620 in 1998, a further slide in copper prices in early-1999 to US$1,440 raised the possibility of large-scale lay-offs later in the year, though the copper price has since recovered.

Electrical And Electronic Equipment

Although Poland lacks a geographic equivalent of Silicon Valley, its information technology (IT) sector is thriving as result of massive investment by the banking and telecoms sectors, and the overhaul of infrastructure in ministries and government agencies. Until the end of communism, Poland was excluded from the computing revolution by the West's ban on exports of electronics equipment with military potential – in practice anything more sophisticated than a calculator – to the eastern bloc. However, the heavy emphasis on science and mathematics in Polish education has made it relatively easy for many Poles to become computer literate. A number of technology parks have been established as Special Economic Zones to attract investment for software development. Computing expenditure in Poland grew by 30% per year over 1993-96, and is estimated to have increased by a further 20% in 1998-2000. Lower costs, legal and cultural insight, and the need for local expertise to provide technical support have enabled a native Polish IT industry to develop despite the global stranglehold exerted by the US computing sector, with more IT stocks listed on the Warsaw Stock Exchange than elsewhere in Central Europe. Hardware sales dominated the Polish IT industry in its early stages of development, but these shrank from 75% to 60% of the total market in 1998, with software services now the growth sector.

Energy

Oil And Petrochemicals: Too Much Product

Privatisation plans for the industry have gone through various permutations of increasing complexity, designed to keep its refining industry intact rather than allowing foreign investors to acquire petrol stations and other outlets for their existing refineries. On paper, the programme has created a vertically integrated industry which the government inherited from its predecessor, and added some changes of its own. At the top of the hierarchy is **Nafta Polska**, the holding company controlling Poland's seven refineries, which together refined 16mn tonnes of crude in 1998, producing 10mn tonnes of diesel and petrol. The largest refineries with the best pipeline connections are: **Petrochemia Plock**, whose profits fell by 24% to PLN607mn in 1998, and **Rafineria Gdanska**, whose 76% profit rise to PLN164.7mn in 1998 was due largely to two months of non-production in 1997. **Centrala Produktow Naftowych** (CPN), the gasoline retail chain controlling 1,400 outlets, was merged with Petrochemia Plock into a new outfit called **Polski Koncern Naftowy** (PKN).

Gas: The Fuel Of The Future

Poland has proven gas reserves of 150bn-160bn m³, and produces around 3.8bn m³ or 35% of its domestic consumption. The remainder is imported, primarily from Russia's **Gazprom**. With gas demand expected to double by 2001, as the use of coal for electricity generation is reduced for environmental reasons, Poland is looking to diversify supplies away from Russia for security reasons. The **Polish Oil and Gas Company (PGNiG),** the state-owned gas distributor, is negotiating alternative supplies with **Gasunie** of the Netherlands for the delivery of a further 2bn m³, and with Norwegian companies for 4bn m³. In May 1999, **Gaz de France** formed an exploration joint-venture with PGNiG. Poland has also signed a declaration of intent with Norway on building a gas pipeline to bring in up to 4bn m³ annually. However, Russia will remain the main supplier because of its proximity. Furthermore, Poland is a transit route for the Yamal gas pipeline, currently under construction, which will transport gas from Siberia to Western Europe. Poland itself will receive 250bn m³ from the pipeline under a 25-year contract signed with Gazprom in 1996.

Electricity Becomes More Competitive

Poland's energy sector, with 17 power plants, 19 combined heat and power plants (CHPs), 33 distribution companies and the national grid, is currently estimated to have a book value of around US$8bn. Poland generated 144,578GWh of electricity in 1998. Coal-fired stations account for 93% of the total output, with hydroelectric plants the remainder, although coal's role is set to decrease as a result of rationalisation of the industry and a progressive switch to gas. In 1997, industry accounted for 55% of electricity sales (as well as generating its own supplies), households 20%, municipal plants 2% and exports 7.5%. Transmission is operated by the **Polish Power Grid Company** (PSE) and distributed by 33 companies, which obtain some 60% of their supplies from PSE and the remainder from local power companies. Poland is integrated into the West European UCPTE and East European CENTREL networks.

Although Poland does not have to comply with the EU's electricity directive until membership is complete, it has started the process of liberalising its energy market. The directive, which demands that at least 25% of a local market is liberalised, itself only came into force in February 1999, and even then Belgium, Greece and Ireland were granted an extension. A new Polish energy law came into effect in 1997, and an independent regulator, the Energy Regulation Office (URE), was subsequently set up to issue licences and approve price increases. It is currently difficult for Poland to rebalance its electricity tariffs fully because PSE is locked into long-term contracts with Poland's major electricity producers, which account for 70% of energy sales. Changes to the energy generation law, to be considered by parliament in 2000, permit the freeing of generation prices. That would leave the government with the task of solving the issue of the long-term contracts, which were often struck at prices higher than free-market prices and used as collateral for loans to modernise plants. The government has proposed cancelling these contracts and compensating plants through a top-up fee to be paid by all end-users.

Plans for privatising the sector have not advanced significantly. The small generating plant, Krakow Leg, was sold to **Electricite de France** in 1997. The PAK power plant, Poland's second largest generator, was set be sold to **National Power** of the UK, but the government cancelled the bid at the end of 1998, and the following spring sold 20% to a consortium led by Polish engineering conglomerate **Elektrim** and **California Energy**. Recognizing that much of the sector is in need of modernization, the government is seeking to finance part of its development by selling stakes in nine energy companies in 2000. These include shares of 25% and 45% in the **Polaniec** and **Rybnik** power plants, and an undecided proportion in one of the country's largest distribution companies, **GZE**. Three CHPs are also to be sold in 2000.

Coal: No Longer King

Poland's main hard coal reserves are located in Upper Silesia in Western Poland, and at Chelm in the east. There are also extensive deposits of lignite, but this is being wound-down as a fuel source for environmental reasons. Once a crucial source of hard currency earnings in the communist years, Polish coal is now increasingly uncompetitive on world markets. Heavy subsidies have invoked retaliatory threats from other coal producing countries such as the UK, which in 1998 complained to the EU about Polish coal entering the British market at 30% below world prices, while Poland itself has imported cheaper coal from Russia and Ukraine. The industry's accumulated debts have also become a drain on the budget. Under the government's plans to rationalise the industry 24 of the 50-plus pits are being closed, and the viable ones privatised. This will slash output from 137 tonnes a year in 1998 to 110 tonnes by 2002. The overall cost of the five-year programme has been estimated at more than PLN14bn, of which the World Bank is to provide PLN3.5bn (US$1bn).

Construction

Industrial Building Has Propelled Growth

The construction industry has enjoyed solid growth, with sales up by 9.0% in 1996, 19.4% in 1997 and a further 10.4% in 1998. Industrial developments, such as new sites for greenfield investments, office developments and financial centres – especially in Warsaw and out-of-town retail outlets – have been the mainstay of construction work to date. In the future Poland's EU requirements to upgrade its transport and energy infrastructure should provide contractors with large projects. In addition, the need to fulfil environmental obligations will result in the rebuilding of power generators and the installation of new waste water and filter plants. Unlike office construction, which has been financed by the private sector, major infrastructure projects will require public financing from the budget and structural funds provided by the EU, World Bank and other bodies. The delays experienced in launching the motorway projects have been due to the inability of private finance to find a profitable way of taking on the entire construction risk. Municipal projects are another growth area. Under the administrative reforms, the regions have a greater share of the central budget and greater powers to approve projects. In February 1999, the government approved a bill providing subsidised funding for the municipalities to develop infrastructure, such as electricity and water, for local housing projects.

Larger Projects Will Demand Bigger Companies

Most of the construction industry has been privatised, mainly by splitting state-owned giants into numerous regional entities, and 14 construction companies are listed on the Warsaw Stock Exchange. Although construction had attracted US$1.7bn of FDI by the end of 1998, Polish companies dominate the market. However, the sector has been highly fragmented, with no company commanding more than a 2% market share, which has created difficulties in bidding for large contracts and left the industry vulnerable to foreign competition. Most bid for projects as general contractors under a fixed or guaranteed maximum price and then subcontract out to specialist companies, although the American system of construction management, involving full site supervision and direct client contractual relationships with subcontractors, is becoming more popular.

The largest Polish construction company by sales is Kielce-based **Exbud**, the former export arm of the region's building industry, with an estimated 2% market share. It built up its position initially through contracts in West Germany, but has since focused its business activities on road, power and other infrastructure projects. Next is **Budimex**, a former foreign trade organisation undertaking overseas projects, with a 1.5% market share and an extensive order book of contracts, including a number of retail projects in Poland's major cities. Its subsidiaries include **Dromex**, Poland's largest road builder. **Mostostal-Export** (with 1% market share), as its name suggests, was the export division of the former Mostostal bridge and infrastructure group, which now specialises in construction, finance and corporate restructuring. Other companies from the group include the general contractor **Mostostal Warszawa** (1%), industrial project specialist **Mostostal Zabrze** (0.6%) and **Mostostal Siedlce** (0.6%), which specialises in steel structures. The main construction company specialising in electrical equipment is **Elektrobudowa**, which supplies the electricity, chemical and mining industries. While most of these companies have already acquired numerous subsidiaries, not all of them are in core businesses. Exbud's proposed merger with Budimex at the end of 1998 was rejected by the smaller company, but the two have since signed a cooperation agreement.

Mortgages Will Boost Residential Construction

The pent-up demand for private housing remains huge. The pace of residential building during the communist era was a national joke, and the space allocation parsimonious. High interest rates and the lack of regulations on private house purchase credits have held back the residential market since the collapse of communism, with the number of completed residential units falling by 12% a year between 1990 and 1996. The market picked up in 1997 when completed dwellings increased by 10%, with a further estimated 20% rise in 1998. The residential construction industry received a significant boost in 1999 with the licensing of mortgage banks. **Bank Rozwoju Eksportu** received the first mortgage licence in February 1999, and others have followed. Muncipal projects are another growth area, partly due to administrative reforms giving local authorities a greater share of overall tax revenues.

Banking And Insurance

Bank Privatisation Is Almost Complete

The privatisation of Poland's complicated banking sector is drawing to a close. In 1998, the government floated a 15% stake in **Pekao**, the former foreign exchange monopoly, and sold a 37% stake in **Bank Przemyslowo-Handlowy** to **Bayerische Hypo Vereinsbank**. In 1999, it sold 80% of **Bank Zachodni**, the last of the nine banks originally carved out of the central bank's commercial operations, to **Allied Irish Banks**, and a further 52% stake in Pekao to a consortium of **Unicredito Italiano** and **Allianz** of Germany.

Though the pace of privatisation has abated, the commercial banking sector still has the potential for strong growth. Despite solid real GDP growth in recent years, Poland is relatively under-banked with less than 50% of the population holding bank accounts. But with EU accession as a backdrop, competition has increased and the range of services on offer broadened considerably. The most significant change in the banking sector over the past decade has been the move away from specialisation bestowed on the former state banks, such as trade finance in the case of **Bank Handlowy** and **Bank Rozwoju Eksportu**, and Pekao's foreign currency transaction function, towards universal banking. This has led to consolidation and foreign bank buy-ins as domestic banks look to develop a customer base. The foreign banking presence has increased, mainly through acquisitions. According to the OECD, 60% of commercial banks' share capital at the end of 1999 was in foreign hands. Poland did not follow the Hungarian pattern fully in selling most larger banks to foreign strategic investors as soon as possible. **Bank Gdanski** was sold to **BIG** (now **BIG Bank Gdanski**), and **Polski Bank Inwestycyjny** (PBI) to **Kredyt Bank**, Poland's two most aggressive local private banks, while Bank Handlowy's privatisation deliberately parcelled out the strategic stake to three foreign institutions to maintain Handlowy's Polish identity.

Polish banks initially assumed that foreign banks were primarily interested in skimming-off the high-margin corporate finance business, but would not be interested in the labour- and capital-intensive retail sector. However, this assumption proved incorrect, with foreign investors either buying into regional banks with established branch networks, or, as in the case of **GE Capital**, smaller banks to establish financial services that do not require networks. Poland, while having some 75 banks, is heavily under-banked in terms of branches and automated facilities, while only a third of the population holds a bank deposit account. All the major commercial banks in Poland are now adopting a similar strategy of opening up large networks of small, automated branches. Retail banks earn higher returns on equity than their more glamorous, but riskier, investment banking cousins. In Poland's case, of the total US$300m of banking sector exposure to Russia after

August 1998 more than 90% was accounted for by three banks. Bank Handlowy, Bank Pekao and BRE Bank.

The move to universal banking, together with relative macroeconomic stability, has resulted in the expansion of consumer credit and mortgage financing. The number of credit cards is expected to increase to 10mn in 2000, from 6.5mn in 1999, and growth will continue as more establishments accept electronic payment. Mortgage banking is widely regarded as a key growth area, but since the law permitting subsidiaries specialising in mortgage banking came into force in 1998, only two banks had started operations by early-2000. Lending policies have been enhanced by the relatively low proportion of non-performing loans (around 10% of total portfolios), a condition attributable to the 1993 law on financial restructuring which facilitated the restructuring of bad loans.

Insurance And Pensions: Healthy Growth

The insurance market in communist times was duopolised by **Powszechny Zaklad Ubezpieczen** (PZU), which handled life and property/casualty business, and **Warta**, which covered foreign business such as overseas travel and reinsurance. Warta became partially privatised in 1994 and rapidly diversified, eating into PZU's market, as did the leading international insurers. PZU, which suffered severe losses on the 1997 floods after failing to purchase adequate reinsurance, is set to be privatised in 2001. The Polish insurance market was liberalised on January 1 1999. Foreign companies from EU, OECD and WTO member states can open an office under the same license procedures as Polish companies without establishing a separately capitalised subsidiary, although their Polish offices must maintain adequate capital within Poland to cover liabilities from policies issued within the country. **Commercial Union Polska** is estimated to write every second life policy. Around 2mn Poles now have life insurance policies, which are increasingly purchased as a savings vehicle rather than a means of protecting dependants, with unit-linked policies the most popular products.

The reformed pension programme, which came into effect in April 1999, is the major stimulus for insurance companies as well as banks and international pension fund managers. Insurance companies have a guaranteed additional line of business as maturing pension funds will be obliged to purchase annuities to fund the benefits. By early-2000, 21 pension funds had received licences, including a mixture of local and international banks, insurance companies and mutual fund managers, as well as some companies and the Solidarity and OPZZ trade unions. The fund managers will be operating in what is regarded as one of the most liberalised systems in terms of investment criteria, but also one of the toughest in terms of disclosure and performance criteria. Comparisons of the full gamut of fees and commissions, including management and custodial charges, will be published regularly, as will performance measures. Funds that fall below a weighted average benchmark will be forced to make-up the shortfall from their own capital, or face takeover by a better-performing pension scheme. The funds will provide a continual source of liquidity for the capital markets, and the sum under management is expected to grow six-fold in 2000 to over US$3bn.

4 Business Environment

Introduction

Competitiveness Needs To Be Improved

The Polish business environment faced a difficult year in 1999. While the 1997 Asian crisis depressed demand in the European Union (EU), Poland's biggest export market, Russia's economic collapse in 1998 had a far more profound effect. It impacted directly on Polish exporters, especially in the food industry, as well as many small businesses, and indirectly by hurting other economies in the region. While Poland still pulled in over US$10bn of foreign direct investment in 1998, the fact that industrial production in Q4 98 fell for the first time since 1992 came as a shock to a country accustomed to high rates of growth.

The effect of 1999's economic downturn was felt across all sectors, although market services fared relatively better than industry and construction. The tougher business environment will force the Polish corporate sector into restructuring their operations. In the case of the state-owned sector, the government has promised faster privatisation, a comprehensive reform of Poland's over-manned and uncompetitive coal and steel industries, and the eventual sale of previous no-go sectors such as the railways. At the corporate level, Polish managers will be forced to rationalise their activities to remain competitive, or find themselves replaced by increasingly restive shareholders.

Many Polish companies are too small to compete effectively against foreign competition in the domestic market, let alone the global one, either in building up new export markets or financing research and development programmes. This phenomenon was already obvious in the banking sector in the mid-1990s, and after various attempts by individual banks to use cross-shareholding to preserve their identity, the government enforced mergers. In the corporate sector shareholders will increase the pressure for mergers and acquisitions. This has already started in the paint, construction and food industries.

Infrastructure

Rethink On Road-Building Programme

Motorway construction is seen as crucial in drawing investment and alternative sources of employment into rural areas, as well as regions such as Silesia, which is set to suffer substantial job losses once the coal and steel sectors are restructured. However, Poland's ambitious motorway construction programme has largely languished on the drawing boards. Under a 1994 law, private contractors are allowed to build some 2,500km of motorways under build-operate-transfer (BOT) schemes. The state will finance 15% of the projects, mainly by purchasing land and preparing surveys, while the private sector puts up the rest of the funds in return for toll concessions of 25-30 years.

The transport ministry is backing the private sector's suggestion for a switch to Public-Private Partnerships (PPP), under which the state would provide 50% of the financing in credits or state guarantees, in return for a greater percentage of toll revenues. The ministry has also proposed a separate highway construction fund within the budget, and an increase in state funding; at present only 30% of fuel excise duties go towards road modernisation and construction. However, these proposals will require time-consuming changes to the law, leading to delays in improving transport links to the EU. The transport ministry has estimated that only 1% of roads currently meet EU standards, and that US$13bn is required to bring the rest up to the required level. At the same time, the number of vehicles is expected to soar by 40% by 2015, putting additional pressure on the existing network. The EU has recognised the problem, and aid for Polish roads is set to increase from EUR80-120mn over 1998-99 to EUR375mn over 2000-02.

The Domestic Market

Population Growth Is Levelling Off

Poland has experienced two significant baby booms, the first at end of World War II, having lost a third of its population, and the second in the early-1980s following the end of martial law. In contrast with other countries in Central Europe, Poland's population has continued to grow since the collapse of communism. Improved living standards have contributed to the population rise. Life expectancy has increased by nearly two years since 1990, while infant mortality has fallen from 19.3 per 1,000 live births in 1990 to 9.6 in 1998. Despite attempts by sections of the ruling Solidarity Electoral Action (AWS) to encourage larger families through tax allowances, the rate of natural increase is levelling off due to a preference for smaller families and easier availability of contraception.

Regional Variations Persist

Although a large proportion of investment inevitably flows into Warsaw, Poland resembles Spain in having its wealth more evenly dispersed among regional capitals. Mazowieckie province, with Warsaw as its administrative capital, and Katowice, the capital of Slaskie province, have the highest levels of GDP; they also have the largest populations and subsequently the lowest per capita GDP. Registered employment rates vary more, with regions in the west benefiting from close proximity to EU markets. The highest unemployment rate is in Warminsko-Mazurskie province on the Kaliningrad border. Some 38% of the population is still rural-based, a relatively high proportion by OECD standards, and one with major implications for Poland's entry into the EU. Successive governments have recognised that the only way to reduce the number of subsistence farmers, without encouraging mass migration to the cities, is to create new jobs and improve infrastructure.

The Labour Market

A Wide Differential In Incomes

Wages were traditionally higher in state-owned industrial enterprises, with miners the best rewarded employees. In contrast, professionals in state sectors such as health and education were, and still are, relatively poorly paid in relation to average earnings. The differential between the private and public sectors is widening, with the former benefiting from improved productivity, and the latter constrained by tighter fiscal policy. As Poland's economy has expanded and reforms have liberalised former state-owned industries, wage differentials with developed countries have narrowed. Although this reduces Poland's attraction as a cheap labour market for multinationals relocating from Western Europe, it also weakens German and Austrian arguments that Polish membership of the EU should initially exclude participation in the free labour market, to avoid a westward migration of Poles seeking better pay.

The Polish Labour Act, last revised in 1996, lays down strict conditions for employment and dismissal procedures in both the public and private sectors, making it difficult for companies to shed employees. The labour code, last revised in 1994, governs industrial relations. Despite the AWS's union roots, the government has faced public sector strikes, particularly by professionals angered not only by below-average wages, but extensive reforms that additionally undermine their job security. In 1999, health workers went on strike, while teachers threatened industrial action at exam times in protest at the education reforms. Unlike industrial disputes, such as the railway strike in 1998, the professional sector's grievances have had widespread public support.

The Education Reforms

As the first European country to establish a dedicated education ministry, Poland has always placed great emphasis on learning. Literacy is nearly universal, and basic standards of numeracy are high, reflecting the bias towards scientific and technical studies. Language skills are also high: after the collapse of communism Russian ceased to be compulsory, with English taking over as the second language. The system adopted in Poland in 1950, while making universal education compulsory, imposed a rigid distinction between academic and vocational secondary education, with the latter geared towards training workers for key economic sectors such as heavy industry, agriculture and mining. Post-communist transition has exposed many skill shortages, especially in information technology, accounting, marketing and business education, although business and commercial studies now account for a quarter of all full- and part-time students. The existing vocational system, meanwhile, continues to train students for increasingly obsolete jobs. The reformed education system, which came into effect in September 1999 and is due to be implemented fully by 2004, extends compulsory education to age 18. From 15 years of age, students will be able (from September 2002) to opt for three years of further secondary education and then university education, or two years of vocational training. University and tertiary technical school students will also have the option of choosing either the existing five year master's degree, or finishing earlier with a three year bachelor's degree. The reforms will prove difficult to implement initially since the plan envisages a reduction in the number of teachers, in line with declining numbers of school entrants.

Corporate Taxation

Further Cuts Planned

The standard corporate income tax rate for 1999 was 34%, down from 36% in 1998. Following last year's tax reforms, it will fall to 30% in 2000 and incrementally to 22% by 2004. Tax rate changes apply as of January 1, to accounting years beginning on or after that date. Under Polish law corporate income tax is defined as gross profits less tax deductible costs. The latter are expenses incurred for the purpose of obtaining profit, such as depreciation of fixed or intangible assets. They specifically exclude expenditures incurred in acquiring fixed assets subject to depreciation, donations and similar contributions, and loan repayments, except capitalised interest. A number of items have limited deductibility, including depreciation and insurance of a passenger car (up to Ecu10,000 in each case) and representation and non mass-media advertising (up to 0.25% of profits).

The 1999 budget law introduced a number of changes to the corporate tax regime. The period over which losses can be offset against tax has been extended from three to five years, and up to half the total loss can be offset in any one year. In addition, companies that change their status from a limited liability entity (ZOO) to a joint stock company (SA) will now be able to retain the loss carry-forward. The advance monthly payments procedure for corporate tax has also been simplified: companies now have the option of using the average monthly profits of the first half of the previous year as the basis for monthly payments in the first six months of the current year.

At present various income tax incentives apply to firms located in the 17 Special Economic Zones (SEZs). For example, in some zones, firms that invest over a certain threshold are exempt from tax altogether. The government plans to phase out the zones by 2017, and under new proposals – which are unlikely to receive parliamentary approval this year – the financial inducements offered to new investors are to be cut back.

Personal Income Tax Stays Unchanged

Personal income tax rates for 2000 remain unchanged from 1999, at 19%, 30% and 40%, although the bands have been adjusted upward for inflation. For 2000, the thresholds are, up to PLN32,736; PLN32,736-65,472; and PLN65,472 respectively. Leszek Balcerowicz's initial proposals to streamline the tax regime by replacing the current progressive system with a flat 22% rate in 2000 (2002 for corporate taxation) have since been modified. The government wanted to reduce the top two tiers to 29% and 35% in 2000, and abolish the top rate by 2002, when the new regime would be 18% and 28%. The immediate revenue loss to the Treasury would be offset by the removal of various exemptions. In addition, from 2003 the government intends to introduce a 5% capital gains tax on unearned income, such as bank deposit interest. A capital gains tax on earnings from shares may come in even earlier. This would mark a further harmonisation of Polish and EU tax policy, and would go some way to deflecting criticism that the government's income tax proposals are only easing the tax burden for the middle-classes and the rich.

European Union Membership

EU Enlargement: A Shifting Timetable

In 1995, the then German chancellor, Helmut Kohl, predicted that Poland would be in the EU by 2000, a view shared by most Poles at the time. Two years later the European Commission recommended that Poland, along with Cyprus, the Czech Republic, Estonia, Hungary and Slovenia, be accepted for early accession talks to the union. Two key reports have charted aspirant countries' progress, while Poland has now pushed the entry date to 2003. The EU steadfastly refuses to commit itself to an entry date for any country. It has not clarified whether it will take all five "fast-track" countries together, along with any others that have made sufficient progress, or allow them to join as and when they satisfy the entry criteria.

Under the phased-entry scenario, the EU accepts Hungary, acknowledged as the country which has made the greatest strides, and one or two of the small countries, Slovenia and possibly Estonia. This scenario assumes that the cost of enlargement to the EU is the overriding factor, in which case Poland, whose population exceeds that of the other aspirant members combined, has virtually no chance of being accepted early. However, this makes little sense politically and would be a diplomatic nightmare should any EU defence issues arise, given that Poland is a member of Nato. There is also a school of thought that believes the younger generation of German politicians, under Chancellor Gerhard Schröder, no longer has any historical obligation towards Poland. This view assumes that the EU's initial conception of creating political stability in Europe has been completely overtaken by economic self-interest. Although successive EU summits have certainly given this impression, the Kosovo crisis refocused attention on the dangers of divisions within the continent. At the other extreme is the assumption that Poland has to be accepted by the EU because of its size and history. This view, which is common among many Poles, took a sharp knock in 1998 when the EU cut Poland's Phare reconstruction fund because it was being squandered on irrelevant projects. A more realistic compromise, administratively cheaper and politically more encompassing, takes in all "fast-track" countries together, provided that they have made sufficient progress, but not necessarily completed the changes recommended in the EC's 1997 Copenhagen report.

The entry date depends increasingly on the EU's ability to reform its internal finances and, in Poland's case, the Common Agricultural Policy (CAP). An unreformed CAP, which already eats up to 50% of the EU's budget, would bankrupt the union if applied to the new members, while a two-tier union would be politically unacceptable to the Poles and would create intolerable pressures within Brussels itself. The EU's ability to contemplate eastward enlargement is not likely before 2005, making 2006 the earliest entry date, although even this assumption errs on the side of optimism, given existing members' preoccupations with rebates and subsidies. Poland's progress in meeting the EU's entry requirements is as follows.

■ **Political Criteria**

Most of these had been fulfilled by the time of the 1997 Copenhagen report, while criticisms about the inadequacies of the civil service and the length of time taken for judicial procedures to be completed are being addressed.

■ **Economic Criteria**

EU membership demands a functioning market economy and the ability to cope with competitive and market pressures in the medium term. Poland meets the EU's definition of a functioning market economy. Outstanding issues include: Polish tariffs on steel, which have been dismantled more slowly than initially agreed in the 1994 Europe Agreement; a large grey economy, which needs to be brought into the formal sector to generate taxes;improved liberalisation of land sales. Poland's ability to cope with competitive pressures within the EU presents it with its biggest challenge as it first needs to restructure its coal and steel sectors, modernise its agriculture and improve its infrastructure. The Commission has singled out the growth of small and medium- sized enterprises as crucial to absorbing workers laid off as a result of restructuring, and urged that this sector get better access to finance and export assistance.

■ **Ability To Assume Membership Obligations.**

Poland's progress in being able to assume the obligations of the so-called *acquis communautaire*, the EU's legal and institutional framework, has been mixed. On the positive side, it has addressed the critical issue of steel reform by drawing up a plan within the EU's timeframe, and markedly improved security on its borders. On the other hand, progress on internal market legislation, state aid and environmental issues has been found wanting.

■ **Administrative Ability To Apply The** *Acquis Communautaire.*

According to the EC, Poland has found it difficult to implement improvements in its administrative structures, especially in strengthening the judiciary, and enforcing intellectual property rights, standards and certifications, and customs procedures, although it has made progress on regional development and financial control.

Industrial Policy

Coal And Steel Sectors Face Massive Restructuring

In 1998, the government launched the most controversial industrial restructuring policy since the end of the communist era, with plans to rationalise the steel and coal industries. The steel reforms are primarily a response to EU pressure on Polish protectionism of a large, but uncompetitive, industry. In return for a delay in postponing import duties, the government has promised to privatise the 12 of the 25 mills still in state hands by 2001, and cut the workforce from 90,000 to 50,000. In the coal sector, nearly half of the pits will be closed and the number of mining jobs cut from 246,000 to 138,000. Miners have been offered voluntary redundancy packages equivalent to 14.2 times annual salaries for those with alternative jobs prospects, and 24 times for those with no job prospects, as well as job-training programmes.

Privatisation Programme Heading Towards Completion

Poland has been relatively slow in privatising its large enterprises. The previous government paid a lot of lip service to the concept, except where banks were concerned, with the co-governing PSL generally hostile to privatisation, especially if foreign buyers were involved. The AWS-UW coalition's programme intended to have the major privatisations completed by 2001. While the UW was ideologically committed to privatisation, AWS support has been more equivocal. However, the sales are expected to progress as the government needs to maintain a high flow of privatisation revenues to finance structural reforms and the budget deficit.

In 1998, only 15 of the planned 50 flotations and strategic sales were completed. The largest were a 15% sale of **Bank Pekao**, raising US$230mn, and 15% in telecoms operator **Telekomunikacja Polska** (TPSA), which fetched US$625mn. The flotation of TPSA succeeded despite appalling market conditions caused by Russia's economic collapse. A further 25-35% of the company is due to be sold to a strategic investor in 2000. During 1999, key privatisations included a stake in state insurer **Powszechny Zaklad Upezpieczen (PZU),** a 52.1% stake in Pekao to a consortium of Italy's **Unicredito Italiano** and German insurer **Allianz** for PLN4.24bn. An 80% stake in **Bank Zachodni,** the last of the regional commercial banks to be privatised, was sold to **Allied Irish Banks** for PLN2.3bn. Other noteworthy sales included 20% of the **Patnow-Adamow-Konin** power generating complex to a consortium led by local conglomerate **Elektrim** for US$88mn, and a stake in **LOT Polish Airlines.**

Foreign Investment Policy

Incentives Are No Longer Necessary...

Most tax incentives, applied in the early post-communist days to induce foreign investors, are being scaled down as part of the general principle of equalising treatment for nationals and foreigners. Generous exemptions were once necessary as investors initially perceived Poland as a politically unstable country which had defaulted on its foreign debt, and opted instead to invest in Hungary and the Czech Republic. Since then Poland has rescheduled its debt, outstripped the rest of the region in economic growth, and driven home the point that, with nearly 39mn inhabitants, it has the largest consumer market in Central Europe. By the end of 1998, cumulative foreign investment had reached US$30.7bn according to PAIZ, the Polish Foreign Investment Office. Investment incentives are to be eliminated as the corporate income tax rate is reduced. Licence and patents implementation, use of recycled waste in inputs, ISO 9000 implementation, employment of handicapped personnel, and investment in the pharmaceuticals industry and areas of high unemployment all qualify for tax relief.

...Except In Special Economic Zones

The bulk of tax exceptions are now directed at Special Economic Zones (SEZ). Designed to create jobs in depressed industrial areas, the SEZs offer incentives such as tax holidays of up to 10 years and a further 50% for another 10 years, or six years in the case of technology parks, as well as accelerated depreciation, on condition that the company fulfils certain investment commitment criteria and creates a specified minimum number of jobs. The investment criteria range from Ecu0.35mn to Ecu2mn, and the number of jobs from 40 to 100. The tax breaks have enabled the zones to attract some significant investors, notably **General Motors**, which established a DM500mn car assembly plant in the Katowicka SEZ. In a number of zones, the tax breaks are negotiable rather than automatic, creating legal confusions.

Foreign Trade Policy

Keeping Up With International Obligations

Poland's foreign trade policy is directed by its international obligations. The 1992 Association Agreement (AA) with the EU obliged Poland to remove most of its industrial tariffs by 1999. The EU reciprocated by eliminating most of its tariffs on Polish goods in 1997. Poland was allowed certain exemptions on sensitive areas such as textiles, steel and food. Polish customs law was harmonised with EU regulations in 1997. Following ratification of its WTO agreement in 1995, Poland committed to reducing industrial tariffs to 10% to 1999 (2005 for textiles). Customs tariff reductions on industrial goods have accelerated, and averaged 7.7% in 1999.

EU Requirements Lead To Hard Bargaining

Poland has progressively dismantled most industrial tariffs within the AA framework with the notable exception of steel. Although originally obliged to reduce import duties to 3% in 1998, Poland instead negotiated an extension (to 4% in July 1998, 3% in 1999 and elimination in 2000) in return for restructuring the steel sector. EU trade in agricultural goods will remain a contentious issue, with Poland operating at a distinct disadvantage. In 1998, Polish dairy products were temporarily banned by the EU for failing to meet hygiene standards. At the end of 1998, after the economic collapse in Russia (hitherto the EU's second-largest food market after the US), the EU diverted subsidised pork into Poland, leading to widespread protests and blockades by local farmers, which the government eventually settled through intervention purchases.

Polish moves to harmonise tariffs with the EU have led to complaints from the US about increasing protectionism. In order to support the American off-road vehicle industry, the US lobbied, with some success, for equal treatment with the EU on import duties for large cars.

Is Cefta Set To Wither?

The Central European Free Trade Agreement (Cefta) was established in December 1992 by the Czech Republic, Hungary, Poland and Slovakia, with Slovenia joining in 1996, Romania in 1997 and Bulgaria in 1998. Cefta's objective was to establish a free-trade zone, with the elimination of all tariffs, by 2001. Members of the bloc subsequently agreed to push the deadline on industrial goods forward to January 2000, and around 80% of tariffs have been eliminated, unlike agricultural goods, where only 50% of tariffs have been removed. Agricultural trade has been a continual source of dispute among Cefta members, which to a large extent compete with each other in the same product markets.

When the European Commission recommended the inclusion of the Czech Republic, Hungary, Poland and Slovenia for early accession to the EU, Cefta's progress on removing outstanding barriers slowed down. EU membership and conditions would supersede those applying to Cefta and other trade agreements, raising the question of whether the bloc will survive once some or all of the four EU "fast-track" countries join up. Hungary is already talking about leaving Cefta, while other countries cited as potential members, for example Lithuania and Croatia, have lost interest. In many respects Cefta has failed to raise trade between member countries to the initially anticipated levels. Cefta's share of Polish trade has grown only marginally, from around 5.4% of exports and 5.6% of imports in 1995, to 7.2% and 6.4% respectively in 1998, while the deficit has increased by 158% to US$978.9mn. However, the trade bloc has given the countries involved practical experience in negotiating with trade partners to increase free trade, experience that could prove invaluable as EU accession approaches.

Bureaucracy And Corruption

Administrative Reforms Will Redistribute Wealth

The controversial 1998 administrative reforms were applauded by the European Commission as a means of redistributing wealth throughout the regions and decentralising government. The reforms replaced the former 49 administrative regions with 16 *voivodships* (provinces), 373 *powiats* (counties) and 2,489 *gminas* or local councils. Between them the three tiers of local government will now get 60% of tax revenues as opposed to 20% in the past. The new system will make the provinces, counties and councils less dependent on ministerial contacts for extracting financing, and one of its objectives was to reduce institutional corruption

Draft Licensing Law Should Reduce Corruption

Poland's licensing law, a long-time headache for companies, previously required licences for 28 types of businesses. As well as being cumbersome, the system was open to abuse. A draft law approved on business activity, approved by Parliament in November 1999, reduced the number of sectors where a licence is required to eight, including: mining and exploration of underground resources, explosives, liquid fuels, security services, air transport and the construction and operation of toll motorways. Some other activities that previously required a licence now only require a permit, for instance tobacco and alcohol producers, telecommunications providers, television broadcasting companies, international freight companies and tourist firms. The requirements for permits are clearly defined and the procedures for obtaining them more transparent than for licences.

Intellectual Property Rights

Enforcement Remains Patchy

Poland is a signatory to most of the international treaties on property rights, including the Paris convention on industrial ownership, the Berne convention on literary and artistic works, the Madrid arrangement on trademarks, the Stockholm arrangement on ownership of intellectual ideas, and the World Institute for Protection of Intellectual Property. Patents and trademarks must be filed with the Polish Patent Office, with foreign companies obliged to use a Polish patents agent. Patents last 20 years from the filing date, while trademarks have a 10-year shelf-life, unless the mark is not used for three consecutive years. Trademarks can also be licensed. The 1994 law on copyrights extended protection to areas such as computer software and audio-visual work, as well as traditional areas such as artistic and literary works. It also brought Poland into line with international norms by extending the period of protection covered from 25 to 50 years. However, according to the European Commission's 1998 report, no significant improvements on copyright legislation have occurred since 1994. Despite the many laws and conventions, enforcement remains weak in a number of areas because of lack of resources and expertise. Infringement is no longer as blatant as was the case in the early-1990s, but remains rampant in areas such as software and audio-visual recordings, which are notoriously difficult to police in any country. The US has estimated that some 75% of software in Poland is pirated, and has frequently registered complaints about infringement of audio-visual rights.

Environmental Regulation

The EU Sets A High Price

Poland suffered substantial ecological degradation during the communist era, when environmental issues were viewed as an obstruction to industrial development or a source of political opposition. Poland's environmental programmes are now driven largely by the need to comply with EU directives, although the European Commission has criticised the lack of progress on improving drinking water and air quality, reducing chemical pollution and lack of regulation on noise pollution. Expenditure on environmental improvement totalled US$2.2bn in 1997, but the environment ministry believes a further US$500mn a year will be necessary if Poland is to meet EU standards by 2010. Since Poland does not have any nuclear reactors, Soviet-built or otherwise, it has at least been spared the decommissioning costs that many of its neighbours face to meet EU, and more specifically German Green Party, demands.

Law On Waste Makes The Polluter Pay

The law on waste management, which came into effect in January 1998, is a landmark piece of environmental legislation, putting the financial onus on the producers of waste rather than the municipal authorities who play host to it. The law's provisions include fees for storing waste, which will be levied according to the nature of the waste and the length of time it is stored. All waste-producing companies must obtain a waste disposal licence, while those producing more than 1,000 tonnes of waste each year will require a licence to continue production. Packaging manufacturers must label their materials. Tax incentives have also been introduced to encourage recycling.

5 Capital Markets

Introduction

Gaining In Strength

The development of stable capital markets and a domestic investor base have been integral parts of economic planning since 1989, with the largest privatisations always involving a flotation on the Warsaw Stock Exchange. Although the size of capital markets in relationship to the economy are still small by Western standards, with total turnover in the equity market equivalent to 15% of GDP in 1999 compared with an average of around 30% in Western Europe, they are providing an alternative to banks in enabling companies to raise finance, and households to channel their savings. There has been a strong emphasis on investor protection and transparency. The Polish Securities and Exchange Commission (KPW), which vets all publicly traded securities, is closely modelled on the US's Securities and Exchange Commission, and is generally regarded as the strictest body of its type in the region, if not Europe itself. Although Polish securities regulations were initially criticised as draconian, and in terms of sheer number of listed stock Poland has never matched the Russian and Czech markets, they have also helped avoid those countries' abuses of corporate governance as well as defaults by listed companies.

The global crises of 1997-98 provided Central Europe with its first major exposure to the volatility inherent in global markets, and the divergent behaviour of equity and bond investors. On the equity market, Poland trades on fundamentals in stable times thanks to good liquidity and high disclosure requirements, but remains an emerging market during crises. Prices were volatile throughout 1997, with sharp falls due to the Czech koruna devaluation in the spring and the Asian crisis in the autumn, followed by rebounds on the back of regionally strong economic growth. A further surge in Q1 98 was wiped out after the Russian collapse in August 1998, which caused a massive exodus from all Central and East European markets, regardless of their relative economic fundamentals. In the bond market, investors have focused on EU convergence and the preparation of the five "fast-track" Central European aspirants for membership of the union and ultimately monetary union. Yields on Polish five-year dollar-denominated bonds shot up from 13% to over 16% in the aftermath of the Russian devaluation, but by the end of the year were down to 10%, a pattern mirrored by Hungarian and Czech bonds. The Polish government even used the temporary fall in debt prices to buy back US$750mn of its Brady bonds and reduce its outstanding debt to international commercial bank creditors. Concern over an economic collapse in Brazil in the early part of 1999 barely made an impression, with Polish debt rising by only 20 basis points. Interest rate hikes from November 1999 to February 2000 have created favourable yield differentials over other European countries and enticed substantial inflows into Polish securities. Unlike stock investors, the bond market has made a clear distinction between countries in danger of default, such as Romania, and those in the clear, such as Poland. This reflects the growing tendency for investors to evaluate each country on its own merits rather than treating emerging markets as a distinct asset class.

Pensions Funds Boost Liquidity

Markets that lack domestic institutional investors are doomed to remain speculative, but post-communist Poland has yet to build up a sufficiently large middle-class to channel savings into institutional funds. The pension reforms, which came into effect in April 1999, will provide a massive stimulus for local capital markets by creating a pool of domestic investors, as well as a compulsory form of savings for employees. Having received around US$975mn in premiums by March 2000, pension funds are expected to grow to US$10bn by 2003. The government bond market will be the first beneficiary of the pensions revolution, since they offer the most secure investments with no limits on how much of its assets a second pillar fund, managing compulsory private pensions investment, can invest in them. The government will also benefit from a cheaper source of financing, since the new pool of demand will inevitably drive yields down. Nevertheless, pension funds can also invest up to 40% of their assets in equities, which is generous by comparison with the Latin American funds that provided the template for Polish pension reforms. Since second-pillar funds that under-perform the weighted average benchmark will be penalised financially, they are expected to follow conservative strategies, opting for larger, more liquid stocks, and using indexing and other passive techniques. Overall, they are expected to stabilise the Polish capital markets, since even in a major crisis they cannot abandon them: only 20% of their assets can go into bank deposits, and 5% overseas.

Equity Markets

Warsaw Stock Exchange Dominates The Region

Founded in 1817 and closed down in 1939 after the Nazi invasion, the Warsaw Stock Exchange reopened for trading in 1991 as a paperless electronic bourse in the former headquarters of the Polish Communist Party. The combined total of listed companies on the main, parallel and free market has increased from 83 at the end of 1996 to 221 at end-1999 – 15 of which are National Investment Funds. Total market capitalisation rose from PLN24bn at end-1996 to PLN123.4bn at end-1999. In addition, the exchange lists futures and warrants and Treasury bonds.

Trading is executed through either single-price auctions, continuous trading of round lots of shares, or off-session block trades of a minimum PLN300,000. Settlement is on a T+3 basis and delivery versus payment through the National Depositary for Securities. All trades must be conducted through licensed stockbrokers and a new law on public securities trading, which came into effect in January 1998, allowed foreign brokers from OECD countries to trade on the exchange. Companies can list on either the main, parallel or free market depending on the issue size and disclosure. The main-market stock indexes, the composite WIG Index and the WIG 20 Index, which represents the largest and most liquid companies, are based on price, while the WRR is a total return index for companies on the parallel market. Main market companies must submit a full prospectus and abide by onerous disclosure requirements that include monthly and quarterly financial reports. With global interest in technology stocks high, the bourse added an all-tech index to its collection of sectoral indices (telecoms, banks, construction and food) in May 2000. In addition, TechWIG index investment units, aimed at smaller investors, are due to be launched by end-2000. Technology and telecom stocks account for over 35% of market capitalisation. To make new issues more attractive, in 1998 allotment certificates were introduced to enable investors who have been allocated rights to new shares but have not yet received the certificates, to sell their rights before the stocks begin trading on the exchange.

Privatisations Supply The Largest Stocks

The supply of stocks depended initially on privatisation flotations, but has subsequently been augmented by private companies and listings from small companies in the Mass Privatisation Programme managed by the National Investment Funds. With bank privatisation moving faster than other sectors in the economy, the exchange was initially overweight in banking stocks. The banking sector at end-1999 still accounted for 28% of total market capitalisation, but its weighting has fallen since the flotation of the telephone giant **Telekomiunikacja Polska (TPSA)**. By number of companies, the construction sector is the largest with 37 stocks. Flotations are an integral part of the privatisation of the larger companies. Of the 28 new companies listed in 1999, oil company **Polski Koncern Naftowy** (PKN) was the largest, boosting market capitalisation by around PLN3bn. The listing of **Agora**, the media conglomerate, which owns *Gazeta Wyborcza*, Poland's best-selling daily, also proved to be popular with investors. The issue raised PLN373mn. Key expected Initial Public Offerings (IPOs) in 2000 include state insurer **PZU**, telecoms company **Netia** and petrochemicals firm **Rafineria Gdanska**.

One concern for the exchange is that foreign companies with majority stakes may de-list their Polish subsidiaries to save themselves the expense and effort of abiding by the regular disclosure requirements, a precedent established in 1998 by **PepsiCo** – which removed its subsidiary **E. Wedel** prior to breaking up the company and selling off its confectionery and biscuits divisions.

NIFs Set To Consolidate

Poland's mass privatisation programme (MPP), which placed 512 smaller companies under the management of 15 National Investment Funds (NIFs), provided investors with additional classes of securities. The certificates, which Poles could acquire for a nominal PLN20, could be traded on the exchange, sold via bank brokerages or exchanged into one share in the 15 NIFs. The certificates expired at the end of 1998, by which time around 25.6mn of the 26mn issued had been converted, although by no means by their original owners, most of whom took advantage of the rapid price rise (to a peak of PLN165 in February 1997) and sold. By the end of 1998, 52 companies in the programme had made it on to either the WSE or the over-the-counter market, while another 133 were sold to strategic investors and 34 liquidated. The NIFs themselves were listed on the WSE in June 1997, but most have not performed well. The NIF index ended 1999 down on 1998's level by 7.6%. Lack of transparency, the complexity of the MPP, quarrels between the NIF's supervisory boards and their fund managers, as well as the fact that the healthier companies in the programme with the fewest restructuring problems have been sold off, all combined to depress prices. At the same time, a few key investors have built up stakes in several funds, including the Polish banks **Pekao** and **Bank Rozwoju Eksportu**, Polish insurer **Powszechny Zaklad Ubezpieczen (PZU)**, the US hedge funds **Everest** and **Baupost**, the US fund management group **Arnold and Bleischroder**, Polish venture capital fund **Copernicus**, and **Credit Suisse First Boston**. With a number of the investors operating in alliance, it is widely assumed that the NIFs themselves are set for consolidation to reduce operating costs and maximise value.

Tech Stocks Drive Bourse in 2000

Although foreign institutional investors have traditionally accounted for only 30% of investments in WSE equities, a relatively low proportion compared with other Eastern European bourses, stock prices still fell victim to the crises that started with the Asian collapse in 1997, and moved closer home in August 1998 when Russia's economy disintegrated. The Russian crisis had the most profound effect in the exchange's short post-communist history. In the two weeks following the August 17 rouble devaluation, the WIG index lost nearly 25% of its value, at one point reaching a low not seen since February 1996.

Equity market sentiment remained indifferent throughout much of 1999. Alongside the overhang of Russia's economic collapse from the previous year, and the likelihood of poor corporate earnings results, the Polish market faced an additional regional factor: a severe economic slowdown throughout Eastern and Central Europe. Apart from dedicated regional funds, institutional investors cut their asset allocation for the region as a whole, without necessarily differentiating among the stronger economies, the weaker ones, and the hopeless. However, Polish stocks made a minor recovery in Q1 99, with the upward trend accelerating during the summer as economic data started to improve. The main WIG index ended the year 41% up on 1998's level, and market capitalisation rose 70%.

Certain sectors – notably banking and telecoms/IT – and stocks have outperformed the market in general. TPSA is an obvious key stock for several reasons. Its large weighting in the main and benchmark indexes inevitably pushes it into any Polish core portfolio, and it is on course to acquire strategic investors and investment in 2000. In addition, Poland's low teledensity means high future growth potential. On the other hand, the coming liberalisation of the telecoms market will expose it to greater competition from private fixed-line operators. IT companies are still a sunrise industry in Poland, with those specialising in services and software development rather than hardware manufacture capitalising on project implementation for numerous ministries, government agencies, local government offices and banks. Indeed, if one sector was firing enthusiasm in H1 00 it was IT and especially those companies with an internet presence. February saw the all-share WIG index leap to record highs on several occasions, fuelled by an injection from pension funds into high-growth sectors, in addition to global interest. However, the latter meant that the market suffered as a result of NASDAQ's wobble in May as investor sentiment for technology, media and telecoms stocks took a turn for the worse.

Mergers and acquisitions play a key part in WSE activity. In 1997, **Carlsberg** acquired **Okocim** via a friendly takeover, while in 1998 nine tenders were launched through the exchange. In 1999, activity revved up, with UK paint manufacturer **Kalon** taking advantage of **Polifarb Cieszyn-Wroclaw**'s languishing stock price to complete a hostile takeover, while Sweden's **Alcro-Beckers** launched a tender offer for **Polifarb Debica** in March 1999. The fragmented construction industry, with 35 companies listed on the WSE, is ripe for mergers.

CeTO Has Been Struggling

Centralna Tabela Ofert (CeTO), the over-the-counter (OTC) stock market, was established in 1996 to enable smaller, dynamic companies to list, including those from the MPP. Unlike the WSE, which demands financial accounts covering three years and a full prospectus for listing, a CeTO quotation requires accounts for only one year and an information memorandum approved by the SEC. The first company, machine-tool manufacturer **Rafamet**, listed in December 1996, but CeTO's growth since then has fallen far short of expectations, with only 14 securities trading by the end of 1997 and 37 a year later. The massive inflow of stock from the NIF-run MPP has yet to materialise. It has taken fund managers longer than envisaged to restructure the companies. It has also proven more cost-effective for the NIF managers to sell companies directly to strategic buyers than incur the expenses of preparing memoranda and marketing campaigns only to risk a flop on a market plagued by poor liquidity and low investor interest. CeTO has broadened its range of offerings to include warrants, convertibles, and treasury and municipal bonds, as well as shares. The quotation of a fixed-rate treasury bond series in July 1998, followed by another in October boosted turnover and pulled CeTO out of financial difficulties, but the market has yet to reach an essential critical mass. IPOs by small IT companies was a key feature of the OTC market in 1999.

Derivatives

Still Emerging

In Poland's highly regulated market, equity derivatives have had a slow and chequered career. In 1995, **Polish Development Bank**, now part of **Bank Rozwoju Eksportu** (BRE), was forced to withdraw its OTC options on the WIG index after objections from the WSE and Polish Securities and Exchange Commission. Ötob, the Austrian futures and options exchange, which has since merged with the Vienna Stock Exchange, beat the Poles by introducing dollar-denominated futures on its own index of Polish equities alongside Hungarian and Czech ones. In January 1998, the WSE finally introduced futures on the WIG 20 index. BRE, as issuer, followed up with European-style (exercisable on the expiry date) call warrants on the NIF index and shares in Poland's largest conglomerate **Elektrim**. BRE also used CeTO to launch American-style (exercisable up to and on the expiry date) call warrants on two separate indexes, on WSE-traded blue-chips and banks. The Polish brokerage **Beskidzki Dom Maklerski** subsequently introduced warrants on **KGHM Polish Copper** onto CeTO. Unlike the CeTO index warrants, the KGHM warrants offered puts (right to sell) as well as calls (right to buy), giving investors the chance to profit from price falls as well as rises, and have thus proved more popular.

Equity market development of derivatives has been hampered by rather basic impediments. Continuous trading for stocks was only introduced in June 1996 as a pilot project for five shares, although an increasing number of the more liquid stocks now trade through this system rather than the single price auction system. More fundamentally, short-selling was still not allowed in 1999. The WSE's WIG 20 index futures have nevertheless proved reasonably successful, outstripping their Austrian rivals despite a later start. Trading volume in 1999 was eight times higher than that in 1998. Futures contracts on the TechWIG index are to be introduced in Q3 00.

Currency and interest rate derivatives have also grown slowly. With the zloty still not convertible for capital account purposes, it has been difficult to develop a liquid market. The new foreign currency legislation introduced in January 1999, while further easing currency convertibility restrictions on the zloty, was a retrograde law in other respects. It rules that banks trading derivatives must obtain a licence, and it failed to allow foreign investors to trade directly. Corporate interest has been hampered by a lack of understanding of risk management, although those that deal in dollar-denominated products, such as the shipbuilders, have run a heavy currency risk exposure, especially in 1996-97 when the zloty appreciated strongly in real terms against the dollar. Non-deliverable forwards and foreign exchange options are traded, largely in London, and are based on a synthetic zloty constructed from its composite basket. A number of Polish banks started trading cash-settled zloty forward rate agreements (short-term interest rate forwards) in mid-1998 fixed against Wibor (Warsaw Interbank Offered Rate) although these are only available to foreign investors. The WSE introduced its own zloty-US dollar futures in September 1998 and plans to launch bond and interest rate contracts. Also in September 1998, a number of banks launched the electronic interbank PGF derivatives exchange. PGF trades 12-month euro and dollar futures as well as three-month contracts on three-month Wibor.

Bonds

Attractive Yields Entice Investors

Since its first treasury bond issue in 1989, the Polish government debt market had grown to over PLN100bn in volume outstanding by the end of 1999. Short-term treasury bills, with maturities ranging from eight to 52 weeks, are used primarily for liquidity management in the banking system by the National Bank of Poland through repo and reverse-repo operations. They are issued as discount securities and settle through the National Bank of Poland. Tradeable Treasury bonds totalled PLN71bn at the end of 1999. The main instruments are two- and five-year fixed rate bonds. In the addition there is a one-year bond indexed to the consumer-price index and three- and 10-year floating rate bonds priced off the average T-bill rate. High interest rates prior to mid-1998 made the issuance of longer-dated fixed rate issues unattractive. However, from mid-1998 to early-1999 the National Bank of Poland embarked on a series of aggressive rate cuts to stimulate the economy, making longer-dated issues feasible. In May 1999, the Finance Ministry issued its first 10-year fixed-rate bond. In addition, the newly created pension funds, as well as existing insurance companies, have created a demand for longer-dated assets to match-fund their liabilities.

Secondary trading of both bills and bonds takes place on the WSE. The major difference is that bills clear and settle through the central bank, while bonds settle through the National Securities Depository and must be transacted by a local broker, a procedure which foreign investors regard as cumbersome. However, the National Bank of Poland is lobbying to take over bond settlement and clearance. Foreign investors can participate in both the bill and bond markets. Investors in countries with whom Poland has not signed a double-taxation treaty are subject to a 40% capital gains tax on income and a 20% withholding tax on accrued interest. Foreign investors were highly active in the bill and bond markets throughout 1997 and the earlier part of 1998, accounting for up to 20% of total investment. Their participation had shrunk to around 10% by Q1 99 as rate cuts pushed yields down, but investors were enticed back into the market in early-2000 by strong yield differentials. Meanwhile, Polish bonds became the first in Central and Eastern Europe to be included in **JP Morgan**'s Government Bond Index in June 2000, with a weighting of 0.1% of the total index.

Corporate Bonds Are Starting To Take Off...

As in other capital markets, a successful treasury bond programme can crowd out non-government issuers. This has been the case in Polish corporate debt, where returns for most classes of investors such as bank and corporate treasuries are taxed as regular income, although pension fund investors will be exempt. However, it will take more than tax incentives to boost the corporate bond market. With several corporate debt laws in place, under either the commercial or civil code, issuers incur high legal costs simply deciding on which structure is the most appropriate. The most successful corporate debt market is commercial paper, which has been issued since 1992, usually for funding short-term working capital. Maturities extend out to one year, and the paper can be issued either with a fixed coupon or discounted, and in denominations of up to PLN100,000. Issuers include a significant number of Polish-based multinationals such as **Ford Motor Credit Europe**, **McDonalds**, **Peugeot** and **Fiat**, as well local entities such as cement producer **Gorazdze** and **Elbrewery**. Robust commercial paper issuance drove outstanding short-term debt up 28% in Q1 00 to PLN8.5bn. Outstanding corporate debt stood at PLN11bn. The outlook for the market is rosy since the legislation covering corporate bonds is being amended in 2000 to ease bond insurance requirements.

...Along With Municipal Bonds

The municipal bond market has been in existence since January 1996 when Gdynia raised PLN28mn through a multi-tranche issue to finance transport development. The number of issuers has increased markedly, as has the size of the bonds. Most municipal bond issues are arranged as private placements. In 1998 Krakow issued the largest municipal bond at the time, for PLN138mn, while later in the year Gdynia broke the record with a PLN206.3mn issue. Both issues were raised to fund road improvement. As a result of the 1998 administrative reforms, municipalities have far greater discretion in raising their finance and numerous environmental, housing and infrastructure projects to fund, which augurs well for the municipal bond market.

Foreign-Denominated Bonds Increasingly Popular

Poland re-entered the international capital markets in 1995 after rescheduling its Paris Club (sovereign) and London Club (international bank) debts. It tapped the eurobond market in 1995 with a US$250mn five-year issue, followed by a DEM250mn five-year bond in 1996 and a two-tranche US$400mn Yankee in June 1997. Further issues were put on ice after the 1997 Asian crisis started pushing yields up. However, a number of non-sovereign borrowers braved the markets in the aftermath of the Russian collapse in August 1998. City of Krakow issued a DEM66mn two-year floating rate note, LOT Polish Airlines a US$100mn five-year floating rate note, and TPSA, which issued US$1bn at the end of 1998, US$200mn as five-year bonds and US$800mn as 10-year bonds. The state returned to the international market in March 2000, launching a EUR600mn bond. Poland has a BBB+ rating from **Standard & Poor's** (uppgraded a notch in May 2000), a Baa1 from **Moody's** and a BBB+ from **Fitch IBCA**.

RUSSIA 2000

Analyst: Ann-Louise Hagger

Editor: Anthony Cooke

Contents

Political Outlook _____ **661**

Domestic Political Outlook 661
Foreign Policy 664

Profile and Recent Developments _____ **666**

Political System And Main Parties 666
Foreign Policy 669

Economic Outlook _____ **671**

Overview 671
Economic Activity 671
Fiscal Policy 673
Monetary And Exchange Rate Policy 675
Balance Of Payments 677
External Debt 678

Profile and Recent Developments _____ **680**

Characteristics Of The Economy 680
Economic Activity 681
Fiscal Policy 682
Monetary Policy 684
Exchange Rate Policy 685
The Balance Of Payments 686
Foreign Direct Investment 687
External Debt 688

Key Economic Sectors _____ **691**

Overview 691
Electricity 692
Gas 694
Agriculture 696

Profile and Recent Developments _____ **698**

Agriculture 698
Energy Sector 699
Metals, Gold & Diamonds 702
Telecommunications 703
Banking And Finance 704

Business Environment _____ 707

Introduction 707
Infrastructure 707
The Domestic Market 708
The Labour Market 709
Corporate Taxation 710
Industrial Policy 710
Foreign Investment Policy 711
Foreign Trade Policy 712
Bureaucracy And Corruption 713
Intellectual Property Rights 713
Environmental Regulation 714

Capital Markets _____ 715

The Equity Market 715
The Bond Market 716

Russian Regions _____ 719

Introduction 719
The Drive Towards Decentralisation 720
The Geography Of Russia 721
The Russian Regions 722

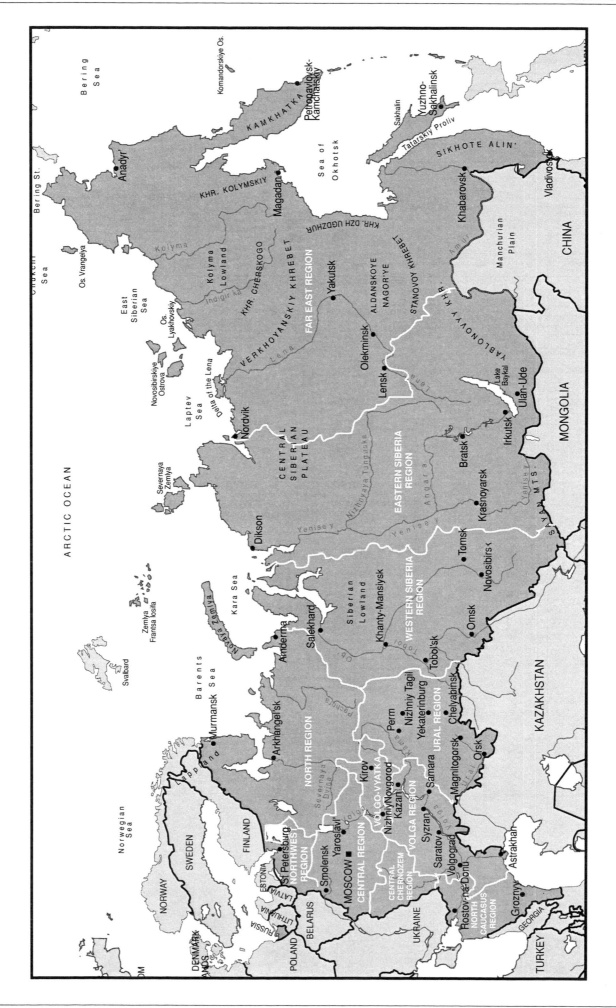

RUSSIA: MACROECONOMIC DATA AND FORECASTS

	1993	1994	1995	1996	1997	1998	1999	2000f	2001f	2002f
Population (mn)	148.2	148.0	148.1	147.7	147.1	146.5	145.8	145.3	144.8	144.3
Nominal GDP (RUBbn)	172	611	1,541	2,146	2,479	2,696	4,546	5,720	6,740	7,840
Nominal GDP (US$bn)	172.9	278.7	337.9	419.0	428.5	277.8	184.6	202.5	221.0	234.0
GDP per capita (US$)	1,167	1,883	2,282	2,837	2,913	1,896	1,266	1,394	1,526	1,622
Real GDP growth, % y-o-y	-8.7	-13.0	-4.0	-3.4	0.9	-4.9	3.2	4.8	2.5	3.0
Industrial production (% y-o-y, period average)	-14.1	-20.9	-3.3	-4.0	2.0	-5.2	8.1	5.5	4.0	5.0
ILO unemployment (%, end period)	6.1	7.8	9.0	10.0	11.2	13.3	12.1	11.5	11.0	14.0
Primary fiscal balance (RUBbn)	-	-	-30.6	-48.8	-65.4	-27.4	88.4	228.8	235.9	196.0
Primary fiscal balance (% of GDP)	-	-	-2.0	-2.3	-2.6	-1.0	1.9	4.0	3.5	2.5
Federal budget balance (RUBbn)	-	-	-85.2	-173.3	-183.2	-134.2	-74.2	0.0	-33.7	-39.2
Federal budget balance (% of GDP)	-	-	-5.5	-8.1	-7.4	-5.0	-1.6	0.0	-0.5	-0.5
Consumer prices (% y-o-y, end period)	839.9	215.1	131.3	21.8	11.0	84.4	36.5	16.0	14.0	12.0
Consumer prices (% y-o-y, period average)	874.6	307.6	197.5	47.7	14.7	27.7	85.7	20.0	15.0	13.0
Exchange rate (RUB/US$, end period)	1.247	3.550	4.640	5.560	5.960	20.650	27.000	29.000	32.000	35.000
Exchange rate (RUB/US$, period average)	0.992	2.191	4.559	5.121	5.785	9.705	24.620	28.250	30.500	33.500
Refinance rate (% per annum, end period)	210.0	180.0	160.0	48.0	28.0	60.0	55.0	30.0	27.0	25.0
Money supply, M2 (RUBmn, end period)	32,601	97,800	220,800	288,300	374,100	448,300	704,700	1,092,285	1,419,971	1,774,964
Money supply, M2 (% y-o-y, end period)	409.4	200.0	125.8	33.7	26.7	19.8	57.2	55.0	30.0	25.0
Customs exports (fob, US$bn)	44.3	67.5	81.1	88.6	88.2	74.2	74.7	89.6	83.3	86.8
Customs imports (cif, US$bn)	32.8	50.5	60.8	68.8	73.7	59.1	40.4	44.4	49.6	57.0
Customs trade balance (fob-cif, US$bn)	11.5	17.0	20.2	19.8	14.5	15.1	34.3	45.2	33.7	29.8
Current account balance (US$bn)	12.79	8.85	8.03	12.45	2.55	1.04	24.96	38.22	25.70	21.45
Current account (% of GDP)	7.4	3.2	2.4	3.0	0.6	0.4	13.5	18.9	11.6	9.2
Foreign debt stock (US$bn, end period)	111.73	121.48	120.44	125.17	125.65	145.00	155.00	149.00	152.00	156.00
Foreign debt stock (% of GDP, end period)	64.6	43.6	35.6	29.9	29.3	52.2	84.0	73.6	68.8	66.7
Foreign exchange reserves (US$bn)	5.8	4.0	14.4	11.3	12.9	7.8	8.5	20.0	22.0	23.0
Import cover (months)	-	0.7	1.9	1.4	1.5	1.0	1.6	4.2	4.2	3.9

e/f = BMI estimate/forecast. Source: CBR/IMF/Russian Economic Trends/Goskomstat/BMI.

1 Political Outlook

Domestic Political Outlook

The New Government Is In Place

The formal transition to the Putin era is now complete, and the new administration has had time to show some of its colours through the policies it has begun to implement. On the economic front, these policies are mildly encouraging, but in the political arena there is cause for concern.

Putin has to a large extent favoured continuity in government, but the cabinet's economic team has taken on an encouraging liberal bent.

Vladimir Putin has favoured a large element of continuity in government. Under the terms of the constitution, the cabinet is obliged to resign when a new president comes to power. As widely anticipated, Putin followed his inauguration on May 7 by naming first deputy prime minister and finance minister, Mikhail Kasyanov, as his candidate for the premiership. After Kasyanov's overwhelming approval by a significantly more pro-president parliament than under Yeltsin, Putin reappointed the defence, foreign, interior, justice and emergencies ministers to their posts. Some fresh faces were brought to the cabinet's economic team, however, in the form of Alexei Kudrin as finance minister and German Gref as minister for economic development and trade.

Kasyanov had already been acting as first deputy prime minister since January, and as finance minister since May 1999 under the governments of both Sergei Stepashin and Putin. He is a 42-year-old technocrat with liberal economic views who is well known in Western circles from his leading role in Russia's foreign debt negotiations in recent years. Along with the appointment of Kudrin – an economist who as deputy minister at the finance ministry had had the run of things there since Kasyanov's promotion to deputy prime minister – and Gref – another economist heading the Strategic Research Centre charged by Putin to devise an economic programme for the country – the cabinet has taken on an encouraging liberal economic bent. The government has already shown its reformist mettle through its firm support for tax reform and by targeting a balanced budget in 2001 for the first time in Russia's post-communist history. The economic programme finally approved by the government at the end of June after much delay is accordingly just the sort of thing investors want to hear (*see Key Economic Sectors*), although its implementation is another matter.

Are The Gloves Off?

The temporary arrest of leading businessman Vladimir Gusinsky on allegations of embezzlement, and his incarceration in Moscow's most notorious prison, has raised questions about freedom of expression and even the future of Russia's fledgling democracy under the new regime. It has also brought to the fore familiar but disconcerting questions about who is actually running the country. Putin, who was on a trip to Western Europe at the time of the arrest, claims to have had no prior knowledge of one of the most dramatic developments of his rule so far.

It is difficult to avoid the conclusion that the Gusinsky affair was designed as an attack on those most outspoken against the Kremlin. Gusinsky is deemed an "oligarch" and at the heart of his business empire lies the **Media-Most** holding company, the country's only independent media group. Media-Most's organs have been unusually critical of the Putin administration, charging it with heavy-handedness and, in particular, opposing the campaign in Chechnya.

If this is the shape of things to come, it may undermine parliamentary support for the government and hinder relations with the West, although the latter have not been too badly affected by the Chechen campaign. Cause for concern though the whole development is, for the moment it is presumptuous to argue that this is the beginning of a drastic whittling away of Russian democracy, flawed though it already is. The substantial backlash to Gusinsky's arrest from various areas of Russian society, including from other oligarchs and from abroad, is likely to have taken its initiators by surprise. Putin was quick to claim that things had gone too far, and Gusinsky was suddenly released from prison after three days, although the charges still stand.

Hot on the heals of the Gusinsky affair, the request from the Moscow prosecutor's office that the 1995 privatisation of metals giant **Norilsk Nickel** – the nub of oligarch Vladimir Potanin's Interros empire – effectively be reversed has raised the prospect that Putin may, against most expectations, be acting on his pledge to crack down on the oligarchs. Yet it is still not clear whether what has undeniably become a succession of *sorties* against individual oligarchs recently is a case of the oligarchs being targeted as a group – which would on the whole send out a positive signal about Russia's political development under Putin – or whether it is just a number of oligarchs

The arrest of businessman Vladimir Gusinsky has raised concerns about an increasingly hardline approach under the new administration. Combined with the Norilsk Nickel affair, it could suggest that Putin is fulfilling his pledge to crack down on the oligarchs, but to date it is not clear whether the oligarchs as a group or just certain individuals are being targeted.

who may have fallen foul of the administration who have cause for alarm. The Norilsk Nickel affair also has possible implications for the business operating environment (*see Key Economic Sectors*).

The issue of who is pulling the strings in Russia achieved particular prominence during the dying days of the Yeltsin regime. The suspicion is that the group of individuals surrounding Yeltsin – the so-called "family" – who had profited from his term in office, plucked Putin from relative obscurity to be Russia's new president in order to safeguard their position. Recent events have heightened the feeling that this very same group is still at work, and some have suggested that Putin's Chief of Staff, Alexander Voloshin, who has retained his influence from the Yeltsin years, may have been behind Gusinsky's arrest. The arrest was also a personal triumph for the most notorious of Russia's oligarchs and a bitter foe of Gusinsky, Boris Berezovsky, who is said to have close ties with Voloshin and be a member of the "family". He is also said to have links with Kasyanov.

Putin Moves Against The Regions

In line with his stated desire to boost the influence of the state, Putin has been quick to define his policy towards Russia's sometimes unruly regions – some of which are more or less run as the personal fiefdom of the local governor. He has issued a decree dividing Russia into seven zones, each under a specially appointed presidential representative. In another sign of the considerably more hardline approach to governance adopted by Putin, only two of the representatives do not have a military background, and they will all sit on the Security Council. In his most decisive move so far, Putin has resolved to deprive regional governors of their automatic entitlement to seats in the upper house of parliament, the Federation Council, and to gain the power to sack them and dissolve regional parliaments.

Putin has moved rapidly to bring the regions under control and has already received the support of the Duma in this.

BMI expects Putin's efforts to rein in the regions to meet with some success. Indeed, it appears that before the presidential election most of the governors had already seen the writing on the wall and resigned themselves to a curtailment of their powers. Putin has considerable room for influence since the centre holds the purse strings. Even those regions which are net donors to the budget will be wary of aggravating him as their terms could still be changed for the worse. Putin's plans for reforming the Federation Council and for allowing him to sack governors have already received the Duma's approval, and although the Federation Council promptly rejected the first proposal, and is likely to do the same with the second, the Duma's support in both cases was in excess of the two-thirds majority which is now required to override the Federation Council's rejection.

There have been a few examples where valuable economic reforms have been introduced by regional governors in contrast to stagnation at the central level, but **BMI** does not expect the change in policy from the centre to undermine these – the point of Putin's policy being not to hinder reform but to tackle Russians' concerns about law and order, and the country's loss of status. However, Putin will need to be careful not to aggravate ethnic tensions as a result of his actions.

Foreign Policy

Putin Is Active On The World Stage

Putin has been busy since his inauguration developing relations with the West and with states nearer home.

At Putin's first summit with end-of-term US President Bill Clinton in early June there was no breakthrough on the key issue at stake – Russia's opposition to amending the 1972 anti-ballistic missile (ABM) treaty to allow the US to create a defence shield system against the perceived threat from "rogue states". Nevertheless, agreements were reached on lesser areas, and there has been talk of a softening from the Russians – who themselves are pushing for larger cuts in nuclear weaponry than favoured by the US. Clinton was also sure to speak in positive terms about Moscow's new economic team, and to voice support for Russia's IMF and WTO bids. Although he pushed for a political resolution to the Chechen conflict and for the international community to be allowed to check up on widespread allegations of human rights abuses there, there was no deviation from the West's generally hands-off approach.

Putin's first summit with German Chancellor Gerhard Schroeder seemed to be imbued with more significance, given that both are likely to be at the helm of their respective countries for a while to come. Both sides were eager to portray the meeting as a new start in Russian-German relations, which have been strained since Russia's 1998 default on its foreign debt. Progress was made in resolving a dispute which has been blocking the reopening of German export credit guarantees and a rescheduling of Russian debt (*see External Debt*), and several important deals were signed between German firms and Russia's gas monopoly **Gazprom**. Germany is already Russia's leading economic partner.

Putin has accompanied reassertion of authority over the Russian regions with the desire to boost Russia's position in the former Soviet Union. In May he visited Turkmenistan and Uzbekistan, reaching an agreement to increase Russia's imports of Turkmen gas in the former, which could have important

economic and geopolitical implications (*see Key Economic Sectors*). In
Uzbekistan, Putin and President Islam Karimov agreed to bolster military
ties in light of the perceived threat to the region from Islamic extremism,
marking a sharp turnaround in the relationship from the Yeltsin years.

Profile and Recent Developments

Political System And Main Parties

Power Is Vested In The President

Russia adopted its present constitution in 1993. It is based around three pillars of government: the president and cabinet, the upper house of parliament (the Federation Council) and the lower house (the Duma). Constitutionally, executive authority is concentrated in the presidency, which has considerable power over the composition of the cabinet and decisions made in the lower and upper houses. The president, for example, is able to appoint a government without taking account of the relative strength of the parties in parliament. The president also appoints the prime minister. Although the president's nominee must then be ratified by a majority in the Duma, if he is not accepted by the third vote, the parliament is automatically dissolved and new elections called. Russia's constitution makes impeaching the president difficult, requiring a two-thirds majority in the Duma to support a motion to pass the charges on to the Federation Council, which will only vote on impeachment if the Constitutional Court agrees that there is a case to answer. Even then, the more conservative Federation Council needs a two-thirds majority of the 178 seats for the vote to carry.

Under Boris Yeltsin, tussles between the president and the Duma were a regular feature of political life. The Duma rejected Yeltsin's nominees for prime minister on more than one occasion, and frequently blocked or amended important legislation, although given its constitutional weakness its bark often proved to be worse than its bite. By contrast, Vladimir Putin, who formally became Russia's new president in May, looks set to enjoy a much better relationship with deputies and the regional governors in the Federation Council. Like Boris Yeltsin, Vladimir Putin is not a member of any political party. However, his backing for the Unity party (*see below*) helped it emerge from nowhere to become a major political force.

Structure Of The Duma

The Duma is comprised of 450 deputies, half of which are elected on a first past the post system, and half taken from party lists. For a party to enter parliament it must have achieved at least 5% of the vote. After the December 1995 Duma election, the Communist Party formed the largest grouping with 157 seats.

The December 1999 Duma election weakened the Communists, although they remain the largest single party with 113 seats. The Unity party, which contested the election on a vague pro-Kremlin ticket, is close behind with 72 seats. Pro-reform economic liberals in the Union of Right Forces did surprisingly well, gaining 29 seats. The Fatherland-All Russia party also did well, with 55 seats. But its leaders, Moscow mayor Yuri Luzhkov and former prime minister Yevgeny Primakov – two of the handful of politicians with a serious national profile to match Putin's – saw their support crumble amid hostile media coverage. Primakov withdrew from the presidential race in February, a gesture widely seen as marking the end of the 70 year-old's political career.

The Party Structure

Russian politics cover a broad spectrum, from the far right to the far left. The country has a wealth of parties, many of which either serve a vested interest or are too small to warrant discussion. Politics remain highly personalised and the fortunes of parties to a great extent revolve around the fate of their leaders. For example, former prime minister Viktor Chernomyrdin's Our Home is Russia, at times the nearest thing to a governing party in the 1996-1999 Duma with 55 seats, was reduced to a handful of seats at the 1999 election. Chernomyrdin and fellow leader Vladimir Ryzhkov subsequently took the rump of their party to join Unity and pledged support to Putin. Indeed, nearly all parties have become much more cooperative with the Kremlin since it became clear that Putin would be elected president.

The Communists still form the most organised party and the one with the most clearly articulated ideological programme. Led by vetaran Gennady Zyuganov, the party's manifesto has become less hard-line and anti-market in order to adapt to the reality of Russia today. However, it still believes in a high degree of state intervention. Its core constituency comprises pensioners and some state employees and industrial workers, for whom it traditionally presses for higher wages and subsidies. How these promises would be funded remains open to question. In recent years, the party has also become more nationalist and a defender of Russia's interest vis-à-vis the West. The failure of the market-led reforms that culminated in the collapse of the rouble and a moratorium on domestic debt payments in August 1998 should have seen the Communist Party increase its power base. Instead, the centre parties have benefited most, at the expense of the extreme parties.

The Liberal Democrats (LDPR), belying their name, represent the far-right of the political spectrum, and are headed by the flamboyant Vladimir Zhirinovsky. This group has ultra-nationalist views and links with far-right parties in Western Europe. However, having seen its popularity rise strongly in the middle years of the decade, support for the party has been on the wane for some time. Western governments were once alarmed at Zhirinovsky's power, but in the last Duma LDPR deputies tended to support the Kremlin and caused little trouble. The LDPR was banned from the last Duma election, but the so-called Zhirinovsky Bloc, which grouped most of the LDPR members along with those of some minor parties, won just 6.4% of the vote.

Yabloko, led by Grigory Yavlinsky, is in favour of democratic principles and the free market, but also emphasises social welfare and the need to control big business. Yavlinsky is an economist who made his name drafting a 500-day plan to reform the Soviet economy in the dying days of the

Gorbachev era. More recently he was one of the only major political figures who dared criticise the war in Chechnya, a position which undoubtedly cost him votes in the presidential election. Yavlinsky declined to participate in any of the Yeltsin governments. This allowed him to successfully avoid being tainted by the unpopularity of economic reforms, but his longevity on the political scene may have in any case counted against him with disillusioned voters. Former prime minister Sergei Stepashin joined Yabloko in 1999, and was selected to head parliament's Audit Chamber in April 2000.

The December 1999 elections saw the emergence of the Interregional Movement Unity (MEDVED) as a new centrist force. Headed by popular Emergencies Minister Sergei Shoigu, it was formed in August 1999, it never laid out its political programme in detail and described its basis for support as "all thinking people". In practice it is a pro-Kremlin party and it received backing from Putin, casting it as "the party of power" and enabling it to take second place in the elections. Other leading figures in the party are former police chief Alexander Gurov and another non-politician, nine-times world wrestling champion Alexander Karelin. Far from being a temporary group, the party has gone from strength to strength since the election.

The Union of Right Forces groups a number of Russia's best-known reformers, most of whom became deeply unpopular as a result of the country's botched privatisation programme. The most famous of them are Sergei Kiriyenko, who as prime minister in 1998 presided over the August crisis, and Boris Nemtsov, who also served in government under Yeltsin. The party favours continued economic reforms.

Fatherland-All Russia, a left-leaning coalition headed by Moscow mayor Yuri Luzhkov and former prime minister Yevgeny Primakov, has a strong support base in the regions and picked up more seats in the Duma via this route than from party lists (36 seats against 30). Both Luzhkov and Primakov were regarded as threat by the Kremlin, and the country's main TV networks gave them extremely negative coverage, suggesting that the 70 year-old Primakov was too infirm to run the country, and alleging that Luzhkov was in league with the Moscow mafia. Since the Unity party captured the centre ground, support for Fatherland-All Russia has waned.

The Oligarchs

Though some "oligarchs" – who, supported by vast financial-industrial groups (FIGs) – exert influence over both Moscow and Russia generally — saw their power wane in the aftermath of the economic crisis, the grip of oligarchs, and even of former criminal organisations, over Russian business remains strong. Many oligarchs accumulated diverse assets during the privatisation process, usually at knock-down prices, but have failed to invest in the underlying businesses and have often channelled earnings abroad. The most notorious oligarch is Boris Berezovsky, who maintained a close relationship with the Kremlin under Boris Yeltsin and helped him to win the 1996 presidential election. Berezovsky's business interests range from aluminium producers to car dealerships and the media. His stewardship of national airline **Aeroflot** is being investigated by Swiss prosecutors, and he was refused a visa to enter Switzerland in early 2000. His stake in national broadcaster ORT has given him further political clout, and he backed Putin's campaign for the presidency. In the election campaign, Putin said that the oligarchs should be cut down to size, but this is easier said than done.

Foreign Policy

Finding A Place In The World Order

Russia's sphere of influence has been diminishing since the collapse of the USSR in the early 1990s. Its empire has been drastically cut back, while its economy has shrunk (Russia now accounts for under 1% of world GDP), and its ability to influence world events has declined. Nowhere was this more apparent than with the air strikes against Iraq in January 1999 and Nato's bombing against Serbia later in the year. Despite vociferous protests and the temporary withdrawal of the Russian ambassadors to London and Washington, Russia's actions in the Iraq conflict proved impotent. Russia's protests during the Kosovo conflict proved equally ineffectual in preventing Nato's campaign, and strained relations with the West, especially when sabre-rattling rhetoric proposed re-targeting nuclear missiles at the countries involved. However, the Kosovo conflict did present Russia with a diplomatic coup, as the peace negotiations were directed through Moscow.

Russia's marginalisation on the world stage has been one factor behind calls for greater cooperation with Russia's near-abroad. The most striking example of this is in the proposed union with Belarus, which is supposed to result in the election of a joint parliament as early as September 2000. However, despite the signing of a union treaty in November 1999, actual union may well not take place. Russia is also fostering closer ties with Ukraine. Three separate accords on the Black Sea fleet, based on the Crimean peninsula, have been agreed. It is envisaged that Russia will lose the Crimea and Sevastopol, but will be allowed to lease Sevastopol for 20 years for the fleet.

The move to strengthen ties with surrounding countries also aims to combat the West's influence in the region. Nato's eastward expansion – which saw Poland, Hungary and the Czech Republic join the alliance in March 1999 and several other Central and South East European countries also eager to join – has led to calls from Russia for a 'red line' to be placed around the borders of the former Soviet Union. The Black Sea fleet agreement with Ukraine effectively prevents one strategic state from joining. Moreover, there are ongoing talks with the US on changing the conventional forces in Europe (CFE) agreement, with Russia keen to limit the size of armed forces that can be deployed in countries that are close to it.

On its southern flank, Russia is alarmed by the spread of Islamic militancy in Central Asia. The region's leaders share these fears, and Russia will continue to extend them military help. In March, it sent more troops to bolster the defences along Tajikistan's border with Afghanistan after fighting flared up there. Uzbekistan also reversed its decision to pull out of a collective security treaty with Moscow, while Russia and Kazakhstan agreed to reimpose mutual visa requirements in a bid to stop "undesirables" crossing the border.

Energy is another crucial issue for Russia and her neighbours. Russia wants to maintain its former grip over energy supplies from oil and gas rich states in the Caucasus and Central Asia, and will continue to oppose any pipeline schemes that bypass it. Relations with Azerbaijan and Georgia, which will benefit from new pipeline projects routed to avoid Russia, will therefore remain cool. To the west, Russia, and in particular gas monopoly **Gazprom**, have a stranglehold over Moldova and Ukraine, whose unpaid energy bills have reached critical proportions. Russia is pressing for debt-equity swaps for stakes in assets included in Ukraine's privatisation programme, while the Moldovans have had their gas supplies temporarily cut off on more than one occasion.

Russia's relations with its former satellite states in Central and Eastern Europe, especially Poland, have a good deal of room for improvement. A spying row with Poland caused the expulsion of several diplomats in Q1 00, and the Polish president openly described ties with Moscow as "poor".

Chechnya War Dominates Foreign Relations In 1999-2000

The dominant foreign policy issue for Russia in Q1 00 was the war in Chechnya, which was launched against suspected terrorist groups and aimed to bring the region back under Moscow's effective control. The Kremlin became concerned by incursions by Chechen rebels into neighbouring Dagestan. A series of bomb attacks on apartment blocks in Russia, which claimed 300 lives, provided the immediate pretext for action in September 1999. Civilians were caught up in the conflict from the start, prompting humanitarian concerns, and by the end of Q1 00 the capital of the region, Grozny, had been reduced to rubble. There is plenty of evidence of unwarranted brutality by Russian troops, including beatings and massacres of non-combatants. The kidnapping of journalist Andrei Babitsky, one of a handful of correspondents who filed reports from the area critical of the government, became a cause célèbre in liberal Russian circles and abroad. But predictably, in their keenness to get their relationship with the new man in the Kremlin off to a good start, world leaders have been muted in their criticism of the war. The most significant exception came in April 2000 when the Council of Europe voted to begin suspension proceedings against Russia.

US President Bill Clinton, his Secretary of State Madeleine Albright and Britain's Prime Minister Tony Blair have all endorsed Putin, and declared that they believe he is a man with whom they can do business. Thus, bilateral relations between Russia and the US and Europe look set to be cordial, albeit subject to disagreements. A change to Russia's national security concept early in January, which reduced the gravity of the circumstances under which Russia would allow itself to use nuclear weapons, was an example of the kind of issue which could periodically arise to cool relations.

2 Economic Outlook

Overview

Prospects Of Renewed IMF Support Have Increased

The chances have increased of agreement being reached later this year to replace the US$4.5bn IMF programme which was suspended in October 1999. Although the current economic upturn has allowed the government to get by without IMF funding, it clearly cannot rely on such good fortune indefinitely given the economy's basically shaky fundamentals. Renewed IMF support will also be necessary to reach agreement on restructuring Russia's Paris Club debt (*see External Debt, below*), and to ease any return to borrowing on the international markets. The authorities' avowed commitment to economic reform has been met with a noticeable change in tone from the IMF, suggesting that the Fund is eager to make the most of Russia's best reform opportunity in some time. Now that the government has announced a satisfactory economic programme, formal negotiations on a new agreement should be able to get under way, but the IMF may want to see further evidence of reforms being implemented before a decision is made, which will in any case take time.

The chances of a resumption of IMF support have increased, with the government's release of a satisfactory economic programme, and the the Fund apparently keen to re-engage the country.

Economic Activity

Economic Growth Outstrips Initial Expectations

Economic activity has been significantly more robust so far this year than previously expected. The 2000 budget assumes real GDP growth of just 1.5%, but in Q1 00 the economy expanded by 8.4% y-o-y, according to the latest estimate from the State Statistics Committee (Goskomstat), up from an initial 6.0-7.0% estimate but more in line with the Economy Ministry's calculations. More recently, Prime Minister Mikhail Kasyanov has claimed that GDP was still up by 7.0% y-o-y in the January-May period.

Industrial production increased by 11.9% y-o-y in Q1 00, growing at a rate

The economy has been expanding more rapidly this year than originally expected, boosted by the international price of oil.

Annual Growth Slows
Industrial production, % change y-o-y

Source: Russian Economic Trends.

Unemployment Has Peaked
ILO unemployment, %

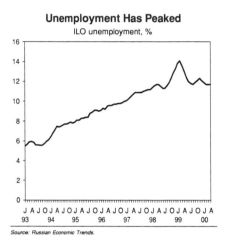

Source: Russian Economic Trends.

The pace of economic growth seen in Q1 00 is not expected to continue during the remainder of the year, but the authorities' current expectation of 4.0-5.0% real GDP growth in 2000 is looking reasonable. Given the temporary nature of the factors boosting 2000 activity, future economic growth will depend on the extent to which structural reforms are undertaken.

similar to that seen in Q4 99, but from a less favourable base of comparison. In y-o-y terms, industrial production growth was on a downwards trend in February-April, slowing to 5.5% in the latter from 13.7% in the former, and is unlikely to return to the pace seen in Q1 during 2000. Nevertheless, in May it was still up by a robust 10.6%.

Although expenditure-based GDP data are harder to come by, figures cited by Russian Economic Trends (RET) put real consumer expenditure on goods and services (akin to household consumption expenditure) up a seasonally-adjusted 7.0% y-o-y in Q1 00, and real fixed capital investment (which gives an indication of gross fixed investment trends) up by 9.0%, seasonally adjusted. But RET estimates that net exports provided the largest spur to economic growth in the period. The economy is continuing to benefit from the effects of the 1998 devaluation, which slashed imports and saw domestic production boosted through import substitution. While the positive impact on exports of the weaker RUB has been limited, exports were driven up in Q1 00 by the rise in the international price of oil to peaks of US$30/b. The first quarter therefore saw the merchandise trade surplus jump again. It more than doubled to US$13.7bn in value terms from US$6.0bn in Q1 99. While imports were up y-o-y by just 2.1%, exports grew by a sharp 51.0%.

Official forecasts for full-year 2000 GDP growth are now falling within a 4.0-5.0% range compared with 3.0% earlier this year. Both the OECD and the EBRD have revised their forecasts upwards significantly to 4.0% from 1.0% late last year. In mid-April, by contrast, the IMF was expecting growth of just 1.5%.

Authorities' GDP Forecasts Realistic, For Now

Developments are not likely to be so upbeat during the remainder of the year. The period of comparison will not be quite so favourable after Q1. In addition, although the international oil price remained surprisingly high in Q2 00, it is likely to moderate later in the year, beginning in Q3. Nevertheless, in light of the strong performance so far, **BMI**'s 3.0% real GDP growth forecast for the full-year is looking modest, and has been revised upwards to

GROWTH AND OUTPUT							
	1996	1997	1998	1999	2000f	2001f	2002f
Nominal GDP (RUBbn)	2,146	2,479	2,696	4,546	5,720	6,740	7,840
Nominal GDP (US$bn)	419.0	428.5	277.8	184.6	202.5	221.0	234.0
GDP per capita (US$)	2,837	2,913	1,896	1,266	1,394	1,526	1,622
Real GDP growth, % y-o-y	-3.4	0.9	-4.9	3.2	4.8	2.5	3.0
f = BMI forecast. Source: BMI.							

4.8%, meaning that we see the authorities' expectations as realistic. Having fallen substantially in 1998-99, consumption of goods and services has been consistently posting positive growth since October 1999, and should continue to see a modest improvement encouraged by real wage growth. Investment should also improve slowly.

The current pace of economic growth is unlikely to continue in the longer run unless further structural reform is undertaken, as this year's impressive growth has been boosted by temporary factors rather than by healthy fundamentals. The average oil price is likely to fall in 2001, while given its impact on the trade balance since the 1998 crisis, import substitution is unlikely to provide such a spur again next year. Although the 2001 budget draft currently assumes the same 4.0-5.0% growth range as is expected for this year, most observers anticipate a slowdown, in the case of the OECD to 3.0%.

Fiscal Policy

Budget Figures Are Positive

Budget figures continue to outperform targets, with the Finance Ministry reporting a surplus equivalent to 2.1% of GDP over the January-May period. The surplus has increased from 0.5% of GDP in Q1 00, and according to Kasyanov, the primary surplus increased to 4.6% of GDP in January-April from 3.8% in Q1. The government is therefore on course to meet its annual budget deficit target of 1.0% of GDP. Figures calculated on the basis of the broader IMF definition show a RUB64.8bn budget surplus in the first four months of the year, compared with a RUB44.2bn deficit in the corresponding period of 1999, while the primary budget rose to a RUB117.5bn surplus from a deficit of RUB2.7bn in January-April 1999.

The latest figures show the budget continuing to outperform its targets, assisted by tax collection efforts and the international price of oil.

The budget is benefiting from improved tax collection, especially from Russia's larger companies, the continuing high oil price and stronger than expected economic growth. Even though oil prices should decline later in the year, the full-year outlook is encouraging.

Balanced Budget Planned for 2001

The new cabinet is targeting a balanced budget in 2001 for the first time in Russia's post-communist history. Targets and assumptions are at this stage preliminary and liable to be revised over the coming weeks (the main budget assumptions were formed in April, but the government is due to present the

For the first time since the collapse of communism, the government is considering a balanced budget for 2001. Progress is being made in passing the tax reform package underpinning it.

budget to the Duma by 1 August). Crucially, however, the government is planning on the assumption that the second part of the tax code will have been approved by parliament in time to come into force next year, and that this will result in a significant rise in revenues in 2001 to RUB1,154.9bn. Without the tax reform, the authorities calculate, revenues will be significantly lower at RUB1,053.9bn, which, if the expenditure target were left unchanged at RUB1,154.9bn, would imply a deficit of RUB101bn or 1.5% of expected GDP.

Part one of the tax code was implemented in 1999, and the second part will establish tax rates. The aim is to rationalise the system. Important measures include the removal of the top income tax rate of 30% and the introduction of a flat rate at the now-standard 13% in order to discourage evasion, and the abolition of certain turnover taxes while raising the profit tax to 35% from 30%. The latter measure aims to eliminate the anomaly whereby companies making a loss are still treated harshly.

The legislative timetable is tight. Encouragingly, however, the Duma has already approved three important elements of the tax reform (concerning income, social and value added taxes) at the second of three required readings, providing further evidence of how much more amenable the new parliament is to the Putin administration's wishes than was the case under Yeltsin. Parliament is due to hold an extra session to discuss the tax code on July 17 (the summer recess is due to begin on July 7). The reform will also need the approval of the Federation Council, which is not particularly well disposed to the government at the moment.

Although the already long drawn-out process of reforming the tax system is undoubtedly essential to setting public finances on a sustainable path, it is, however, an entirely different matter whether the government's revenue projections for next year will be realised even if the reform is passed in time.

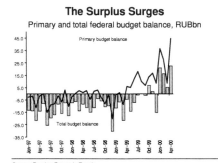

The Surplus Surges
Primary and total federal budget balance, RUBbn

Source: Russian Economic Trends.

	FISCAL DEFICIT						
	1996	1997	1998	1999	2000f	2001f	2002f
Primary fiscal balance (RUBbn)	-48.8	-65.4	-27.4	88.4	228.8	235.9	196.0
Primary fiscal balance (% of GDP)	-2.3	-2.6	-1.0	1.9	4.0	3.5	2.5
Federal budget balance (RUBbn)	-173.3	-183.2	-134.2	-74.2	0.0	-33.7	-39.2
Federal budget balance (% of GDP)	-8.1	-7.4	-5.0	-1.6	0.0	-0.5	-0.5

f = BMI forecast. Source: BMI.

Monetary And Exchange Rate Policy

Inflows Boost Rouble And Money Supply...

The economy disinflated more quickly than anticipated by most in the first four months of 2000. In April, the y-o-y inflation rate stood at 19.9%, and has declined consistently from 120.9% in August 1999, assisted by the RUB's greater stability. This led the Economics Ministry to forecast that the rate could be as low as 12.0% by end-year, significantly below the 18.0% projected in the budget. This was a view endorsed by new Finance Minister Alexei Kudrin, who argued that inflation would not be above 12.0%. However, trends have not been so positive since May. The y-o-y rate still declined again in that month, but only to 19.3%, and the latest word from Goskomstat is that m-o-m inflation probably picked up to 2.5-2.7% in June. According to **BMI**'s calculations, this would take the y-o-y rate upwards once again to around 20.0%.

The latest forecast from the Economics Ministry is for inflation of 15-17% at end-2000, and Kudrin has also raised his expectations to 15-18%, although the IMF is more optimistic, saying that inflation should not be above 15%. We have revised our end-2000 inflation forecast downwards to 16.0% from 21.0%. The government has been using an 11.0% end-year rate in the preparation of next year's budget, but in line with the less upbeat expectations for this year, it has indicated recently that inflation is now expected to be nearer 12-15% in 2001.

...Posing An Upside Risk To Inflation

The danger is that inflation is beginning to be boosted by money supply growth. There has been strong upwards pressure on the RUB this year, resulting from a combination of buoyant export-related foreign exchange inflows and a slowing of capital outflows (capital flight is estimated to have fallen to US$300mn a month from around US$1bn earlier this year). The Central Bank of Russia (CBR) has engaged in unsterilised intervention to combat this pressure and also to boost its reserves, with the result that gross international reserves excluding gold had reached US$15.9bn by the end of May. Reserves have risen consistently from US$6.6bn in September 1999. In May alone, they increased by US$2.5bn. This has boosted the money supply. In April, y-o-y growth in M2 (which measures currency in circulation and demand and time deposits) was running at 54.6%, not that much lower than the 57.2% rate at the end of 1999. However, the full impact on inflation of the rise in the money supply has not been felt because of the low

Recent inflation developments have been unfavourable, and the danger is that prices could be boosted by the money supply growth associated with strong foreign exchange inflows.

The Surge Is Stemmed
Consumer price inflation

Source: Russian Economic Trends.

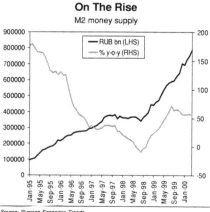

On The Rise
M2 money supply

Source: Russian Economic Trends.

level of lending activity in the economy which has seen commercial banks' excess reserves with the CBR mount. The banks' correspondent accounts rose to around RUB80bn in early July from RUB70bn at the end of 1999. The possibility of this money being released into the economy is a cause for concern. Perhaps as a sign of concern over inflation, CBR Chairman Viktor Gerashchenko said at the end of June that the refinance rate might be reduced in the summer, whereas in early June he had suggested a reduction was imminent.

Next year, the situation should not be so extreme given that the price of oil is likely to fall, but nevertheless, sentiment has improved, capital flight is falling, and Russia is making progress in alleviating its debt servicing obligations, suggesting that over the longer run upwards pressure on the RUB will continue to be a factor, barring a change in sentiment or the global outlook. Inevitably, the situation poses a problem for the CBR in its conduct of monetary policy – especially given the lack of monetary tools at hand. The CBR cannot, for example, employ sterilisation as the domestic debt market has yet to recover from the 1998 crisis. However, not only is there the concern about money supply growth; Kasyanov has said that any further strengthening of the RUB would harm the economy (the RUB has depreciated by only 2.6% in nominal terms so far this year, according to our calculations, despite the CBR's intervention). This has prompted Gerashchenko to speak out against what he calls an artificial weakening of the RUB and to say that exports would still be competitive even at an exchange rate of RUB25/US$. The differences between Gerashchenko and Kasyanov have been enough to set the rumour-mill going that the former could be on his way out in the next few months.

The IMF argued recently that a real appreciation of the RUB was probably unavoidable in the coming period, assuming that the government's economic policy was acceptable. It said that the economy should be able to cope with a gradual appreciation, but advised that a sharp strengthening be avoided.

On The Mend
Gross international reserves (excluding gold), US$bn

Source: Russian Economic Trends.

INFLATION AND EXCHANGE RATES							
	1996	1997	1998	1999	2000f	2001f	2002f
Consumer prices (% y-o-y, end period)	21.8	11.0	84.4	36.5	16.0	14.0	12.0
Consumer prices (% y-o-y, period average)	47.7	14.7	27.7	85.7	20.0	15.0	13.0
Exchange rate (RUB/US$, end period)	5.560	5.960	20.650	27.000	29.000	32.000	35.000
Exchange rate (RUB/US$, period average)	5.121	5.785	9.705	24.620	28.250	30.500	33.500

f = BMI forecast. Source: BMI.

Balance Of Payments

Current Account In Huge Surplus

Q4 99 balance of payments data from the CBR showed an even bigger current account surplus than we had expected. The surplus reached US$10.24bn, taking the full-year surplus to US$24.96bn, or 13.5% of GDP, up from US$1.04bn or 0.4% of GDP in 1998. It was therefore by far the largest surplus seen since the end of communism. Indeed, it was roughly twice as large again as any other surplus seen during the period. An almost doubling of the trade surplus to US$35.30bn from US$17.10bn was largely responsible for the sharp improvement in 1999. Exports were virtually unchanged from the previous year, declining by 0.3% to US$74.66bn from US$74.89bn. With this following from the large 15.9% y-o-y contraction seen in 1998, it is clear that exports failed to derive a significant gain from the devaluation. However, the narrowing of the merchandise trade deficit was propelled by a 31.9% y-o-y drop in imports as demand for foreign goods collapsed following the devaluation.

The improvement in the merchandise trade surplus in y-o-y terms started to moderate in Q3 99 as the period of comparison became less favourable, although the surplus was still up by over a quarter in Q4 99. However, Q1 00 saw the merchandise trade surplus jump again, more than doubling to US$13.7bn from US$6.0bn in Q1 99. While imports were up by just 2.1% y-o-y after growth of 19.1% in Q4 99, exports grew by a sharp 51.0% y-o-y, boosted by oil prices. In April, according to the most recent figures, the trade surplus was still up on the year-previous period by around half to US$4.7bn from US$3.1bn in April 1999.

The growth in real wages and the recovery in domestic demand should see imports continuing to rise this year, but we are still expecting their growth to be relatively modest. Moreover, oil prices are proving to be higher than

In 1999 Russia posted its largest current account surplus since the end of communism, and 2000 will be an even stronger year.

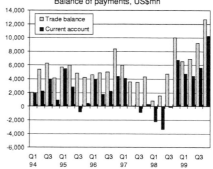

In Massive Surplus
Balance of payments, US$mn

Source: Central Bank of Russia.

CUSTOMS TRADE AND BALANCE OF PAYMENTS							
	1996	1997	1998	1999	2000f	2001f	2002f
Customs exports (fob, US$bn)	88.6	88.2	74.2	74.7	89.6	83.3	86.8
Customs imports (cif, US$bn)	68.8	73.7	59.1	40.4	44.4	49.6	57.0
Customs trade balance (fob-cif, US$bn)	19.8	14.5	15.1	34.3	45.2	33.7	29.8
Current account balance (US$bn)	12.45	2.55	1.04	24.96	38.22	25.70	21.45
Current account (% of GDP)	3.0	0.6	0.4	13.5	18.9	11.6	9.2
f = BMI forecast. Source: BMI.							

anticipated, and we are expecting the current account surplus to be even stronger in 2000 than last year.

FDI Remains At Low Levels

The latest balance of payments data also reveal that foreign direct investment (FDI) in Russia picked up slightly in 1999 to US$2.89bn from US$2.76bn in 1998. At 1.6% of GDP, it remains at a very low level, but anecdotal evidence of increased foreign interest in Russia bodes well for a further rise this year. If a law to allow for production-sharing agreements in the oil industry is passed in Q4 00, as many expect, then Russia could begin to receive far more FDI from 2001 onwards.

External Debt

Government Tones Down Paris Club Hopes

Following the restructuring deal which Kasyanov clinched with the London Club of commercial creditors in February, the government appears to have shelved its hopes of working out a similar restructuring with Russia's sovereign creditors for this year at least. A temporary rescheduling agreement was reached with the Paris Club in August 1999, according to which around US$8bn due in the remainder of 1999 and in full-year 2000 was reduced to US$620m, with US$880m due in 2001-05. It was also agreed that negotiations on a restructuring proper would begin in autumn 2000. The Russians are likely to air their wishes for a restructuring, which include a demand for a more than 50% write-off of the Paris Club debt, at the G8 summit summit in July. However, they feel that their case is not particularly strong at the moment, given that a deal with the IMF is unlikely to have been reached by then and that the government has only just released its economic programme. Kasyanov has said recently that a further transitional rescheduling agreement may be signed later this year with the Paris Club rather than a full restructuring. What form more comprehensive restructuring might take is as yet unclear. Russia's debt write-off hopes continue to meet opposition, most recently from Japan, which has said that although a rescheduling is an

FOREIGN RESERVES							
	1996	1997	1998	1999	2000f	2001f	2002f
Foreign exchange reserves (US$bn)	11.3	12.9	7.8	8.5	20.0	22.0	23.0
Import cover (months)	1.4	1.5	1.0	1.6	4.2	4.2	3.9
f = BMI forecast. Source: BMI.							

option, it sees no need for debt reduction. Although Putin's recent visit to Germany made progress towards the implementation of Germany's side of the rescheduling agreed last year, the country – Russia's largest creditor – remains adamantly opposed to debt relief.

Profile and Recent Developments

Characteristics Of The Economy

Transition Set Back Again In 1998

The Russian economy has faced a difficult transition from communist central planning to a capitalist market. Between 1992 and 1998, the only year in which GDP rose in real terms was 1997, and that was a mere 0.8% increase. Hopes that 1998 would see a continuation of the modest gains made in the previous year were dashed by August's economic crisis, and instead nominal GDP shrank to US$276.6bn, a paltry amount given the size of the country and its rich natural resources. By comparison, US GDP for the same period was US$8,681.2bn. The decline of the economy in recent years places Russia on a level comparable with poorer countries, and is ranked as a lower-middle income economy on the World Bank's GDP per capita scale. In 1999 GDP began to rebound, recording 3.2% growth on the previous year's low base and raising hopes that the economy had finally bottomed out after a decade-long decline, but it is widely accepted that only a fundamental restructuring of the economy holds out the hope of sustainable growth.

Russia's greatest strength remains its wealth of natural resources. The country is rich in oil and gas, metals, minerals and precious stones. It is the world's third largest oil producer and has the seventh largest oil reserves. At 48trn m³, its gas reserves are the largest in the world. Russia also has significant deposits of copper, aluminium, iron ore, nickel, platinum, palladium and other metals. Its mineral wealth includes substantial diamond deposits, making it the world's second largest producer. This resource base dominates exports, with over 60% of all exports being commodities, while oil and gas provide half of all hard currency export earnings. Although this resource wealth provides a ready means for economic growth, it also suffers from the disadvantage of making the country susceptible to fluctuations in world commodity prices. Moreover, the focus on resource extraction rather than refining or using resources further up the manufacturing chain restricts the ability to add value and growth potential.

The industrial sector remains a key component of economic activity, but suffers from outdated machinery, lack of investment and low-quality products. Moreover, Russian industry continues to produce goods for which there is limited demand. In the Soviet era, much industrial capacity was oriented, for example, to producing military hardware. Iron and steel, oil, gas and manufacturing are major components of the industrial sector. Agriculture also has its problems, not least the 46.1% decline in the grain harvest in 1998, Russia's worst for 40 years. The sector suffers from low investment, poor productivity and high import penetration, and staged only a modest recovery in 1999. While the service sector could be expected to fill the gap left by industry and agriculture, relatively low income levels (real wages have declined by roughly 50% since the beginning of the 1990s) mean that, to date, service-based industries have tended to locate within the Moscow and St. Petersburg areas. The financial sector, a key component of services, is underdeveloped and suffered badly as a result of the 1998 economic crisis.

Economic Activity

Reversing Hard-Won Gains

In 1998 Russia's economy experienced the worst crisis since its shift from central planning to market-led policies in the early 1990s. Real GDP contracted by 4.6%, the worst performance for four years. The rouble ended the year 71.74% below its end-1997 level. Inflation, which had been on a declining trend, soared to 84.5% y-o-y by December from only 5.6% in July. The greatest decline in output was seen in agriculture, construction and financial services, the latter hindered by the virtual breakdown of the payments system that followed the rouble devaluation.

The crisis stemmed from the government's inability to service its debt obligations and increasing capital flight from the rouble. In turn, this was due to the spiralling interest rates facing the government in the domestic bond market, caused by poor investor confidence in the running of government finances. The rouble collapse and the subsequent domestic debt default saw Russia cut off from international financing and the payments system grind to a halt. Banks no longer had sufficient liquidity to fulfil their obligations, and many became technically bankrupt in the process. As a result, economic activity suffered a sharp decline, not just in the financial sector, but across all industries. As inflation soared and wages failed to keep pace, so real incomes began to decline, further deepening the economic crisis.

Government policy initially tried to limit the impact of the economic slowdown by reducing wage arrears wherever possible, attracting new investment into the country, keeping inflation under some control by limiting monetary emissions, and increasing the share of expenditure going to the regions. However, the extreme difficulties in financing the budget and the need to meet budget criteria laid down by the IMF meant that the government was unable to provide any degree of fiscal stimulus to the economy. Indeed, spending was reined in wherever possible in order to maintain a substantial primary budget surplus.

In many ways, however, the devaluation was beneficial. From early 1999, the weaker rouble helped bolster export competitiveness and reduce import demand. Overall imports declined by more than 47% in 1999 on a balance of payments basis, and in some sectors the fall was even greater, helped by the high income elasticity of many imported products. Cheaper domestic products, despite being lower quality, made significant gains by filling the gap in the market. GDP growth was 3.2% in 1999, led by 8.1% growth in industrial output. Agriculture grew 2.4%.

Fiscal Policy

The Seeds Of The Crisis

At the heart of Russia's budget problems is the government's inability to collect sufficient tax revenue to finance desired expenditures. At times in 1998 tax revenue as a percentage of GDP fell below 10%, forcing the government to use the domestic bond market as a vehicle to make up the shortfall. This policy worked so long as investors had confidence that the government was managing the situation properly and that it was sustainable. However, with the crisis in Asia to the forefront of many investors' risk assessment, this confidence began to wane, in spite of a US$22.6bn IMF-inspired rescue package. The nature of the domestic debt market, with the majority of the issues of very short duration, meant that the government needed to continuously roll over maturing debt and issue additional bonds if it was to finance the budget gap. The situation came to a head in August, by which time yields had risen to such an extent that it became clear that the government could no longer attract sufficient funds at interest rates it could afford.

In the months following the crisis, the government tended to spend less than envisaged, helped by the facts that prior to the passing of the 1999 budget the previous year's spending targets were used, and that the authorities were concerned not to let monetary emissions spiral out of control. However, revenue collection was patchy, and the government's ability to increase tax collection rates remained poor. Although collection rates were higher than the very low levels seen shortly after the crisis they remained subdued, and this continued to be an area of concern for multilateral lenders. In the past, the government has found it impossible to sustain higher rates of tax collection and a clear policy to both simplify and improve the tax system to facilitate sustainable collection rates is needed. Moreover, actual cash collection is often only 70% of revenues, the remainder taking the form of barter goods.

Aiming To Keep The IMF On Side

With the Communists fighting a constant battle against the presidency, negotiating the budget was a drawn-out process during most of Yeltsin's second term. The fact that the 1999 budget was quickly passed by both chambers of parliament partly reflected an awareness of the difficulty of Russia's economic position. Another key factor dictating events was the need to obtain further assistance from the IMF and wider international community. The budget therefore focused as much on trying to meet IMF criteria as it did on addressing the issues facing the domestic economy.

By forecasting an annual inflation rate of no higher than 30% and a relatively stable RUB21.5/US$ exchange rate for 1999, the budget's assumptions were criticised as unrealistic at the time, although they turned out to be not so far off the mark. The budget initially targeted a primary surplus of 1.7%, although this was later raised to 2.3% in an attempt to meet halfway the IMF criterion that a surplus of at least 3-4% be targeted. The government believed that this would at least provide grounds for continued dialogue with the Fund, if not fully satisfy its demands. Indeed, channels of communication remained open, and the IMF dropped its insistence on a high structural surplus.

While the economy was in deep recession and unemployment on the rise, the personal sector offered little scope for improvement in revenue. The government turned increasingly towards the corporate sector to raise money, arguing that the rouble devaluation delivered substantial benefits to certain sectors. The oil industry was a prime target, the government introducing floating tariff on oil exports, which was still in place (albeit with some modifications) in early 2000. However, policy is heavily influenced by vested interests. A proposed 5% tariff on gas exports was rescinded following lobbying from **Gazprom**. In all, the energy sector contributes approximately 40% of total government revenues. Other areas which saw tariffs imposed were coal, nickel and copper ores and products, and natural gas and oil products.

The tripling in the international price of oil from lows of under US$10/b at the end of 1998 to over US$30/b in around a year also greatly boosted government income. Each dollar change in oil prices has a direct impact on oil revenues of about US$1.0-1.5bn, and up to US$2bn if the gas sector is included. There was also an upturn in the fortunes of the large manufacturing companies upon which the budget relies heavily, and the government received a greater share of taxes in cash, especially from the energy companies. Revenues were 25% higher than planned and fiscal results consequently the best in a decade, despite the lack of fundamental reforms to the system. The federal budget recorded a deficit of just 1.7% of GDP, down from 5.0% in 1998, and below the 2.5% target. The administration was also able to remain current on its external obligations, despite not receiving IMF funding following its suspension in September 1999 on the grounds that Russia had failed to meet the terms of its agreement, not just in economic performance but in relation to the reforms it had pledged to carry out, for example in the banking system. Getting back to an agreement with the Fund was initially seen as critical for Russia to maintain its balance of payments, but as the oil price improved over the latter half of 1999 and early 2000, the urgency diminished.

Monetary Policy

Initially Undermined By Lax Fiscal Policy

Monetary policy is the domain of the Central Bank of Russia (CBR).The CBR's independence is guaranteed by law, but in practice the government enjoys considerable leverage over it, and the Duma can dismiss the central bank chairman at the request of the president.

Following the break-up of the Soviet Union, Russia experienced an inflation explosion and a collapse in the value of the rouble. At the end of 1992 inflation was 2,508.8%, falling to 839.9% the following year. This difficult transitionary period saw monetary policy initially accommodate the freeing of prices and the shift to a market-led economy, but it was subsequently tightened in an attempt to rein in the consequent rampant inflation. The policy was successful in this, with inflation declining steadily to only 11.0% by end-1997. The CBR's control of monetary emissions limited the decline in the rouble and was successful in allowing interest rates to fall and capital markets to develop, providing the government with a source of budget financing without the need to resort to money creation, albeit at the price of a significant decline in output and real income.

This benign trend changed in 1998. The rouble devaluation caused an immediate surge in inflation once again, with the annual consumer price inflation rate ending 1998 at 84.4%. However, inflation results were much better than many had feared, especially given the reputation of Viktor Geraschenko, who was re-appointed CBR chairman in the wake of the crisis, a post he had previously held when monetary emissions were high. The CBR has, for example, often favoured monetary expansion to increase the level of credit to industry (in the form of subsidies) and stimulate production. In fact, the authorities resisted the temptation to print money to ease the budget situation. The growth in M2 matched the rate of inflation over the first three quarters of the year at around 3.1% m-o-m, and the growth in the monetary base was lower, at 2.4% per month. The sale of a 2.5% stake in Gazprom to Germany's **Ruhrgas** for US$660mn provided some much-needed revenue, while the rising oil price and a gradually recovering economy also helped. At the level of the consumer, prices also rose less steeply than expected due to the sweeping substitution of imported goods by local production, which became instantly more competitive on price, if not in quality. Consumer price inflation peaked at 126.5% y-o-y in July 1999, but by the end of the year had dropped back to 36.5%. Producer price inflation increased more rapidly in 1999 to end the year at 57%.

Exchange Rate Policy

Struggling To Support Rouble Stability

After the rouble declined significantly in the years immediately following the break-up of the Soviet Union, the period between May 1995 and August 1998 saw the currency stabilise and follow a path of gradual and controlled depreciation. This situation changed abruptly in the summer of 1998. The central bank attempted to stem the flight from the currency by both raising interest rates further and intervening in the foreign exchange market. The IMF disbursed US$4.8bn of an additional US$11bn package, designed to bolster investor confidence, much of which was spent trying to defend the rouble. All this proved to no avail, as Russia found itself unable to attract enough financing to cover the budget deficit, and without sufficient reserves to support the rouble. The inevitable result was a domestic debt default and rouble collapse.

A new floor for the rouble of RUB9.5/US$ was initially announced, but it quickly became apparent that a sustained defence at this level would not be possible. The authorities had little option but to allow the currency to find its own level, with policy geared to smoothing the decline rather than defending a rate. The central bank attempted to slow the pace of the decline by forcing exporters to repatriate 50% of export earnings back into roubles, a figure that was later raised to 75%. By the end of 1998, the currency had fallen to RUB20.65/US$, a 70% fall on its end-July level.

There were fewer surprises for the currency in 1999. It depreciated by 30.8% during the year to RUR27.000/US$, indicating a recovery in real terms against the dollar. The CBR is not pursuing an explicit inflation or exchange rate target. It did not intervene to support the rouble in the currency markets, instead buying dollars during the course of the year to meet foreign debt repayments. While external confidence in Russia's economic policies remained limited, the currency benefited from a sharp rise in the oil price, which boosted hard currency inflows sharply. The CBR also raised reserve requirements for commercial banks twice during the year to prevent excess rouble liquidity in the banking system from impacting on the exchange rate.

The Balance Of Payments

Returning To A Large Surplus

The depreciation of the rouble from August 1998 resulted in a significant turnaround in Russia's trade balance. The decline in the rouble produced a significant rise in export competitiveness, both in actual and real terms, as the pace of producer price rises and other import costs lagged behind the currency's decline. However, the major factor at work was the collapse in imports as the economy entered a sharp recession, real incomes declined and unemployment rose. In the first eight months of 1998, the average customs trade surplus was just US$26mn, compared to an average surplus of US$719mn in the seven months following the devaluation. On a balance of payments basis, the trade surplus more than doubled in full-year 1999 to US$25bn from US$17.1bn in 1998. However, exports were virtually unchanged on the previous year at US$74.66bn, with the increase in the oil price, from an average of US$12.28/b for the Opec basket in 1998 to US$17.47/b in 1999, partly offset by Russia being forced to sell a considerable share of its oil at a discount price (ranging from between 35-44% of the world price) to its beleaguered customers in the CIS. Overall exports to the CIS countries fell 22% y-o-y. Imports, however, fell by 31% to US$39.4bn from US$57.8bn in 1998.

The Direction Of Trade

The pattern of Russia's external trade is gradually shifting westwards, a process hastened by the difficult economic conditions in most of the CIS countries since the rouble crisis. In 1998, 37.6% of Russian exports went to emerging European economies, 7.5% to Asia (of which over half was accounted for by China) and 48.7% to industrialised countries. The US was the largest individual market for Russian exports, accounting for 8.4% of the total, while Germany, Ukraine and Belarus were close behind with shares of 7-8% each.

Capital Flight Is Still A Problem

Despite the significant improvement in Russia's merchandise trade performance from August 1998, foreign exchange reserves remained under considerable pressure until the third quarter of 1999, when they began to rebound sharply. At the end of July 1998, reserves including gold stood at US$18.4bn, boosted by the US$4.8bn IMF cash injection, but by year-end they had fallen to US$12.2bn (including gold reserves valued at around US$4bn). They reached a low point of US$11.2bn in September 1999. The situation was symptomatic of continued capital flight, a major concern for both the government and the IMF. Wary of being charged with sending good money after bad and bailing out private sector investors, the IMF adopted an irregular method of disbursement, with any loan tranches being shifted to Russia's account at the IMF rather than being transferred to the CBR. This is to guarantee that funds are used to refinance payments to the Fund, and are not redirected or misused.

The CBR has stepped up efforts to combat capital flight by cracking down on the use of certain

Pacific tax havens, with some success. The rate of the outflow eased over the course of 1999, but nevertheless the CBR estimated capital flight at US$15bn in total in 1999, compared with US$25bn in 1998. The Ministry of Finance, using a wider definition, put the figure at US$23-25bn in 1999. In Q4 99 reserves began to increase more steeply, a pattern which continued in Q1 00. With Yeltsin gone and the presidency apparently in safe hands, the confidence of Russian business in the economy appeared to undergo an improvement. The fall in inflation also lessened the imperative to convert rouble earnings into dollars. As of Q1 00, the restrictions on exporters requiring them to sell 75% of their hard currency earnings on the domestic market were still in force.

Foreign Direct Investment

Unfulfilled Potential

Despite being the largest country in the world, with vast natural resource potential, Russia has found it hard to attract foreign direct investment (FDI). FDI is a vital lifeline for developing countries, providing fresh investment, new and more efficient production techniques, jobs, technical know-how and expertise. Moreover, FDI is long term, as companies make a commitment to the country for a number of years. This contrasts with portfolio investment, which, although usually greeted with open arms, can create as many problems as benefits. Very strong portfolio inflows into both the equity and debt markets in 1997 were seen as a sign that the reform process was proceeding on track, and that the economy was entering a recovery cycle. In direct contrast, 1998 saw capital inflows turned into huge outflows, leading to the rouble collapse and debt default.

The European Bank for Reconstruction and Development (EBRD) estimates that Russia's cumulative FDI per capita between 1989-97 was just US$63. This contrasts with US$1,667 for Hungary, US$823 for the Czech Republic, US$695 for Estonia, US$425 for Azerbaijan and US$365 for Kazakhstan. Indeed, of the 25 Central and East European, Baltic and CIS countries surveyed, only four had a worse FDI record over the period. Taking 1997 alone, and looking at FDI as a percentage of GDP, only the Slovak Republic had a worse figure than Russia. In 1999 Russia attracted US$2.89bn of FDI, up slightly from US$2.76bn in 1998, but well down on 1997's US$6.64bn level. The FDI that Russia does attract tends to be focused on industry and, to a lesser extent, the oil and gas sectors, and has a distinct regional pattern. Moscow takes the lion's share of inflows along with oil-producing areas such as Sakhalin. The US accounts for roughly half Russia's FDI, and the EU is another important source.

The failure of the Russian economy to attract significant levels of FDI has held back growth and development. The relative lack of FDI can be put down to many factors, some of which the government is trying to address. FDI got off to a poor start following the privatisation programme in the early 1990s. Foreigners were barred from participation in the initial wave, while later privatisations saw domestic interests take precedence over foreign investors. Limits on foreign investment also remain in a number of sectors. For example, no more than 12% of the banking system's assets can be owned by foreigners. The majority of Russia's major corporates have only allowed the sale of minority stakes to foreign investors. In too many respects Russia provides a business environment that deters FDI. While, for example, the oil and gas industries are an obvious target for FDI, this has been held back by the delay in passing enabling legislation for production sharing agreements (PSAs). Recognising this deficiency, Primakov's government pushed the PSA law through the Duma during the first quarter of 1999, but it had not yet passed into law by the end of Q1 00. The tax system is also cumbersome, complicated and open to abuse and manipulation, while widespread crime and corruption present an immediate problem to those looking to invest. For many foreign companies Russia is seen as a place where – unless you know the way the system works – it will be difficult to prosper. The lack of international accounting standards makes analysis difficult and further muddies the waters, as does the level of bureaucracy that still affects the country. Meanwhile, Russian law is not sufficiently strong enough to effectively protect property rights. Until these issues are addressed the country will continue to struggle to attract sufficient levels of FDI inflows.

External Debt

No Shortage Of Creditors

Russia's external debt at the beginning of 2000 totalled US$158.8bn. External debt can be split into two categories: debt taken on by the Russian Federation following the break-up of the Soviet Union, and that accumulated by the Russian Federation. Of the former Soviet debt, US$31.8bn was in the form of eurobonds which were repackaged commercial debts owed to London Club creditors. These included the well-known PRINs and IANs, or principal and interest arrears notes. The other major component was US$40.2bn in outstanding bilateral loans to the Paris Club of creditor nations. Of the post-Soviet debt, the sum owed to the multilateral organisations – the IMF and World Bank – totalled US$21.8bn, while there were US$9.2bn in Paris Club bilateral loans and US$16bn in Russian eurobonds which were issued in 1996 and 1997. The government has remained current on Russian (i.e. post-Soviet) obligations in order to safeguard access to international markets in the future, but defaulted on some Soviet-era debt in the wake of the economic crisis.

London Club Rescheduling Agreement Reached

In February 2000 Russia reached agreement with the London Club of creditors to restructure the Soviet-era commercial debts that it inherited from the former Soviet Union. The London Club restructuring is a major step forward in allowing Russia to resume a normal relationship with international lenders following the crisis. Investors agreed to write off an average of 36.5% of the US$31.8bn outstanding in the form of PRINs and IANs, originally issued by the state-controlled Vneshekonombank. Most of the debt will be packaged into 30-year Eurobonds, with a US$2.8bn 10-year bond to include missed interest payments. The conversion of the debt into eurobonds raises the seniority of the obligation, giving bondholders a greater degree of security in return for assuming the write-off.

Ratings agency **Standard and Poor's** responded to the debt deal by upgrading the rating on Russia's senior unsecured foreign currency debt from CCC to CCC+. The restructuring gives Russia some breathing space by deferring the start of repayments until 2007, but the amortisation schedule will see payments step up considerably in the medium term. Kasyanov views US$11-12bn annually as a sustainable level of repayments going forward. The 2000 budget sets aside US$10.5bn for foreign debt repayment.

Tackling Paris Club Debt

The question now is whether a similar restructuring can be applied to Paris Club debt, as the Russians would like. Repayments on this debt were rescheduled in 1996 and 1999 following on from earlier restructurings in 1993-95, cutting the payments due from US$8bn in 1999 and 2000 to just US$600mn. Germany, which is owed around half of this sovereign debt, has said that it believes Russia should mobilise resources more effectively and does not need to write off any of its debt. By 2000 the huge surplus being recorded in Russia's balance of payments was undermining its case for debt reduction, though it was still expected to proceed.

3 Key Economic Sectors

Overview

A Tentative Step In The Right Direction

The new government's economic programme has been generally welcomed as targeting some of the structural reforms likely to eventually pull Russia out of the post-Soviet crisis. But a certain caution as to its implementation, given Russia's track record of failed reforms, remains. The programme aims to improve Russia's business environment, with measures to assist competition, reduce government interference, protect property rights and foster the use of bankruptcy proceedings. Economic policy will focus in particular on reforming the tax system – the process is already underway (*see Economic Outlook*) – and introducing zero deficit budgeting. Indeed, a balanced budget is being targeted for 2001 (*see Economic Outlook*). Specific sectors of the economy singled out for reform are banking and the "natural monopolies" (electricity, gas and railways). With regard to the latter it is proposed to improve the respective companies' financial transparency and to make further efforts to tackle the non-payment of bills by, for example, increasing the number of customers who can be cut off for failing to pay up. The programme also aims to undertake land and pension reform, and to oversee a completion of the privatisation process.

The government's economic programme has been welcomed as having the right intentions. But given Russia's track record, there is still caution as to how far it will be implemented.

Norilsk Nickel Affair Raises Questions

Unfortunately, the programme's release has been overshadowed by the **Norilsk Nickel** affair, which has once again highlighted the very uncertain operating environment for virtually any sector of the economy. The affair does not constitute the beginning of a wider campaign to reverse the privatisation process *per se* (as displayed by its economic programme, the new administration wants to push the Russian economy closer to, not further away from, a market economy). However, the simple fact is that the oligarchs as a group derive their current wealth and influence precisely from their shadowy involvement in Russia's flawed privatisation process. A wide range of privatisations could be challenged, if the authorities so choose, as part of an assault on the oligarchs.

However, the government's declared intentions on the economic front have been overshadowed by the Norilsk Nickel affair and its possible implications for the business environment.

A crack-down on the oligarchs as a group could be interpreted as signalling a more favourable business environment under Putin, with Russia's "crony-capitalism" seen by many, especially foreign investors, as a key obstacle to investment. However, the very suggestion that past privatisations, in effect supposedly done deals, are open to examination and reversal, is bound to be unsettling, especially given the potential for large-scale disruption of the economy. However, it seems more likely that the oligarchs as an institution are alive and kicking under Putin, but that the balance of power between them is shifting. This scenario does not offer scope for optimism about the business environment on any front.

Electricity

Sector In Dire Straits...

Without reform, the outlook for the electricity sector is grave. This has prompted a restructuring proposal from UES and the new government to make electricity one of the priorities of its economic programme.

The electricity sector is facing severe problems. Giant electricity provider **United Energy Systems** (UES) is suffering from an impossible working environment. The electricity sector was partially privatised in 1992, but the state still retains a 53% stake in UES. Under a system in which prices are set artificially low for political reasons, investment in the sector has been so meagre since the collapse of communism that there are warnings that Russia could become a country dependent on energy imports by 2005, and that only an entire overhaul of the sector will be sufficient to tackle the problem. The sector's difficulties are compounded by the wider payments problem which is crippling the Russian economy. Even when bills are paid, there is still a reluctance to pay in cash (although UES has made good progress in boosting the level of cash collection to 68% in April, and hopes to see this rise to 75% by end-2000). UES is estimated to be owed over RUB130bn, and is said to owe natural gas monopoly **Gazprom** around RUB50bn. This led to a dispute earlier this year when Gazprom cut gas supplies to federal power plants by around 60%, and UES warned of a 25% drop in electricity production.

The electricity sector is likely to receive attention from the new administration. An appreciation of the sheer scale of the problems facing the system, and therefore the economy as a whole, no doubt prompted the government to make electricity one of the priorities of its recently released programme. A strategy for the sector's reform has already been penned by Anatoly Chubais, veteran economic reformer, who became UES CEO in 1998. Under a programme approved by UES' board of directors in April, it was forecast that as much as US$70bn will need to be invested over the 2000-10 period, and that the only way to raise this much money would be through making

UES an attractive option for investors. It was therefore proposed to sell off UES' generation and supply capabilities while maintaining control of transmission.

...But Reform Will Not Be Straightforward

Reform is not going to be easy. Indeed, Chubais' programme has already run into trouble from UES' foreign minority shareholders (foreigners own about a third of the company), who have been alarmed more by questions to do with the implementation of the reform than the reform itself. Their central concern is that sell-offs will be made before the value of assets can be boosted by, for example, raising tariffs to cover costs, solving the non-payments problem and establishing an acceptable regulatory regime for the sector. Another concern is that UES' assets will be broken down into too many companies, which will be, because of their size, unattractive to foreign investors, and that they could end up being sold to the local elite – with the airing that suspect state sell-offs are currently receiving in the media adding grist to the mill.

UES has said that it is keen to involve the minority shareholders in formulating the restructuring strategy, and has set up a special advisory board to address their concerns. Nevertheless, doubts persist. Crucially, Chubais is saying that sell-offs could begin as early as next spring, while the minority shareholders have argued that a three-year timescale is necessary. Moreover, the government, as the largest shareholder in the company, is measuring its words, suggesting a quick decision on the form of restructuring is unlikely. The government's economic programme aims to break up the electricity monopoly, and Chubais has claimed that, in essence, it is exactly in line with UES' plans. However, the government has indicated recently that a number of unresolved issues remain. UES now appears to be working on a more specific restructuring plan with the advice of **Deutsche Bank**, **PriceWaterhouse Coopers** and **JP Morgan**, and Deputy Prime Minister Viktor Khristenko said recently that and that this would be discussed by the government in September. The EBRD and World Bank, for their part, have on the whole expressed their support for Chubais' proposals, and suggested that the minority shareholders are being overly demanding.

This is not to mention the problems which could be caused in the future by more traditional sources of opposition to electricity reform. Opposition has in the past been particularly strong in parliament, and there is also resistance from the regions, where prices are set by local regulators who can, in turn, be in the sway of local politicians. That said, the new Duma is considerably more amenable than the last, and the regions are currently on the back foot. It could also be significant that the former fuel and energy minister Viktor

In a first sign of the difficulties ahead, Chubais' programme has already come up against considerable opposition from foreign minority shareholders. While supporting a break-up of the electricity monopoly, the government is also measuring its words, suggesting a quick decision on the form of restructuring is unlikely.

Kalyuzhny, who had been particularly obstructive, was dropped from the new government, although his replacement, Alexander Gavrin, is something of an unknown quantity.

Gas

Gas Sector Reform Is In The Air

Talk of restructuring the gas sector is also in the air, but the issue is at a very early stage, and longer term it is difficult to see Gazprom bowing to fundamental reforms, such as giving up its grip on export routes, without a fight.

Another key sector that the new government is proposing to restructure is gas, but the issue is at a far earlier stage than in the case of electricity. At present, the sector is dominated by the country's largest company, **Gazprom**, which has a virtual monopoly of production and supply. Like UES, Gazprom complains that a difficult operating environment – including artificially low domestic prices, non-payment and the government's taxation policy – has led to insufficient investment and the use of imports to make up for a shortfall in domestic production. However, Gazprom sits on the largest reserves of natural gas in the world, benefits from substantial exports, and has fared significantly better than most other companies in the post-Soviet era. There has therefore not been the same pressure to reform the sector as with electricity. The unwillingness to change is heightened by the company's political importance, which extends as far as its use as a foreign policy tool.

Nevertheless, pressure for reform has been mounting. In addition to the advice of international lenders, the government is facing demands from the oil companies that they be permitted to exploit the gas potential of their fields. And the underlying assumption of the economic programme drawn up for the government by minister for economic development and trade German Gref is that investment needs to be encouraged in the sector. To begin with, however, the government's intentions appear to focus on financially separating Gazprom's transport and distribution facilities, and in the longer run it is difficult to imagine the company bowing to more fundamental reforms, such as giving up its grip on export routes, without a fight.

Progress Continues On Major Investment Projects

Gazprom continues to make progress on its substantial investment undertakings, with its "Blue Stream" project to supply the Turkish market recently receiving a key boost against the rival TCP.

Meanwhile, Gazprom is making good progress on the substantial investment projects it has already undertaken. In particular, the "Blue Stream" project – which aims to construct, in collaboration with Italy's **ENI**, an underwater pipeline under the Black Sea to supply the key Turkish market – received a boost when it was agreed that Russia's imports of Turkmen gas would be increased. Although the deal has not yet been finalised (the price remains a sticking point), it could not only provide a cushion against any domestic gas production shortfall, but, due to the amounts of gas involved, could prove to be a key blow to the TransCaspian Pipeline (TCP) project, which plans to build a pipeline to Turkey from Turkmenistan. The latter project is, incidentally, favoured by the US, largely because it would bypass Russia. Work on the Blue Stream began in early 2000, and the aim is to have one line in operation in late 2001 and a second the following year.

Gazprom is also continuing to make progress in the construction of a pipeline from Yamal in the Arctic to Europe, with the Belarus-Poland stretch of the route opened in September 1999. Longer term, the company is reportedly considering building a pipeline beneath the Baltic Sea to Europe. Gazprom's plans highlight expectations of an encouraging outlook for the company in Europe, but the company would also like to get involved in the exploitation of the Kovykta field in east Siberia, which could serve the Chinese market. Unusually, the licence to develop the deposit was won by a company in which Gazprom has no part, **Rusia Petroleum** (in which a subsidiary of BP Amoco is the main shareholder).

Foreign Stake May Be Boosted

Gazprom has also signalled that it may allow foreign investors to play a larger role in the company. Currently the share of foreign investors in the company is around 6%. Germany's **Ruhrgas** owns 4%, and 2% is traded in the form of American Depository Receipts (ADRs). Earlier this year, Gazprom said that it planned to sell a further 14% of the company to foreigners via ADRs by 2003. Ruhrgas may also be interested in increasing its stake.

Gazprom may allow foreign investors to play a greater role in the company over the next few years.

It is worth noting that Gazprom's chief executive Rem Vyakhirev is an oligarch who in the past at least has been considered suspect by the Putin administration. It is said that Gazprom has a significant stake in Vladimir Gusinsky's Media-Most empire (*see Political Outlook*), and Vyakhirev was suspected of supporting Yevgeny Primakov's candidacy for the presidency. Boris Berezovsky has also spoken out against Vyakhirev in the past.

Agriculture

Still In The Doldrums

Agriculture's share of GDP has declined more sharply in Russia than in virtually any other former Soviet state. There is still a chronic lack of investment, and although production is expected to grow this year, this is from a low base.

Agriculture continues to suffer from chronic problems. It has always been less important to the overall Russian economy than in other former Soviet states, but nevertheless, its share of GDP has seen a decline over the last decade unparalleled anywhere but in Kazakhstan. According to figures from the Interstate Statistical Committee of the CIS, agriculture accounted for just 6.0% of Russian GDP in 1998 compared with 14.0% in 1991, while in Kazakhstan its share had fallen to 9.0% from 29.0%. A dearth of investment in the sector continues. Overall investment in fixed capital is reported to have increased last year for the first time since the end of communism (albeit by a meagre 1.0%, and with the level still being 20% of that seen in 1990), but investment in agriculture still fell by 4.2% after a 15.9% fall in 1998. It has been estimated that farmers have only 40-60% of the machinery they need.

Agricultural output has at least expanded in 2000, but by an extremely modest 1.2% y-o-y in January-April, and this from a low base of comparison: output had contracted by 4.6% y-o-y in the equivalent period of 1999. The agriculture ministry is expecting the grain harvest to exceed last year's 54.7mn tonnes, but it has revised its expectations downwards to 62-63mn tonnes from its previous 70-75mn forecast. The Economics Ministry has said that it is expecting growth in agricultural production this year of no more than 3% because of the generally unfavourable situation in the sector, especially in livestock.

Land Reform Comes To The Fore...

Land reform, including legislation to allow the private ownership and sale of land, is seen as key to reviving the sector's fortunes.

Against this inhospitable background the question of land reform is seen as crucial to reviving agriculture's fortunes. The lack of an adequate legislative framework allowing for the private ownership and sale of land is seen as the greatest immediate obstacle facing agriculture, the reasoning being that if these were allowed, farmers would be able to borrow from banks using land as collateral. A land market would also develop, allowing land which is currently disused to pass into productive hands. While the Russian constitution does allow for the private ownership of land, and up to 90% of land is officially considered to be in private hands, the appropriate legislation has not been approved by parliament. A draft Land Code has been stuck in the legislature for years.

The issue of land reform has been pushed into the realm of public debate recently by the highest levels of the administration. Putin himself signalled that he would like to address the issue, saying before the presidential election that a referendum might be called on whether to allow private ownership of land, and creating a land market is one of the aims of the government's economic programme.

...But Putin Remains Cautious

However, Putin has on the whole pursued a cautious line. Land reform is, after all, an exceptionally sensitive issue politically. The Communist and Agrarian parties are those most vehemently opposed to a land market, but many others are also concerned about whose hands land would fall into if it were open for sale, and for what purposes it would be used. Indeed, the draft Land Code currently in parliament is the work of the leftists and, as a result, puts strong limits on the conditions under which land can be owned. An alternative draft has been put forward by the Union of Right Forces, which specifies only that the land should be used for agricultural purposes. Even if Putin does decide that he wants to move forcefully on land reform now he is firmly ensconced in the Kremlin and parliament is showing an unusual willingness to cooperate, it would be unwise to believe that it would be plain sailing for the agricultural sector from then on. It is estimated, for example, that at least 20 other laws would need to be passed to accompany the Land Code, and it is a big assumption to make that Russia's banking system would be up to the task of helping to restore agriculture.

The issue of land reform is highly sensitive politically, and Putin has so far been moving cautiously.

Profile and Recent Developments

Agriculture

Suffering From Underinvestment

In the Soviet era the agricultural sector could be characterised as inefficient, heavily subsidised and incapable of producing enough to prevent food shortages. The sector saw little need to use resources efficiently or to modernise, working instead to meet the state plan. This often involved the setting of artificially low targets that the sector could then meet. The cold winds of competition that blew across the country in the early 1990s saw a dramatic swing in fortunes, with subsidy levels – sometimes as much as 60-80% of the price of a product – dramatically reduced. The sector was unprepared for the changes that were taking place, and as a consequence output declined and the industry suffered at the hands of a surge in imported products. Although often more expensive than domestic products, these did not experience the inconsistencies of supply and poor quality associated with domestic output, and therefore gained an extensive foothold within the market place.

The second half of the 1990s saw the agricultural sector coming to terms with the new environment. As distribution networks improved and companies began to use inputs more efficiently, output began to recover, and domestic producers began to at least hold their own in the face of foreign competition. Across the sector as a whole, 1998 was relatively favourable. However, this disguised considerable discrepancies between sub-sectors. The main problem came in the grain harvest, which saw a decline in production to 47.8mn tonnes in 1998 from 88.6mn tonnes in 1997. This was the worst harvest for forty years, and also came at the worst possible time for the country as it entered a deep economic crisis. The result was an acute shortage of grain, despite food aid from the US and EU.

1999 saw another low grain harvest of 54.7mn tonnes. Real growth in agriculture is impossible without investment, but until a proper system of private land ownership is in place few Russian farmers, and even fewer foreign investors, will consider committing large-scale investment. President Putin has said that he wants to see land reform, but the Duma has backed away from it on a number of occasions in the past.

Energy Sector

An Important Revenue Provider

The energy sector plays a key role in both the overall economy and in providing resources for the government in the form of budget revenue and valuable hard currency earnings. For example, **Gazprom**, the state supplier of gas, has the largest gas reserves in the world and provides one-quarter of government revenues. The gas sector's size, importance and capacity to provide budget revenues has opened it up to state interference through the restructuring of the companies within the sector and the imposition of export tariffs on output.

Oil Sector: Higher Revenues Boost Producers

Oil prices rose from around US$10/b at the beginning of 1999 to peaks of US$30/b in Q1 00. This provided a huge shot in the arm for Russian producers, who enjoy some of the lowest fixed costs in the world. A meeting of Opec oil ministers at the end of March authorised the partial reversal of price-supporting production curbs, letting around 1.5mn barrels per day of extra oil onto the market. In expectation of this, the price of Brent crude had dropped back to around US$25/b. **BMI** expects the price to fall gradually to US$20-25/b during 2000. Even so, this is far above what much of the industry, and the Finance Ministry, would have dared hope a year ago. Analysts believe that the stock market valuation multiples of the Russian majors should converge towards those of their Eastern European counterparts during 2000.

Step Up In Investment Required

Russia's traditional oil-producing territories in the Volga and West Siberian regions have been poorly-managed since Soviet times, and the decline in oil production can only be reversed by large-scale investment in exploration in new areas and in enhanced recovery techniques in existing fields. Even in the absence of either of these, oil production is expected to rise in 2000 by 1-3%, and while still at low levels, investment will rise more quickly. As part of a stepping-up of investment in Russia in 2000, the European Bank for Reconstruction and Development (EBRD) plans to make a US$150mn loan to the biggest oil producer **Lukoil**, subject to the ironing out of various transparency concerns. Lukoil needs capital to help develop a huge new offshore find in the Severny field in the Caspian Sea, which was unveiled in Q1 00. The find is estimated to contain as much as 2.2bn barrels, a significant addition to the company's already-massive 14.4bn barrels. Third-biggest producer **Yukos** listed once again on the Moscow Interbank Currency Exchange (MICEX) in March, although it will need to combat its poor reputation among Western investors before it can raise significant capital via this route. January crude export figures posted an increase of 2.8% month-on-month and 6.1% year-on-year to 2.24mn barrels, suggesting exports will grow in 2000. The great boost to profitability given to Russian oil companies by the combination of the rouble devaluation and the near-tripling of oil prices will continue to show its effects throughout the forecast period. Oil companies receive major export earnings in dollars but most of their costs, from wages to pipeline tariffs, are denominated in roubles. This has given the industry more money to invest without calling on foreign capital. However, just as important as the oil price, and not much less volatile, is the attitude of the Russian government itself.

Crude Export Tax Hits Oil Industry

In principle, Putin says he wants to restrict the state's role to that of enforcing the rules of the game. In practice, he appears to favour proactive moves by the tax authorities. Starting at the beginning of 1999, the government has sought to tap into the oil companies' windfall with a floating rate export tax. This was later replaced with a fixed rate. At the beginning of March, the Ministry of Energy raised the rate from EUR15/tonne to EUR20/tonne. These taxes will raise revenue but such changes do little to help investors plan ahead. In this context, it is to be hoped that the extension of production sharing agreements for oilfields where foreign investors are active participants continues. These contracts, such as the one recently signed by **Tatneft** in the Romashkinsoye field, give investors more certainty over the level of taxes. Another problem is the tendency of the authorities to limit exports from particular projects. Such decrees, aimed at guaranteeing supplies to the domestic market, where prices are lower (although they are rising to more realistic levels) have resulted in numerous setbacks for foreign oil companies in Russia. Revenues have failed to compensate for the investments made in these cases.

Corporate Restructuring Keeps Analysts Guessing

A long-standing plan to merge the remnants of the state-owned oil industry, including **Slavneft** and **Onako**, may become less of a priority. There is ongoing speculation that Gazprom's monopoly of gas transport may be broken by splitting the management of the giant pipeline network away from the production arm. If so, this would give private oil companies access to markets for their gas for the first time, enabling them to export it rather than flare it. The process of trying to create a new state oil company would become an unnecessary distraction amid such a huge venture.

The announced consolidation of **Surgutneft**, a major producer based in Western Siberia, was cautiously welcomed by the markets in Q1 00. It would constitute a takeover of the production subsidiary (in which most foreigners have holdings) by the holding company. The process is expected to be completed during 2000. It would make the company's shares more liquid. Surgutneft managed to raise production by 6.8% to 37.6mn tonnes during 1999, and is well-regarded by investors for concentrating on its core business rather than asset-stripping other enterprises.

Gas Sector: A Global Player

Gazprom, the gas monopoly accounting for more than 95% of gas production, is Russia's largest company. Based on the US$660mn paid by **Ruhrgas** of Germany for a 2.5% holding in the company at the end of 1998, it would be worth more than twice the value of the top 50 Russian companies put together. The company is not just large in Russia – it holds the largest reserves of natural gas in the world and has a 20% share of the European gas market. Indeed, it is towards Europe that the company is looking to generate sales growth over the forecast period. Russia accounted for 37% of European gas imports in 1998, and in April 2000 it said that exports to Europe could double by 2020 to 250-270bcm per year as European countries open up 20% of their gas supply markets to international competition.

The link with Ruhrgas makes sound commercial sense, allowing Gazprom increased access to the West European market. Foreigners own around 6% of the company, as well as a proportion of the openly-traded shares. The law forbids foreigners from taking more than a 20% stake in Gazprom, while a presidential decree cut the limit further to 14%. Gazprom has said it plans to issue new ADRs up to this lower limit. These currently make up 2% of the share capital, while the Russian government owns a 38% stake.

Gazprom is also embarking on some impressive capital spending programmes. Not least of these is the 'Blue Stream' project to construct the deepest underwater pipeline in the world, running from the port of Dzhubga on Russia's Black Sea coast to Samsun in Turkey (396km). Work has already begun on the line, which will supply 16bcm per year to Turkey. German-Russian company **Wingas** is ready to start on a 225km stretch of pipeline to supply Russian gas to Rueckersdorf in Thuringia.

However, 1998 saw Gazprom record a loss of approximately US$2bn due in no small measure to the decline in the rouble. The company made RUB37bn from the sale of gas, but lost RUB82bn from the exchange rate fall. It was owed RUB132bn in payment arrears from domestic gas users.

Electricity: Dominated By UES

The electricity sector is dominated by national power utility **Unified Energy System** (UES). The company has stakes ranging from 16-100% in 71 out of 73 regional power utilities, and owns the transmission grid along with several large power stations. UES is 52.7% owned by the state. Headed by former first deputy prime minister Anatoly Chubais, the company vies with Gazprom for dominance of the corporate sector. Like many utility companies in Russia, UES faces difficulties in obtaining payment for the services it provides. In 1998 payment was received for only 80% of the electricity supplied, and of that only 20% was made in cash, although there was an improvement in 1999 with the cash component rising to 49% in December and to 39% for the year as a whole. This enabled some improvement in UES' relations with Gazprom, but the two companies still publicly rowed in early 2000, when Gazprom cut supplies of gas to power stations in protest at UES non-payment.

Both companies are hampered by being forced to supply non-paying customers which the government wants to see kept afloat for social or strategic reasons. The share of cash in payments to Gazprom was just 33% in 1999, even lower than at UES. The payment indiscipline does not stop with domestic sources – CIS countries are heavily in debt to UES, with some in consultations with the company over restructuring payments. To counterbalance this, the company has plans to step up exports to (solvent) West European customers such as Finland.

Metals, Gold & Diamonds

Iron And Steel: Looking For New Markets

With domestic demand estimated to have fallen by at least 20% in 1998, and a huge competitive gain arising from the decline in the rouble, producers looked to overseas markets to make up the shortfall. However, this led to trade tensions, particularly with the US, which accused Russian companies of dumping. Under threat of punitive dumping duties and restrictions, Russia agreed to halt exports of basic steel products to the US for six months, and to sharply reduce exports in 16 other categories. The export of hot rolled steel was limited to 1996 levels and a minimum price imposed on Russian exporters. Exports of this type of steel are not to exceed 750,000 tonnes per year under a new agreement. This is a setback for Russian steel producers, but will encourage the search for other export markets to replace the US. Europe stands out as a prime candidate, given the decline in demand from Asia (**Severstal**, the largest Russian steel producer, used to send more than half its exports to Asia, but this has dropped to 10%).

Platinum Group Metals: Hit By Low Prices

Other metals producers in 1998 faced an equally difficult environment. Low world prices were a heavy financial burden. **Norilsk Nickel**, the dominant producer in the sector accounting for 99% and 70% respectively of nickel and copper exports, cut production in 1999, partly to allow modernisation of its plant. However, low world prices are likely to have been an equally important consideration, although these improved in the second half of 1999 and early 2000. Meanwhile, the company is not planning to raise platinum group metals production in the next 10 years, reflecting the demand/supply imbalance on the world stage. Norilsk was also scathing of the 5% export tariff imposed on nickel and copper ores and related products for the first six months of 1999. The company would have preferred a floating tariff similar to the one agreed with the oil industry, but suffered in part from the industry's less effective lobbying power.

Gold: Further Output Declines

Russia's gold producers are facing a hard time in a low-price environment compounded by high taxation and a lack of government support. The government decided in December 1999 to maintain a 5% gold export tariff, imposed in April to tap windfall profits from the rouble devaluation. Goskomstat stopped publishing gold output figures in 1998, making accurate data hard to come by. However, the Gold Industrialists' Union has said that gold mining output increased in 1999 to 113.9 tonnes from 105.2 tonnes in 1998, reversing the declining trend seen in recent years. The industry lacks the necessary investment in plant and equipment to boost output, suggesting that Russian gold companies face a period of consolidation rather than growth. Illegal production remains high.

Diamonds: Extended De Beers Deal

Russia is one of the world's largest producers of diamonds. South Africa's **De Beers**, which accounts for two-thirds of global sales, estimated 1999 output at US$1.6bn, just behind first-placed Botswana on US$1.8bn. The diamond market was boosted by an increase of over 10% in global jewellery sales as retail demand picked up. **Alrosa** (Almazy Rossii-Sakha), the largest diamond producer in Russia with a 99.7% domestic market share and the second largest in the world, signed a three-year extension to their agreement signed with De Beers in October 1997, commiting Alrosa to sell a minimum US$550mn of diamonds through De Beers' Central Selling Organisation (CSO). Alrosa's actual sales through the CSO are expected to significantly exceed the minimum provision. The company is allowed to sell up to a maximum of 26% of De Beers' group sales, which totalled US$505bn in 1999.

Aluminium: Surviving By Tolling

Aluminium has become Russia's most significant export after oil and gas, earning around US$3.12bn in 1999. The industry relies heavily on a tax-avoiding mechanism known as tolling which allows processors to import raw material and export refined aluminium without paying tariffs. The future of the industry hinges on whether the government allows this to continue. Over 60% of capacity is situated in three regions in East Siberia, where the industry was located in the Soviet era to take advantage of plentiful hydroelectric energy sources, but most of the raw material is imported from Ukraine. During the 1990s Trans-World Corporation tried to acquire control of a majority of the aluminium industry but has since sold its assets. In early 2000 shareholders in oil company **Sibneft** and **LogoVaz** acquired a major chunk by buying plants in Achinsk, Bratsk and Krasnoyarsk.

Telecommunications

Limited By Weak Economy

The events of 1998 produced a negative backdrop for telecom companies' outlook. These companies suffer from high debt levels, the inability to set their own tariffs and falling demand due to the general economic background. The providers of cellular equipment have been particularly hard hit, given the higher prices of mobile communications and the fact that a mobile telephone is seen as a luxury rather than a necessity. Mobile operators had to switch to a mass-market strategy as free-spending business customers grew harder to come by. 1998 saw a 25% stake in cellular operator **Vimpel-Communications** sold for US$160mn to state-owned Norwegian company **Telenor AS**.

Telephone penetration remains low by international standards. In 1997 the International Telecom-munications Union (ITU) estimated the number of main telephone lines per 100 inhabitants at 18.3, compared with over 30 in many other transition countries. As a result, there is significant potential for future growth. The sector is dominated by **Svyazinvest**, a government-owned holding company which has controlling stakes in nearly all the regional telecom companies. A 25% plus one share stake in Svyazinvest was sold to private investors in 1997, with the remainder of the company being held by the state. The authorities had intended to sell a further 25% holding during 1999 in an attempt to plug government finances, but this was blocked in 1998 by the impact of the financial crisis. The long-standing plan may be revived again in 2000 or 2001. The restructuring of the company got underway in early 2000 with mergers between some of the 90 regional operators, starting with a three-way merger between the companies serving St. Petersburg. The deal amounts to a takeover of the other two by local operator, St. Petersburg Telephone. The merger process is intended to increase efficiency and investor interest.

Tariffs Remain Fixed, Despite High Inflation

The telecommunications sector overall faces a difficult environment due to its inability to set its own tariffs. These are controlled by the government, and have not been raised on domestic lines in the wake of the 1998 crisis despite the rapid rise in inflation. The government is keen to limit price pressures wherever possible, and this is one area where there has been scope. However, this hinders profitability within the sector. Only **Rostelekom** has been able to raise tariffs for international lines, blaming the weak rouble. In contrast to the poorly-run Svyazinvest, it has managed to attract much more investor interest. A further hindrance is the level of debt the industry carries, in particular foreign currency denominated debt. This was issued in better times, and at more favourable exchange rates, and the rouble's fall since 1998 has led to a significantly higher debt-servicing burden for the telecom companies. It is estimated that equipment-related liabilities for companies connected to Svyazinvest amounted to US$200-250mn in 1999, double 1998's level. The company managed to reschedule US$100mn in debt to **Merrill Lynch** in Q1 00.

Banking And Finance

In Need Of Major Restructuring...

Russia has a very underdeveloped banking system, a factor which limited the impact of the 1998 financial collapse on the real economy. By the end of 1999, banking sector assets were 14% of GDP, compared with 25% pre-crisis, a level already low by emerging market standards. Public mistrust of the banking system has only been increased and there is thought to be as much as US$30bn in mattress savings outside the banks.

Before the 1998 crisis the sector was already showing signs of poor management and structural weaknesses, which massively exaggerated the effects of the rouble's collapse. Not least of these was a reliance on the government with large exposure to government securities, particularly short-term t-bills (GKOs). It is estimated that over 10% of the banking system's assets were held in these instruments by mid-1998, and for some institutions the proportion was considerably higher. The collapse of the GKO market produced a serious decline in banking sector liquidity as well as a severe overnight decline in asset values. The impact was to effectively bankrupt many institutions. To a great extent, the focus on the government debt market derived from the poor opportunities to lend elsewhere in the economy and inadequate risk assessment, with the result that many banks entered the crisis with a high proportion of bad loans. The CBR estimated bad loans as a percentage of total loans at 7% in September 1998, although this number may well have underestimated the true picture. More importantly, half of the bad loans were on the books of the top five banks which accounted for one-third of lending in the economy. The banking sector had additionally undertaken a large volume of off-balance sheet forward contracts. These were unhedged exposures, the value of which plummeted with the collapse in the rouble. This further exacerbated the liquidity crunch and the viability of many institutions. Furthermore, the banks had borrowed heavily in hard currencies (mostly US dollars) and had also provided deposits in hard currencies. Without corresponding foreign assets to match these liabilities, the rouble collapse left many institutions unable to cover foreign obligations.

Realising that the banking system was in trouble, investors and deposit holders attempted to remove their money from the banks in the weeks after the August crisis. This served to heighten the liquidity shortage, with many institutions unable to provide all or part of the funds demanded. The CBR has estimated that by the end of August 1998 44% of the banks were experiencing liquidity problems. To boost liquidity it allowed reserves to be drawn down and extended loans to institutions. Moreover, any bank with deposits of more than RUB300bn was forced to transfer them to state-owned and CBR-controlled **Sberbank**. By the end of November 50% of rouble deposits and 10% of foreign currency deposits in six major commercial banks had been transferred. The low transference of foreign currency deposits reflected the RUB9/US$ exchange rate Sberbank offered for the transaction. In addition to these measures, the CBR provided liquidity to institutions it considers to have 'potential'. Unfortunately, this process lacked any transparency in qualifying criteria. Some viable institutions were overlooked while other, less sound banks, were favoured. This led to accusations that the CBR is pursuing its own agenda due to political factors or the desire to favour certain individuals. Domestic savings have gravitated towards Sberbank, which accounted for 80% of deposits by the end of 1999.

...But Plans Fall Short

The authorities realised that the banking system was not viable and needed restructuring. To this end they set up the Agency for Restructuring of Credit Organisations (ARCO) – 51% of which is owned by the government and 49% by the CBR – with a capital base of RUB14bn. The agency will oversee the restructuring process, taking stakes in those banks seen as viable, managing bad assets, initiating bankruptcy proceedings where appropriate, and raising funds necessary to complete its activities. In 1998, the number of banks fell from 1,675 to 1,468.

The plan, although laudable in the context of the economic crisis, is not without its drawbacks. The failure to press ahead with large-scale bankruptcies and the provision of near-term liquidity raise questions both about the timeframe of the restructuring and the capacity for misappropriation of funds. Supporting bankrupt institutions that would be better closed immediately is likely to be inefficient and costly. This also applies to the CBR's decision to support some of the banks deemed too large to fail. Meanwhile, the CBR's plan does nothing to solve the underlying problems of bad debts and poor management.

The ability to restructure the banking system is further compromised by the behaviour of the CDR. Widely distrusted by politicians, it has been under investigation for corruption. In 1999 it was revealed that Russia transferred part of its foreign exchange reserves to an obscure fund management company in Jersey, called **FIMACO** between 1993 and 1997.

Foreign Investment Remains Minimal

One logical answer to the current problems would be for the Russian banking market to be opened up to foreign banks for investment. Unfortunately, the business and regulatory environment is antithetical to significant investment in the industry, and many foreign bankers will not even consider committing money. In August 1998 only 4% of the banking market was controlled by foreign banks, compared with a permitted ceiling of just 12%. While governments have in the past made welcoming noises about foreign access to the sector, xenophobia still reigns supreme. Jingoistic legislators tend to view the banking sector as "strategic", believing that foreign participation would endanger national security.

4 Business Environment

Introduction

Uncertainty Clouds Business Decisions

The 1998 crisis cast a long shadow over the business environment in Russia. It put in jeopardy the gradual move to a market economy and therefore resulted in a substantial rise in the level of uncertainty and the difficulty of business planning. For foreign investors the most pressing questions concerned Russia's relationship with the outside world – how far it would accede to IMF demands and remain part of the international community. By early 2000 the situation had improved markedly, with IMF support having become less important as a guarantee of stability. In a key development for domestic enterprises, the rouble devaluation delivered a strong competitive boost to export-orientated companies, and drastically improved the competitiveness of local products against imports. The demise of the high-yielding government debt market also brought an end to easy speculative profits, and spurred firms to step up productive investment instead.

For companies looking to invest in Russia, the most attractive opportunities are still in the key strategic areas such as oil and gas projects, and oil and gas companies have proved the most willing to run the risk, lured by the promise of big profits. But although Russian assets are cheap – and certainly much cheaper than at the start of 1998 – the degree of uncertainty, over policy direction if nothing else, has so far kept Russia off the investment horizon for many potential investors.

Infrastructure

Infrastructure Spending Limited

The state of most of Russia's infrastructure is poor. There has been some investment in ports, telecoms and railways, but a worrying area is the electricity industry. Power cuts are becoming more frequent and the situation has not been helped by disputes between gas giant **Gazprom** and state electricity holding company **UES,** which owes it RUB130bn. UES chairman Anatoly Chubais has said that the industry needs US$5bn a year in investment, whereas it can only raise US$500mn a year. Renewed belt-tightening in the wake of the financial crisis further reduced the government's ability to spend money on infrastructure. In early 2000 it approved a 20-year plan to improve the road network in the north-west of the country. One aim is to improve transport links with the rest of northern Europe. Longer-term, Russia is keen to develop an alternative land route for trade between Europe and the Asia-Pacific region.

Within the industrial sector, oil and gas have the most scope for new infrastructure investment. **Gazprom** and Italian energy giant **ENI** have started on the US$3bn 'Blue Stream' underwater gas pipeline. The project will link Dzhubga on Russia's Black Sea coast with Samsun in Turkey at depths of up to 2,200m, 30% deeper than any existing subsea pipeline. Although at odds with US government schemes for an 'energy corridor' from the Caspian Sea region to Turkey, the project started in 1999. Gazprom is in the process of routing its exports to Europe away from the Ukrainian transit system (where Gazprom has long alleged that theft is taking place), directing more throughput via Belarus and Poland. In the oil sector, a feasibility study is under consideration for a US$10bn gas pipeline between Russia and China. **Sidanco**, the Russian oil company that underwent bankruptcy proceedings in early 1999, and **China National Petroleum Corporation** are behind the proposed pipeline. Meanwhile **Yukos**, the second largest oil company in Russia, is holding discussions with the Chinese authorities over pipeline proposals. In March 2000, oil transport company **Transneft** began work on pipeline to Primorsk on the Gulf of Finland, which will enable an increase in oil exports of 240,000 b/d once it is completed in around two years.

The Domestic Market

Use Of Barter Starting To Fall, Slowly

The decline in economic output coupled with the rise in unemployment and poverty has contributed to a steady fall in the Russian population and produced a difficult background for business operations. The Economy Ministry estimated that Russians' standard of living dropped 15% in 1999, while the number of people living below the official poverty line increased to 50mn out of a population of 147mn. Nevertheless, such was the gain in competitiveness following the rouble collapse that Russian companies sourcing inputs from domestic suppliers can exploit the fall in import demand. However, Russian enterprises remain inefficient. A study of 10 major industries by the **McKinsey Global Institute** published in 2000 found that Russian productivity levels were approximately 19% of those seen in North America, while GDP per capita is just 15% of the US level. The report estimated that a quarter of all industry was unviable and would eventually need to be closed. Underemployment is a serious problem. Local administrations frequently channel subsidies to loss-making companies in order to prevent job losses, or for corrupt reasons. This undermines competition from profitable and more efficient competitors.

The use of barter increased following the 1998 economic crisis to account for over 50% of all transactions. Barter proves effective at keeping businesses operating during times of financial chaos, banking sector illiquidity and payment arrears. Gazprom, for example, obtained only 18% of its revenue in cash in 1998, while less than 40% of its tax was paid in cash. The downside is that it allows companies and individuals to avoid tax payments, facilitates corruption and creates inefficiency. As time and resources are wasted trying to match up goods, the market mechanism cannot operate properly and resources are misallocated. By the start of 2000, there was more liquidity in the financial system and the use of barter to settle transactions was falling. The recovery in industry was also accompanied by a fall in enterprise arrears.

The Labour Market

A Change Of Policy Direction

Primakov's coming to power saw a change of emphasis in labour policy. Where previously employees had taken the strain for the inefficiencies of government and industry, usually via wage arrears, Primakov realised that this option would not be sustainable. The extent to which the economy and financial system had collapsed, together with the need to pull the strands of the diverse political parties together, meant that it was imperative to placate the workforce as much as possible. This would help to reduce social tension, show that the government was working on the people's behalf, and lessen the impact of the economic decline. Wage arrears have been reduced, with the overall wage debt of the state sector falling to RUB10.2bn in Janaury 2000 from RUR19.4bn in January 1999. However, this still does not mean that all wages are being paid on time, including those of soldiers in Chechnya. The potential to remove wage arrears altogether is limited. In April 2000 the government instituted a 20% public sector pay rise and increased the meagre standard pension.

The economic crisis saw unemployment rise to 13.3% at the end of 1998, before moderating to 12.3% a year later. Although government data considerably understates true employment within the economy, there is also the level of underemployment to be taken into account. Sustained growth will require the subsidising of inefficient and outdated industries to be abolished – under such a scenario unemployment is likely to rise before it comes down again. The decline in the manufacturing economy in favour of the service sector has been partially halted by the improved price competitiveness of Russian goods over foreign competitors following the rouble's collapse, but not permanently.

Corporate Taxation

A Precarious Balancing Act

The administration has been faced with conflicting objectives in the field of corporate taxation. The need to promote business at a time when the economy was suffering badly contrasted with the desire to increase budget revenues as much as possible to meet IMF targets. The approach adopted was to accommodate both strands by reducing the corporate taxation rate to 30% from 35%, and by imposing additional taxes on those areas considered able to sustain them, including the oil and gas sectors, which gained considerably from lower operating costs. But the tax system relies too much on the resource sector, which was hit by export taxes in 1999, raised again in 2000. Major inconsistencies remain, however, with different companies in the same sector paying taxes at different rates. In 1998 Gazprom paid US$1.57bn in a year in which it made losses of US$5.5bn, while in 1999 – a far more profitable year for the company – it handed over just US$457mn. The tax authorities' periodic raids are suspected to be motivated as much by political pressures on certain businessmen as by the efficient collection of tax.

Industrial Policy

Promoting Domestic Producers

The continued decline in the rouble created an opportunity for Russian industry which the government was keen to foster. This not only included the export sector, where Russian products enjoyed a clear competitive price advantage, but also the domestic sector, where imports were effectively priced out of the market. The government has tried to provide as benign an environment as possible for the industrial sector, since this is one way to limit the extent of the economic fallout and reduce social and political tensions. One method is to clear the tax and wage arrears clogging up the payments system, making companies work more efficiently and limiting the use of barter. This requires work on two fronts. Firstly, the financial system, and the banks in particular, are in need of reform. The collapse of the rouble left many banks facing an acute shortage of liquidity that effectively rendered them bankrupt. The authorities realise that a substantial number of Russia's banks will need to disappear, either through mergers or bankruptcy. The Agency for Restructuring Credit Organisations (ARCO) is the body charged with managing this process. Prime Minister Mikhail Kasyanov was named to chair it in early 2000. The IMF and World Bank suggested that the selection process for which institutions should be allowed to go under should be based on the institutions' importance and the consequences if they were to fail. Unfortunately, evidence suggests that this policy is not being followed. Indeed, some banks are being supported on the basis of who owns them or who has vested interests in them. This is not a healthy signal for overall reform of the system, and the failure of the government to promote reform in the financial sector was a major reason why the IMF decided to suspend Russia's loan programme in 1999. The second element for clearing the payments system is to reduce government arrears and help promote the greater use of cash in society. Success in the former has been partly achieved, while the latter has been more of a challenge.

Foreign Investment Policy

Looking To Boost Foreign Direct Investment

Attracting funds from overseas is a high priority. Indeed, Putin and his advisors appear to be particularly keen to attract FDI, given that such inflows tend to be long-term and improve both economic growth prospects and infrastructure. This contrasts with the short-term capital inflows that Russia has tended to attract in recent years, the majority of which went into the domestic debt (GKO) market. These inflows just as quickly reversed in times of trouble, a characteristic which helped to precipitate the 1998 economic crisis.

The main barriers hindering foreign investment have traditionally been an unpredictable political outlook, uncertainty surrounding the economic climate (economic nationalism is a greater force in Russia than in many emerging markets), and Russia's relationship with the international community, including the IMF. The government's need to secure agreement with the international community goes much further than merely solving the short-term economic crisis, and as such has far reaching long-term implications. However, even with the greater certainty in the political sphere brought by Putin and a more buoyant economy, matters are still being made difficult for foreign companies by the lack of transparency in both the law and the way business is conducted in Russia. Without a clearer set of laws which look after the interests of foreign investors in an open manner, attempts to attract foreign investment will be confined to those areas where companies can see a clear advantage and are willing to take the risk – for example within the oil and gas sector. Even here, investment has been hampered by the lack of production-sharing agreement legislation.

Foreign Trade Policy

Trade Tensions Rise

While Russian producers have found themselves at a competitive advantage due to the rouble devaluation, trade tensions have risen both with the Central Asian region – an important market for Russian products – and more widely, particularly with the US. Although the Central Asian countries experienced currency falls associated with the declining rouble, the movements have tended to be of much smaller magnitudes and, therefore, still favoured Russian companies. Some countries tried to limit their exposure to Russian products without having to see their own currencies devalue. Kazakhstan struck the first blow by imposing a unilateral ban on Russian foodstuff imports in early 1999. Russia is keen to limit any rise in protectionism, given that it is in its best interest to keep as many trade routes open as possible, and indeed, it is in the process of strengthening ties with some of its neighbours. A pact has already been signed with Belarus, opening the door to tax harmonisation, full-scale monetary union and a single currency in the future. Although the latter is contentious, and likely to be put on hold for the time being, it does demonstrate Russia's desire to maintain close ties with, and influence over, surrounding states. This trend was reinforced by the friendship pact with Ukraine. However, tighter security at borders prompted by concerns over Islamic terrorism is hampering cross-border trade within the CIS.

Developed markets also felt the impact of cheaper Russian goods. In February 1999, in response to accusations of dumping by the US authorities to suspend its exports of hot rolled steel to the US for six months, Russia agreed to restrict exports in other areas, and raise prices. The alternative was the unilateral imposition of import duties by the US (similar to ones imposed on Japanese and Brazilian steel), which would have significantly reduced Russia's export capabilities. Had Russia been a member of the World Trade Organisation (WTO) such action would not have been possible.

Bureaucracy And Corruption

A Barrier To Investment

The communist system became a breeding ground for both bureaucracy and corruption, the legacy of which has stayed with Russia in its move to a free market. The situation does not appear to be improving. The Interior Ministry announced in March 2000 that the number of crimes committed by public officials in 1999 had risen by 35.6% on the previous year to 53,700, with a cost to Russia in the region of US$1bn a year. A number of high-profile foreign investors, including **BP** and **Ikea**, have suffered well-publicised setbacks to their investments in Russia as they battled with local administrations and courts. With low pay endemic throughout many public and private institutions, corruption is one way for individuals to supplement meagre incomes, meaning that an element of corruption often comes into the equation for those wishing to do business effectively in Russia. The administration acknowledges the problem. However, tackling is not easy, especially as many people see it as a natural way of doing business rather than something that is inherently wrong. Moreover, the extensive use of barter within the economy further blurs the line between legitimate and non-legitimate payments. An improvement in political stability and in fair enforcement of rules is a precondition for corruption to be reduced. Some companies benefit unfairly from lower tax rates, lower energy prices and enhanced access to government contracts, for example, which constitute unfair advantages. At the policymaking level, there were few concrete steps against any of the so-called "oligarchs" in the first few months of Putin's rule as prime minister.

Intellectual Property Rights

Turning A Blind Eye

Russia lags behind in a world where the protection of intellectual property rights is coming to the fore. One of the most common breaches is in the music industry, where illegal copies of copyrighted material are widely available, for which the owner receives no income. The authorities have not shown a strong desire to crack down on this practice or enforce the intellectual property rights accorded to such material. The organisations running these illegal operations usually have considerable financial clout.

Environmental Regulation

Regulations Are Lax

Compared to its counterparts in the West, Russia continues to have lax environmental standards. The desire to keep industry functioning, provide jobs and support the economy, comes ahead of environmental considerations. The authorities are keen not to overburden companies with a host of extra costs aimed either at cleaning up the environment or reducing the level of environmental pollution. This does allow more leeway than would be the case in Western economies. For example, Lada cars have had to be withdrawn from some markets in the West due to poor emission levels, but suffer no such restrictions in the domestic market. Catalytic converters, now mandatory in the West, are not required by law in Russia.

However, this does not give companies the right to pollute without regard. Industries do have to adhere to environmental controls. A recent law aimed at making producers more accountable states that companies which produce waste products are considered their legal 'owner' and are responsible for their safe disposal. However, the extent to which laws are enforced often leaves much to be desired, and the potential to bypass them, probably via illegal means, is high. As long as public health is not obviously suffering as the result of an industrial operation, it may be allowed to continue. The price for this policy is high. The level of air pollution has been said to exceed the country's maximum permitted levels in over 200 cities. The State Environmental Protection Committee has been charged with drawing up an "environmental security" document to outline how the environment is to be protected.

The most worrying environmental threat comes from decaying nuclear installations, especially those related to the military. Large parts of the aging nuclear-powered fleet are in need of decommissioning, the cost of which will be too much for the authorities, but the international community is willing to provide assistance. The arrest for treason of former navy captain Alexander Nikitin, who divulged to a Norwegian environmental group that Russia had dumped contaminated materials in the sea, demonstrated that the environmental issue is pressing and that the authorities do not like to air their dirty washing in public. Nikitin was finally acquitted of charges of divulging state secrets in December 1999.

The conflict in Chechnya has caused major environmental damage. The most serious aspect of this has been the destruction of oil refineries and the setting ablaze of numerous oil wells. Alleviating the consequences for the environment will form a huge part of any future reconstruction effort.

5 Capital Markets

The Equity Market

Dominated By Commodity Producers

The Russian equity market is dominated by resource-based companies, reflecting both the high concentration of natural resources within the country and the paucity of opportunities in manufacturing and services companies. The most popular traded shares include **Gazprom**, **Lukoil** and **UES**, along with **Rostelecom**, **MTS** and oil company **Surgutneftegaz**. As a proportion of the IFCG index for Russia (which notably excluded some large stocks such as oil company **Sibneft** and telcos **Golden Telecom** and **Vimpelcom**), oil and gas companies accounted for 62.8% of market capitalisation as of February 2000, compared with 13.6% for telecoms and 14.8% for utilities.

The collapse of the rouble and the sharp decline in Russian stock prices took a heavy toll on Russia's standing in the financial community. At the start of 1998 the top 10 companies by market capitalisation in Eastern Europe were all Russian, led by **Gazprom**, **Lukoil** and **UES**. By the start of 1999, only five companies of the top 10 were Russian, and only one – Lukoil – made it into Europe's top 500 companies. The first quarter of 1999 saw the equity market improve significantly, with the RTS index producing a gain of 36.36%. This strength reflected several factors. While there was the inevitable rebound following drastic overselling at the end of 1998, and the growing optimism that Russia would not be isolated from the world community, the main driving force was the realisation that the equity market would benefit from GKO restructuring. As part of the debt restructuring deal to enable the GKO market to begin trading again, funds are permitted to leave the country only on a very strict basis. This limitation on converting roubles into hard currency meant that monies were held 'captive' in the country, and that some of it would find a home in the equity market.

The plan to redirect monies from debt restructuring into equities would be conducted through the MICEX market, which comprises 48 companies, on the grounds that only this market has sufficient controls in place to police the scheme. Gazprom is not included on the list of companies on this market, leading both Gazprom and Lukoil to suggest issuing corporate bonds and allowing the proceeds of the restructuring to be invested in these issues as well as in equities. **Tyumen Oil** and **Surgutneftegaz** have also said they would like to issue bonds. Therefore, GKO restructuring is expected to help boost both the equity and corporate bond markets. The IFC investable index for

Russia rose by 197% in 1999, and by the end of Q1 00 had put on a massive 460% from its lows in October 1998. In the year to March 2000 the relative performance of the sectors in the equity market varied widely. Telecoms came out best, but other sectors showed equally dramatic variation between different stocks.

The Bond Market

The Debt Market Remains Sidelined

The August 1998 decision to impose a moratorium on domestic debt maturing up to the end of 1998 marked the beginning of Russia's economic crisis. The moratorium affected RUB282bn (US$44.3bn) of debt, approximately one-third of which was held by foreign investors. Investors lost the majority of their money, with much of it frozen in so-called S-accounts. Trading in the bond market was effectively ended and attention became focussed on Russia's ability to maintain payments on its foreign debt, including older Soviet-era obligations and more recent eurobonds. The Russian bond market, according to the JP Morgan index, produced a return of –84.9% in 1998.

Domestic Debt Restructuring

Although the Russians were quick to devise a plan to restructure the domestic debt market, the restructuring negotiations dragged on until spring 1999 as deadlines came and went and foreign investors held out for better terms. Even then, not all foreign investors agreed to the terms offered. Throughout the negotiations the Russian position stayed broadly constant and few concessions were made. Sweeteners were given in the form of allowing equity investment with some of the proceeds of the restructuring, and the possibility of investing in new corporate bonds, but that was all. Having tried to negotiate from a common standpoint, by February 1999 the group of foreign banks who had lost as a result of the moratorium began to disintegrate. **Deutsche Bank**, the head of the group, and **Chase Manhattan** decided to accept the deal the authorities were offering on behalf of the bank's own holdings. This led to the sacking of Deutsche Bank as head of the group and considerable disarray within the group as a whole. With the Russians having gained the upper hand in the debt negotiations, the ability to push for further concessions was compromised.

The restructuring option which most of the investors took gave them around 37% of the rouble value they had invested, or allowing for the collapse in the exchange rate, around 7-8% of their original investment. Even this could only be repatriated after a year as the Russians sought to minimise the impact on the exchange rate. All non-resident proceeds of the restructuring, with the exception of a 3.33% cash dispersal, were placed in special 'transit' accounts. These are labelled repatriation, investment and depository accounts. The repatriation account allows a limited amount of money to be exchanged for US dollars and repatriated. The CBR originally envisaged allowing US$550mn into these accounts, following 11 monthly foreign exchange auctions of US$50mn. However, this was subsequently reduced to US$200mn over four currency auctions. The investment account allows for the purchase of government bonds (new or old), equities and new corporate bonds. These instruments must trade on MICEX to be allowed. Finally, newly purchased bonds or stocks will be held in the depository account.

In the first quarter of 2000 the government began to test the water pending a return to the domestic capital markets. The sole debt issue made by the authorities, worth RUB3.52bn, was sold at a premium and yielded –0.54%, demonstrating investors' eagerness to quit the market. The amount of domestic debt is still small and debt issues are not yet being used as a tool of monetary management.

6 Russian Regions

Introduction

Shifting Power To The Regions

Soviet-era centralisation was reversed under Yeltsin, when the ability of the regions to influence their own affairs was greater than ever before. The process began when Yeltsin guaranteed greater regional autonomy under the March 1992 Federal Treaty, with the result that local politicians rather than central government have largely determined the development of regions outside Moscow. Only now is Putin seeking to reverse this trend.

Russia is a country of great diversity, in which the economic and cultural make-up of the regions varies significantly. This makes it impossible to talk about the regions as a whole, but rather requires an individual examination of each area. While some regions are able to stand alone, needing little assistance from Moscow and, indeed, make a net contribution to central government coffers (the 10 so-called 'donor regions'), others rely on the central government for subsidies and transfers. The regions have several sources of funding, including taxes shared with the federation, regional taxes, non-tax revenues, and transfers and subsidy payments from the federal government and municipalities. In general, the donor regions receive most of their income either from shared taxes or taxes they have raised themselves. The greater degree of independence has also seen an increase in social and municipal responsibilities for the regions. Whereas in the past the central government controlled many local services, these activities have been passed on to the regions. However, in many cases the additional funds needed to finance such expenditures are not forthcoming from the central government.

The decentralisation has caused problems for the government in recent years, with the regions increasingly setting their own agendas rather than following the federal government's line. The economic crisis of August 1998 made the problem significantly worse. With little help coming from federal agencies and the central government, at times, not in a position to provide support, the regions started to solve their own problems. This has seen some of them refusing to pay federal taxes, restrictions on goods entering some regions, and other attempts to wrest control away from Moscow. Putin campaigned on the need for a strong central state and for law and order and has made reforming centre-region relations a centrepiece of his first year in power.

The Drive Towards Decentralisation

Regions Take Responsibility For Budget Setting

Today the regions are, in many cases, responsible for social policy and to some extent setting revenue and expenditure plans. Although the central government has in the past been keen to allow greater regional autonomy on the grounds that the individual areas will know what best suits them, in part the change of policy was forced on it. The government has many calls on its resources, but at the same time has proven particularly inefficient at increasing available resources. One solution was therefore to transfer the problem to the regions. This has had two effects. Firstly, income distribution has become more uneven between regions. The relatively cash- and resource-rich regions have the means to finance the additional expenditure passed on by the central government, while others are considerably poorer and therefore unable to provide the same level of income and services. Secondly, the extra responsibilities forced onto regional governments has seen them get bigger, while the federal apparatus is getting smaller. This has increasingly led to confrontation and heightened the risk of a breakdown in control.

As a result of the economic crisis of 1998 and 1999, the need for central government to control spending and increase revenue placed further pressure on the regions to come up with funding solutions. The situation was further aggravated by the fact that most regional spending is socially oriented, leading to higher demand for transfer payments, and resulted in barter and other non-market mechanisms coming to the fore. Credit notes and barter, for example, came to play an important role in the day-to-day running of local government. The use of non-money means of payment in some regions reached as high as 80% of transactions.

Following the federal government's virtual paralysis following the August economic crisis and Yeltsin's sacking of then prime minister Sergei Kiriyenko, and with a difficult winter ahead, several regional governments moved to protect their interests and seized the opportunity to widen their power base. Kalmykia on the shores of the Caspian Sea refused to hand over federal tax payments, and in the Volgograd region at the heart of Russia's grain belt, restrictions were imposed on the transport of grain outside the region's borders.

The economic crisis also saw business and industrial policy being constructed along regional rather than national lines. The banking sector has seen the large national banks falter and regional institutions benefit. Meanwhile, the regions often impose their own taxes and levies and, given the breakdown of the cash system, can often determine which businesses succeed and which fail.

The Geography Of Russia

Endowed With Natural Resources

At 17,075,400km², Russia is by far the largest country in the world, dwarfing all others. Canada is only 9,976,999km², China 9,651,000km² and the US 9,363,000km². The country covers 11 time zones and occupies one-eighth of the world's land surface, while its borders stretch from Europe's Finland and Norway in the west to China and Mongolia in the east. The country's size was reflected in its superpower status. While this still applies, Russia's financial problems have forced a scaling down of aspirations, although Russia still has a formidable military presence, including a large nuclear arsenal.

Russia is endowed with significant natural resources. These range from oil and gas to metals, gold and diamonds, and commodities account for well over 60% of exports. Russia has over 60bn barrels of recoverable oil reserves, equivalent to 30 years of production at current rates. In all likelihood, however, this probably significantly understates the extent of oil reserves. There remain large tracts of Siberia and the Caspian Sea that have yet to be fully explored. Russia has the largest gas reserves in the world, estimated at over 48trn m³, equal to the combined reserves of the Middle East. **Gazprom** already has a 20% share of the European gas market and has the potential for further gains.

The bulk of Russia's natural resources are located in the Siberian regions. However, the sparse population there combined with climatic conditions makes extraction harder, and tends to increase operating costs. Indeed, the majority of Russia's 147mn population is located away from the resource-rich north and east in the (relatively) milder western regions. This mismatch of factors of production is repeated in many Russian industries, where central planning allocated production on the basis of social needs rather than economic criteria.

Agriculture forms an important component of many regional economies. However, due to Russia's northern geographical position and poor climatic conditions – including extreme cold and relatively frequent droughts – agricultural yields are low. The 1998 harvest, the worst for 40 years, was a clear demonstration of the climate's impact. Due to the climate and soil structure, only one-seventh of the total land area is given over to agricultural production. Approximately three-fifths of farmland is used for crop production, with the rest used for pasture and meadow. Grain is the most important crop produced, including wheat, rye, barley and oats. Other crops grown include sunflowers, sugar beet, flax, potatoes and other vegetables.

The Russian Regions

The Regional Structure

In a continuation of the Soviet system the Russian Federation is broken into 11 regions. Three are in Asia, east of the Ural mountains, and eight are in Europe. These regions are in turn subdivided into 89 republics, oblasts, krais and okrugs, as well as the two largest cities, Moscow and St. Petersburg. The 89 subdivisions are referred to as 'subjects of the federation' – a legal concept which regulates relations with the federal centre. However, although the Federal Treaty of 1992 provides a formal framework, numerous exceptions exist regarding the degree of fiscal and economic freedom, and some subjects even enjoy considerable autonomy in foreign relations.

The North Region

The sparsely populated North Region produces 4.7% of Russia's output and hosts 4.2% of its population. Economic activity is focused on forestry and timber. The region produces 25% of the country's cut timber, 47% of its pulp and 46% of its paper products. Four of Russia's largest pulp and paper companies are located within the region (**Kotlas**, **Syktyvar**, **Kondopoga** and **Segezha**). Oil, gas, fertiliser, iron ore, steel and shipbuilding in the Arkhangel Oblast are also important. The Pechora coalfield is located in the Komi republic, which also contains the Komi-Ukhta oil and gas deposits. Approximately 3% of Russia's oil is derived from this region. The Murmansk Oblast is rich in mineral deposits that are used in the production of fertilisers. Vologda Oblast produces 16% of Russia's steel and 17% of its rolled ferrous metals.

The Northwest Region

Despite a lack of natural resources the Northwest Region is highly industrialised, containing both light and heavy industrial plant. It is known for its precision engineering and production of heavy electrical power equipment and optical instruments. St. Petersburg, Russia's second largest city, is located within the NorthWest Region, which is home to 5.6% of Russia's population. St. Petersburg itself is a city of 4.7mn inhabitants, over half the region's population. Novgorod, the region's second largest city (250,000 inhabitants) is dwarfed by comparison. St. Petersburg does not depend on the central government for subsidies, generating sufficient revenue itself. However, it carries a large debt burden that proved difficult to manage following the economic crisis. The adjacent Leningrad Oblast managed to attract FDI from the mid-1990s onwards as it pursued investor-friendly legislation, including tax breaks. Novgorod Oblast has also successfully attracted foreign investment, again with the help of investor-friendly legislation.

The Central Region

The Central Region lies at the heart of European Russia and is home to 20.4% of the population. Of this, 10.5% live in Moscow and the Moscow Oblast. The region is the most developed in Russia, and accounts for a significant proportion of output (12.8%). There are limited supplies of natural resources available in the area and no coal, oil, or natural gas, so it relies on energy supplied from elsewhere in the country.

In the northern part of the region the focus is on industry. In towns such as Kirov, Yaroslavl and Rybinsk, production is concentrated on machinery, car components and engines. In the south, the focus switches to agriculture, producing meat, wheat and vegetable oils. Textiles are a key industry for the Central Region, producing over 70% of Russia's output. The Central Region as a whole also produces 18% of Russia's electricity, 16% of its cement and 20% of its bricks, as well as 13% of its fertilisers and 9% of its timber products.

Moscow

With a population of approximately 8.7mn people, Moscow is the largest city in Europe, as well as being Russia's largest city and capital. A further 6.3mn people live in the Moscow Oblast. The city covers a wide range of sectors: industry, distribution, services, banking and finance are all located there. The city is the hub of the country, being both home to the central government and Russia's leading intellectual and cultural centre. As such, the infrastructure that the city enjoys eclipses that generally available elsewhere. Moscow is also home to Russia's newly rich – the business class which has prospered since the introduction of market reforms – and this is reflected in the availability of luxury goods in the shops. In 1997, Moscow's GDP per capita was 55% above that of the Russian Federation, while the average monthly wage was 39% higher.

Moscow Oblast

Moscow Oblast benefits from the business generated by the capital. From a diverse economy the oblast contributed 5% of GDP in 1996. Major industries are ferrous metals, chemicals, engineering (rolling stock), construction equipment, consumer goods and services. The airports of Domodyedovo and Bykovo, serving domestic flights, are located here. In the Soviet era, the oblast focused on defence and heavy manufacturing industries, but these were hard hit by the transition to a market economy. The region is heavily dependent on **Mostransgas**, which accounted for 36% of tax revenue in 1996. The close connection with the City of Moscow should help ensure that Moscow Oblast retains its development potential. However, since the economic crisis, it has lost out to the city in terms of investment, which has restricted growth and led to a widening of income differentials.

Volga-Vyatka Region

Volga-Vyatka is a highly industrialised region in which much of the Soviet Union's military-industrial production was located, and accounts for 5.7% of Russia's population and 4.2% of its industrial production. The military connection meant that many cities were closed to foreigners – Nizhny Novgorod Oblast was only opened to outsiders in 1992. The region is also a centre for car production (14% of vehicles are produced there) and is home to **Gorky Avtomobilny Zavod (GAZ)**, the second largest car factory in the country. This company produces the Volga range of cars. GAZ has formed a US$850mn joint venture with **Fiat**, although production was delayed owing to the economic crisis.

Nizhny Novgorod Oblast

Nizhny Novgorod Oblast is the most developed part of the region, accounting for some 3% of national GDP and housing 3.7mn inhabitants. Its capital, Nizhny Novgorod (previously Gorky), is the third largest city in Russia with a population of 1.44mn. Also included in the region are Kirov Oblast and the republics of Mordovia, Mary El and Chuvash.

In the Soviet era the city of Nizhny Novgorod was renamed Gorky in honour of the famous writer Maxim Gorky. Several large-scale enterprises were established, including GAZ, the **Sokol** aircraft assembly plant, the **Bor** glass factory, the Gorky machine building plant, and the **Balakhna** pulp and paper enterprise. In wartime, Gorky was the production centre for tanks and a major supplier of armaments. This role continued after the war with the production of MiG jet fighters. By 1991, the defence sector accounted for 25% of the oblast's production, although this figure had fallen to only 8% by 1995. While the remainder of the defence industry is likely to remain in the hands of the state, the oblast is keen to attract new customers, and has set up a consultancy. It also helps former defence enterprises convert to civilian production as well as providing 'tax exempt production zones' in unprofitable enterprises. The region is well supported by infrastructure. It has a good road network and three rivers, allowing connection to Russia's system of navigable waterways.

The oblast is at the forefront of liberal economic reforms. Boris Nemtsov was appointed governor in 1992 in return for helping Yeltsin during the August 1991 coup attempt, and brought in liberal reformer Grigory Yavlinsky to plan economic development. This led to a reform of communal services (particularly housing), privatisation of state enterprises, free registration for private enterprises, land reform and the sale of land to individuals. Over the 1991-96 period 4,111 enterprises were privatised, raising RUR178bn, of which RUR27bn went to the oblast's budget. This background has attracted considerable foreign investment and support from foreign bodies. 77% of the region's output is produced by privatised firms (against a national average of 67%), while for Nizhny Novgorod itself the figure rises to 88%. Nizhny Novgorod Oblast maintains good relationships with international bodies including the World Economic Forum, the EBRD and the British Know-How Fund. The latter has a technical assistance centre in Nizhny Novgorod city.

The oblast is more industry-based than most (industry employed 36.1% of the population in 1995 compared with a national average of 27.1%) and less dependent on agriculture (which accounted for 10% of employees against 15.4% for Russia as a whole). Important industries include oil refining, auto production, machine building, metallurgy, diesel engines, ships, aeroplanes, domestic electrical appliances, food processing, chemicals/petro-chemicals, and pulp and paper. The Norsi oil refinery in the city of Kstovo is Russia's largest, accounting for approximately 10% of total crude processed in the country. With regard to agriculture, the oblast is an efficient producer of 2.6% of Russia's cereals, 2.9% of its potatoes, 2.6% of its vegetables and 2.7% of its meat. It was quick to adopt a programme of land reform to voluntarily re-organise the former collective farms into new, privately-owned units. Members could choose the form of ownership, which included cooperatives, partnerships and sole proprietorships. Moreover, an effort has been made to establish clearly defined property and management rights. This so-called Zerno, or grain programme, has become a model for reform elsewhere in Russia. In consequence, 55,000 agricultural labourers have become landowners and 294 state enterprises have been privatised.

The Central Black Earth Region

This region is named after the "chernozem", or black soils, which cover the area. The soils are rich and fertile, allowing the easy cultivation of many crops, making this the dominant sector. However, cattle-rearing, meat processing and the cultivation and processing of sugar, dairy products and vegetable oils are also important.

The region is home to 5.2% of Russia's population and accounts for 4.1% of its industrial output. Industrial growth only took hold in the 1960s and 1970s, as iron ores from the **Kursk Magnetic Anomaly** were used in the new steel plants at Lipetsk and Stary Oskol, as well as supplying ore to other regions. Metals remain important today: 17% of smelted steel production is from the region, while 19% of rolled ferrous metals are produced in the Lipetsk Oblast alone. Other non-agricultural production includes 13% of Russia's cement output.

The Volga Region

The Volga region contains three major industrial cities – Samara, Saratov and Vologda – as well as the republic of Tatarstan, which under President Mintimar Shaimiyev is the most independent of Russia's republics. The Volga region accounts for 11% of Russia's population and 9.2% of industrial production. It covers a belt 300-500km wide that stretches along the Volga river for 1,750km. The Volga is connected to other river systems, allowing trade between the Baltic, Caspian and Black Sea.

The region only began to develop in the 1950s following the exploitation of local oil and hydroelectric power (HEP) energy resources. The focus on HEP resulted in the region producing 10% of Soviet electricity. The Volga-Ural oilfield extends from the western Urals through the Volga valley to the Caspian Sea. It became the Soviet Union's main producer of oil, with output of 100mn tonnes per annum by 1960, 70% of the country's production. This earned the region the title of 'Second Baku'. Although it was subsequently surpassed by the discovery of oil reserves in Siberia, it still remains an important source of oil products. Russia's largest car manufacturer, **AvtoVAZ**, is located in the Volga region, in Togliatti in Samara Oblast, where Fiat began a joint venture to produce cars for the domestic market in 1970. AvtoVAZ accounts for over 75% of car production and is owner of the **Lada** marque.

The Republic of Tatarstan also has considerable hydrocarbon reserves. Its oil company **Tatneft** produces 8% of Russia's oil output. The republic has pursued a largely independent line and in 1994 secured full ownership of oil reserves and industrial enterprises, the right to pursue an independent foreign economic policy, and the right to retain the majority of tax revenues. Tatarstan has been less keen to embrace market reforms, retaining significant regulation and subsidy payments. This has in turn restricted the area's development. Tatarstan is home to Russia's largest truck manufacturer, **KamAZ**. The company was in trouble even before the August 1998 crisis and then defaulted on bank loans provided by the EBRD.

The North Caucasus Region

This region is important as a link between the oil deposits in the Caspian Sea and the Black Sea and Turkey, and then onto Europe. As oil production in the Caspian area increases, so the region's importance should also rise in the years ahead. Currently it is underdeveloped, being home to 11.8% of Russia's population but producing only 3.7% of industrial production. Politically, the area is unstable. Russia fought a bitter civil war against Chechnya from December 1994 to September 1996 to prevent it from seceding from the federation. A deal brokered by former presidential hopeful Alexandr Lebed ended the violence, but Moscow once again sent in the troops in September 1999 to secure the region and hunt down insurgents. The leading sectors in the North Caucasus Region are agriculture, food processing, cement (it produces 11% of Russia's cement) and bricks (14%). The region still sees strong state influence and low rates of privatisation.

The Ural Region

The Ural Region lies to the east of the Ural mountains, the traditional boundary between Europe and Asia, and became heavily industrialised during World War II when factories were transferred to the east of the Urals to escape the reach of the advancing German army. It produces 16.8% of Russia's industrial output and is home to 13.8% of the population. The region is rich in natural resources – a major part of the Volga-Ural oilfield is in Perm and Orenburg Oblasts. The Ural Region produces more oil and gas than any other region with the exception of Western Siberia. It accounts for 14% of the country's oil production and 6% of its natural gas.

With over 20 steel-producing centres in the region, 10 of which have fully-integrated plants, the region accounts for 44% of Russia's smelted steel and rolled ferrous metal output. Five of these steel centres (Magnitogorsk, Nizhny Tagil, Chelyabinsk, Novotroitsk and Serov) account for 50% of the output. Located within the region are major deposits of ferrous and non-ferrous metal ores from which nickel, chrome, cobalt, manganese, aluminium ores, copper, gold and iron are produced. Ore processing, metallurgy and engineering activities on the basis of these ores are carried out in the above five cities. Given the region's reliance on industry and natural resources, the economic crisis and the decline in world commodity prices have hit the local economy more than most. This is putting additional strain on the budget and the regional government's ability to provide the full range of services.

The Ural Region contains Russia's fifth largest city, Yekaterinburg – or Sverdlovsk as it was known during the Soviet period – with a population of 1.4mn people. The cities of Chelyabinsk, Perm and Ufa also have populations of just over 1mn. Sverdlovsk Oblast has tended to be a leader in economic reform (over 6,000 firms have been privatised) and has been keen to foster relations with foreign investors to help exploit the natural resources on offer. In 1997 there were over 500 joint ventures from 63 different countries in operation. The oblast was also the first of Russia's 89 local administrative bodies to implement free elections. It has a population of 4.7mn people (the fifth largest in Russia) and is dominated by heavy industry, though it also holds substantial natural resources in the form of iron, nickel, chrome, manganese and copper. As a result of its well-developed structure, the oblast enjoys a higher than average level of income and a larger service sector than the national average.

Siberia

Siberia, a vast region covering 12,766,000km², can be divided into three separate regions: Western Siberia, Eastern Siberia and the Far East. Even with this division, each region is still larger than any other in Russia. Natural resources dominate in Siberia and manufacturing is poorly represented. However, many of the resources are located in the sparsely populated extreme north, which incurs high production costs due to the difficult climatic conditions and extensive transport links needed to bring products to market (the northern area has four significant towns – Norilsk, Yakutsk, Magadan and Petropavlosk – although the population of each is under 300,000. Simeria has abundant supplies of hydroelectric power using the large rivers that flow through the region). The bulk of the population is located in the southern area, which also contains most of the agricultural land. While oil and gas industries are the key resources, large deposits of gold, diamonds, nickel, platinum and palladium are also found in Siberia, which in fact accounts for most of Russia's production of these commodities. Coal is produced in Siberia, while molybdenum, tungsten, tin, lead and zinc are extracted in the Buryat Republic and Chita Oblast, and tin in the Khabarovsk and Maritime Krais.

Siberia's development was helped by the opening of the Trans-Siberian railway, built between 1892 and 1916. In the Soviet period the region began to develop its abundant natural resources, although wages needed to be high to attract labour. This pool of labour has, to some extent, become trapped following the collapse of the old order as workers saw the value of their savings wiped out almost overnight.

The Western Siberia Region

The Western Siberia region contains the largest oil and natural gas reserves in the country, accounting for 68% of its oil production and 91% of natural gas output. At 7.4%, Tyumen Oblast, occupying most of the Western Siberian plain and an area of 1,435,200km², accounts for the largest share of output of any one region. This is home to most of Russia's major oil companies and also produces 38% of the nation's coal. It was only in the 1960s, with the opening of major oil deposits along the River Ob, that development of the oblast began to take shape.

Located within the oblast is the Yamalo-Nenets Autonomous Okrug, covering an area of 750,000km² and home to a population of 491,000. Autonomous okrugs are accorded the status of independent subjects of the federation. Yamalo-Nenets contains 30% of the world's proven gas reserves and 30% of Russia's oil reserves. 91% of Russia's gas and 10% of its oil are produced there, with the Urengoi and Medvezhye fields the most important. Gazprom dominates gas production in the okrug, accounting for 99% of total output, while oil is produced by **Noyabrskneftegaz** and **Purneftegaz**. The Yamalo-Nenets Okrug remains a net contributor to the federal budget. The fact that most of Russia's oil companies have been privatised, albeit partially in some cases, means that the Western Siberia region can be classed as one of the more reform-oriented areas. 78% of enterprises have been privatised, compared with the national average of 67%. In Tyumen, Yemal and Khanti-Mansi, the figure is as high as 99%.

With a population of 1.5mn people, Novosibirsk is the largest city in Western Siberia. It developed as an industrial centre during World War II, and also has important research facilities, including Akademgorodok (Academic Town). This was established under Nikita Khrushchev and was the Siberian Centre for the Academy of Sciences of the former Soviet Union. The concentration of scientific and computer skills in the area has begun to make Novosibirsk a focus for the software industry.

The Eastern Siberia Region

The River Yenisey separates East from West Siberia. The Eastern side occupies more than 25% of Russian territory, but only accounts for 6.7% of its population and 6.4% of its industrial output. It produces 22% of Russia's timber products, mainly in Irkutsk and Krasnoyarsk, and 33% of Russian pulp, mostly in the Irkutsk Oblast. Some 75% of the region's enterprises have been privatised.

Krasnoyarsk Krai

Half of Eastern Siberia's output is produced in Krasnoyarsk Krai, which accounts for 13.6% of total Russian Federation production and has a population of just 3.5mn. Its governor is Alexandr Lebed, the popular general who was a former aide to President Yeltsin. Lebed's presidential ambitions crumbled after he received considerable bad publicity surrounding allegations of corruption and poor financial management in his running of the Krasnoyarsk region.

Krasnoyarsk contains vast natural resources and houses the four largest metals companies in Russia. These are **Norilsk Nickel**, the **Krasnoyarsk Aluminium Factory**, the **Sayansk Aluminium Plant** and the **Bratsk Aluminium Factory**. Norilsk Nickel is the largest enterprise and taxpayer in the krai, and is an important producer of nickel, platinum, palladium, cobalt and copper, both in Russian and global terms. The geographical location of the krai presents problems both in terms of the climate and high transport costs. Norilsk, for example, home of Norilsk Nickel, lies 200 miles north of the Arctic Circle. The area is one of the poorest in Russia, and the economic crisis only hastened a trend of falling incomes, rising unemployment and regional emigration. Norilsk is also part of Vladimir Potanin's business empire, which also includes the troubled **Uneximbank**. The latter became the first Russian entity to default on eurobond debt, demonstrating the extent of problems faced by Potanin at this time. Nevertheless, Norilsk Nickel remains a going concern and should continue to be a source of revenue for the region as a whole.

The Far East Region

This sparsely populated area, occupying 34% of Russia's territory yet accounting for only 4.9% of its population, is one of the least developed in Russia. Its main activities are shipping, fishing, timber products and gold and diamond mining. Khabarovsk and Primorsk (or Maritime) Krais are important as trade and transport centres, while the major ports in Vladivostok and Nakhodka link up with the Trans-Siberian railway.

The Sakha Republic

The Sakha Republic, formerly known as Yakutia, is about the size of India and is the largest republic in the Russian Federation. Rich in diamond and gas reserves, the region has reached agreement with the central government on sharing revenues from diamond sales and the ownership of diamond deposits. Sakha produces nearly one-fifth of the world's diamonds by value, making it the second largest producer, and is Russia's dominant supplier. Its output is sold through the **De Beers** organisation. The region is set to see further development of its natural resource base due to abundant gas and oil deposits. The region relies on transfers from the federation to supplement tax income. However, the high debt level of the region is proving a problem in the present circumstances. Indeed, the region has already defaulted on an agrobond – RUB52.04mn was paid after the deadline – and RUB48mn of domestic bonds, and has turned to restructuring of foreign currency debt.

Sakhalin Island

Sakhalin is in Russia's Far East Region and has a population of 700,000. Although fishing is the most important industry on the island, accounting for 40% of its commodity output, oil, gas and coal are set to take over as the dominant primary products. Oil and gas reserves are estimated to be of a similar magnitude to those available in the North Sea, at some 29bn barrels. While the island's high latitude means that the sea surrounding it is frozen over for more than six months of the year, the reserves are not inaccessible, being only 10-30km offshore and in relatively shallow water (10-50m). Offshore projects at Sakhalin-1 and Sakhalin-2 are already under way, while **Exxon Corporation** has reached agreement with Russia's state-owned oil company **Rosneft** and a related company to develop two blocks in the potentially giant Sakhalin-3 field. The shareholders in Sakhalin-2 include **Marathon** of the US (37.5%), **Mitsui Sakhalin Holdings** of Japan (25%), **Royal Dutch Shell** (25%) and **Diamond Gas**, a subsidiary of **Mitsubishi of Japan** (12.5%). Phase two of the Sakhalin development also saw international funding amounting to US$177mn coming from the European Bank for Reconstruction and Development, the US government-owned OPIC (Overseas Private Investment Corporation) and the **Export-Import Bank of Japan**. This was the first funding made to Russia on the basis of a production sharing agreement. Sakhalin's oil should find a ready market in the Far East as the "tiger" economies of South East Asia continue to recover from the regional recession. Looking further ahead, China will also provide a market for the oil.